The Alexander Scriabin Companion

The Alexander Scriabin Companion

History, Performance, and Lore

Lincoln Ballard
Matthew Bengtson
with John Bell Young

ROWMAN & LITTLEFIELD
Lanham • Boulder • New York • London

Published by Rowman & Littlefield
An imprint of The Rowman & Littlefield Publishing Group, Inc.
4501 Forbes Boulevard, Suite 200, Lanham, Maryland 20706
www.rowman.com

86-90 Paul Street, London EC2A 4NE

Copyright © 2017 by Lincoln Ballard, Matthew Bengtson, and John Bell Young
Paperback Edition 2024

All rights reserved. No part of this book may be reproduced in any form or by any electronic or mechanical means, including information storage and retrieval systems, without written permission from the publisher, except by a reviewer who may quote passages in a review.

British Library Cataloguing in Publication Information Available

Library of Congress Cataloging-in-Publication Data
Names: Ballard, Lincoln, 1975– | Bengtson, Matthew | Young, John Bell.
Title: The Alexander Scriabin companion : history, performance, and lore / Lincoln Ballard, Matthew Bengtson, with John Bell Young.
Description: Lanham : Rowman & Littlefield, [2017] | Includes bibliographical references and index.
Identifiers: LCCN 2017011438 (print) | LCCN 2017011542 (ebook) | ISBN 9781442232624 (electronic) | ISBN 9781442232617 (cloth) | ISBN 9781538198889 (paper)
Subjects: LCSH: Scriabin, Aleksandr Nikolayevich, 1872–1915—Criticism and interpretation.
Classification: LCC ML410.S5988 (ebook) | LCC ML410.S5988 B335 2017 (print) | DDC 786.2092 [B]—dc23 LC record available at https://lccn.loc.gov/2017011438

Contents

Foreword		vii
Preface		ix
Acknowledgments		xv
1	En Garde or Avant-Garde? Exploding the Scriabin Myth	1
Part I:	**Encountering Scriabin**	
2	Life, Legacy, and Music	15
3	The Solo Piano Music	33
4	Symphonies and Orchestral Works	74
Part II:	**Topics in Reception History**	
5	Madness and Other Myths	113
6	On Synaesthesia or "Color-Hearing"	131
7	Scriabin's Russian Roots and the Symbolist Aesthetic	158
8	The Revival in 1960s America	182
Part III:	**In Performance**	
9	From Musical Text to the Imagination	207
10	Technique	218

11	Line and Melody	239
12	Harmony	251
13	The Scriabin Sound	282
14	Rhythm	306

Notes	327
Glossary and Pronounciation Guide	381
Bibliography	391
Index	397
About the Authors	421

Foreword

Some composers lead interesting lives, others don't, but no other composer has a more multidimensional allure than Scriabin. It's not just that the music on the page and its vibrations in the air is only the beginning of an understanding of the Russian composer, but the force of the artist behind the notes draws us into a beguilingly strange world where music and mysticism, sense and spirit blur and blend.

From an ephemeral one-minute *Poème* whispered on a drawing room Bechstein to the mighty ambition of the "*Mysterium*," a projected weeklong work designed to be performed at the foot of the Himalayas as the world dissolved in bliss, Scriabin's inspiration was as much color and perfume and philosophy as simple notes of the scale. And that musical scale itself was constantly expanded, its tonal implications massaged into strange shapes and intoxicating harmonies, their overtones spiraling upward like so many exotic petals unfolding on a rare flower. If Wagner's yearning endlessly seeks resolution, Scriabin is on a search for the yearning itself: Who needs a resolution when the longing provides such ecstasy?

And eroticism. There is barely a bar in Scriabin's entire output which does not aim to seduce with the voluptuousness of its harmonies or the beguiling line of its melodies. It is a celebration of the power of sound to arouse—the fingers caressing the keys, the ear trembling with sympathetic, sensual delight.

This book is the fruit of decades of either writing or playing at the highest level by three musicians who have immersed themselves in this composer's extraordinary world. How to handle Scriabin? At the keyboard he requires consummate virtuosity on every level—fingers, pedal, sound, nuance, rubato; in print he needs someone with imagination, flare and daring . . . and perspective. As we observe the centenary of his death, this book brings Scriabin back to life once more, although do I hear the composer's voice? "Ah, but I never died in the first place."

—Stephen Hough

Preface

Lincoln Ballard

My journey into the strange and wondrous world of Alexander Scriabin's life and music began in the summer of 2000. Having moved from the heartland of Ohio to pursue a master's degree at Florida State University, I rented an apartment close to the FSU campus and befriended a French horn player who lived in the same complex. I was an aspiring pianist in those days, but I started playing far too late in life to ever be competitive. None of that soured my love for playing the piano and learning new repertoire. I will never forget the day my friend handed me an all-black CD with a shadowy figure on the cover who gazed dreamily into the distance and proudly displayed his starched collar and handlebar moustache. "I think you're going to like this," he said. That night, I found myself captivated by the mysterious rumblings and thundering climaxes I heard pouring through my speakers, played by the American pianist Ruth Laredo on the Nonesuch label. It was a profound musical experience that led me down the rabbit hole of studying Scriabin, his music, and all of its associated influences.

Since that incredible moment of discovery, I have devoted myself to learning everything I could find out about Scriabin's life and legacy. I have scoured a broad range of sources and saved morsels of information wherever I could locate them.[1] My curiosity about all things Scriabin has not diminished since my graduate school days, and today I am well versed in the myths, legends, and historical issues that have enveloped this fascinating composer, whom the pianist and musicologist Jonathan Powell described in the 2001 *Grove Dictionary* (the gold standard of music history) as "one of the most extraordinary figures musical culture has ever witnessed."[2] In writing this book, I am fortunate to have had the assistance of two of the top Scriabin-playing pianists in the world, John Bell Young and Matthew Bengtson. Their decades of experience performing and interpreting Scriabin's music at the keyboard complements my fifteen years of historical research.

The year 2015 marked the centenary of Scriabin's death at age forty-three in Moscow, Russia. This important anniversary occasioned the writing of this book and was celebrated worldwide through various tributes in print and performance. Among the all-Scriabin concerts that took place, notable events occurred at Cornell University, Ohio State University, and at the New England Conservatory, where the complete piano music was performed over seven nights. Pianists Dmitry Rachmanov, Garrick Ohlsson, and Matthew Bengtson toured the country separately performing all-Scriabin lecture recitals, and the Scriabin Association in England (www.scriabin-association.com) hosted several concerts. At the Proms concerts in London, conductor Oliver Knussen performed the *Poem of Ecstasy*, and Vladimir Jurowski conducted the *Divine Poem* and Knussen's own *Scriabin Settings*, which are orchestrations of five of Scriabin's piano miniatures. In Florence, Italy, the students and professors of Conservatorie Luigi Cherubini held a four-day festival and performed a broad range of Scriabin's solo piano music. Italian scholars like Luigi Verdi lectured on Scriabin's significance for twentieth-century music. Related publications that appeared during Scriabin's centennial year included an 18-disc collection of the complete recordings issued by Decca Records, and a facsimile of the autograph manuscript of the Seventh Sonata published by G. Henle Verlag, with a preface written by Valentina Rubtsova.

This surge of publications provides clear evidence of Scriabin's rising stock among scholars and the academic community. This has been especially true with regard to Urtext publications, which compare all known versions of a musical score and their original manuscripts to produce the most authoritative edition. A few years ago, Bärenreiter published critical editions of Scriabin's complete sonatas and posthumous works (in four volumes) under series editor Christoph Flamm. Henle now features Urtext editions of Scriabin's Piano Sonatas Nos. 1–10, as well as the Prelude and Nocturne for Left Hand Alone Op. 9, the 24 Preludes Op. 11, *Vers la flamme* Op. 72, and the nearly forgotten Romance for Horn and Piano. The Bärenreiter and Henle scores both include insightful prefaces and critical commentary on the history, reception, and performance of the music. For those interested in consulting original manuscripts of Scriabin's late works, several high-quality digital scans of Opp. 59 and 60–64 are available online through the Juilliard Manuscript Collection.[3] These incredible artifacts bring Scriabin's holographs out of the dusty archives and straight to your laptop. The astounding calligraphy and preciseness with which Scriabin notated these pieces is a true visual feast.

Scholars and music lovers alike celebrated Scriabin's centenary with several events. European and American academics recognized the composer's centenary with a conference at the Scriabin Museum in Moscow during April 24–27. Later that year, an event hosted by the Musicology Department at the University of California Los Angeles titled "Scriabin Among the Symbolists" positioned the composer's activities and creative thought well within the cultural context of his era. Simon Morrison, professor of music at Princeton, delivered public lectures throughout the year 2015 that explicated the history and meaning behind the mystic chord.[4] No Scriabin-related event in the centennial year of 2015, however, rivaled the magnitude and grandeur of a multimedia festival organized by British photographer Jarek Kotomski, called "Scriabin in the Himalayas." Billed as a modern-day realization of Scriabin's fabled *Mysterium*, this multisensory extravaganza combined dance, performance, colored lights, and customized perfumery in the timeless setting of the Thikse Monastery in Ladakh, India. Coauthor Matthew Bengtson performed the opening recital. Scheduled to coincide with the summer solstice, this historic event was captured on film and is slated to be released as a feature-length documentary.[5] These worldwide tributes make it evident that Scriabin's music enjoys a strong band of followers in our modern times.

The goal of this book is to help readers appreciate the cultural and musical traditions that Scriabin upheld and upended, and to identify defining qualities that the finest interpreters of his music share. No formal musical training is needed to follow the discussion, and technical terminology is kept at a minimum.[6] One might assume that in a musical performance, a pianist or conductor simply follows the score, and that any rendition of a piece should sound the same from one performer to the next. But such variables as the tempo at which a piece is played, the way notes are attacked (articulation), gradual fluctuations in volume (dynamics), and a thousand other nuances significantly impact the overall performance. It is these intangibles that make pianists like Sofronitsky, Richter, and Horowitz (among others) exemplary in this repertoire. To borrow a baking analogy, Scriabin's music is like a delicate pastry that requires the perfect proportion of ingredients and technique to achieve the ideal texture and shape; an amateur chef might be able to follow the recipe and produce a passable product (or have it collapse entirely), but only a master chef can elevate it into something extraordinary and refined. The authors do not presume to cover all of the existing knowledge and sources on Scriabin, as such a wealth of information could not be contained within a single volume. We also do not include all of the methodologies and analytical approaches that have been applied to this music in recent decades, such as gender studies, hermeneutics, and even neuroscience. But we do hope that this book serves as a compendium of modern information for the growing legion of Scriabin fans, and for those who have already been bitten by the Scriabin bug.

This book is divided into three sections. John Bell Young's opening essay, "En Garde or Avant-Garde? Exploding the Scriabin Myth," takes a critical stance against formalist views of Scriabin's music, which consider it as pure structure divorced from its cultural context. Such an approach to Scriabin's art, Young argues, eviscerates its cultural meaning and sociological relevance. As an alternative example of how Scriabin's music can be more meaningfully understood, Young proposes the art of engaged listening, or *intonatsiia*, as derived from the theories of Boleslav Yavorsky. Part I of this book, "Encountering Scriabin," is written by Lincoln Ballard and provides background information on the composer's life, influences, and musical style. Part I also offers overviews of his major works for orchestra and for solo piano, with brief sketches of each piece, and information on its performance history and compositional background. To help the reader sort through the dense catalogue of recordings that now exist for Scriabin's music, each piece profiled in these chapters is accompanied by a list of recommended recordings.[7] Part II, also written by Ballard, offers critical commentary and summaries of the literature on four major topics in Scriabin's reception: the myths generated by his biographers, his alleged synaesthesia or "color-hearing," the accusations of anti-Russianness leveled against his music, and his revival in 1960s America as a proto–Flower Child.[8] In part III, Matthew Bengtson discusses the challenges and solutions to performing Scriabin's music at the piano. He approaches this topic from a variety of angles, and partitions Scriabin's complex art into more manageable chunks. Each section of this book, then, examines a different theme or topic in Scriabin's music and legacy, and these topics are cross-referenced between chapters. Readers need not read the entire text sequentially, as the chapters are arranged in a way that encourages readers to thumb through the different sections to learn more about their chosen topic.

Another noteworthy feature is the glossary of names found at the end of this book. Many of the names encountered in the text will be well known to readers, while others may be less familiar. This pocket guide explains each figure's role in history and relationship with Scriabin. More importantly, this glossary is intended to teach non-Russian speakers how to correctly pronounce the names of these figures who played such important roles in Russian music history. The beginning student of the Russian language quickly learns that accents in names such as Safonov, Isakovich, and Sabaneev fall in places that elude the intuition of native English speakers. These encyclopedic entries will allow readers to more easily recognize these names.

Most importantly, this book offers a corrective for the misinformation that has saturated the English-language literature on Scriabin. Over the last century, an aura of mystique has surrounded Scriabin and glamorized his life and creative aspirations, but obscured certain facts of his life and legacy. Sifting through the literature, readers are hard pressed to distinguish truth from fiction when they read that he was mentally ill, a genuine synaesthete, autistic, an alcoholic, predatory toward women, a hypochondriac, or an artistic recluse. Such myths infiltrate the media that most directly feeds the public perception about such matters, namely, CD liner notes, program notes at concerts, and performance reviews.

The factual errors and misinformation in the literature often originated from Scriabin's biographers, especially Faubion Bowers (1917–1999), who wrote two major studies on the composer, *Scriabin: A Biography* (in 2 volumes, 1969) and *The New Scriabin: Enigma and Answers* (1973). Anyone reading the literature cannot escape Bowers' influence because he was the first to publish a modern biography of the composer in English. His books provided colorful anecdotes about Scriabin's personality and translations of primary sources that were otherwise inaccessible to those who could not read Russian. Quotes from his books are deeply woven into the secondary literature on Scriabin. Unfortunately for students and scholars, Bowers' books are both a blessing and a curse. Having no proper index makes information hard to find, short of physically searching through his books, and the absence of citations makes it nearly impossible to know the original sources of many of the quotes and information that he included.

In short, Bowers' books on Scriabin are blighted by serious problems of scholarship that undermine his authority. The British musicologist Gerald Abraham summed it up best in his review of Bowers' 1969 two-volume biography: "Mr. Bowers has had access to an unprecedented amount of rare material, and he has made an incredible mess of it."[9] Bowers invents conversations as if he were present in the moment and transcribed every spoken word straight from the source. His attempts at musical analysis unleash a torrent of poetic descriptors and buzzwords that dazzle the senses, but only scratch the surface in their descriptions of how the music works and what it means. To his credit, Bowers' evocative descriptions of Scriabin's music reveal his fondness for this repertoire. But his cultural insights are often risible and blur the line between fact and fiction. Take, for example, his description of the cultural climate that Scriabin encountered in America during his tour of the country in the winter of 1906–1907: "New York City was pretty much of an opera town. One night in December, 1906, someone counted that at that moment, 6,702 people were listening to opera."[10] Such fly-by-night observations are a common ingredient in Bowers' writings. Yet the concerns voiced by Abraham and other reviewers over Bowers' standards of scholarship have done little to diminish the immense presence his writings have had in the literature. Until the definitive biography of Scriabin appears, Bowers' books are not going away anytime soon. If approached with the proper precautions, however, his books can be useful guides for chronicling Scriabin's life. But the astute researcher will take Bowers' anecdotes, quotes, and claims with a grain of salt, and independently verify each and every one of them.

Keeping the problems with Bowers' books squarely in mind, we have made every effort to verify the original sources of quotations and other facts contained in this book, and properly cite them. The endnotes at the end of this book contain references for many important primary sources, and serve as bread crumbs to guide future investigations. Indeed, plenty of stones remain unturned for the modern historian who is interested in studying Scriabin. The current view of the composer has evolved considerably from the image that persisted of him around mid-century; that of an eccentric figure whose flights of fancy derailed what otherwise would have been a promising career. Today, Scriabin is hailed as an innovative pioneer of modern harmony and multimedia art, and the demand for new studies of his creative process and output is greater than ever.

Finally, this book aims to close the gap between rigorous and often daunting scholarly studies and journalistic yarns. Modern insights about Scriabin's life and music gained traction in the West during the 1970s, when the composer underwent a tremendous revival of interest due to the centenary of his birth in 1972. Since that era, a deluge of writings has appeared in English, especially among graduate students writing dissertations and theses. This extensive body of scholarship has focused on three areas of study: theory and analysis, performance practice, and cultural context.

The unfortunate reality is that much of this literature is written for specialists, and years of training are required to benefit from such writings. Few enthusiasts outside of the academic community even seem aware of this vast repository of literature, or know how to access it. The polarity between these two bodies of writings has hindered the widespread understanding of Scriabin's music. The time has come for a new approach that does not misrepresent historical facts for the sake of sensationalism, or exclude readers due to the specialized nature or technical language of the text. This book is meant to be one such offering, which occupies a middle ground between scholarly research and publicly accessible information on Scriabin.

Scriabin will always remain a secondary figure in classical music history. Never will he attain the name recognition of Bach, Beethoven, or Brahms. Scriabin is a protean figure whose music can mean many different things to many different people. His multifaceted legacy exemplifies the triumphs and perils of changing cultural and political tides, and precarious personal tastes. We are finally on the path to judging the true measure of his historical significance by understanding more clearly how his contemporaries saw him, and what his music means in the context of his age and our own age. Scriabin's music will reward the curious listener who looks past the canonized works of the common practice period, and seeks to discover what treasures lie in the annals of music history. There they will find a rare form of escapism in Scriabin's music and be transported into a colorful world full of imagination and mystery. To experience Scriabin's music in its full glory requires a leap of faith into the wondrous unknown. Let this book be the beginning of that journey.

Acknowledgments

Writing this book has been a labor of love, and I am very thankful for the assistance of several people who helped me in its creation. In particular, I would like to thank the editorial team at Rowman & Littlefield and especially Bennett Graff for his constructive feedback and the organizational tips he offered in the early stages of this manuscript. I am also sincerely grateful for my editor, Natalie Mandziuk, and her assistant editors, Mary Malley, Monica Savaglia, and Kathleen O'Brien, for being on hand to answer my many questions along the way.

Individuals working at various businesses and academic institutions helped me obtain the permission rights to reproduce historic images and quote passages from important sources, and including these documents has immeasurably enriched this book. These sources bring this rich history to life, making mythic events seem more tangible. I am especially appreciative of the efforts of the following people: Sally Childs-Helton at Butler University in Indianapolis, who sent me information about the Festival of Romantic Music that was inaugurated in the late 1960s; Rob Hudson and Kathleen Sabogal at the Carnegie Hall archives, who dug up the original concert bill from the world premiere of *Prometheus* with colored lights; Donald Minildi and Maxwell Brown at the University of Maryland, who scanned photos of Raymond Lewenthal from their archives; and David McKnight at the University of Pennsylvania, who allowed me to reproduce an image from Leopold Stokowski's personal score of the *Poem of Ecstasy*. Thanks also extend to Maira Canzonieri at the Royal College of Music in London, who provided me with important biographical information on the British pianist and Scriabin devotee, Edward Mitchell. Teresa Hale and Gene Zacharewicz of Universal Music Group generously granted me the rights to reproduce the "First Flower Child" decal featured in Hilde Somer's first recording of Scriabin's piano music. I would also like to thank Kathleen Blind from Dover Publications for granting me and my coauthors permission to use published material from

Faubion Bowers' revised second edition of his biography of Scriabin (1996). Finally, dozens of librarians across the country patiently answered my research inquiries, and pointed me in the right direction in my searches for sources and leads.

Numerous friends, family members, coworkers, and peers also lent their time and energy reading over early drafts of these chapters. The final manuscript is immeasurably richer and smoother due to their suggestions. Chief among these readers were Sandra Ballard, Matthew Bengtson, Ellon Carpenter, Anna Gawboy, Matthew Groves, Rebecca Mitchell, Jerome Stanley, and Xenia Tashlitsky. Ms. Tashlitsky deserves special praise for her eagle-eyed proofreading and her many insightful suggestions on matters of style and content. As my chief Russian-language consultant, Ms. Tashlitsky also ensured accurate translations of primary source materials, and assisted with the pronunciation guide found in the glossary. I would also like to express my immense gratitude for the unwavering support of my wife, Lisa Tsai.

Finally, I would like to express my appreciation for my coauthors, John Bell Young and Matthew Bengtson, who lent their unique insights, time, and energy to this project. I could not be more fortunate in having such experienced and knowledgeable collaborators. In closing, I would like to recognize the Scriabin Society of America as a vitally important institution that in recent years has fallen inactive and needs to be revived as a focal point for the thousands of Scriabin enthusiasts in North America. In its place, the newly formed Scriabin Association has been recently founded in England, and this organization will hopefully encourage international collaboration between Scriabin scholars and enthusiasts across the globe.

—Lincoln Ballard

The quality of my writing, and indeed all of my work on Scriabin, would have been greatly compromised without the great assistance of many people. I am indebted to readers who have volunteered their time and energy to offer many helpful suggestions, both minute and large-scale, on these chapters. These include especially Marcus Blunt, Jay Reise, Sharon Levy, Aleksandra Vojcic, and Dayton Hare.

I would like to thank my numerous and knowledgeable Scriabin-loving friends, who have enriched my substantive understanding of this composer via both printed word and personal discussion. In addition to the two coauthors, these include Jay Reise, Marcus Blunt, Anna Gawboy, Rebecca Mitchell, and Arthur Greene.

Many librarians have come to my aid at crucial moments in this project. Thanks to Jamuna Samuel for helping with access to materials at an important time, and to Jason Imbesi for his assistance with locating hard-to-find scores in a timely manner. Thanks to Jane Gottlieb from the Juilliard Library for permissions to reprint portions of the Juilliard Manuscript Collection.

I owe a great thank-you to all my piano teachers with whom I have had the good fortune to study, all of whom in their own way encouraged and developed my Scriabin enthusiasm in its various stages, especially Maryanne Dalton, Patricia Zander, and Ann Schein. Thanks to Robert Levin for having carefully read my first undergraduate writings on *Prometheus*, offering both encouragement and substantive critique.

I would like to thank numerous concert presenters who offered their enthusiastic support of my performances of Scriabin's music. Especially, a big thank-you and hats off to Jarek Kotomski for the vision and energy it took to organize and bring off the extraordinary "Scriabin in the Himalayas" festival in Ladakh, India.

I owe special thanks to my family for their essential support of all these endeavors, without whom none of these events could have come to pass. I owe special loving thanks to both my parents for having gotten to know this music over so many years, for reading my chapters and offering many good suggestions on them. I owe a big thank-you to my wife Seohee for her selfless help with technical matters, and to both her and my children for putting up with all the time and care I have devoted—especially in many long evenings—both to the editing of recordings and to the writing of these pages.

Finally, I owe special thanks to coauthors John Bell Young and Lincoln Ballard. For John's extraordinary kindness and support, his many bits of sound advice, and his faith in my work on this project, I am both honored and deeply grateful. And to Lincoln, without his endless resources of Scriabin information, his hundreds of e-mails and phone calls, patience and careful reading, my work would surely be much the weaker in many respects.

—Matthew Bengtson

I am indebted to the staff of the Scriabin Museum in Moscow for their help in assembling much of the research material for this book, and for allowing me to examine Scriabin's autograph scores, correspondence, and personal library. Among my many friends and colleagues in Russia, I would especially like to thank the late professor Margarita Fyodorova of the Moscow Conservatory, who was not only one of the greatest interpreters of Scriabin, but a remarkable teacher and scholar.

For their help in tracking down rare scores, biographies, and letters of Scriabin, my thanks to the late musicologist Rostislav Zdobnov in Moscow; V. V. Rubtsova, editor of Muzyka publications and Russia's preeminent biographer of Scriabin; the late pianist and professor emeritus Nathan Perelman of the Leningrad Conservatory; Sergei Dzhevanovsky, director of the Glinka Choir College in St. Petersburg; professors Ekaterina Murina and the late Sofia Khentova of the Leningrad Conservatory; and in the United States, the pianist Dmitri Rachmanov and Dr. James Baker, chairman of the Brown University Department of Music; and especially the late critic, pianist, and editor of Scriabin's earliest compositions, Donald Garvelmann. Thanks, too, to the St. Petersburg Composers Union, and to the Scriabin Society of Russia and its director, Alexander Serafimovich Scriabin, for their generous help. Warmest thanks, too, to Scriabin's late daughters, Marina Scriabine of Cap d'Ail, France, and Elena Scriabin Sofronitsky in Moscow, for their generous help and for providing me not only with many rare materials, but also their personal recollections.

This study would not have been possible without access to materials and documentation at the following libraries: the Leningrad Conservatory Music Library; the Moscow Conservatory Music Library; the library of the St. Petersburg Institute of Culture; the Lincoln Center Library for the Performing Arts; the Pierpont Morgan Museum; the Library of Congress; the Orwig Music Library at Brown University; and the Firestone Library at Princeton University. I am indebted to the Staffordene Foggia Library of Hernando County, in Spring Hill, Florida, which lent me the use of its computer, and a much-needed Interlibrary loan system, to complete much of my research at a time when I sorely needed it.

—John Bell Young

1

En Garde or Avant-Garde? Exploding the Scriabin Myth

John Bell Young

> *Facts don't exist until man puts into them something of his own, a bit of free human genius—of myth.*
>
> —Boris Pasternak, *Dr. Zhivago* (1957)
>
> *In those mysteries of antiquity there was real transfiguration, real secrets and sanctities... all our little saints of today have forgotten their power of old.*
>
> —Alexander Scriabin

In the century that has passed since he composed his last work, the fragile and desolate *Poème* Op. 74 No. 2, Alexander Scriabin has remained an enigmatic figure in the history of music. He has been sanctified and demonized, extolled and condemned, revered and ridiculed. Vilified as a decadent in the early years of the Stalin regime, his works were resurrected in the early 1930s as the subject of a State-sanctioned theoretical study by a group of Bolshevik-era intellectuals, the GIMN (Gosudarstvenii Institut Muzikalnoi Nauki—The State Institute of Musical Science). Public sentiment in the USSR, however, had turned against Scriabin by the 1930s. Even Shostakovich, the darling of early Soviet realism, shunned Scriabin as "our bitterest musical enemy" in 1931, citing publicly his distaste for the music and thus legitimizing to this day a rejection of Scriabin's compositional language in certain circles of the musical avant-garde. "But it's all one chord!" protested one acquaintance of mine, a Soviet conductor, on more than one occasion.

Attempts to reconcile the principal elements of Scriabin's creative personality—compositional technique and spiritual aspirations—have met with varying degrees of success. Even theorists favorably disposed toward the music have chosen to toe academia's official party line: the music, not the mysticism, is all that matters. A whole matrix of compositional analyses has fathomed the instability of Scriabin's harmony of saturated dominants. These analyses, for all their variety and sophistication, are perhaps no less rich than Scriabin's compositional vocabulary, and have enhanced the overall appreciation for his work. Figuring prominently among the theoretical literature are works by Varvara Dernova, James Baker, Gottfried Eberle, Hanns Steger, and George Perle.[1] Manfred Kelkel's radical approach to an analysis of chordal complexes in Scriabin's late works formed the subject of his 1971 essay, "Les esquisses musicales de l'Acte Préalable de Scriabine," which caught the eye of the Scriabin Museum.[2] Twenty years later, the Museum put Kelkel's article on display, under glass, as part of the 1992 Scriabin Festival in Moscow.

Still, the majority of musicologists and biographers, upon whom the world has depended to decipher Scriabin's aesthetic, have dismissed his mysticism as pathological, egocentric, and unworthy of serious discussion. Even the most important narrative biographies—notably, those of Faubion Bowers, Igor Belza, and V. V. Rubtsova—while acknowledging the impact of Scriabin's spiritual beliefs on his aesthetic disposition, have supported prevailing theoretical opinion.[3] Still, other philosophically oriented studies such as those of Martin Cooper, Richard Taruskin, Ralph Matlaw, Manfred Kelkel, and Malcolm H. Brown, have substantially enriched the literature by combining theoretical analysis with cultural exegesis.[4] In these writings, Scriabin is viewed as a product of his time and national environment. Only one book, by Scriabin's friend and brother-in-law Boris de Schloezer, a would-be philosopher, attempted to evaluate with any seriousness Scriabin's mystical philosophy and its effect on his compositional approach.

What, then, remains to be written about Scriabin? In the absence of a psycho-semiology or a cinematic treatment, a fresh approach is needed; a critique that refuses to pigeonhole Scriabin as one thing or the other, as mystic or composer, but as a systole of a relatively new musical tradition that had its roots in ancient cultures, languages, and religions. Leaving aside for a moment the relevance of a performer's perspective, the time has come, in my view, to challenge traditional musicology with regard to the music of Scriabin. Thus do I indict the inflexible position that summarily rejects Scriabin's mysticism as materially irrelevant to his compositional techniques. I also question the wholesale dismissal of his music as having any relation whatsoever to ancient forms of Russian liturgical music. His works, to the extent that they symbolize his faith in the transfiguration of man, form a kind of hymnography in their own right. From this perspective, the music he composed in the final years of his life can be viewed as a single unified text, and an opportunity for personal and communal transcendence.

Whatever its allegiances, on one point musicology suffers no dissent. Nothing short of unimpeachable evidence is acceptable to demonstrate the influence of one musical style upon another. To establish the existence of such evidence, comparative analysis demands a taxonomy of technical procedures. Its plausibility relies on demonstrable parallels that unite methods of articulation, harmonic language, and rhythmic characterization across diverse compositional genres. Comparative analysis legitimizes appropriation as it conforms to the prevailing theoretical ideology that dictates its standards.

Yielding to the complexity of Scriabin's harmonic language and the importance of mysticism in the formulation of his aesthetics, theory has been compelled to reconsider the notion of influence as an instrument of musicological archaeology. It has been asked to gauge the relation between musical and nonmusical structures. This has provoked a certain academic reluctance to express the dialectic of the music's psychological dimensions, and led to the somewhat dismissive attitude that too often prevails among theorists to this day. Even attempts by musician-philosophers such as Theodore Adorno and Jean-Jacques Nattiez to elaborate on the sociology of music or a reception theory along semiological lines have been greeted with cynicism by pragmatists.

But there is no need to abandon hope where traditional methods fail to determine the relationship between aesthetic and social phenomena. The source of musicology's lack of confidence is a model of historical interpretation that characterizes history as linear and continuous. It interprets progress as the legacy of derivation, influence, and technique. Forgetting Grandfather Hegel, empiricism holds court at the sight of reified expectation: it refuses to divest itself of litanies, facts, targets, or descriptions. It extinguishes the sensual embers of musical experience in favor of sustaining a fiction *about* that experience. The domain of theory is abstract, not practical; it has no need for performers. As it disparages unsubstantiated opinion and assassinates intuition, musicology mocks initiative and settles for what it can deduce, not what it can discern. How it drags its feet behind philosophy and psychoanalysis in its campaign to ostracize discourse in favor of documentation! Not even Nietzsche, perhaps the most musical of all writers, whose iconoclasm compelled an anxious world to reevaluate the way it looked at art, has shaken musicology from its general malaise.

Scriabin was barely cold in his grave when musicology began to reinvent him for posterity. The Promethean vision that had inspired an entire generation was not to be tolerated in the new socialist state. Ironically, what had been the emblem of Promethean dignity—the free spirit enchained—was transformed by communism into a symbol of conformity. Firing the first volley in 1923, the Soviet musicologist I. I. Lapshin waxes ruthless in his indictment of apologists sympathetic to Scriabin's mysticism:

> Stupid proponents of Scriabin during his lifetime were inclined to wrap him in the mantle of a prophet, or better put, in the cloak of a charlatan . . . They preferred above all else his theosophic delirium, theurgic tricks and thaumaturgic manipulations. This was nothing less than consummate ignorance and a salon type of snobbishness. Scriabin's philosophical world-understanding was merely a convenient platform from which he fleshed out his artistic, intuitive world-view. We must look at his works for the key to his artistic feelings about the world, and not to his philosophy. Music alone is expressible in sounds. No system of thought is.[5]

Unless the world of twentieth-century art has missed something, music is nothing if not an expression of thought. An affective gestuary of wish fulfillment, music is an expression of a composer's psychological condition. This is nowhere more true than in the works of Scriabin. To ascribe "artistic feelings" solely to the products of his musical imagination ignores the *Weltanschauung* that made them possible. Worse yet, it shows a glib disregard, even contempt, for the thoughtful—and artistically wrought—conceptual scaffolding that supported Scriabin's philosophical doctrine. For all their shortcomings, his mystical beliefs were carefully considered. But Lapshin's conceit has its place, because it begs the question: What does Scriabin's music express?

This remarkable bit of musicological myopia is not limited to the dusty textbooks of Stalinist-era scholarship. In his *History of Russian-Soviet Music*, James Bakst writes:

> Scriabin's concern with the irrational reduced his musical imagery to vague allusions or hints. He attempted to describe emotional experiences divorced from reality. His music expressed purposeless, ecstatic intoxication and emotional energy without emotion. . . . When separated from its philosophical bases [Scriabin's music] is the creation of a refined ecstatic intellectual. . . . When one disregards Scriabin's fantastic ideas, there is left in the balance art whose heroic strivings represent a unique phenomenon in Russian music.[6]

Bakst's breathtaking generality of thought, so blithely alienated from the core of Scriabin's artistic aesthetic, would be laughable were it not for the fact that it proffers such a serious misunderstanding and thus perpetuates a false consciousness. When was the last time anyone ever heard of an emotional experience, whatever its etiology, divorced from reality or, at the very least, from its perception as reality? Evidently, Bakst labors under the impression that through-composed music by any composer worth his salt from Beethoven to Shostakovich can be effortlessly separated from the very "philosophical bases" that at once inspire it and inform its construction. What he fails to recognize is that to disregard Scriabin's "fantastic ideas" is to obliterate precisely that which makes his music (if not his philosophy) unique in the first place. Nor can the music's implicit teleology, to the extent it reflects the intentions of its composer, be characterized as purposeless. But the absurdity of Bakst's position, and others like it is exposed, as we shall see, by Vavara Dernova and Richard Taruskin, the most provocative of all Scriabin theorists, each of whom persuasively elaborates the near mathematical precision and psychological specificity of Scriabin's compositional vocabulary.[7]

Exemplifying musicology's late twentieth-century disposition, James Baker, in the afterword to his deftly detailed micro-analysis of Scriabin's harmony, *The Music of Alexander Scriabin*, writes:

> As we become more separated from the era in which he flourished, it is increasingly difficult to comprehend the grandiose self-image as a high priest of an art which would bring about the end of the world, uniting all mankind in an ecstatic and all-consuming burst

of energy. Although his visions were the primary motivation for his experimentation and innovation, what remains today is his music. Scriabin's art survives because he was a master of the craft of musical composition. Much as he might have been disappointed, it is through the study of his musical structures that we can best know him today.[8]

But is it really? An interpretation that pays homage strictly to the autonomy of compositional structure as the definitive measure of Scriabin's creative process ignores the breadth of his aesthetics. Where technical analysis is regarded as a panacea for meaning, a historically informed evaluation of Scriabin as a true child of his culture is dismissed as irrelevant. Aesthetic exegesis is here supplanted by an appreciation of craft.

But the mechanical character of this view attenuates what it expects to redeem. Of course, Adorno's obiter dictum that "[musical] meaning is revealed essentially in technical categories" is no less true for Scriabin than it is for Schoenberg or Beethoven.[9] Music's polemical nature, the destiny of its inner relations and the integration of its parts within the whole reveal a world that speaks for itself. A through-composed work satisfies its own logic while amplifying the psychological proclivities of its creator. Nevertheless, Scriabin's music demands more than lip service; it requires the elucidation of extra-musical dimensions that not only coexist with, but migrate into the corpus of the music itself. It is a sacramental sphere where music assumes a votive function that emulates prayer, and thus fulfills its own concept as the prolongation of a private epiphany. Not even the elegant and avuncular prose of critic Paul Henry Lang, musicology's answer to Gibbon, dares admit the cultural implications of Scriabin's art. Indicting him as a tragedy for whom experimentation was the final aim, and as "an artist not interested in national or social aims, in the music of the people, not even in the purely technical or formal problems."[10] Lang not only betrays a puerile distaste for the composer, but a spurious grasp of Russian history and culture. Scriabin was a product of Russia's Silver Age, and the roots of his occultism are implicitly social. It is all too easy to attribute Scriabin's beliefs to an escapist mentality, attenuated by societal instability, in a turbulent, pre-Revolutionary Russia.

Thus when Lang ridicules Scriabin for his experiments with sound and color, he misses the point. "Nor was the already immensely rich color scheme of the modern orchestra sufficient," he wrote. "Scriabin and his followers wanted actual light and actual color."[11] For all his erudition, Lang fails to observe that the notion of combining color with music has its origins in Greek Music Drama. The concept was also a metaphor for the Symbolist doctrine of correspondences that expressed itself as synesthesia, a mélange of the senses where tone is perceived as color. Synesthesia itself was a subtext of Greek dramaturgical practices. As Nietzsche observed:

> The music that was written [in antiquity] ended by pleasing not the ear but the eye. The eye was to admire the composer's contrapuntal skill; the eye to recognize the fitness of the musical expression. How was this accomplished? The written notes were actually colored, to correspond to the colors of the objects spoken in the text: green for plants, fields and vineyards, purple at the mention of the sun. It was literary music, music to be read.[12]

What this amounts to is a sort of affective animism that invested individual tones and modalities with associative meanings. Romanticism held no monopoly on the idea, which enjoyed a long life in the household of Symbolism; it is echoed in the musical "speech" and proportion theory of the Baroque era as well.[13] Even in those days, components of a composition were assigned moral values or imbued with an ersatz naturalism. And who can forget that chromaticism, tonality's calling card, is a derivative of the Greek word for color? As for Paul Henry Lang, one can only surmise that his omission was deliberate, given the smoldering repugnance he harbored for Scriabin. Then again, Lang's distortion of historical perspective is characteristic of one who disparages atonality as unmusical and Mahler's *Das Lied von der Erde* as "a lack of cohesion and aesthetic unity."[14]

In the intransitive and frequently unstable hover that characterizes his harmony, Scriabin invented the technical means to exploit an act of cultural solidarity. With this he fully expected to consummate the relation between philosophy and music. Musicology's determination to sever the connection between them in the interest of technical exposition is to disavow Scriabin's voice in the Russian cultural ethos, and to negate its communal intimacy. Although he straddled the threshold of theurgic symbolism, Scriabin declined to commit himself to its doctrine, preferring to create his own. But he was hardly the anomaly whose art, as some believe, evolved mysteriously on the outside of his culture, but the locus of its aesthetic sensibilities. "Is it possible that 1 am not a Russian composer merely because I don't write overtures and capriccios on Russian themes!?" he once complained to his publisher, Mitrofan Beliaev.[15] Given the historical burden he was compelled to bear, perhaps he had no choice but to go his own way and express himself in the context of a false piousness.

No doubt this critical positioning of Scriabin within a discursive chain creates a parallax for his interpreters. But no amount of musicological strong-arming can dislocate him from the aesthetic orientation of his historical orbit. The extent to which his spiritual ideology distracts contemporary theory is indicative of *transitive significance*, where meaning is interpreted to conform to the prevailing tastes of an era. Perhaps for musicology the symbolic meaning of Scriabin's music, as well as its "authorial intent" have grown cold.[16] Writing on language and literature, the distinguished Soviet semiologist Mikhail Bakhtin observes the following with prescient intuition:

> Yet the artwork extends its roots into the distant past. . . . Trying to understand terms of the conditions of its most immediate time will never enable us to penetrate into its semantic depths. Enclosure within the epoch also makes it impossible to understand the work's future life in subsequent centuries; this life appears as a kind of paradox. Works break through the boundaries of their own time, they live in centuries, that is, in great time, and frequently (with great works, always) their lives there are more intense and fuller than are their lives within their own time. . . . It is frequently the case, however, that a work gains in significance, that is, it enters great time. . . . But the work cannot live in future centuries without having somehow absorbed past centuries as well. If it had belonged entirely to today (that is, were a product of its own time) and not a

continuation of the past or essentially related to the past, it could not live in the future. Everything that belongs to the present dies along with the present. . . . It seems paradoxical that . . . great works continue to live in the distant future. In the process of their posthumous life they are enriched with new meaning, new significance: it is as though these works outgrew what they were in the epoch of their creation.[17]

It is no longer reasonable to assume that Scriabin's creative development in the midst of revolution and immanent social collapse provides sufficient data to evaluate the man or define his art. Nor does the rejection of his mystical conviction by a phalanx of theorists hail the end of perspective. Reliance on technical means alone to provide a sense of psychological and spiritual significance represses the vibrancy of the symbolic. Scriabin can no more be known by the prolixity of notes in a text or the complexity of his language than a man by his vital organs; any first-year medical student—or any reasonable person, for that matter—is bright enough to recognize the difference between a cadaver and a human being. The morgue into which a formalist analysis throws everything that Scriabin symbolizes reveals the essential poverty of its understanding. One gains an advantage over musicology and its self-appointed expertise where listening becomes dialectical, that is, a measure of discourse, and where criticism collapses, like light into a black hole, directly onto its object.

Where Bakhtin reckons no one is the origin of his own meaning—a heady thought indeed—the conductor and baroque music authority Nikolaus Harnoncourt configures the same idea, in an essay on baroque music, as practical advice for performers:

> If the music of the past epochs is in any way relevant to the present in a deeper and wider sense, if it is to be presented with its total message intact . . . [then] the understanding of his music has to be relearned from the principals that underlie its essence.[18]

Scriabin's message, febrile and symbolic, fathoms chaos as it tangos with Shiva. What socialism couldn't deliver in human relations—authenticity—Scriabin did in music. But its site is sound, its population counterpoint, and thus it encapsulates a paradise where a "society of freedom and love rises phoenix-like from the fires of revolution."[19]

* * *

If the prevailing view that Scriabin's mysticism is pathological and irrelevant to his music is to be exploded, the opinion of the formalist rear guard invites rebuttal on at least two fronts: (1) that his compositional language, which musicology envisions as technical rather than strategic, is substantially unrelated to ancient forms of liturgical music, particularly medieval Byzantine and Russian chant; and (2) that the spiritual dimensions of his aesthetic, which is mortgaged in part to Greek Music Drama, resist codification in compositional categories. Implicit in a critique that dares challenge the normative view is a threat to dissolve, like sugar in coffee, the formalist position that rejects Scriabin's mysticism as unnecessary to understanding, interpreting, and performing his music. Scriabin is an heir to the estate of Russian culture; his aesthetic is a descendant of the ceremonial structures of sectarian ritual, liturgical music, and Orthodox pageantry. The deftness and complexity of Scriabin's musical imagination inspires this critique. It relies on a tissue of critical strategies that draw on a broad range of musical elements (harmony, rhythm, form), and extra-musical disciplines (psychoanalysis, semiotics, history), while owing allegiance to none of them in particular. It is a movement away from chronological narrative, such as that of a biographical treatment, and toward an explicative approach that invites the reader to "jump" into the text at any place, any time.

But rest assured that obscure motivic parallels which evoke a superficial resemblance of compositional genres, or between unrelated classes of experience, are rejected as an oversimplification and find no sympathy here: comparative analysis is exiled as a tool of musical excavation. Moreover, any suggestion that would beatify Scriabin's music as something more "meaningful" than art is likewise banished. To do otherwise diminishes the integrity of its immanent structure and artistic value. That certain conclusions drawn by musicology are not uniformly convincing where Scriabin is concerned hardly justifies a complete abandonment of its methods. After all, analysis frees an interpreter to trace a work's formal components, to contemplate the inner logic that relates its parts, and to map out its performance. It also provides a model for a musical grammar that compels a performer to disentangle, contemplate, and reintegrate complex compositional structures. And yet, while theoretical models may describe music, they do not necessarily explain it. For the nonexpert, theory wraps a language around music and fails to deliver him into musical experience, into its inner sanctum of expressive conflicts, enigmas, and digressions. If Scriabin is to reward the listener, his music requires a fresh approach to interpretation that assimilates idiosyncrasies and looks behind the notes toward the vast cultural mosaic that engenders them. Imagine, then, a critique that intervenes in the dynamic that identifies music with mystical revelation. What drives such an analysis, to the extent that it is nonidentical with that experience, is an action (*dyeistviye*) or willfulness that propels the listener into the work, allowing him to "think along with what he hears."[20]

Action, a central concept in Scriabin's creative lexicon, resides in the domain of affective orientation, that is, in an interpreter's disposition toward music. Like Greek Music Drama, action solicits participation in the unfolding of compositional events. It inscribes intuitive responses within the living body—the performance—of the musical text and thus becomes a part of the counterpoint. Action is the defining moment of musical cognition when idea, sound, and flesh unite and engrave themselves in compositional texture, significance, and destiny. Past, present, and future converge, fade, and disperse in a sonic matrix where each moment is pregnant with the next, where every pitch is engorged and bursts with the cumulative energy that sired it. For Scriabin, action is not the limit of musical experience, but a fertility rite all its own.

As Nietzsche pointed out, in Greek Music Drama "the emphasis is on undergoing rather than doing, on pathos rather than action."[21] This philological expansion of the concept is no cause for alarm. On the contrary, toward the end of the candle flicker by which a life can be measured, action, by Scriabin's definition, embraces consciousness and nirvana, humanity and artistic synthesis, apocalypse and Armageddon. Enlightenment at last achieves embodiment in the corporeal as the defining (or at least, the ideal) principle of his aesthetic. In this realm, musical criticism, if it is to do justice to his work, becomes explicative, not descriptive. It navigates the seas of Scriabin's aesthetic strategies and harvests the "grain of his voice," to paraphrase Rolande Barthes.[22] It is an X-ray that irradiates the sinewy prism of his harmony, oscillates in the kingdom of the verb, shuns the adjective, and celebrates the rhythmic vitality of the active voice.

In Scriabin's cosmos of harmonic paradox, symbolism is ambiguous and does not aspire to fixed, immovable values. The motive—a rhythmically organized, compositionally integrated, and purposely designed unit of affect—is no longer maintained by Scriabin solely in the service of structural integrity. In his music the motive assumes a heightened symbolic function, one that cathects his works with emotional energy and languor; will and desire are reproduced as a reservoir of dynamic tensions, which the listener experiences as affect. Thus it is the phenomenal world that becomes a metaphor for his music, and not the reverse. Sequential streams of dominant quality harmonies, transpositionally invariant and enharmonically juxtaposed, express ambiguity and destabilize his music. In this sense Scriabin had more in common with the Russian Imagists and their doctrine of variable meaning than he did with the theurgic symbolists, who shaped the arts and philosophy in Nicholavean Russia.

INTONATSIIA

Indispensable to any interpretation of Scriabin's music is Russian intonation theory, or *intonatsiia*. Though documented at the turn of the twentieth century by a musicologist, Boleslav Yavorsky, as a tool of compositional process and interval theory, *intonatsiia* embraces something broader: the principles of linguistic theory. As early as 1860, Modest Mussorgsky embraced the musical properties of speech as an opportunity to exploit new avenues of artistic expression: "If we could register an emotional intonation with absolute accuracy and artistic instinct," he confided to a colleague, "then perhaps we could capture our thought processes as well."[23] In its attempt to adapt one genre (music) to another (speech), *intonatsiia* provides a mechanism for the expression—and experience—of musical affect. The concept proposes an aesthetic connection between musical expression and speech, and refers to the dynamic tension between notes. While its domain is that of microdynamics, *intonatsiia*'s aim is to sculpt the musical line and assimilate the inflections in speech. From this perspective, *intonatsiia* is an interpretive tool that allows the performer to illuminate the psychological dimensions of a composition.

The interval, or distance between two pitches, is the breeding ground of *intonatsiia*. Viewed as the science of musical articulation, *intonatsiia* refers to the attraction one tone has for another. The nature of that attraction is precisely what we've been speaking of all along, namely, an affect. Yavorsky aptly described this phenomenon as the principle of *auditory gravitation*.[24] When two or more pitches are horizontally arranged and sequentially distributed, they form independent units of rhythm, or motives, which articulate, drive, and cumulatively give shape to a work. They inform a composition's unique design as they impart sense to its form. These are, in effect, the musical cells of a composition. In the rhythmic play of these tiny compositional motors lurks the source of all musical declamation: here music whispers, cajoles, sighs, rages, ponders, shouts, seduces.

In *The Structure of Musical Speech* (1908), Yavorsky, one of Scriabin's earliest propagandists and theorists, describes *intonatsiia* as "the smallest basic tonal form in time," and its role in "the disclosing of the expressivity of a tonal cell, that is, the unfolding in time of the potential energy of a system."[25] Equally significant is his observation that "the comparison of two tones (or moments) . . . that have different gravitations [suggests] the expressiveness of speech, the transfer of its sense and character."[26] But in the view of Yavorsky's colleague, Boris Asafiev, *intonatsiia* was also a distillation of social conditions that could be expressed symbolically in music. As Asafiev noted:

> The people, the culture and the historical epoch define the states of intonations, and through intonation are determined by both the means of musical expression, and the selection and inner connection of musical elements. The musicians must hear and evaluate intonations . . . as music of a concrete social environment, constantly changing its formations.[27]

Divorced from the word, as it is in instrumental music, *intonatsiia* is the realm of innuendo and bridges the gap between music and social (behavioral) conventions. Asafiev's observations anticipate, by several decades, the theory of the renowned Russian semiologist Mikhail Bakhtin (1895–1975), whose concept of "great time" owes allegiance to that of intonation theory.[28] What concerns us are not the notes themselves, but what occurs between them. Intervallic space is rarely if ever empty, but a kind of gravitational field in which tones emerge, collide, and resurface. If I may indulge a parallel with the world of physics, such intervallic space can be viewed as the "dark matter" of music. Each pitch is a repository of cumulative energy, pregnant with the one that follows. Like the neural network of the brain, *intonatsiia* is a synaptic process that telegraphs meaning across distance. Purged of the word, which in speech plays host to intonation, music gives sanctuary to affect and inflection. Silence and distance, while properties of *intonatsiia*, are not identical to it, but a measure of its inflective potential. Thus *intonatsiia* is to music what light and shadow are to painting: a means of determining perspective. It relies on an exponential procedure that gauges dynamic perspective and renders affective expression intelligible.

As a concept that accounts for the relevance of musical expression, its historical locus, and the development of a culture, *intonatsiia* may provide a key to understanding and performing Scriabin's music in the context of his strongly held personal beliefs and aesthetic philosophy. It is in this spirit—where *intonatsiia* informs the analysis of musical expression—that the extra-musical dimensions of Scriabin's art can be evaluated, and the principles of a performance practice can be articulated. That Scriabin embraced mysticism as a measure of his creative vision is no reason to dismiss his extra-musical beliefs as invalid. In any case it is unlikely that his harmony evolved in a vacuum. Though often characterized as "perfumed" or "exotic," he rejected Russian folk music as a source of motivic inspiration, although this alone would have been enough to distinguish him from his Western European contemporaries. But upon closer investigation, his harmonic and rhythmic language had religious roots which beg the question: Did the ceremonial practices of Russian Orthodox Christianity, together with the Byzantine and medieval liturgical chant that ruled Russian musical life for centuries find a sympathetic (and perhaps secret) admirer in Alexander Scriabin?

For Scriabin, *intonatsiia* was a musical field theory of perpetually expanding and contracting sororities, a "continuous expansion of all musical parameters."[29] A vestige of its archaic heritage, the Scriabinian motive, is an enigma, an intonational archetype, an ontological emblem of his culture. He elevated it to the status of an icon, an expressive systole of an aesthetic philosophy so grand it was capable of satisfying its own concept within and beyond compositional categories. There is something egalitarian about the cozy comradeship of Scriabin's intonational and motivic universe. His late works have not so much been shorn of their individual character as purged of anything that might threaten to differentiate them. "Music," he said, "takes on idea and significance when it is linked to one, single plan within the whole of a world viewpoint."[30] This provided him fertile ground upon which to sow the seeds of his Promethean ideology. Here, Scriabin, the fervid antirationalist, could play God in his field of dreams. "One is all, all is one" might well have been his properly panenhenic credo.[31] "I am but the translator," he proclaimed; thus spake Scriabin, the pied piper of nature mystics.[32]

A strict, non-dualist interpretation of Scriabin's solipsism, particularly in the context of the Eastern philosophies and theologies to which he aspired, would likely expose his failure to annihilate the ego through music and thus transcend the phenomenal world, insofar as he conceded its existence at all. At the same time, his much-publicized longing for the transfiguration of man through artistic synthesis evoked an autochthonous formation, a Supreme Being or "act" (*dyestviye*). While seeking God, Scriabin also aspired to His omnipotence. But Scriabin's view of himself as God was not so much a contradiction in terms as it was an abstraction, a mask for what he really felt: at-one-with-the-world. If it was by means of some abstract multiplicity that he fulfilled (expressed) himself, personally and aesthetically, and if the characteristic fullness of that experience mistook itself for omniscience, it also provided the principal source of his creative energy: delusion.

Here then was the dynamic *idée fixe* of a refractive consciousness that distilled panenhenic experience and configured meaning into the innumerable shades of affect that constitute musical substance. Invested with magisterial potency and symbolic power, each of his late works—those composed after 1905 (perhaps not coincidentally in the wake of the tragic events that very year at the Winter Palace, which eventually led to revolution)—can be interpreted as an individuated vibration in a vast musical space that risks emasculation if disembodied from the all-embracing spiritual ideology that informs it. Thus, a unification theory that seeks to connect Scriabin's late works motivically has provocative implications for interpretation and performance.

Imprisoned by traditional approaches that attempt to distinguish the mystic from the musician, and a narrow perspective that holds history hostage to continuity, Scriabin has been suffocated, by his apologists as well as his detractors, in a labyrinth of theoretical abstractions and picturesque narrative biography. With all the short-sighted bravado of Kutuzov's army at the Battle of Borodino, musicology beats no retreat from its entrenched position: a reluctance to acknowledge, unequivocally, that in the household of symbolism and psychology, Scriabin's music is inseparable from the spiritual ideology that informs it. Mystery, sanctity, myth, and transfiguration seek symbolic expression in the music of Scriabin. These are the metaphors of his legacy. Perhaps the "oohs" and "aahs" intoned by the chorus at the close of *Prometheus: Poem of Fire*, Scriabin's last complete work for orchestra, are more than a prescient echo. They form a motivic mantra, an archaic shudder that sings to the Russian soul. Thus, when Andrei Bely resonates the collective unconscious in the eerie alliteration of *St. Petersburg*, he too alludes to the shadowy origins of the creative spark, to the gift of Prometheus:

> Those who ventured at nighttime into the open suburban spaces heard a persistent moan with stress on the note "Oo." "Oo-oo-oo-oo" sounded in the open spaces. It was a sound from some other world and it attained a rare strength and clarity. "Oo-oo-oo-oo" . . . such was the sound that came, not too audibly from the fields on the outskirts of Moscow, Petersburg and Saratov . . . Did you hear this October Song of the year 1905?[33]

I

ENCOUNTERING SCRIABIN

Lincoln Ballard

# 2

Life, Legacy, and Music

If any classical music composer fits the profile of a mad genius, it would be the Russian pianist Alexander Nikolaevich Scriabin (1872–1915). He had one of the most colorful personalities in music history, and he interpreted his Christmas Day birth as a sign of his divinity. Scriabin's insistence on the strength of his creative powers, however, left him subject to ridicule, and hindered the widespread acceptance of his music. After all, a man who asserted, "I am God. . . . I am the instant illuminating eternity, I am the affirmation, I am Ecstasy" could never write any music with substance, or so his detractors have argued. The composer's friend, Leonid Sabaneev, a distinguished music critic in his own right, argued that in order to understand Scriabin's music, "one had to believe that he was a prophet, and that his music was a sort of tonal pharmacopoeia on the subject of the premature production of the end of the world."[1] Whatever one's approach to this music may be, there is little doubt that Scriabin was a singular Russian artist whose art brilliantly reflected the cultural climate of his era.

The web of mystery that hangs over Scriabin's music and legacy has made it difficult for audiences to get comfortable with this music. Many of the myths and misunderstandings that have plagued his legacy are explored in this book. Even by 1954, the English writer and composer Terence White Gervais admitted in his *Grove Dictionary* entry on the composer that, "To discuss Scriabin's work is difficult at the present time, for very few have any detailed (or even general) knowledge of it."[2] Times have changed. A vast sea of recordings, literature, websites, and other media await the curious listener who is interested in Scriabin. But the difficulty in relating to his music remains, and is partly a product of the radical stylistic evolution that Scriabin underwent during his career. Scarcely can the listener believe that the same composer who wrote the charming waltzes and mazurkas of Scriabin's youth produced the near-atonal works of his final years. But such was the steady development of his art.

STYLISTIC INFLUENCES AND EVOLUTION

Scriabin's creative output is traditionally split into three periods. While such broad divisions of the creative estate make it convenient for historians to classify a lifetime's worth of music, they can be limiting in scope. Scriabin's stylistic evolution was gradual and organic; rarely can the listener discern any abrupt stylistic shifts between successive opus numbers. Nevertheless, such parsing of Scriabin's music helps differentiate his student works from his mature compositions, and illustrates his steady stylistic evolution during his foreshortened career.

From early in life, Scriabin was on a path to becoming a professional musician. He was the only child in an aristocratic (but untitled) family with a strong military background. His mother, Lyubov Petrovna Shchetinina-Scriabina (1849–1873), was a distinguished pianist and student of Theodore Leschetitsky. Such famous musicians as Tchaikovsky and Anton Rubinstein praised her musical talent. Lyubov died of tuberculosis only a year after her son's birth. Alexander's father, Nikolai Alexandrovich (1849–1914), was an interpreter and diplomat for the Russian embassy; he traveled frequently during Alexander's youth, never bringing along his family. Scriabin never knew his father well. In his father's absence, Alexander was raised by his aunt Lyubov (1852–1941), two grandmothers, and a great-aunt, all of whom endlessly pampered the boy. A modern biographer could discern a great deal about Scriabin's mannerisms and sensitivity during these formative years. Scriabin learned melodies by ear and could improvise by the age of five. Later, he studied at the Moscow Conservatory (1888–1892). His first serious compositions for piano were published in 1893 by Pyotr Jurgenson; they included the Valse Op. 1, three Morceaux Op. 2, ten Mazurkas Op. 3, two Nocturnes Op. 5, and two Impromptus Op. 7.

These early works showed promise, but Scriabin had yet to shed his idols' influences. The music of Chopin and Liszt exerted particularly strong holds over his early- and middle-period works. From these two composers, Scriabin gleaned their inventive treatment of motives and melodies, and their techniques for creating unique timbres and textures at the piano. So dominant were these two composers' influences that many commentators could not see past them when evaluating Scriabin's music.

The strongest early influence on Scriabin was Frédéric Chopin (1810–1849), whose stylistic fingerprint is evident in the lyricism and melancholic tinges that pervade Scriabin's adolescent works. Scriabin's early solo piano works use the same dance forms that dominated Chopin's music: preludes, etudes, waltzes, mazurkas, and polonaises. At times, this reliance on Chopin overshadows Scriabin's unique compositional voice. Vyacheslav Karatigin was a St. Petersburg critic and modern music advocate, and he was one of several commentators who noticed how much Chopin's influence had stifled Scriabin's personal voice. In his estimation, this influ-

ence "shows all too clearly through the wrapping of the Chopinized sound world
... here a convulsively compressed rhythmic figure, there a nervously, morbidly soft
suspension, now an explosion of pathos from heaven knows where, which in a flash
attains extraordinary intensity before petering out."[3] In his early, Chopin-inspired
works, Scriabin wears his heart on his sleeve. His music has all the trappings of the
late romantic style: lush and colorful chords, sentimental melodies, and traditional
forms. Despite Chopin's dominant influence on Scriabin's earlier compositions, it
lends these works a high degree of accessibility.

Also casting a shadow over Scriabin's compositions was the Hungarian pianist
Franz Liszt (1811–1886), arguably the greatest virtuoso pianist of the nineteenth
century. Nearly every pianist-composer after Liszt was indebted to his prodigious and
inventive technique, and Scriabin was not least among these. But Liszt was so much
more than a piano virtuoso; his bold experiments in form, harmony, and programmatic content and design left a decisive impact on music history. Scriabin studied
Liszt's works as a student at the Moscow Conservatory, and taught Liszt's music while
serving as a piano professor at the same institution. He also shared Liszt's flair for the
sinister side of life, as demonstrated by such works as the *Poème satanique* Op. 36 and
"Black Mass" Ninth Sonata Op. 68. For Sabaneev, Liszt's influence on Scriabin was
less apparent in pianistic textures; he saw Liszt's influence as manifested strictly in
music transcendentalism. "Unlike Liszt," Sabaneev wrote in a 1911 article, "Scriabin
did not become a spiritual composer, but was a composer of the spirit; he went down
the path of conscious theurgy."[4] The distinction here is between music that lifts the
spirit into a higher state of consciousness, versus music that serves the glory of God,
such as Liszt and Bach wrote. Those learning about Scriabin's works for the first time
may find these broad comparisons with Chopin and Liszt useful for getting their
bearings in the Russian composer's music. At the same time, one should not ignore
the individual talent that shines through in each page of music that Scriabin wrote
during his early years.

The professors who taught at Scriabin's alma mater, the Moscow Conservatory,
and its sister institution, the St. Petersburg Conservatory, must also be counted
as influences on Scriabin's style. The music of the Mighty Five was certainly very
much in Scriabin's ears, though few scholars have yet posited stylistic and topical
semblances. In particular, the exotic or fantastical element in these composers' works
found its way into Scriabin's music. In contrast to the stereotype of Scriabin as being antinationalist, as explored in chapter 7, much of his music has a distinctively
Russian flavor, in terms of its rich and colorful orchestration, repetition of themes,
and expansive melodies.

The year 1903 was a watershed in Scriabin's compositional and personal maturity.
He resigned from his teaching position at the Moscow Conservatory and separated
from his wife, Vera, to live with his mistress, Tatyana, who encouraged his philosophical interests and compositional focus. Through these life changes, Scriabin found
greater compositional assurance and maturity. That fateful year also saw the death
of his longtime publisher and mentor, Mitrofan Beliaev. Not coincidentally, around

the same time, Scriabin invested considerable energy into studying the writings of philosophers such as Nietzsche, Kant, and Schopenhauer, all of whom imparted strong influences on his musical development. His middle-period music pushed the boundaries of harmony and form in an attempt to express bigger and bolder ideas he had picked up from these philosophers. The musical influences of Chopin and Liszt were replaced by that of Richard Wagner, especially in his use of chromatic harmony to symbolize intense emotion. The pieces Scriabin wrote during this second period are characterized by rhythmic energy, chromatic inflections, and modulations to remote keys. Scriabin also abandoned the generic titles he preferred earlier in his career in favor of poetic titles such as *Poème tragique* (Op. 34), *Divine Poem* (Op. 43), *Fragilité* (Op. 51 No. 1), and *Danse languide* (Op. 51 No. 4).[5] "Poème" became his preferred designator for a musical composition, the notion of which suggested an extra-musical content that sought to express a philosophical ideal. The boundary between the composer's middle and final periods falls on his *Feuillet d'album* (Album Leaf) Op. 58 (1908).

The final phase of Scriabin's career gained traction when he returned to Russia in January 1909 after living abroad for five years in Switzerland, France, Italy, and Belgium. (He returned to live in Russia permanently in 1910.) The return of Russia's prodigal son was celebrated with several "Scriabin weeks" of public concerts that witnessed the Russian premieres of the *Divine Poem* and *Poem of Ecstasy*. The composer also delivered several critically acclaimed recitals of his newest piano pieces around Russia in the 1910s. So fervent was the support for Scriabin's music that several societies formed across Russia in an attempt to make his music better known and understood; these organizations flourished after his death in 1915.[6] Listeners were as enthralled as they were baffled by his late works. Scriabin had now established himself as the leading modernist of his generation.

This final period of the composer's career ends with the Five Preludes Op. 74 (1914), and these works represent a stylistic turn away from the mystic chord-based harmony of Op. 58. Despite earning the admiration of critics and becoming the darling of Russian musical culture, Scriabin's world shrank to an intimate circle of friends, and artistically he retreated into his private sphere. He had always been fiercely devoted to his own cause, and had not played other composers' music since his student days. But by the 1910s, no trace of any other composer's influence remained. He had successfully cultivated an original style that would be frequently imitated, but never matched.

MUSICAL IDEOLOGY AND AESTHETIC AGENDA

Just as poetry and philosophy were strong influences on two of Scriabin's musical idols, Liszt and Wagner, Scriabin turned to the writings of the poets and philosophers of his era to understand his role in the world and validate his theories of art. His coupling of music and philosophy proved to be one of the most controversial aspects of his reception. Philosophical ideas were often promoted as inseparable from his music, especially in his final three symphonies: the *Divine Poem*, the *Poem of Ecstasy*, and *Prometheus: Poem of Fire*. For these works, written programs were made available to audiences, either in the form of pre-published articles or concert program notes. The plot inevitably featured a protagonist who overcomes adversity and achieves communion with the divine. Scriabin's outspoken views on the importance of philosophy made it nearly impossible to ignore this aspect of his art. He was adamant that philosophy and, later, Theosophy were vital tools that helped him achieve his artistic goals. In many respects, these philosophical ideals formed the basis of his critical reception, especially in the West.

Many critics thought that Scriabin was either arrogant or insane. Eventually, this aversion to his philosophy led to its total removal from aesthetic consideration, and a rally cry to evaluate only the "music itself." To cite a few representative samples, in 1926, the British critic Alexander Brent-Smith offered this typical assessment:

> Has, then, Scriabin's work any permanent value? Until he fettered himself with theories to prove his independence of theories—Yes. Afterwards his work was . . . sterile and futureless. . . . He strutted in the garments of a fashionable philosopher, but his mind was made for small emotions and not for great thoughts. . . . It is because he offered muddle-headed reasoning seriously that the value of his later work is being suspected.[7]

Such was the general tenor of opinion toward the composer's philosophy, and in many respects that attitude persists today. In a 1957 article in the *Musical Times*, the English critic Rollo Myers averred that, "Scriabin's hysterical, almost maniacal outpourings offend our twentieth-century canons of taste, and we are right to question the propriety of trying, as he did, to mix music and metaphysics."[8] Similar assertions are rife in the literature. The critic William Mann explained the pall that was cast over Scriabin's reputation due to the importance he placed on philosophy:

> Over Scriabin's posthumous reputation hung the terrible accusations of Egotist, and Mystic, which more or less forbade actual examination of his work in strictly musical terms. If he had regarded himself as the new Messiah, his music could not possibly be real or good. The reasoning was false: if music is eloquent, the pretext for composing it, however unwelcome, is of no matter.[9]

But as John Bell Young points out in the opening chapter of this book, to ignore the cultural background that inspired Scriabin, and consider his music only in the abstract, limits our understanding of it. One should at least appreciate the fact that Scriabin highly valued philosophy in his creative ideology, even if one believes that an understanding of philosophy is not necessary to comprehend the music. Several scholars have produced insightful studies on the relationship between Scriabin's philosophy and music.[10] Only one study has dealt strictly with Scriabin's metaphysics: Boris Schloezer's *Skriabin: Lichnost, Misteriia* (Scriabin: Personality, Mystery [Berlin: Grani, 1922]), which was translated into English in 1987 by Nicolas Slonimsky, and published under the title *Scriabin: Artist and Mystic*. It comes as no surprise that Schloezer's book received mixed reviews, and several reviewers even questioned the value of its publication.[11]

Scriabin never subscribed to any one theory or principle; instead, he borrowed ideas from various philosophers. Two German philosophers left a decisive impact on his creative thinking: Arthur Schopenhauer (1788–1860), whose most important book was *The World as Will and Representation* (1818), and Friedrich Nietzsche, whose two writings, *The Birth of Tragedy from the Spirit of Music* (1872) and *Thus Spoke Zarathustra* (1883), also deeply impressed Scriabin. From Schopenhauer, Scriabin seized upon the idea of controlling one's fate and the world around one through personal will, and interpreting the creative act as a sexual metaphor. From Nietzsche, Scriabin viewed the world as a balance of Apollonian and Dionysian forces, the latter of which was an essential element of creativity. Scriabin saw himself as a Nietzschean Superman who possessed extraordinary powers that could alter human history. What he admired most about these philosophers was the pride of place they granted music in culture. Music was the highest of all art forms, and the only artistic medium capable of transforming life. A belief in music's transformative properties was espoused most notably by the Russian Symbolists, an artistic group of Scriabin's generation that the composer found eminently sympathetic to his creative ideas. Later in his life, Scriabin took credit for philosophical ideas he claimed were original, but he essentially recycled and blended theories that he had gleaned from the intellectual history of the past. There is little doubt, however, that Scriabin gained conviction in his powers as an artist from the writings of these two German philosophers.

Scriabin's philosophical outlook evolved substantially to arrive at his view of music as a vehicle for spiritual transcendence. Initially, he adhered to the teachings of the Russian Orthodox Church in which he was reared. At the age of twenty, however, he experienced a profound spiritual crisis that was triggered by a physical injury. In a brash attempt to prove that he was the best pianist in his class at the Moscow Conservatory, Scriabin prepared two fiendishly difficult works: Mily Balakirev's *Islamey* and Liszt's *Réminiscences de Don Juan*, the latter being the personal showpiece of his rival, Josef Lhevinne. But Scriabin nearly crippled his right hand by over-practicing, or perhaps exacerbating an old injury.

From this physical trauma came two results. Scriabin wrote his first Piano Sonata, complete with a Funeral March that recalls the Funeral March in Chopin's Sonata No. 2 in B♭ minor. The second consequence was that Scriabin questioned the omnipotence of God. Once he renounced God's all-encompassing power, he discovered within himself a creative potential that formed the basis of his new religion—the religion of art. In his private journal, Scriabin declared:

> Whoever it was who mocked me, who cast me into a dark dungeon, who raised me aloft only to hurl me down, who gave me gifts only to take them back, who lavished caresses on me only to torment me, I forgive you, I do not reproach you. I am still alive, I still love life, and I love humanity. . . . I will go forth to announce to everyone my victory over you and over myself. I will go forth to warn them not to place their hopes in you,

not to expect anything from life, except what they can create for themselves. I thank you for all the trials and tribulations to which you subjected me, for you gave me the knowledge of my endless power, my unbounded strength, my invincibility.[12]

Such confessions of self-empowerment appear throughout Scriabin's philosophical musings. These ideas at first found expression in his private journals, but gradually coalesced with his music and entered the public sphere. With the exception of the First Symphony, these writings never took the form of sung lyrics, and were instead ancillary ruminations about music's metaphysical meaning. Throughout his life, Scriabin felt compelled to articulate the *raison d'être* of his creative impulse, in music and in prose. Certain universal themes form a binding thread through his literary output, including divine will, individual effort, and the search for spiritual truth through Dionysian ecstasy. While some of these literary efforts, such as his accompanying poem for the *Poem of Ecstasy*, were initially presented alongside the music, eventually the composer suppressed these writings and let the music stand on its own merits.[13]

Around 1903, Scriabin's music became inextricably linked with philosophical ideas. In a conversation with Leonid Sabaneev, Scriabin remarked upon his new sense of purpose: "I cannot understand how to write *just* music now," he said. "How boring! . . . The purpose of music is revelation. What a powerful way of knowing it is!"[14] By "just music," Scriabin meant music intended for pleasure or entertainment, and lacking any deeper meaning or purpose. His philosophical orientation turned to *solipsism*: an idealist/subjectivist belief that posits that the self is all that can be known to exist. One essentially identifies oneself as the Godhead of one's own universe, the creator of all things. Scriabin wrote in a notebook from 1905–1906 that, "I am nothing. I am only what I create. All that exists, exists only in my awareness. All is my activity, which in turn is only that which my activity produces."[15] The Fourth Piano Sonata (1903) was a breakthrough composition of this period. A poem that accompanies the sonata describes the hero's striving toward a flickering star—a symbol of divine beatitude.

Scriabin's exposure to German philosophy and occult religions deepened when he met Prince Sergei Trubetskoi (1862–1905), the president of the Moscow Religious-Philosophical Society and a professor of philosophy at the Moscow University. This scholarly figure was an ideal guide for Scriabin's explorations of philosophical thought. Through his conversations with Trubetskoi and his interactions with other intellectuals, Scriabin came to regard solipsism as a limiting point of view. He refocused his efforts on achieving a sense of collective unity, or *sobornost*. It was the task of poets and composers to elevate humanity to a higher plane of existence and achieve a collective unity among the people. Through Trubetskoi, Scriabin also fed his fascination with the occult, and he attended lectures and séances by mystics and mediums in his search for a higher truth. Historian Martin Cooper observed that many early twentieth-century intellectuals turned to mystical and supernatural modes of inquiry to comprehend the world around them.[16] Participants rarely broadcast such activities because of the negative social stigma associated with them. But the occult lore that has surrounded Scriabin's legacy has allowed it to gain significant traction in popular culture, from the witchcraft said to be practiced in the Sixth and Ninth Sonatas, to more kitschy interpretations of the composer's occult associations found in works of popular fiction and other entertainment media.[17] Indeed, Scriabin's alleged associations with the occult have provided rich fodder for countless recordings, advertisements, and mass marketing of his music.

Mysticism was another powerful force on Scriabin's creative thought and aesthetic outlook. Of all the labels that writers have bandied about in their descriptions of Scriabin, "mystic" is surely the most ubiquitous. Most writers use this term to refer to a general interest in spirituality and a curiosity about Eastern religions like Buddhism and Hinduism. Briefly defined, mysticism is the intuitive sense that all things stem from a single source. To adopt a mystical point of view is to pursue the breaking down of material barriers and false constructs to apprehend the spiritual world that is thought to lie beyond the facade of reality. Mystics believe that the Ultimate lies within them, and that the union of the inner self with the Ultimate is the pinnacle of spirituality. Nothing mediates between reality and personal experience. The two are drawn together in an intimate encounter that is often described in sexual terms. In John Ferguson's classic text on mysticism, *An Illustrated Encyclopedia of Mysticism and the Mystery Religions*, he quotes French philosopher Victor Cousin (1792–1867), who defined mysticism as "substituting direct information for indirect, ecstasy for reason, rapture for philosophy."[18]

The mystical aspect of Scriabin's legacy took direct representation in his signature sonority, the "mystic chord," which is built from six notes (C-F♯-B♭-E-A-D) stacked in intervals of fourths instead of thirds. Scriabin's mystic chord defies the laws of major-minor harmony; its denial of the tonal system is a metaphor for the transcendence of consciousness, the surmounting of the little "I" for the greater "I." When applied in the context of his music, this chord leaves an impression of harmonic ambiguity or eerie stillness. As described by Matthew Bengtson later in this book, Scriabin's mystic chord is an enactment in musical terms of his philosophical ideals in the language of tension and release, and a foundational element of his mature compositional style. The mystic chord exemplifies Scriabin's interest in exotic modes of thought as well as nontraditional approaches to approximating an extra-sensory experience. One merely needs to play this unusual chord to conjure up Scriabin's exotic sound world.

Scriabin's thinking was very much a product of his time and place. His participation in philosophical inquiry was a fashionable pursuit shared by many of his contemporaries, especially the Russian Symbolist poets. Members of the *fin de siècle* intelligentsia were fascinated by new theories being proposed about individuals and their roles in society; these theories offered insights into the mysteries of the human mind and its untapped potential.[19] Having never received a formal education, Scriabin was self-conscious of the gaps in his knowledge, and wanted to appear erudite among his peers and maintain his upward mobility in social status. By exchanging ideas with others and absorbing various philosophical concepts and theories of his era, he became ever more focused on the quest to justify his artistic aims.

THE ALLURE OF THEOSOPHY

While German philosophy and mysticism exerted strong influences on Scriabin, his most public endorsement was to a spiritual philosophy that combined ancient wisdom with modern science and philosophy, called Theosophy. The *Oxford American Dictionary* defines Theosophy as "any of various philosophies professing to achieve knowledge of God by spiritual ecstasy, direct intuition, or special individual relations, especially a modern movement following Hindu and Buddhist teachings and seeking universal brotherhood."[20] Scriabin's participation in Theosophy and its influence on his music has been a popular topic, as discussed in numerous articles, websites, and recording liner notes.[21] Just as certain works by Mozart, such as *The Magic Flute*, featured Masonic symbols that reflected the composer's involvement with Freemasonry, so too Scriabin's late works have been thought to reflect his interest in Theosophy, especially *Prometheus: Poem of Fire*, which Faubion Bowers described as "the most densely Theosophical piece of music ever written."[22] Most writings on the connection between Scriabin's music and Theosophical principles provide no specific theoretical or stylistic details on how Theosophical principles are represented in his music, but a few scholars have provided clearer insights into this topic, most notably Anna Gawboy and James Baker.[23] Whatever the exact degree of influence, there is little doubt that Theosophy provided Scriabin with a rich lexicon of metaphysical concepts and New-Age buzzwords, such as "astral planes" and life cycles called "Manvantara," that codified his hazy philosophical notions into something resembling a doctrine. But as we explore in further detail in chapter 5, Theosophy was only one of several influences that left their mark on the composer's creative ideology.

Helena Petrovna Blavatsky (1831–1891) served as Theosophy's public figurehead, and along with Colonel Henry Steel Olcott, she founded the Theosophical Society in America in 1875 in New York City. The Theosophical Society flourished across Europe in the 1880s and 1890s. The Society is still active today, and boasts over 4,000 members worldwide. At a time when organized religion was being overshadowed by scientific advancements, modern psychology, and Eastern spiritual practices, Theosophy strove to synthesize the best qualities of each of these fields of thought. Following Blavatsky's death, the Society's figureheads in the United States became Annie Besant (1847–1933), who undertook several lecture tours up the East Coast and across the Midwest in the early 1900s, and Katherine Tingley (1847–1929), who presided over affairs on the West Coast. In 1900, Madame Tingley founded a Theosophical commune called Lomaland, which is perched on the shores of the Pacific Ocean in modern-day San Diego, California.[24] Scriabin never visited Lomaland, but had he traveled that far west during his tour of America in 1906–1907, and he might well have considered Lomaland a suitable alternative site for his intended mystical rite, the *Mysterium*.

Scriabin read and admired Blavatsky's Theosophical writings that had been translated into French, including *La Doctrine Secrète* (The Secret Doctrine, 1888) and *La Clef de la Théosophie* (The Key to Theosophy, 1889). Sabaneev and Schloezer recalled that the latter of these two volumes was a fixture on the composer's worktable. After reading this text in Paris in 1905, Scriabin revealed to his brother-in-law, Boris Schloezer, that through his readings of Blavatsky, he gained insights into an "interpretation of the cosmos." Scriabin confessed to Schloezer that, "I know that Mme. Blavatsky's ideas helped me in my work and gave me power to accomplish my task."[25] In addition to these quotes, evidence of Scriabin's interest in Theosophy is provided in his subscription to the Theosophical journals, *Le Lotus Bleu*, *Teosofskii Zhurnal*, and *Revue Théosophique Belge*. Historian Maria Carlson noted that members of the Russian intelligentsia used Theosophy's "cosmogenetic paradigm and its syncretistic doctrine to justify their own theories that true art was religious creativity, and that the true artist was a being in touch with the divine, and a high priest."[26]

However much Scriabin's involvement with Theosophy was touted in the popular press, the degree to which he seriously studied and understood Theosophical teachings, let alone incorporated its principles into his music, is doubtful. One website about the composer claims that Theosophy was "the intellectual foundation of Scriabin's musical and philosophical efforts."[27] Such statements are common in public sources, which tend to portray Scriabin's spiritual influences in a narrow light. In his writings on Scriabin, Faubion Bowers privileged Theosophy as a primary influence on the composer and downplayed other important influences, such as Russian Symbolism. A comprehensive look at Scriabin's aesthetic ideology must account for a broader range of influences. Boris Schloezer noticed that even though Scriabin read Theosophical publications, he only skimmed their contents, and that the journals to which he subscribed were left unopened for many months. Scriabin was especially dissatisfied with the minor role that music played in Theosophical teachings, as compared to those of Schopenhauer and Nietzsche. This contradicted his belief in music's exalted function. Nor should one believe that Scriabin's supporters subscribed to Theosophical ideas by default. The British biographer Arthur Eaglefield Hull confessed his ignorance on the subject, and concluded that, "Scriabin would hardly expect one to judge of Theosophy by his music. Still less is one able to estimate his music in terms of Theosophy."[28] Like his studies of Nietzsche and Schopenhauer, Scriabin's readings of Blavatsky were cursory. From these writings, Scriabin selected only what he needed to justify his own theories. But from Theosophy, Scriabin seized upon a central tenet: the transmission of esoteric knowledge gained from ancient wisdom. That principle would form the creative thrust of his last great creative project, of which many of his late piano works function as a giant mosaic or canvas of sound.

Life, Legacy, and Music

THE *MYSTERIUM*

Prometheus may be the most famous example of Scriabin's alleged application of Theosophical principles in his music, but a far more illustrative composition that borrowed ideas from Blavatsky's writings was a work that remained unfinished. Indeed, no project encapsulates Scriabin's career quite like the *Mysterium*. First conceived in 1902, around the time that Scriabin began studying philosophy, the *Mysterium* was to be the crowning achievement of his dream to create a collective artistic experience that would unite humanity. So grandiose was his conception that it could only have existed in the imagination. But what a fascinating concept it was, and it has been duly publicized since the composer's lifetime. Even now, the tale of Scriabin's *Mysterium* continues to fascinate us with its impossible dimensions and sheer impracticality, leading many to wonder whether this work was just a sign of the times or irrefutable proof that the composer had succumbed to megalomaniacal madness.[29]

The *Mysterium* was to be far more than a musical performance; it was to be an apocalyptic rite of Biblical proportions that would bring about the total destruction of the material world and spiritual transcendence of humanity. Scriabin imagined that the *Mysterium* would take place at a spherical temple in the foothills of the Himalayas, where attendees would be summoned to the event by clanging bells suspended by the clouds. The proceedings would have incorporated every available artistic medium—dance, theater, poetry, architecture, visuals, and even perfumes and odors—for a weeklong spiritual rite. Pillars of incense would glow and transmogrify, and performers and spectators would exchange looks and caresses. At the end of the seven-day cycle of events, matter would dissolve into spirit; the material world would be annihilated, and humanity would achieve spiritual communion with the divine. Thus Scriabin's *Mysterium* would surmount the limitations of art and become a religious act.[30]

In its timeline of seven days, the *Mysterium*'s cycle of events was borrowed from Blavatsky's teachings, as detailed by the musicologist Simon Morrison in his book, *Russian Opera and the Symbolist Movement* (2002). Blavatsky attached deep symbolic significance to the number seven. In her cosmology, there are seven planes of existence that correspond to the seven States of Consciousness in man. Many Theosophical principles follow a sevenfold pattern. Morrison pointed out that Scriabin's *Mysterium* sought to realize "the central task of Theosophical doctrine . . . to enable humanity to recognize that the material world is illusory and to commence the journey back into spirit."[31] He detailed how Scriabin's idea for the project accorded with the types of Symbolist mystery plays that such poets as Vyacheslav Ivanov discussed as an abstract possibility, but never actually planned to execute, as Scriabin did. Blavatsky was hardly the sole influence on Scriabin for his *Mysterium*. The initial idea for the piece also owed a debt to Wagner in his idea of a *Gesamtkunstwerk*, or "total art work," that would reunite the separate art forms into one powerful, potent whole. In his self-appointed role as a messiah, Scriabin believed that it was his destiny to create this mystical fusion of all the arts and senses, which was to bring about a spiritual catharsis for humanity. "He regarded himself as a solitary figure standing outside history, a mystical exception," wrote Schloezer.[32] Although Scriabin spent many hours discussing the *Mysterium* with his friends, deciding where the event was to be held (Scriabin even purchased land in Darjeeling, India), no musical score or stage directions were produced upon his death in 1915. Aside from a batch of sketches and a lengthy poetic text, the work existed only in Scriabin's mind as a great, unrealized possibility.

The only physical remnants of the *Mysterium* were thirty unedited pages of poetic text and fifty-four sketch pages for a related project that Scriabin titled *Acte préalable* (Prefatory Act). Around 1913, the composer declared that humanity was not spiritually prepared for the *Mysterium*, and he determined that a preparatory event was necessary before the *Mysterium* could be fully experienced. To some degree, he also realized the impossibility of what he had proposed. As a result, Scriabin began composing the Prefatory Act in the spring of 1914. Schloezer explained that Scriabin "felt that he had to accomplish something tangible, here and now, and so the *Acte préalable* became an abridged version of the *Mysterium*."[33] Scriabin not only convinced himself that the *Acte préalable* was attainable and imminent, but also that its creation was essential to create a new life in place of the crumbling existence around them.

The *Acte préalable* consists of three sections: Part I—*Universe*: the history of the cosmos and the appearance of humankind; Part II—*Mankind*: the history of humanity, the establishment of the harmony of the universe, and its degeneration as a result of greed and evil; Part III—*Transfiguration*: the evildoer is banished to the desert and encounters Death, who transforms his negativity into optimism, and encourages the evildoer to return to the world and enlighten the masses. Unfortunately, Scriabin's busy concert schedule left him with little time to work on the piece, and upon his death, the *Acte préalable* also remained incomplete. Several passages in his sketches for the Prefatory Act, however, show Scriabin working with chords that contain all twelve pitches of the chromatic scale. Although the *Acte préalable* was left in a fragmentary state, the Soviet composer Alexander Nemtin (1936–1999) dedicated twenty-eight years of his life to completing a version of what this work could have become. Starting in 1970, Nemtin fleshed out the skeletal sketch pages Scriabin had left behind. In 2000, Vladimir Ashkenazy recorded Nemtin's realization of the *Acte préalable* for the Decca label under the title, *Preparation for the Final Mystery*.[34]

In its extremism, the apocalyptic fervor of Scriabin's music and his pursuit of transcendental art was symptomatic of his age. Several other artists from that era in history were also engaged with creating huge musical canvases that commented on the history of time and the spiritual evolution of humanity. Like Scriabin's *Mysterium*, these colossal works were left unfinished by their authors, perhaps intentionally. Examples include Stephané Mallarmé's *Le Livre*, Charles Ives' *Universe Symphony*, and Arnold Schoenberg's oratorio, *Der Jacobsleiter*, to name a few. Scriabin's promise of spiritual renewal amid the turmoil of cultural and societal upheaval must have seemed like a new religion during its time. His message especially appealed to young artists working in societies that were left ravaged after the Russian Revolution and World War I. As fantastical as Scriabin's plans for the *Mysterium* were, it took a special force of conviction to enact ideas that had only been dreamed of by his contemporaries.

PRINCIPAL BIOGRAPHERS AND POSTHUMOUS RECEPTION

Few composers' receptions have been so sharply divided as Scriabin's. Even in his lifetime, his music provoked visceral hostility from some listeners and rabid enthusiasm from others. The battle lines between his dissenters and defenders are not easily drawn; many commentators revised their views on his music and historical significance as they aged and cultural values changed. The literature on his life and legacy spans multiple languages and includes biographies, memoirs, concert and record reviews, articles in scholarly journals and popular publications, music history surveys, blog posts, and personal websites.[35] A brief survey of Scriabin's posthumous reception and the writers who chronicled its vicissitudes will afford readers an appreciation for the extreme shifts in popularity his music has experienced over the last century.

The first books published on Scriabin were occasioned by his sudden death in April 1915. These studies have never been translated into English, but they laid the bedrock of knowledge that virtually all English-language writers before 1950 consulted for their own biographies of Scriabin. Leading the charge was Scriabin's fellow pianist-composer and close companion from 1912–1915, Evgeny Gunst (1877–1950). His 1915 book, *A. N. Skriabin i ego tvorchestvo* (Scriabin and His Creative Work), set a reverential tone for future writers by celebrating "the greatest genius of the twentieth century." Gunst supplied readers with rare details about Scriabin's childhood and education, and he promoted the composer's historical significance as equal to that of J. S. Bach, Beethoven, Chopin, and Wagner. Despite his book's hagiographic tone, it remained one of the early twentieth century's seminal texts on Scriabin.[36] The next year, the Moscow critic Yuli Engel (1868–1927) published extensive biographical material in a memorial issue of the journal, *Muzykal'niy sovremennik* (Musical Contemporary). Engel hailed Scriabin as a bold pioneer into "untold vastitudes, new worlds where no one had set foot before him."[37] That same year saw the publication of a biography written by Scriabin's close friend, Leonid Sabaneev. Combined with numerous adulatory articles in arts journals of the era, these publications established the composer as the leading modernist of his generation in Russia.

Until the mid-1920s, Scriabin's music reigned supreme in Russia as a paragon of pre-Revolutionary culture, and younger Russian composers jealously imitated his harmonic mannerisms. Yet an undercurrent of nationalistic pride threatened its hallowed reputation. As explored in chapter 7, many critics and Russian composers condemned Scriabin's indifference to setting folk tunes and Orthodox chant melodies, and considered it tantamount to antinationalism. The tide turned against Scriabin in 1923. In the newly formed USSR, his cosmopolitanism led ideological pundits to brand him as a decadent whose moody scores and opaque musical language were anathema to the spirit of the working class. Realism reigned supreme as the new aesthetic standard. Typical was the rebuke of a key member of the RAPM (Russian Association of Proletarian Musicians), Mikhail Ivanov-Boretski, who reviled Scriabin as an "intolerable example of bourgeois culture" whose art was "counterintuitive to proletarian ideology." Citing the irreconcilable contradiction between the composer's style and communist ideology, he contended that, "Scriabin's art forms, no matter how new and revolutionary they may seem, are not only inadequate for revolutionary psychology, but are endlessly far from it. . . . The face of our revolution will be the music of New Artists who will demonstrate in their art the psychology of their own class."[38]

The composer whose steely rhythms and affirmative vitality provided the antidote to Scriabin's moody subjectivism was Sergei Prokofiev, and in some circles, Stravinsky.[39] In his *Book About Stravinsky* (1926), the distinguished Soviet critic Boris Asafiev commented on the aesthetic shift from Scriabin to Prokofiev, whose music was seen as:

> a product of robust social health, and a counterbalance to the sterile aestheticism, refined exaltation, and convulsive lyricism of Scriabinism, and to the erotic intoxication that had captured almost universal attention. Of course, Scriabin, who rose head and shoulders above those immediately around him, dreamed of going even higher, whence no one could follow him. That made a clearing of the atmosphere all the more necessary.[40]

Even Scriabin's erstwhile advocate, Vyacheslav Karatygin, welcomed Prokofiev as the "antithesis to Scriabin—and thank God that antithesis has appeared."[41]

Although Scriabin's music had fallen out of favor in Russian culture, it was still considered sacrosanct, as evidenced by its prevail through the infamous *Zhdanovschina* trials (1946–1953), so named after the secretary of the Central Committee of the Communist Party, Andrei Zhdanov (1896–1948), whose policies of cultural reform led to public persecutions of many of Russia's greatest living composers, including Shostakovich, Khachaturian, and Prokofiev. This dark age of Russia's cultural history was documented by Alexander Werth in his book, *Musical Uproar in Moscow* (1949). Had Scriabin lived through this era of political turbulence, he would have surely suffered the same fate that befell these composers. The irony of his exoneration by state officials was not lost on Werth, who cited the composer's case as a prime example of its double standards:

> If ever there was a composer who suffered from *all* the vices which Zhdanov attributed to Shostakovich, Prokofiev, Khachaturian, and Myaskovsky, it was surely Scriabin; harmony, acute and morbid "neuropathic" egocentricity, totally un-Russian in his themes, and who was, in fact, more "anti-People" than anything in the whole of Russian music. But no! Scriabin was sacrosanct—a classic, who was lucky enough to die in 1915, two years before the Revolution. Had he been still alive to-day, one shudders to think what Zhdanov would have said.[42]

Several anniversaries after Scriabin's death punctuated his significance as a national treasure, and these dates were marked by scholarly publications and public performances of his music. The twenty-fifth anniversary of his death was commemorated by a memorial volume of essays by notable scholars of the era.[43] For the seventy-fifth anniversary of Scriabin's birth in 1946, Vladimir Sofronitsky (1901–1961) and other Russian pianists delivered all-Scriabin recitals, and the USSR Radio Committee under Nikolai Golovanov performed the orchestral works with "great success."[44] The centennial of Scriabin's birth in late 1971 offered Soviet officials an expansive platform to publish several laudatory articles and mount celebratory concerts. The composer's visage was even emblazoned on a state-issued stamp. Soviet cultural officials cemented Scriabin's status as a national treasure who had proven that Russian culture was every bit as progressive and culturally refined as its Western counterparts. Today, his name and music is familiar to the Russian people, in contrast to his relative obscurity in the West, even among pianists.

In England, Scriabin reaped success when he visited that country in the spring of 1914. He performed his piano concerto, *Prometheus*, and late sonatas to critical acclaim. A few years prior, Koussevitzky had introduced London audiences to Scriabin's symphonies. A final preparation for Scriabin's visit came on 18 October 1913, when Sir Henry J. Wood performed the *Divine Poem* at Queens Hall. The English public's rapturous reception of Scriabin's late music is remarkable considering their brief exposure to a smattering of his music before hearing the ultra-modern *Prometheus*, which premiered in England in 1913. Even today, *Prometheus* astounds the ear with its wrenching harmonies and dense orchestration, and it is a testament to the English public's willingness to give new music a chance that they applauded it.[45] So great was the composer's popularity in Europe after World War I that in 1919, the German journalist Alfred Kalisch forecasted, "It looks as if we are on the eve of a period of Scriabin worship."[46]

American critics similarly appreciated what little they knew of Scriabin's music by the early twentieth century, although they remained skeptical about his metaphysics. Their opinions lent credibility to Scriabin's music at a time when it was relatively unknown in the United States. Powerhouse American critics like Olin Downes of the *New York Times* and Paul Rosenfeld, who wrote for literary periodicals like the *New Republic* and *Vanity Fair*, sung Scriabin's praises as one of the leading "futurist" or "ultra-modern" composers. Rosenfeld defended Scriabin against accusations of being an ersatz Chopin or Liszt, and published a glowing account of his creative evolution in a 1917 article published in *Seven Arts*. Rosenfeld wrote his final Scriabin essay nearly twenty years later (1936) and remained steadfast in his support of the composer's music. By then, however, he admitted that Scriabin's "glory remains fairly complete in its eclipse."[47] Yet another trusted critic was Lawrence Gilman (1878–1939), who reviewed the American premiere of the *Divine Poem* in 1907, which had failed to impress him.[48] Within a few years, however, Scriabin's music won Gilman over. He considered Scriabin to be among the finest and most fashionable of the "ultra-modernist" composers, but he valued the composer strictly for his musical ability, and dismissed any claims of Theosophy and metaphysics as "spurious." These and other critics were prominently featured in newspapers and journals, and they helped shape the composer's public image every bit as much as performers.

Lending weight to these critics' laudatory reviews were a constellation of star performers who promoted Scriabin's music in America, including the pianists Katherine Ruth Heyman in New York and Djane Lavoie-Herz in Chicago, and the conductors Serge Koussevitzky (Boston), Frederick Stock (Chicago), Leopold Stokowski (Philadelphia), and Albert Coates (Los Angeles). These performers lionized his orchestral and piano works in the first decades of the twentieth century, and cemented his reputation as one of the leading composers of the era.

Although Scriabin enjoyed the support of critics and performers, by the mid-1920s a shift in tastes was under way in the West. War-ravaged audiences had grown weary of his utopian dreams of spiritual transcendence, and his musical style conflicted with the values of rationality and emotional restraint that dominated the cultural landscape. Writing from Paris in 1924, Boris Schloezer explained that Scriabin appeared "old-fashioned, a *démodé* anarchist. [His] restlessness, his over-reaching desire, his ecstaticism are felt as vain agitation, weakness and lack of discipline."[49]

In England, more homespun works like William Walton's *Façade* suite (1922) and jazz-tinged overture *Portsmouth Point* (1925) captured the public sentiment more successfully than Scriabin's hyperactive scores. A *London Times* critic reported in 1923 that, "The popularity of Scriabin seems to be on the wane" now that the "real poverty of the music" had been exposed.[50] For an unnamed reviewer, Alfred Swan's 1923 biography of the composer illustrated just how far Scriabin's stock had fallen: "There is a decided slump in Scriabin just now," he observed. The reasons were obvious: "His early works too obviously derive from Chopin, and his later ones suffer from a triple defect; they are either invertebrate, or harmonically monotonous, or they attempt to express ideas for which music is an inadequate medium."[51] With such condemnations emanating from critics, the floodgates of criticism flung wide open.

With the exception of a few passing mentions in historical surveys, no other major English-language publication on Scriabin emerged for another four decades, and this dry spell was only broken with the arrival of Faubion Bowers' two-volume biography in 1969. English critics noted the composer's precipitous decline. Ernest Fennell observed in 1926 that Scriabin's music was "out of fashion" and Terrence White could well write in 1932 that, "Scriabin is now, by artist and layman alike, almost entirely neglected."[52] British commentators such as Gerald Abraham attacked Scriabin on musical and personal grounds, asserting that his late works amounted to little more than "paper music." With smug satisfaction, Abraham wrote in a 1933 article that, "Scriabin is now thought very little of." In hindsight, he considered the composer's harmonic developments, such as the mystic chord, as "a mere side-track in the history of music as a whole."[53] British conductor Sir Adrian Boult refused to conduct the Scriabin selections recommended by BBC program director Edward Clark (who headed that organization from 1924 to 1936), sneering that it was "evil music."[54] Boult further issued a ban against broadcasting Scriabin's music on British airwaves during the 1930s.[55] Confirmation of Scriabin's lagging popularity emanated from multiple sources. Writing from England in 1934, Martin Cooper noted that, "Neither Scriabin nor Liszt have been great favourites with the concert-going public in England in the last few years." English critic Robert Hull observed that same year that, "During recent years Scriabin's orchestral works have been rarely heard in London."[56]

The middle decades of the twentieth century saw Scriabin's music fall into almost total neglect, as conservative values and modern sensibility ran counter to his idealistic theories of transcendental art. Despite the efforts of a few performers, Scriabin's music sank to its nadir in popularity. Russian-born pianists Simon Barere (1896–1951) and Maria Safonov (1897–1989, the daughter of Vasily) played all-Scriabin recitals in America into the 1940s, but they faced critical opposition. Even Scriabin's strongest supporters from his golden age in popularity, such as Serge Koussevitzky, turned their backs on the composer and argued that his music had fallen out of sympathy with the modern aesthetic of realism and rationality. Koussevitzky presents an illustrative example of a figure whose complicated relationship with Scriabin's music exemplifies its extreme shifts in popularity. His history with the composer is explored in chapter 4.

Such was the anti-Scriabin sentiment until the 1960s, when a revival of interest in romantic music in the West coincided with the rise of the counterculture movement. This wave of rebellion and freedom of expression swept across the United States, and in its wake, Scriabin was recast as a proto–Flower Child whose radical ideas about performing music to the accompaniment of colored lights and aromas found an eager and receptive audience that sought enlightenment through the arts. The tale of this revival of interest in Scriabin's music is told in chapter 8. To be suited to the Aquarian Age, however, proved to be a double-edge sword; as the Flower Power movement faded into history, so did Scriabin's second heyday in the West. Western performers and audiences may have lost interest in his music by the mid-1970s, but the revival inspired academics to launch a new wave of research on his music, cultural milieu, and philosophical beliefs. Music theorists offered a new spin on the composer's legacy by replacing the well-worn image of Scriabin as a half-mad, dreamy improviser with that of an ingenious craftsman who devised some of the most advanced harmonic combinations in twentieth-century music. In many circles, this image of the composer as an innovative pioneer prevails in the public imagination. This enthusiastic reappraisal of his legacy has endured through the present day, and continues to inspire new research on his cultural context, critical reception, and performance practice.

Today, Scriabin's solo piano and orchestral music maintains a stable, if modest, standing in the repertory. Many of its leading interpreters, both past and present, are profiled in this book. His music has also earned the respect of critics, and attracted a great deal of scholarly attention. Scriabin's music is better represented now than at any other time during his posthumous reception, and as we shall see, it has officially crossed over into the pop culture mainstream in the West. But he will always remain a polarizing figure. Many of the fundamental and controversial issues that have defined his legacy are explored in this book. Although the historical essays are segregated from the discussions of performance, these two disciplines should be considered in tandem. Historians and performers can learn much about one another's craft through a careful study of these essays. Just as any informed historical reading of a composer's reception must take performance into account, so too should performers base their interpretations of Scriabin's music on a proper understanding of its historical background. After a consideration of the issues, the reader is able to weigh the evidence and make an informed judgement of Scriabin's daring genius.

3

The Solo Piano Music

The piano was Scriabin's first love and the medium through which he most intuitively expressed himself in music. So enamored was he with the instrument that as a child he built miniature pianos to scale to painstaking detail. Small wonder, then, that his compositional output is dominated by solo piano pieces. In 1906, when Scriabin made his first and only tour of the United States, American newspapers announced the arrival of the "Russian Chopin." It was a fitting, if partial description, but American audiences knew almost nothing of Scriabin then. It is true that as a youth, his adoration of Chopin's music was so great that he slept with the Pole's scores beneath his pillow. As a composer, he naturally favored the same forms and genres as Chopin, especially dance pieces like mazurkas, polonaises, and waltzes, as well as popular nineteenth-century genres like preludes and impromptus. Like Chopin and Liszt, Scriabin also turned his attention to the etude and piano sonatas. In this genre, however, Scriabin made developments that were leaps and bounds over his pianistic idols. His Piano Sonatas Nos. 1–10 are the pinnacles of his legacy and rank among the most original contributions to the piano sonata in twentieth-century music. This chapter covers the gestation, performance history, and recommended recordings of Scriabin's most famous works for solo piano.

Writers usually approach Scriabin's pre-1905 piano works with an attitude of impatient anticipation; accolades are bestowed upon passages where hints of the "real" or "future" Scriabin style appear with regard to form, rhythm, and harmony. The rest is dismissed as ersatz Liszt or Chopin. The Russian composer César Cui, an original member of the Mighty Five, famously snubbed Scriabin's music as "bits filched from Chopin's trousseau," and this derogatory remark speaks to the overtly feminine quality of Scriabin's music as well as its perceived unoriginality.[1] Similar dismissals of Scriabin's music as "nothing but diluted Chopin" abound in the literature.[2] I personally believe that each phase of Scriabin's creative development should be appreciated on its own merits. If we can look past the obvious affinities with the music of Liszt and Chopin, Scriabin's unmistakable voice can be heard in his earliest pieces, like the hauntingly beautiful Canon in D minor from 1883, written when he was only eleven years old. Other published guides provide useful information for those who want to learn more about the history and recorded legacy of this rich body of solo piano music.[3]

EARLY MASTERPIECES

Nocturne for Left Hand Alone Op. 9 No. 2
Date of Composition: 1895

A bounty of piano music exists for the left hand alone, with examples of solo works and concertos written by composers such as Alkan, Korngold, Strauss, Saint-Saëns, Prokofiev, Britten, and Ravel.[4] Many of the most famous works for left hand alone were commissioned by the Austrian pianist Paul Wittgenstein (1887–1961), who lost his right arm to an injury he sustained in World War I. Wittgenstein went on to become one of the greatest performers of left hand piano music. His virtuosic technique electrified audiences and fired the imagination of composers. A name equally synonymous with left hand piano music is Leopold Godowsky (1870–1938), whose transcriptions and arrangements (including fifty-three paraphrases on Chopin's etudes) earned him the title of the "Apostle of the Left Hand." Scriabin's signal contributions to this literature were his Prelude and Nocturne Op. 9 Nos. 1 and 2. Of the two works, the Nocturne has achieved distinction as one of Scriabin's most famous compositions, and it sealed his early reputation, much as Rachmaninov's C♯ minor Prelude Op. 3 No. 2 had achieved for him early in his career.

The story of Scriabin's left hand alone works is an often repeated, if romanticized, tale. When Scriabin was a student, he envied the technique of his classmate Josef Lhévinne, who was the top pianist at the Moscow Conservatory. Over the summer of 1891, Scriabin strained his right hand in an attempt to match Lhévinne's feats of speed and strength. Although he recovered from this nearly career-ending injury, his right hand never regained its full power. The fact that these two pieces were published in 1895, four years after Scriabin's injury, suggests that they were not borne of physical necessity, as legend tells, and were instead compositional exercises inspired by this period of convalescence. Yet another version of the story was offered by pianist and critic Evgeny Gunst in 1914, and was repeated by Arthur Eaglefield Hull in his 1921 biography, *A Great Russian Tone Poet: Scriabin*. Gunst suggested that Scriabin's first experiments in playing with the left hand alone came ten years before the Op. 9 set was published, and were prompted by an accident. Scriabin had absentmindedly wandered into the street and was struck by a passing open-air carriage, or *drozhky*. In his fall, he broke his right collarbone. Faubion Bowers recounted a similar tale of this accident, and dated the incident to April 1885. While the exact gestation point for the Op. 9 works is debatable, these pieces demonstrate the composer's early fascination with demanding left hand passages, which are on display in so much of his piano music.[5]

Chopin is the clear model for the Nocturne; in fact, it is surprising that Scriabin did not write more pieces with this title. Op. 9 No. 2 is in the classic Chopinesque key of D♭ major (Cf., the "Raindrop" Prelude Op. 28 No. 15 or the "Countess" Nocturne Op. 27 No. 2). It could be considered an etude due to its dual challenges of texture and tone; the pianist must sustain the melody line, and lend the impression of two hands playing instead of one. The Nocturne is deeply introspective and traverses an expansive range of moods in a few short minutes. Each time the heavier, brooding B material is presented, it is marked *marcato sempre* (always accented), and it concludes with a Lisztian cadenza-like passage. An authoritative version of the published score was edited by Nikolai Zhiliaev in 1935. Fittingly, one of the best recordings of this work is a Welte-Mignon piano roll recorded in 1906 by Josef Lhévinne.

Recommended Recordings: Heinrich Neuhaus (Russian Disc 15004, 1993); Leon Fleisher (Sony Classical 48081, 1993); Alexis Weissenberg (Philips Great Pianists of the Twentieth Century, Vol. 97, 1999); Josef Lhévinne (Pierian 0018, 2003).

Fantasie in B minor Op. 28
Date of Composition: 1900
Premiere: 24 February 1907 in Moscow, by Alexander Goldenweiser

The B minor *Fantasie* caps off Scriabin's early stylistic period. Although his distinctive compositional voice is salient in its triplet figures and cross-rhythms, there is no denying the Lisztian figurations and Chopinesque turns of mood and phrase. Written in the grand romantic tradition, the piece is indebted to Chopin and Wagner in its harmonic texture and epic sweep. The *Fantasie* was written in 1901 during Scriabin's tenure as a piano professor at the Moscow Conservatory (1897–1903). Owing to his teaching duties, it was one of the few solo piano works of any significant length completed at that time, aside from the Third Sonata and nine Mazurkas Op. 25. The free-form nature suggested by the piece's title belies its tight formal construction. Like most of his early works, the triplet subdivision is a foundational rhythmic cell, much as it is in Chopin's music. The left hand figurations are particularly emblematic of his early style, with their repeated chords in the middle register, reminiscent of the D♯ minor Etude Op. 8 No. 12, and in their repeated-note arpeggios that use the doubled pitch as a physical pivot point.[6] The brooding and portentous opening theme in B minor is complemented by one of Scriabin's most ravishing themes in the relative major key of D. A typical performance of the work lasts around ten minutes, and it remains a brilliant, if underplayed, concert showpiece for virtuosos. It still ranks as one of Scriabin's most difficult pieces for solo piano, and at times its technical demands overshadow the musical effect. Sabaneev and Bowers both related an apocryphal story that Scriabin had forgotten that he even wrote the *Fantasie*, but this tale seems dubious considering the piece's uniqueness in his output and its substantial size. More likely, he had outgrown its inflated rhetoric and turned his back on it for good.

Recommended Recordings: Sviatoslav Richter (Live Classics LCL441, 1994); Heinrich Neuhaus (Russian Piano School RCD 16247, 1996); Lazar Berman (Aura Classics, 0161, 1999); Vladimir Sofronitsky (Denon COCQ-83669-70, 2003).

PIANO SONATAS NOS. 1–10

Scriabin's ten published sonatas for solo piano rank as his most visionary artistic statements, and many of them remain integral works in the standard repertory. Arthur Eaglefield Hull, Scriabin's first biographer in English, predicted in 1921 that the composer's sonatas were "destined in the future to occupy a niche of their own, together with such treasures as the Forty-Eight fugues of Bach, the Thirty-Two Sonatas of Beethoven, the Pianoforte Works of Brahms, and the music of Chopin."[7] Time has borne out Hull's presumption. Scriabin's sonatas showcase his assured handling of larger forms and structures, as well as his intuitive grasp of pianistic sonorities. They also lend a distinctive Russian stamp to a genre that had been dominated by European composers. Indeed, Scriabin's sonatas epitomize the mood of heady anticipation and world-weariness of the early twentieth century. Most attention from critics and performers has been focused on the late sonatas. As Scriabin's creative vision became more focused on his *Mysterium*, his compositional focus narrowed. Smaller works like impromptus and preludes preoccupied his attention far less after 1903, and from the Sixth Sonata Op. 62 through the Tenth Op. 70, every other opus number is a piano sonata. Three earlier sonatas without opus numbers were published posthumously: a Sonata-Fantasie in G♯ minor from August 1886, a Sonata in C♯ minor from September 1887, and a Sonata in E♭ minor from 1887–1889, the first movement of which became the *Allegro Appassionato* Op. 4.

Historical Background

Piano sonatas have been a staple of classical music since the days of Italian keyboardist Domenico Scarlatti (1685–1757), who was a contemporary of Johann Sebastian Bach. Traditionally, a sonata was a multi-movement instrumental piece that *sounded*, versus a cantata, which was sung. Each of the great composers brought new innovations to their chosen genre, and few composers accomplished that better than Scriabin with the piano sonata. A genre's evolution in the hands of a master composer is less a matter of musical progress than it is a total rethinking of its function and purpose. Consider Joseph Haydn's "conversational" string quartets, Mozart's politically tinged and revolutionary operas, such as *Le Nozze di Figaro* and *Don Giovanni*, Beethoven's monumental symphonies, and Chopin's and Liszt's exquisite etudes for solo piano, which refined technical exercises into high art. The modifications made by these composers included longer movements, dramatic shifts in key and tempo, nontraditional scoring (e.g., choir and vocal soloists in Beethoven's Ninth Symphony), and a new depth of expression hitherto absent or rare in a work. Even if Scriabin's contemporaries did not understand his sonatas upon their initial hearings, they nonetheless recognized their superior craftsmanship and individuality.

In Russia, the piano sonata was almost completely ignored by composers before 1850. A few scattered examples exist before 1870 by composers whose names are now forgotten. The first sonatas of any significance were written by Anton Rubinstein (1829–1894), who founded the St. Petersburg Conservatory in 1862. His eleven piano sonatas demonstrate his assured command of the instrument, but are decidedly cosmopolitan in style. Heavily influenced by Chopin and Liszt, Rubinstein had no interest in cultivating a nationalist style, and his piano sonatas bear few distinctive Russian traits. Tchaikovsky wrote two piano sonatas, but these works also failed to plant the seed for the modern Russian piano sonata.

Scriabin led the charge for the Russian piano sonata in the early twentieth century. By 1903, he had published four piano sonatas, just as many of his peers suddenly took to the genre. Glazunov produced his only two sonatas in 1901 (issued by Scriabin's publisher, Beliaev), and Rachmaninov wrote his first sonata in D minor Op. 28 in 1908. Nikolai Medtner (1880–1951) produced the first of his fourteen sonatas in 1902–1903, which was heavily indebted to Scriabin. Subsequent sonatas written in imitation of Scriabin appeared between 1900 and 1914 by Nikolai Myaskovsky, Sergei Prokofiev, and Anatoly Alexandrov.[8] There is no doubt that many Russian composers struggled to find their own style under Scriabin's spell. It took courage and conviction for Scriabin to modernize this traditional genre, and make it one of the premiere genres of early twentieth-century music.

To the casual observer, the most innovative aspect of Scriabin's sonatas is the single movement design used in Nos. 5–10. Single-movement sonatas were unusual in Scriabin's day, but not without precedent. Scarlatti wrote over 500 single-movement sonatas for harpsichord. In formal terms, Scarlatti's pieces differ from Scriabin's sonatas in their binary or two-part design, which was common for Baroque keyboard suites. The sonata form that was current in Scriabin's time was a three-part design. In his sonatas Nos. 5–10, Scriabin compressed these three parts into one movement, yet he preserved the basic formal outline of a traditional sonata form. Throughout his career, he never abandoned this tried-and-true sonata form design, which led American composer Aaron Copland (1900–1990) to pillory Scriabin's "fantastic idea of attempting to put this really new body of feeling into the straight jacket of the old classical sonata form." To Copland, Scriabin's attachment to the sonata form, despite his harmonic advancements, was "one of the most extraordinary mistakes in music."[9]

The wellspring for the single-movement sonata, however, was Liszt's Sonata in B minor (1853), a work so daring that it challenged all known formal designs and physical demands.[10] So formidable was the B minor Sonata's technical hurdles and compositional approach that it would require the rest of the nineteenth century to earn its rightful place in the classical canon. Considering the dominant influence of Liszt's keyboard style on Scriabin, the importance of the B minor Sonata cannot be underestimated as a model for the Russian composer's own single movement sonatas.

Complete Sonatas
Recommended Recordings: Vladimir Ashkenazy (London 452579-2, 1989); Ruth Laredo (Nonesuch 73035, 1996); Vladimir Sofronitsky (Classound 001-023, 2001); Roberto Szidon (Deutsche Grammophon 431747, 2004); Vladimir Stoupel (Audite 21.402, 2005); Matthew Bengtson (Roméo 7232/7308, 2015).

Sonata No. 1 in F minor Op. 6
Date of Composition: 1892–1893 in Moscow
Premiere: 23 February 1894 in St. Petersburg, by the composer
This is the longest sonata Scriabin ever wrote, in four movements instead of the usual three. It is full of grand, assertive gestures in the Beethoven and Brahms traditions, fitting for a headstrong twenty-one-year-old. It is no coincidence that the key of this work (F minor) is the same key that Beethoven and Prokofiev chose for their first piano sonatas, and Brahms for his third.[11] When it was written, sonatas had been mostly abandoned as a genre. But as a recent graduate of the Moscow Conservatory, the conventions of tradition loomed large in Scriabin's mind. This sonata displays his compositional craftsmanship and confidence in large-scale forms. A virtuoso technique, athleticism, and a keen sense of keyboard topography are required to execute the left hand leaps, which demonstrate the kinds of figurations that became hallmarks of Scriabin's playing style. The first movement is marked *Allegro con fuoco* (Fast with fire) and features furious octaves in both hands that propel the music forward. The rising motive heard in the first three notes (F-G-A♭) provides a germinal motive for the entire sonata. Despite the initial outburst, a hint of gloom hangs over this opening movement. Scriabin wrote this sonata not long after he had injured his right hand. Physicians feared he would never perform again, and the funeral march in the final movement conveys the composer's submission to his sad fate. A two-measure recitative passage in the bell-like *Quasi niente* (As if distant) section is marked *a piacere* (ad lib.), and represents the hero's solitary cry against his misfortune. Interestingly, this same melodic line reappeared years later as the secondary theme in the Seventh Sonata Op. 64.[12] The notes may be the same, but the moods of these two passages are worlds apart.

The second, slow movement is a chorale-like theme that is reminiscent of Russian plainsong or chant. Droning, resonant sonorities are treated to ornamentation, but never extend past the middle register. The virtuosic third movement features scampering left hand figurations evocative of Liszt and Chopin. The ghost of the latter especially looms in the 12/8 time signature and driving right-hand accents. Already in this first sonata, we see the sort of technical demands that make Scriabin's music so brilliant, yet so intimidating for amateurs. After debuting the work in 1894, Scriabin rarely played it in public. The only documented exception was when he performed the Funeral March at a concert in Paris at the Salle de Journal on 10 July 1900. Today, this piece is seldom heard in concert programs, but it remains one of the outstanding sonatas of its time period.

Recommended Recordings: Lazar Berman (Columbia/Melodiya M 34565, 1978); Vladimir Ashkenazy (London 452579-2, 1989); Marc-André Hamelin (Hyperion CDA67131/2, 1996); Wojciech Kocyan (Dux Records 389, 2003); Roberto Szidon (Deutsche Grammophon 431747, 2004).

Sonata-Fantasie (No. 2) in G♯ minor Op. 19
Date of Composition: Originally sketched in 1892 in Genoa; revised 1897 in Crimea
Premiere: 5 May 1896 at the Salle Erard in Paris, by the composer

Cast in two movements, this sonata features an introspective and dreamy introduction that leads to a brisk *moto perpetuo* finale. The binary design of Slow-Fast mirrors that of an earlier, unpublished sonata Scriabin wrote in 1886, a *Sonata-fantasie* for solo piano also in G♯ minor.[13] The gap in time between these two movements was unusual. Scriabin wrote the second movement four years before the first, and the two parts were welded together in 1897. It took some cajoling from Scriabin's publisher, Beliaev, to put the sonata into finished form. Both parties also had financial interests at stake, since large-scale genres commanded higher prices than stand-alone pieces. Scriabin's decision to title it a "Sonata-fantasie" pays homage to Beethoven's famous "Moonlight" Sonata Op. 27 No. 2, subtitled *Quasi una fantasia*. The nod to Beethoven is not just in name; the two-part form of Scriabin's sonata also follows the plan laid out in several of Beethoven's sonatas, including Op. 90 in E minor and Op. 111 in C minor. Whereas most composers balked at the idea of following in Beethoven's footsteps, Scriabin embraced the challenge. This sonata is dedicated to Scriabin's first sweetheart, Natalya Sekerina, and is one of his only compositions to bear such an inscription.

Op. 19 presents, in the composer's words, "an image of the wide, turbulent expanse of the sea," a Romantic metaphor for the human psyche.[14] More specifically, Scriabin took as his inspiration the Black Sea on the shores of Crimea, which he visited during his honeymoon with Vera in the fall of 1897. The first two bars present a three-note call that echoes into the distance. This triplet figure serves as a prominent feature of Scriabin's early works; for instance, it pervades the Piano Concerto Op. 20. From a performance standpoint, the leisurely pacing and lyrical quasi-improvised sections of this introductory movement make for an interpretive challenge. The pianist can easily feel lost at sea, as it were, in an undifferentiated swamp of sound. Emphasizing the variety of the tone combined with a well-judged lyrical rubato are the keys to sustaining the musical line in this movement. The development section portrays growing storms, after which radiant moonlight glows in the key of E major. The second movement (Presto) features brilliant but difficult passagework, and the opening theme returns in various guises. In the Coda, for instance, the tightly interlaced treble lines are not merely decorative, but are motivically derived. Informed pianists will highlight these motivic connections in performance. Brilliant and succinct, this sonata was one of Scriabin's favorite pieces, and he even recorded it on a piano roll for the Hupfeld company in 1908.

Recommended Recordings: Vladimir Sofronitsky (Melodiya D-19639, 1960); Sviatoslav Richter (Music & Arts 878, 1972); Samuil Feinberg (Russian Disk R10 01071-4, 1992); Wojciech Kocyan (Dux Records 389, 2003); Yevgeny Sudbin (BIS SACD 1568, 2007); Daniil Trifonov (Deutsche Grammophon 4793795, 2014).

Sonata No. 3 in F♯ minor Op. 23
Date of Composition: 1897–1898 in Paris, Maidanovo, and Moscow
Premiere: 6 March 1900 in Moscow, by Vsevolod Buyukli

The Third Sonata is the crown jewel of Scriabin's early sonatas. It ranks among his most popular and enduring works. Its rich themes and piquant harmonies display a sense of individuality that is less prevalent in his first two sonatas. Scriabin began writing his Third Sonata almost immediately after publishing his *Sonata-Fantasie* Op. 19. It was a time when his professional and personal life were taking off astride, and he was expecting his first child with Vera. His ambition as a composer was rapidly outgrowing the salon preludes and etudes he had been producing. His attention now focused on large-scale multi-movement forms, like his Third Sonata and First Symphony.

It comes as no surprise that this sonata displays a greater sophistication of thematic development, controlled counterpoint in the inner voices, and an epic sweep to the dramatic trajectory. Preoccupied as he was with squeezing the greatest meaning and expression into his music, this sonata was appended with a poetic program that describes the progression of events. Scriabin's common-law wife, Tatyana, wrote the programmatic text (just as Liszt's longtime lover, the princess Carolyne Sayn-Wittgenstein, wrote many of the programs to his works).[15] But there is little doubt that Scriabin approved of its content, even if he did not necessarily want audiences to rely on it to understand the music.

> *Soul States (Etats d'Ame)*
> a) The free, untamed soul passionately throws itself into pain and struggle.
> b) The soul has found some kind of momentary, illusory peace; tired of suffering, it wishes to forget, to sing and blossom—despite everything. But the light rhythm and fragrant harmonies are but a veil, through which the uneasy, wounded soul shimmers.
> c) The soul floats on a sea of gentle emotion and melancholy; love, sorrow, indefinite wishes, indefinable thoughts of fragile, vague allure.
> d) In the uproar of the unfettered elements, the soul struggles as if intoxicated. From the depths of Existence arises the mighty voice of the demigod, whose song of victory echoes triumphantly! But, too weak as yet, it fails, before reaching the summit, into the abyss of nothingness.[16]

Each of these descriptions roughly corresponds to the sonata's four movements. The first line of the text, for instance, describes the music of the opening "Drammatico" in F♯ minor. Rhythmically assertive and declamatory, the main theme consists of leaping figures in the bass followed by unfolding melodic replies. The individual phrases and components of this first movement are seamlessly combined, yet their formal divisions are plainly evident. Scriabin's balance of formal traditions and personalized expression in this first movement displays a fine sense of craftsmanship and artistry. The principal theme from this opening movement and its rhythmic permutations return throughout the remaining three movements, thus tying together the individual movements in a cyclical fashion reminiscent of the works of Liszt or César Franck.[17]

The second movement (Allegretto) is in the key of E♭ major and serves as the dance movement. It is an Intermezzo with a trio. The reference to the "momentary, illusory peace" in the poetic text cited above is expressed through the mode mixture between major and minor (G to G♭) heard in the opening phrase, and in the trio section marked *con grazia* (gracefully), which bounces along with delightful turns of phrase that are tastefully ornamented. This coquettish music has not a care in the world. The gorgeous third movement (Andante) in B major is among the most soulful pieces of music that Scriabin ever wrote. He likened it to the stars singing. It is a lullaby, and its drowsy effects are offset by the meandering *doloroso* (painful) section. Gradually this music pulls itself out of its slumber and restates the opening theme with added filigree. The opening bars from the first movement are recalled at the end of the Andante before plunging into the turgid and frenetic *Presto con fuoco* (Fast with fire). After a fiery finish, the opening tag motto is heard once more to conclude the work. The thematic integration and large-range design of this sonata shows that Scriabin's compositional technique had evolved past the piano preludes and etudes of his youth.

The Third Sonata is one of the most frequently recorded and performed of Scriabin's sonatas, surpassed only by the Fourth, Fifth, and Ninth Sonatas. The composer played the work for the first time in public at the Salle de Journal in Paris on 10 July 1900, and again in Moscow in 1902. He played selected movements of the work throughout his concertizing career, and even included it in his final public appearance, in St. Petersburg on 15 April 1915. Horowitz's two live recordings from 1953 and 1965 set a benchmark standard. Glenn Gould turned in a particularly thought provoking, if unidiomatic, reading, while other pianists such as Vitaly Margulis have waxed notable interpretations that deserve a close listen.

Recommended Recordings: Vladimir Horowitz (RCA GD86215, 1956); Samson François (Columbia SAXF 220, early 1960s); Vitaly Margulis (Inak 8707, 1986); Glenn Gould (Sony Classical SM2K 52 622, 1995); Emil Gilels (The Giant RCA 75523, 2000).

Sonata No. 4 in F♯ major Op. 30
Date of Composition: 1903 in Moscow

The Fourth Sonata marked a radical departure from Scriabin's previous efforts due to its innovative form and harmonic ingenuity. Like the Sonata-Fantasie Op. 19, the Fourth Sonata is divided into two movements with a tempo plan of Slow-Fast. The two movements are linked thematically, and the sonata established what would become a pattern for Scriabin of stating a slow melody at the beginning of the piece and transforming it into a triumphant final theme. The balance that had been observed between the first and second movements in the Sonata-Fantasie Op. 19, however, is shifted here so that the second movement is the weightiest, and is preceded by an introduction.

The shortest of his piano sonatas, the Fourth was first sketched as early as 1899. This early draft was abandoned, however, and when Op. 30 was published in 1903, it bore little resemblance to the original sketches from 1899.[18] The sonata's final version was produced in the summer of 1903, a period of great industry when Scriabin wrote the piano works Opp. 30–42 and orchestrated the *Divine Poem*. Like the poetic description associated with the Third Sonata, the Fourth Sonata also bears a literary text that describes the artist's ascent from earthly trammels to the eternal divine. Cosmic bliss is symbolized by a pulsating star—an early instance of Scriabin's fascination with representing light in music. F♯ major serves as the central key of the Fourth Sonata. Throughout his middle-period works (1902–1908), F♯ major is the key in which Scriabin expresses his most ecstatic musical emotions, just as Liszt did before him and Messiaen after him.

The laconic melody at the work's beginning is one of its most unusual qualities. Typically a sonata's opening movement begins with a vigorous theme that establishes a decisive rhythm. But in this sonata, the fragmentary melody at the outset outlines a widely spaced and mildly dissonant chord structure voiced in fourths. Only gradually does the work gather energy. According to Hull, the composer told Evgeny Gunst that the opening melodic ideas in this work symbolized the "striving upwards towards the Ideal Creative Power." The secondary theme consists of a falling figure with a rising scale as its consequent statement; this figure, in Hull's words, represents the "resultant Languor or Exhaustion after effort."[19] These sorts of metaphysical moods with musical themes would serve as a leitmotif for Scriabin in his middle-period works. The opening melody is heard a second time with a rich accompaniment that requires three staves to notate. Here are the first and most palpable strains of eroticism in Scriabin's music.[20] The opening segues directly into the second movement, which sets a brisk pace. The triumphant coda recalls the opening motive from the first movement and transforms it into an ecstatic finale.

The Fourth Sonata remains one of the most frequently performed pieces of Scriabin's solo piano repertoire. It still sounds as fresh and modern as it did over a century ago. In 1904, Scriabin won the Glinka Prize for this sonata, and although it was an honor and brought a financial windfall, everyone knew that the "anonymous" donor of the annual Glinka Prize was Scriabin's publisher, Beliaev.

Recommended Recordings: Andrei Gavrilov (EMI, 1C 067 EL 27 0090, 1984); Vladimir Ashkenazy (London 452579-2, 1989); Samuil Feinberg (Arlecchino ARL 50, 1996); Ruth Laredo (Nonesuch 73035-2, 1996); Stephen Hough (Hyperion CDA67895, 2015).

Sonata No. 5 in F♯ major Op. 53
Date of Composition: August–December 1907 in Lausanne, Switzerland
Premiere: 1 December 1908 in Moscow, by Mark Meichik

The companion piece to the *Poem of Ecstasy*, the Fifth Sonata in F♯ major was the first of Scriabin's piano sonatas to be compressed into a single movement. Each of his sonatas thereafter would be cast in one movement. Legend has it that this piece came to Scriabin in a flash of inspiration in late 1907, and that its actual composition required only six days. In reality, the initial sketches for its themes were inscribed in notebooks from 1905 to 1906, and its genesis unfolded over the course of several months, from August to early December 1907. Once Scriabin realized the final form that the piece would take, however, the sonata came together quickly.

Like Sonata No. 4, Scriabin's initial ideas for the Fifth Sonata were jettisoned. Maria Nemenova-Lunz was the composer's pupil and heard him perform the sonata in its early stages. On 8 December 1907, Tatyana Schloezer wrote to Nemenova-Lunz in astonishment, marveling that, "Sasha has succeeded in finishing . . . the 5th Sonata! I don't trust my ears, for it is so unbelievable! The Sonata flowed out of him like a river. What you have heard is nothing . . . the Sonata is unrecognizable, and is not to be compared with anything."[21] Scriabin believed that the music existed outside the material world, and he saw himself as a translator who captured this divine vision into crude notated form. The actual writing down of the piece even discouraged him at times, as its rendering into notated form failed to capture the spiritual revelation that the composer experienced when he first envisioned it. Upon its completion, he wrote to his benefactress, Margarita Morozova, expressing in equal parts exhaustion and amazement, exclaiming, "I do not know by what miracle I accomplished it."[22] Scriabin self-published this sonata at a considerable expense in Lausanne in the spring of 1908. His former publisher, Beliaev, had died in 1904, and the composer's relationship with the executors of Beliaev's publishing estate was strained. Koussevitzky's firm, Édition Russe de Musique, published a second edition of the work in 1910, which corrected many of the errors in the first edition.

Like Scriabin's previous two sonatas, a poetic text is appended to the Fifth Sonata. It is an excerpt from a lengthy poem Scriabin wrote in tandem with the music for the *Poem of Ecstasy*. Most editions of this sonata print the excerpt at the top of first page, which reads: "I call you to life, oh mysterious forces! / Buried in the obscure depths / Of the creative mind, sketchy / Outlines of life, to you I bring my proud spirit." The words capture in prose the subterranean rumblings and whoosh of sound that opens and closes the sonata. These fleet-fingered passages nearly leap off of the page and reappear at various points throughout the music. Halting and fragmented themes present vague melodic outlines, as if in a dreamlike state. The exposition starts with one of Scriabin's most invigorating rhythmic combinations, a 6/8 pattern in the right hand against four beats in the left, marked *Presto con allegrezza* (joyfully fast). Like the *Poem of Ecstasy*, the Fifth Sonata is an ideal balance of form and content. The music is richly expressive, and its themes and sections are clearly delineated. The final pages contain some of the most expansive keyboard writing in the modern literature, with an ecstatic presentation of the initial slow theme transformed into a soaring and luminous celebration of life.

Since its premiere in Moscow by Mark Meichik on 1 December 1908, the Fifth Sonata has been a favorite among concert pianists and audiences alike. It is an ideal piece to acquaint audiences with Scriabin's mature style because of its relative brevity (a typical performance clocks in around 10–12 minutes) and its unbridled energy, which makes palpable the feverish inspiration from which it was produced. Its technical virtuosity is breathtaking. Sviatoslav Richter described it as the most difficult piece in the solo piano repertory.[23] Rachmaninov delivered some of the most notorious performances of the Fifth Sonata in history during his concert tour in the fall of 1915, which memorialized the recently deceased composer. His grounded reading of the work infuriated Scriabin's devotees, leading some audience members in the provincial towns to angrily curse at him using the Russian word *pórcha*, which means "spoiling" or "bewitchment." It is a hex used to wish evil upon someone.[24]

The Fifth Sonata's fame has allowed it to transcend the world of classical music and earn recognition in popular culture. Among other sources, the sonata is mentioned in Jim Tushinski's 2004 novel *Van Allen's Ecstasy*, whose protagonist suffers a nervous breakdown and sudden amnesia.[25] In the course of recovering his memories and regaining his identity, the main character becomes obsessed with the Fifth Sonata. Through Scriabin's ebullient and explosive score, Van Allen discovers a sonic analogue to his own inner reality, and the music empowers and enlightens him toward self-awareness.

Recommended Recordings: Walter Gieseking (Live, Music & Arts, CD 1070, 1947); Sviatoslav Richter (Music & Arts 878, 1972); David Bean (ABC Westminster Gold WGS 8306, 1975); Vladimir Horowitz (RCA 6215-2-RG, 1989); Thomas Schumacher (Elan 82242, 1995); John Bell Young (Americus 1013, 1999); Roberto Szidon (Deutsche Grammophon 431747, 2004).

Sonata No. 6 Op. 62
Date of Composition: 1911–1912 in Beatenberg and Moscow
Premiere: 19 March 1912 in Moscow, by Elena Bekman-Shcherbina

The Sixth Sonata was first sketched at Scriabin's summer dacha in Kashir in 1911. By early December of that year, the composer wrote to the pianist Alexander Siloti to announce that the sonata was complete, aside from a few minor details. Since its genesis, this music has earned a reputation as the most diabolical piece in Scriabin's catalogue. The composer never performed it in public, and was reportedly terrified by the dark spirits conjured up by its evil harmonies, which (according to Faubion

Bowers) were "nightmarish... fuliginous... murky... unclean... mischievous."[26] In his *Reminiscences*, Sabaneev recorded that Scriabin "liked to play the second theme and the gloomy, unsettling storm bells, adopting a terrified look on his face and even expressing with gestures a certain shock, as though confronted by visions of ghastly phantoms."[27] The music's ceremonial atmosphere and dissonant, unsettling harmonies certainly impart a sense of ritualistic gloom.

Occasionally listed in the key of G, the Sixth Sonata has no key signature and opens with a gonglike sonority that has no reference point in functional harmony, and does little to establish G as a tonal center. The opaque harmonies are widely spaced and reverberate in this texture. This work inhabits a new tonal universe for Scriabin. It was his first systematic exploration of a pitch collection with strong Russian roots, known as the octatonic scale.[28] This eight-note scale proceeds by alternating half and whole steps. In its formal layout, the piece retains a traditional sonata-allegro design.[29] Scriabin's lifelong allegiance to sonata form has drawn critical censure, but here is a case in point for retaining certain traditional elements to balance out his more innovative ideas, especially in the realm of harmony. To capture the essence of this otherworldly harmonic environment, the composer used poetic performance descriptions almost exclusively in French. Critics and commentators scoffed at the poetic indicators that Scriabin wrote into the scores of his late piano pieces, but these verbal cues serve as important formal signposts that identify the major themes.

Two themes are introduced on the first page: an archlike rhythmic motive heard at the outset, and a contrasting lyrical theme marked *avec une chaleur contenue* (with a restrained warmth). These themes are repeated before a third idea is introduced, *le rêve prend forme—clarté, douceur, pureté* (the dream takes shape—clarity, sweetness, purity). The music soon turns sinister and builds in intensity before erupting in a profane frenzy, marked *l'épouvante surgit* (the terror rises up). Trills assume tremendous prominence in this sonata, as they represent flashes of light or clanging alarm bells. The music is physically demanding and requires three staves to notate in some sections. The pianistic textures are quite new in this sonata, with wide stretches and dramatic uses of silence. Stylistic traits from the Fourth and Fifth Sonatas appear in the repeated note chord clusters marked *joyeux, triomphant*. The recapitulation arrives after a set of repeated chords marked *effondrement subit* (sudden collapse), and the musical material is developed in roughly the same order in which it was originally presented. The final pages of the piece climax in a vertiginous dance that ends in halting, skipping gestures before finally releasing into a dense chord cluster that leaves a sense of suspense and irresolution that befits this nightmarish work.

Recommended Recordings: Sviatoslav Richter (DG London, 1961); Anton Kuerti (Monitor 2134, 1972); Igor Zhukov (Melodiya/Angel 40218, 1972); Vladimir Ashkenazy (London 452579-2, 1989); Roger Woodward (Etcetera KTC 1126, 1991); Matthew Bengtson (Roméo Records 7308, 2015).

Sonata No. 7 Op. 64, "White Mass"
Date of Composition: 1911–1912, Kashira, Beatenberg, and Moscow
Premiere: 5 March 1912 in Moscow, by the composer

Sketches for the Seventh Sonata date from 1910–1911, but the remaining parts were drafted outside Moscow in Kashira in 1911, and completed the following year in Beatenberg, Switzerland. The "White Mass" Sonata was given its nickname by the composer and was one of his favorite works. Musically, the pious Seventh Sonata provides antidotal relief from the terrifying Sixth. Structurally and in terms of their harmonic content, these two sonatas are closely related, much closer in fact than the "White Mass" and "Black Mass" (No. 9) Sonatas, which are typically regarded as siblings. Op. 64's nickname refers to a pagan ritual of exorcising demons and purifying the soul. Sabaneev wrote that the Seventh was a "Light-filled Mass—a liturgical sacrament with solemn, radiant elements. This Sonata, which is filled with powerful exclamations, with bell- and trombone-like sounds, and at the same time, with the most subtle nuances of mystical experience (second theme) . . . [also] contains an element of severity, holiness, even a certain cruelty."[30]

Scriabin believed that the Seventh Sonata represented "purest mysticism" and a "total absence of human feeling"; it was the most "holy" or "saintly" music he ever wrote, yet distinctively non-Christian.[31] One reason for its purity was its harmonic vocabulary. The core harmony is a seven-note matrix set that differs only slightly from the mystic chord (D natural is lowered to D♭, and G is added). These pitches are selected for their ability to generate symmetrical collections like whole tone and octatonic scales (that is, groups of notes that are equidistant from one another and which maintain their harmonic relationship when transposed to different pitch levels). The actual presentation of the material (in a melody or chord, in thirds or fourths) is irrelevant since the composer made no distinction between chords and scales in the set transpositions. Scriabin was immensely proud of the result, and remarked that this sonata exemplified "the highest complexity within the highest simplicity."[32] It is far more accurate to describe Scriabin's late harmonic practice in these terms rather than the traditional explanation that his harmonies were stacked in fourths or atonal; indeed, quartal harmonies are almost nowhere to be found in this piece.

Bell sounds figure prominently in this sonata, and many of its themes were intended for the *Mysterium*. John Bell Young has suggested that the bells in the Seventh Sonata are closely related to the bells in the Coronation music from Mussorgsky's opera *Boris Godunov*, and specifically the bells that peal out in Yegoryevsk, an industrial city that lies roughly 70 miles southeast of Moscow.[33] Tolling bells are heard at the beginning and end of the sonata, and the repetitiveness of this opening idea and other themes lend the work a ritualistic atmosphere. Bell-like passages in this sonata are almost invariably marked with the words *mysterieusement sonore* or some variation thereof, which lends a certain consistency to Scriabin's poetic descriptions. These performance markings in French freely intermingle with more traditional tempo and interpretive indications written in Italian.

The Seventh adheres to sonata form, but includes a second recapitulation of the opening material. Four main ideas are presented: the opening Allegro theme in triplets; a middle-register idea also based in triplets and marked *avec une somber majesté* (with a somber majesty); a contrasting, lyrical secondary theme, marked *avec une céleste volupté* (with a celestial pleasure); and a related archlike idea in pentuplets, marked *le mélodie bien marquee* (the melody well marked). The opening clanging chords return periodically with heightened intensity, and there is a palpable sense of dramatic escalation in mood despite the work's separation from traditional tonal mores. At its explosive climax, the music jolts into a vertiginous dance and tears a hole in the fabric of the universe with a huge rolled chord. Perhaps recalling his visit to New York in the winter of 1906–1907, here Scriabin writes a 25-note "skyscraper" chord, a stairway to heaven. The effect is akin to a space-time warp that transports the listener from their everyday reality into a parallel dimension. The work's final bars feature ghostly trills over the mystic chord, lending the effect of an out-of-body experience that captures the moment the ego's spirit dissolves and becomes one with the divine.

Recommended Recordings: Roland Pöntinen (BIS CD-276, 1987); Joseph Villa (Dante PSG 8801, 1988); Vladimir Ashkenazy (London 452579-2, 1989); Sviatoslav Richter (AS Disc 346, 1995); John Bell Young (Americus 1013, 1999); Arcadi Volodos (Sony Classical 56887, 2009).

Sonata No. 8 Op. 66
Date of Composition: 1912–1913, in Moscow
Premiere: 18 November 1915 in St. Petersburg, by Elena Bekman-Shcherbina

Scriabin started writing his Eighth Sonata in Moscow during the winter of 1912 and completed it by the early summer of 1913. This piece was written concurrently with the Ninth and Tenth Sonatas, the latter of these being completed first. The Eighth Sonata exemplifies Scriabin's compositional philosophy that "melody becomes harmony and harmony becomes melody."[34] Gone is the traditional leading melody with supportive chordal harmonies. But the dissonant textures of this piece are not bereft of melody. This equalization of melody and harmony is apparent in the opening bars, which present no less than five separate melodic strands in dense counterpoint. These incandescent harmonies are one of Scriabin's most brilliant examples of projecting light through music. He must have considered the music to be pure or absolute, in no need of the kinds of poetic descriptors that one finds throughout his other late sonatas. Only a few sparse Italian tempo designators are in the published score, with the exception of a single theme marked *Tragique*. This lengthy composition is full of dark colors and episodic twists and turns of mood. The Scriabin researcher and pianist Donald Garvelmann described the Eighth Sonata as "a walk through a crystalline floral labyrinth . . . trying to find one's way around may be confusing, but the view is always bewitching and beautiful."[35] Indeed, this moody music churns and glows like a bubbling cauldron of molten lava.

Like all of Scriabin's late sonatas, key signatures are absent, although this piece is sometimes listed in the key of A. It follows a sonata-allegro form, but is in no way formulaic. A brief prologue is followed by the exposition, which begins with descending parallel fourths marked *Allegro agitato*. Themes mix and intermingle in phantasmagoric fashion. The American pianist Katherine Ruth Heyman delivered the U.S. premiere of Op. 66 in New Orleans in 1916. She interpreted the sonata's five basic motives as the base elements of fire, water, earth, air, and atmosphere. "These five short motivs [sic]," she wrote in her 1921 book, *The Relation of the Ultramodern to Archaic Music*, are the runes according to tradition given to Scriabin from one source or another, of the five elements."[36] These five motives are laid out in succession on the first page of the score, and though the casual observer might glance over these slight figures as decorative turns of phrase, they are important structural motives. In similar fashion, the Soviet critic Boris Asafiev associated the Eighth Sonata with the natural world and the laws of energy and matter. Such observations are corroborated by the composer's own views on the sonata, as reported to Sabaneev and translated by Bowers. To Scriabin, the Eighth Sonata's harmonies had been inspired by nature, like the bells in the Seventh Sonata, and this music spanned "bridges between harmony and geometry, life visible and unseen."[37]

Like its sibling work, the Tenth Sonata, the Eighth Sonata has a fearsome reputation. Not many pianists have the courage to perform it in public. Scriabin never played it in public, presumably because its considerable length (nearly 500 bars) and technical mazes make it challenging to memorize, let alone execute in front of a live audience. Texturally, the sonata has incredibly difficult passagework that spans an enormous range and occasionally lies awkwardly under the hands. For most of the twentieth century, few pianists played this sonata. By 1974, even in the wake of the Scriabin revival, Donald Garvelmann could name only Martha Anne Verbit as the lone pianist who kept the Eighth Sonata in her active repertoire. Today, the Eighth Sonata remains by a wide margin the most rarely performed of Scriabin's sonatas.

Recommended Recordings: Vladimir Sofronitsky (Arlecchino ARL 119, 1958); Roger Woodward (Etcetera 1126, 1991); Vladimir Ashkenazy (London 452579-2, 1989); Matthew Bengtson (Roméo Records 7308, 2015).

Sonata No. 9 Op. 68, "Black Mass"
Date of Composition: 1911–1913, Beatenberg and Moscow
Premiere: 25 October 1913 in Moscow, by the composer

Sketched over two years and completed in 1913, the "Black Mass" is Scriabin's most famous sonata. Its nickname came from the composer's friend and fellow Theosophist, Alexei Podgaetsky, who contrasted the sonata's demonic qualities with the saintliness of the "White Mass" Sonata. The composer beamed with pride at this suggestion and the name stuck. Like all of Scriabin's sonatas from the Fifth, the Ninth Sonata was cast in a single movement and served as preliminary sketch material for the *Mysterium*. More economical in form than the other late sonatas, the "Black

Mass" is less than half as long as the Eighth Sonata, at least in terms of page length. Poetic descriptions are applied generously in the published score, offering some corroboration that the composer had a specific vision in mind for this piece.

Op. 68 begins with an ominous, slow, tolling four-note motto that is exchanged between both hands. This plodding motive soon breaks down and is interrupted by a mysterious vocal-like idea in triplets, marked *mysterieusement murmuré*. The opening theme returns throughout the movement, but the music dissolves into dark murmurings and haunting trills. One of the sonata's most remarkable aspects is its transformation of this opening four-note motto into various themes, including a final vertiginous dance fit to shake the heavens. The musical effect is akin to Berlioz's deliciously evil twist on the *idée fixe* in his "Dream of a Witches' Sabbath" from the *Symphonie fantastique* (1830). As a fitting end to Scriabin's Ninth Sonata, the sepulchral motto that appears at the beginning of the piece reappears in the same guise in the last bars, bringing the events full circle. In Hull's words, in this reprise of the opening motto, "The mist of the nightmare dispels—the painful memories fly away—leaving the pure semi-luminosity of the atmosphere of the opening bars."[38]

In addition to its musical merits, the Ninth Sonata has achieved its notoriety due to its associations with Satan and the occult. In his *Reminiscences*, Sabaneev asked Scriabin to compare its evilness to the *Poème satanique* Op. 36, to which the composer replied, "In the Ninth sonata I came into contact with the Satanic more profoundly than ever before. There [in Op. 36] Satan is a *guest*; here he is *at home*."[39] The link between the Ninth Sonata and the occult is bolstered by popular sources like the 1943 horror novel *Conjure Wife* by Fritz Leiber, which tells the story of a small-town college professor who discovers that his wife is a witch. In one scene, the professor becomes consumed by his ruminations, and in a moment of ritualistic meditation, he puts on a record of the "poisonous" Ninth Sonata, a "perfidious" piece that "rasped the nerves." As if executing a ritual or ceremony, the professor outfits the record player with a clean, unused record needle specifically for the occasion:

> Faster and faster it went. The lovely second theme became infected, was distorted into something raucous and discordant—a march of the damned—a dance of the damned—breaking off suddenly when it had reached an unendurable pitch. Then a repetition of the droning first theme, ending on a soft yet grating note low in the keyboard.[40]

Regrettably, this creepy scene was omitted in British director Sidney Hayers' 1962 film adaptation of Leiber's book, titled *Night of the Eagle*. Such references to the Ninth Sonata in popular lore have long bolstered Scriabin's reputation as having ties to the occult and black magic. This public image of Scriabin is reinforced by such works as the *Poème satanique*, *Vers la flamme*, and the apocalyptic *Mysterium*, all of which fueled speculation that Scriabin had dabbled in occult practices.

The Ninth Sonata has never fallen outside the concert repertory owing to its notoriety, brevity, and technical approachability. Its proper interpretation, however, is another matter, but it is the key factor in the work's public success. According to Sabaneev, Scriabin once remarked that he was "practicing sorcery" while playing the Ninth Sonata, and that ideal is realized by such master interpreters as Vladimir Horowitz, whose smoldering version in his comeback concert at Carnegie Hall in 1965 makes "the sulfurous smell of evil . . . reek in every measure," as David Dubal described it.[41] The Ninth Sonata is a powerful work that tests the mettle of even the best performers. Several talented pianists have recorded definitive interpretations of this work, yet its many opportunities for interpretive liberties will allow for future generations to filter their own interpretive genius through this masterwork.

Recommended Recordings: Vladimir Horowitz (Columbia Masterworks M2L 328, 1965); Vladimir Ashkenazy (London 452579-2, 1989); Sviatoslav Richter ([live] Music & Arts 878, 1995); Vladimir Sofronitsky (Phillips, Great Pianists of the Twentieth Century, 1169796, 1999); Yevgeny Sudbin (BIS-SACD-1568, 2007); Alexander Melnikov (Harmonia Mundi HMG 501914, 2014).

Sonata No. 10 Op. 70, "Trill"
Date of Composition: 1912–1913 in Moscow
Premiere: 25 December 1913 in Moscow, by the composer
The Tenth Sonata is the pinnacle of Scriabin's accomplishments in the genre. Although it was written concurrently with the last three piano sonatas, it stands apart from the earlier sonatas in its stark originality and shimmering harmonies, which have been compared to the fiery textures of *Prometheus: Poem of Fire*. Both works demonstrate Scriabin's fascination with light as well as his desire to create transcendent Symbolist art that would cause a temporal shift in the material world. As in *Prometheus*, light and color are symbolized by tremolos that reverberate through this piece, and are marked *lumineux, vibrant*. The Tenth Sonata has been popularly nicknamed "Trill," but that moniker was bestowed posthumously and gained currency due to its simplicity. In this atmospheric piece, trills are anything but decorative ornaments. The symbolic and gestural functions they served in Scriabin's previous five sonatas, which symbolized quivering or light, are transformed here into "palpitation . . . trembling . . . the vibration in the atmosphere," in the composer's words.[42] The Tenth Sonata shows Scriabin working with tone clusters of the sort that contemporary composer-pianists like Béla Bartók, Charles Ives, and Leo Ornstein were exploring, not to mention Stravinsky in orchestral works like the *Rite of Spring* (1913). Although these composers are often regarded as pioneers of harmony, their interest in tone clusters was driven less by the desire to radicalize traditional harmony, and more by the urge to create new sounds and musical effects. Tone colors and dissonance, then, were new ways of expressing emotions for a modern age, and Scriabin's Tenth Sonata is a definitive statement toward that artistic aim. Indeed, the apocalyptic tones of this sonata leave us wondering what he had in mind for his *Mysterium*.

Like the basic four-note motto that opens the "Black Mass" sonata, the Tenth Sonata starts with basic intervals that form the nucleus of the core harmonies, in this case a major third followed by a minor third. In spite of its dense harmonic fabric, the Tenth Sonata follows a conventional formal plan in its use of a prologue followed by a sonata-allegro form. As the musical lines unfold at the sonata's opening, a new, descending chromatic melody is added to the top line. Instead of traditional melodic themes, its motives are boiled down to small intervals and sparse gestures. Listeners who expect traditional themes with strong melodic and rhythmic profiles may feel lost in the cascading climaxes and brilliant colors of this piece. Among the many changes of meter and harmonic vagaries, trills remain one of the only consistent elements to guide listeners through this piece. This is some of the most transcendental, ecstatic music that Scriabin ever wrote.

Interpretively, the Tenth Sonata ranks among the most difficult of Scriabin's sonatas, not only due to its physical challenges, but also because the dense harmonic material lacks the tonal familiarity and steady pulse of Scriabin's middle-period music.[43] Pianists and listeners can easily lose their way in the surging tide of trills and abbreviated themes. Given its heavenly overtones, it is appropriate that the composer delivered its world premiere on Christmas Day, 1913. Despite its technical and interpretive challenges, this sonata is one of the most popular of Scriabin's late pieces. Many pianists consider it their favorite of Scriabin's sonatas once they get to know their way around the piece. Since the early twenty-first century, it has been given inspired readings by Jonathan Powell, Arcadi Volodos, and Garrick Ohlsson, among others pianists.

Recommended Recordings: Vladimir Horowitz (Historic Return Sony Classical 53461, 1965); Roberto Szidon (Deutsche Grammophon 2543 816, 1971); Arcadi Volodos (Sony Classical 60893, 1999); Mikhail Pletnev (Virgin 45247, 2010); Matthew Bengtson (Roméo Records 7308, 2015).

MAZURKAS FOR SOLO PIANO

Opp. 3 (1887–1889), 25 (1899), and 40 (1902–1903)

The mazurka is a Polish dance in triple meter. When properly performed, the inequality of beat stresses can blur whether the music is in a triple or duple meter. But it is ideal for fitting in the heel clicks of the dance. The mazurka has its origins in folk music, specifically the slow *kujawiak* and the fast *oberek*. In Polish, the form is known as a "Masur" or "Mazurek," which is derived from the tribe of Masures who lived on the eastern plains of Poland. The rhythmic peculiarity of the dance brought it to European ballrooms, and classical composers took this folk form and subjected it to classical techniques such as counterpoint and fugue. Chopin is the composer most closely associated with the mazurka due to his sixty examples of the genre. For Chopin, mazurkas were experimental pieces that functioned as both folk tradition and folk mythology.[44] Their exotic harmonies and off-kilter rhythms had historical roots in Polish culture, but these pieces were exemplary for invoking a faraway land or a time that existed only in the imagination. The exotic strains of the mazurka endeared it to many nineteenth-century composers, including Tchaikovsky, Borodin,

Glinka, and of course Scriabin, who was the first composer-pianist after Chopin to publish mazurkas of any great distinction. (Karol Szymanowski and Alexander Tansman later followed suit with highly original mazurkas of their own.)

Scriabin's attraction to the mazurka ran deeper than his desire to emulate Chopin's achievements. The genre's basis in dance music, profusion of maudlin melodies, and bold harmonic shifts also attracted him. But surely he sensed the opportunity to surpass his idol in one of his signature styles. John Bell Young explained that, "What inspired Scriabin was Chopin's vivid imagination and compositional finesse. What challenged him was the potential for reinventing the mazurka on Russian terms, translating its trochaically structured musical prosody—so characteristic of the speech rhythms of the Polish language—into its lush Russian equivalent."[45] For pianists, these works are not technically challenging, but the push and pull of the rhythmic pulse must never be lost in performance. The composer premiered Nos. 1, 3, and 4 from the Op. 25 set in Moscow on 18 March 1902, but throughout the rest of his career, he played only selections of his mazurkas.

Scriabin wrote a total of twenty-three mazurkas (two were published posthumously), starting with the *Ten Mazurkas Op. 3* (1888–1890). It was the first collection of pieces he published, through the Jurgenson firm in 1893. As some of Scriabin's earliest compositions, these works are often considered derivative, but they demonstrate his keen assimilation of the genre's stylistic nuances, especially its harmonic quirkiness and sense of adventure. Scriabin preserved the basic formal design of several sections of contrasting character and key. It is significant that nine out of these ten works are in minor keys. To enhance their exotic, folksy flavor, Scriabin favored remote keys such as G♯ minor, B♭ minor, and D♯ minor. Given their kinship of character and mood, only highlights of the Op. 3 set are discussed below.

No. 1 in B minor was written in November 1887, when the composer was only sixteen. It sets the stage for the set with its melancholic mood and episodic structure. The long flowing lines of No. 4 make it one of the more extended works of Op. 3, and this sense of an unraveling melodic line is a common element among the melodically driven pieces. No. 5 in D♯ minor is marked *Doloroso* (painful), and its flowing melodies share commonalities with the archlike, compound melodies of No. 8 in B♭ minor. No. 6 is a Beethovenian bagatelle in C♯ minor. Marked *scherzando*, this impish piece features a poignant middle section with a sighing and dripping chromatic melody line. The descending chromatic lines of No. 7 offer a natural segue from No. 6, and provide pianists with ample opportunities to draw out the sinewy inner parts. No. 10 in E♭ minor is more than twice as long as any other piece in the set, and is also the richest in its variety of moods. This final work in the Op. 3 set brings this group full circle with its emphasis on the flattened sixth scale degree (C♭), which is enharmonic with the pitch B—the tonal center for the first piece in the set.

Scriabin wrote the *Nine Mazurkas Op. 25* (1898–1899) early in his teaching tenure at the Moscow Conservatory, when he was short on both time and inspiration. It shows in these pieces, which display a greater concern with harmonic complexity and formal development, but at the expense of pure invention. Perhaps to counteract the stress of his teaching duties, these works portray a more graceful and playful spirit than the Op. 3 set, yet many of them exhibit a lack of individuality. It is strange that Scriabin returned to writing mazurkas after a break of nine years, but being surrounded by the music of other composers had a mimetic effect upon his creativity, much to his consternation. The obligation of sending new works to Beliaev for publication also surely motivated him.

Op. 25 No. 1 in F minor is less formally compartmentalized than pieces from the Op. 3 set, and is almost rhapsodic in design. Yet some formal congruity holds the piece together; the *scherzando* middle section in A♭, for instance, returns at the end in the home key. No. 2 recalls the salon style of Scriabin's youth. It is delicate and refined, and ornamented in an almost Baroque manner. A noticeable lack of a dance pulse distinguishes No. 3 in E minor, which is Schumanesque in its styling. Its introspective and halting phrases seem to search for meaning in the ineffable mysteries of life. No. 4 in E major shows Scriabin on the cusp of his middle-period style, with passages that foreshadow the graceful melodic turns of the *Poème* Op. 32 No. 1. No. 5 in C♯ minor recalls the Third Sonata in its dramatic mood and octaves in dotted rhythms. Its secondary theme marked *Molto tranquillo* is cut from the same cloth as the secondary theme of the Third Sonata's first movement. No. 7 in F♯ minor is the most extended piece of the Op. 25 set. It features an abundance of tugging half steps and sinewy chromaticism, yet the music's overall mood remains tranquil. The scope and harmonic wanderings of this piece cause it to drift away from the basic dance feel, until a decorated and almost hopping melody reminds us that this is indeed a mazurka. No. 9 in E♭ minor is sensitive and refined in its twisting modern harmonies. Scriabin's singular compositional voice is heard more clearly here than in any other piece in the Op. 25 set.

The relative obscurity and rhythmic idiosyncrasies of these mazurkas have dissuaded pianists from performing them with any regularity. The gentle nature and idyllic quality of the Op. 25 set is especially unrepresentative of Scriabin's burgeoning middle-period style as compared to other works from this period, such as the Third Sonata and *Fantasie* Op. 28. Samuil Feinberg set the standard for these mazurkas' interpretation with his recordings made in the 1950s, which brilliantly capture their elusive metrical pulse. The mazurkas Opp. 3 and 25 have enjoyed even greater popularity in arrangements other than for solo piano, including violin and piano, string quartet, and solo guitar. Opp. 25 Nos. 3 and 4 were recently treated to a series of improvisations by the jazz pianist David Gordon. With his Trio, Gordon recorded a tribute to the Scriabin centenary, called *Alexander Scriabin's Ragtime Band* (Mr. Sam Records SAMCD 004, 2015). The stylistic mashup that Gordon brings to Scriabin's music merges classical music with ragtime, Latin music, and modern jazz. The Mazurka Op. 25 No. 3, for instance, is transformed into a Brazilian choro. The mazurkas are but one genre of Scriabin's solo piano music that has enjoyed a second life in alternate arrangements, but these pieces have been especially well served by this process.

Recommended Recordings: Artur Pizarro (Collins 13942, 1993); Boris Bekhterev (Camerata Records 28222, 2012); Samuil Feinberg (MEL CD 1002192, 2014).

ETUDES FOR SOLO PIANO

Scriabin published twenty-six etudes (literally *studies*) throughout his career, grouped in sets of twelve (Op. 8), eight (Op. 42), and three (Op. 65). Like the piano sonatas, this collection of etudes illustrates a wide range of moods and technical demands. Of these twenty-six etudes, several stand out from the group and have stood the test of time. Three of Scriabin's most famous etudes were choreographed by the legendary American dancer Isadora Duncan (1877–1927) in a set of dances written in between 1921 and 1924: Op. 8 No. 12 in D♯ minor ("Revolutionary"), Op. 42 No. 5 in C♯ minor ("The Crossing at St. Petersburg"), and Op. 2 No. 1 in C♯ minor ("Mother").[46] The last of these works is one of Scriabin's first published pieces and was written when he was only fifteen. Its evocative depiction of loneliness calls to mind images of the vast Russian steppes, and its searching melody and meditative middle section in E♭ major add to the sense of soulful expression. This etude is quite approachable for amateurs, and its sonorous use of the piano's natural resonances make it one of Scriabin's most memorable compositions.

Op. 2 No. 1
Recommended Recordings: Vladimir Horowitz (Columbia Masterworks M2L 328, 1965); Émile Naoumoff (Live at the Théâtre des Champs-Elysées, Thesis 582018, 1989); Vladimir Sofronitsky (Saison Russe RUS 788032, 1997); Michèle Gurdal (Challenge Classics, #CC 72640, 2014).

Twelve Etudes Op. 8
Date of Composition: 1894–1895 in Moscow
The Op. 8 Etudes are an early manifesto of Scriabin's pianistic and compositional prowess. The impressive range of emotion and technical demands in these works display a degree of sophistication that belies their low opus number. There is no denying that the influence of Chopin and Liszt hovers over these works; from these two composer-pianists, Scriabin learned to elevate the musical content above the technical challenges. After all, these etudes are meant to please the ears more than the fingers. These works have appealed to pianists and non-pianists alike, and nearly every one of them has been arranged for various instrumental combinations. As the first organized set of published works that Scriabin produced, he understandably labored long and hard before releasing them for public consumption. In a letter of 20 March 1895 to his publisher, Beliaev, Scriabin admitted their tortured gestation:

> I am working literally all day long. I start writing right after getting up and keep composing until evening without even taking a walk. Do you think that I am writing anything new? Absolutely not, still the etudes. Several of them you will not recognize—so much they were altered. For example, the A♭ major [No. 8] was completely re-written as well as the B♭ minor [No. 7], D♯ minor [No. 12], and the middle part of the other B♭ minor [No. 11]. I think I will also revise and correct the octave etude [No. 9], which still does not satisfy me.[47]

Scriabin sent them off to Beliaev for publication in late March 1895. However, the composer was so indecisive over the final form for the capstone of the set, No. 12 in D♯ minor, that he wrote two versions, although the original version is far more often played.[48] The alternate version was published posthumously and is rarely performed. The chairman of Beliaev's publishing house, Rimsky-Korsakov, rendered the final decision for the version of Op. 8 No. 12 that is so well known today, lest the composer vacillate further on which version to publish.[49]

Op. 8 is divided into two parts and organized according to key. Like Chopin's Op. 10 and Op. 25 sets, as well as Liszt's Transcendental Études, Scriabin's Op. 8 is in a set of twelve. The key signatures of the first three selections proceed by fourths (C♯-F♯-B minor). At No. 4, a shift from minor to major tilts the trajectory, which continues its progression of fourths to complete Part 1 (B major-E-A).[50] The key of C♯ major for the energetic No. 1 is unusual and signals Scriabin's fondness for remote keys, duly noted by contemporary critics.[51] The influence of Schumann is also evident in this piece. No. 2 in F♯ minor presents a variety of demanding polyrhythmic patterns between the hands. This is one of the more original pieces of the set. It exudes a sense of reckless passion and is appropriately marked *a capriccio, con forza*. No. 3 in B minor is a *moto perpetuo* work in a Chopinesque vein that challenges the right hand to constantly alternate between single notes and octaves, among other physical obstacles. The sinuous melody of No. 4 in B major includes some interesting coloristic effects and surprising chromaticism in its middle section, but overall the mood is airy and carefree. No. 5 in E major is one of the most charming in the set. Its compound melody features octave leaps in the right hand, and the piece has a wistful sense of nostalgia, which lightens in mood when the opening melody is heard in triplets in the concluding section. The basic pulse of triples segues into No. 6 in A major, an off-kilter waltz that seems to flow in free time. The right hand melody is harmonized in sixths, but technically this piece is more approachable than Chopin's own study in sixths, the Etude Op. 25 No. 8.

Part II of Op. 8 starts with No. 7 in B♭ minor, which has strong affinities with Chopin's Etude Op. 25 No. 4 in A minor, but ventures into new territory in its middle section. The right and left hands are written in different meters at the opening. No. 8 is set in A♭ major, a classic key of love and tenderness. It is an ode to Scriabin's childhood sweetheart, Natalya Sekerina.[52] The work makes a technical study of sustained sonority and prolonged phrases, symbols of the strength and longevity of their love. No. 9 in G♯ minor is driving and impetuous from its opening bars.

It is the lengthiest etude of the set with a heading of *alla ballata* (in the style of a *Ballade*). This study in octaves summons the spirit of Liszt in its opening material, and the middle section marked *Meno vivo* (less animated) could have been lifted straight from Chopin's *Ballades*. No. 10 in D♭ major focuses on chromatic double notes in the right hand and features an incredible range of motion in the left hand. The syncopated middle section provides sonic relief through consonant thirds. It is one of the most charming works of the set and was arranged for violin and piano by Joseph Szigeti in 1953. No. 11 in B♭ minor echoes the spirit of Rachmaninov in its pathos and emotional appeal. It has long enjoyed recognition as one of Scriabin's most beloved slow pieces. The melancholic cantilena played against repeated chords paints a poignant mood.[53]

The last and most famous etude of the set, No. 12 in D♯ minor, was an international hit for Scriabin, surpassing even the left hand Nocturne in popularity. For newcomers to Scriabin's music, the D♯ minor etude is an ideal introduction to his Russian romantic style. Marked *Patetico*, this visceral piece exemplifies the brooding intensity of late nineteenth-century music, and features surging octave runs in the right hand that press upward. The furiously repeated chords heard at its climax became a favorite device of Scriabin's, and they can be heard in the finales of his Fourth and Fifth sonatas. Like Chopin's "Revolutionary" Etude, the D♯ minor Etude has become a warhorse for pianists. Scriabin recorded it in February 1910 on a Welte-Mignon piano roll, and it was a favorite encore for many twentieth-century virtuosos, from Horowitz and Van Cliburn to Lang Lang.

Op. 8 Etudes
Recommended Recordings: Morton Estrin (Newport Classics NCD 60067, 1990); Piers Lane (Hyperion 66607, 1992); Mikhail Voskresensky (Kvadro KTL02-601, 2002); Yuki Matsuzawa (Pianissimo PP 10394, 2004); Vladimir Sofronitsky (Le Chant du Monde LDC 278 765).

Eight Etudes Op. 42
Date of Composition: 1902–1903
Premiere: 15 March 1906 (Nos. 1 and 5) in Moscow, by Vera I. Skriabina
The Op. 42 Etudes were published in 1904, during one of the most bountiful periods of Scriabin's career. In the pieces he wrote around 1903, including the Symphonies Nos. 2 and 3, he developed a distinctive compositional voice that focused on achieving ecstasy through music. The harmonic language of the Op. 42 etudes is post-Romantic and highly chromatic. Phrases are strung together in periodic fashion, but consistently avoid harmonic resolution. Polyrhythms are a core element of the Op. 42 set, which seems to achieve a sense of hovering, swirling sounds.[54] No. 1 in D♭ major presents a typical Scriabinian rhythm of nine against five in a *Presto*

tempo, which lends the effect of nervous energy or flight, the latter of which was one of Scriabin's preoccupations in the mature works. Here, melody and harmony are dissolved into one amalgam of sound. The music passes through several keys before the main subject returns in a nine against six rhythm. Although less of a mathematical puzzle than nine against five, this basic pulse is still difficult to maintain in the light and dexterous articulation that Scriabin prescribes. The next three selections all take F♯ as their key center. Op. 42 No. 2, however, is introspective, with ascending groups of five in the left hand against a sparse melody in the right. A polyrhythm of five against three predominates. No. 3 in F♯ major is a long, measured trill, and its fluttering, buzzing runs earned it the nickname "Mosquito." The challenge of sustaining the steady right-hand trill is made more difficult by the *Prestissimo* tempo and constant *ppp* dynamic. No. 4 in F♯ major is highly erotic, yet soothing in its tenderness and introspection. It shares a common mood with the Prelude Op. 37 No 1. Contrapuntal balance and a consistent tempo are demanded in this piece, as its sentimental nature tempts one to savor the delicate beauty of these sumptuous harmonies.

No. 5 in C♯ minor is marked *Affanato* (breathless, or agitated), and its intensity and enormous power has made it the most celebrated piece of this set. The music is probing and knotty, lofty and ecstatic. Scriabin declared that this etude "excelled the Third Symphony in power and sublimity."[55] Independence of the fingers and sustained tension are put to the test in this work, which was a favorite piece for the composer to perform, as well as such virtuosos as Horowitz and Evgeny Kissin. The Viennese pianist Hilde Somer remarked that, "Performing this etude is a physical endurance test—the sinewy bass develops a rotating left arm of herculean strength and snake-like flexibility."[56] No. 6 in D♭ major recalls the rhythmic contortions of the five against three rhythm heard in Op. 42 No. 2, as well as the independence of the top line, carried by the fourth and fifth fingers. Wide stretches of both hands also present complications of agility due to the awkward hand positions. No. 7 in F minor returns to the world of Chopin (especially his *Trois nouvelles* études) with a rhythm of three against four, and single- and double-notes in the right hand. No. 8 in E♭ major recalls the five against three heard elsewhere in this set, but the quintuplets are confined to the right hand in a compound melody. The middle section returns to F♯ major for the kind of interlude one might encounter in a Chopin sonata or Scherzo. The reprise of the opening material brings closure to this etude and the set as a whole.

Op. 42 Etudes

Recommended Recordings: Lazar Berman (Melodiya D 8677/8, 1963); Arthur Greene (Supraphon 3324, 1998); Garrick Ohlssohn (Bridge 9287, 2009); Joseph Villa (Piano Classics 30, 2012).

Three Etudes Op. 65
Date of Composition: 1911 and summer 1912, Beatenberg and Moscow

Aside from the Etudes Op. 49 No. 1 in E♭ major (1905) and Op. 56 No. 4 (1908), eight years elapsed after the Op. 42 set was published before Scriabin turned his attention once again to writing a set of piano etudes. In 1911, when the Op. 65 works were first sketched, Scriabin's technical and conceptual approach to the piano had evolved far past his previous efforts. The idea of writing study pieces like the Op. 8 group—with its focus on technical hurdles and plotted traversal of key centers—was now foreign to his concept of music. But the idea of conveying spiritual uplift was more imperative than ever. He was living at the time in Beatenberg, Switzerland, far removed from contemporary musical life in Western Europe. Scriabin had also secured a new contract with Jurgenson, the same firm that published his early works.

The iconoclastic Etudes Op. 65 thumb their nose at tradition and objectify some of the most forbidden intervals for well-mannered composition: minor ninths (No. 1), minor sevenths (No. 2), and perfect fifths (No. 3). Scriabin wrote on 3 August 1912 to his friend Leonid Sabaneev, beaming with pride over his irreverence:

> I inform you of news that is rather pleasant for me, maybe not indifferent to you, and quite unbearable for some proponents of classicism: a composer you know has written three etudes! In fifths (oh horror!), in ninths (what depravity!), and . . . in major sevenths (the final fall!?). What will the world say?[57]

Scriabin's single-minded focus on these intervals was not a way of simplifying the compositional process, but rather a self-imposed limitation that forced him to be inventive in other ways. The preoccupation with spiritual ascent, for instance, is conveyed through ascending scales in all three etudes, each with its own character or personality according to interval. Some critics, however, took offense to the exploitation of these taboo intervals, and even supporters like Edwin Evans in England shunned these etudes as "frankly mechanical, and the harmonic justification of the sequence . . . the merest sophistry. This rather paradoxical coincidence of an acutely 'cérébral' phrase with a period of intense imaginative fervour is the most baffling problem Scriabin has set us."[58] For pianists like Katherine Ruth Heyman, however, these innovative etudes were "sharp [and] scintillant, like bright bits of broken glass."[59]

Like the late piano sonatas, the Etudes Op. 65 were originally published with key signatures, but over time, modern scores have omitted any key designations. No. 1 exploits major ninths in the right hand, an oddly dissonant interval that just surpasses the octave, but which raises the technical difficulty level of this piece exponentially. The ninths lend a distinct bell-like sonority to the piece. The wide stretch in the right hand makes this etude virtually off limits for pianists with anything less than an expansive reach, and it is for this reason that the composer never performed the work in public. Like the quiet, sustained trills in the "Mosquito" Etude Op. 42 No. 3, the *pp* dynamic in Op. 65 No. 1 complicates the physical execution of these ninths. No. 2 in major sevenths has a strange, liturgical sensibility, but mystical or paganistic instead of Christian. The contrasting material is marked *Impérieux* and is declamatory with repeated chords in the bass. The opening material interjects in these bold phrases, but is overcome by the driving insistence of this new idea. As in *Vers la flamme*, chords pounded out in the piano's highest register evoke flashes of light. No. 3 adopts a typical Scriabinian mood with its triplet phrases that suggest flight. Its final phrase brings formal closure to the set by directly quoting the opening phrase of Op. 65 No. 1, but in fifths instead of ninths. These three etudes were orchestrated by Alexander Nemtin as part of his realization of Scriabin's unfinished *Acte préalable*.

Recommended Recordings: Roger Woodward (Etcetera KTC 1126, 1991); Arthur Greene (Supraphon 3324, 1998); Sviatoslav Richter (Andromeda ANDRCD 5134, 2008); Dmitri Alexeev, Complete Etudes (Brilliant Classics 94439, 2015).

PRELUDES FOR SOLO PIANO

A *prelude* is an introductory piece borne of inspiration and improvisation. Its appearance in music history was a matter of practicality. Preludes allowed musicians to tune and adjust their instruments and warm up their fingers. Historically, preludes consisted of extended, unmeasured flourishes for the right hand, supported by skeletal bass lines. Their composers fully expected performers to extemporize on the basic material. As the genre evolved, left hand parts gained greater independence, especially in the harpsichord preludes written in France and Germany during the eighteenth century by Jean Philippe Rameau and Francois Couperin.[60]

It was Johann Sebastian Bach, however, master organist, composer, and improviser, who elevated the prelude to a new level of refinement in his two books of the *Well-Tempered Clavier* (1722 and 1742, hereafter WTC). Unlike the free-form, improvisatory nature of earlier preludes, Bach's preludes demonstrated the single-minded working out of a compositional idea. This musical objective formed the basis for the prelude as a genre. In his WTC I and II, Bach paired preludes and fugues in every major and minor key, thus retaining the prelude's function as a prefatory piece while demonstrating its ability to stand as an independent work. In the nineteenth century, the prelude evolved yet another degree in the hands of Chopin, who distilled intense expressivity into concentrated and highly economic musical forms. To this day, Chopin's 24 Preludes Op. 28 remain quintessential examples of the poetic potential of the genre in the nineteenth century.

Determined to emulate and eventually surpass the Polish master, Scriabin completed a total of ninety preludes throughout his career. For all of his grandiose works like the *Divine Poem* or *Poem of Ecstasy*, Scriabin was an equally gifted miniaturist, and throughout his career he endeavored to compress his musical ideas into ever-more concise forms. What his preludes lack in duration they compensate for in poeticism and concentrated intensity, and his contributions to the genre marked the first significant piano preludes in Russian music. Perhaps influenced by Scriabin's successes, Rachmaninov soon followed suit by writing piano preludes of his own (Opp. 23 [1901–1903] and 32 [1910]). Like Scriabin's development of the piano sonata, his preludes demonstrate him bringing an older genre into the modern era.

24 Preludes Op. 11
Date of Composition: 1888–1896

Scriabin's Preludes Op. 11 offer a diverse sampling of his youthful, late-romantic style. It is the largest collection of his works contained in a single opus number. It is a mistake to dismiss these finely wrought miniatures as ersatz Chopin, since Scriabin's voice shines through in the distinctive melodic turns, rhythmic skips, and harmonic tinges.[61] In its traversal of every major and minor key in the chromatic scale, Scriabin's Op. 11 took Bach's *Well-Tempered Clavier* as an obvious model (or target), but an even greater influence was Chopin's twenty-four Preludes Op. 28. Legend has it that Chopin had Bach's WTC Books I and II by his side while writing his Op. 28 preludes in Majorca, Spain, in 1839. Most of Scriabin's Preludes Op. 11 were written during the years 1895–1896, when concert tours took him to Paris, Dresden, Heidelberg, and Amsterdam. But eleven of the twenty-four works were written in Moscow, and many of them strike a classic, bleak Russian mood. Each of these musical postcards in Op. 11 bears an inscription of the city where it was conceived.

The large-scale organization of this set reflects the guiding hand of Beliaev, who wrung as many works as he could from his protégé, and assembled them into published form. Scriabin and Beliaev made a wager in November 1895 that Scriabin could not deliver forty-eight preludes by the following April. Although Scriabin completed only forty-seven pieces by the deadline, he declared himself the winner, as he had revised the terms of their agreement and had intended (in his mind) to complete forty-six total pieces.[62] Twenty-four of these works went into the Op. 11 set, while the remaining twenty-three pieces were distributed among the Preludes Opp. 13, 15, 16, and 17. Despite grouping the twenty-four pieces in a complete set, Scriabin resisted the idea that Op. 11 was a unified cycle that should be performed *in toto*. Typically, these works are performed in selected groups, as the composer often did at his own concerts. He also recorded several of these Preludes on Welte-Mignon piano rolls (Nos. 1, 2, and 13). Rachmaninov played several of the Op. 11 Preludes during his memorial tour for Scriabin in the fall of 1915, and they are still regularly heard today. In recent years, the Latvian-born pianist Dina Yoffe (b. 1952) has been delivering performances of Scriabin's Op. 11 and Chopin's Op. 28 preludes intertwined on the same program.

A number of stylistic similarities can be observed between Scriabin's Op. 11 and Chopin's works. Op. 11 No. 1 in C major was originally marked *ondeggiante, carezzando* (undulating, caressingly), and it features arpeggiated chords in contrary motion between the hands, like Chopin's opening number of Op. 28. The ending of No. 1 evokes the clanging of Moscow's church bells. No. 2 in A minor is a wistful, chromatic waltz. Scriabin's use of the French sixth harmony here is significant, as it would become a distinctive harmonic fingerprint of his later style.

No. 4 in E minor was based on an early *Ballade* in B♭ minor that Scriabin wrote when he was sixteen (1888). Its persistent falling melody suggests a heavy burden, and recalls Chopin's Etude Op. 25 No. 7, which has a similar three-voice texture and descending melody line. The bel canto melodies that drive Scriabin's early works are on display in No. 5 in D major, a nocturnelike piece that features a rolling accompaniment in the left hand against an unfolding melody in the right. No. 6 in B minor is an etude in octaves, driven by two ideas: the hands fill in one another's spaces while the melody ascends in its calling phrase, then falls in its responding phrase. This work shares some traits with No. 18, another octave study with a characteristic two against three rhythm. No. 7 in A major is in the style of a barcarolle, or Venetian gondolier song, with octave pedal points and the effect of fading away at its close through ever-decreasing dynamic markings. No. 9 in E major avoids the tonic harmony until the end of the piece, and recalls Chopin in its mazurka-like character. The left hand figurations in No. 11 in B major also recall Chopin's Etude Op. 10 No. 9.

The second half of the Op. 11 set starts with a nocturne in G♭ marked *Lento* (slowly), which recalls the texture of No. 5. No. 14 was inspired by the famous rock formation called Bastei in the Elbe Sandstone Mountains of Germany. Its bristling energy depicts the water crashing against the rocks. No. 15 is an etudelike piece that focuses on double-note patterns. Its modal harmony recalls the music of the Mighty Five and is notable for having no accidentals. It also evokes Chopin's Op. 28 No. 22 in its texture. Scriabin's individual voice shines through in Nos. 16 and 19, which include some unique rhythms and haunting moods. No. 20 is an octave study, while No. 21 is folklike in its shifting meters. No. 23 in F major is in the style of a mazurka and strongly recalls Chopin's Prelude in F major from his Op. 28 set. The repeated chords of No. 24 in D minor again introduce a Scriabinian hallmark, as do the wide-ranging left hand octaves. In its heroic repose, it makes an effective conclusion to the cycle, although the climax of the Op. 11 set as a whole comes with Nos. 18–20.

Recommended Recordings: Gina Bachauer (Capitol G-7110, 1958); Igor Zhukov (Melodiya C10 14251/2, 1980); Gordon Fergus-Thompson (ASV 919, 1995); Piers Lane (Hyperion CDH55450, 2000); Mikhail Pletnev (Virgin 45247, 2010).

Middle-Period Preludes Opp. 31, 33, 35, 37, 39, 45, 48, 49, 51, 56, and 59
Date of Composition: 1903–1905
These eleven batches of page-long preludes constitute the bulk of Scriabin's middle-period works, written from 1903 to 1905. These preludes often allowed the composer to work out in miniature the harmonic schemes that he employed in his symphonies. The aphoristic nature of these preludes makes them akin to visions or prophecies. Sustained development defeats their purpose and meaning. While the phrase lengths and formal designs remain conservative, the real advancements are in the harmonies. Richly decorated dominant chords proliferate the musical texture to

the extent that they no longer require resolution. Scriabin's modus operandi in these middle-period preludes is to prolong the dominant (or tension) harmony as long as possible, sometimes even from the opening bar, to create a sense of heightened suspense. The effect is employed to such an extent that the triadic endings in these middle-period preludes can seem ad hoc and necessary only to the point that they provide an obvious signal of closure. Comparatively speaking, the middle-period preludes have received less scholarly attention than the Op. 11 and Op. 74 sets.[63] But nevertheless, they are hugely important for tracing the development of Scriabin's compositional vocabulary in his middle period.

Although all of the preludes that Scriabin wrote from 1903 to 1905 are richly expressive, the Four Preludes Op. 48 (1905) offer illustrative examples of Scriabin's harmonic advancements in his middle period. It is misleading to call this music atonal; the chords are dominant sevenths with chromatic alterations that do not immediately resolve. Scriabin wrote these Op. 48 Preludes during the same time period when he was working on the *Poem of Ecstasy*. Like that symphonic poem, they feature richly descriptive performance and tempo indications. The snapping triplet rhythm heard in the exposition of the *Poem of Ecstasy*, for example, appears at the opening of No. 1 in F♯ major, marked *Impetuoso fiero*. The wide reaches of a ninth in the right hand must have taxed the composer in performance (he could barely reach an octave). The musical terrain pushes out from the middle register of the keyboard to its outer reaches, and the clanging, bell-like harmonies of this piece obscure the tonal center. No. 2 in C major uses tendency tones that dance around the tonic and dominant harmonies and deftly avoid the home key until the last bar. Voice leading remains crucial to the proper performance of this piece, marked *Poetico con delizio*. No. 3 in D♭ major demonstrates an early example of the archlike gestures that reappeared in Scriabin's later works, like the Seventh Sonata and Prelude Op. 59 No. 2. These wavelike ideas provide rhythmic momentum that carries through to the last bar of the piece. This prelude contains the most diatonic harmonies of the set. No. 4 in C major is the most popular piece of the group, and it begins with the same kind of fiery keyboard fanfare heard in No. 1. It maintains the harmonic tension that Scriabin picked up from Wagner, with relief provided only by the abrupt final cadence in C major. The Op 48 set continues to challenge pianists in its dissonant harmonies and wrenching rhythms, to say nothing of its emotional impact, which is more opaque and abstract than earlier sets. The composer delivered the premiere of the Op. 48 Preludes in Brussels on 21 November 1906.

Middle-Period Preludes
Recommended Recordings: Valeri Kastelsky (Melodiya C10 26485 006, 1988); Paul Komen (Globe GLO 5098, 1993); Piers Lane (Hyperion 55451, 2000); Boris Bekhterev (Camerata Tokyo CMCD 15139-40, 2015); Anthony Hewitt (Champs Hill CHRCD072, 2016).

Five Preludes Op. 74
Date of Composition: 1914

Scriabin's Five Preludes Op. 74 are like finely crafted gems or Fabergé eggs. Each of them explores a compositional principle that relates to octatonic harmony. In the composer's hands, the dissonant sonorities take on a refractory or prismatic quality. As his last completed works, these preludes were originally intended for the *Mysterium*. They offer a glimpse into Scriabin's inner world—that of upheaval due to the Russian Revolution and World War I as well as the devastating reality of his own mortality. They march us to the precipice of atonality and reveal a frightening vision of the future. Yet these works possess a strange malleability that allows them to take on different moods based on the manner in which they are played. Scriabin compared them to a crystal, since "the same crystal can reflect many different lights and colors."[64] Op. 74 No. 1, for instance, can be played quickly as Paul Komen does, or slowly like Emil Gilels; accordingly the mood shifts from nervousness to weightlessness. Scriabin played No. 2 in two different ways for Sabaneev; the first time was radiant, scorching like the desert sun, while the second version, according to Sabaneev, lost "every trace of caressing eros which once shadowed it. The warmth was gone."[65]

Some measure of the cultural value of this set in Soviet life is witnessed by an anti-Communist story written by Yevgeny Zamyatin in 1920 titled *Peshchera* (The Cave). The protagonist Martin Martinych, and his wife, the terminally ill Masha, suffer through a brutal winter in a Spartan apartment in St. Petersburg, which is compared to a prehistoric cave. They kneel at the altar of the insatiable stove that keeps them from freezing to death, gathering whatever goods allow them to survive, "like in Noah's ark."[66] Their sole possessions consist of a desk, books, hardened pancakes, five potatoes, an iron, bedsprings, an axe, firewood, and Scriabin's Five Preludes Op. 74. Eventually these musical treasures, once so rife with the promise of a new future, are shorn of their cultural import and valued only for the paper on which they are printed, and the warmth they can provide. For Zamyatin, Scriabin's Preludes Op. 74 represented an artistic treasure of the past whose brilliance was set into stark relief under these harsh conditions. They rank among Scriabin's best-known works, and there have been numerous adaptations and transcriptions for various instrumental combinations.

In the Op. 74 preludes, Scriabin's systematic approach to harmonic organization is at its most refined level of application. No. 1 is marked *Douloureux, déchirant* (excruciating, gut-wrenching), and it couches the romantic idea of anguish in modernist language, as Strauss had done in *Salome* and *Elektra*, and Schoenberg in *Pierrot Lunaire*. The main motive of the prelude is an unsettled, running gesture. The daring harmonies of No. 1 blend pitches drawn from the octatonic scale. F♯ serves as the foundational pitch. In the brief span of sixteen bars, Scriabin creates an active and strictly controlled harmonic environment that evokes a highly affective emotional state. No. 2's interminable weariness recalls Chopin's A minor Prelude Op. 28 No. 2 in its droning oscillation of dyads in the left hand and minimalistic melody. Scriabin told Sabaneev that Op. 74 No. 2 was an "astral desert . . . here is fatigue, exhaustion.

See how this short prelude sounds as if it lasts an entire century? Actually it is all eternity, millions of years."[67] No. 3 picks up the pace with the tempo marking of *Allegro drammatico*, and in one section, Scriabin indicates that it should be played "like a cry" (*comme un cri*); but this scream is indignant and defiant, without a hint of sadness. The limpid harmonies of No. 4 clash a minor third against a major third at its opening and close. Most pianists exaggerate the tempo marking of "Lent, vague, indécis" (slow, indefinite, uncertain), and play it lethargically, losing the basic pulse. The main compositional formula is on interval cycles of minor thirds, as Richard Taruskin has demonstrated in his brief analysis.[68] The set concludes with the savage No. 5, marked "Fier, belliqueux" (proud, warlike). Here too, octatonic harmonies dissolve the traditional polarity between major and minor, tonic and dominant. This piece exemplifies his compositional approach of developing set material by transposing it to different pitch levels. The character and pacing recalls the Seventh Sonata, especially in its arched figures that respond to the opening fanfare. The music is stripped to its bare elements; nothing extraneous is added.

Recommended Recordings: Raymond Lewenthal (Westminster XWN 18399, 1956); Anton Kuerti (Analekta 9202, 1982); Vladimir Kastelsky (Melodiya C10 26485, 1988); Paul Komen (Globe GLO 5098, 1993); Mikhail Rudy (Calliope 9692, 1994).

POÈMES FOR PIANO

The first piece of music to be called a "poem" was written in the early nineteenth century, when the German composer Carl Loewe (1796–1869) wrote his little-known "tone poem for piano," *Le Printemps* (The Spring, 1824). While other examples can be found in the literature, Franz Liszt is generally recognized as the progenitor of the musical tone poem, with his symphonic poem for orchestra, *Les Préludes* (1848).[69] In Russia, the Mighty Five's admiration for Liszt led them to write symphonic poems of their own, and by the early 1900s, the Russian Symbolists advanced this idea a step further. The Russian Symbolist poet Andrei Bely wrote a series of literary *Symphonies* in 1902, and Lithuanian painter Mikalojus Ciurlionis painted meditative canvases he titled "Prelude" and "Sonata." Scriabin continued this tradition with his musical "Poèmes," which to him designated an artwork that transcended pure music and became life itself. Throughout his career, poetry was an integral aspect of his creativity in addition to music, and he experimented with reconciling poetry and music in forms other than song. But words never came as easily for Scriabin as music, and his *poèmes* for piano or orchestra were never intended to be programmatic in a literal sense.

Scriabin published a total of twenty *poèmes* for piano between 1903 and 1915, and he also invoked this special word in the titles of his Symphonies Nos. 3–5, the *Divine Poem*, *Poem of Ecstasy*, and *Prometheus: Poem of Fire*. After 1903, *poèmes* became as important as sonatas for his creative ideas. Scriabin's concentration on the piano *poème* is especially apparent after the Sixth Sonata (1911–1912), as his works are almost exclusively titled either *poème* or sonata. It was inevitable that these two genres would eventually coalesce, as they did in *Vers la flamme* Op. 72, which was originally sketched as Scriabin's Eleventh Sonata. Other late works like the *Poème-Nocturne* Op. 61, which is detailed below, display a similar concern with hybrid genres. These *poèmes* for piano allowed Scriabin to work out in miniature the same compositional ideas he applied to his *poème*-titled symphonies. Today, these solo piano pieces remain some of his most popular and enduring compositions.

Poème satanique Op. 36 *(Satanic poem)*
Date of Composition: 1903
Premiere: 15 March 1906 in Moscow, by Vera I. Skriabina

Written in between the Fourth Sonata and the *Divine Poem*, the *Poème satanique* ranks as their equal in compositional drama and design. Its mood is much more sardonic or ironic than pure evil. The demonism of the *Poème satanique* is theatrical, and distanced from the menace of the Sixth and Ninth Sonatas. Scriabin was amused by literal interpretations of the title; to Sabaneev he confessed, "My *Poème satanique* isn't true evil. It is an apotheosis of insincerity. Everything in it is hypocritical and false . . . Satan is not really himself there. He's just a little devil, not in earnest. He's genteel and rather sweet."[70] Yet a diabolical streak is palpable in this piece, and the influence of Liszt is particularly regnant, especially in its virtuosity, piquant harmonies, and abrupt shifts between tenderness and ferocity. More than one writer has observed affinities between Scriabin's *Poème satanique* and Liszt's Mephisto Waltz No. 1 (1859), also written for solo piano. In a 1965 interview with Faubion Bowers, the Soviet pianist Sviatoslav Richter pinpointed the decisive influence that Liszt's waltz imparted:

> "Do you know where all of Scriabin comes from . . . in one single passage? Guess." He raced to the piano and played the sinister, sickly-sweet, singing middle-section tune of Liszt's Mephisto Waltz. "Yes," I thought, "it was Liszt who first put the devil in music." "Hear how it's all there," Richter sang, "the indefinitely held suspensions of ninths and elevenths, the building of chords not in thirds but in fourths and fifths."[71]

Poème satanique depicts Satan mocking two lovers in an attempt to destroy their bond, much as Liszt's waltz represents Mephistopheles tempting Faust and the villagers at a wedding dance into debauchery. Beliaev was delighted when Scriabin first played the piece for him, and he implored the composer to repeat the ending three times.[72] Its immediate appeal is not hard to fathom. The devil's chortling laughter is portrayed through descending staccato chords marked *riso ironico* (ironic laughter). Appended to this main theme is a questioning melody marked *dolce, appassionato* (sweet, passionate), which is a sarcastic parody of tenderness. The two lovers' lyrical theme is marked *dolce, cantabile, amoroso* (sweet, singing, affectionate), and features intertwining legato melodic lines. The lovers' chromatic inner parts represent their unstable emotions of passion and doubt. The upward leap from E to D in the melody at m. 17 symbolizes their hope, with the top note of this figure (D) resolving from the dissonant minor seventh to the more harmonious interval of a sixth (C), suggestive of their compatibility. These contrasting themes of the devil and the two lovers are in constant battle, and they are nearly fused into an indistinguishable whole at times, as if the devil's influence had overwhelmed their senses to the point of unconsciousness. The raucous harmonies in this work are balanced by traditional elements, which lend the piece a high degree of accessibility, such as a rhythmically assertive main theme and a contrasting lyrical theme. The polar attraction between these traditional "masculine" and "feminine" roles forms the essence of the sonata principle, and is a core element even in Scriabin's most harmonically advanced music.

Scriabin's wife, Vera, premiered the *Poème satanique* in 1906, and the composer performed it often at his concerts. Rachmaninov included this piece in his 1915 memorial tour after Scriabin's death. The conductor Modest Altschuler, whose power and influence over musical affairs in New York paved the way for the composer's success there, proposed an orchestral version of the *Poème satanique* that never came to fruition. This work remains one of the lesser-played *poèmes* for piano, but it deserves greater recognition due to its stunning power, economy of form, and unique character.

Recommended Recordings: Margarita Fyodorova (Melodiya CM04267, 1980); Vitaly Margulis (Aurophon 11174, 1986); Vladimir Sofronitsky (Melodya MELCD1002237, 2014); Michael Ponti (Dante PSG 9329, 1977–1980 Live).

Poème-Nocturne Op. 61 (1911)
Premiere: 23 December 1912 in St. Petersburg, by the composer

Like the *Poème satanique,* the *Poème-Nocturne* Op. 61 is one of Scriabin's longer *poèmes* for piano. This desolate, atmospheric piece is redolent of his later, mystical style. Considering it falls between *Prometheus: Poem of Fire* (Op. 60) and the Sixth Sonata (Op. 62), it shares many characteristics with these works, but its harmonic vocabulary has more in common with the Sixth Sonata than with *Prometheus*. The work's harmonies borrow elements from the mystic chord and octatonicism.[73] Formally, sonata form principles are observed, although the languorous quality of both the first and second themes blurs their formal division. This piece strikes a mood of sensual eroticism or mystical desire, as if groping toward some undefined goal that is never quite achieved. Performance indications in French are used profusely in this piece, as if to compensate for its vagueness, including some poetic gems like *comme un murmure confus* (like a confused murmur), *avec une soudaine langueur* (with a sudden languor), and *cristallin, perlé* (crystalline, pearly), which as Hugh Macdonald noted of this last marking, fits the music superbly.[74] The best performances and recordings of this piece likewise cast a sheen over the music that lends it a quality of light. There is a delicious ambiguity about this music, which is hazy and veiled in its expression, perhaps explaining why Scriabin called it a Nocturne. It has a dreamy weariness, as if trapped between a waking and a dreamlike state.

Recommended Recordings: Vladimir Sofronitsky (Melodiya D 19641/2, 1960); Vitaly Margulis (In-Akustic, Inak 8707, 1986); Sviatoslav Richter (Live Classics LCL 441, 1992).

Vers la flamme Op. 72 (**Toward the Flame**)
Date of Composition: 1914
Premiere: 14 March 1915 in Kharkiv, by the composer
Composed in 1914, *Vers la flamme* was originally intended to be Scriabin's Eleventh Piano Sonata, but it soon became a stand-alone piano *poème*, and one of his most famous works. This powerful work depicts the spirit's evolution from darkness to the purifying fires of redemption, or as Scriabin once described it to Sabaneev, "from the fog to the blinding light."[75] It would be a mistake, however, to think of this music in strict programmatic terms, as its beauty and brilliance lies in its multiplicity of meanings. From its suggestive opening, the music carries the listener along a steady path from bleakness to spiritual release and divine consummation. Trills and tremolos dominate the musical texture. As it becomes more animated, Scriabin marks these passages *Éclatant, lumineux* (Bright, luminous). Intervals of a fourth are particularly prominent, especially in the flashes of light in the right hand passages. These characteristic spacings of a fourth lend a hollow, gonglike resonance to the harmonies. Scriabin's idea of spiritual uplift is also conveyed by shifting his thematic material into successively higher-pitched notes, so that by the end of the piece, the flashes of light in the right hand are heard in the piano's highest, most iridescent register.

Vers la flamme is a tour de force of pianistic color and rhythmic propulsion. Only the briefest melodic fragment of a semitone is offered as a stable element for the listener. Among its most challenging technical hurdles are the frequent hand crossings, tricky polyrhythms of nine against five, and a careful balance of sound and rhythmic momentum. Like the Ninth Sonata, *Vers la flamme* is one of Scriabin's more technically accessible late works, but achieving the proper accumulation of explosive energy requires a masterful touch. In this respect, the recordings of Horowitz and Richter are unmatched.

With regard to the work's pianistic textures, the musicologist Ryan Rowen has observed strong stylistic affinities between *Vers la flamme* and Louis Brassin's (1840–1884) famous solo piano transcription of the "Magic Fire Music" from Wagner's *Die Walküre*.[76] Brassin's transcription was wildly popular in the nineteenth and early twentieth centuries, and almost certainly passed through Scriabin's hands at some point. Metaphorically, both works focus on the mystical properties of fire and magic, and their music conveys the idea of an eternal flame that never burns out. A disturbing sense of obsession hovers over this music, which has attracted many to its mysteries, and contributed to Scriabin's reputation as being involved in the occult. For some pianists, the music of *Vers la flamme* has literally pushed them to the breaking point.[77] The solo piano score has been adapted for several productions, including an orchestrated version in 1954 for a ballet by Hungarian composer Rudolf Bella based on Oscar Wilde's *Picture of Dorian Gray*, and a 1999 production by American theater artist Martha Clarke that adapts five short stories by Anton Chekhov, which featured pianist Christopher O'Riley playing roughly thirty selections of Scriabin's music, including the title piece.

Recommended Recordings: Ruth Laredo (Nonesuch 73035, 1973); Vladimir Horowitz (Sony B00000DS85, 1990); Christopher O'Riley (Image Recordings IRC9902, 2001); Sviatoslav Richter (Live Classics LCL 441, 1992).

* * *

SCRIABIN'S CHAMPION PIANISTS: A BRIEF HISTORY

Setting aside all aesthetic preferences, Scriabin's piano music has not enjoyed the popular appeal among pianists that the works of Beethoven, Liszt, or Chopin have received for two reasons. Its technical demands can be fearsome; players might be called upon to execute algebraic cross-rhythms, navigate treacherous leaps and demanding passages in the left hand, or project a sense of eroticism, hyperactivity, or languid introspection that may be foreign to their natural temperament. What's worse, the real virtuosity in Scriabin's works is often buried in the music. There are relatively few bravado passages, such as one finds in Liszt's works, for instance, that automatically translate into audience appeal. The physical demands of Scriabin's music are towering, but its intellectual and interpretive challenges outstrip any technical concerns. Performing his piano music requires a vivid imagination, rhythmic plasticity, and a genuine understanding of and sympathy for the culture and music. Not every pianist has it in their bones to play Scriabin well. Critical and audience approval, however, rests squarely upon the performer's capacity to deliver the total package. Simply put, there is an X-factor or intangible quality that is needed to perform Scriabin's piano music with conviction.

Pianists are well aware of its formidable reputation, and for many, the risks outweigh the rewards. Anatole Leikin touched upon the perils of playing Scriabin's music in a 2008 review of a recital by Chinese sensation Yuja Wang:

> Playing Scriabin is always fraught with danger. There is a special Scriabin spirit that appears only in an atmosphere of exaltation and impulsiveness, even explosiveness. It requires an extraordinary, mesmeric delivery, with a special tone quality, pulse, and rhetorical verve. One French music critic, enthralled by Scriabin's performance in Paris, said the composer was "all nerve and a holy flame." Without these qualities, Scriabin's music ceases to be unique and becomes merely pleasant.[78]

Cautionary tales abound to dissuade even the most intrepid pianists. Consider the case of Rachmaninov, one of the early twentieth century's great pianists. He undertook a memorial tour in 1916 to raise funds for Scriabin's family after the composer's death the previous year. But his well-intentioned tributes outraged audiences because the revelatory quality they had sensed in Scriabin's own performances was sorely missing from Rachmaninov's interpretations. In a review of one of Rachmaninov's memorial concerts, critic Grigorii Prokofiev of the *Russkaia muzykal'naia gazeta* dismayed that, "You should have seen the disappointment with which the admirers of Scriabin's later piano works looked at each other as they heard the innocuous and prosaic interpretation of the *Satanic Poem*, or the academically chilled treatment of the Second and Fifth Sonatas."[79]

Several factors conspired against the would-be Scriabin interpreter, not the least of which was an almost unattainable standard of interpretation, as well as a hostile attitude borne of a sense of protective duty on the part of his devotees. The Russian American pianist Alexander Borovsky (1889–1968) performed his own memorial concert for Scriabin in 1915. In the early decades of the twentieth century, Borovsky was one of the finest interpreters of Scriabin's music in England and in Russia, although his lack of commercial recordings made him relatively unknown in the West until recently.[80] Borovsky left an account of the unwelcoming environment that greeted any pianist who played Scriabin's music publicly soon after his death. Failure to honor the legacy of the great composer with a worthy performance, he observed, might lead to "personal alienation [caused] by the jealousy of the composer's nearest friends and of his mistress [Tatyana], who never learned to tolerate hearing anyone praised for playing Scriabin, save Scriabin himself."[81] Other examples of pianists whose performances of Scriabin's works in the wake of his death left something to be desired are not hard to find.[82]

Such circumstances are unfortunate when we consider that Scriabin's greatest asset was his intuitive understanding of the piano: its timbral colors, contrapuntal possibilities, and dynamic range. Yet Scriabin's music did not die out along with the physical death of the composer. His music held a foothold in the repertory after his death due to those gifted pianists who grasped its architectural scope, and could communicate its emotional verve. These figures built a posthumous legacy for his music in Russia and the West, in terms of its historical importance and performance practice. I will not attempt to explain the myriad nuances needed to achieve that standard of excellence in performing Scriabin's piano music, as Matthew Bengtson lends his expertise to that subject in part III of this book. But those performers who left their inimitable stamp on Scriabin's solo piano music and endeared it to Western listeners deserve recognition. Aspiring pianists of today and tomorrow who wish to perform Scriabin's music can learn best from those who were closest to this music, whether through their personal connections or an intuitive understanding of Scriabin's unique sound world.

There may be some merit to the idea that pianists with a streak of madness in them play Scriabin's music best. Some of the twentieth century's most colorful artists ranked among the composer's most eloquent spokesmen. The matriarch of the Scriabin cult in America during the first half of the twentieth century was Katherine

Ruth Heyman (1877–1944). Born and raised in Sacramento, California, Heyman was well known on the West Coast. A trailblazer in her time, she delivered all-Scriabin recitals in New York in 1924 and 1927, and Europe in 1927, 1934, and 1935. Known as the "high priestess of the Scriabin cult," Heyman's beguiling self-publicity lent her recitals a mark of authenticity and distinguished her in a male-dominated profession. Her New-Agey sensibility and stage theatrics, however, struck some critics as kitschy, and likely hindered critical respect for Scriabin as a serious composer. Of the same era, but of a more rational mind-set was the English pianist Edward Mitchell (1891–1950). Mitchell was one of the leading interpreters of Scriabin's music in England from the 1910s through the 1940s. He delivered numerous all-Scriabin recitals in the 1920s–1930s. In his campaign to make the music more intelligible to the public, he often gave lecture-recitals. Mitchell taught at the Royal College of Music from 1921 until his death in 1950, and he published a short guide to the composer's works in 1927, *Scriabin: The Great Russian Tone Poet*.[83]

Fast-forward later into the twentieth century, and Scriabin's music had been out of favor for decades and was being reintroduced to audiences in the mid-1960s by a flamboyant pianist named Raymond Lewenthal (1923–1988). Fashioning himself as a modern-day Liszt, Lewenthal would sashay onto stages bedecked in a top hat, red-lined cape, and cane, as seen in figure 8.1. His recitals featured highly virtuosic and obscure nineteenth-century works, and were often held in near total darkness to heighten the séance-like atmosphere. Another Scriabin-playing pianist of the 1960s and 1970s who plunged headlong into madness was John Ogdon (1937–1989). Ogdon became an overnight sensation after sharing first prize with Vladimir Ashkenazy at the 1962 Tchaikovsky Competition. A powerful and erratic performer, Ogdon possessed a prodigious memory and expansive repertoire, and he recorded Scriabin's complete sonatas in 1971, just in time for the composer's centenary revival. A mere two years later, however, he suffered a mental breakdown that was first thought to be schizophrenia, but was later diagnosed as bipolar disorder.[84] Several suicide attempts followed, and Ogdon coped with his depression by channeling his dark thoughts and emotions into his piano playing, often with mixed results.[85] His championing of the Russian Romantic repertoire was commendable, and his dedication to Scriabin's music helped bolster his reputation among Western audiences. Among his other achievements, Ogdon arranged for solo piano Scriabin's early *Poème symphonique* in D minor (1896–1897). These three performers possessed the interpretive finesse and commanding techniques to communicate Scriabin's transcendent vision to the public, and their personal quirkiness only added to the composer's mystique.

Throughout the twentieth century, Russian pianists were the preeminent interpreters of Scriabin's works, by virtue of their birthright, cultural upbringing, temperament, and training. In a league of his own was the composer's son-in-law, Vladimir Sofronitsky (1901–1961). He never met his famous father-in-law in person or heard Scriabin perform. Yet Sofronitsky communicated the rhetorical gestures and emotional intensity of the composer's works better than anyone. He almost never performed outside the USSR, but his recorded legacy is a treasury. Tall, lean, pale, and never smiling on stage, Sofronitsky possessed an enigmatic air that enveloped his live performances. The Soviet émigré pianist Mark Zeltzer recalled how Sofronitsky would "walk to the piano with a slow, distracted gait, then, before playing, apply a black handkerchief to his nose. In musical circles there were rumors about what was on Sofronitsky's handkerchiefs, or in them."[86] But the musical result was unparalleled; the Ukrainian pianist Dmitri Paperno recalled that "Sofronitsky's playing was a brilliant display of dialectics in performance art: indestructible logic, an almost architectural modeling of musical images, but at the same time a free and almost improvised manner of expression in which unexpected subordinate voices and timbres were brought out."[87]

Nearly as influential as Sofronitsky was Heinrich Neuhaus (1888–1964), who taught piano at the Moscow Conservatory from 1922 until his death. For his debut recital in Moscow, Neuhaus performed Scriabin's complete sonatas to critical acclaim. Neuhaus was an admirable and sensitive interpreter of Scriabin's works who recorded the Piano Concerto, Seventh Sonata, and several smaller works. Neuhaus's greater legacy, however, was as an instructor. Two of his pupils proved especially talented and committed to Scriabin's cause: Sviatoslav Richter (1915–1997) and Margarita Fyodorova (1927–2016). Richter's interpretations and gripping sense of musical tension are unparalleled by any artist. No technical problem hindered his single-minded vision of the music, which he communicated with a rare intensity. Although Richter seldom focused on any single composer's music, he played all-Scriabin concerts in 1945, 1957, and 1972. When the poet Boris Pasternak died in 1960, Richter stayed up all night, playing Scriabin's music from memory next to the open coffin. Richter's intellect radiates through his performances and communicates the musical structure with unquestioned clarity. His recordings of the Fifth and Seventh Sonatas are unmatched for their intensity and musicality. Fyodorova recorded Scriabin's works for the Melodiya label in Russia and was one of Scriabin's leading interpreters.[88] Her only commercial release available in the West was a collection of the piano *poèmes*, but her recorded version of the Piano Concerto and *Poème tragique* (available on YouTube) demonstrates her keen musical intuition for this repertoire. Fyodorova may not be as well known in the West as Richter, but she was a musical giant who did much to champion Scriabin's legacy.

Members of the so-called Russian Piano School, especially those who trained and taught at the Moscow and St. Petersburg Conservatories in the early twentieth century, were also strong exponents of Scriabin's music. Elders of this generation had known the composer personally, heard him play, and assimilated nuances of his style. In turn, they passed along important performance secrets to their pupils. To this day, their recordings of Scriabin's music remain definitive. One of these patriarchs was Samuil Feinberg (1890–1962), who taught at the Moscow Conservatory in the 1920s along with Heinrich Neuhaus and Alexander Goldenweiser, the latter of whom was a distinguished Scriabinist in his own right. Feinberg was known for his interpretations of Bach's keyboard music, and his acuity for polyphonic textures infused his performances of Scriabin's music.[89] His interpretation of Scriabin's Fourth

Piano Sonata even impressed the composer.[90] Like Richter, Feinberg possessed an encyclopedic memory and inexhaustible stamina, even in his golden years. Perhaps the greatest product of the Russian piano tradition was Vladimir Horowitz (1903–1989). Horowitz was a thunderous, breathtaking performer who made Scriabin's music a cornerstone in his repertoire. He released an all-Scriabin album in 1956, well ahead of the revival crowd. In mid-century, at the nadir of the composer's reception, he called for a "re-hearing of Scriabin's music, which has so vastly enriched our piano literature." Horowitz's close kinship to this style and commanding presence put Scriabin's legacy in a positive light. He made the music speak to listeners, and took seriously his mission to communicate its message to the masses. He well recognized that Scriabin's music is "difficult for the general public even though it's Romantic. This is supersensuous, superromantic, supermysterious. Everything is 'super'—it is all overboard. From the spiritual and emotional point of view, it is one of the most difficult chunks of music in the literature."[91] Horowitz's performances of the Ninth Sonata during his so-called Historic Return recital in 1965 and of *Vers la flamme* remain gold standards.

Among other interpreters, Vitaly Margulis (1928–2011) left behind a recording of the Third Sonata that to some critics surpassed even the recordings of Horowitz and Sofronitsky. Vladimir Ashkenazy (b. 1937) has produced lucid and authoritative readings of Scriabin's scores that draw out every detail without excessive liberties. He interpreted Scriabin's scores in a literalistic manner, but his lucid account of the music never lacks the prerequisite atmosphere. Ashkenazy's recording of the complete sonatas for Decca remains one of the best on record. Other notable Russian interpreters of Scriabin's works include Igor Zhukov (b. 1936), a student of Neuhaus who in the 1960s recorded the complete Preludes Op. 11 and all ten piano sonatas. Zhukov's keen sense of lyricism and ironclad command of structure and form make his accounts worth seeking out.

Scriabin had numerous exponents in the West as well, especially during the revival that developed in the late 1960s and early 1970s around the centenary of his birth. This anniversary inspired several pianists to take up his cause in the hopes of carving out a niche for themselves, and capitalizing on a booming market. Among the leading revivalist performers of this era were Ruth Laredo and Hilde Somer. Laredo is generally recognized as the better Scriabin player, although to her credit, Somer's prowess in marketing and theatrics (incorporating light shows in her recitals, for instance) attracted throngs to her recitals and enticed the younger demographic. The American pianist Michael Ponti (b. 1937) was another major player in the revival years. Ponti provided an honorable service when he recorded Scriabin's entire catalogue of piano music in 1972–1974, which Vox remastered and rereleased on compact disc in 2002. To delight of completist collectors, Ponti's recordings provided the first commercial recordings of Scriabin's complete piano works. Ponti used a bright-sounding Bechstein piano for his Scriabin recordings, just as the composer had favored (Zhukov did the same). Ponti shines in the earlier Scriabin sonatas, especially in the finales to the first three sonatas. But the nebulous and mystical late works seem beyond his reach, and his performances are far from note perfect. The tinny, brittle sound of the Vox recordings also failed to supply the necessary breathlike quality and rich tonal spectrum that Scriabin's late music deserves.[92] For some listeners, however, Ponti's reckless abandon and shrill sound complements the neurotic quality of the music.

While Scriabin's music thrived for many years after his revival, his posthumous legacy suffered a serious blow in the late twentieth century with the deaths of several Russian pianists who ranked among its best interpreters, including Emil Gilels (d. 1985), Horowitz (d. 1989), and Richter (d. 1997). Critics took notice of the changing of the guard, and voiced concerns over the drying well of Russian pianism. Donal Henahan of the *New York Times* wondered, "now [that] the postwar heroes of Soviet art are just about gone . . . who will be nominated to carry the banner of Soviet pianism?"[93] Virtuoso pianists were a dime a dozen, but technique alone was no guarantee that they understood the finer nuances of music making. The dean of American music critics, Harold Schonberg of the *New York Times*, served as a juror in international piano competitions during the 1980s and grumbled, "All this talent, all this preparation and dedication—and so little to say! . . . Pianist after pianist would come with their Chopin or Liszt or Schumann with virtually no idea of how the music should go."[94] Flaws that Schonberg complained of would have proven disastrous in Scriabin's music. In his seminal tract, *Pianism as Art*, Samuil Feinberg observed that, "With Scriabin, harmony and timbral coloring are inseparable . . . In his late-period compositions, the smallest upsetting of balance and accurate distribution of force . . . may be perceived as falsity or excessive nervousness."[95] In recent years, however, the tide seems to be turning, with increasing numbers of pianists genuinely interested in the music, the history and ideas behind it, its proper performance practice, and the man himself.

Scriabin's music still has something to say to us in the hands of the right pianist. The strongest interpreters grasp the cultural context and historical significance behind the music, and can project the poetic lyricism that courses through all of Scriabin's works, no matter how dense the harmony and texture. While his piano music may never be a concert staple, save a few hits like the D♯ minor Etude Op. 8 No. 12 and the Fifth and Ninth Sonatas, it has nevertheless maintained a strong foothold since the dawn of the new millennium. The inherent beauty and craftsmanship of Scriabin's solo piano works will continue to compel performers to take on its technical and interpretive challenges. This personal investment is necessary to tap into its full expressive potential. In the process of playing this resplendent music and delivering it in performance, pianists may discover something about themselves.

4

Symphonies and Orchestral Works

With the exception of the *Poem of Ecstasy*, Scriabin's most famous composition, his orchestral works have been overshadowed in popularity by his solo piano pieces. Even Scriabin's most daringly original symphonies have been belittled by many critics, who claimed that these masterworks were simply piano improvisations stretched onto a symphonic canvas. Typical of this tribe is a comment from British composer Robin Holloway, who carped that Scriabin "was basically a pianist-composer; even in the *Poème de'extase* it is apparent that the characteristic textures and spacings have been conceived at the keyboard."[1] Scriabin's former professor at the Moscow Conservatory, Alexander Glazunov (1865–1936), also sensed that his pupil used the same compositional methods in his piano miniatures as in his symphonies.[2] Countless other critics have contended that Scriabin's intuitive grasp of the keyboard limited his musical invention to ideas that were inherently pianistic.[3] Thus, Scriabin's orchestral works, each filled with pages of highly original and expressive music, became neglected in the repertory and targets of critical derision.

Those who enjoy Scriabin's symphonic works, however, appreciate how these works reveal a different side of his creativity. This chapter offers insights into the history of Scriabin's orchestral works and stylistic observations on each piece. As we shall see, each of his orchestral works reveals an imaginative and colorful side of Scriabin's creativity that rewards close inspection.

Symphonies are among the most venerated genres in classical music, with roots dating back to the 1700s, when the Italian operatic *sinfonia* (derived from the Greek word meaning "sounding together") gained an independent existence outside of the opera house as a stand-alone concert piece. A three-movement design of Fast-Slow-Fast was established, and the format proved wildly popular with audiences. The dramatic potential of symphonies reached new heights under Johann Stamitz (1717–1757), whose martial leadership of the court orchestra in Mannheim, Germany achieved a new standard of precision in performance, including uniform bowing in the strings and a stunning dynamic range nicknamed a "Mannheim Steamroller," which blended a crescendo with an accelerando. Stamitz was no slouch as a composer, and his symphonies introduced a four-movement format (Fast-Slow-Dance related-Fast) that became standardized by Haydn, Mozart, and Beethoven.

In the hands of these masters, symphonies became the pinnacle genre for self-expression and compositional technique. By the 1850s, the symphony had attained such a degree of sophistication that composers such as Johannes Brahms faced paralyzing fear at the prospect of writing a worthy successor to Mozart's "Jupiter" Symphony or Beethoven's Ninth. It took Brahms twenty years of tinkering with his Symphony No. 1 in C minor Op. 68 (1876) to get it just right, and not surprisingly, critics dubbed it "Beethoven's Tenth."[4] Twenty-three years later, Scriabin joined the ranks of these composers with his First Symphony, which was undoubtedly written with these historic precedents squarely in mind.

As a student at the Moscow Conservatory (1888–1892), Scriabin studied under some of the greatest orchestrators and composers in history. He absorbed much knowledge during those years, but was lackadaisical about completing his assignments, and squandered opportunities to learn more from the distinguished faculty, whose authority he resisted by nature and who found him curiously aloof despite his obvious gifts. Scriabin's principal teachers were Vasily Safonov (1852–1918) in piano, the aforementioned Glazunov in harmony and form, and Sergei Taneyev (1856–1915) in counterpoint and theory. Taneyev was the conservatory director the year that Scriabin matriculated (he stepped down in 1889). Another instructor who left a strong impression on Scriabin, in spite of their mutual antipathy, was Anton Arensky (1861–1906), who taught harmony and composition. Ten years Scriabin's senior, Arensky resented his star pupil's arrogance and indiscipline, and their bitter clashes resulted in Arensky's infamous refusal to sign Scriabin's diploma. A final figure of inestimable value was Nikolai Rimsky-Korsakov (1844–1908), a master orchestrator who taught at the nearby St. Petersburg Conservatory, but who met Scriabin regularly at the home of his patron and impresario, Mitrofan Beliaev, for weekly musical gatherings that were nicknamed "Quartet Fridays."[5] Rimsky-Korsakov begrudgingly recognized Scriabin's talents, and tempered his praise of this "star of first magnitude" by adding that Scriabin was "somewhat warped and self-opinionated."[6] Scriabin graduated from the Moscow Conservatory in 1892, headstrong and eager to earn a name for himself. But he lacked practical experience in orchestral writing. Only one piece predates any of his published orchestral works: a *Symphonic Allegro* in D minor (June 1896), the only fruit of an abandoned early symphony.

Exactly what makes Scriabin or any composer a great symphonist or orchestrator is hard to define. Generally speaking, it refers to a composer's ability to generate musical ideas that are ripe for large-scale development, and to give life to those ideas by assigning them to the right instruments. This skill requires a keen understanding of instrument ranges, color combinations, and playing techniques. Choosing the right orchestration demands every bit as much creativity and training as conceiving the melodies, rhythms, and forms. In one of his lectures for the "Young People's Concerts" series, the American conductor Leonard Bernstein (1918–1990) observed that, "good orchestration means not only the clothes that you put the music into, the way you wear a dress or a suit to keep yourself warm. It's got to be the right suit or the right dress. Bad orchestration would be something like putting on a sweater to go swimming."[7] In another lecture titled "What Makes Music Symphonic" (13 December 1958), Bernstein explained that, "the key to it is *development*," i.e., exploiting the full dramatic potential of a musical idea.[8] He illustrated his points with examples borrowed from the symphonies of Tchaikovsky, Brahms, Haydn, Mozart, and Beethoven and added that, "the basis of all development is repetition—the less exact the repetition is, the more symphonic it is." As we shall see, Scriabin excels in his ability to generate and vary his basic materials, and transform their character by assigning them to the appropriate instruments.

Scriabin's symphonies remain endlessly rewarding to study and contain passages of sumptuous beauty that are unequaled in the orchestral repertory. Particularly noteworthy in these works is his natural tendency to write in triple meters, a carryover from his love of dance forms, which as we shall see, are perfectly at home in the genre of the symphony.

Piano Concerto in F# minor Op. 20
Date of Composition: October 1896–May 1897
Premiere: 23 October 1897 in Odessa, cond. by Vasily Safonov with Scriabin as soloist

Any pianist-composer who was determined to forge a career in the nineteenth century needed to compose a solo concerto in order to market themselves and showcase their technical and compositional ability. There was no shortage of inspiration or models. A rich legacy of solo concertos stretched back over a century. Solo concertos were brought to early perfection by the Baroque violinist Antonio Vivaldi (1678–1741). His contemporary, Johann Sebastian Bach (1685–1750), wrote several noteworthy keyboard concertos of his own. The concerto earned a new distinction in the Classical Era in the works of Haydn, Mozart, and Beethoven. These composers finally put the keyboard on equal ground as the violin in terms of its expressive capacity and virtuoso technique. By the nineteenth century, the piano concerto became the instrumental equivalent of a theatrical drama due to the development of larger orchestras, more powerful pianos, and greater stylistic contrasts between soloist and orchestra.

European musical developments were slow to reach Russia, and before 1850, most Russian concertos lacked the polish and sophistication of their European counterparts. By 1870–1880, however, Russia came into its own as a powerhouse for great piano concertos, starting with those of Rubinstein and Tchaikovsky and continuing through the concertos of Scriabin, Rachmaninov, Prokofiev, and Shostakovich. Scriabin's Piano Concerto demonstrates his inheritance of this rich legacy and his assured command of the genre, even if it does not break much new stylistic ground. Despite its understated reputation, it contains many passages that are sensitive, mercurial, and even childlike in character. It is a snapshot of the composer's personality at a formative time in his career.

Ideas flowed easily for Scriabin during the writing of his Piano Concerto, which evolved at a time when he was still emerging from his idol's shadow. Scriabin's first mention of his Piano Concerto comes in a letter of 27 October 1896 to Beliaev, in which he reported his rapid progress on the piece.[9] A month later, Scriabin announced that the Concerto was finished and only needed to be orchestrated, a task that proved far easier said than done. The manuscript was forwarded to Rimsky-Korsakov for evaluation, who was so incensed at the careless orthography and rough state of the score that he fired off a scathing letter to Scriabin. He deposited the manuscript with Anatoly Liadov and attached a covering note that bellowed, "Look at this filth I have! There is much I don't understand. . . . I have no time to scrub Scriabin."[10] (As a side note, Scriabin relied heavily upon his wife, Vera, in the preparation of this score, as well as the four-hand version, yet she received little credit for her efforts.) Rimsky-Korsakov's opinions finally softened once he heard the work performed in St. Petersburg a year later. In all likelihood, the manuscript had been riddled with errors, since Scriabin had worked feverishly to get it into presentable form.

Several unusual qualities distinguish this underrated piece. Its hushed intimacy at times approximates chamber music. Its avoidance of bombastic gestures and flamboyance sets it apart from the warhorses of his contemporaries. Very few big gestures or flashy moments are found in its three movements, which are all in the key of F♯. Instead of front-loading the opening movement, when the audience has the most patience and attention, Scriabin bulks up the final movement, which equals the length of the first two movements combined. He eschews the typical bright scoring of brass and strings in favor of muted horns and soft reeds. As Jeremy Norris described it, Scriabin's Op. 20 "is sketched in pastel shades rather than the strong primary colors of, say, the concertos of Tchaikovsky or Rachmaninov."[11] There are also no cadenzas, usually a staple of the genre that grants the soloist an unaccompanied moment of glory in the first (and often third) movements.

The opening bars are tonally ambiguous and highlight a solo muted horn that plays a falling melody of three notes. Scriabin's use of a horn at the opening recalls Brahms' Piano Concerto No. 2 in B♭ major (1881), the first movement of which starts with a slow horn call that is answered by the soloist. The basic motive that Scriabin presents with this sighing horn melody—three falling notes—becomes the melodic nucleus for the entire movement. Scriabin draws attention to the importance of this motive each time it appears by marking it with accents called *tenutos*. These accented notes are clearly visible in figure 12.1b, found in chapter 12 on harmony. Years later, in a discussion with Sabaneev, Scriabin cited this relationship between this motive and the Piano Concerto's overall design as illustrative of his compositional "principle":

> "Thought must always be present in the composition and creation of themes. It is expressed through the presence of a principle, which directs creativity. My themes, for the most part, I wrote always guided by some principle. And only for that reason do they

differ in harmony. . . . For example, take my Piano Concerto. The bedrock here was the descending succession, against which bloomed the whole theme." And he played me the theme of the Concerto, which through these accented descending passages took on a completely different meaning.[12]

The profusion of triple meters and dance rhythms contributes to the Concerto's light mood, and recalls Scriabin's love of Chopin, whose basic creative impulse naturally expressed itself through mazurkas, waltzes, and other folk dances in triple meters. To draw attention to Chopin's influence on this music is to state the obvious. But less attention has been paid to how Scriabin develops this borrowed material into original ideas. To take one illustrative example, the contrasting, secondary theme of the opening movement is a jaunty, skipping tune that is light on its feet and possesses a childlike innocence. It is the kind of figure that would fit perfectly in a waltz or mazurka, as seen in figure 4.1. Set in the warm key of A major, Scriabin develops this fleet-footed theme later in the opening movement, recasting its rhythm as a countermelody that is heard first in the strings, and then transferred up through the winds and reeds.

Figure 4.1. Jaunty second theme from the Piano Concerto in F♯ minor, Mvt. I, mm. 59–66.

The slow movement is an Andante in F♯ major, and it features a chorale-like theme played by muted strings (*con sordino*), followed by four variations. The chorale theme is thought to be a melody from Scriabin's childhood, although its exact provenance is unknown. The stately theme's inner voices tug and pull, adding a rich and expressive range of emotion. His choice to write a *Tema con variazioni* was unusual. By 1896, only Mozart's Piano Concerto No. 21 in C minor, K. 491 (final mvt.) stands out as an exception to the general avoidance of a theme and variations form for any movement of the solo concerto. Variation I features brilliant and relaxed passagework for the soloist, who is content to remain in the background and accompany the main theme's restatement by the clarinets, cellos, and violas. Variation II (Allegro scherzando) springs back to life with middle-register chordal melodies and octave leaps, foreshadowing the sort of pianistic figures that Scriabin would use to great effect in his Fourth and Fifth Sonatas.

Chopin's influence is unmistakable in Variation III, where dark clouds appear and turn the chorale melody into a haunting memory. Figure 4.2a shows the last bars of this variation, where Scriabin evokes a funeral march that recalls Chopin's C minor Prelude Op. 28 No. 20, a work that is known to every amateur pianist. Many composers favored the key of C minor for their most solemn music; countless examples are found in works by Haydn, Mozart, and Beethoven. For Scriabin, however, the ultimate pathos was expressed in D♯ minor, the relative minor of his favorite, "mystical" key of F♯. It is in the key of D♯ minor that Variation III languishes. Comparing the final bars of Chopin's prelude in figure 4.2b and Scriabin's variation shows the stylistic affinities: a dotted-rhythm melody set atop block chords, while octaves in the left hand descend chromatically. The gloomy clouds dissipate in Variation IV, bringing streaming sunlight and chirping birds. The soloist signals their joy over this celebration of life through trills, turns, and ornaments. By the end of this movement, Scriabin repeats the stylistic figurations of the first variation to bring a sense of closure to the movement, which maintains the frolicsome interplay between soloist and orchestra. Overall, this middle movement is redolent of nature, and Scriabin celebrates not only the simplicity and grandeur of Mother Nature, but also her quicksilver changes in mood.

Figure 4.2. (a) Final bars of Variation III, Piano Concerto in F♯ minor, Mvt. II. (b) Chopin, Prelude in C minor Op. 28 No. 20, mm. 9–13.

The final movement is the longest of the Concerto and made the greatest impression on audiences when the composer performed it live. Its exuberant main theme features an arpeggio that scampers up into the keyboard's highest registers before scaling back down again. This recurring idea ties the movement together, as per typical rondo form, pulling the music back on course to its final goal after its peregrinations. Listeners can make good use of this athletic arpeggio as a musical guidepost. Scriabin ties together all three movements by recycling rhythmic patterns from the first two movements in the finale, including some of the variation techniques used in the second movement. A later section within this finale is cast in the grand romantic piano tradition, and this passage foreshadows the kind of pianistic writing that Rachmaninov used to great effect in his own piano concertos. Not surprisingly, this radiant theme is eventually developed into the movement's climax. After so many beautiful moments, the final movement concludes unusually with unsettling and exclamatory chords.

Scriabin's Piano Concerto has never held a secure position in the repertory. A few of his contemporaries even refused to perform it; Sergei Prokofiev's well-known dismissal of the piece as "lackluster" and a waste of time for him to bother learning should be weighed against his characteristic impudence (Prokofiev similarly disparaged the music of Rachmaninov and Medtner).[13] The first pianist to champion the work was the composer, and even though Scriabin tended to dismiss his earlier works as he matured artistically, his Piano Concerto remained a perennial favorite throughout his career. Especially noteworthy were his performances of the piece on 20 December 1906 at Carnegie Hall under Safonov (its U.S. premiere),[14] his performances under Koussevitzky during the Volga tour of 1910,[15] and his appearances in London under Sir Henry J. Wood in March 1914.[16] Another unlikely champion of the piece was Rachmaninov, who performed it in 1915 for his own memorial series for Scriabin, and then repeated it again for the statewide anniversary of the composer's death in 1916.[17] By mid-century, the Concerto was tossed into cold storage and forgotten. But in recent years, modern pianists such as Evgeny Kissin, Garrick Ohlssohn, and Yevgeny Sudbin have brought the piece back into concert halls.

Recommended Recordings: Nikolai Golovanov, Grand Radio Symphony Orchestra with Heinrich Neuhaus, piano (Melodiya D 19635/6, 1946); Alexander Gauk, USSR Radio Symphony Orchestra with Samuil Feinberg, piano (Melodiya D 418/9, 1950); Lorin Maazel, London Philharmonic Orchestra with Vladimir Ashkenazy, piano (Decca 641461, 1971); Andrew Litton, Bergen Philharmonic with Yevgeny Sudbin, piano (Bis B00OMEJ8JE, 2015).

Rêverie in E major Op. 24
Date of Composition: Autumn 1898 in Moscow
Premiere: 17 September 1898 in St. Petersburg, cond. by Nikolai Rimsky-Korsakov
Often mistaken as Scriabin's first orchestral composition, this charming miniature was written soon after Scriabin completed his Third Piano Sonata, in 1898. Strictly speaking, it is his first purely symphonic work with no designated part for piano. It predates his First Symphony by roughly a year. For Scriabin, the years 1893–1897 were filled with international concert tours that took him to Berlin, Dresden, Paris, and other artistic hubs across Europe. These years of travel witnessed the growth of Scriabin the artist and the man, and this newfound freedom was documented in the dozens of piano miniatures he wrote wherever and whenever the mood struck

him. Nearly every miniature Scriabin composed during these years of wanderlust (including the Preludes Opp. 11, 13, 15, 16, and 17) bears the name of the city that inspired it. Although there is no particular city associated with the *Rêverie*, we can think of it in similar terms, as a fleeting thought captured in time, an idyllic summer daydream, *une Rêverie*.

Rêverie was written soon after Scriabin joined the Moscow Conservatory faculty as a piano professor in the fall of 1898. Considering the doubt and anxiety that plagued him during the writing of his Concerto—correcting mistakes, setting tempo and dynamic markings, and other editorial tasks—he must have set a goal to prove his independence in orchestration. The proud composer presented *Rêverie* as a gift to Beliaev, who was so touched by the gesture that he nearly forgave Scriabin for the past months' delays and empty promises in sending other new works. Titling a piece of music a "reverie" was a generic term, and part of the nineteenth-century tradition of writing character pieces bearing such names as Impromptu, Fantasy, Moment Musicale, etc. Scriabin and Beliaev deliberated over exactly what to call the piece, since the working title had been "Prelude." Ideas for its title (in Russian), included *mechty* (daydreams) and *gryozy* (musings).[18] They settled on *Rêverie*, and it was the first of Scriabin's orchestral works to be performed in America, where it was heard on 2 December 1900 under Frank Van der Stucken (1858–1929) and the Cincinnati Symphony Orchestra; he repeated the work in 1905 and 1906.[19]

In terms of style, Op. 24's themes are distinctly symphonic rather than pianistic. Although known primarily as a pianist-composer, Scriabin's keen understanding of orchestral timbre and textures is evident by his elegant treatment of *Rêverie*'s main theme, which is transferred throughout various instrumental sections, as opposed to varying the idea through filigree, ornamentation, and textural changes, as one would expect from a pianistic treatment. The main melody is intoned first by the clarinets and flutes, while the strings accompany them with tremolos and trills. (In 1926, the Russian composer Alexander Winkler [1865–1935] published a four-hand piano transcription of *Rêverie*, and the accompaniment parts are treated as a series of measured tremolos and trills.) What makes this work sound quintessentially Scriabin is the aching melody, with its chromatic tinges that sound like musical sighs and add a touch of world-weariness. A pang of melancholy pervades the work, prompting Rimsky-Korsakov to remark that Scriabin's *Rêverie* "called to mind Pushkin's words, "*Mechty, mechty, gde vasha sladost*" (Daydreams, daydreams, where is your sweetness?). Indeed, this was not a "daydream" but a kind of black melancholy.[20]

The work's formal structure is simple: A-B-A-Coda. Despite its brevity (an average performance lasts four minutes), the work builds impressive climaxes in a brief span of time, making it an effective insert on concert programs. The most salient aspect of *Rêverie* is its dreamy atmosphere, which creates a floating sensation that is consistent with the title of the piece. This mood is most evident in its unsteady pulse. Instead of providing a steady beat, the phrases slur across the barline, fooling the listener as to its actual meter (it's in 3, like a waltz). Like the Piano Concerto, *Rêverie*'s sounds are veiled and shadowy. Listeners familiar with the sound world of French Impressionism, epitomized by such works as Debussy's *Prélude à l'après-midi d'un faune* or *Nuages*, can bask in the evocative soundscapes that Scriabin conjures in this work. Considering the composer's travels in Europe, and especially Paris, in the years before he composed this work, Scriabin must have been exposed in some measure to French Impressionism, either in the visual or musical arts. Yet these influences are assimilated into Scriabin's unique Russian voice.

Recommended Recordings: Neeme Järvi, Scottish National Orchestra (Chandos 8462, 1986); Vladimir Ashkenazy, Deutsches Symphonie-Orchester (Decca 473 971–2, 1991); Yevgeny Svetlanov with the USSR Symphony Orchestra (Russian Disc RD CD 11 057, 1993).

Symphony No. 1 in E major Op. 26
Date of Composition: 1899–1900 in Darino and Moscow
Premiere: 24 November 1900 in Moscow, with Anatoly Liadov (minus the choral finale); first complete performance on 29 March 1901 in Moscow, cond. by Vasily Safonov

The romantic tradition of writing symphonies that burst at the seams in size and scope was seized by Scriabin with characteristic aplomb in his Symphony No. 1 in E major Op. 26 (1900). Cast in a late romantic idiom, the work features six movements instead of the standard four, and reaches its apotheosis with a choral finale that worships at the altar of art. The historical precedent for his choral finale was Beethoven's Ninth Symphony (1824), a work that set a new standard for the symphony by introducing voices into its finale. Friederich Schiller's appeal for universal brotherhood in the "Ode to Joy" text sealed the Ninth Symphony's permanence in popular culture. After Beethoven's Ninth, the symphony was no longer limited to all-instrumental forces. Even so, adding voices to a symphony as late as the year 1900 was still an audacious move, even if Gustav Mahler (1860–1911) did just that in his Second Symphony, "Resurrection" (1888–1894). Like Scriabin's First Symphony, the symphonies of Bruckner, Mahler, and Beethoven are notable for expanding the basic four-movement design and introducing a new intensity of self-expression. Scriabin's attempts to follow in their footsteps won him the Glinka Award of five hundred rubles in 1900, but the negative criticism that has surrounded this symphony since its premiere was a chain around Scriabin's neck for much of his career. Even Faubion Bowers kicked it to the curb, calling it a "paper-thin suite structured on flimsy bits and pieces . . . like musical shorthand."[21] With such endorsements from Scriabin's apologists, it is no wonder his First Symphony remains underrated.

Each movement of Op. 26 is written in a conservative style that could never offend the ear. Peace and calm pervades the prologue (Lento in 3/4), which basks in a radiant glow of E major. A solo clarinet and solo violin rise above the murmur and sing melodies that are echoed by the strings in a cinematic sweep. Winds and reeds trill like birdsong, and the lithe texture is anchored by gently rocking figures in the lower strings. An agitated theme for strings animates the second movement in E minor (Allegro dramatico in 3/4), and this theme resolves with a characteristic skipping or tripping rhythm that Scriabin favored so often to end his phrases. This movement traverses a rhapsodic sea of moods, alternating between full textures with the string orchestra and chamberlike passages with solo highlights. In the slow movement in B major (Lento in 6/8), a solo clarinet adds dashes of color that recall the prologue's placid mood. A contrasting second theme momentarily disrupts the calm, but the storms soon dissipate. Movement IV in C major is a Scherzo in 9/8 that maintains an air of calm, despite its bustling melodic and rhythmic activity. The galloping pace returns, but the forced re-transition to the main theme sticks out like a seam in the structural fabric, showing Scriabin's lack of polish. Movement V (Allegro in E minor) is cast in the late romantic orchestral style of Strauss or Bruckner. The dramatic verve of this movement offers a satisfying conclusion to the symphony, should conductors choose to omit the finale.

The choral finale (Movement VI) features tenor and mezzo soprano soloists singing Scriabin's self-composed text that celebrates the sovereignty of art. Despite Russia's rich operatic legacy, writing for voices never appealed to Scriabin. Upon submitting the score to Édition Russe de Musique, the Beliaev-appointed editorial committee (Liadov, Glazunov, and Rimsky-Korsakov) deemed the finale "unperformable" and refused to publish the work. Eventually they acquiesced, but in its initial performances, the symphony failed to win over critics. Vyacheslav Karatigin observed in 1914 that select members of the musical community believed Scriabin to be "an unusually deft smuggler," a charge that Karatigin fully endorsed: "the whole symphony contains not a single bar, not a single harmony or counterpoint which could not be explained by this or that paragraph in school textbooks."[22] Despite passages of sumptuous beauty, much of Scriabin's First Symphony sounds like a pastiche of other composers' styles, as Karatigin observed.

Once Safonov and company finally mustered the resources to mount Scriabin's First Symphony with its choral finale, the overwrought style set against Scriabin's ecstatic text must have made an already lengthy piece seem interminable. An excerpt from the choral text reads as follows:

> O wondrous image of the divine
> The pure art of harmony!
> Together we bring you praise
> Of the rapturous light of life
> I am a dream, you are celebration, you are respite
> Like a gift you bring your people mystic visions . . .
> Come all nations of the world
> Sing to the glory of art![23]

These words celebrate art's power to transform life, and this theme that Scriabin turned to so often has clear influences in the writings of Nietzsche, notably in his *Birth of Tragedy* (1872). As noble and uplifting as this text may be, a choral finale proved impractical from a performance standpoint. Even the premiere under Liadov omitted the last movement due to difficulty in securing the necessary performing forces. Well aware of this fact, Beliaev allowed his protégé to reach for the stars in his first symphony. But when Scriabin proposed similar performing forces for his next symphony, Beliaev put his foot down. In a letter of 5 May 1900, he stated frankly:

> Forgive me (as a layman), but even your finale with duet and chorus seems to me a pretension to the Ninth Symphony (although it is your first). Write for the piano, for the orchestra, for voice or other instruments, but do not plunge immediately into such complex works, which demand large musical resources and monetary expenditures for their execution.[24]

Beliaev's reprimand persuaded Scriabin to abandon such ambitious schemes and focus on more practical endeavors, at least for the meanwhile. For all the criticism surrounding the choral finale in the First Symphony, it remains one of the most memorable parts of the symphony, not only for its unusual addition of voices, but also for its eminently hummable melodies.

Several classic compositional techniques are featured in the finale of Symphony No. 1. The tenor and mezzo-soprano soloists sing in a call and response style known as *imitation*. When the main vocal melody is heard again, the orchestra (especially flutes and oboes) echoes its sentiments. A declamatory middle section intervenes before the chorus introduces a new melody that serves as the main subject of a strict style of composition called *fugue*. The rules and procedures of fugues surpass the scope of this chapter, but a basic definition is that they feature multiple independent melodies of equal interest woven together in a contrapuntal texture called *polyphony* (many voices). Strict laws govern the precise intervals and entrance points of each musical line. Fugues reached their perfection in the music of J. S. Bach, and the fugue technique signified high art or the *stile antico* by virtue of its association with church music.

For a composer like Scriabin, who sought to establish a reputation as a musical innovator, writing an old-fashioned fugue was an odd musical choice. Indeed, much of the criticism leveled at this piece has focused on the chorale finale. Even devotees like Arthur Eaglefield Hull panned it as a "'school fugue' on a very ordinary subject . . . it smells too much like the Academy."[25] One explanation for Scriabin's decision to evoke the *stile antico* was that it served as retribution for those skeptics who believed he was undisciplined. Rachmaninov was rumored to have jested after hearing his classmate's First Symphony that, "I thought Scriabin was simply a swine, but it seems he is a composer after all," although he denied uttering the remark.[26] Recall Scriabin's fallout with Arensky in his last year at the Moscow Conservatory; to make up for incomplete assignments, Arensky gave Scriabin the choice of writing ten perfect fugues over the summer or failing the program. Scriabin returned to school that fall with one "Fugue-Nocturne" and narrowly avoided expulsion.

Another interpretation for Scriabin's fugal finale is that he observed high art traditions, or the "learned style." Eighteenth-century composers like Mozart and Beethoven were well attuned to the correlation between music and rhetoric. Classical rhetoric established a wide range of topics, or *topoi*, that orators used to construct arguments using common tropes like puns and metaphors to engage their audiences. Likewise, eighteenth- and nineteenth-century composers drew from a stockpile of well-known musical *topoi*, including folk dances, pastorales, military marches, hunting calls, and other stock devices that aroused specific emotional states in their audience.[27] The learned style was one such *topos*, and it was especially effective in finales because it approximated a sublime experience. Theories on the sublime preoccupied eighteenth-century philosophers such as Immanuel Kant and Edmund Burke, who were fascinated with experiences that wrested them out of everyday existence and represented the height of emotion. The musicologist Elaine Sisman wrote that, "Appealing as it does to both intellect and imagination, learned style thus works particularly well in the peroration, the final part of the oration or piece, in which arguments are summed up in a last attempt to secure the emotions of the audience. It is no accident that full-movement fugues appear most often as the second of a pair of movements and in finales."[28] Theories of musical *topoi* and the sublime help explain Scriabin's decision to compose a fugal finale for his Symphony No. 1, which glorified the transcendent powers of art.

The Symphony No. 1 has been rarely performed over the last few decades. When it is heard, the finale is often omitted out of time constraints or lack of performing forces (soloists and a chorus are not inexpensive to retain and rehearse). The symphony debuted in America under Modest Altschuler with his Russian Symphony Orchestra Society in New York on 28 February 1907, with the composer in attendance. Safonov often guest conducted with the New York Philharmonic, and he performed the work on 13 and 14 December 1907. It premiered in England on 13 March 1913 with the Royal Philharmonic Society (without the final movement) again under Safonov, where it was paired with Beethoven's Ninth. In recent years, the Symphony No. 1 has appeared on the Chicago Symphony Orchestra's programs under Riccardo Muti, who brought the score to the CSO for the first time in its history. Among other champions of this piece are the Russian conductor Valery Gergiev, whose masterful recordings of Scriabin's orchestral works have earned critical acclaim, and the pianist and conductor Mikhail Pletnev, who recorded the work in 2015 for the Dutch label, Pentatone.

Recommended Recordings: Nikolai Golovanov, The Great Symphony Orchestra and Choir of the All-Union Radio and Central TV (Boheme Music CDBMR 907081, 1948); Riccardo Muti, Philadelphia Symphony Orchestra (EMI Classics B000002RS6, 1991); Mikhail Pletnev, Russian National Orchestra (Pentatone PTC5186514 SACD, 2015).

Symphony No. 2 in C minor Op. 29
Date of Composition: January–September 1901 in Moscow
Premiere: 25 January 1902 in St. Petersburg, cond. by Anatoly Liadov with the Russian Symphony Society Orchestra

Within weeks of completing his First Symphony and having it performed, Scriabin wasted no time plunging into writing its successor, dissatisfied as he was with his artistic goals and the critical reviews for the First. Once again, his creative ambitions outgrew the four-movement design, but the Second Symphony's five movements amount to three large sections. Like the Symphony No. 1, Op. 29 is cast in a lush romantic style, but its cyclical form is innovative, and its dissonant chromatic transitions sound refreshingly piquant today. In both form and content, this symphony demonstrates Scriabin flexing his compositional muscles and discovering his personal flair for orchestration. It is a pity that this work has been largely neglected in the repertory. If the First Symphony demonstrated Scriabin's fluency with late romantic style, then the Second shows his assimilation of the symphonic techniques of Tchaikovsky, Wagner, and Strauss, with a glimpse of the future. The performing forces required for Op. 29 are modest, but Scriabin's treatment of thematic development shows a significant step forward in his handling of large-scale forms.

The Second Symphony was mainly written in Paris, where Scriabin spent the summer of 1901 to escape his domestic obligations with Vera in Moscow, and allow his creative juices to flow free of distraction. He was so excited with his initial progress that he wrote to Beliaev of his intention to conduct it himself (his reservations about Liadov's renditions of his music were another factor). Considering Scriabin's lack of experience in conducting, wiser heads thankfully prevailed. His natural tendency for *rubato* (an elastic stretching and compressing of tempo) would have made him ill suited to the task of leading an orchestra. Beliaev fielded Scriabin's suggestion delicately: "a conductor must be very stable in rhythm . . . I have not felt this requisite rhythmicality in you."[29] By the fall of 1901, the Second Symphony reached its completed form, and any doubts that had plagued Scriabin about writing for orchestra had been eradicated. In 1903, Beliaev entrusted Vasily Kalafati (1869–1942), a music professor at the St. Petersburg Conservatory and pupil of Rimsky-Korsakov, to arrange a four-hand piano transcription of the Second Symphony.

Movement I in C minor is in cyclical form, with periodic restatements of the principal theme and its variations. The opening bars set a serious tone and present the movement's main motive. It is heard on a clarinet in its bottomed-out *chalumeau* register, spotlighting that instrument as a protagonist in the drama. Two aspects of this main theme warrant closer inspection. Its contour suggests a motive of languor, with its leap downward of a sixth and slow climb back up to its starting pitch, as shown in figure 4.3. The falling sixth interval is a trope of world-weariness or *Weltschmerz*. The gravity of this falling sixth interval can be sensed by singing the opening two notes of the popular spiritual "Nobody Knows the Trouble I've Seen." Like the falling sixth in this spiritual (no-*bo*-dy), the opening motive in Scriabin's symphony provides a basic idea from which the rest of the themes grow throughout the piece. The solo violin offers a lyrical counter-theme, and this idea is heard in the opening movement and finale. The first movement segues directly into Movement II, set in the relative key of E♭ major, which traditionally serves as the heroic antipode to C minor. This energetic movement is propelled by furious string figures and imperious brass that summon the spirit of Wagner. Later in the movement, the solo clarinet theme returns, climbing higher and higher in its melodic contour, as if to reassure listeners of its resiliency in the face of such tumult.

Figure 4.3. Second Symphony in C minor Op. 29, Mvt. I, opening theme.

The slow Movement III is evocative of nature, replete with birdcalls in the flutes and swaying breezes in the strings. A rich tradition of nature-themed slow movements can be found in nineteenth-century symphonies, including Beethoven's Sixth ("Pastoral"), Berlioz's *Symphonie fantastique*, and Mahler's Third. But to write off this poetic and expansive movement as a Disneyesque ode to nature, as many writers have, undervalues its grandeur and depth of expression. This poignant Adagio (marked *Andante*) signals Scriabin's emergence as a serious symphonist, not only because its radiant orchestral colors anticipate moments in the *Poem of Ecstasy*, but also for its ability to sustain the listener's interest over a lengthy period.

The symphony's climax arrives in Movement IV (Tempestoso, F minor), which features swirling strings driven by timpani and brass. A contrasting theme in the first violins offers a brief respite from the storm, but the whirling winds return before the movement modulates to the major mode and recapitulates the first movement's ending. The finale (Movement V) brings a transfiguration of C minor tragedy to glorious C major (à la Beethoven's Fifth and Tchaikovsky's Fifth). Scriabin set out to write a finale that would strike at the hearts of the common people, but in the end he jested that all he ended up with was a "military parade." Despite his disappointment, the final movement of this symphony provides a satisfying conclusion for modern audiences. Ever focused on his next big idea, the composer often dismissed his earlier compositions as inferior to his current projects. Such was the case with the finale to this symphony.

No other symphony of Scriabin's has received fewer performances than his Second, and only in recent years has it gained a greater appreciation. It remains his most neglected work for orchestra; even Rêverie crops up occasionally on concert programs. The Second Symphony's premiere in St. Petersburg under Liadov in January 1902 was far from an unqualified success, even though Liadov was the natural choice for conducting it. It is odd that Liadov agreed to the task, considering his negative opinion of the score when Scriabin first sent him the opening movement. In a note to his comembers on Beliaev's editorial committee, Liadov wrote, "Scriabin boldly stretches out his hand to clasp Richard Strauss. But gentlemen, where is the music?"[30] Liadov still conducted the piece at the premiere, but a riot nearly broke out. Scriabin's aunt Lyubov Skriabina left a vivid account of the premiere in St. Petersburg in January 1902:

> Half of the audience made their way to the stage with roaring applause. The other half remained in their seats. There was a terrible clamor, hissing, whistling, an unbelievable noise rocked the house. The applause was so strong that Alexander had to come out on

the stage, and so did Safonov. Pale, but absolutely calm, even smiling, Alexander Nikolaevich stared down his audience.[31]

Arensky naturally sided with the dissenters, and in a letter to Taneyev, he bellowed, "One dissonance after another piles up without a single thought behind any of it."[32] Today, these grinding dissonances do not perturb as much as they did a century ago, but listening to the chromatic transitions of this opening movement will bring a smile to one's face with Arensky's pothers in mind. In its day, the Second Symphony had plenty of enthusiasts. Safonov conducted its premiere in Moscow on 21 March 1903, and was so bowled over by the work that when he brought it to the musicians of the New York Philharmonic, he waved the score in their faces and excitedly shouted, "Gentlemen, here is the new Bible!" Arthur Nikisch also performed the Second Symphony at the Season of Russian Music Concerts in Paris in May of 1907, and this celebrity conductor's endorsement of the work raised Scriabin's stock as a symphonist.

After Nikisch's historic performance in 1907, the Second Symphony was virtually abandoned. It was heard again in England on 14 September 1921, when Sir Henry J. Wood debuted it for the Promenade Concerts (or "Proms," as they are known) at Queen's Hall. The first performance of Op. 29 on American soil was at Town Hall in Manhattan on 12 March 1935, with Musicians from the New York Philharmonic (an independent coalition) being led by Viennese conductor Gertrud Hrdliczka in her New York conducting debut. The Second Symphony would have been heard earlier in America, had it not been for Scriabin's reluctance to having it performed because of his dissatisfaction with the finale. Its American premiere with a full professional orchestra waited until 6 December 1968, when the Boston Symphony Orchestra resurrected it at Symphony Hall under Georg (Jerzy) Semkow (1928–2014).[33] Semkow brought the work to the New York Philharmonic for the first time the following year, but after that, the Second Symphony disappeared from the programs of major American orchestras for nearly forty years. Not until 29 January 2009 did public audiences enjoy the ebullient strains of the Second Symphony once again, when Riccardo Muti exhumed it from its tomb with the New York Philharmonic.[34]

Recommended Recordings: Neeme Järvi, Scottish National Orchestra (Chandos 8462, 1986); Yevgeny Svetlanov, USSR State Symphony Orchestra (Russian Disc B000001L0F, 1992); Igor Golovschin, Moscow Symphony Orchestra (Naxos 8.553581, 1995); Vladimir Ashkenazy, Deutsches Symphonie-Orchester Berlin (Decca B000002RS6, 2003).

Symphony No. 3 in C minor Op. 43, Le Divin Poème (Divine Poem)
Date of Composition: 1902–1904 in Moscow, Obolenskoye, Lausanne, and Beatenberg
Premiere: 29 May 1905 at the Théâtre du Châtelet in Paris, cond. by Arthur Nikisch

The year 1903 was pivotal in Scriabin's life. In his personal affairs, he reached an impasse in his marriage to his wife, Vera, and confessed to Safonov his decision to leave her and their children (she refused to grant him a divorce) and take Tatyana Schloezer as his mistress. Tatyana was the niece of Pavel (Paul) Schloezer, who had been Vera's piano instructor at the Moscow Conservatory. Scriabin's scandalous affair with Tatyana ruptured his friendship with Safonov, and cost him a powerful ally in his career.[35] Changes were also underfoot in Scriabin's professional life. He resigned from his teaching post at the Moscow Conservatory to focus on composition. Despite the allure of a steady paycheck, the exposure to other composers' music had proved distracting and was drowning out his inner creative voice. Scriabin had informed Beliaev of his intention to leave the Conservatory the previous year and requested a raise in his annuity, to which his benevolent patron obliged after reminding the composer of debts owed. By year's end, however, tragedy struck when Beliaev's poor health exacted its enervating toll, and he died from heart failure on 4 January 1904 while recovering from a surgery for recurrent ulcers. Beliaev's death stunned Scriabin and left him without a benefactor and mentor.

Scriabin's saving grace in this time of need was Margarita Morozova (1873–1958), a former pupil and wealthy widow of a Moscow arts collector. Like Beliaev, Morozova established herself as an important patron of Symbolist artists, and she generously supplied Scriabin with an unconditional annuity. This arrangement lasted until 1908, when relations between Scriabin and Morozova deteriorated over what he perceived as a lack of enthusiasm for his career (her commitment to Scriabin was not nearly as dutiful as Beliaev's), as well as her sympathy for Scriabin's estranged wife, Vera. In spite of, or perhaps due to these profound changes, 1903 was one of the most fruitful years of Scriabin's life, which saw a spate of new music, including the Fourth Piano Sonata, over thirty preludes and character pieces, and the bulk of the work on his Third Symphony.

The *Divine Poem* is the longest work Scriabin ever wrote, and its three movements are performed without pause for roughly fifty minutes. In this and later symphonies, all traces of Chopin's influence have been eradicated, although the specters of Wagner and Berlioz still linger. The orchestral forces are extensive, with heavy brass, percussion, and frequent *divisi* strings. The impulsive, unbridled intensity of the music belies its fine craftsmanship and careful construction, especially in its use of thematic transformation and developing variation. Scriabin started writing the piece in 1902, and finally completed it in November 1904 after laboring on it for nearly three years. Much of the symphony was fleshed out in Obolenskoye, where Scriabin spent his summers. In mid-1903, Scriabin's second summer there, his neighbor was the Russian poet and the future–*Doctor Zhivago* novelist Boris Pasternak (1890–1960), who was then an impressionable thirteen-year-old and who became entranced by the composer's magnetic personality. He recalled hearing the emerging strains of the *Divine Poem* being pounded out on an old upright piano, which echoed through the thickets that divided their dachas:

> Just as light and shadow alternated in the woodland and birds called and flew from bough to bough, so the pieces and fragments of the Third Symphony, or *"Divine Poem"*

carried and reverberated to it as they were composed at the piano in the neighboring dacha. Lord, what music it was! The symphony constantly collapsed and fell in ruins like a city under shell-fire, and then it was built up and grew again from its own fragments and destruction.[36]

The three-year gestation for the *Divine Poem* is a testament to the effort Scriabin exerted to advance his symphonic technique. His efforts paid off when the work earned rave reviews and the Glinka Prize in 1906. Lev Konyus, a classmate of Rachmaninov and piano professor at the Moscow Conservatory until 1918, transcribed the *Divine Poem* for two pianos in 1905, and Sergei Pavchinsky arranged it for solo piano in 1954.

The *Divine Poem* rose from the ashes of an abandoned opera that had occupied Scriabin since 1900. Its hero was a "Philosopher-Musician-Poet" (in that order) who interacted with other allegorical characters in a quest to attain universal brotherhood. Scriabin's compositional gifts ultimately proved ill-suited to the dramatic demands of theater, but the ideological remnants of this opera spilled over into the *Divine Poem*. The philosophical narrative that underlies the *Divine Poem* is the evolution and liberation of the human spirit and its communion with the divine. The words and text he felt necessary to convey his artistic intentions in the First Symphony were incorporated into his Third Symphony by way of descriptive titles and idiosyncratic performance indications. In the first movement alone, we find such performance markings as *Mystérieux, mystique, légendaire* (predating its appearance in the Ninth Sonata), *tragique, avec abandon*, and *sublime*. Of this last marking, Taneyev famously quipped, "You are the first composer who, instead of indicating the tempos, writes praise of his own compositions."[37] As risible as these expression marks may seem, they indicate the composer's desire to express something more than just music, or to vouchsafe a glimpse of an alternate reality.

The introduction in 3/2 is headed by the words *Divin, grandiose*. This unorthodox marking describes a stately theme in D♭ major played by the brass and lower strings. This six-note motto serves as the thematic crux of the entire symphony, and it reappears in various guises in all three movements. After its initial statement, the harmony falls to an unstable, sustained chord, over which the trumpets leap up a sixth in a fanfare motive that declares, *Ya Yest'*, or "I am!"[38] A reduction of this famous opening is shown in figure 4.4. These opening bars were salvaged from Scriabin's abandoned *Symphonic Allegro* from 1896, but another famous work may have influenced its original design. The musicologist Richard Taruskin has advanced a compelling case for a connection between the openings of the *Divine Poem* and Richard Wagner's Prelude to *Tristan und Isolde* (1859). A reduction of Wagner's Prelude is shown in figure 12.4 in chapter 12. Both passages consist of a one-measure introduction with a leap of a sixth, which settles on a dissonant chord that resolves in such a way as to disorient the listener as to its key. The melodies and harmonies of their respective openings provide the compositional basis for the rest of the work; from the acorn, to the oak.

Figure 4.4. *Divine Poem* opening motto with "I am" theme, mm. 1–3.

In terms of music theory, the chords in Wagner's and Scriabin's works both contain a sonority known as an augmented sixth chord, and the dissonant, tonally ambiguous properties of this chord allow it to resolve in two different ways. Space prohibits an analysis of the theoretical implications of Scriabin's harmonies, and readers are referred to Matthew Bengtson's discussion of augmented sixth chords in chapter twelve on harmony. Suffice it to say that the *Divine Poem* represented a compositional breakthrough for Scriabin, regardless of its stylistic debts. It was his first systematic application of a method for prolonging the dominant function for long stretches of music without sacrificing a sense of musical line and forward momentum.

Following the introduction, the first complete movement is titled *Luttes* (Struggles, in 3/4), and is a sonata-rondo form in C minor that recasts the opening six-note motto as an Allegro theme, as shown in figure 4.5.[39] For Scriabin, the struggles in this grandiloquent movement refer to the common man's search for his inner-God. It is an episodic movement with quicksilver changes in mood and multiple themes, including several reappearances of the "I am" theme, heard each time on the trumpet. With each appearance of this theme, the harmony resolves to a new key that thwarts its expected course, symbolizing an unforeseen challenge that the protagonist faces on his quest. Among its many evocative episodes is a diabolical passage marked

Figure 4.5. Allegro theme from "Luttes," *Divine Poem*, mm. 1–8.

écroulement formidable (sudden collapse) that is horror music akin to the famous Wolf's Glen scene from Carl Maria von Weber's opera, *Der Freischütz*, or Berlioz's "Dream of a Witch's Sabbath" from the *Symphonie fantastique*. This expansive first movement of Scriabin's symphony encompasses roughly half of the entire work, and it concludes by restating the opening motto in the home key of D♭ major.

Luttes segues directly into the slow movement, *Voluptés* (Sensual Pleasures), which depicts the worldly pleasures that tempt the hero before he surrenders to divine will. The freewheeling abandon of this music belies its tightly integrated motivic construction. The opening motto is crafted into a lyrical melody in the key of E. Soft strings and light winds dominate the opening section, which offers tranquil repose from the drama of *Luttes*. The music moves at a much slower harmonic rhythm and is mainly diatonic. A few mildly dissonant pitches rub up against one another in a delectable approximation of physical sensuality. Solo instruments spotlight important material, such as fluttering birdcalls in the flutes that recall the slow movement of the Second Symphony, and the "I am" theme, now played by the violin.

The finale, *Jeu Divin* (Divine Play), is a sonata-allegro form that celebrates the soul's transcendence from the earthly to the divine. The violin and flute offer solo passages that sparkle with trills and ostinatos, and the orchestra builds to an incredible climax while the musical texture remains utterly weightless. Motives from the first two movements are intricately woven into this multilayered finale, including a recapitulation of the first theme from *Luttes*. The final moments of delirium are depicted with breathless, circular melodies in the winds and strings, until the nearly hour-long journey reaches its peroration when C minor releases its pent-up energy into C major, which marks the moment when humanity finally unites with the divine (marked *avec ravissement et transport*). With this finale, Scriabin seems to have finally solved the problem of composing a satisfying ending, which had plagued him in his first two symphonies.

Since its publication by Beliaev in 1905, the *Divine Poem* has been well represented on concert programs, at least among Scriabin's symphonies. Critical approval of this work, however, was not easily won. Its U.S. premiere in New York under Modest Altschuler and the Russian Symphony Society on 14 March 1907 was a major event attended by top critics. Program notes for the evening noted that the work's opening theme symbolized "the affirmation of conscious existence, the coexistence of matter and spirit in the Ego."[40] But the symphony failed to measure up to its rhetorical hype. Although critics like Lawrence Gilman (1878–1939) defended the *Divine Poem* against naysayers who ridiculed its philosophical program and overblown orchestra, Gilman admitted that Scriabin "does not command the scope and fertility and eloquence of inspiration which are needed for the adequate musical realization of such a subject. He has essayed a theme which would have taxed the genius of Wagner or of Richard Strauss, and has quite naturally met defeat."[41]

Undaunted by the poor reception the piece had received, a resolute Leopold Stokowski brought the *Divine Poem* to the Philadelphia Orchestra in 1915. Albert Coates followed suit soon after, and was the first to conduct it with the New York

Philharmonic, on 5 January 1922. One of the most dedicated evangelists for the *Divine Poem* was Frederick Stock, who performed it annually with his Chicago Symphony Orchestra from 1923 to 1941.[42] In England, it premiered with the Queens Hall Orchestra under Sir Henry J. Wood on 18 October 1913. Hamilton Harty performed it with the Hallé Orchestra on notable occasions in March 1920 and December 1921.

The technical complexity and breadth of the score likely contributed to the hostile reception that greeted the *Divine Poem* in its initial performances. It must have presented a supreme challenge to Altschuler's orchestra and other ensembles at the turn of the century. Such errors as misplaced notes and rhythms and a slackening of the musical pulse could have disastrous effects on the overall performance. In his 1956 coming-of-age novel, *Comfort Me With Apples*, the American humorist Peter De Vries (1910–1993) gave some indication of the fine line between a great and an average performance of Scriabin's music. The main character's best friend, Nickie Sherman, upon returning from a concert at Tanglewood, offhandedly remarked, "They played Scriabin rather badly I thought. But then how can you tell when Scriabin is being badly played?"[43] Dozens of recordings of the *Divine Poem* have appeared over the last twenty years, some of which use the Kalmus edition of the score, which adds cymbal crashes and auxiliary instrumentation that Scriabin never authorized, and which do not appear in the Beliaev edition.

Recommended Recordings: Riccardo Muti, Philadelphia Orchestra (EMI Classics 567720, 2001); Nikolai Golovanov, Grand Symphony Orchestra of USSR (Music Online, 2007); Valery Gergiev, London Symphony Orchestra (LSO, LSO Live LSO0771, 2014); Vasily Petrenko, Oslo Philharmonic (Lawo LWC 1088, 2015).

Poème de l'Extase (Poem of Ecstasy) in C major Op. 54
Date of Composition: 1905–1908 in Beatenberg, Geneva, Lausanne, and Paris
Premiere: 10 December 1908 in New York, cond. by Modest Altschuler with the Russian Symphony Society at Carnegie Hall

Ecstasy as a philosophical idea first captured Scriabin's attention around 1905. In private journals never meant for public consumption, he wrote that ecstasy represented "the utmost increase of activity, ecstasy is a peak. Ecstasy is the total synthesis."[44] For Scriabin, ecstasy meant spiritual transcendence and sensory stimulation. His understanding of the term is rooted in Nietzsche's theory of the Dionysian sublime as expounded in *The Birth of Tragedy*. The *Poem of Ecstasy* was a public declaration of Scriabin's philosophy, and a celebration of music as a gateway to the divine. The overall style and design of the music was a departure from his previous symphonies, so much so that he dispensed with the idea of calling it a symphony altogether, although it is sometimes referred to as his Fourth. For Scriabin, ecstasy was not personal, but cosmic or universal. His outlook on ecstasy has a rough analogue with the utopian communes or "Love-Ins" of the American counterculture. This association with an era of sexual freedom is even more resonant in light of the work's original title, *Poème Orgiaque* (Orgasmic Poem). There is no mistaking the overt eroticism of this music, and its palpable sensuality has contributed to its reputation as Scriabin's most famous composition. The American writer Henry Miller captured its intoxicating quality when he wrote in his 1961 book, *Nexus*:

> That *Poème de l'extase*? Put it on loud. His music sounds like I think—sometimes. Has that far-off cosmic itch. Divinely fouled up. All fire and air. The first time I heard it I played it over and over. . . . It was like a bath of ice, cocaine and rainbows. For weeks I went about in a trance.[45]

There are two *Poems of Ecstasy*, one musical and one poetic. Both roughly convey the spirit's ascendance from earthly struggles to the eternal divine. Scriabin wrote a 369-line poem at the same time he composed the music, but the text was never meant to be sung. He was so enraptured with his poem that he had five hundred copies printed and distributed. Eventually, he suppressed the poem from performances, and insisted that the music stood on its own terms. His poem mused on such esoteric ideas as the "rays of celestial suns," "spirits caressing," and "divine play." While the literary poem is often dismissed as rhetorical fluff, the music speaks for itself. The titles of the symphony's three main parts roughly describe the narrative progression of events: (1) the soul in the orgy of love; (2) the realization of a fantastic dream; and (3) the glory of one's own art. These sections were conceived as separate movements, but were eventually condensed into one uninterrupted flow.

In terms of genre and form, the twenty-minute piece is akin to a Strauss or Lisztian symphonic poem, but its German influences are far less prominent than its French. It's no coincidence that Scriabin's use of French instructions proliferates in this score, including such markings as *très parfumé* (very perfumed), *charmé* (enchanted), and *avec une volupté de plus en plus extatique* (with increasingly ecstatic pleasure). Further emphasizing its French influences is its use of whole-tone scales, which lack any leading tone to indicate the root harmony. These whole-tone passages create harmonic ambiguity and fluidity between key centers. The harmonic tension steadily builds, teasing a climax that comes only in short bursts. The music stubbornly avoids resolution and its passages are fortified with "color" notes that evade any sense of a solid harmonic anchoring. One aspect that makes the *Poem of Ecstasy* so effective is its masterful balance of form and content. The orchestration is eminently modern in its use of instrumental sonorities and effects. In this respect, Scriabin owed a debt of gratitude to Altschuler for offering his advice in matters of orchestration. The *Poem of Ecstasy* features several solo passages for violin and trumpet, the latter of which typically receives credit as a soloist. The performing forces require an enormous roster of 110 players to achieve its magical nuances and sensational power.

The *Poem of Ecstasy*'s themes are notable for their brevity and individual character. They consist of small motivic fragments with distinct rhythmic profiles, each of which represent a condition or emotional state. They are presented in clear succession before being sliced up and combined in inventive ways. Arthur Eaglefield Hull was the first writer to lend distinct monikers to these melodic fragments, and his

Symphonies and Orchestral Works 95

Figure 4.6. "Human striving after the ideal," *Poem of Ecstasy*, mm. 1–4.

imaginative descriptions have stuck. The prologue presents the first of three ideas. A flute melody is heard at the outset over hovering whole-tone chords. The melodic outline lies on the note B, heard as the first, middle, and last pitch of the idea. This note of B functions as the *leading tone*, i.e., the note that leans most toward the home pitch of C and imparts a sense of yearning or striving for a goal. Hull christened this idea "human striving after the ideal," and this melody is shown in figure 4.6. This idea is heard next in a higher key and builds to a climax before the music settles and a solo clarinet offers a new theme, Hull's "Ego Theme gradually realizing itself," shown in figure 4.7 in its reduction for two pianos as transcribed by Lev Konyus in 1908. The exposition (Allegro volando) begins with an upward-skipping melodic idea in 2/4 played by the flutes, the "soaring flight of the spirit," seen in figure 4.8. This theme is developed briefly before a contrasting secondary theme enters on the solo violin. Marked *carezzando* and representing "human love," this chromatic melody shown in the bottom system of figure 4.9 symbolizes the mercurial nature of emotions. The final theme of significance is allotted to the brass, which offer up a summons motive that Hull identified as the "Will to rise up," as shown in figure 4.10. This theme is carried by the brass and guides the *Poem of Ecstasy* to its smoldering conclusion. The final, resplendent C major climax affirms the ego's quest for transcendence, and envelops its listeners in a blinding supernova of sound.

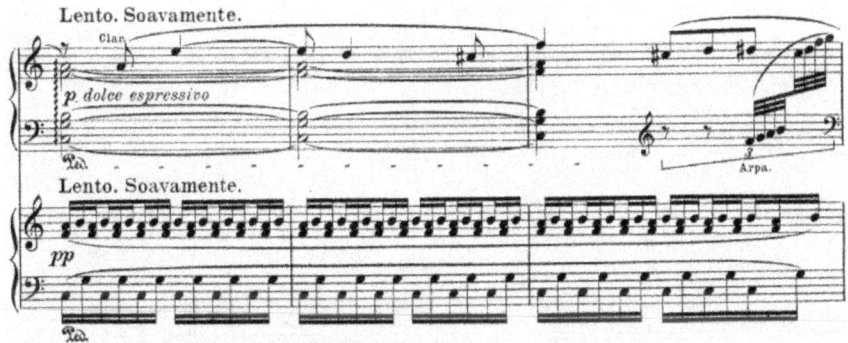

Figure 4.7. "Ego Theme gradually realizing itself," *Poem of Ecstasy*, mm. 19–21. *Four-hand piano transcription by Lev Konyus. Leipzig: Beliaev, 1908.*

Figure 4.8. "Soaring flight of the spirit," *Poem of Ecstasy*, mm. 40–41. Trans. Konyus, Leipzig: Beliaev, 1908.

Figure 4.9. "Human love," solo violin, *Poem of Ecstasy*, mm. 71–76. Trans. Konyus, Leipzig: Beliaev, 1908.

Figure 4.10. "Will to rise up" (solo trumpet), *Poem of Ecstasy*.

The world premiere of the *Poem of Ecstasy* was originally scheduled for 16 February 1908 in St. Petersburg, but the performance was cancelled because Maestro Felix Blumenfeld ran short of rehearsals to overcome the score's complexities. The challenge of being the first to conduct it was then accepted by Modest Altschuler, whose Russian Symphony Society premiered the work on 10 December 1908, an evening that also marked the American debut of Jewish violinist Mischa Elman (1891–1967). On that night at Carnegie Hall, Elman's electrifying performance of Tchaikovsky's Violin Concerto upstaged Scriabin's *Poem of Ecstasy*. Henry Krehbiel of the *New York Tribune* commented that Scriabin's tone poem lacked a "firm melodic framework. It had its rapturous moments, but it left the hearers unconvinced."[46] William J. Henderson of the *New York Sun* similarly grumbled that Scriabin's tone poem

> conveyed a sense of eeriness and uncanny connotation. Most of the time, the violins were whimpering and wailing like lost souls, while strange undulating and formless melodies roved about in the woodwind. A solo violin spoke occasionally, growing more and more plaintive, and finally being swallowed in a chaos of acid harmonies with violins screaming in agony overhead. . . . It was many things far from ecstasy.[47]

Within only a few years, however, the *Poem of Ecstasy* vaulted into the top ranks of the modern repertory, thanks to charismatic conductors who adopted it as their pièce de résistance.

The Russian premiere of the *Poem of Ecstasy* took place on 1 February 1909 in St. Petersburg with the Court Orchestra under Hugo Warlich, although several sources cite Felix Blumenfeld as the conductor. Critical reactions were divisive, and many attendees left the concert hall stupefied. A nervously excited Scriabin asked of his former teacher, Taneyev, what he thought of the piece, to which Taneyev replied, "I felt as if I had been beaten by sticks."[48] The younger generation of Russian composers, such as Prokofiev and Myaskovsky, felt very differently and left the concert awestruck by the tone poem's modern harmonic language and expressive power. Serge Koussevitzky premiered the *Poem of Ecstasy* in England on 4 April 1910 with the London Symphony Orchestra, and it went on to become one of his signature works. Arthur Lourié wrote in his biography of the conductor that in his hands, the *Poem of Ecstasy* "rose to such a high level of tenseness and creative saturation that the 'professional' character was completely dissolved away and an impression of almost 'noumenal' music produced."[49]

The *Poem of Ecstasy* remains one of the most frequently recorded works in Scriabin's orchestral catalogue. It took Second Prize at the annual Glinka Awards when it was published in 1908. Several transcriptions for solo piano and piano duet exist, as well as an adaptation for ballet, which was written by John Cranko for Dame Margot Fonteyn (1919–1991), who was among the greatest classical ballet dancers of the twentieth century.[50] Cranko's ballet debuted on 24 March 1970 with the Stuttgart Ballet and garnered critical acclaim. The *Poem of Ecstasy*'s enduring popularity has also earned it several references in twentieth-century films and novels.

Recommended Recordings: Leopold Stokowski, Houston Symphony Orchestra (Everest EVC 9037, 1959); Claudio Abbado, Boston Symphony Orchestra (Deutsche Grammophon LP 2530 137, 1971); Yevgeny Svetlanov, USSR Symphony Orchestra (Angel/Melodiya SR-40019, 1977); Giuseppe Sinopoli, New York Philharmonic (Deutsche Grammophon 427 324–2, 1988).

Prometheus: Poem of Fire in F♯ major Op. 60
Date of Composition: 1908–1910 in Brussels and Moscow
Premiere: 15 March 1911 in Moscow, cond. by Serge Koussevitzky (orchestra and chorus only); 20 March 1915 in New York at Carnegie Hall, cond. by Modest Altschuler with the Russian Symphony Society (with full orchestra, chorus, and color organ)

Scriabin's rising fame reached new heights in January 1909, when he made a celebrated return visit to Russia after living abroad for five years. Several "Scriabin Weeks" in Moscow were devoted to public performances of his newest works, which established him as the leading modernist composer of his generation. In April 1910, Scriabin moved back to Moscow permanently. Once there, he created his fifth and final symphony, *Prometheus: Poem of Fire*. The piece stunned the world with its dissonant harmonies, Theosophical program, and *clavier à lumières*, or color organ. Early information about *Prometheus* came from Rosa Newmarch (1857–1940), England's resident authority on Russian music. An article she wrote in 1914 offered a cogent analysis of the music and program of *Prometheus*, which depicted how in ancient times, Lucifer, Satan, and Prometheus harnessed their active energy to create the cosmos. Scriabin's concept of Prometheus was not the primordial Titan who stole fire from the gods to enlighten humanity, but "one of that class of adepts symbolized at a much later date by the Greeks under the name of Prometheus. These 'Sons of the Flames of Wisdom' . . . were alone able to impart to humanity that sacred spark which expands into the blossom of human intelligence and self-consciousness."[51]

In putting a modern spin on the myth of Prometheus, Scriabin joined the ranks of other romantic composers who had reinterpreted this ancient legend. In 1801, Beethoven wrote incidental music for the ballet *Creatures of Prometheus* and recycled its themes in the finale to his Third Symphony, "Eroica" (Heroic, 1803). Franz Schubert composed a dramatic art song in 1819 on the Prometheus myth with text written by Johann Wolfgang von Goethe, and in 1850, Franz Liszt titled the fifth of his symphonic tone poems "Prometheus." Add to this short list other Promethean-inspired pieces by Camille Saint-Saëns, Gabriele Fauré, and Hugo Wolf, and readers can appreciate the rich history that the Prometheus legend commanded in nineteenth-century music (to say nothing of the visual arts) when Scriabin turned his attention to it in 1910.[52]

Prometheus is often regarded as Scriabin's most public testimony of his involvement with Theosophy, a spiritual philosophy that seeks to reconcile scientific, religious, and philosophical practices and beliefs into one compatible worldview. Scriabin particularly admired the writings of Helena Blavatsky, who wrote of the

Prometheus legend in her Theosophical tome, *The Secret Doctrine* (1888). She posited that the fallen Titan was one of the first descendents of divine disciples, a first-generation Higher Race of enlightened beings from whom modern humanity descended. Theosophists believe that a few chosen adepts are endowed with ancient wisdom, and Scriabin believed that he was one such enlightened being. The Theosophical program for *Prometheus* was included in program notes and many reviews.

Any ambiguity about its Theosophical origins was laid to rest by the striking frontispiece of the score, illustrated by Belgium artist, occultist, and Theosophist Jean Delville (1867–1953). In this striking illustration, shown in figure 4.11, an androgynous face peers out from a lyre that is adorned at the bottom by the Star of David (an ancient symbol of Lucifer). At the top, a plume of fire reflects the rays of the sun and refers to the "Sons of the Flames of Wisdom," which Blavatsky prophesized were ancient messengers who imparted divine wisdom to humanity. James Cousins wrote of the fateful meeting between Scriabin and Delville, and the inspiration for Scriabin's orchestral masterpiece:

> [Scriabin] asked Delville, in the same room where we heard the story, what was behind his attitude to life, and how he, the questioner, could reach a similar attitude. Delville produced two large volumes and put them before Scriabine. "Read these—and then set them to music," he said. Scriabine read the books—*The Secret Doctrine*. He went on fire with their revelation. The result was his immortal masterpiece, "Prometheus." . . . While Scriabine composed the Symphony, he came excitedly at intervals into Delville's drawing-room and played for the painter the musical ideas that were crowding in on him. At the same time Delville painted his wonderful picture of Prometheus falling from the sky with the gift of fire for the earth. He showed us the great canvas in his studio.[53]

Another Theosophical reference is found in the choral finale, in which a chorus dressed in all white robes sings a text of mainly vowel sounds. Critics first thought that the vowel sounds had no specific meaning, but musicologist Anna Gawboy has traced these vocalisms to Blavatsky's *Secret Doctrine*, which posited that the vowel sound "Oeaohoo" represents "the septenary [sic] root from which all proceeds. In one sense, Oeaohoo is the 'Rootless Root of All,' and in another sense it is a name for the manifested one life, the Eternal living Unity."[54] These influences upon *Prometheus* are well known today, but it is a mistake to chalk up this magnificent tonal canvas to a work that worships at the altar of Theosophy. As we shall explore in later chapters of this book, Theosophy was but one influence on the composer late in his career.

Prometheus is scored for a huge orchestra, including full percussion, solo piano, solo violin, auxiliary brass, organ, and mixed chorus. Its most famous instrument, however, is the *tastiera per luce*, or color organ, which is notated as two melodic strands at the top of the score. This "color organ" was meant to bathe the concert hall in colored lights that corresponded with the music. Heeding Beliaev's earlier warnings about writing pieces that were too costly to mount, Scriabin specified in the score that the color organ and chorus could be omitted from performances. As for its genre, *Prometheus* is a modern hybrid of a piano concerto and a symphonic poem.

Figure 4.11. Jean Delville, cover illustration for published score of *Prometheus*. First published by Édition Russe de Musique (Moscow, 1911). *Courtesy of the Library of Congress Prints and Photographs Division, LC-USZC4–14462.*

Prometheus won the Glinka prize in 1911, much to Liadov's chagrin, and Leonid Sabaneev published a four-hand piano transcription of the piece in the same year.

One of the most novel aspects of *Prometheus* is its harmonic basis, which avoids major-minor harmony and is founded on Scriabin's signature sonority, the "mystic" chord, or Prometheus chord. It is used to great effect to represent the inchoate void of the cosmos at the beginning of *Prometheus* (marked *Brumeux* [misty]). The murky orchestration adds to the hazy, unsettling effect. The solo piano (marked *imperieux*) symbolizes mankind crashing through space to announce its presence in the world. As the work progresses, various solo instruments introduce motivic ideas that represent allegorical tenets that are familiar from Scriabin's previous symphonies, such as the Creative Principle, Joy for Life, and Will. The brevity of these symbolic motives and the dense harmonic language can it make it difficult for listeners to feel oriented in this opaque sound world, but one should not approach *Prometheus* with the same set of stylistic expectations as say, Beethoven's Fifth Symphony or Mozart's Symphony No. 40. There are no nature scenes or summer idylls in *Prometheus*, as there are in Scriabin's Second and Third Symphonies. This is music of the cosmos, or *musica universalis*.

The world premiere of *Prometheus: Poem of Fire* took place in Moscow on 15 March 1911, with Scriabin as soloist and Koussevitzky conducting. Considerable media hype surrounded the premiere, and Koussevitzky held an unprecedented nine rehearsals for its preparation. But the Maestro's limited conducting skills were no match for the score's technical demands, and he prevailed upon Eduard Nápravník (1839–1916), the longtime conductor at the Imperial Mariinsky Theater in St. Petersburg, to assist with the performance. To what degree Nápravník guided the actual performance remains uncertain, but Koussevitzky apparently learned what he needed from this experience, since he later led the Boston premiere of *Prometheus* on 27 March 1925, with Alexander Lang Steinhart as the pianist (repeated by popular demand on May 1 of that year). Like the Moscow performance, the Boston concert omitted the color organ, as did later performances in Bremen, Paris, and Chicago. The U.S. premiere of *Prometheus* occurred on 5 March 1915 with the Chicago Symphony Orchestra under Frederick Stock. The most infamous early performance of *Prometheus* (*sans luce*) occurred at Queen's Hall in London on 1 February 1913 under Sir Henry J. Wood, who boldly performed it twice to aid the audience's comprehension.[55] Critical reactions were predictably hostile. The English conductor Frederick Corder accused Scriabin of "mental derangement," and a critic for *Staats Zeitung* complained, "I really do not know how one can call this orgy of cacophonies and grotesque combinations music. All the horrors of the most modern modernists were surpassed and the ear vainly sought a resting place."[56] The press buzz generated over Wood's double performance turned it into the stuff of legend, and only steepened the mystery and allure of this ultramodern score.

Recommended Recordings: Nikolai Golovanov, USSR Radio Symphony Orchestra with Alexander Goldenweiser, piano (Boheme CDBMR 908087, 1952); Lorin Maazel, London Philharmonic Orchestra with Vladimir Ashkenazy, piano (Decca 417-252-2, 1989); Claudio Abbado, Berlin Philharmonic with Martha Argerich, piano (Sony 53978, 1994); Nikolai Gergiev, Kirov Orchestra with Alexander Toradze, piano (Phillips B00000DBUS, 1998).

* * *

SCRIABIN'S CHAMPION CONDUCTORS: A BRIEF HISTORY

No discussion of Scriabin's symphonies would be complete without recognizing the conductors who lent their talents and imagination to his orchestral music, and who campaigned on its behalf, even when it was unfashionable to do so. Performances of Scriabin's music not only supported the composer's cause; they also benefited these conductors' careers, as many of them made his symphonies signature works in their repertoire. The first champions were Vasily Safonov (1852–1918) in Moscow and Anatoly Liadov (1855–1914) in St. Petersburg. Safonov served as a guest conductor for several major orchestras around Europe before he left Russia after the 1905 Revolution and settled in the United States. From 1906 to 1909, he was the principal conductor of the New York Philharmonic. Safonov successfully promoted new Russian music during his tenure, and bemused New York critics by conducting without a baton. Back in Russia, Liadov led the premieres of Scriabin's first two symphonies. Of his performance of the First Symphony, critic Alexander Ossovsky praised him as "a truly gifted conductor" whose rendition of the work was "strong, nervous and delicate. . . . Scriabin's symphony acquired in his loving, caring, and nobly exalted interpretations both graphic elegance of form and expressive vitality."[57] These early champions brought critical recognition for Scriabin's gifts as a symphonist, and established him as a composer of international repute.

In America, no conductor fought harder to promote Scriabin's music in the first decades of the twentieth century than Modest Altschuler. A cellist by training, Altschuler studied at the Moscow Conservatory and graduated in 1890. It was there that he first met Scriabin, and they bonded over their mutual passion for modern music and their diminutive statures (both men barely stood over five feet in height). Scriabin and Altschuler remained friends long after Altschuler settled in America in 1895. In 1903, he founded the Russian Symphony Orchestra Society, which established itself as a cultural powerhouse in New York, even stirring competitive jealousy from the New York Symphony's directors. Altschuler's ensemble offered unique performance opportunities for Russian émigrés. His organization thrived due to the patronage of wealthy entrepreneurs such as George Westinghouse and Charles Schwab. Altschuler and the Russian Symphony Society delivered dozens of premieres of new Russian compositions, including the U.S. premiere of Scriabin's *Divine Poem* in March 1907, and the world premiere of the *Poem of Ecstasy* on 10 December 1908, the score of which Altschuler personally imported to the United States after visiting the composer in Interlaken, Switzerland. Altschuler performed every symphony Scriabin ever wrote, but his most spectacular production was the world premiere of *Prometheus: Poem of Fire* with colored lights on 20 March 1915 at Carnegie Hall (Margaret Volavay, piano). Despite the failure of the performance from a technical standpoint, the event sealed Altschuler's name in the annals of music history. The Russian Symphony Society disbanded in 1922 when Altschuler moved to Los Angeles to write film music. But its achievements raised the stock of

Russian music in New York, and lent invaluable credibility and exposure to Scriabin's music by bringing it to American audiences at the highest professional standards.

In Chicago, the torch for Scriabin's cause was hoisted by Frederick Stock (1872–1942), the music director for the Chicago Symphony Orchestra from 1905 until his death in 1942. In the decades before World War II, Chicago ranked second only to New York City as a musical epicenter in America, and Stock's affinity for late romanticists like Wagner and Strauss led him to conduct Scriabin's works.[58] Chicago proved an ideal environment to disseminate Scriabin's gospel in the 1910s–1920s, as it was a hotbed of activity for devotees of Theosophy and mysticism. Stock presided over musical affairs in the Windy City, and his dedication to Scriabin was evident. He delivered the U.S. premiere of *Prometheus: Poem of Fire* (without the *luce* or mixed chorus) on 5 March 1915, and repeated it in 1930 and 1937.[59] It was the *Divine Poem*, though, that was Stock's calling card; he performed it annually from 1922 to 1941.[60] In a memorial article on Stock, *Chicago Tribune* reporter Cecil Smith pinpointed one of the key traits that allowed the famed maestro to excel at Scriabin's scores: "[Stock] was a consummate master of what is known as rubato conducting. He knew precisely how much rhythmic resiliency and freedom to allow a melody, in order to make it sing its song with the greatest eloquence. Yet there was a firmness in his rhythmic pulse which kept this freedom from slopping over into sentimentality."[61] Stock's polished technique was augmented by his magisterial personality. By the end of his tenure with the Chicago Symphony Orchestra, he had gained mastery over the complexities of the *Divine Poem*, leading critics to gush over his nearly annual performances.

A third U.S. city where Scriabin's music boasted a powerful ally was in Philadelphia, where from 1915 to 1932, the charismatic conductor Leopold Stokowski (1882–1977) led several performances of Scriabin's last three symphonies. Long before he was immortalized as the wild-haired maestro in Walt Disney's animated classic, *Fantasia* (1940), Stokowski carved out a reputation as a staunch defender of modern music. His star status (he dated Greta Garbo and married a Vanderbilt) added a touch of glamour to Scriabin's burgeoning popularity in the United States, akin to a celebrity endorsement. Stokowski adopted the *Poem of Ecstasy* as one of his trademark pieces, which he performed in Philadelphia as early as 1916. Fortunately, he lived long enough to capture his inimitable interpretations in an age of high quality sound recording.[62] As the cultivator of the sumptuous orchestral texture known as the "Philadelphia sound," Stokowski basked in the radiant, fluttering textures of the *Poem of Ecstasy*, leading one critic to effuse that his readings of the piece "brushed volcanic fires into rainbows."[63] Figure 4.12 shows the first page of Stokowski's personal conductor's score of the *Poem of Ecstasy*, illustrating the phrase divisions he sought to achieve between the winds and reeds in the top half, and the slower pulse heard in the lower strings.

Stokowski held a sense of protective duty over Scriabin's legacy that surpassed his own career interests, as well illustrated by a colorful episode from a February 1919 concert in Philadelphia. At intermission, a bulk of the audience left the hall in order

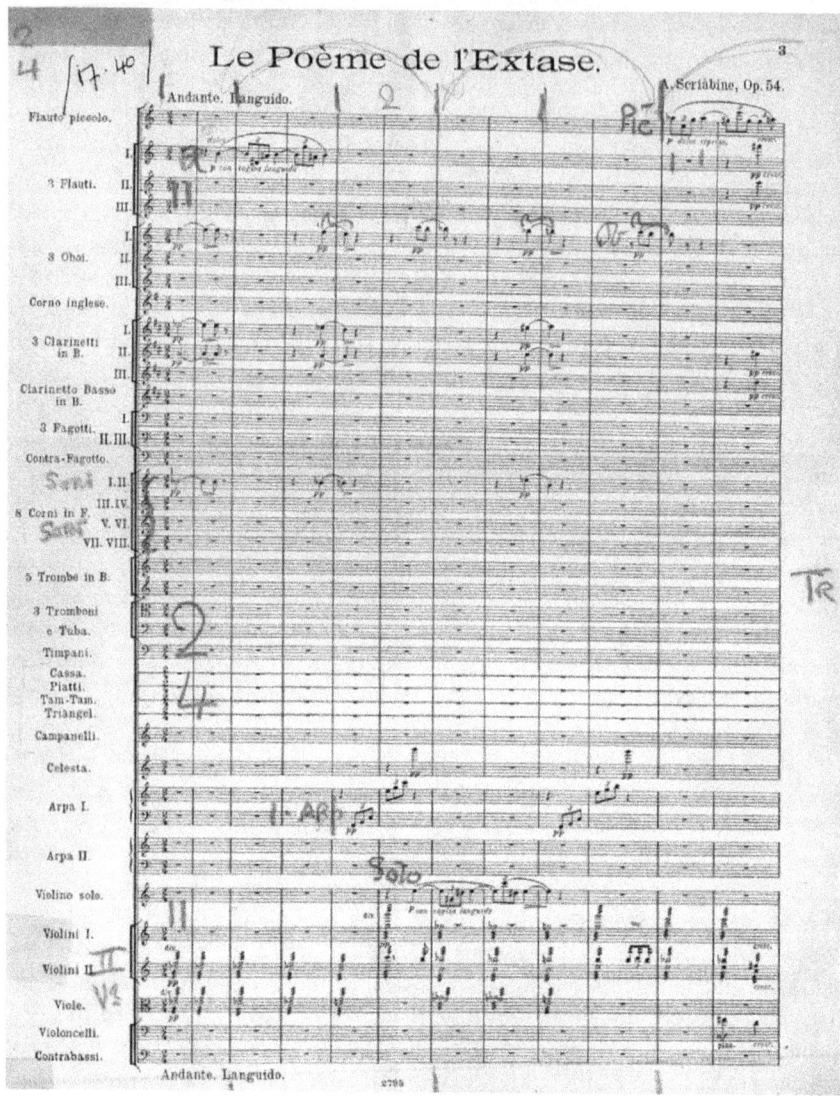

Figure 4.12. Leopold Stokowski's marked-up conductor's score for the *Poem of Ecstasy*. Leopold Stokowski Collection of Scores. Kislak Center for Special Collections, Rare Books and Manuscripts, University of Pennsylvania Libraries.

to avoid the modern strains of the *Poem of Ecstasy*. This cowardly retreat so incensed Stokowski that he bellowed at the remaining audience members that, "Whenever we present music of a novel sort to audiences in this city, the people here fail to give us a chance to do any justice to the music. It is impossible for any orchestra to do its best work in such an atmosphere of hostility." He vehemently defended the *Poem of Ec-*

stasy as a masterpiece; in an interview three years later, his opinion had not softened: "It is useless to speak to many people of Scriabin's *Poème d'Extase* . . . they dismiss this remarkable work with a contemptuous muttering of 'decadent' or 'immoral.' On the contrary, it is one of the most highly organized and complex pieces of orchestral polyphony which exists."[64]

In England, Scriabin's music flourished during the 1910s and 1920s under London's preeminent musical spokesman, Sir Henry J. Wood (1869–1944), best known for his long association with London's annual promenade concerts, or "Proms." Wood's industrious nature and tenacity (refusing to stop performing Wagner's music, for instance, during an air raid on London during World War I) made him a national icon. Londoners' first taste of Scriabin's music began with his most advanced works, including the late piano pieces and *Prometheus*. Yet miraculously, the English public embraced his music, at least in part due to Wood's authoritative readings. In August 1912, Wood aspired to mount the first performance of *Prometheus* in England, and he wrote to Scriabin to enlist his help directing rehearsals for the piece at the 1912 Birmingham Festival. Scriabin declined due to financial constraints, and *Prometheus* was withdrawn from the program. Undaunted, Wood mounted his own rehearsals for the piece and performed it on 1 February 1913 with Arthur Cooke playing the piano part.

To improve comprehension of the ultramodern score, *Prometheus* was heard twice on the same program, a risky stunt that polarized audiences. But the event has lived in infamy, and the double performance approach was adopted by latter-day conductors such as Modest Altschuler in New York in 1915, and James Dixon at the University of Iowa in 1975. Even Scriabin objected to double performances. In a letter of 7 June 1913 to Beliaev, he insisted that, "It is impossible to give equal inspiration twice over."[65] London *Daily News* critic E. A. Baughan reported that, "Between the two performances many people left the hall, giving it to be understood by their manner that their musical morals had been outrageously assaulted by Scriabin's music."[66] Critic Ernest Newman confirmed that "not more than half of the people who heard the first performance remained for the second," but he commended Scriabin for uttering "things that have never been expressed in music before."[67] Members of the press speculated that the British intelligentsia appreciated *Prometheus* not for its musical brilliance, but for its Theosophical program. Regardless of the reasons for its rapturous reception, *Prometheus* enjoyed immense success in England. Wood accompanied the composer on his visit to London in 1914, and on 14 March he conducted *Prometheus* and the Piano Concerto with the composer playing the solo piano part. This legendary performance persisted in public memory long after the last notes faded away, and closely associated Wood's name with Scriabin's enduring popularity in England during the first decades of the twentieth century.

Equally allied to Scriabin's cause in England and America was Russian-born conductor Albert Coates (1882–1953). Coates earned his bona fides as a Russian music specialist by studying with Rimsky-Korsakov, and he appeared with major orchestras like the London Symphony Orchestra (1919–1922), Rochester Philharmonic

(1923–1925), and Los Angeles Philharmonic in the 1920s–1940s. Coates' infectious energy and mayoral presence at the podium led critics to regard him as the natural successor to his teacher, Arthur Nikisch. Coates was Scriabin's personal friend, and had even provided him with financial aid that allowed him to quit teaching at the Moscow Conservatory and focus exclusively on composing. The *Poem of Ecstasy* was his pièce de résistance, and after numerous live performances of the work on tour in England and in London, Coates waxed his inimitable interpretation as his initial offering for Columbia Records in 1920. It was the first of many recordings of Scriabin's tone poem. In his final appearance with the New York Philharmonic on 2 January 1921, Coates capped his program with the *Poem of Ecstasy*. The force of conviction that he delivered in this performance even moved the implacable Henry Krehbiel, no great admirer of Scriabin, to applaud his "clarity and force," which "came near to persuading the hearers [that] this intense expression of things earthly and things mystical is absolute music."[68]

A priceless anecdote illustrates the sheer excitement aroused by Coates' interpretations of the *Poem of Ecstasy*. British composer Cyril Jenkins had organized a two-day festival in 1920 at Mountain Ash, Wales, and engaged the London Symphony Orchestra to perform. Coates' rendition of the *Poem of Ecstasy* that particular day left the audience in such raptures that the orchestra was nearly compelled to repeat the twenty-minute work in full:

> 5,000 to 7,000 people, most of whom were of the so called working classes—miners, engineers, and the like. One would have expected that so novel and hectic a composition as Scriabin's *Le Poeme d'Extase* would leave such a gathering bored and contemptuous; but the exact contrary proved to be the case. Mr. Albert Coates's interpretation whipped his listeners to an enthusiasm that found vent in a physical demonstrativeness such as the Albert and Queen's Halls can never have witnessed: at one point it appeared as though the complete work would have to be played a second time.[69]

Even Coates was shocked by the mania that greeted this career-defining performance, about which he remarked that it "so astonished me (I had never dreamed that they would understand it) that I turned to a sailor who was yelling fit to burst his lungs and asked him what he liked so much about the work. 'Ah,' he said, 'I'm of course not wise enough to understand it, but it makes me feel like a young horse. I should love to kick out, and then run around a field for an hour.'"[70] Such esteemed interpreters as Coates and Stock cemented the composer's reputation as a legitimate heir to the venerable symphonic traditions of the nineteenth century.

No other conductor illustrates Scriabin's shifting fortunes in popularity better than the double bassist-turned-conductor Serge Koussevitzky (1874–1951). Koussevitzky came into Scriabin's life in June 1908, when the composer found himself in financial dire straits. Koussevitzky had married a wealthy heiress to a tea merchant, and he offered to publish the composer's works through his Édition Russe de Musique and provide the struggling composer with a princely stipend. Koussevitzky was an upstart to conducting when he took an interest in Scriabin's music, but he had picked up a few tips from observing Nikisch. Despite his technical limitations, Koussevitzky earned a reputation as a compelling interpreter of Scriabin's symphonies. His passion for the music combined with just the right amount of vulnerability and recklessness made his renditions sensational. The German artist Robert Sterl (1867–1932) created several iconic images of Scriabin when he accompanied the party that participated in the Volga River tour of 1910, including a snapshot of Scriabin and Koussevitzky in fine form during a performance of the Piano Concerto Op. 20, as shown in figure 4.13.[71]

Figure 4.13. Scriabin performs his Piano Concerto with Serge Koussevitzky. Oil on wood, by Robert Sterl, 1910. Berlin: Galerie Neue Meister, photo by Jürgen Karpinski. Courtesy of Art Resource, New York.

This musical partnership initially proved beneficial for both men's careers. But the honeymoon came to an abrupt end in February 1911 after their Volga tour. Scriabin and Koussevitzky had a falling out over financial compensation and artistic differences that was so acrimonious that neither man could even bear to utter the other's name. Koussevitzky continued to perform Scriabin's music long after the composer died, since his reputation largely rested upon his compelling interpretations of this music. He conducted performances of Scriabin's symphonies across the United States in the 1910s and 1920s, and even debuted the *Poem of Ecstasy* in England in 1910.[72] Koussevitzky emigrated from Russia in 1920, and was appointed the principal conductor of the Boston Symphony Orchestra (BSO) in 1924, succeeding Pierre Monteaux. Like an importer of rare jewels, Koussevitzky specialized in exotic and colorful gems of Russian orchestral music, and his reputation in America was forged on the strength of his interpretations of such works as the *Poem of Ecstasy*. In his debut as the Music Director for the BSO on 10 October 1924, he capped the program with Scriabin's famous tone poem. Olin Downes, then a new critic for the *New York Times*, fell under Koussevitzky's spell and captured the overwhelming effect of his performance of the *Poem of Ecstasy* that night:

> Under Koussevitzky the mounting ardors and exultations of what is essentially a bacchanale, a Venusberg if there ever was one in tones, are held in superb control. They advance and recede, but always advance further. And when at last the great climax came with a brilliancy, with a drenching richness of color, it had almost the effect of blinding light on the eyes. Every choir of the orchestra contributed its tint to the rainbow, and there stood Mr. Koussevitzky, his features and his nervous hands betraying his own excitement in the music.[73]

Before long, however, Koussevitzky grew disenchanted with Scriabin's music, and after the 1920s, there were only eight performances of Scriabin's orchestral works. Eventually, the famed conductor abandoned this music, which had been such an integral part of his repertory. When pressed about this neglect of his former métier, Koussevitzky's temper ran short.[74] By 1939, Koussevitzky confessed, "Scriabin? I tell you frankly, it is now hard for me to play him at all."[75] Reflecting in 1939, Koussevitzky mused that:

> The exalting theme of "*Le Poème de l'extase*," vaulting skyward, used to stir me immeasurably, and I would brood long hours upon the manner in which it should be announced by the orchestra. . . . The music doesn't stir me as it did, and when one's convictions grow weaker it is time to stop attempting an interpretation designed to convince an audience.[76]

Koussevitzky knew that his reputation rested on his choice of repertoire, but his decision to stop performing Scriabin's orchestral works was at least as personal as it was professional. Symbolic of his aversion to the music was his silver anniversary program in 1949 with the Boston Symphony Orchestra, which mirrored his 1924 debut with the exclusion of the *Poem of Ecstasy*. Despite Koussevitzky's disenchantment with Scriabin's music and the sour end to their personal relationship, the composer's posthumous legacy benefited tremendously from this conductor's lionizing of this music.

Of all the modern conductors who lent their talents to Scriabin's orchestral music, no one produced more controversial interpretations than Pierre Boulez (1925–2016). Boulez's involvement with this music began during the revival of the early 1970s, when the Russian was considered the "composer-in-residence to the Age of Aquarius."[77] During that decade, Boulez occupied posts as a conductor with the Cleveland Orchestra (1970–1972), BBC Symphony (1971–1975), and New York Philharmonic (1971–1977). With the latter ensemble, he recorded the *Poem of Ec-*

stasy in 1972. His reputation as an ultra-rational, even mathematic musician makes his association with Scriabin's hyper-emotional scores surprising. Boulez freely admitted his distaste for Scriabin's music, with the exception of the piano sonatas. In a 1996 interview, he even argued that aside from works by Mussorgsky and Stravinsky, Russian music was devoid of any effective pieces for modern orchestra, an extreme opinion that attests to his tendency for polemics:

> I've conducted Scriabin, too, but I don't care much for his orchestral works; I find them badly constructed. There again, certain passages in [Stravinsky's] *The Firebird* are far better than Scriabin's symphonic poems, because the musical thought is more profound. Scriabin is very interesting when he writes for the piano, less so where orchestral literature is concerned.[78]

Boulez's solution was to perform Scriabin's music *his* way, by emphasizing precision of sound, scaled-back dynamics, and proportionate tempi in service of analytical clarity. With the Chicago Symphony Orchestra, he recorded the Piano Concerto, *Prometheus* (Anatol Ugorski, piano), and the *Poem of Ecstasy* (Adolph Herseth, trumpet). His performances of these works are marked by diaphanous textures, controlled tempi, and attenuated dynamics.

Boulez's formalist approach to Scriabin's music accorded with the performance practice ideology of the 1990s, which eschewed the hazy textures and exaggerated tempi and dynamics that had been established for Scriabin's music by hot-blooded interpreters like Coates and Stokowski. Exactly how this change in attitude developed requires some historical context to appreciate. The Scriabin revival of the 1970s inspired a spate of new scholarship, especially on the composer's harmonic formulae. Studies by such theorists as Varvara Dernova, George Perle, and Anthony Pople argued that Scriabin's systematic approach to harmony was highly rigorous, and even proto-serialist in its approach. As a result, scholars came to regard Scriabin as a forgotten avant-gardist who independently kept pace with Strauss and Schoenberg in the race to advance musical style into the modern era. This revisionist perspective shifted the public image of the composer from a dreamy-headed improviser to a clear-eyed theoretician, and performers responded to this shift in attitude with restrained, almost clinical approaches to his music that stressed clarity of tone, balance, and emotional restraint. To employ terms used by Stravinsky in his *Poetics of Music* (1959), formalist performers like Boulez aimed for precise "executions" of Scriabin's scores rather than "interpretations."[79] Like their music theory counterparts, performers focused their attention on structural aspects of a work, and their formalist approaches attest to modernism's enduring influence on late twentieth-century performance practice.

Boulez's recording of Scriabin's orchestral works was released in 1996 by Deutsche Grammophon and ignited a firestorm of controversy. Some critics argued that his rational intellect had refreshingly revealed the modernist spirit of Scriabin's music. "The slightly mad find their most eloquent spokesmen in the ranks of the eminently sane," wrote Bernard Holland of the *New York Times*. He applauded Boulez for revealing the "method in the madness. . . . Here is indirect proof that Scriabin's ravings, like Messiaen's religious deliriums, are founded not on raving or delirium, but on sophisticated and original grammars."[80] John von Rhein of the *Chicago Tribune* agreed that Boulez's "elucidating intelligence as an interpreter kept the Promethean fires from consuming the performance: Madness, in art, must be based in reason." Other commentators who upheld the performance traditions of the past were far less sympathetic. American pianist and critic John Bell Young blasted Boulez's "mathematically inspired" approach to the orchestral scores as "dispassionate, unimaginative, and cold-blooded. . . . He gives us Scriabin sorely in need of a Viagra fix."[81] In a letter to the editor of the *New York Times*, Kevin Lenaghan agreed that Boulez's performances "although note perfect, are academic and disappointingly boring."[82] What a contrast it would be to compare the Chicago Symphony Orchestra's performances of Scriabin under Boulez versus Stock, all considerations of time and personnel aside! Boulez's attention to Scriabin's music was not marked solely by controversy; *Prometheus* had been absent from the CSO's repertoire since 1938 until Boulez revived it in 1999. Whether or not Boulez's interpretations appeal to one's personal tastes, his efforts to reveal a different side of Scriabin's art are commendable, and the clout he carried in the classical music world brought international attention and respect to Scriabin's music.

The conductors discussed above are hardly the only figures who sustained Scriabin's legacy in the twentieth century. A full exegesis of these music directors' legacies is beyond the scope of this chapter, but we would be remiss not to mention a few additional names. Vassily Sadasky founded the International Symphony in 1930 and lent an imaginative touch to the *Divine Poem* on many memorable occasions, as did the Polish conductor Artur Rodzinski while he served as music director for the Los Angeles Philharmonic (1929–1933). Yevgeny Mravinsky was a loyal supporter and persuasive interpreter of Scriabin's music in the USSR during the 1930s and 1940s. The Scriabin revival of the early 1970s led esteemed maestros such as Eugene Ormandy, Seiji Ozawa, and Claudio Abbado to rally for Scriabin's cause and perform his symphonies, especially the *Poem of Ecstasy*. Russian conductors active in the 1970s–1980s who often conducted his works included Nikolai Golovanov (1891–1953), Yevgeny Svetlanov (1928–2002), and Kirill Kondrashin (1914–1981), whose parents were string players in Koussevitzky's orchestra. Honorable mention also goes to Giuseppe Sinopoli (1946–2001), whose enthusiasm for Scriabin's symphonies was so great that he occasionally placed two of them on the same program.

The most vigilant modern champion of Scriabin's symphonies has been Riccardo Muti, who has served Scriabin's cause for nearly three decades. He started regularly performing Scriabin's symphonies during his tenure with the Philadelphia Symphony Orchestra (1980–1992), and has continued this trend with the Chicago Symphony Orchestra, both on the concert stage and in the recording studio. A century's worth of performance traditions for Scriabin's orchestral music is also in the hands of modern music directors like Valery Gergiev, Vasily Petrenko, and Kirill Petrenko. The commendable efforts of these men will hopefully inspire newer generations of Scriabin enthusiasts to delve deeper into the mysteries and wonders of his orchestral works.

II

TOPICS IN RECEPTION HISTORY

Lincoln Ballard

5

Madness and Other Myths

In the 1993 documentary *Horowitz: A Reminiscence*, viewers are given a rare glimpse inside the private world of Vladimir Horowitz (1903–1989), one of the greatest virtuoso pianists of the twentieth century, and one of Scriabin's devoted champions in the West.[1] An octogenarian when much of the original footage was shot for the 1986 documentary *The Last Romantic*, Horowitz still bubbles with youthful charisma as he recounts tales of famous musicians he knew throughout his life, including Sergei Rachmaninov and Horowitz's father-in-law, the Italian conductor Arturo Toscanini. Basking in the limelight of the cameras and recording engineers that crammed into his Upper East Side apartment, Horowitz clowns around between takes and serves up bits of concertos, waltzes, and other staples of his expansive repertoire. "You see, I remember *everything*!" he repeats with a beaming grin while his wife Wanda presides over the scene with watchful eyes. A soulful rendition of Scriabin's Etude Op. 2 No. 1 in C♯ minor brings to Horowitz's mind his fateful audition for the composer in 1914. As he tells the story, "I played for Scriabin, one year before he died. He wanted to be nice to my uncle" [Alexander Horowitz (1877–1927), piano professor at the Kharkov Conservatory]. "My uncle told him, 'we have a nephew who is so talented, you have to hear him.' So I come to him, and he was like [acts out nervous twitches and facial tics], Scriabin . . . he was crazy, you know!"

Horowitz's unforgettable impression encapsulates the popular image of Scriabin as deranged, regardless of one's opinion of his abilities as a composer. This portrayal of Scriabin as a borderline madman has been an integral aspect of his legacy, from his lifetime to ours. Scholars have not been intimidated by Scriabin's madness. Many simply rejected the mysticism and highfalutin rhetoric that was tied to Scriabin's artistic ambitions. Scholars are usually so focused on other aspects of his music, such as its harmonies, that they overlook or even embrace the oddities of Scriabin's personality. For the average listener, though, the situation is quite different, since they often struggle to understand the music. This air of impenetrability has fostered many myths, not the least of which is the idea that Scriabin was insane. After all, only a crazy person could write music of such histrionic cacophony and masquerade it as art. Such attitudes have also bred the belief that Scriabin's music is high-strung, intense, and nervous, like the composer himself. Lest we subscribe to this biographical fallacy, the Scriabin enthusiast knows how charming and beguiling these works can be, not only in his early pieces, but also throughout his entire output.

Twentieth-century critics never minced words when explaining why Scriabin's mature music eludes the average listener. In a 1915 review of *Prometheus: Poem of Fire*, the English composer Frederick Corder wrote in the *Musical Quarterly* that his music was "the product of a once fine composer suffering from mental derangement. . . . You cannot expect either a journalist or his public to see any difference between a lunatic and an idiot."[2] That same year, the London journal *Critical Opinion* was up in arms over the same work and printed Scriabin's photo with the caption, "Genius or madman?"[3] A century later, many still believe that this question is just as relevant now as it was then.

The accusations of historians and critics have greatly shaped the public perception of Scriabin's music. Let us take a moment to appreciate the chorus of protests against the composer's mental health, and by extension, his historical insignificance. British musicologist Gerald Abraham railed against Scriabin's "insane imagination" and "incredible egomania," which he believed had led Scriabin astray creatively.[4] In the 1930s, the musicologist Michel-Dimitry Calvocoressi denigrated Scriabin's "music of colossal self-aggrandizement," and the British composer Constant Lambert pleaded for relief from the "angry waves" of the *Poem of Ecstasy*, which "beat vainly at the breakwater of our intelligence."[5] In 1941, the American musicologist Paul Henry Lang remarked that Scriabin's "whole art, nay, whole life, was a mere experiment, a supernatural dream, and whose mind, possessed by demonic forces, penetrated deeper and deeper into the mire of mystical speculations, hallucinations, and dementia."[6] Antagonism against the composer's mysticism reached a fever pitch by the mid-twentieth century in the West. Not until the mid-1970s did Scriabin's fortunes improve, but a strong faction of dissenters has always been on hand to cast derision on the composer's mental clarity, and by extension, the quality of his music.

The myth of Scriabin's insanity is but one strand in the web of mistruths that surrounds the composer. This mythology has fascinated and frustrated scholars and music lovers alike. In his liner notes for Michael Ponti's 1974 recording of Scriabin's complete solo piano works, Donald Garvelmann took stock of the myths that had trickled down over time about the composer:

> Scriabin is supposed to never have worn a hat, never to have sat on the grass (photographs prove otherwise); we are told he hated Beethoven's music (actually, he particularly loved the "Tempest Sonata"); we are advised there is a "Russian school of Scriabin playing" (yet Horowitz, Richter and Sofronitsky—great Russian Scriabinists—are each stylistically quite different); we read that Scriabin could only compose after alcoholic or

sexual stimulation (physiological principle alone crushes this statement) and that he was a homosexual (this is no way supported by biographical fact).[7]

Garvelmann was careful to shoot down each of these claims, but being a lone voice among a chorus of busybodies was not enough to overturn fifty years worth of gossip. These same popular myths are recycled in today's concert program notes, recording liner notes, and countless other forms of public media. They have lent an aura of mystique to the composer's legacy, but they have distorted the facts of his life and legacy, and transformed a highly original personality into a caricature.

Fifty years after Garvelmann wrote those words, popular fiction has provided us with a contemporary source to summarize the myths and legends that swirl around Scriabin. It comes from a recent book written by Stephen Deutsch (b.1945), an author and film composer who studied at Juilliard and the Royal College of Music. Set in the early 1970s, his novel, *Zweck: A Novel and Mostly Reliable Musical History* (2015) follows an American named Bernard Robins who moves to London to make his mark as a professional musician.[8] While abroad, Robins encounters a long-lost great uncle who was almost a great composer several decades ago, and who had rubbed shoulders with the legendary musicians of his age. Zweck's riotous tales of these composers and his unabashed irreverence toward their seemingly unimpeachable legacies offers an amusingly candid take on classical music history. At one point in the book, the topic of conversation turns to Scriabin, and Zweck offers his recollections:

> A little fellow; very frail. In fact, he died of blood poisoning from a shaving cut, I am told, which doesn't surprise me. You could call him a walking factory of bizarre misfortune. And he just couldn't sit still for long, maybe a nervous tic. Anyway, the main reason he interested me was because of his work on synaesthesia. This interests me because certain keys show me different colours; in my mind's eye, anyway. . . . So all this colour business came to nothing. But he was extremely famous while he was alive, and then almost completely forgotten after his death. Today he's just a curiosity whose piano music is difficult to play and whose orchestral music is impenetrable to most people. Of course, he goes crazy in the end, because he was seduced by all sorts of mysticism and also very serious about Nietzsche, not to mention metaphysics. Such a cocktail could turn anyone loopy. Now this is interesting: he had a younger cousin called Vyacheslav Scriabin, who at the time of the Russian revolution changes his name because the Scriabins come from an aristocratic family. So he changes it to Molotov! Scriabin's music has visions of hell in it.[9]

This priceless passage is a veritable laundry list of rumors that have followed Scriabin, and as such, it provides many threads to pull on. We will consider each of these myths throughout this chapter.

The time has come to more fairly consider Scriabin's legacy. A logical starting point is Scriabin's biographers, several of whom were prime perpetrators of these myths, despite their good intentions. Three biographers in particular have shaped the public perception of Scriabin, yet each writer put his own unique spin on the composer. Collectively, the writings of Leonid Sabaneev, Boris Schloezer, and Faubion Bowers have formed a composite image by which Scriabin's art and personality have been perceived by the Western public. Later in this chapter, we will tackle some of the mini-mysteries that linger about Scriabin, as enumerated by Zweck, and lay to rest some of these long-standing legends.

MYTHMAKING BIOGRAPHERS

Leonid Sabaneev

Among Scriabin's biographers, an early instigator of several myths that beclouded his legacy was Leonid Sabaneev (1881–1968). A Boswellian figure of central importance to Scriabin scholars, Sabaneev was the composer's close friend, and the author of several books and articles. His writings on music originally appeared in Russian and were often translated into English by S. W. Pring, a talented linguist whose translations of articles on Russian music were ubiquitous in the 1920s–1930s. From 1910–1915, Sabaneev paid almost daily visits to Scriabin and was a key member of his inner circle. His 1916 biography, *Skriabin*, was not the first to appear on the composer, but his books and articles on Scriabin's music became cornerstones in the literature, especially his *Vospominaniia o Skriabine* [Reminiscences of Scriabin, 1925].[10] While his 1916 biography focused on ideological principles that inspired Scriabin, his 1925 *Reminiscences* drew upon diary entries that Sabaneev recorded during his nearly daily interactions with Scriabin after 1912. Sabaneev's pedigree as a professional critic and close friendship with Scriabin earned him public credibility. His writings depict the composer as a megalomaniac who was full of contradictions—a rationalist yet a mystic, a romanticist and a modernist—and whose music embodied the hysteria and mania surrounding the *fin de siècle* atmosphere in Russia and Europe.

Sabaneev's relationship with Scriabin may have lent his writings an aura of unquestioned authority, but he was hardly the detached and objective observer he portrayed himself to be. Trained in mathematics and physics at Moscow University, Sabaneev's positivistic approach to the world led him to devise quasi-scientific explanations for Scriabin's artistic experiences, including his harmonic vocabulary and color-hearing. In many cases, Sabaneev's theories led him down the wrong path, but his headstrong nature compelled him to publish his findings anyway. From this self-assurance came his advocacy of a system of equal-tempered tuning that squeezed fifty-three notes into an octave (which he argued was the future of music). Furthermore, he argued that Scriabin's mystic chord contained every consonant triad of functional harmony (major, minor, augmented, and diminished), and that its individual notes were derived from the overtone series. While the composer never thought of his famous sonority in these terms, Sabaneev advanced this theory of the overtone series as the source of the mystic chord as early as 1910 in the Russian art journal *Muzyka*, and he further developed the theory in an article published the following year in the modernist journal *Der Blaue Reiter*. Like many of Sabaneev's claims, however, the overtone series has long been discredited as the source of Scriabin's mystic chord, yet even today it persists as a nagging narrative.

One of the prime myths perpetrated by Sabaneev to make Scriabin seem larger than life was that he died on Easter. This link with the Messiah has sanctified the composer in the eyes of his disciples. The false claim that Sabaneev asserted in the *Reminiscences* has been repeated by countless writers. A careful examination of the dates in question proves the falsity of this claim. Using the modern Gregorian dating system (thirteen days ahead of the old Julian style), in 1915, the year that Scriabin died, Easter Sunday fell on April 4 and Scriabin died on April 27. (Using the Julian style, Easter Sunday fell on March 22, and Scriabin died on April 14.) Either way, over three weeks passed between Easter Sunday and Scriabin's death, illustrating how far Sabaneev had stretched the truth. The confusion between the two dating systems and the commonly repeated point that Easter came early that year (which indeed it did) has contributed to the misunderstanding over Scriabin's Easter death. But the provenance of this myth can be traced to Sabaneev, who conflated the dates to sensationalize his subject.

Sabaneev was a talented writer who was well positioned to offer insights into the artists and stylistic developments of Scriabin's generation. But his credibility was questioned on more than one occasion.[11] According to the composer's great-grand niece, Alina Ivanova-Scriabina, a faction of critics who distrusted Sabaneev coined the Russian term "Sabaneevschina" (the era of Sabaneev) to describe the period in the early twentieth century when his writings on Scriabin were almost universally accepted as gospel.[12] An infamous incident in Sabaneev's career exemplified his propensity to prevaricate. In 1916, the year after Scriabin died, Sabaneev published a condemnatory review in the Moscow newspaper *Novosti sezona* (News of the Season) of the premiere performance of Sergei Prokofiev's *Scythian Suite*. Unbeknownst to Sabaneev, Prokofiev's *Suite* had been withdrawn from the program; thus, Sabaneev reviewed a performance that never occurred. The cunning Prokofiev would never miss such a golden opportunity for a moral victory, and he published an open letter in local newspapers, publically challenging Sabaneev's review of this imaginary concert. Sabaneev was forced to admit his mistake, and the opprobrium he suffered from the incident led him to resign from his post two years later as music critic for the *Musical Contemporary*. This embarrassing episode blighted his career; once the specter of mistruth had reared its ugly head, it was not easily dismissed. Sabaneev's achievements in music criticism notwithstanding, he would be remembered primarily in history for his close friendship with Scriabin and this ignominious episode with Prokofiev.

The question of Sabaneev's veracity is further complicated by the fact that his views on Scriabin wavered throughout his life. In a candid conversation with pianist Vladimir Sofronitsky (Scriabin's son-in-law), the pianist and pedagogue Heinrich Neuhaus (1888–1964) pointed out Sabaneev's tendency to vacillate in his opinions, however strongly they may have been asserted. Neuhaus aptly described Sabaneev as "a remarkable musical scholar, but, unfortunately, a man of 'flexible morality.'"[13] No other relationship in Sabaneev's life highlighted this tendency more than his friendship with Scriabin. In her recent book, *Nietzsche's Orphans: Music, Metaphysics, and the Twilight of the Russian Empire,* historian Rebecca Mitchell suggested that Sabaneev first experienced disillusionment with Scriabin around 1915. In the months leading up to the composer's death that year, Sabaneev gradually distanced himself from the group that gathered almost daily at the composer's apartment. His fever for all things Scriabin had broken, and now freed of the spell that Scriabin had cast over his admirers, Sabaneev lost his faith in the transformative power of art and his view of the composer as a spiritual guide.[14]

Political and cultural strictures in the USSR led Sabaneev to defect from Russia in 1926 and move to Paris, where he enjoyed a successful, if low profile, career as a music critic. From 1928 to 1940, he wrote articles for the *Musical Times* and the *Russian Review,* and contributed several articles on Scriabin for these publications. Distanced from the intoxicating atmosphere and poignant memories stirred by the sights and sounds of Moscow, "the musical Jerusalem of the Russians," Sabaneev took a sober view of his former idol. Embarrassed over his former "extreme enthusiasm for Skryabinism," Sabaneev's opinions of his erstwhile idol hardened even further after he emigrated from Russia. He emphasized the disturbed, psychotic tendencies of Scriabin's music, and criticized it as diabolical and satanic.[15] After he published his *Reminiscences of Scriabin,* all sides seemed to turn against Sabaneev. Soviet authorities regarded him as *persona non grata,* even writing him out of the history books.[16] These developments fed his bitterness and dissolution with his former life in Russia. In a 1928 letter to the Soviet composer Alexander Krein, Sabaneev remarked on the psychic distance that now separated him from his former life: "I must admit that all of them [Scriabinists] are 'strange' somehow, and they appear not old, but extraordinarily antiquated."[17]

One of the topics on which Sabaneev took a particularly harsh view after he moved abroad was Scriabin's madness. In the *Reminiscences,* he argued that the "hysterical and psychopathic nature of [Scriabin's] music . . . did more than a little damage to his musical career."[18] As time wore on, Sabaneev likened this fatal flaw to something far more sinister and destructive, akin to "musical appendicitis in the life of the composer." In his 1927 book *Modern Russian Composers,* Sabaneev addressed the issue of Scriabin's insanity head-on and concluded that he was "the first 'consistent paranoiac' to reduce musical insanity to a peculiar sort of scheme and even to a theory." He compared Scriabin's tendency for schematization and rhythmic dissolution to artwork produced by psychiatric patients.

In Sabaneev's mind, Scriabin's obsessions led him down two dead ends; the first was in his imagination and was epitomized by his *Mysterium,* an unfinished and impossible project that made his "fate truly tragic, for having devoted his whole life to dreaming only a single dream, and having sacrificed everything for its sake, he never succeeded in carrying out that one thing." The second dead end was the stylistic cul-de-sac that Scriabin had backed himself into with his mystic chord.

Sabaneev recoiled at Scriabin's obsession with an "acid chord" that "fills almost the entire contents of Skryabin's last compositions, giving them the character of a sort of enclosed, narrow, isolated and sequestered musical sphere, something like a tonal hothouse wherein grow only orchids of a single species and where no other plant can survive."[19] He lamented that despite Scriabin's desire to elevate art above the realm of entertainment and to become something greater than a mere composer, in the end "he was regarded merely as a musician, and a poor one at that."[20] These opinions marked a dramatic reversal for the man who once described himself as "a Scriabinist in the fullest sense of the term."

Sabaneev's turn of opinion against Scriabin shocked his friends and fellow Scriabinists. Members of the then newly formed Scriabin Society, of which Sabaneev was a founding member, cursed him as a "heretic."[21] Varvara Lermontova, a founding member of the Scriabin Society in Russia after the composer's death, wrote directly to Sabaneev after he published his biography, *Skriabin*, and inquired in accusatory tones, "If you truly took Scriabin as you claim, then it becomes unclear why you maintain the image of a passionate friend and admirer. . . . What convinced you to write this book?"[22] Sabaneev's condemnation of Scriabin's art and legacy became commonplace in his writings after the 1920s. He came to see Scriabin as a figure of marginal importance in music history, and attributed this failure to a fundamentally weak compositional technique and the "hysterical and psychopathic nature of his approach to music."[23] In his final article on the composer, published two years before his own death, Sabaneev remained intransigent in his distaste for Scriabin's "morbid megalomania," which had transformed the composer into a "mad dreamer, a psychologically sick man even in his appearance."[24] Modern scholars like Ivanova-Scriabina have framed Sabaneev's reversal of opinion more in intellectual terms than emotional ones when she reasoned that Sabaneev had "rebuilt" Scriabin "in his hierarchy of values."[25] But the tale of Sabaneev's betrayal of his former friend remains one of the great controversies in Scriabin's legacy. Sabaneev will always rank as an important and informed source on the composer, but his personal biases must be considered when reading his views on Scriabin. It is only one man's opinion, but it is a strong voice.

Boris Schloezer

In contrast to Sabaneev's depiction of Scriabin as dark and disturbed, the composer's brother-in-[common]-law Boris Fedorovich Schloezer (1881–1969) wove his own myth of Scriabin as a beacon of light. To Schloezer, Scriabin was an Orphic figure whose message of redemption through art immortalized him as a source of inspiration for humanity. Schloezer took offense to Sabaneev's slanderous depictions of Scriabin, and the two men's adversarial relationship led them to criticize one another in their respective writings.[26] Schloezer's publications helped construct an image of Scriabin as a paragon of ideological and artistic values. Especially in Russia during the 1910s and 1920s, the composer was praised as a national icon that the people should respect and admire as a role model. This whitewashed view of Scriabin as a positive, healthy influence has been lost in contemporary culture, but in the early days of post-Revolutionary Russia (and oddly enough, in the 1970s among the American counterculture), Scriabin's music and legacy were passionately promoted as a positive influence. In the newly formed Soviet Union, politburo leaders like Anatoly Lunacharsky and Arthur Lourié touted Scriabin's historical significance, as did writers residing outside the Soviet Union. At present, modern culture is incapable of sustaining such a reverential attitude toward Scriabin's music and legacy, which makes it difficult to relate to such fanaticism. Nevertheless, an understanding of where and how these archetypes originated—including Schloezer's depiction of Scriabin as an "Artist and Mystic," to quote the Anglicized title of his book (translated by Nicolas Slonimsky)—can only enhance our appreciation for the composer's place in contemporary culture.[27] Make no mistake, these archetypes of Scriabin are alive and well today.

What drove Schloezer to proselytize on Scriabin's behalf throughout his long life was their intellectual kinship and family bond. Nine years Scriabin's junior, Schloezer was raised in a cultured household that prized the arts and philosophical debate. He studied philosophy at the University of Brussels, and music theory and aesthetics at the Paris Academy of Music. This education prepared him for the verbal sparring that Scriabin was so fond of, and which strengthened the friendship between them. It also led Schloezer to give more credit to Scriabin's abilities as a thinker than most would allow. They first met in 1896, when Boris was at the impressionable age of fifteen. The composer's affair and cohabitation with Boris's sister, Tatyana, brought them into almost daily contact, and Scriabin regularly engaged him in philosophical debate. Schloezer eagerly accepted these provocations, and through them he gained a better understanding of the composer's thought process. Schloezer was deeply impressed with the originality of Scriabin's music and his commitment to his role as an artist for the people. When Scriabin died, Schloezer and the Scriabinists scrambled to make sense of the sudden loss of their hero. Schloezer fled Russia in 1920 and relocated to France, where he wrote criticism for the Russian émigré journal, *Les Dernières Nouvelles*. Once abroad, he added a "de" to his name, and occasionally a "von," in order to fit into post-Revolutionary European society. Like Sabaneev, Soviet critics treated Schloezer with contempt due to his defection, and only in the last few decades has his legacy been rehabilitated.

Whereas Sabaneev and other critics ridiculed Scriabin's philosophical ideals and metaphysics, Schloezer argued that understanding the philosophy behind the music was essential to grasping its significance. But Schloezer's idolatry for the composer blinded him to the imperfections of his subject. He refused to concede the irrationality of Scriabin's schemes, especially the impossibility of his plans for the *Mysterium*. On this topic, he and Sabaneev were forever at odds, and Schloezer was the main target of Sabaneev's vitriol in the *Reminiscences*. Many of Schloezer's writings after the 1910s were produced against the backdrop of wartime, and perhaps as a way to shield himself against the horrors of war, he remained steadfastly devoted to pre-Revolutionary ideals. His eternal optimism is salient in his evaluations of Scriabin, many of which justify the composer's less desirable traits. A case in point is his defense of Scriabin's condemnations against other composers' music, which were usually based on a superficial familiarity with the works in question. In his *Reminiscences*, Sabaneev recorded many of the composer's snap judgements for posterity, including his pet phrase, "*minimum tvorchestvo*" (minimum creativity). Schloezer, however, chalked up Scriabin's tendency to find fault in other composers' music to his need for precision and clarity, adding that "He was repelled by anything that was disordered or inconsistent within itself, any sign of sloppiness in thinking, feeling, and acting."[28] Such justifications are all too common in Schloezer's writings. His interpretation of the composer represents a polar opposite view from that Sabaneev's—that of the benevolent artist whose few trivial flaws should be overlooked in light of the greater good that he brought to humanity.

Schloezer's advocacy for the composer appeared in several articles and one book, *Skriabin: Lichnost, Misteriia* (Personality, Mystery). Schloezer wrote the book in 1919, and it was published in 1923 by a German émigré press, Grani. He originally wanted to write two volumes, the first a study of Scriabin's creative ideology and the second containing theoretical analyses of his music's chords and formal structure, but he only completed the first volume. What resulted is a biography-memoir, or what historian Caryl Emerson referred to as both a primary and secondary source.[29] From its opening pages, readers are well primed to give serious consideration to metaphysics as they encounter an astrological study on Scriabin's natal chart prepared by his daughter, Marina, the last surviving offspring of Scriabin and Tatyana. The English translation of this book in 1987 by a prestigious university press was risky, but it filled an important void in the literature despite its lack of an index and discursive style. Like Sabaneev, Schloezer addressed Scriabin's "madness," but to him, madness represented a state of intoxicated delirium that he experienced in the composer's presence, "a sublimation of those forces in our subjective life which, stirred to a high state of tension, sweep us forward in their frenzied state."[30] Perhaps in line with his view of the composer as an exalted figure, Schloezer also supported the idea that the mystic chord was based on the overtone series.

In addition to glossing over or justifying the more outlandish and bizarre aspects of Scriabin's personality and philosophy, Schloezer also identified Theosophy as one of the major influences in the composer's ideological scheme. In his *Artist and Mystic* book, Schloezer wrote unequivocally about Theosophy's impact on Scriabin's thinking, stating that, "here we can definitely speak of an influence." His emphasis on Theosophy overshadowed other influences on the composer, especially Russian Symbolism and the theories of nineteenth-century philosophers aside from Blavatsky. Numerous critics and biographers gleaned a few central ideas and choice quotes from Schloezer's writings, and these writers subsequently granted Theosophy pride of place as an all-encompassing influence on the composer's late music.[31] In popular lore, Theosophy remains a ubiquitous reference in liner notes and program notes as Scriabin's principal philosophical influence, thus providing a perspective that represents only a single piece of a much larger puzzle.

According to Schloezer, Blavatsky's writings made a strong impression on Scriabin, although he lost his passion for Theosophy only a few years after discovering it. Blavatsky's *Secret Doctrine* (1888) consistently ranked among Scriabin's favorite books, and in his personal copy he underlined several passages in pencil. Scriabin admired the *Secret Doctrine* mainly because it reinforced his preconceived notions. Having very little formal education, he was quick to lapse into philosophical debate as a pretense for erudition. Schloezer reported that when he pressed the composer to expand upon a point of view in a debate, or explain a contradiction, the composer would wave aside such challenges. He refused to discuss Theosophical principles with Schloezer until he read the texts for himself. Scriabin told him, "I will not discuss with you the truth of Theosophy, but I know that Mme. Blavatsky's ideas helped me in my work and gave me power to accomplish my task."[32] When Schloezer familiarized himself with the texts, he realized that "Scriabin used theosophical terms quite loosely. He adapted them to his own ideas, aspirations and yearnings and employed theosophical postulates as formulas to describe his own experiences."[33] In truth, Scriabin borrowed ideas from various philosophical teachings and assembled them piecemeal, but his understanding of these fields was superficial at best.

A final point that puts to rest any notion that Theosophy formed the cornerstone of Scriabin's thinking was the superfluous role that music played in Theosophical teachings. Schloezer explained that Scriabin was "shocked by the lack of appreciation of the fine arts among Russian and foreign theosophists and by their unwillingness to give music its rightful place in their writings." "Can you imagine," Scriabin exclaimed in horror, "they adore [French opera composer Jules] Massenet!"[34] As for the notion that Scriabin's music expressed specific Theosophical ideals and principles, Schloezer noted that on one occasion, two English women put Scriabin's music in service of "theosophical propaganda," much to the composer's chagrin. Afterward, Scriabin despaired that, "they don't understand, they do not love art." Despite the Theosophical Society's lofty aims to uplift humanity through their teachings, Scriabin regarded their goals as superficial and self-serving. One can imagine how Scriabin would have decried latter-day apologists who took his commitment to Theosophy in literal terms and posed explicit linkages between his works and Theosophical principles.[35]

Schloezer was an incredibly important source of primary information about Scriabin, but like Sabaneev, his interpretations of the composer were filtered through his own personality. In their constant attacks on one another's character, Scriabin unwittingly became a casualty of their great war. Neuhaus observed that, "Such mystics and obscurantists like L. Sabaneev and B. F. Schloezer have done Scriabin enormous damage."[36] Had Neuhaus lived long enough to read Faubion Bowers' biography of the composer and witness the effects of his interpretations, he might well have added Bowers' name to that ignominious list.

Faubion Bowers

Embracing the role of Scriabin's modern-day mythmaker was Oklahoman biographer Faubion Bowers (1917–1999). Bowers aspired to become a concert pianist, and even studied with Katherine Ruth Heyman and at Juilliard. In his youth, he succumbed to the Scriabin fever that afflicts many pianists, and performed several all-Scriabin recitals. Fearing that he lacked the raw talent to succeed as a concert pianist, Bowers moved to Asia, where he polished his language and writing skills, and immersed himself in a culture he had always admired from afar. Before writing his Scriabin biography, he published several books in the 1950s on Japanese theater and Indian dance, and wrote criticism in the 1960s for popular publications like the *Village Voice*, *Harper's Magazine*, and *The New Yorker*. Bowers had a natural propensity for hyperbole in his writing and speech, and when listening to his interviews or reading his writings, one can immediately sense the dramatic flair he added to his subjects, casting himself and those he admired in an almost mythic light.[37] Consequently, nearly everything that he wrote about the composer must be weighed against this tendency. Bowers became the leading authority on Scriabin by virtue of his experience as a critic and by saturating the literature with his writings on a figure who was long overdue for reappraisal.

In Bowers' career as a writer, Scriabin became his meal ticket. Capitalizing on the relative obscurity and timeliness of the composer's story (the centenary of his birth was in 1972), Bowers wove a sensationalist narrative loaded with armchair psychoanalysis and historical gossip about the personal feuds and sex lives of Russian artists. To his credit, Bowers had found in Scriabin an ideal subject for a psychoanalytic reading of his music and personality. As he matured, Scriabin formed his closest ties to older males. Bowers noted that Scriabin's "deepest attachments were with huge, massive, gruff men, totally contrasting from himself. All his six known heterosexual affairs were marked with undue publicity and scandal, as if to advertise himself . . . and counterbalance."[38] Bowers was hardly qualified to interpret the nuanced ways in which Scriabin's personality was filtered through his music, and he shrugged off his controversial theories by claiming that his book was a compilation of raw materials and not a proper biography. But the damage had been done. Scriabin's interests in mysticism, which were directed toward the musical expression of his aesthetic ideals, were exploited by Bowers to fit the machinations of 1960s pop culture. His interpretation of Scriabin as a neurotic whose creativity was fueled by sexual impulses was widely accepted as the honest truth. It is a shame that his biography, which was published nearly fifty years ago, and even then was below scholarly standards, remains one of the primary sources of information on the composer. Books on Scriabin's contemporaries such as Rimsky-Korsakov, Rachmaninov, and Stravinsky have never been in short supply. But the fact that no better English-language biography of Scriabin has come along to replace Bowers' books is a testament to the composer's marginalized position in music history, or perhaps the challenging nature of the subject.

One of Bowers' greatest faults was that he lacked the restraint or judgement to temper the floridity of his writing. Fiction is often conflated with fact. At times his biography reads more like a novel than a historical account of a famous figure. It is entertaining, but anything but a reliable source. Consider the following passage from his original two-volume biography, which fueled so many of the myths that crop up in the popular literature. No evidence exists to support any of these assertions, and we can only surmise that he included such observations to sensationalize his subject:

> Scriabin was a nest of nervous gestures and compulsive habits all his life. He washed his hands constantly, often after merely shaking hands. He wore gloves inside the house. He feared bacteria, contagious germs, everything ... He fidgeted, fretted, fussed, fumed and drummed his fingers. He jiggled his knees, pinched the bridge of his nose as if sinus pained him, shuddered if any food fell from the plate to the tablecloth and refused to eat it even if it was bread. If a doctor prescribed medicine, he invariably took beyond the dose.[39]

Such characterizations of Scriabin are rife throughout Bowers' writings on the composer, which appeared not only in his books, but also in record liner notes, concert program notes, and entertainment magazines. Thus while Scriabin's music made a strong comeback in Western concert halls during the early 1970s, the image of the composer that greeted his new audience was a tangled mess of nervous compulsions, hypochondria, and raging hormones. It is perplexing that Bowers cast Scriabin in such a negative light considering his reverence for the music. But sensationalism and sex sells, and he was likely more motivated to boost sales than to provide an accurate historical account of his subject. Not surprisingly, he also recycled Sabaneev's claim that Scriabin died at Easter. Such glosses on historical facts are prevalent throughout his books, and these mistakes have been well enumerated in numerous reviews.[40]

Playing up the myth of Scriabin's madness, Bowers first provides seventy pages of historical background on the "Kaleidoscope of Russian Music," its origins, atmosphere, and history, before introducing Scriabin in a discussion of the "malaise" that afflicted pre-Revolutionary Russian composers. Depression, alcoholism, hypochondria, neuroticism, misogyny, and homosexuality were rampant among this group, or so Bowers argued. Bowers airs the dirty laundry of nearly every major composer of the era, including Mussorgsky's demise in an alcoholic stupor (poignantly captured in Ilya Repin's stirring portrait of Mussorgsky, painted only days before his death), and Rachmaninov's debilitating depression after the disastrous premiere of his First Symphony, the recovery from which only came after therapy sessions with Dr. Nikolas Dahl. (As a gesture of gratitude, Rachmaninov dedicated his comeback piece, the Piano Concerto No. 2 in C minor Op. 18, to the good doctor.) In Bowers' depiction of Scriabin as effeminate and borderline homosexual, he interpreted much of the composer's music as overtly erotic, and in some cases downright pornographic. While the idea of sexual desire certainly played a major role in Scriabin's compositional ideology, as it did for many Romantic artists, it cheapens his music to interpret it on the level of crude sexual metaphors. Yet Bowers brought much attention to himself through such exploitative readings. Latter-day psychologists entered the discussion and explored the composer's pathology with a greater sense of historical responsibility. A fascinating body of literature has subsequently developed that analyzes Scriabin's eccentricities from the standpoint of modern psychology.[41]

The most controversial aspect of Bowers' interpretation was his claim that Scriabin was homosexual. To level such accusations based on a few passing references and pure conjecture was highly provocative. Bowers' views on Scriabin's sexual orientation were driven in part by the amateur psychoanalysis that came into vogue during the 1960s. As the puritanical values of the 1950s loosened, Freud's psychosexual theories of repressed desires and animal instincts reached the mass consciousness through numerous books and popular magazines. The popularity of Freudian thought in the 1960s encouraged candid discussions about sexual desire and frustration, and Bowers cashed in by portraying Scriabin as having an insatiable sexual appetite and repressed homosexual tendencies. This effeminate image of the composer spawned the idea that he was nicknamed "Pussy."[42] Very little evidence or self-admissions of homosexuality exist from that era that could verify such accusations. In Russia during Scriabin's lifetime, homosexuality was considered a crime punishable by death. For anyone who failed to read between the lines, Bowers put the matter bluntly: "it would be recreant to shirk a rather homosexual interpretation of Scriabin's life."[43] Even without proof, the mere suggestion of Scriabin's homosexuality provided a spark that ignited the flames of controversy.

Bowers' interpretation of Scriabin's homosexuality was also conditioned by his own struggles over his sexual orientation. Bowers admitted his own homosexuality, even though he married the Indian writer Santha Rama Rau in 1951. (She is known principally for writing the screenplay to *A Passage to India*, based on the book by E. M. Forster.) They divorced in 1966. In an interview in 2003, Rau recalled of her partnership with Bowers that, "We were married for fifteen years—ten years of bliss, and five years of hell."[44] Bowers campaigned to normalize homosexuality in his criticism, and in addition to using Scriabin's biography as a platform to openly discuss homosexuality, wrote several pieces on the subject, including a major article in 1972 for the *Saturday Review*.[45] He identified homosexuality as a prominent yet secretive trait in Russia's musical culture. In a revealing 1969 interview with Donald Garvelmann, Bowers even considered homosexuality an essential trait for effective Scriabin playing. The shoe fits when one considers such master Scriabinists as Sviatoslav Richter or Vladimir Horowitz, the latter of whom once quipped, "there are three kinds of pianists—Jewish pianists, homosexual pianists, and bad pianists." These observations are not included to defame Bowers, but to shed light on his influences and perception of Scriabin. Just as Sabaneev's and Schloezer's views on the composer were conditioned by their personal experiences, Bowers' interpretation of Scriabin as a homosexual was filtered through his personal belief system and values.

These three biographers left an indelible mark on Scriabin studies in Russia and the West, and their interpretations went a long way toward constructing Scriabin's public image over the course of the twentieth century. However pointed their opinions were, they represent only one side of the story. Scriabin's Soviet writers told an entirely different version of Scriabin's story. Their interpretations valorized the composer as a pioneering innovator who anticipated such late twentieth-century technological developments as stereo sound and space travel. Principal among these

Soviet writers were the musicologist Boris Asafiev, and the biographers Viktor Delson and Mikhail Mikhailov.[46] The composite images of Scriabin advanced by the writers described above have shaped our opinions of the man and his music. But these portrayals must be understood in light of the individual influences and backgrounds of their writers.

* * *

MINI-MYSTERIES

The Afterlife of Scriabin's Music

One of the most egregious myths regarding Scriabin's legacy is that his music sank into obscurity after he died in 1915. Nothing could be further from the truth. During the first seven years after his death, Scriabin's music experienced its zenith in popularity, in England and in Russia. So frequently was his music performed during this era that critics pleaded for relief from the "overdose" on Scriabin by the early 1920s. Unfounded claims of Scriabin's dwindling popularity lurk in every corner of the literature. To cite a few examples, consider critic Charles Stuart's remark from the early 1950s that, "Overnight the balloon deflated. Scriabin dropped from the programmes and from our minds." Likewise, the Russian historian Boris Schwarz asserted in his widely read book on Russian music history that, "Whatever influence Scriabin exerted on Russian music, it evaporated rather soon."[47] As time wore on, the waters of historical accuracy were muddied even further, and this recursive myth became entrenched in the literature. Faubion Bowers similarly stated that, "After the October Revolution of 1917, a reaction set in against Scriabin."[48] These writers could not have been more misguided in their assumptions.

Scriabin's music was wildly popular after his death. The sudden loss of Russia's leading modernist composer sent shock waves through the musical community, and the outpouring of sympathy and reverence allowed the composer to achieve immortal status. As befitting Scriabin's legacy, performers were the most public supporters of the composer's cause after his death. Sergei Rachmaninov undertook a concert tour to memorialize Scriabin and raise funds for his near-destitute family. The conductor Serge Koussevitzky mounted public performances of the orchestral works, including the Piano Concerto, with Rachmaninov as the soloist. Scriabin's complete piano music was also performed by the students and professors of the Moscow Conservatory. As the years passed and Russia underwent a cultural and political upheaval after the 1917 Bolshevik Revolution, Scriabin was not forgotten, especially on anniversaries. For the five-year anniversary of his death in 1920, Koussevitzky delivered all-Scriabin orchestral concerts in Moscow, and conductor Emil Cooper followed suit in Petrograd (present-day St. Petersburg) with his own all-Scriabin series. So strong was the composer's presence in the Russian repertory that during the 1922–1923 Moscow

Philharmonic season, only the works of Beethoven and Tchaikovsky enjoyed more performances than Scriabin's works.[49]

Scriabin's posthumous legacy in Russia also thrived thanks to the support of several nonperformers who eulogized him as a national icon whose significance for Russian culture equaled that of Tolstoy and Pushkin. Influential in this regard was Anatoly Lunacharsky (1875–1933), the first People's Commissar of Education. From 1917 until 1920, Lunacharsky organized Bolshevik festivals in which Scriabin's music was regularly featured. Lunacharsky believed that the proletariat should have access to the cultural treasures of the past, which had been exclusive to the bourgeoisie. Exposure to high art, Lunacharsky reasoned, would strengthen the proletariat's intellect and patriotism, and dissolve the boundary between the upper and lower classes. Lunacharsky's support for the composer was generous, and he even allocated state funds to restore Scriabin's final residence and convert it into a state museum after a fire nearly destroyed it in 1919. Lunacharsky portrayed Scriabin as a crusader for a benevolent cause that superseded everyday concerns and individual needs in service of a greater good. Historian Isaac Deutscher remarked that Lunacharsky "combined in himself the qualities of the guardian of the heritage and those of the innovator."[50] To the masses, Lunacharsky portrayed Scriabin as a cultural icon and the musical voice of the people.

Also rallying for Scriabin's cause in early Soviet Russia was avant-garde composer Arthur Lourié (1892–1966), whom Lunacharsky chose to oversee the music division (called Muzo) after Koussevitzky had declined the post. In Lourié's eyes, Scriabin's ability to synthesize traditional and modern styles made him a national genius. He asserted that, "as far as the Russian symphonic music of that period is concerned, only two men count—Tchaikovsky and Scriabin."[51] In his enthusiasm for avant-garde music, Lourié aggressively promoted Scriabin and other modernist composers until he was dismissed from his post in 1921. The steadfast support of these figures allowed Scriabin's music to remain in circulation until well after his death, and raised his cultural stock in Soviet-era Russia.

In England, support for Scriabin's music also remained fervent for many years after his death. British audiences were treated to a series of public performances by the composer in 1914. From its first exposure abroad, his music was enthusiastically received. The composer's merits were also applauded by influential critics such as Arthur Eaglefield Hull, who published numerous articles on Scriabin and made no attempt to temper his unabashed reverence for the composer. Such enthusiasm for the composer's music must have made a strong impression on readers. Hull opened his article "Survey of the Pianoforte Works of Scriabin" by breathlessly asserting:

> No revolution in musical art—perhaps in the whole history of the arts in general—is more striking than that effected by Alexander Scriabin, the great musical genius of the Russia of to-day. His innovations were so many-sided, so far-reaching, and so completely revolutionary, that I cannot hope to do any sort of justice to them in a single article.[52]

Equally committed to Scriabin's cause in England were the critics Alfred Swan and Rosa Newmarch. Swan (1890–1970) represented an academic perspective and was a generation younger than Newmarch. Despite his youth, he was an established authority on ancient Orthodox chant and folk song. Swan's enthusiasm manifested itself in the form of unrestrained hyperbole: "Let us rejoice in the heritage left to us by this Messiah among men," he wrote in his 1923 biography of the composer. Fifty years later, his support for the composer had not diminished: "All of us who have been drawn into [Scriabin's] orbit feel grateful for such a great and privileged experience."[53] Newmarch (1857–1940) was a regular contributor in the popular press on Scriabin's music and ideology. An expert on Russian music and culture, Newmarch had met Scriabin in person and the composer had authorized her to write the program notes for the 14 March 1914 performance of *Prometheus*. She identified Scriabin as "the most discussed of all the contemporary representatives of the musical art in Russia."[54] Newmarch also published on Scriabin's music and background, including the composer's obituary and the 1937 *Grove Dictionary* entry. These talented writers helped make Scriabin's music and ideas well known to the British public, and their publications mark the cresting peak of Scriabin's fame in England in the 1920s.

Scriabin's music retained its popularity into the 1920s, leading to an inevitable reaction against his works. Writing in late 1922, an unnamed critic for the *Musical Courier* acknowledged that Albert Coates' powerful rendition of the *Poem of Ecstasy* still intoxicated listeners, although he admitted that "We Londoners have rather overdosed with Scriabin, truth to tell, but the flaming and the smoky clouds made a great impression here."[55] Critic Robert Hull similarly expressed relief in 1926 that, "For the moment [Scriabin's] writings are out of fashion, the almost inevitable result after an overdose in the last few years."[56] Only after this total saturation did audiences seek relief from the ardor of Scriabin's music.

Clearly Scriabin's music did not disappear with the 1917 Bolshevik Revolution or even World War I. From his death in 1915 through at least 1923, Scriabin's music enjoyed a degree of popularity that went unmatched until his centenary revival.

Felled by a Pimple?

It is an amusing and ironic twist of fate for Scriabin's detractors that a man who claimed to possess the power to alter human history through his music should perish from a trifling pimple. Icarus could not have fallen further. This factoid gave countless writers the license to add Scriabin's name to the short list of the strangest and most ignoble deaths in classical music history. Details of his death by an infected pimple were spread by newspaper obituaries from the first days after his demise. The odd tale of Scriabin's death from a pimple provides a striking contrast to his larger-than-life persona, and also serves as a cautionary tale for acne-ridden teenagers. Stravinsky's mother Anna, a lifelong admirer of Scriabin's music and mystical aesthetics, often chided Igor for not composing in Scriabin's manner, much to Stravinsky's chagrin.[57] Her constant needling knew no bounds, and when once she caught Stravinsky tending to his blemishes, she admonished him to not pinch the affected area because "that's how poor Scriabin died." The apocryphal tale of Scriabin's death due to a common pimple is widespread and has persisted for well over a century. It is long overdue for some modern medical clarification.

More accurately, Scriabin developed a boil or furuncle, which is larger and more painful than a pimple, and is the result of bacterial contamination that forms from an infected hair follicle. By contrast, a pimple is the superficial blockage of a hair follicle that is clogged with dirt, oils, or skin cells trapped beneath the skin's surface. Left untreated or improperly treated, boils can exact an enervating toll on the body. A furuncle can be excruciating and is often accompanied by a fever of the type that Scriabin complained of in his letters to Tatyana from abroad, when he first noticed the painful bump on his upper lip in March 1914 during his concert tour of London. Scriabin could scarcely have believed that the small sore that appeared beneath his right moustache near the nose, over which he was more embarrassed than concerned (his famous moustache needed to be trimmed), would cause his death barely a year later.

An easily treatable condition today, several factors conspired to make Scriabin's case deadly, not the least of which was the fact that the discovery of penicillin by chemist Alexander Fleming lay fourteen years into the future. Scrawny his entire life, Scriabin's immune system was surely weakened from an unbalanced diet and lack of exercise. Fastidious about his personal appearance and hygiene (Sabaneev compared Scriabin's daily primping to a teenage girl in love), Scriabin was also likely not careful enough about cleaning the skin beneath his officer-like moustache, the ends of which he waxed into sharp points on concert days. His initial attempts to squeeze out the pus in the boil (or perhaps he nicked it while shaving), and the eventual lancing of the area on advice from a local doctor worsened his condition.[58] Once the skin around the affected area was broken and not properly sterilized, pathogens penetrated deeply into the hair follicles of the skin, causing a purulent inflammation of the subcutaneous tissue and blood vessels. In the modern age, someone suffering from this condition would immediately consult a surgeon or dermatologist, since a boil not only brings about intense pain, but also life-threatening complications such as the development of an abscess.

The most serious complication of an improperly treated furuncle is a blood infection, which is what happened in Scriabin's case. A deadly storm brewed inside his body, and his weakened immune system could not fight off the infection. When the offending sore returned a year later in the same spot, as boils are wont to do, it appeared in the area of the face that encompasses the nose and upper lip, colloquially referred to by physicians as the "triangle of death." Sepsis set in and Scriabin died a painful and prolonged death due to blood poisoning. Such cases were not entirely unheard of in the late nineteenth and early twentieth centuries, but Scriabin's unfortunate demise ranks as the most notorious, if not entirely accurate, example of someone perishing from a pimple.

The Molotov Mystery

A final myth in the Scriabin literature that needs to be addressed is the notion that the composer was related to the Soviet politician Vyacheslav Molotov (1890–1986), who was well known in the West as Stalin's minister of foreign affairs during the Cold War. Molotov was the namesake of the so-called Molotov cocktail, a crude incendiary weapon that consists of a glass bottle filled with gasoline or some other flammable accelerant that is ignited with a makeshift wick, usually of cloth. Molotov the man was born in Kukarka (now Sovietsk) with the last name "Scriabin," but rumors that he was related to the famous Russian composer are patently untrue. Molotov's mother was allegedly the composer's half sister, but some sources identify him as the composer's second cousin or nephew. Close examination of each figure's family history, however, reveals divergent lineages. It is worth noting that the composer's father, Nikolai Alexandrovich (1849–1914), was a diplomat who traveled widely and fathered at least six known children, possibly more. Modern books of both history and fiction perpetuate the idea that Scriabin and Molotov were related, but it is high time that this myth was debunked.

Molotov's adopted name carries some political meaning. Just as Stalin abandoned his original surname (Dzhugashvili) and adopted a brawny nickname that translated to "Man of Steel," Molotov gave himself a new nickname that translated to "The Hammer." (In Russian, the word *molotok* means "hammer.") It was a fitting description for a man described in his obituary as a "humorless, round-faced man with a bristling moustache."[59] Diplomats devised their own nickname for Molotov—"Iron Pants"—because of the hardball tactics he used in political negotiations. It was rumored that Molotov dropped his given surname because the composer came from a family of aristocrats, and Molotov wanted to depict himself as an authentic proletariat. An alternative interpretation was that he was ashamed of the composer's poor reputation and wanted to distance himself from this disgraced figure.[60] At any rate, both interpretations are false. In his memoirs, *Molotov Remembers: Inside Kremlin Politics* (1993), Molotov confided to biographer Felix Chuev that his brother Nikolai Scriabin, who was also a composer, adopted the name Nikolai Nolinsky (1886–1966) to distinguish himself from the famous composer. It is likely that this reference to Molotov's brother was conflated with the politician's own story.

Myths such as Scriabin's death at Easter, his death from a pimple, or his dwindling popularity after 1915 will never entirely cease to circulate. Whispered rumors and half-truths about Scriabin have always added a mysterious, enigmatic quality to his legacy that has by now become a defining aspect of his life.[61] But those who appreciate Scriabin and want to understand his life and music deserve to have the record set straight. Let us hope that this brief exegesis will set an example for future generations and demonstrate that truth is stranger and endlessly more rewarding than fiction.

6
On Synaesthesia or "Color-Hearing"

In thy Music, we will see Music. In thy Light, we will hear Light.

—Olivier Messaien

Alexander Scriabin was a man of many talents, but his most unusual gift was surely his color-hearing, or *synaesthesia*, a subject of great debate in his legacy. It is hard to fathom the media frenzy that has surrounded this topic over the last century. As a starting point, let us begin our tale at Carnegie Hall on Saturday 20 March 1915, a night when the air was chilly, but public enthusiasm was at a fever pitch in anticipation of the world premiere of Scriabin's *Prometheus: Poem of Fire* with colored lights. *Prometheus* had already been performed in Russia, England, Germany, and Chicago, but never with the color organ, or *tastiéra per luce*, as Scriabin designated it in the score. The atmosphere that night was electric over the unveiling of this new instrument, which had been designed specifically for the premiere, and which promised a spectacle of colors the likes of which the world had never seen. The concert program for that historic evening advertised "The Most Talked of Musical Composition of the Twentieth Century," thus promising an event that any well-to-do society person would not want to miss. The concert bill from that historic evening is reproduced below in figure 6.1. That night in Carnegie Hall saw the birth of multimedia art. A correspondent for *Musical America*, the musical voice for the public, reported that:

> The current season has witnessed no event as sensationally bizarre as the first New York production of Alexander Scriabine's "Prometheus." Great secrecy was maintained prior to the performance. There was plenty of excitement and cynical anticipation when all the lights of Carnegie Hall, except those above the exits and the musicians' desks, were put out and a drab colored curtain at the back of the stage was drawn aside revealing a sort of diminutive moving picture screen.[1]

12th Season   CARNEGIE HALL   1915
Final Subscription Concert of the Season

RUSSIAN SYMPHONY SOCIETY Of New York (Inc.)

MODEST ALTSCHULER, Conductor

(Orchestra of 100)

Saturday Evening, March 20th, 1915, at 8:15 o'clock

Soloists:
　　MISS LOUISE COX, Soprano, of the Metropolitan Opera House.
　　MISS MARAGARET VOLAVY, Pianiste

PROGRAM
1. Fantasie "The Sea" .... *Glazunow*
   Dedicated to Richard Wagner
   (First time)
2. Letter Scene from the Opera "Eugene Oniegin"... *Tschaikowsky*
   MISS LOUISE COX AND ORCHESTRA
3. Allegro Moderato Pastoral from the "Symphonietta"
   .... *Ippolitow-Ivanow*
4. Fantasie "Night on the Bald Mount" .... *Musorgsky*

PART II
The World Premiere
of

Scriabine's Poem of Fire "PROMETHEUS"

The Most Talked of Musical Composition of the Twentieth Century

Introducing the New
TASTIERA PER LUCE (A Colored Light Keyboard)

This will be the first time anywhere in the world Scriabine's work will be given a hearing completely embodying the composer's wishes. The arrangements for producing the color effects have been developed with the kind co-operation of the ELECTRICAL TESTING LABORATORIES.

By numerous requests it will be repeated after a short intermission in order to give the audience an opportunity to acquaint themselves with the intricate score of *"PROMETHEUS."*

Miss Margaret Volavy will play the Solo Piano Part, and Mr. Harry Rowe Shelly will be at the organ.

Steinway Piano Used

Seats: $2.00 to 25 cents.　　　　　　　Boxes: $20.00 and $15.00
Now on Sale at Box Office

Figure 6.1. Carnegie Hall program for the world premiere of *Prometheus* with colored lights. *Used by kind permission, Carnegie Hall archives.*

But the bubble burst; the color organ was deemed a flop, and critical reviews of the event were overwhelmingly negative. Most argued that the mishmash of colored lights only added another layer of disorder to the already chaotic music. *Musical America* deemed the *tastiéra per luce* "a silly, childish and annoying device which hurt the eyes, detracted attention from the orchestra, and perplexed the beholder with the inconsistency of its application." A month later, the composer (who was unable to attend this historic performance) suddenly died at age forty-three, leaving behind a legacy filled with as many myths as truths.

Since that night at Carnegie Hall, controversy has raged over the artistic value of adding lights to Scriabin's music, especially pieces he never designated for colored lights. Of even greater debate is the question of whether or not Scriabin actually saw colors when he heard music, especially his own. In 1915, few questioned his claims, but times have changed. Critical discourse, both then and now, has focused on whether or not a combination of lights and music enhances the music or cheapens it. This chapter explores this controversial topic. It summarizes the major literary milestones, and concludes that although Scriabin was not a synaesthete in physiological terms, a broadened definition of the term, such as that which was current during his lifetime, might account for his experiences. We will also examine the approaches taken by performers who incorporated colored lights into their performances of Scriabin's works, and the reception that their artistic decisions have received. This information will allow us to build a framework for understanding the techniques that Scriabin used in his piano and orchestral music to symbolize light. Regardless of one's opinion of the composer's synaesthetic abilities, listening to his works with these associations in mind affords a greater appreciation for his light-inspired music.

First, let us take a moment to define synaesthesia. For synaesthetes, stimulating one of the five primary senses produces an involuntary response in another sense. Color-hearing is only one form of synaesthesia; this cross-modal sensory perception manifests itself in a variety of ways according to the individual. Other forms of the condition can be surmised by the titles of two popular books on the subject written by neurologist Richard Cytowik: *The Man Who Tasted Shapes* (1993) and his follow-up title, *Wednesday Is Indigo Blue* (2009). Other forms of the condition might include spoken words triggering taste sensations or even inducing visual hallucinations of colors and/or shapes. A synaesthete may read a musical score in colors or even see numbers in color, no matter what context ones encounters it. Only in recent decades have scientists gained a deeper understanding of the condition. As late as 1933, a study led by scientist Otto Ortmann concluded that a young synaesthetic girl suffered from "an interlacing of the [nerve] fibres."[2] (Ortmann may be familiar to readers as the scientist who studied muscle movements in piano playing, as cited in Reginald Gerig's 1974 book, *Famous Pianists and Their Technique*.) We now know that the physical hardwiring of people afflicted with synaesthesia is no different than the rest of us, and that the subtle firing of their neurons triggers their cross-sensory experiences. With regard to synaesthesia and music, colors are often visualized according to three different types of stimuli: a specific pitch, a general *tonality*, or even the word of a particular note name (e.g., A, C♯, F, etc.). Famous synaesthetes who were musicians include Duke Ellington, violinist Itzhak Perlman, and popular songwriters Stevie Wonder and Pharrell Williams, among others. For non-synaesthetes who are curious to understand the effects of this condition, the writer and neurologist Oliver Sacks (1933–2015) has suggested that Walt Disney's classic film *Fantasia* (1940) offers one of the best approximations of its effects.

The idea that music can induce profound physiological reactions in listeners is nothing new, but the individual ways in which synaesthesia expresses itself distinguishes it from the Doctrine of Affections (*Affektenlehre*), which was a system of thought that governed eighteenth-century Enlightenment aesthetics. The Doctrine of Affections held that particular tonalities aroused specific emotional states within listeners. Composers like Beethoven and Mozart used them with regularity in their instrumental works to get their musical points across without the aid of a verbal text.[3] The key of D minor, for instance, represented tragedy or pathos, whereas D major symbolized triumph and rejoicing. Various rhetorical gestures rendered in melodic or rhythmic figures further enhanced the desired mood, such as chromatic dips to represent a musical sigh, hunting calls on the horns, stately waltzes, rousing military marches, and so on. These devices established a tradition of associative gestures in music, that is, symbolic ideas that represented extra-musical content. With synaesthesia, however, the connections are autonomic, and in some cases, even displeasing for the afflicted person, not unlike someone endowed with perfect pitch who listens to a performance by out of tune instruments. The strange and wondrous condition of synaesthesia has fascinated scientists for over a century, and only in recent decades have they better understood its neurological basis.

DISCOVERY AND DEBATE

Scriabin first gained awareness of his color-hearing (the most common form of synaesthesia) in 1907 after attending a concert with Nikolai Rimsky-Korsakov, professor of composition at the St. Petersburg Conservatory, and Sergei Rachmaninov, his former classmate from the Moscow Conservatory. After the concert, the three musicians reflected on the evening at the Café de la Paix in Paris. Their conversation turned to the relationship between music and color, and Rachmaninov was astonished to learn that his two companions agreed upon this correlation, if not the exact color-chord combinations. (C major, for instance, was red to Scriabin and white to Rimsky-Korsakov.) Rachmaninov protested its existence, but Rimsky-Korsakov countered that, "I will prove to you that we are right by quoting your own work. Take, for instance, the passage in *The Miserly Knight* (1905) where the old baron opens his boxes and chests and gold and jewelry flash and glitter in the light of the torch . . . well?" Rachmaninov conceded that the passage in question was indeed in the key of D major, which Rimsky-Korsakov and Scriabin both agreed was yellow. A wry smile crept across Scriabin's face as he said to Rachmaninov, "You see, your intuition has unconsciously followed the laws whose very existence you have tried in vain to deny."[4] From that day forward, Scriabin began to work out the laws that governed his color-hearing. His impulse to quantify his intuition into a system of universal laws was consistent with the ideology of an age that witnessed the scientific discovery of radioactivity as well as Max Planck's quantum theory, Einstein's Theory of Relativity, and Niels Bohr's theory of atomic structure—all topics that Scriabin's brother-in-law Boris Schloezer tells us were discussed in the Scriabin household.[5] It is not too much of a stretch to imagine that color-hearing was also regarded as another natural phenomenon, the existence of which merely needed to be quantified to be proven as fact.

Leonid Sabaneev was an important early witness to Scriabin's evolution of thought regarding his color-hearing. His publications form the bedrock of knowledge from which countless other writers have drawn their own conclusions about Scriabin's synaesthetic experiences. Sabaneev's first writings on the subject first appeared in January 1911 in the Soviet arts journal *Muzyka*; they were advertisement for the recent publication of the score to *Prometheus: Poem of Fire*. A second, more comprehensive discussion appeared in a 1916 memorial issue of *Muzikal'niy sovremennik* (Musical Contemporary), which was dedicated to the late composer. Further observations are found in Sabaneev's *Vospominaniia o Skriabine* (Reminiscences about Scriabin, 1925).[6] In these writings, Sabaneev purveyed the notion that color-hearing is an associative, rather than a physiological condition, but he argued that it is rare and exclusive to individuals with a sensitive ear and active imagination. Sabaneev observed that Scriabin divided the color spectrum on a tonal axis between "spiritual" keys (F♯ major—azure blue) and those that were material or earthen (C major—red). Scriabin's color wheel is reproduced in figure 6.2.[7] Only three key areas presented themselves to the composer in vivid colors—C (red), D (yellow) and F♯ (blue); the rest of the color spectrum he derived "theoretically," that is, by association according to the circle of fifths.

Unlike Sabaneev, Scriabin believed color-hearing was not a specialized ability, but an innate trait possessed by everyone. "It can't be personal," Scriabin told Sabaneev, "there must be a principle, must be unity."[8] Whether or not the average person could harness its potential, however, was another matter. His thoughts on the subject were influenced by Theosophical texts, which not only preached a synthesis of science, philosophy, and religion, but also taught that humans produced colored auras that reflected their emotional states (red for anger, blue for sadness, etc.).[9] Understood in light of Theosophical teachings and the romantic ideal of synthesizing the arts, or *Gesamtkunstwerk*, Scriabin's desire to incorporate colored lights as well as scents and other sensory stimulation during performances of his music do not seem so unusual. Scriabin, however, overestimated what he believed was an obvious connection between the music for *Prometheus* and the colored lights, and he left few specific instructions in the score of exactly how the *luce* was supposed to be realized. As we shall explore later in this chapter, numerous attempts have been made to realize the *luce* part in conjunction with the music. But the degree to which these additions have

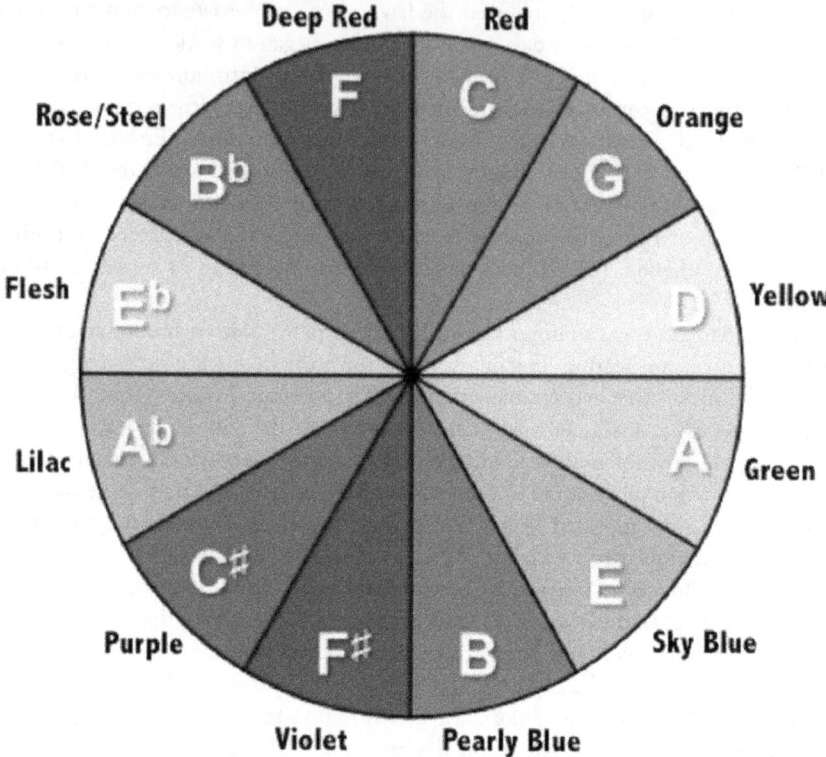

Figure 6.2. Scriabin's color-tonal correspondences. *Based on Bulat Galeyev's chart from the Prometheus Institute, Kazan.*

enhanced audiences' appreciation for the music has been a contentious issue. Until recently, most disapproval has raged over the technical limitations of the lighting, which disappointed listeners with its underwhelming effects. Thus, it seems that the affinities between color and music were not as intuitive and universal as Scriabin had believed.

Today, most scholars believe that Scriabin was not a real synaesthete, since aspects of his account of his experiences raise doubts about his claims. It is odd, for instance, that he discovered his abilities at such a late stage in life, since most synaesthetes gain awareness of their gifts in childhood (Scriabin was 35 years old at the time of his conversation with Rimsky-Korsakov and Rachmaninov at the Café de la Paix). Additionally, the composer's systematic arrangement of color schemes based on the circle of fifths is uncharacteristic of documented cases of synaesthetic correspondences, which are usually unique color-tonal equivalents that lack any systematic order. Refuting Scriabin's account, historian Kevin Dann attested in his book, *Bright Colors Falsely Seen: Synaesthesia and the Search for Transcendental Knowledge*, that "no true chromasthete has such a systematic arrangement of color-tone equivalences."[10] Genuine synaesthetes, in fact, have even expressed bewilderment at Scriabin's arrangement of colors and tonal areas. But these charges of charlatanism hold true only if we limit our understanding of the term to autonomic physical responses. Musicologist Anna Gawboy observed that a century ago, synaesthesia included a broad range of cross-sensory phenomena, regardless of whether such mappings arose through neurological, psychological, pathological, artistic, intellectual, or spiritual means. She clarified that, "It is perhaps most accurate to say that Scriabin *was* a synaesthete according to the way the phenomenon was framed during his own time period, but according to current definitions he was not."[11]

Despite these conclusions by Gawboy and other researchers, many advocates still perpetuate the myth of Scriabin's synaesthesia in printed literature and online. Commentary has come from writers of all stripes, including trusted authorities and nonprofessionals. To illustrate a few examples, in Richard Cytowic's book, *Synesthesia: A Union of the Senses* (1989), he accepts Scriabin's claims to synaesthesia without question, and argues how this phenomenon influenced his creative direction.[12] Corroboration from the scientific community comes from prominent figures like Daniel Levitin, professor of psychology and behavioral neuroscience at McGill University, and author of the best-selling book *This Is Your Brain on Music: The Science of a Human Obsession* (2006). In 2010, New York's classical music station, WXQR interviewed Dr. Levitin, and he asserted that Scriabin was an authentic synaesthete, telling his radio audience that, "Scriabin would see in his visual field colors in association with certain pitches of the musical scale."[13] However, from Sabaneev's writings we know that this statement is wrong on two counts. Scriabin only "felt" colors or associated them with his compositions, and definitely *not* with individual pitches of a scale, but within large-scale key areas. Prominent corroboration from such leaders in the field as Dr. Levitin has contributed greatly to the gross misperception on this matter. As with other topics attached to Scriabin's legacy, readers are encouraged to review the facts on Scriabin's color-hearing and decide for themselves what they believe.

LITERATURE ON SCRIABIN'S SYNAESTHESIA

The first major publication on Scriabin's synaesthesia was written by the physician and psychologist Charles S. Myers (1873–1946) from the University of Cambridge. His study was significant because it took Scriabin's color-hearing from the tabloids and into the scientific arena. In the spring of 1914, Scriabin undertook a concert tour of England, and while abroad, Myers invited the composer to share his insights into synaesthesia in a personal interview, although their only common language was French (Alexander Brianchaninov translated). Myers rushed into print to share the details of his brush with a celebrity in an article obliquely titled "Two Cases of Synaesthesia."[14] Although brief, Myers' report provided an early account in favor of

Scriabin's synaesthesia by insinuating that his claims had been scientifically tested. Reading his report a century later, one senses that Myers was starstruck around the famous composer, and his inexperience in music is also evident, although some salient points emerge. Just as Scriabin told Sabaneev, he informed Myers that the color-chord combinations he devised "must be shared by all who are endowed with coloured hearing." He also held that the strongest colors were produced by his favorite keys, especially F♯ major.[15] The remaining colors were derived by association. Myers strikes at the heart of the matter in his observation that, "when listening to music, [Scriabin] has only a 'feeling' of colour; only in cases where the feeling is very intense does it pass over to give an 'image' of colour." Genuine synaesthetes respond involuntarily to sensory stimuli, and not simply stimuli that is anticipated or conceived. In physiological terms, Scriabin's experiences do not correspond with the type of perception reported by actual synaesthetes.

From his conversation with Scriabin, Myers broadened his definition of synaesthesia to include the idea of color *thinking*, and with this criteria in mind, Scriabin's claims could be construed as legitimate. Considering how little information was available about synaesthesia in the 1910s, Myers likely focused on documenting the phenomenon in all of its manifestations. A parallel example of this type of synaesthesia is also linked to the French composer Olivier Messiaen (1908–1992), who closely related colors and music. "I see colours when I hear sounds," Messiaen explained to the French critic Claude Samuel in 1988, "but I don't see colours with my eyes. I see colours intellectually, in my head." Comparing his experiences with the synaesthetic responses experienced by his friend, Swiss "musicalist" painter Charles Blanc-Gatti (a genuine synaesthete), Messiaen admitted that, "I see [colors] inwardly; this is not imagination, nor is it a physical phenomenon. It's an inward reality."[16] Although Scriabin and Messaien did not experience the autonomic responses commonly associated with synaesthesia, the affinities they perceived between music and color profoundly impacted their creativity and should not be disregarded just because they do not conform to the clinical definition of synaesthesia.

Other details of Myers' report expose inconsistencies in Scriabin's account compared to typical synaesthetic experiences. It is odd that the composer insisted that "a single note has in itself no colour," since synaesthetes often visualize colors with a single note. Even more improbable is the composer's claim that he anticipated changes in color before they even happened in the music. He also decried any associations with the actual name of each note, and dismissed these claims as less authentic than his own experiences. (Scriabin insisted, for instance, that C major was associated with white only because that chord is played with only the white keys of the piano; similarly, Rimsky-Korsakov saw F major as green because that key is often used in pastoral music, a classic holdover from the Doctrine of Affections.) Scriabin further attested that music in minor keys evoked no color associations for him (he told Sabaneev the same thing), and that just as "colours have their over-colours, [so too] tones have their overtones." The most startling revelation in Myers' report is Scriabin's claim that "older" works, such as Beethoven's symphonies, lacked sufficient changes in tonality and were "too intellectual in character" to produce colors. To Scriabin, Beethoven's compositions lacked the "psychological basis of modern music" and were the equivalent of an old black-and-white movie. To assert that Beethoven's symphonies are harmonically monotonous and underutilize the full palette of colors available through the modern orchestra is an extreme position to say the least, and it betrays Scriabin's prejudice against the German master. Bowers reports in his biography of the composer that Scriabin found Beethoven's music "unbearably monotonous . . . the work of a muscle man with biceps."[17] So much for automated physiological responses divorced from all reasoning.

Not until 1985 was the next milestone in the literature on Scriabin's synaesthesia laid by Kenneth Peacock, professor of music at New York University. Like Myers and Levitin, Peacock unconditionally accepted Scriabin's claims to synaesthesia and set out to validate them through scholarly research.[18] In his article, he examined the phenomenon's broad range of symptoms and focused on its application in music. Peacock pointed out that synaesthetes often visualize colors based on compositional style, timbre, pitch, and/or tonality. He cited several examples from clinical studies and fictional literature that document the full range of synaesthetic experiences (obligatory is his inclusion of E. T. A. Hoffmann's famous description of Dr. Johannes Kreisler in *Kreisleriana* [1813] as "the little man in a coat the color of C♯ minor with an E major colored collar").[19] After presenting several case studies, Peacock identified affinities between Scriabin's symptoms and the common traits of those endowed with the condition, and argued that Scriabin's experiences were well within the normal range of synaesthetic experience. The remainder of his article featured a theoretical analysis of the *luce* part in *Prometheus*, and argued that the *luce* makes intelligible for the audience the overall tonal plan. As Peacock put it, the combination of color and music presented a "powerful psychological resonator for the listener." Peacock's article was notable because it regarded Scriabin's synaesthesia as worthy of modern academic study, lending this subject the credibility that it lacked for most of the twentieth century. Peacock argued that there was a method behind the madness, and that there was a concrete, rational, and musical connection between the *luce* part in *Prometheus* and its music. Yet this systematic organization was incongruent with normal synaesthetic experience; the very fact that Scriabin viewed synaesthesia in this way is evidence against his natural experience of the condition.

Since the *luce* part in *Prometheus* was the most explicit realization of Scriabin's synaesthesia, let us examine its properties more closely. The *luce* consists of two separate melodic lines; the faster moving top line outlines the root of the harmonies, and the slower moving lower part ascends through the notes of a scale and symbolizes the evolutionary states that humanity undergoes en route to spiritual purification.[20] In the months leading up to the first Russian premiere, Scriabin worked closely with his friend, engineer Alexander Mozer, to create a *clavier à lumières*. Scriabin ultimately withdrew the instrument before the Moscow premiere due to unspecified technical difficulties, but a prototype is still on display at the Scriabin Museum in Moscow. Information about the genesis of the *luce* part can be found in several sources, including an article cowritten by Scriabin scholar Anna Gawboy and lighting designer Justin Townsend, who collaborated on a stunning production of *Prometheus* with colored lights in February 2010 at Yale University's Woolsey Hall, which adhered to the composer's original prescriptions as faithfully as possible.[21] Gawboy based her research on a forgotten score of *Prometheus* that is currently archived in the Bibliothèque Nationale in Paris, and which contains Scriabin's handwritten notes about the shades of color and lighting effects he imagined would accompany performances of the tone poem.[22]

In Scriabin's homeland, two Russian scholars devoted their careers to studying the composer's pairing of colors and music, and their insights have afforded scholars a deeper understanding of that relationship as Scriabin imagined it. Irina Vanechkina (b. 1942) and Bulat Galeyev (1940–2009) were longtime colleagues at the Prometheus Institute in Kazan, which Galeyev founded in 1962, and which was the site of some of the most innovative experiments in music and colored lights to take place anywhere in the world. It was established in the heady days of the early Soviet space program, when the triumphs of Sputnik inspired Russians to pursue the limits of their imagination. The Prometheus Institute adopted the composer's final symphony as its namesake and developed several color-music instruments, one of which was utilized for the first performance ever in the Soviet Union of *Prometheus* with colored lights, which took place in Kazan in 1962.

Among their publications, both individually and as a research team, their 2001 article "Was Scriabin a Synaesthete?" marked the first time that Russian scholars openly cast doubt on Scriabin's claims to synaesthesia. In this article, the authors paid deference to Sabaneev and Myers, and took as their starting point the fact that "Scriabin has been mentioned without fail as first in a list of such synaesthetes . . . as Rimsky-Korsakov, Kandinsky, Ciurlionis, and Messiaen."[23] They determined that Scriabin's color-hearing was associative rather than physiological, and in later publications they argued that the modern (Western) definition of synaesthesia is too narrow because it does not admit correspondence schemes constructed for aesthetic purposes. Their work attempts to account for the artist's perception, which may not have an exact scientific explanation. Since then, countless other writers have included their findings in their own investigations of associative synaesthesia. A final important point the authors advanced, and one to which we shall return later in this chapter, was Scriabin's concept of music in terms of color or light. According to the authors, it was the latter of these two elements that he prized most highly in his compositional ideology. "Scriabin regarded his 'color-sound synaesthesia' (or 'color-hearing') as less important than his 'light-sound synaesthesia' ('light-hearing'); the latter allowed him to attain an effect of 'effulgence' or 'luminosity' in the music itself even without real light." We will return to this idea later in this chapter in a deeper discussion of exactly how Scriabin achieves luminous effects in his music.

The last noteworthy article that explores Scriabin's synaesthesia was written by music theorist James Baker, who focused on the world premiere of *Prometheus: Poem of Fire* with colored lights at Carnegie Hall on 20 March 1915.[24] To Baker, that performance was a "culminating event in the history of attempts over the centuries to combine music and color, but it also served as an important stimulus to further work in 'color-music.'" He detailed how the colored lights and otherworldly music fueled speculation about the composer's mystical-spiritualism as well as his mental stability. Although the performance was a failure from a technical standpoint, the event ranks as one of the most important performances of the twentieth century. Baker supplied several reviews from contemporary critics, who were less than sympathetic, and he provided rich details about the immense preparation that went into the premiere, including rehearsing the music, and designing and constructing the *tastiéra per luce*.

Baker situated the *Prometheus* premiere in a historical panorama, from developments taking place around New York City to artistic events happening across Europe. He traced the history of synaesthesia in art, music, and literature, and drew particular attention to Scriabin's influences and interests in Symbolist poetry, philosophy, and Theosophy. Baker convincingly argued how *fin de siècle* artists were preoccupied with synthesizing the arts, and he makes a compelling case that Scriabin's interest in color-music was part of a larger cultural fascination with the interplay of the senses. As Baker contested, Scriabin "was simply a creature of a time when the notion of appealing to all of the senses was pervasive in all fields of artistic endeavor." Baker's article is exemplary for its broad range of sources and scholarly rigor, and it is refreshing in its objectivity compared to some of the hagiographic treatments left to us by Scriabin's admirers. It is an interesting departure from his usual recondite analyses of Scriabin's music, which have been criticized for their overly analytical approach and failure to adequately account for Scriabin's cultural context.[25]

These four articles represent important contributions to the literature about Scriabin's color-hearing and synaesthesia in music, and the ideas they advanced and sources they cited make them excellent starting points for anyone who is interested in investigating this topic further. There are other publications that address Scriabin's synaesthesia and the lights in *Prometheus*, and these have appeared over the years in various arts and music journals and newspapers.[26] Among the most notable contributions in recent years is an article coauthored by Anna Gawboy and Justin Townsend on their collaboration at Yale in 2010, titled "Scriabin and the Possible."[27] This chorus of commentators makes for interesting reading, and it provides readers with a deeper appreciation for the diversity of opinions on this subject.

ILLUMINATING THE PERFORMANCES

Although *Prometheus: Poem of Fire* is the only example of Scriabin's music where colored lights are designated in the score, others of his solo piano works have also been staged with colored lights, despite the fact that they were not originally scored as such. Predictably, these realizations have drawn mixed reviews. However, since *Prometheus* has drawn the lion's share of attention from lighting designers, critics, and scholars, our discussion naturally begins with that work. Scriabin drew inspiration for *Prometheus* from the writings of Helena Blavatsky, the figurehead of a mystical religious philosophy known as Theosophy. Blavatsky recast the famous myth of the Titan who stole fire from the gods as an allegory for the most important moment in human history: the acquisition of thought and reason. Like Blavatsky, Scriabin associated the "sacred spark" of intelligence with both celestial lights and earthly electricity.[28] Attempts to translate this almost biblical message through multimedia has led to more than a few lackluster displays that have little bearing on Scriabin's aesthetic code. These miscues underscored the perceived disparity between the music and colored lights. A typical result is gleaned from critic Edward Rothstein's review of a 1983 performance of *Prometheus* with the Baltimore Symphony Orchestra under Sergiu Comissiona: "A few half-hearted streams of smoke emerged from the balconies, and the sketchy color patterns amateurishly extended off the screen onto the curtain and ceiling."[29] Over the years, though, other attempts have fared better and delighted critics and audiences alike, exposing Scriabin's music to an entirely new population.

What better starting point for this discussion than the world premiere of Scriabin's *Prometheus: Poem of Fire* with colored lights? Altschuler's realization at Carnegie Hall with his Russian Symphony Society (Margaret Volavay, piano) may have been a failure from a technical standpoint, but the interest that it aroused in the musical community created a powerful ripple effect that inspired countless artists, then and now. This critical "failure" became a popular success in part due to the publicity that surrounded the event. Before its New York premiere, *Prometheus* had been performed in Chicago on March 5 (without the colored lights), where it elicited a divisive reaction from the audience, and even prompted a portion of the audience to hiss in disapproval. But this controversy only aroused greater interest in the piece. *Musical America* primed its readers with "dire rumors from Chicago regarding the monumental ugliness of the thing and its monstrous capacity for offending the ears." The audience that evening in Carnegie Hall was "the largest to which the Russian Orchestra has played in many a moon."[30] To give the public its money's worth and to aid comprehension of this ultramodern music, Altschuler performed *Prometheus* twice that evening, an idea he probably picked up from British conductor Sir Henry J. Wood, who had used the same tactic on 1 February 1913 in London when he introduced British audiences to *Prometheus* (*sans luce*).[31] The Old Guard of New York critics at Carnegie Hall that evening in March 1915, however, had their patience tested with a single performance of *Prometheus*, let alone two. In his typical sardonic tone, William J. Henderson of the *New York Sun* grumbled, "I did not stay for the repetition, but I am certain that if I had done so, I would have known less than after the first, for if I had watched another round of those lights, I would have lost my vision."[32]

The color organ that debuted at the legendary 1915 performance was christened the "Chromola" and was designed by Preston S. Millar, general manager of the Electrical Testing Laboratories in New York City. Millar worked closely with Altschuler for several years before unveiling the final design of the device, which featured fifteen keys that operated tungsten lamps with color filters, and two foot pedals that controlled a rheostat which allowed the user to vary the intensity of the colors.³³ Many critics at Carnegie Hall had complained of a lack of varying intensity to the colors, so it remains unclear whether user error or technical limitations (or a combination of both) led reviewers to this conclusion. Instead of bathing the concert hall in a rainbow of colors, as Scriabin had imagined, the projections blobbed in a murky haze on a screen raised behind the orchestra, which consisted of "two series of gauze strips about eight feet by ten, hung at the back of the stage ten feet from the floor, and presenting to the eye simply a white rectangle in about the position of a picture suspended on the back wall."³⁴ William J. Henderson concluded that, "just once in the composition there was a glimmering of sane artistic purpose. The rest was gibberish in tones and a garish glitter of colors which had about as much significance in the whole scheme as a string of signal flags communicating the morning coal report of a battle fleet would have in Rubinstein's 'Ocean' Symphony."³⁵ Other critics were even less flattering. As with other attempts before the 1970s to approximate Scriabin's visions, the limitations of modern technology simply could not realize the ambitions that performers and lighting designers had to bring the composer's ideas to life. Even Altschuler and Millar were left dissatisfied by the results they achieved in 1915. But even in its ineffectiveness, the Chromola served as a beacon of modernity.

Prometheus has been staged many times with colored lights since 1915, and these performances have met with varying degrees of success. In Russia, it was fully realized with colored lights for the first time at the Bolshoi Theater in 1917, on the eve of the Bolshevik Revolution. On this occasion, Leonid Sabaneev performed the *luce* part, but just as in New York, audiences were left disappointed. A year later, the renowned scene designer Aristarkh Lentulov (1882–1943) offered his guidance and achieved more satisfying results. After that, however, over forty years elapsed before anyone else in Russia mustered the courage and resources to try again. Finally on 6 April 1962, the aforementioned Prometheus Institute mounted a performance that projected the two color lines onto a large screen. The following year, the Prometheus Institute unveiled a newly constructed lighting instrument called "Prometheus-2" that produced 120 points of light, each of which could blend five different colors. Today, fifty years after its initial founding, the Prometheus Institute remains at the forefront of education and research toward light-music in Russia.

Since the 1960s, several performances of *Prometheus* with colored lights have taken place in Russia and the West, most of which have rejected Scriabin's original color-tonal scheme in favor of their own arrangements. Consider a performance of *Prometheus* in 1969 with the New York Philharmonic under Seiji Ozawa. Lighting designer Peter Wexler created his own color scheme, which adopted the psychedelic style in vogue at the time. Faubion Bowers had choice words for the artistic decisions behind this event. Not only did Ozawa hastily breeze through the piece, thereby turning this earth-shattering work into a casual affair, but the overall effect of the lights and the music struck Bowers as "rather disrespectful to Scriabin. What [Wexler] did was bring the Electric Circus to Philharmonic Hall."³⁶ As an example of a more successful production, Bowers hailed a 1967 performance of *Prometheus* with the

Rochester Philharmonic under Lázló Somogyi as the "most definitive light display, coming closest to Scriabin's vision." The lighting apparatus for that production was designed by film producer Alex Ushakoff, who rigged twenty-eight projectors with color filters and modified a synthesizer to create a modern-day *luce*.[37] Several scholars have documented all of the known performances of *Prometheus* with colored lights, and readers interested in this complete listing can refer to several reliable sources.[38]

By the 1970s, technology finally caught up with Scriabin's futuristic visions. Laser light shows at rock concerts and counterculture "happenings" paved the way for similar spectacles in the concert hall. All manner of lighting methods were used for these performances, including inflating weather balloons, stretching large canvases across the stage, and projecting colored lights onto an all-white robed chorus. The most notorious production of *Prometheus* with colored lights took place at Yale University's Woolsey Hall on 20 February 1971, under the direction of John Mauceri. As the musicologist Hugh Macdonald recalled, "tinfoil reflectors [were] handed around to every member of the audience and aromas of doubtful legality filled the auditorium."[39] Part of what made this performance so successful was the interactive component. Edward Rothstein described the concert hall as "flooded with smoke, and colored stage lights were set up in the aisles and balconies. Each listener was provided with a metallic strip of reflective Mylar so the shafts of light would scatter against each body into the smoky mists."[40] So noteworthy was this event that it transcended the world of classical music and registered on the pop culture radar, even earning recognition in *Life* magazine. Its venerable reputation must have loomed large in the mind of Anna Gawboy, who, as mentioned earlier, mounted a spectacular production of *Prometheus* with colored lights in collaboration with lighting designer Justin Townsend at Yale University in February 2010, and repeated the performance in 2012 with the Cape Cod Symphony, and in 2013 at Utah State University.

Among other notable performances in the 1970s, Professor Emeritus Lowell Cross of the University of Iowa built a device that he called the Video-Laser III, for a performance of *Prometheus* with colored lights on 24 September 1975 under the baton of James Dixon. An engineer and instrument builder, Cross left behind a venerable legacy in the world of electro-acoustic music. Faubion Bowers turned to parlance more typical for comic books than concert reviews when he reported of the event that, "Cross flashed his krypton-argon laser beams in giddying patterns on a huge scrim screen which translucently hid the one hundred-member orchestra on stage."[41] The audience turnout far surpassed the capacity of the hall, and hundreds of concertgoers were turned away due to lack of space. In England, *Prometheus* was first performed with colored lights on 4 May 1972 with the London Symphony Orchestra under Elyakum Shapira at the Royal Albert Hall. With seating for over five thousand, the immense performance space understandably dictated some artistic decisions. A parachute was draped across the stage and was illuminated as a backdrop for the colored light projections, but in this massive hall it seemed tiny and tame. The production crew compensated for this shortcoming by spraying Floris perfume throughout the seating stalls to incorporate scent into the show. Hugh Macdonald documented two other performances in which *Prometheus* was treated to colored lights, in 1973 at Residentie Orkest under Michael Gielen, and in 1979 with the Oxford University Orchestra under his own direction.[42] His account of the supreme effort that went into these events makes it clear that devising adequate and aesthetically pleasing lighting to accompany performances is no simple matter. Indeed, the mixed reviews these performances received, in spite of their inspired spirit, have only sustained the skepticism that lingers around the topic of Scriabin's music and colored lights. The philosophical program about the origin of the cosmos, and the Theosophical aura of *Prometheus* made it an easy target for ridicule. Any deficiencies that were perceived in the music or its program were, by nature, extended to the lighting.

No discussion of light projections with Scriabin's music in the 1970s would be complete without recognizing Viennese pianist Hilde Somer (1922–1979). Somer toured the United States from 1969 to 1972 delivering all-Scriabin recitals with lighting effects by Pablo Lights and Thomas Shoesmith of the Joshua Light Show.[43] Here was a classical performer who broke down art music's barriers by forging alliances with the lighting experts who honed their craft in the hallowed halls of rock music, including Fillmore West, Fillmore East, and Winterland (all owned by rock impresario Bill Graham). Somer carved a niche for herself in the male-dominated world of classical pianists by aligning herself with the occult mystique that was an integral part of Scriabin's reputation among the American counterculture in the early 1970s. "It was just like never, never land," Somer recalled of her light shows. "All the elements—heaven, fire, stars, the sun . . . water—were combined in the Scriabin recital. Truly the Scriabin spirit."[44] Somer's use of colored lights to accompany her recitals of Scriabin's music was driven as much by artistic considerations as it was market demands.[45] In her campaign to champion Scriabin's music during his revival, Somer issued her first all-Scriabin record in 1968 with a psychedelic decal depicting Scriabin as the "First Flower Child" (see figure 8.2 in chapter 8 on the 1960s revival). Her follow-up album in 1970, *AΩ* (Alpha Omega), continued to capitalize on Scriabin's occult reputation, and the liner notes to her album featured images of mythical beasts and otherworldly androgenic faces. Somer's ability to capitalize on the spirit of the times, in addition to her technical chops, earned her distinction as one of the leading proponents of Scriabin's music in the 1970s, with or without the colored lights.

In contrast to the aesthetic of the 1970s, modern-day performers have favored more subtle color variations. A case in point is Georgian pianist Eteri Andjaparidze, who mounted a production in November 2011 called "Spectral Scriabin" that was featured as part of Lincoln Center's White Light Festival. The annual event is a community arts extravaganza that celebrates music's ability to enrich life. Her hourlong program featured Scriabin's solo piano music being played without pause to the accompaniment of background lighting projections designed by Jennifer Tipton (b. 1937), whose lighting artistry has earned her recognition in theater, dance, and opera.[46] Tipton closely studied the composer's color-tonal scheme, but eventually abandoned any strict observance of Scriabin's ideas simply because they didn't match the mood she wanted to convey during the performance. Tipton is also steadfast in her preference for incandescent bulbs over LED technology, since older bulbs project a warm glow that softens the luminescent effect. In contrast to the bigger and bolder approaches of the past, Tipton's projections featured slowly shifting geometric patterns that blended colors in highly subtle shifts that were nearly imperceptible to viewers, and intentionally so. These subtle moods were complemented by Andjaparidze's musical selections, which emphasized the ethereal side of Scriabin's music. Their collaboration pleased the festival organizers and audiences, and was successful enough to be repeated by popular demand in subsequent years.

Critics, however, were predictably reserved in their praise for Andjaparidze's show. Anthony Tommasini of the *New York Times* found the projections "fairly tame" despite his realization that Tipton had deliberately downplayed the lighting effects. Mark Swed of the *Los Angeles Times* was similarly unmoved by the lighting as well as by Andjaparidze's piano playing, which he found overly theatrical and lacking expressive depth.[47] Just as with Somer's performances, however, voices of the popular press waxed lyrical over the possibilities. Theodore Bell of *Culture Spot LA* remarked that Andjaparidze and Tipton produced "a powerful multisensory synesthetic simulation that continued to shine in my memories long after the music stopped. . . . The Gestalt was truly mesmerizing as the color and sound combined to evoke an elevated emotional response, especially interpretative with Scriabin's more esoteric moments."[48] These critics voiced both sides of a debate that still rages on today, especially among professional music critics, whose tastes do not always represent that of the average concertgoer.

Andjaparidze's decision to refer to Scriabin's style as "spectral" was not by chance, as it accords with modern research on the composer. The prolific new music pianist Marilyn Nonken, professor of music at New York University at Steinhardt, recently published a book titled *The Spectral Piano: From Liszt, Scriabin, and Debussy to the Digital Age* (2014), in which she discusses a lineage of composers who followed in the footsteps of Hungarian pianist-composer Franz Liszt. These composers, Scriabin chief among them, shared an overriding concern with instrumental timbre as a guiding ideology for their compositions. Spectralism, she argued, is more an attitude than a compositional approach, and it is equally influenced by technological developments as it is by the natural sounds of living creatures and the environment. The spectral style is primarily associated with compositional approaches of the 1970s, when computer software was developed to isolate sound waves, and composers elevated timbre and space over harmony and form. Nonken identified Scriabin as one of the key progenitors of spectralism, and she argued that an understanding of this historical heritage should guide performers' approaches to that repertoire. When performing spectral music, Nonken advised that, "pianists must preoccupy themselves with the projection of harmonic-timbral complexes: creating highly specific kinds of resonance and controlling their projection in time. . . . To approach performance with a spectral attitude, the pianist must interpret the score embracing the idea that work is about nothing except the sound itself."[49] With such an approach in mind,

Scriabin's philosophical programs and extra-musical ideas become considerably less important.

Considering the ubiquity of laser light shows and other visual props at popular music concerts, it is only natural that these devices would find their way into classical concerts. In today's visually oriented world, with its emphasis on sensory over-stimulation, it is not surprising that contemporary audiences would enjoy and be enlightened by a sophisticated and tasteful application of colored visuals to classical music. Performers and stage technicians are poised now more than ever to take advantage of modern technology, and collaborate to add another sensory dimension to their performances. But critical reception on this issue will always remain divided. Old habits die hard, and the tastemakers of high culture still consider it a curious experiment or unwelcome intrusion to include colored lights in performances of classical music, and certainly not the wave of the future.

For those performers who include colored lights in their performances of Scriabin's music, a clear distinction must be made between entertainment and historical accuracy. If the intent is to educate audiences about Scriabin's original ideas, then historically informed performances should remain faithful to the composer's instructions, even if they disagree with the color-tonal correspondences. But if the goal is to entertain audiences, then that initiative should be made clear, and critics and audiences will likely be more sympathetic to their cause. We would do well to recall the words of critic Allen Hughes, who reviewed Hilde Somer's December 1969 concert at Alice Tully Hall at Lincoln Center and remarked frankly that, "This listener and watcher cannot honestly say that [the colored lights] seemed to bear any special relation to Scriabin's music, that they enhanced it, or that they would not have gone just as well with, say, compositions by Chopin, Debussy, or Schoenberg. The projections were pretty, and that was enough."[50]

THE CONSTRUCTION OF LIGHT

No evidence has supported Scriabin's claims to synaesthesia, and most performances of his music with colored lights have met with a mixed reaction at best and derision at worst. So should we ignore this defining aspect of his legacy? Is it only a distraction from the natural beauty of the tones themselves? Or could the *idea* of representing color and light in Scriabin's music lend new insights into his art? Scriabin certainly cared enough about his color-hearing to consider it a guiding principle in his creative ideology. That alone should persuade us to entertain the possibilities of using the idea of light in music as a lens through which to interpret his art. As we shall see, many of his works feature explicit references to light, and understanding the compositional techniques that Scriabin developed to create these luminous effects will enhance an appreciation for his art.

Let us first examine how Scriabin's predecessors represented light in music, since he follows their examples in many respects. One common tactic composers have used is a shift from the minor to the major mode (e.g., C minor to C major). This technique is particularly effective when accompanied by a change in register, instrumentation, texture, and/or dynamics. A prototypical example of this minor-major jolt is found in Beethoven's Fifth, the most famous symphony in the world. Its stormy home key of C minor dominates most of the piece before the final movement dawns in the radiant key of C major, a tonal shift that even Beethoven compared to a flood of light after a storm. He remarked, "Many assert that every minor piece must end in the minor. *Nego!* Joy follows sorrow, sunshine—rain. It affects me as if I were looking up to the silvery glistening of the evening star."[51] Beethoven used even more imaginative compositional techniques to depict light in his next symphony, "Pastorale" Op. 68 (1808). In the fourth movement, a violent thunderstorm erupts in F minor, unleashing thunder, howling wind, and flashes of lightning that still astound in their realism. Eventually, the storm soon passes and brings streaming sunlight in the key of F major, the so-called pastorale key in the Doctrine of Affections. The shift from the minor to the major mode—achieved by raising a single note one half-step—casts a resplendent sheen over the music, thus breeding the "happy and thankful feelings after the storm" that Beethoven referred to in his title for the final movement.

One of the quintessential representations of light in music is found in Joseph Haydn's oratorio, *The Creation* (1796–1798), a sort of opera without acting that tells the story of the creation of the universe, as described in the book of Genesis and Milton's *Paradise Lost*. Like the opening bars of Scriabin's *Prometheus*, Haydn's *Creation* begins with harmonically unstable chords, which symbolize the inchoate state of the universe. The absence of a rhythmic pulse and the dissonant harmonies disorient the listener, lending the effect of stumbling around a dark room. Soon the chorus lowers to a whisper, and on the text, "And God said: Let there be light, and there was *light!*" the chorus and orchestra erupt in a blaze of glory that beautifully captures God's creation of the first light. The strings cast off their mutes, the brass blast away, and the chorus resounds. What makes this moment such a masterstroke of genius is that the sudden shift in dynamics from soft to loud not only represents light illuminating the darkness, but also the shock and awe that greeted the appearance of the first light. Scriabin surely knew these works by Haydn and Beethoven, as all music students do, and he borrowed their techniques of scoring and dramaturgy to create the impression of light in his own music, perhaps even unconsciously.

Prometheus: Poem of Fire is the most famous example of Scriabin's depiction of light through music, but many other of his works also simulate light, although the connection may be less obvious. According to Faubion Bowers, the idea of light in music became one of the composer's guiding principles in his mature works. Bowers wrote that Scriabin believed that "the gods communicated by emitting lights and flashing sparks. As his music advanced, he dropped programmatic 'imitation' or 'description' of light. He was concerned with actually reproducing light in music palpably and visibly—like gods talking."[52] For Scriabin, optic light symbolized spiritual enlightenment. His first breakthrough in this quest to create light in music came in his Third Symphony, the *Divine Poem* (1902–1904), a programmatic work about humanity's ascent from the earthly to the divine. The finale to the *Divine Poem*, titled *Jeu divin* (Divine Play), marked the first time that Scriabin felt he had created light in music. He told Sabaneev that it was "the first time I knew intoxication, flight, the *breathlessness* of happiness."[53] To make his extra-musical ideas explicit, the light-emitting passages in the score are marked with performance directions such as "*lumineux*" (bright), and "*lumineux de plus en plus éclatant*" (light becoming brighter). The encouraging results of these early experiments of imitating light emboldened Scriabin to test the limits of this idea in later compositions, the ultimate result being the actual pairing of a color organ and music in *Prometheus*.

Flushed with success from constructing light in the *Divine Poem*, Scriabin set out to develop techniques to represent light in his music for solo piano, his natural medium. The first breakthrough came in his Piano Sonata No. 4 Op. 30 (1903). Not surprisingly, it was the first of his sonatas to abandon the traditional three-movement design in favor of a two-part structure. The creative inspiration for the music was a beacon of light—specifically, a distant star, a symbol of divinity and beatitude. To make explicit his vision for the music, Scriabin wrote a poem that describes how the artist is irresistibly drawn to a gleaming star. Gradually its beauty overwhelms him, and he longs to reach it, until he finally unites with the star. Here are excerpts from Scriabin's poem:

> In the light, gentle mists, lost in the distance,
> The bright light of a star twinkles softly. How beautiful it is!
> It rocks me to sleep, caresses me,
> The secret of its wonderful, blue rays entices me,
> Oh, to be near to you, distant star!
> To drown in your trembling rays, you magnificent star!
> O deep, mad yearning! O sweet delight of desire!
> I wish only to desire eternally, yearning itself is my only wish,
> But no! My elated flight takes me ever higher,
> Mad dance! Joyful rapture!
> May my flight lead me to you, wonderful star!—
> To you, whom I freely created, [. . .]
> In your glittering waves I drown,
> And I drink you, o sea of light,
> Light, I devour you![54]

How does Scriabin transform this flowery verse into music? The Fourth Sonata opens with a languid melody supported by unstable harmonies, as if the music has no direction or orientation. The fragmentary melodies and diaphanous textures in its opening bars depict the "light, gentle mists" mentioned in the poem's opening lines. As the music gains momentum, verses that describe how the celestial light "rocks me to sleep" and causes the stargazer to "drown in your trembling rays" are set musically when the right hand intones softly repeated chords against the melody, which is played by the left hand. These chords are marked with *portato* articulation—groups

Figure 6.3. Halos of light with portato chords in Sonata No. 4 in F♯ major Op. 30, mm. 40–45. *Leipzig: Beliaev, 1904.*

of notes played with space between them, as designated by staccato dots, as seen in figure 6.3. With the proper pedaling, these translucent chords bathe the melody in a radiant glow, providing a sonic analogue for the pulsating star. Soon the piano's right hand breaks off into decorative filigree in the highest register, dancing like flecks of sunlight bouncing off the water. The unusually wide expanse on the keyboard in this section presents a new kind of piano writing for Scriabin; for the first time, he expands his notation from two staves to three. As quintessential as this style of piano writing is for middle-period Scriabin, it also elicits parallels with the music of the French Impressionist style, most notably Claude Debussy's water-inspired works, such as *La Mer* (The Sea, 1903–1905), in which Debussy depicts light glinting off rolling waves, and *Reflets dans l'eau* (Reflections in the Water, 1905), the first of three piano pieces from Book I of *Images*. Scriabin was notoriously disinterested in the music of other composers, but upon his death, a copy of *La Mer* was found among his personal library, and we might assume that he picked up a few tips on orchestral color from Debussy. The "mad dance" and "joyful rapture" mentioned in Scriabin's poem is represented at the start of the second movement, marked "Prestissimo volando" (as fast as possible, as if flying).

Scriabin amplified the effect of light illuminating darkness in his next orchestral work, the *Poem of Ecstasy*, his most popular composition. This tone poem traverses a maelstrom of moods before reaching its conclusion in the purifying gleam of C major. This visceral release is achieved by prolonging the dominant harmonic function, which presents harmonic tension that demands release to the home key. Scriabin masterfully sustains this dominant function throughout the entire piece, and this denial of harmonic resolution lasts until the final moments, which feature the only complete consonant triad in the entire work. When the release finally comes, it is underscored by the orchestra's full participation, which unleashes a wall of sound that never fails to leave a strong impression on audiences. Many famous conductors adopted this piece as a signature work in their repertoires. The Russian-born conductor Albert Coates (1882–1953), who was a champion of Scriabin's orchestral music during the 1920s, launched his recording career with the *Poem of Ecstasy* (its first commercial recording), and elevated its popularity in England and America through numerous rousing live performances. Coates keenly sensed the work's light-emitting properties, and sought to convey this aspect of the music in his performances. He observed that in the *Poem of Ecstasy*

> we find Scriabin's love of light. In the great climax representing the very height of ecstasy, he had the picture in his mind of the human being, now freed from the fetters and trammels of everyday life, standing on the mountain-tops, with arms flung wide and head thrown back, bathed in a radiant splendor of dazzling golden sunlight.[55]

Scriabin never left any programmatic description of the work that matches Coates' vision, but according to Faubion Bowers, he did tell the Moscow critic Ivan Lipaev (1865–1942) that, "When you listen to *Ecstasy*, look straight into the eye of the Sun!"[56] It may be odd to think of music as having a quality of luminescence, but hearing the *Poem of Ecstasy* performed live by a first-rate orchestra will highlight the sharp glare of the horns, the rich resonance of the organ, and the shimmering harmonies played by the strings in this resplendent peroration. So stunning is the effect created in this moment that one must nearly shield their eyes from the intense sound.

Scriabin's literary impetus expressed itself through ancillary poetry in his earlier works, and it gradually became incorporated into his later scores by way of poetic performance markings. These function as musical signposts that identify passages where the composer expressly sought to represent light through music. One such moment is found in his Seventh Sonata, the "White Mass." This scintillating passage is marked "*très doux, joyeux, étincelant*" (very soft, joyful, sparkling). Its fleeting grace notes surround the melody like wispy filigree. Even its notation resembles a roman candle spitting sparks as it twirls through the air, as shown in figure 6.4.

Figure 6.4. Twirling sparkles of light in Sonata No. 7 Op. 64, "White Mass," mm. 119–21. *Ausgewählte Klavierwerke, Band 6: Sonaten 6–10.* **Leipzig: Edition Peters, 1972. Used by permission.**

This moment marks the first appearance of an important theme that will eventually guide the sonata to its apotheosis, a proverbial light at the end of the tunnel. The quality of lightness in this passage might also refer to the sparse distribution of the notes, which offers a strong textural contrast from the thick clusters of dissonant chords heard up until this point in the work. The Seventh Sonata passes through a variety of mystical moods, including a delirious section marked *avec une joie débordante* (with an overflowing joy), before it reaches its vertiginous finale. The étincelant theme makes a final appearance near the end of the sonata, where it is marked "*fulgurant*" (flashing like lightning). The sonata climaxes with a massive twenty-five-note cluster, and this bolt of lightning marks the moment we are transported to another dimension, something akin to a space-time warp (see figure 13.4 on The Scriabin Sound, four bars from the end). In Russian Symbolist terminology, this gesture is known as a *poriv*, or transporting burst.[57] A gripping rendition of the Seventh Sonata should leave audiences breathless after this torrential release of energy, leaving behind billows of smoke emanating from the stage, and a sense of disorientation in both time and space.

In addition to using mode mixture and distinctive figures to represent luminosity, Scriabin also uses trills. Especially in his late period works, trills were elevated from mere ornamental or decorative devices to a level of key significance in his works.[58] Trills serve as important rhetorical gestures for Scriabin; according to Bowers, trills represented to the composer trembling or quivering, and the "vibration of the atmosphere."[59] Not since Beethoven had a composer exploited the thematic and dramatic potential of the trill so innovatively as Scriabin did in his Piano Sonatas and late piano pieces. Naturally, Scriabin also used trills in the conventional manner, which is to sustain a pitch or chord, and even probed their technical possibilities in his Etude Op. 42 No. 3, nicknamed "Mosquito" (1903). Its *moto perpetuo* style recalls Rimsky-Korsakov's *Flight of the Bumblebee* (1899–1900), with its swirling figures and endless stream of fast-moving notes. The history of the trill and its performance practice in piano music has a rich and extensive history that exceeds the scope of this chapter, but recognizing the extra-musical significance of trills in Scriabin's later works will enhance an appreciation for the drama that they symbolize in his music.

Trills assume a special prominence in the Sixth and Ninth Piano Sonatas, which the composer considered his most profane in that genre. In these sonatas, they produce an effect of nervous excitement and add lustrous, coloristic effects. Trills are particularly important in the "Black Mass" Ninth Sonata Op. 68, where they bubble up from the musical texture like glints of flickering light. As the music builds in intensity, these figures bubble and rise to the surface, only to dive down again into the murky depths, as shown in figure 6.5. Rarely have trills been used so effectively to create such a spooky, eerie atmosphere as in Scriabin's Ninth Sonata.

Trills and luminosity achieve their fullest expression in the Tenth Sonata (1913), the so-called Trill Sonata, although Scriabin never sanctioned that nickname. In this titanic piece, trills of every manner are exploited; they are adorned with grace notes, appoggiaturas, three-note tremolos, and other *fioratura*, as seen in figure 6.6.

Figure 6.5. Trills as bursts of light in Sonata No. 9 Op. 68, mm. 27–28. *Moscow: Jurgenson, 1912.*

Scriabin expands the basic two-note trill into fistfuls of notes, and these shimmering tremolos radiate light, as shown in figure 6.7. Scriabin makes his extra-musical intentions explicit with such poetic indicators as "*crystallin*," "*lumineux vibrant*," "*de plus en plus radieux*" (over a series of single-note trills), and at the climax, "*Puissant, radieux*" (Powerful, radiant). Scriabin imagined that this music would emit vibrations into the atmosphere, and shake the heavens. The composer commented that in his Tenth Sonata, "Here is blinding light as if the sun has come close. Here is the suffocation one feels in the moment of ecstasy."[60] As strange as it may be to think of this clangorous music as symbolic of nature, the bird calls in its opening bars and sheets of sound within its pages recall a prehistoric time when the earth underwent volatile changes in its landscape and formation. The Tenth Sonata is music of the universe. The composer believed that it represented "the sounds and moods of the forest . . . joyously radiant and earthy."[61] Hearing these pealing clusters of dissonant chords can overwhelm listeners if they are well played and especially well pedaled, as such dense chords trigger overtones from the piano's sympathetic strings and enrich the sound color. Pianists must strive to maintain control of the sound, lest these heavenly overtones devolve into a noisy din. Like Haydn's representation of the first

Figure 6.6. Trills as bursts light in Sonata No. 10 Op. 70, mm. 260–62. *Moscow: Jurgenson, 1913.*

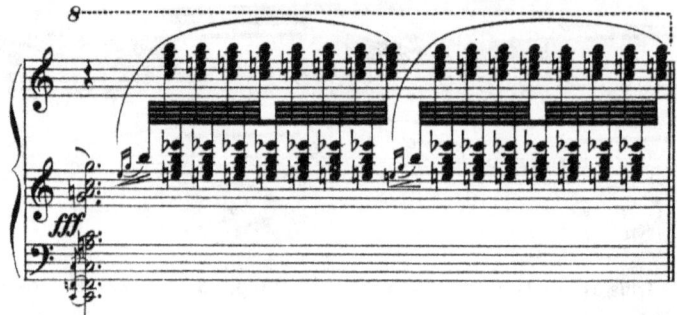

Figure 6.7. Luminous tone cluster trills in Sonata No. 10 Op. 70, m. 221. *Moscow: Jurgenson, 1913.*

light in *The Creation*, Scriabin's depiction of blinding light through these tone clusters creates a stunning effect.

The final example of Scriabin's depiction of light in music is found in *Vers la flamme* Op. 72 (Toward the Flame). This piece is notable because it combines multiple light-making techniques found in earlier works. With the exception of *Prometheus*, no other work in Scriabin's catalogue so explicitly worships the purifying properties of fire like *Vers la flamme*. Its searing intensity is palpable from its opening bars. This music is devoid of human emotion. In addition to using poetic performance cues like *Éclatant* and *lumineux* (Bright, brilliant), Scriabin combines two light-making techniques discussed earlier. Figure 6.8 shows how tremolos in the left hand are played against repeated *portato* chords in the right hand, both of which create glowing effects similar to moments highlighted in the Fourth and Ninth Sonatas. Used in conjunction, their radiance is twofold. The composer places these chords in a high register for maximum brightness of tone. As the music builds in intensity, he repeats the effect. The repeated chords are like flashes of lightning in a storm. Adding to the intensity is Scriabin's obsessive dwelling on the smallest pos-

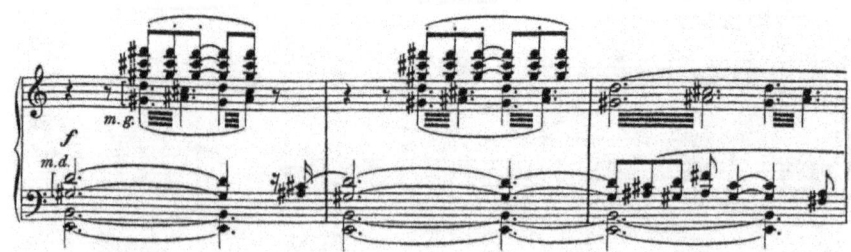

Figure 6.8. Portato chords combined with tremolos in Vers la flamme Op. 72, mm. 107–09. *Moscow: Jurgenson, 1914.*

sible interval—a minor second. The rocking, hypnotic rhythm to which this interval is set is both dazzling and disturbing.

These lighting effects may be written into the score, but it requires a sensitive and gutsy performer to help the audience see the light in these passages, so to speak. Like the "Mosquito" etude, *Vers la flamme* is a study in measured tremolos, and its restless churning propels the piece to its smoldering conclusion. It is no easy task for pianists to master this work's tricky cross-rhythms and unbridled intensity. To the Russian virtuoso Vladimir Horowitz, *Vers la flamme* reflected Scriabin's belief that a steady accumulation of heat would eventually destroy the universe (which is not too far fetched considering the effects of global warming). Eteri Andjaparidze took a different approach in the aforementioned "Spectral Scriabin" series, and interpreted *Vers la flamme* more like a spiritual journey from darkness into light. It was the first work on her program, which started by plunging the stage into darkness. Lighting designer Jennifer Tipton focused a single beam of light on Andjaparidze's hands in order to accentuate the ominous mood of the opening bars, and gradually this darkness evolved into luminescence. For any performer, the individual interpretation is what makes the performance truly effective. One need only contrast the intimate, personal interpretations of this piece delivered by Sviatoslav Richter with the volcanic performances of Horowitz to see that there is more than one way to interpret this music.

These examples offer a few illustrative passages of Scriabin's luminous imagination, and readers are encouraged to use them as models to identify other passages in his music that use these techniques to represent light. A natural extension of this investigation would be to explore how certain colors are represented through tonal shadings and other techniques. Scriabin's light-emitting techniques are an integral part of his musical vocabulary, and it is little wonder that he counted those works that use them among his personal favorites. Just as we do not need to subscribe to the composer's mystical or philosophical outlook to appreciate his efforts to elevate art above the realm of entertainment, so too can we recognize the importance of light in his creative artworks without believing he was an authentic synaesthete, at least in today's physiological terms.

CONCLUSIONS

We have come a long way from accepting Scriabin's synaesthesia on faith alone, as many people did when Modest Altschuler debuted *Prometheus* with colored lights at Carnegie Hall in March 1915. The natural curiosity for the composer's color-hearing that resulted from this event was laced with a healthy dose of skepticism, and this skepticism bred contempt. Thus an important source of inspiration for the composer became regarded as a dispensable accessory, or even an embarrassment to some critics, not unlike the philosophical programs of the *Divine Poem* or the Fourth Sonata. Having faced his own struggles to construct a functional color organ, Scriabin was well aware of the challenges presented to performers by the *luce*, and he wisely indicated in the score to *Prometheus* that the work "may be performed without color organ and without chorus." His decision to make these parts optional, however, was based on practical considerations, and not aesthetic concerns. Scriabin would have scornfully rejected any ad hoc arrangement of the color wheel that deviated from his own prescriptions, especially for entertainment purposes. Considering that something so fundamental to his creative ideology is so easily discarded explains much of the mystery and confusion that has hung over the composer's legacy for over a century. It is no wonder that many listeners are content to ignore all the controversy and simply bask in the sounds alone. Personally, I am not opposed to performances of Scriabin's music with colored lights, as long as they are tastefully applied. That being said, I also believe that the music stands on its own merits, and does not need colored lights to achieve its full luminous and coloristic effects.

Performers and lighting designers who incorporate Scriabin's color schemes into their performances will surely face opposition as well as enthusiasm, regardless of whether they follow the composer's original key-color pairings or devise their own arrangements. Finding the proper balance is crucial, and not easily attained. Producing a satisfactory colored lights display to accompany Scriabin's music is clearly a difficult task, in terms of practical and technical considerations as well as aesthetic appeal. Even Scriabin enthusiasts might take umbrage with theatrical displays like those of Hilde Somer. If the assumption has been that colored lights enhance an appreciation for the music, then the results of the last century do not support that belief. Make no mistake; the odds are stacked against any performer who incorporates colored lights into their performances. On the other hand, the time is ripe now more than ever to explore the limits of modern technology and realize Scriabin's futuristic visions through its power. LED projections and computer programming have made the possibilities limited only by the human imagination. Considering Scriabin's commitment to experimentation in his music, performers who seek to pair colored lights with his music owe it to the composer to put forth their best efforts.

Interest in Scriabin's synaesthesia continues to thrive, and aside from the studies covered in this chapter, other notable contributions have appeared in the form of recent dissertations by such scholars as Anna Gawboy and Christopher Dillon.[62] Outside of the field of musicology, Lazaros Triarhou, Professor of Neuroscience from the University of Macedonia, recently self-published a book that examines Scriabin's synaesthesia from a neurological perspective.[63] Popular commentators whose opinions appear in CD liner notes, blogs, and concert program guides will undoubtedly perpetuate the myth of Scriabin's faux-synaesthesia, as such tales only add to the composer's mystique. Discoveries made over the last several decades by scientists and scholars, however, have removed the veil of mystery that has hung over Scriabin's synaesthesia, and essentially called his bluff. Other avenues of research surely await further study, and future generations of scholars will continue to discover new insights into Scriabin's associations between music and color.

In the early twentieth century, Scriabin's interests in color-hearing and extrasensory abilities were not unique, and were shared by his contemporaries in art, music, and science. The breakthroughs of that era opened up new vistas of understanding about the mysteries of the universe and the wonders of the human mind. Developments in the soft sciences like psychology and perception were accompanied by equally impressive leaps forward in industry and technology, and this potent fusion of idea and practice made the possibilities seem limitless. In that period of scientific advancement, it must have seemed old-fashioned and narrow-minded to *not* entertain the idea that nearly anything was possible. Wanting to believe in Scriabin's claims to synaesthesia was a part of the ideology of the era. Artists of that time concerned themselves with breaking down traditional boundaries and seeking new modes of expression, and synaesthesia was another way of tapping into new realms of thought and experience. One merely needs to gaze upon a 1920s-era canvas by Mondrian or Kandinsky to recognize these artists' shared concerns with blending abstract forms and vivid colors into a strange kind of modern beauty. Today, over a century after the world premiere of *Prometheus* with color organ, Scriabin's theories about color, light, and music continue to amaze us and spark controversy. But thinking of his compositional language as expressions of light and color will hopefully allow a new generation of listeners to experience his music in new ways.

7

Scriabin's Russian Roots and the Symbolist Aesthetic

> *Scriabin, a contemporary of Rasputin, was a loner, emotionally, temperamentally and stylistically removed from the last Tsarists to whose number he belonged historically.*
>
> —Ates Orga[1]

This ill-considered remark, written by a classical music writer and record producer who ought to know better, encapsulates Scriabin's public image. It comes from the liner notes of a CD issued in 1997, but Orga's opinions could have easily appeared in the liner notes or concert programs of today. In a few words, he touches on several of the biases that have beleaguered Scriabin's legacy for over a century. Orga makes two key points: first, he depicts Scriabin's music as the product of a bygone age that died out along with the fall of the Romanov dynasty, and second, he claims that the composer was an artistic recluse among his peers. Each of these allegations warrants closer inspection, but the second point is particularly misguided, and will occupy our attention in this chapter. At the heart of this matter are two fundamental questions asked by so many: How did Scriabin's music and ideology fit in with the cultural movements of his time, and what are the qualities that make Russian music sound uniquely "Russian"? Neither question has a simple answer, but both are overdue for reconsideration, especially with regard to Scriabin.

In the eyes of Orga and those who share his point of view, very little has changed over the last century with regard to Scriabin's position as an outsider in music history. These pundits have ignored the wealth of literature that has emerged since the 1970s, which situates Scriabin's music and creative thinking well within the cultural climate of *fin de siècle* Russia and Europe. But like many myths about Scriabin, old habits die hard, and much work remains to overturn the received wisdom that he was an outsider to the cultural currents of his time. Have we learned nothing from a century's worth of scholarship? Consider this estimate of Scriabin written in 1915, which could have been written today:

> A strange man was Scriabin! No composer of our day held a more isolated position. In his later works he went solely his own way and the strangest part of his career as a composer is the fact that he was not in the slightest degree influenced by the Russian composers who preceded him, Glinka, Rimsky-Korsakov, Mussorgsky, Borodin, or Tschaikowsky [sic].... He stood on an island, as it were, quite alone. He threw all classical traditions to the wind, and his harmonic system in his later symphonic works had nothing at all to do with the great symphonic epoch that ended with Brahms.[2]

These assumptions have been implanted deep into the public's imagination over the last century. Even in the midst of the Scriabin revival in the early 1970s, the *New York Times* critic Harold Schonberg, who was an avid supporter of Scriabin, upheld this romanticized image of the composer as an isolated genius: "When he died, in 1915, he bestrode a no-man's land, living in a world of his own devising."[3] Such statements cast Scriabin in a mythic light, but they ignore his cultural background and harmonic developments. They also obscure the fact that Scriabin was one of the most representative artists of his era, a shining star among a galaxy of like-minded artists and poets. Even Stravinsky saw Scriabin as an outsider to Russian art and questioned, "Is it possible to connect a musician like Scriabin with any tradition whatsoever? Where does he come from? And who are his forebears?"[4] As it turns out, they are many of the same traditions that influenced Stravinsky and the other composers of his generation. Our temporal distance from this time period, however, makes this situation more difficult to appreciate.

Two central concepts reinforce this image of Scriabin as a rogue artist. Both operate under the assumption that his music developed independently from other musical styles. The first perspective adopts a *synchronic* point of view (a cross-sectional look at something as it existed at a single point in time), and considers how his music related to the works of other composers of his era. As we shall see, critics and historians have portrayed Scriabin as a lone wolf whose art was disconnected from the stylistic developments of his time. The second perspective is *diachronic* (the historical development of something over a period of time), and concerns Scriabin's fidelity to Russian musical traditions. Being a Russian composer came with an expectation to uphold the musical traditions that put Russian classical music on the international stage. This celebration of national identity through music manifested itself in several ways. One of the established methods that audiences came to expect from Russian composers was the use of musical quotations, either of folk melodies or church chants from the Orthodox liturgy. To make one's nationalist allegiance apparent, Russian composers could feature an indigenous instrument like the balalaika or the gusli, the latter of which Rimsky-Korsakov used in his opera, *Sadko* (1895–1896). These stylistic markers were particularly prominent in stage pieces like operas and ballets, which commanded prestige in Russian music. Composers could feature dialogue in their native tongue, or use set scenery full of glittering costumes and onion-shaped domes that captured the colorful landscape of Russian life. Stravinsky did just that in his ballet *Petrushka* (1911), which is set at St. Petersburg's Shrovetide Fair, and which overflows with quotations of folk tunes. But Scriabin never deigned to follow any of these folkloric traditions, and he never produced anything for the stage. Although he expressed his Russian heritage in his own way, perhaps even unintentionally, he paid the price for not following established conventions.

It is odd that we have regarded Scriabin as an outsider, since his contemporaries saw him very differently. In Russia after 1910, Scriabin was the quintessential figure of his era, and his music was the voice of the revolution. The Marxist philosopher Georgi Plekhanov (1856–1918) observed that Scriabin's music "was his era transposed into sound . . . it so fully expressed the mood of a very significant part of our intelligentsia at a particular period in history."[5] The first People's Commissar of Education, Anatoly Lunacharsky (1875–1933), was equally enthusiastic in his view of Scriabin as "the representation of the Revolution . . . he was its musical prophet, and therein lies his social significance."[6] To latter-day historians like Donald Grout, however, who operated outside the influence of Russian history and culture, Scriabin was an "unclassifiable Russian composer," an enigma or problem that one encountered by applying the conventional methods of historiography.[7] Grout's view offers a resonant example of this phenomenon, as his *History of Western Music* (the source of this quote) was for many years the standard text used by music students since it was first published in 1960. To a large degree, historians like Grout shaped how Scriabin has been viewed in the West. I will not attempt to expound upon the complicated matter of writing the history of Russian music, as other writers have addressed that issue with authority.[8] But it stands to reason that Scriabin's art can be best understood in the context of his era. Taking a broader look at his position in history also demonstrates how similar his reactions were to the cultural, historical, and political influences of his time in comparison to his contemporaries. We will tackle the Russian question first, since it directly relates to Scriabin's exclusion from his peers.

THE ONUS OF NATIONALISM

A (not so) simple reason explains why Scriabin's music has been considered outside the mainstream of Russian traditions. In writing the history of early twentieth-century music, historians have grouped together composers who cultivated so-called "nationalist" styles that are particular to certain geographical regions, and that promote the values and traditions of those locales. Any figure who did not belong to a group of nationalist composers was marginalized. In music, this nationalistic index typically appears in the form of quotations from folk tunes or church chants, references to cultural landmarks or customs, or similar artistic displays of patriotism. In music history books, one finds the usual couplings of composer and country that uphold the nationalist narrative in music: Sibelius in Finland, Smetana in the Czech Republic, Debussy and Ravel in France, Copland and Ives in America, Albéniz and de Falla in Spain, and Glinka and the Mighty Five in Russia. By the 1880s and 1890s, when Scriabin emerged onto the international scene, such nationalistic indexes had become compulsory. Absent a figure like Gustav Mahler (1860–1911), who earned fame as much for his skills as a conductor as for his abilities as a composer, very few early twentieth-century composers received recognition as major players in music history without being card-carrying members of a fraternity of composers like the Russian nationalists.

The historiography of early twentieth-century music has been dominated by these "isms" or "schools" of composers: impressionism, neo-classicism, expressionism, serialism, and nationalism. To take a contemporary example of a school of composers, consider the Second Viennese School, headed by the German composer Arnold Schoenberg (1874–1951). (The First Viennese School consisted of Haydn, Mozart, and Beethoven, three composers who never studied together and who cultivated unique styles, but are also considered a triumvirate.) Schoenberg was two years younger than Scriabin, and independently developed a method of organizing pitches that was not based on the tonal system. His prize pupils were Alban Berg and Anton Webern, and although each man developed a distinct style, collectively they are known as the Second Viennese School. Although Scriabin's music inspired many imitators, especially his late works, no figure developed his style to a degree that historians recognized as a bona fide compositional school.[9] The surfeit of Scriabin imitators was so rampant by the mid-1920s that the critic Carl Engel bemoaned, "Whether it be Leonid Sabaneiev [sic], or A. Shaposhinko, or D. Melkikh, or E. Pavlov—everywhere the same perfumed grief and impotent raving, the chromatic worming of inner voices and the furious assaults that come to naught."[10] The Russian musicologist Boris Asafiev believed that Scriabin's style was so utterly original and fully developed that following the path he laid could only lead to blind imitation. Nicolas Slonimsky translated Boris Schloezer's monograph on the composer, and similarly believed that the composer's genius was inimitable: "Scriabin remains an isolated figure in modern music. Not a single composer, in Russia or elsewhere, has picked up the musical thread of Scriabin's unique art."[11] But without the distinction of being associated with an ism or founding a school of his own, Scriabin was seen by latter-day historians as an outlier among the tastemakers.[12]

It is hard to underestimate the pressure that Russian composers of Scriabin's generation faced to uphold nationalist traditions in the late nineteenth century. Few scholars have articulated the prejudices of nationalism in Russian music as perceptively and candidly as the musicologist Richard Taruskin, professor of music scholarship at the University of California, Berkeley. Taruskin's interpretation of the nationalist paradigm in Russian music takes as its basis the anthropological ideal of the noble savage:

> A Russian composer in the art music tradition is assumed (or rather, doomed) to create, because he is Russian, in the manner of a peasant singer—not by effort or art but by instinct. . . . While one can affect admiration, even a sort of envy, for such an artist

on the romantic or neoprimitivist assumption that what is unmediated by civilization is imbued with spontaneous authenticity, such admiration is laced with condescension. Mr. Natural, with his biologically inherited attitudes, can have only a group identity. Stripped of that identity, he is stripped of all authenticity.[13]

In no body of art was the nationalist paradigm applied with such severity as in Russian music. In his 1939 Charles Eliot Norton lecture at Harvard, Stravinsky reproached this long-standing bias when he protested, "Why do we always hear Russian music spoken in terms of its Russianness rather than simply in terms of music?"[14] Yet as we saw at the beginning of this chapter, Stravinsky is guilty of the same nationalist prejudices about Scriabin.[15] Nearly sixty years later, the historian Marina Frolova-Walker questioned, "Is there some peculiar shortcoming afflicting Russian music that prevents us from discussing it except in terms of nationality?"[16] The reason is that the progenitors of Russian music propagandized a nationalist ideology that by Stravinsky's day had become dogma. Its founding fathers were Mikhail Glinka (1804–1857) and a group of composers known as the Mighty Handful, Mighty Five, or *Moguchaya kuchka* (occasionally shortened to just *kuchkists*). Glinka set the tone for Russian composers by using nationalistic themes long before Socialist Realism demanded it in the 1930s. The composition that became the touchstone for Russian musical style is Glinka's *Kamarinskaya*, a theme and variations based on two folk dances. Likewise, Glinka's *A Life for the Tsar* (1836) is a heroic-tragic opera that celebrates the sacrifice made by an actual historical figure to save the first tsar-elect of the Romanov dynasty. Composers working in the generation after Glinka continued these traditions and drew from their cultural heritage to distinguish themselves from their European counterparts. John Bell Young wrote of the stylistic glue that bonded this group: "the Five espoused pan-orientalism as the measure of their cultural heritage. Though they harvested the folk music of Turkestan and Kirghizia, Georgia and the Caucasus for melismatic models, they were careful not to neglect the vast reservoir of Slavic liturgical music."[17] There was no question that these stylistic markers would be observed by Russian composers. Anything less would be a betrayal of one's national roots.

Understandably, Scriabin's disinterest in adopting these cultural traditions drew accusations of antinationalism, or at least cosmopolitanism, especially in his homeland. In 1909, only a year after the *Poem of Ecstasy* had been published, the Moscow critic Yuli Engel (1868–1927) marveled that Scriabin's music contained "not even a vestige of so-called 'Russian style.'" Whereas "a symphony by [Vasily] Kalinnikov gives away the country where it saw the light of day all by itself," a symphony by Scriabin "tells you nothing on that subject. When listening to it, one is just as entitled to suspect that it carries the stamp 'Made in Germany' as 'Made in Russia,' or for that matter any other stamp."[18] While Engel's critique speaks more on Scriabin's cosmopolitanism than on his antinationalism, other critics like the Russian-born German Lovtsky were less objective in their assessments. Lovtsky took issue with

Scriabin's deficient Russianness in the Soviet journal *Sovremennye zapiski* (Contemporary Notes, 1921). Lovtsky's vitriol demonstrates the sort of reductive reasoning that led to Scriabin's castigation as an outsider:

> There was not in him even an imitation of nationalism, as was the case with Tchaikovsky, and he stood apart—and probably felt himself so—among the composers of the purely nationalist Russian school who were grouped around M. P. Bielaeff [*sic*]. The Russian folk-songs, that inexhaustible treasury of great national spirit, did not exercise upon Scriabine even an indirect influence. The Russian nature was alien to him; he never attempted to paint it in sounds. What remains of the national in Scriabine then? Only the circumstance that he was born in Russia.[19]

The lack of specific compositional techniques associated with Russian style is what dissenters like Lovtsky found fault with in Scriabin's music. Even supporters like Engel could not deny the composer's stylistic similarities with Wagner, which did little to promote a Russian nationalist agenda. Once it had been applied, the antinationalist label stuck.

Scriabin deeply resented any accusations of antinationalism. In a heated exchange with Beliaev, he screamed, "Is it possible that I am not a Russian composer merely because I don't write overtures and capriccios on Russian themes!?"[20] Scriabin also defended himself to Boris Asafiev, Russia's preeminent musicologist, arguing that, "Russian music is not confined to the narrow ranks of 'nationalism,' in the sense that Western Europe means the word. It is of course nationalistic, but all the same it has to breathe the atmosphere of internationalism."[21] Scriabin saw nationalism not as a tradition to faithfully uphold, but as a barrier or constraint to surpass and overcome. So strong was his desire to overcome the bonds of nationalism that it led him to criticize his former idol, Chopin, in a 1910 interview as limited in artistic scope because the Pole had been "crushed by nationalism."[22] His critics and his peers did not agree, however, and many jumped on the bandwagon of antinationalism. In a 1919 interview, Rachmaninov scoffed that, "Scriabin is quite un-Russian" and argued that his late works "belong to a musical 'No-man's-land.' While they have added notably to his reputation for eccentricity, they have not enhanced his repute for true musical constructiveness."[23] These were harsh words from a man who only four years earlier had toured throughout Russia performing Scriabin-only recitals in tribute of his former classmate, who had died suddenly in 1915. When handed an opportunity to voice his opinion, however, Rachmaninov revealed his true feelings, or perhaps just sided with the majority opinion. Similar snipes came from Stravinsky, who famously snubbed Scriabin as a renegade artist "without a passport."[24] Sabaneev took issue with Stravinsky's glib dismissal of Scriabin, and retorted that, "there is far more of the typical Russian in [Scriabin] than in the precise and calculated creative work of Stravinsky."[25] The fact that these countrymen who knew Scriabin personally thought of his music in this way shows how deeply entrenched the nationalist bias had become.

In the Western literature on Russian music and on Scriabin in general, such insults and dismissals are even more derogatory. Historian Richard Leonard cast some of the most vicious aspersions against Scriabin, in full compliance with nationalistic biases:

> Scriabin is hardly a Russian composer at all, so strongly is his music turned away from nationalism and toward the West. He had little affinity for the nationalist movement, ignored almost totally the use of folk song, and was at the opposite pole aesthetically from the concept of realism in art.[26]

Gerald Abraham likewise considered Scriabin's music "outside the main current of Russian art."[27] Latter-day scholars like Robert Morgan were also puzzled by the composer's disinterest in nationalist traditions. In his 1991 survey of twentieth-century music (another popular text in music history courses), Morgan seemed surprised that, "Curiously, Skryabin was not himself nationalist in orientation."[28] Even Scriabin's apologists could not recognize the Russian spirit in his music. The British music historian Alfred Swan wrote a heartfelt tribute in his 1923 book, but inexplicably concluded that Scriabin "could scarcely be called a Russian composer at all" because, "strangely, there are no typical Russian idiomatic expressions anywhere, either from folk-song or from chant." Although Western critics and historians were not confined by the same ideological constraints as Russian critics and composers, they were among the worst perpetrators of the nationalist bias against Russian music. By using the conventional methods of categorizing Russian music, these commentators were at a complete loss as to how to classify Scriabin's art.

Not everyone held such narrow views of Scriabin. Native Russians have long considered Scriabin as a national icon whose music is one of Russia's greatest treasures. Like most Russian-trained pianists, Sviatoslav Richter (1915–1997) studied Scriabin's music as a part of his education at the Moscow Conservatory. In a 1965 interview with Faubion Bowers, he spoke of Scriabin's music as a balsam for the soul and the lifeblood of his artistic heritage: "In Russia [Scriabin] is part of the mainstream of musical life . . . our heritage. We grow up with him, are nurtured by him, nourished by him. [Russians] absorb him, as soon as we are born."[29] Richter understood that Scriabin's Russian musical roots ran deeper than folk tunes and chant melodies. He also recognized that Russian nationalism was a historical fallacy that only served those who created it. A few latter-day writers shared Richter's perspective and recognized that Scriabin's Russian heritage shone through in other ways. Historian Larry Sitsky, for instance, identified Scriabin's fascination with the unexplained mysteries of life and the occult as key markers of his Russian roots: "The problem with Scriabin was that he was Russian not musically, but mystically."[30] Yet it was this quality of his music that Soviet policy makers frowned upon and scholars overlooked. These voices of reason, however, were drowned out by the prevailing orthodoxy of antinationalism.

One way of demonstrating the inherent Russian quality of Scriabin's art is to examine in closer detail the stylistic markers that have defined Russian music, and compare these identifiers to Scriabin's music. His music features many distinctive

Russian traits that are often overlooked by critics and historians. By highlighting these stylistic qualities, we can put the composer's historical position and legacy in a more appropriate and favorable context, and frame it as a product of a specific time and place in history.

EMBLEMS OF RUSSIAN MUSIC

What are the qualities or characteristics that make Russian music sound uniquely Russian? Providing a clear and concise definition can be a slippery slope, as it often leads to oversimplification. We can start by identifying the nonmusical elements commonly associated with Russian style. More often than not, Russian music is identified by these subjective descriptors more than by actual musical elements. Pervasive in Russian music is a fascination with myth and folklore, and the celebration of culture and place. There is a pronounced tendency for autobiographical confessionalism, especially in the music of romantics like Tchaikovsky and Rachmaninov. This sentimentality and melancholia stem from a longing for a distant past that exists only in the imagination. These qualities are rife in the poetic and musical literature, as well as in many Russian operas. Supernatural and folkloric elements also figure prominently, as exemplified in such works as Stravinsky's ballets, *Firebird* and *Petruschka*. Russian music is also routinely associated with heightened emotion, but in an early essay titled "Elements of Russian Music" (1928), Gerald Abraham argued that Russian music was marked by an overt *lack* of emotion. Abraham contended that "very little [Russian music] is inspired by erotic (or other) emotion, and still less by psychological self-analysis."[31] In this respect, Scriabin's works (along with those of Tchaikovsky and Rachmaninov) are clear exceptions to the rule. But other quintessential Russian traits that Abraham identified, including brevity and directness of expression, are prominent in Scriabin's music.

The musicologist Anatole Leikin identified other distinctive Russian qualities found in Scriabin's music, including references to the occult and folklore, and the *bytovoi romans*, or urban romance style. The *bytovoi romans* was popular in Russia in the late nineteenth century, and was a domestic art song that depicted real-life subjects. In using this term, Leikin had in mind the salon works of Scriabin's youth, which were delicate and refined, and which displayed a markedly indoor quality. Russian critics like Engel also remarked upon its salonlike style. To Engel, Scriabin's music represented "The city, four walls, the refined and complicated moods of the 'upper most ten thousand'—that is the sphere of [Scriabin's] art."[32] Leikin pointed out that Scriabin's "later compositions lost their connection with Russian romance-like vocalism, a fact that has provided additional ammunition to those who have argued for Scriabin's lack of Russian character."[33] Matthew Bengtson, however, would have us believe otherwise. In chapter 11 on line and melody, he presents a compelling case for melody as one of the building blocks of Scriabin's compositional approach, even in so-called atonal works like the Prelude Op. 74 No. 4. These aspects of Scriabin's Russianness were intrinsically linked to his creative impulse; he simply expressed it in nontraditional ways.

In musical terms, we have seen how Russian music has been defined by superficial qualities like the modal melodies and rhythms of folk tunes and Orthodox chants. But other stylistic markers are readily apparent, including colorful and brilliant orchestrations, odd-length phrases and quintuple meters (e.g., the Bridal Chorus in Glinka's *A Life for the Tsar*, or the Promenade from Mussorgsky's *Pictures at an Exhibition*). Also of great significance is a compositional principle known as voice-leading, which refers to the smooth transitions between notes in the melodies and inner voices. Scriabin mastered the voice-leading technique during his studies at the Moscow Conservatory with Glazunov and Taneyev, and his adeptness at this technique is displayed in such works as the *Divine Poem* and *Prometheus: Poem of Fire*.[34] These stylistic markers are ubiquitous in Scriabin's music, but they are often buried beneath the musical surface and less obvious to the casual observer. Nevertheless, these Russian qualities permeate Scriabin's works.

Richard Taruskin has also pointed out Russian composers' tendency to repeat ideas, a quality that is pronounced in Russian music and poetry, and which Taruskin refers to as *drobnost*, "an untranslatable Russian word that denotes the quality of being a sum-of-parts."[35] Scriabin's teacher, Rimsky-Korsakov, was roundly criticized for using the sort of patterned repetition one finds throughout Scriabin's music, such as even-length phrases of two or four bars that are transposed to another key, but otherwise replicated wholesale. Compared to the Austro-German method of composing, which is prized for its techniques of developing variation and the "composing out" of motivic fragments, Scriabin's tendency to repeat sections and transpose large stretches of musical material to a different key struck many critics and scholars as a simple cut and paste job.[36] But Gerald Abraham explained that "Such thinking in sound—*progressive* thinking—is not the Russian's way of going about things; his mental process is more akin to brooding, a continual turning over of ideas in his mind, viewing them from different angles, throwing them against strange and fantastic backgrounds, but never evolving anything from them."[37] Hugh Macdonald similarly identified Scriabin's "characteristically Russian tendency to pursue an idea, once embraced, with unswerving ardor . . . His Russianness is inescapable."[38] Such an approach to composition was not simple laziness or ineptitude on the part of Russian composers, but a systematic approach and compositional aesthetic they learned from training in Russian conservatories. Yet even these descriptions offer limited information about what makes Russian music sound truly unique.

To gain a better understanding of what makes Russian music sound the way it does, we must wade briefly into the waters of music theory. One harmonic peculiarity that is distinct to Russian music, and which supplies Scriabin's middle-period works with their strange evocative quality, is the use of the sharpened fifth in a dominant chord. In a 1939 book, Abraham drew attention to this harmonic element as a uniquely Russian trait, and he traced the roots of this harmony to Glinka, Russia's first great composer. This Russian spice lends works like *Kamarinskaya* (1848) their exotic flavor, and it is prominent in the music of noted Russians like the Mighty Five.[39] Examples of the sharpened fifth abound in Scriabin's middle-period works like the *Poem of Ecstasy* and *Désir* Op. 57 No. 1. In these pieces, the signature sonority consists of a dominant ninth chord with a raised fifth, anchored over a tonic bass, as shown in figure 12.9 in chapter 12 on harmony. To play this chord on a piano (in the key of C major), play a C octave in the bass, and with your right hand, strike a dominant ninth chord with the raised fifth (D♯), consisting of the notes G-B-D♯-F-A. (N.B. The chord sounds best with the A as the top note.) This delicious mixture of tension from a dominant harmony and resolution (tonic in the bass) supplies works like the *Poem of Ecstasy* with their titillating emotional quality and distinct Russian flavor.

Two other essential Russian scales are common to Scriabin's late music, and can be traced to the *kuchkists* as well as Scriabin's teacher, Rimsky-Korsakov. These are the octatonic scale, which alternates half and whole steps, and the whole-tone scale.[40] Rimsky-Korsakov was the first Russian composer to explore the potential of the octatonic scale. So prevalent was this symmetrical collection among the St. Petersburg composers who gathered around Rimsky-Korsakov that it became known as the *Korsakovskaya gamma*, or Korsakovian scale. Not surprisingly, the octatonic scale is used to great effect in Stravinsky's rambunctious and colorful ballets like the *Rite of Spring* and *Petrushka*. Scriabin discovered the octatonic scale through his encounters with the St. Petersburg composers who worked with Rimsky-Korsakov, and it lends such works as the Seventh Sonata Op. 64, his Prelude Op. 74 No. 4, and other late works their otherworldly quality.[41] Much the same could be said of the whole-tone scale, which is typically thought of as a French trait due to its use in Debussy's so-called Impressionistic works. But it is also a predominant element of Russian musical style, and dates back to Glinka. It is typically used in operatic passages to denote sorcery or fantasy, and thus functions as a trope of musical exoticism.[42] Scriabin's preoccupation in his later years with symmetrical scales like the octatonic and whole-tone collection could be cited as another typical Russian trait. An abundance of theoretical literature goes into greater detail about Scriabin's use of these scales, but this cursory coverage offers specific examples of quintessential Russian traits that Scriabin used in his music.

Scriabin was a distinct product of his unique time and place in history. In spite of his cosmopolitanism and the European influences of Wagner, Liszt, and Chopin, he naturally fell under many of the same cultural influences as his contemporaries Rachmaninov, Medtner, Stravinsky, and Prokofiev, both in terms of style and technique. To some degree, the influence of Russian culture was inescapable, yet each composer filtered these influences in unique ways. A man of few words, Rachmaninov simplified this matter: "I am a Russian composer, and the land of my birth has influenced my temperament and outlook. My music is the product of my temperament, and so it is Russian music."[43] Although we have no such sworn statement from Scriabin, the same rule applies. Recent scholarship has started to overturn this long-standing bias in Scriabin's reception. Taruskin confirmed that, "Although it is customary to regard

Scriabin as an anomalous outsider to Russian 'national' traditions in music—even to think we have somehow characterized him by categorizing him so—in fact his music was morphologically akin to that of his Russian contemporaries to an extent that has yet to be adequately measured, but was undoubtedly very great."[44] To follow Taruskin's directive and recognize these pervasive influences, we must look beyond purely musical influences and poetic descriptors, and consider more subtle markers of Russian culture that stem from the atmosphere where these composers lived, breathed, and worked.

OMNIPRESENT RUSSIAN BELLS

We have outlined many musical traits that distinguish Russian music, but perhaps the quintessential Russian quality in Scriabin's music is his evocation of bells. A rich tradition of bell sounds permeates Russian culture and dates back to the fifteenth century. These chiming, clanging sonorities resonated in Russian life during Scriabin's lifetime, and they punctuate his orchestral and piano music. The music historian Boris Schwarz observed that for Russians, bells signify all that is "joyous, ominous, alarming, and beautiful—part of the gamut of emotions the spirit or soul must pass through before the final attainment of ecstasy."[45] Since instruments are forbidden in the Orthodox Church, bells provide the only sonic medium between humans and the divine. They were not merely musical instruments, but the sounds of the heavens. Bells hold deep spiritual significance for Orthodox Russians. Every major function, whether social, political, religious, or secular was heightened in importance by bell ringing. Struck bells symbolize memory or nostalgia; consider the saying that something "rings a bell" when you recall its significance or meaning. Bells also signify the passing of time by marking events like births, deaths, and weddings, and passage into the afterlife. They were even used to ward off evil spirits. Bells function as a general symbol of human experience, but they are given particular weight in Russian culture. As a monument to the importance of bells in Russian life, on the Kremlin grounds sits the largest bell in the world, Tsar Kolokol (Tsar's Bell, completed in 1735), which measures twenty feet high by twenty-two feet wide, and weighs in at 216 tons of pure bronze. Tsar Kolokol was never rung, but it honors the rich tradition of bell founding and bell ringing in Russian culture. The sheer ubiquity of bells in Russian life made them an inescapable influence for every Russian composer.

Nowhere did the sound of pealing bells saturate the Russian air more than in Scriabin's birthplace of Moscow. By the late nineteenth century, over 1,600 onion-shaped belfries dotted the Moscow skyline. Bells pealed out all day, lending an aural pulse to Russia's capital city. In his recollections, Rachmaninov recalled the strong impression that bells left upon him while growing up: "The sound of church bells dominated all the cities of the Russia I used to know: Novgorod, Kiev, and Moscow. They accompanied every Russian from infancy to the grave, and no composer could escape from their influence. . . . This love for bells is inherent in every Russian."[46] For the first seventeen years of the twentieth century in Russia, the period in which Scriabin lived and worked, bells experienced a golden age in production and usage. After the Bolshevik Revolution of 1917, however, much of that cultural heritage met with a violent end. During the war years, many priceless and historic bells were destroyed or melted down for raw materials, and lost forever. Years later, some bells were tracked down by preservationists and returned to their rightful positions alongside their companion bells. The tumult and upheaval of the political transitions in Russia temporarily diminished the importance of bells in Russian life. Those who survived these difficult times, like Rachmaninov, drew strength and courage from their rich memories of these clanging church bells, which had provided the soundtrack to their childhood.

In musical terms, Russian bells differ in many ways from their Western counterparts. European bells are tuned on a lathe to produce a specific pitch in the tempered scale, but Russian bells are cast to elicit an individual sound. Russian bells can approximate pitches in the tempered scale, but the most interesting and unique bells have tones that lie in the cracks between the notes. Timbre is of prime importance in bell founding. The more individual the quality of tone, the more it is valued. The emphasis placed on uniqueness of tone is evidenced by the fact that Russian bells are often given proper names and treated as animate objects. Russian bells are typically cast in bronze, which lends each bell a deeply resonant sound that is enriched by the overtones of the fundamental tone. The process of ringing Russian bells is an art form that involves different rhythmic patterns and groupings of bells, depending on the occasion. Russian bells are rarely heard alone, and their collective sound, or *zvon*, emits pulsating waves of sound, from rapidly repeating high-pitched bells to slower moving gongs. This unique counterpoint of sound has a hypnotic effect. The *zvon* is considered one of the most important properties of Russian bells. Considering the importance of bells in Russian life, it is improbable to imagine that Scriabin could not have been influenced by their religious and cultural symbolism as well as their constant clattering in Moscow.

Listening to nineteenth-century Russian music with this bell association in mind lets us hear some familiar passages in new ways. Many famous works in the Russian orchestral catalogue include prominent parts for actual bells, like the Coronation scene in Mussorgsky's opera *Boris Godunov* (1873) and Alexander Borodin's perennially popular opera *Prince Igor* (1890). In both works, struck bells draw the listener's attention to major events in the plot and heighten the musical drama. Similarly, in Rimsky-Korsakov's opera, *The Legend of the Invisible City of Kitezh and the Maiden Fevroniya* (1905), struck bells heard on and off stage symbolize the opposing worlds of reality and fantasy. Among Russian composers, Rachmaninov readily admitted the enduring influence of bells on his music. One of his most beloved compositions (and his personal favorite) was the symphonic poem *The Bells* Op. 35 (1913), with text based on a poem by Edgar Allen Poe and translated into Russian by the Symbolist poet Konstantin Balmont. Scriabin included bells into his First Symphony, but omitted them in his Second and Third Symphonies. With *Poem of Ecstasy* and *Prometheus*, however, bells assumed an even greater role, and added a distinctly Russian touch to his music. The ubiquitous presence of bells in Scriabin's music shows his adoption of common cultural traits from the society in which he lived. Indeed, these traits may have even been unconsciously adopted.

Bell sounds on the piano will always be imitative, and that limitation inspired composers to devise some ingenious solutions. Liszt's solo piano showpiece, *La Campanella* (Little Bell, 1851), is a transcription of a work by the virtuoso violinist Niccolò Paganini (1782–1840), and it offers a classic example of bell imitations. The "little bell" referred to in the title of this theme and variations is the memorable pinging of a high D♯ repeatedly struck by the pianist's right-hand pinky. Often the intrinsic musical beauty of these passages is so striking that the association with bells goes unnoticed. A case in point is the opening bars of Rachmaninov's Second Piano Concerto in C minor Op. 18, where the pendulum-like oscillation between fistfuls of notes in the piano's middle register and deep low F's in the left hand evokes tolling bells, as shown in figure 7.1. In this passage, one of the most famous in the concerto repertoire, Rachmaninov carefully marks *tenutos* over each chord and over the low F's in the bass, instructing the performer to bring out the maximum sustain from these tones.

Figure 7.1. Tolling Russian bells in Rachmaninov, Piano Concerto No. 2 in C minor, Mvt. I, mm. 1–8.

Taking stock of the techniques other pianist-composers used to imitate bell sounds provides a historical context for Scriabin's use of this mimetic device in his solo piano music. One of the most well-known evocations of bells in Russian piano music is in the final movement of Mussorgsky's *Pictures at an Exhibition*, "The Great Gate of Kiev," which begins and ends with jubilant church bells. Two other techniques used by nineteenth-century pianist-composers to imitate bells include a rocking metrical pulse like a timepiece, and imitations of echoes or reverberations. Not surprisingly, examples of these are found in the music of Liszt, one of Scriabin's pianistic idols. *Les cloches de Genève* (Bells of Geneva, 1855) is a product of Liszt's Swiss years from his musical travel logs, *Années de pèlerinage* (Years of Pilgrimage). *Les cloches de Genève* is a Nocturne or night piece. Bells are imitated by the chiming grace notes that decorate the main melody as well as offbeat chords struck in a low

Figure 7.2. Clocklike bells in Liszt, *Les cloches de Genève*, mm. 23–27. *Musikalische Werke*, ed. José Vianna da Motta. Leipzig: Breitkopf & Härtel, 1916.

register, complete with the reverberating effect of echoes fading into the distance (see figure 7.2).[47] Rachmaninov used a similar registral technique in his immortal Prelude in C♯ minor Op. 3 No. 2 (1874), a work that drips with Russian melancholia and which brought the composer overnight fame. Dubbed the "Bells of Moscow" by a publisher, the work's foreboding opening foreshadows the opening of the Second Piano Concerto, with its thick middle-register chords punctuated by low notes in the bass, as shown in figure 7.3.[48]

Figure 7.3. Russian bells in Rachmaninov, Prelude in C♯ minor Op. 3 No. 2, mm. 1–4. "Bells of Moscow." Moscow: Muzyka, eds. Pavel Lamm and Konstantin Igumnov, n.d.

Scriabin was no different from these composers in his fondness for bell sounds and his incorporation of them into his piano music. Bell sounds found their most natural expression in his solo piano music, especially the piano sonatas, and these bell sounds make their appearance in the First Sonata in F minor Op. 6. The piece was written during a spiritual crisis when the composer injured his right hand and feared that his performing career was over. Tolling bells dominate the fourth movement, a funeral march for the death of his bright future. Low octaves in the left hand provide a droning, insistent beat that suggests a forced march, and a repeated figure oscillates between two notes a half step apart, adding to the sense of foreboding gloom, as shown in figure 7.4. Tinkling bell sounds also appear in the Third Sonata Op. 23, especially in the captivating third movement, which pianist Mark Meichik

Figure 7.4. Tolling bells in Piano Sonata No. 1 in F minor Op. 6, Mvt. IV, mm. 16–19.

(who delivered the world premiere of Scriabin's Fifth Sonata) had the privilege of hearing the composer perform. Meichik noted that when the composer played this movement, "the melody carried in the left hand sounded exactly like ringing silver bells glinting in light."[49]

Bell-like sonorities complement other works, such as the secondary theme of the Fifth Sonata Op. 53, where a clangorous sonority is struck on a cadential point and the resultant notes spill over in a wash of sound in the manner of Liszt's *Les cloches de Genève*, as shown in the third and fourth bars of figure 12.12 in chapter 12 on harmony. Other early piano works of Scriabin's that feature bell sounds include the Prelude Op. 11 No. 1 in C major, which features a joyous clattering of repetitive falling notes that flutter above booming bass gongs. A similar impression of bells clanging in panoramic fashion is found in the final phrases of Scriabin's Prelude Op. 37 No. 2 as well as his Prelude Op. 13 No. 1, which is designated "Moscow, November 1895" and sounds like a festival of bells. Similar moments of resounding bell sounds are found in the Impromptu Op. 12 No. 2 and the Mazurka Op. 25 No. 8, particularly in the *sotto voce* section. His unfinished *Mysterium* would have been the ultimate application of bells in his music. Participants from across the world were to be summoned to this apocalyptic rite in the Himalayas by bells hanging from clouds. But the bells in the *Mysterium* not only served as a proverbial call to prayer. In their ability to mediate between the material and spiritual planes, they served as key elements in the composer's scheme to transfigure humanity through his art. Sabaneev tells us that Scriabin also intended bell sounds to be used at the opening of his Prefatory Act, which he described as a "Brassy, sinister, and fateful harmony, like a 'final warning' before the end of humanity, prepared for the terrible and ecstatic hour of ultimate reunion."[50]

Scriabin invariably labels bell-like passages in his scores with characteristic identifiers, which makes them easy to spot. His later sonatas all contain imitations of bell sounds in various guises, and invariably he marks these passages with the words "*mysterieux*," "*mystérieusement sonore*," or some variant thereof. The Sixth Sonata, that house of horrors, takes as its foundational sonority a widely spaced gonglike chord and its echoing afterthought. Fittingly, Scriabin marks this chord "*mystérieux*," as shown in figure 7.5. Scriabin uses dissonance to suggest the clanging of Russian bells, much

Figure 7.5. Clanging bells in Sonata No. 6 Op. 62, mm. 1–5. Berlin: Édition Russe de Musique, 1912.

like Mussorgsky did in the "Great Gate of Kiev." But instead of a jubilant celebration, bell sounds in Scriabin's Sixth Sonata are séancelike, and summon spirits from other worlds. Of Scriabin's ten sonatas, the Seventh Sonata Op. 64 is the most evocative of bells sounds. John Bell Young suggested that this music specifically evokes the bells of Yegoryevsk, an industrial city that lies roughly seventy miles southeast of Moscow. The composer's son-in-law, Vladimir Sofronitsky, described the opening pages of the Seventh Sonata as "the last bell ring, the universal catastrophe. The bells forebode this, in these is the Apocalypse. And the tempi should not be that fast. The Sonata is a most threatening one."[51] Other late works, like the first of *Deux Poèmes* Op. 71 and (to some people's ears) *Vers la flamme* Op. 72, also evoke clanging bell sounds, which adds to the mystery and mysticism of these late piano pieces.

There are many riches to explore in the tradition of bell sounds in Russian classical music, and in Scriabin's music in particular. Samuel Randlett, an authority on Scriabin's piano music, observed that, "Russian bells and Oriental gongs seem to pulsate through much of Scriabin's piano music; the Seventh Sonata treats the piano essentially as a kind of gamelan orchestra, a family of gongs."[52] Such sonic analogies allow us to hear his music in new ways, provided that the performer emphasizes this aspect of the music in their interpretation. In many ways, bells are the quintessential Russian sound, and they embody the contradictions of Russian life, with its contrast between centuries-old religious traditions and practices, and the frantic pace of modern life.

Accusations of antinationalism may have blighted Scriabin's legacy, but today we can recognize that the composer adapted earlier traditions and built upon them in order to discover his unique compositional voice. Scriabin's music strove for denationalization, or perhaps even supra-nationalization, but that is not necessarily a fault or shortcoming. Scriabin simply filtered these stylistic traits and influences to arrive at his own interpretation of the modern Russian sound.

* * *

RUSSIAN SYMBOLISM AND IVANOV

Establishing Scriabin's Russian roots also lends context to another virulent myth in his reception, noted at the beginning of this chapter. We have seen the remarks of non-Russian critics and historians who portrayed Scriabin as a lone wolf who was lost in his own world. This image of Scriabin working in isolation from his peers ignores a rich body of literature that has emerged since the early 1970s, which conclusively demonstrates his affinity with the Russian Symbolist poets and painters of his era.[53] These findings normalize Scriabin's belief in an underlying social unrest from which he sought salvation, as well as his conviction that redemption could only come via art, especially his own music. Many other Symbolists in Russia and Europe held similar views of art and aesthetics in the early twentieth century. A greater awareness of Scriabin's affinities with the Russian Symbolists of his generation provides a more comprehensive view of his creative thought and artworks than citing Theosophy as a lone influence. Examining the key figures of Russian Symbolism and their philosophical aims will illuminate Scriabin's unique place in the history of Russian culture.

During the Russian Silver Age, the era in which Scriabin lived, Symbolism ranked as one of the most influential aesthetic movements. The Silver Age roughly spanned the years 1898, when the arts journal *Mir Iskusstva* (World of Art) was first published, to 1914 when World War I broke out. Symbolism's practitioners were poets, philosophers, and painters. Scriabin was the only professional musician among the group, which explains why he is not often aligned with that movement in history. Its main figureheads were poets, the foremost of whom was the Russian poet Alexander Blok (1880–1921). The Symbolists of Scriabin's generation were divided into the materialists and the mystics. Given his admiration for Nietzsche, it is no surprise that Scriabin sided with the mystic Symbolists. He developed close friendships with the Symbolist poets Konstantin Balmont (1857–1918), Vyacheslav Ivanov (1866–1949), and Jurgis Baltrušaitis (1873–1944), and he gave serious consideration to their opinions of poetry and philosophy. In turn, the Symbolist poets thought of Scriabin, in the words of the musicologist Richard Taruskin, as the "most potent, and most 'essentially Russian' of them all."[54] Scriabin's compatibility with the Russian Symbolists was well recognized by his composer contemporaries, which makes it all the more curious that latter-day historians took so long to make the connection.[55]

What united the Russian Symbolists in spirit and purpose was their desire to transform life through art. In this theurgic aim, Scriabin's bond with the Symbolists was undeniable. They saw the creation of art as a religious act and believed that it was the only path to spiritual enlightenment. The Russian Symbolists considered artists to be high priests, and they wanted to elect them as societal leaders. In the Symbolist code of values, the artist is a prophet who reveals the "more real" world that is unseen by the uninitiated. This notion of a "more real" world can be traced to ancient Greek times, when Plato first proposed that the material world was an approximation or imperfect copy of a better world, which he referred to as the "really real." The clues and symbols of this veiled world, which Plato wrote about in *The Republic* around

360 B.C.E., are deeply woven into the fabric of everyday reality, but the common man was ill-equipped to apprehend this higher plane of existence. Anyone who has seen one of the *Matrix* films written by Lilly and Lana Wachowski can appreciate this idea of our world as a projection of a false reality. Revealing this hidden or "more real" world was the core aesthetic of Russian Symbolist art and the primary thrust of Scriabin's mature music.

Scriabin embraced Russian Symbolism shortly before he returned from Switzerland to live in Russia in 1910. After being exposed to various philosophies that were fashionable across Europe, including Theosophy, Rosacrusianism, Nietzscheism, and Freemasonry, he discovered in Russian Symbolism "the compatible doctrine he craved," according to the historian Malcolm Brown.[56] Scriabin's approach to art after 1910 featured symbolic motives and figures that were modified from Wagner's leitmotif technique. These musical symbols were designed to trigger unconscious responses in his listeners.[57] Such a desire to transcend reality through a syncretic approach to art was common among the artists of his age. The first decades of the twentieth century witnessed anxiety and excitement over the dizzying development of technology and civilization. Eschatological beliefs and doomsday prophecies foretold the death of God and the end of the human race. Maria Carlson explained that during this time in history, "there was a frantic attempt to cope creatively with the decay of old cultural values, to escape creatively from the impending crisis of culture and consciousness, [and] to bridge the growing chasm between science and religion, reason and faith."[58] Symbolist artists seized the moment like a call to arms, and in this intense psychological climate they vowed to lead the people through this spiritual crisis to the next phase of human evolution. Symbolist art demanded apocalyptic, earth-shattering, all-or-nothing projects. Historian Louis Marvick explained that for mystic Symbolists such as Scriabin and Ivanov, "the apocalyptic work of art is the only one which it is possible to undertake; the completion of the true work of art *must* coincide with the end of the world."[59] According to Marvick, apocalyptic Symbolism was "the first truly modern aesthetic—a synthesis in the dialectic of intellectual history."[60]

Just as the poems of the French Symbolists Charles Baudelaire, Stéphane Mallarmé, and Paul Verlaine left an indelible mark on French art music (especially in the works of Debussy and Fauré), the writings of the Russian Symbolist poets Vladimir Solovyov (1853–1900) and Vyacheslav Ivanov had a decisive impact on Scriabin's music and creative ideology.[61] Particularly resonant for Scriabin was Solovyov's theory that art harnessed Divine Will. Solovyov prophesized that "Art must have a real force, enlightening and regenerating the entire human world."[62] In creating transcendent and redemptive art, Russian Symbolist artists utilized ancient languages, codes, and symbols to reveal unknown or hidden realities. Painters created intensely personalized interpretations of scenes from literature, mythology, and their own nightmares to project a hyper-real vision of the world. Scriabin referred to this state of mystic transcendence as "ecstasy." This metaphysical uplift blurred the lines between spiritual and physical love. Ecstasy became a central theme in Scriabin's philosophical musings and public artworks like the *Poem of Ecstasy*. Scriabin's concept of ecstasy is closely associated with Dionysian eroticism, and it is experienced most viscerally in his harmonies, which ratchet up the tension of the dominant-tonic relationship to dramatic heights.[63] Suggestions of ecstasy are also represented in the poetic performance markings in his scores. For Scriabin, achieving ecstasy meant breaking through the material world and accessing this higher reality, where his inner godlike power could be fully realized.

The leader of the mystic poets of Scriabin's generation and the composer's close friend was Vyacheslav Ivanov, who coined the rally cry for the Symbolist movement: *a realibus ad realiora* (from reality to a higher reality).[64] In a 1910 essay, Ivanov articulated a credo for the Russian Symbolist aesthetic. It served to clarify the movement's aims and focus his thoughts on the subject. In his view, mystic Symbolist art revealed a

> parallelism between the phenomenal and noumenal, consciously expressed by the artist; a harmony between what art depicts as external reality (realia) and what it sees through the external, as an internal and higher reality (realiora); the naming of correspondences and relationships between the appearance (which is "only a parable," "nur Gleichnis") and its essence (comprehended rationally or mystically), which casts a shadow of the visible event.[65]

In taking as starting points the introspective views of truth and spirituality, as well as the betterment of the human condition, the Russian Symbolists departed from the positivists who trusted empiricism and science to verify their understanding of the world around them, and the Impressionists who were inspired by nature. To achieve life-altering Symbolist art, the artist must sacrifice himself to his art, and to this impossible ideal Scriabin became a "prophet and martyr to the cause," in the words of the musicologist Simon Morrison.[66]

Scriabin and Ivanov first met in December 1909, when the composer performed a recital at the offices of *Apollon*, a Symbolist journal that championed classical clarity, and was published from 1909–1917 in St. Petersburg. Ivanov was so enraptured with Scriabin's performance that he presented him with an inscribed copy of his new collection of writings, *Po zvezdam* (By the Stars, 1909).[67] From this initial meeting, Scriabin and Ivanov enjoyed a close camaraderie based on their mutual admiration of Wagner, the Dionysian/Apollonian duality, and ancient theater.[68] Ivanov was the person with whom Scriabin felt closest, and who best articulated the Symbolist message of transformative art. Scriabin confessed to Sabaneev that, "He's so close to me and my thought—like no one else."[69] Ivanov likewise considered his friendship with Scriabin a "profound and luminous event in my spiritual development."[70] It is not hard to imagine why Ivanov was so thrilled with Scriabin's performance that day in the offices of *Apollon*. The transcendent strains of his music combined with the composer's magical aura must have left a deep impression. The poet Nina Serpinskaia described the hypnotic effect that Scriabin's performances left upon listeners in these intimate settings: "with his music, Scriabin made everything around purer, deeper, more meaningful. Triviality fell silent and vanished. People who had grown cold, already unfit for any expansiveness in life, unwillingly opened themselves to the pathos of the author of the *Poem of Ecstasy*."[71]

Scriabin's magical playing and magnetic personality were not the only reasons Ivanov was so captivated. In the Russian Silver Age, music was considered the highest form of creativity, and the art form that held the greatest hope for social unity and spiritual salvation. Ivanov equated it with language and religion as one of the building blocks of civilization. He thought that music was the most synthetic of the arts due to its ability to accommodate speech, religion, dance, and virtually every other artistic medium. The music that Scriabin was writing around the time he met Ivanov, including the later sonatas and *Prometheus: Poem of Fire*, struck Ivanov as possessing the kind of Dionysian quality that could lead the Russian people to spiritual redemption.[72] Ivanov believed that music, and specifically Scriabin's music, was the key ingredient to ushering in spiritual renewal. Breaking down the boundaries that separated the arts and reuniting them into a collective whole was a topic of endless fascination among Silver Age artists. Scriabin and Ivanov would often spend long hours discussing the meaning of art and the role of the artist in society. The idea of reuniting the arts had been popularized by the German opera composer Richard Wagner, who posited his theory of a *Gesamtkunstwerk*, or total artwork, that would combine the various art forms into a transcendent art. Scriabin's unfinished *Mysterium* was to be the ultimate realization of that idea. Ivanov's idea of the Mystery or Symbolist apocalypse was based on Greek tragedy, whereas Scriabin adapted the Theosophical idea of spiritual evolution through seven astral planes. Another major difference of opinion between Scriabin and Ivanov is that Scriabin concerned himself very little with the practical considerations of his *Mysterium*. Scriabin's friends like Ivanov and Sabaneev had serious reservations about its feasibility and the composer's mental state, but most of their concerns were offset by their sheer fascination over his ambitious plans.

Far from depicting Scriabin as an isolated genius who was out of touch with reality, Ivanov believed that Scriabin's art defined the essence of the Russian spirit. He heralded Scriabin's arrival as the spiritual glue that would reunite the socially divided Russian people. Scriabin and Ivanov both agreed that humanity was on the cusp of a cosmic transfiguration that would bring about a collective unity, or *sobornost*. This idea of achieving social unity or solidarity was one of the key concerns in Russian life after the 1905 Revolution, when it became evident that the old social and political structures would soon collapse. When World War I broke out in the summer of 1914, their suspicions about the coming apocalypse seemed to be confirmed. For Ivanov, Scriabin's desire to bring salvation to the people through his art symbolized "the moment of universal self-determination on the part of the national Russian soul."[73] Far from seeing Scriabin as an "unclassifiable Russian composer," to repeat the words of Donald Grout, Scriabin's contemporaries considered him to be the quintessential artist of his generation.[74]

Ivanov's dream of social renewal was interrupted when Scriabin died suddenly in 1915. In true Symbolist fashion, he reasoned that Scriabin had fulfilled his Orphic mission to ascend to a higher plane of reality.[75] As a tribute to his late friend, Ivanov founded a memorial society called "Venok Skriabina" (Scriabin's Wreath), and delivered dozens of lectures at concerts and Scriabin Society meetings in the mid- to late 1920s. Five essays and eight poems flowed from Ivanov's pen after Scriabin's death. He took it as his personal mission to proselytize on the composer's behalf. Ivanov was an ideal spokesperson for Scriabin because of his eloquence and profundity. He well recognized the elusive quality of Scriabin's art, and likened it to "the flight of an arrow that has been shot right over the visible horizon and disappears so far away that we are powerless either to encompass or to measure with our eye the distance that has buried it."[76] He endeavored to make Scriabin's ideas and music more comprehensible to the common man. Ivanov's speeches made a profound impact on everyone who heard them. The esteemed St. Petersburg critic Vyacheslav Karatygin attended one of his lectures and marveled, "How could we expect that a pronouncement about a musician made by a person who has little to do with music would be nearly the most significant and meaningful thing that has been said or written so far about the creator of the *Poem of Ecstasy* and *Prometheus*?"[77] Ivanov's tireless efforts to maintain respect and enthusiasm for Scriabin's music and ideas while living in Russia and abroad kept the composer's memory alive and spread his life-affirming message. Ivanov earned permission to emigrate from the Soviet Union in 1920, and he eventually settled in Rome. He never returned to the USSR, but his reputation in his homeland remained in good standing. Fortunately, Ivanov never suffered the character defamation that befell other Russian emigrants like Sabaneev.

RELATED SYMBOLISTS: VRUBEL, CIURLIONIS, AND MALLARMÉ

Ivanov was hardly the only Symbolist of Scriabin's generation who pursued the ideal of transcendental art. Several Symbolist painters strove to create interdisciplinary artworks that rejected past standards and pushed the boundaries of self-expression. The outstanding Symbolists of the first generation of Silver Age painters (1890–1910) were Alexandre Benois (1870–1960) and Konstantin Somov (1869–1939), whose canvases focused on the historical (Benois) and the homoerotic (Somov). The second generation of Russian mystic Symbolist painters included Mikhail Nesterov (1863–1942) and the troubled painter and sculptor Mikhail Vrubel (1856–1910). Vrubel is probably the best known artist among this group, and his personal idiom blends elements of ancient Christian art and modern style. Yet each of these figures created Symbolist art that portrayed an inner reality and higher truth, and their activities provide illustrative parallels to Scriabin's own artistic endeavors.

In keeping with the apocalyptic fervor of the age, Scriabin and Vrubel were both fascinated by demonic forces, as evidenced in such works as the *Poème satanique* and the Sixth and Ninth Piano Sonatas. Scriabin and Vrubel both used the Devil as an important symbol in their work, and they envisioned Lucifer not as an evil antichrist, but as a positive force. For Scriabin, Lucifer was a Promethean light-bringer; for Vrubel, the Devil represented the human soul struggling against its instinctively rebellious nature.[78] Vrubel earned notoriety for a series of devilish canvases, the most celebrated of which are *Seated Demon* (1890), *Flying Demon* (1899), *Fallen Demon* (1901), and *Demon Downcast* (1902). The first of these paintings was inspired by a poem by Mikhail Lermontov titled "Demon" (1829–1839). It tells of an omnipotent demon who wanders a desolate forest, unable to use his miraculous powers. He attempts to gain redemption through the love of a mortal woman, but his kiss proves deadly and he realizes he can never escape his solitary fate. Such themes played into the popularity of satanic imagery in the late nineteenth century. Eroticized images of the Devil appeared regularly in publications. The famous operatic baritone Feodor Chaliapin built a stage career from his legendary portrayals of the Devil in Gounod's *Faust* (1859), Boito's *Mefistofele* (1868), and Anton Rubinstein's *Demon* (1871). Like Scriabin's mature music, Vrubel's infernal canvasses depict fantastical visions, dreams, and otherworldly scenes that seem to transcend reality.

The common aesthetic shared by Vrubel and Scriabin was their depiction of inner strength and a sense of the godlike within oneself. Such ideals were held up by Scriabin's Soviet biographers, who emphasized his progressive, robust spirit. In his 1971 biography of Scriabin, Viktor Delson drew explicit parallels between Scriabin's Second Symphony and Vrubel's *Demon* paintings, writing that "the first bars of the [Second] symphony immediately call to mind the tragic or severe image of hidden or bound mighty strength."[79] Indeed, the similarities between their artistic paths are striking. The Russian poet Alexander Blok spoke at Vrubel's grave on the day of his death, and he could have just as easily been eulogizing for Scriabin: "He left us his Demons to exorcise the violent evil and the night. What Vrubel and those like him reveal to mankind once a century, makes me tremble with awe. We don't see the worlds they have seen." In their mutually eccentric visions of an alternate reality and their embrace of the Devil as an allegorical figure who symbolized humanity's modern plight, Scriabin and Vrubel both created Symbolist artworks that testify to the intense psychological pressures faced by modern artists, who sought to reconcile past traditions with an avant-garde sensibility.

Just as the Russian Symbolist poets emphasized the rhythm and phonetic timbre of their verses, Symbolist painters created dynamic canvases that bore titles more commonly used for music. Exemplifying this trend was the Lithuanian painter, composer, and author Mikalojus Ciurlionis (1875–1911). Ciurlionis moved to St. Petersburg in 1909, and his fellow Symbolists embraced him as an innovative artist. Scriabin knew and admired Ciurlionis' works, but no evidence exists to support the opposite. A musical prodigy, Ciurlionis wrote around four hundred works for solo piano and was an excellent sight-reader (unlike Scriabin). Just as Scriabin titled his short piano pieces "Poèmes," Ciurlionis conceived of his visual artworks in terms of rhythm and tone color, and he "composed" paintings with titles like "Sonata,"

Fugue," and "Prelude." Ciurlionis and Scriabin also both admired the music of Chopin and explored systematic approaches to modal harmony, placing them at the vanguard of modern harmony. Owing to their similar artistic purpose and kinship, works by these two Symbolist artists are often paired together in galleries and concerts. Along with Ivanov's poems, the artworks of Ciurlionis demonstrate that Scriabin was not alone in his quest to create a synthetic art that would resonate with the society and culture in which he lived.[80]

A third and final contemporary who shared Scriabin's creative ambitions was the French Symbolist poet Stéphane Mallarmé (1842–1898). Mallarmé spent the last thirty years of his life working on a magnum opus that he called *Le Livre* (The Book), which was the culmination of his personal style and a testament to the power of Symbolist art. Like Scriabin's *Mysterium*, *Le Livre* was meant to be a performance rite lasting several days that would synthesize the various art forms into a unified whole. Its climax would bring about spiritual nirvana for its participants. Originally sketched as a Symbolist bible, Mallarmé later imagined it as a drama or "open" work of performance art. An obsession with the impending apocalypse was not the only commonality between Scriabin and Mallarmé. Like Vrubel, both men also closely linked colors and numbers, and they believed that the right combination of these two elements could unlock the secrets of the universe. Ultimately, the colossal scope of their visions and the authors' lack of mastery over all the art forms they wished to incorporate prevented them from completing their ambitious projects. But the similarity of their artistic aims leaves little doubt as to their kinship of thought and expression.

Symbolism had all of the guises of an ism or school of composers, but as the only professional musician among them, Scriabin was not seen by historians as a representative of that group. Insofar as crossing over from music into verse, Scriabin's attempts to write poetry in the Symbolist tradition never surpassed an amateur level. The contempt that the Symbolist poet Andrei Bely held for Scriabin shows that the Symbolists hardly thought of themselves as kindred spirits.[81] But the remarkable compatibility between Scriabin's creative ideology and that of other Symbolist artists of his generation shows him to be anything but a lonely spirit of his times. This network of like-minded artists and thinkers gave Scriabin a theoretical framework in which to base his ideas, to debate with others, and to refine his thoughts. Most importantly, situating his aesthetics among the Symbolists of his age lends a richer context to the Russian composer's experimental ideas, and shows him to be a distinct product of his time and place in history.

Two final takeaways conclude this chapter. First, we should not limit our focus to only Theosophy and Symbolism as major influences on Scriabin's music and ideas. Many other influences shaped his artistic reactions to the cultural events and political developments of his era. These topics await further exploration in future studies. From the Hindu philosophy of Vedanta to Rosicrucianism and Russian Orthodoxy, untold areas of investigation remain to be explored in order to supply a complete picture of Scriabin's musical and philosophical inspirations. Second and most importantly, instead of condemning Scriabin for his nonconformity to an ad-hoc historical group, or even for his eccentricity, we should celebrate his bold individuality. His unique brand of Russian Symbolism made a distinct contribution to early twentieth-century music. Perhaps now, a century after his death, Scriabin can rightfully hold a secure position in the historiography of Western music as a distinguished composer in the Russian Symbolist tradition.

8

The Revival in 1960s America

> *It would be terrible to remain nothing more than a composer of sonatas and symphonies
> . . . To be regarded merely as a musician would be the worst fate that could befall me.*
>
> —Alexander Scriabin[1]

Scriabin's supreme confidence in his creative powers convinced him that he could change the world through his art. While this megalomaniacal streak gave him the courage and conviction to create some of the twentieth century's most monumental compositions, it has long challenged writers to provide impartial assessments of his output. In his 1978 book, *Skryabin*, the musicologist Hugh Macdonald wrote on behalf of rationalists everywhere in his observation that, "It would be a pity if appreciation of the music required us to follow Skryabin into this world of cosmic hocus-pocus, but there will always be those who value the mystical element in his music as its prime virtue."[2] For Macdonald, the music should stand on its own merits. But this extra-musical dimension of his music has been such a decisive factor in his reception that it cannot possibly be ignored in a full consideration of his legacy. The tendency to separate Scriabin's music from its extra-musical ideas has been particularly pronounced in the West, where the composer underwent extreme shifts in popularity over the last century. Olga Tompakova and Gareth Thomas have each catalogued the enthusiastic reception his music enjoyed in England during the 1910s and 1920s, but his reception in the United States during those decades remains less documented.[3] Scriabin's music may have been performed more often in Russia and England than in the United States before 1930, but it enjoyed a concurrent vogue in America, especially due to his interests in Theosophy and synaesthesia. Once spiritualism and occult practices fell out of fashion in the later 1920s, though, Scriabin's popularity sank, and his legacy became a cautionary tale of an artist whose fringe interests damaged his reputation. Scriabin's reception offers a powerful lens through which to examine the individuals and organizations that promoted Russian music in the United States, as well as tastemaking critics' views on modern style.

Contempt for Scriabin's self-aggrandizement and his restricted harmonic vocabulary prevailed well into the twentieth century, especially among Western critics and scholars. Scottish music critic Cecil Gray was no fan of the Russian composer, and wrote in his 1927 *Survey of Contemporary Music* that Scriabin "suffered from megalomaniac delusions concerning his own importance. . . . His artistic achievement, apart from a few little piano pieces, is virtually nil."[4] Thirty years later, public opinion had not changed. Martin Cooper observed in 1957 that, "Today Scriabin's harmonic 'innovations' appear as no more than the exploiting *ad nauseam* of a single chord, while his mystical beliefs are regarded as psychological fantasies of purely clinical interest."[5] American commentators tended to agree. In a 1960 essay, musicologist Joseph Kerman scoffed that "Scriabin, who would have added Indian mysticism, color, and scent to the already bulging *Gesamt* of Wagnerian orthodoxy, came to nothing."[6] Expressed in an era when rationalism and positivism dominated art music and its scholarship, these writers' reproaches are unsurprising, and their opinions accorded with the widespread view of Scriabin as an ephemeral product of his time. By the early 1960s, Scriabin's music was rarely performed in public and woefully underrepresented on recordings. It is understandable, then, that Joseph Machlis had assured readers of his *Introduction to Contemporary Music* (1961) that, "We shall never again view Scriabin with the enthusiasm he aroused among certain sections of the intelligentsia forty years ago."[7] Little could these writers have imagined that a full-scale Scriabin revival would soon develop in the midst of the American counterculture movement of the late 1960s, which would renew an appreciation for this abandoned body of music, and all its extra-musical baggage that seemed so risible to critics and historians for much of the twentieth century.

FIRST IMPRESSIONS IN THE UNITED STATES

The pianists and conductors who introduced Scriabin's works to American audiences are names both familiar and forgotten. In March 1898, the pianist Josef Hofmann impressed audiences at Carnegie Hall with a batch of Scriabin's preludes and the volcanic D♯ minor Etude Op. 8 No. 12.[8] On 2 December 1900, Frank Van der Stucken, the founder of the Cincinnati Symphony Orchestra, conducted Scriabin's short orchestral Rêverie at Music Hall, and repeated it in 1905 and 1906.[9] At Josef Lhevinne's Carnegie Hall debut in January 1906, he encored with the left hand Nocturne Op. 9 No. 2, and in recital programs he delivered across America over the next year, Lhevinne added the Etudes Op. 42 Nos. 4 and 5.[10] But for Scriabin's music to reach a wider public, it behooved him to tour the United States, and in the winter of 1906–1907, he finally made the journey. Potential fame and fortune lured the cash-strapped composer, and salvation came via his former Moscow Conservatory classmate Modest Altschuler (1873–1963), who proffered the services of his newly founded Russian Symphony Orchestra Society. J. E. Francke, a veteran stage manager at Steinway Hall, handled Scriabin's concert bookings, but as of the composer's arrival in Hoboken, New Jersey, on 11 December 1906 via the liner *Ryndam*, only one concert date had been confirmed.

Some indication of the first impressions that Scriabin made on American critics is provided by an article published on 22 December 1906 in the *Boston Evening Transcript*:

> From beyond the closed door came the peculiar muffled roar of a piano being played vigorously with the lid down. The visitor's knock was lost in the music. A mad rush of octaves and the invisible pianist paused. Again the visitor knocked. This time the door was opened. "It is too bad to interrupt you just at this moment," said the intruder. The player courteously demurred at this suggestion, and waving his visitor to a chair submitted without further ado to that strangely American ordeal of being interviewed. There he stood, the "Russian Chopin," short, slim, pale, the delicate mould of his features half lost in the full brown beard, but distinctly Slavic in cast. This was the Alexander Scriabine who wrote the nocturne that is so dear to all pianists who have both will and technique to obey literally the Scriptual injunction touching the knowledge of the left hand. . . . Scriabin did not altogether welcome the idea that he should be a Chopin of any sort. "Of course Chopin influenced me at first," he admitted [likely through a translator] and my piano concerto belongs to my Chopin period. But with Opus 23 [Third Piano Sonata] came a change. I am now in my fifth period as a composer and working out a musical and aesthetic ideal of my own."[11]

Even from his first meetings with the American press, Scriabin spoke of his philosophy or aesthetic agenda as eagerly and readily as he discussed his music. And that is how most Americans were introduced to Scriabin's music: as inseparable from its philosophy.

Critical acclaim was not easily won for Scriabin in the United States. He did, however, boast an influential connection with his erstwhile Moscow Conservatory Professor Vasily Safonov, who was then music director of the New York Philharmonic. Safonov conducted a successful performance of Scriabin's Piano Concerto with the composer at the piano and the Russian Symphony Orchestra on December 20 at Carnegie Hall. The composer also played his D♯ minor Etude, a mazurka, and the left hand Nocturne.[12] Like the impression left by his Mendelssohn Hall recital on 3 January 1907, his youthful compositions bore few marks of originality, and critics found his keyboard technique lacking a proper singing tone or richness of color.[13] Desperate for a lucrative opportunity (in his letters he frets that the cost of living in the U.S. is five times higher than in Europe), Scriabin performed his Piano Concerto under Van der Stucken in Cincinnati on 10 and 12 January 1907, and then returned to New York to deliver a second Mendelssohn Hall matinee recital on January 30.[14] Despite the lukewarm reviews, Scriabin and Altschuler forged ahead with even more ambitious fare: Scriabin's Symphony No. 1 Op. 26, which was presented at Carnegie Hall on 28 February 1907. The work's choral finale, a glorification of art and a nod to Beethoven's Ninth Symphony, was omitted to conserve resources and avoid immodesty, but critics' expectations of originality, thematic development, and skilled orchestration were largely unmet.[15]

Sentinels of the Old Guard of New York and Boston critics remained implacable to Scriabin's efforts. The most unforgiving was William J. Henderson (1855–1937) of the *New York Sun*, who belittled Altschuler's attempt to present Scriabin as a piano virtuoso as "one of the most ludicrous failures of the season."[16] Circumstances were admittedly unfavorable for Scriabin's appearance with that orchestra, as Henderson considered Altschuler's organization "devoted to the propagation of a taste not necessarily for good music, but for Russian music . . . the truth is that nine-tenths of the Russian music which the Russian Symphony Society has introduced to us has not been worth the trouble of rehearsal."[17] Like other senior music critics such as Richard Aldrich (1863–1937) of the *New York Times* and Henry Krehbiel (1854–1923) of the *Daily Tribune*, Henderson upheld the harmonic and formal traditions of common practice music as inviolable standards.[18] "Mr. Scriabine is a gentleman and a scholar and doubtless a good judge of vodka, but as a composer he is open to the suspicion of drinking cream of violets and smoking Turkish cigarettes," Henderson wrote. Historian Mark Grant has described how these Old Guard critics rose to power to become tastemakers during the height of late Romanticism. They judged early twentieth-century "futurists" like Scriabin with extreme skepticism.[19] Without these critics' imprimatur, Scriabin's success in America was greatly hindered.

Determined to establish himself as a serious artist and thinker, Scriabin conspired with Altschuler to present a work that expressed his new philosophical orientation even more directly than his Symphony No. 1: the *Divine Poem* (Symphony No. 3, Op. 43). Program notes for the 14 March 1907 concert at Carnegie Hall disclosed the composer's desire to express "the emotional side of his philosophy of life," with themes symbolizing "the affirmation of conscious existence [and] the coexistence of matter and spirit in the Ego."[20] Stormy passages in C minor depict the self-torment and worldly temptations the protagonist wrestles with before surrendering to divine will in the radiant key of C major. The work's philosophical program, huge orchestra, and sustained dramatic tension reflect the lingering influence of German romanticism and the budding seed of Russian Symbolism. Although Scriabin's aesthetics were loose knit, he and other mystic Symbolists sought to create art that could enact a spiritual transformation, and these ideological aims were made explicit in the program notes to the *Divine Poem*. For better or for worse, this formula of music-cum-philosophy established Scriabin's early American reputation as an artist who tested music's formal and expressive limits. This aspect of his legacy would experience a parallel period of success by attracting acolytes in the 1920s and revivalists in the late 1960s through the early 1970s.

Despite Scriabin's ambitious efforts, critics argued that the musical structure of the *Divine Poem* had buckled under the weight of its philosophical pretense. In *Harper's Weekly*, Lawrence Gilman lamented that despite "moments of splendor," the symphony "afflicts by its monotony of mood, its lack of variety and contrast, its amorphous structure, and the weakness of its fundamental ideas."[21] Program music's fashionability had also worn thin, as evidenced by Krehbiel's remarks that the work was "obviously designed to out-Liszt Liszt and out-Strauss Strauss, the Richard."[22] Scriabin's U.S. tour wrapped up hastily in March 1907, and although he ultimately failed to win over critics, he managed to carve out a modest reputation in America.[23] Altschuler continued to perform Scriabin's symphonies after the composer had returned home, and led the American premiere of the *Poem of Ecstasy* at Carnegie Hall on 10 December 1908.

Scriabin's philosophy was not the only extra-musical aspect of his legacy that captured the American public's attention. Of equal fascination were his interests in Theosophy and synaesthesia. Theosophists believe that seven cosmic planes encompass the spectrum of consciousness, and that only the chosen few gain gnostic wisdom. Scriabin considered himself as one such enlightened being. The work that most explicitly established his Theosophical convictions was his Symphony No. 5, *Prometheus: Poem of Fire* Op. 60. Altschuler performed its celebrated world premiere with the color organ, or the *tastiera per luce* on 20 March 1915. The color organ was designed to bathe the hall in iridescent hues that corresponded to Scriabin's synaesthetic experiences. The program notes for *Prometheus* were written by Leonid Sabaneev and described how Satan, Prometheus, and Lucifer struggle against one another before transcending to a higher plane of existence. To represent spiritual transcendence, Scriabin based *Prometheus* on the "mystic chord" (C-F♯-B♭-E-A-D), an unconventional sonority with no common practice equivalent. This sonority's deviance from conventional harmony represents an alternate reality, just as the *luce* represents what Scriabin hoped his audiences would experience: synaesthesia, or a union of the senses. These sensational associations earned Scriabin and his color symphony significant press coverage. Indeed, Altschuler's full realization of *Prometheus* with colored lights ranked as the most important performance of the composer's music in the United States during his lifetime.

Unfortunately, news of this multimedia extravaganza reached readers along with reports of Scriabin's untimely death at age forty-three. Instead of hastening the composer's decline in popularity, however, his death inspired celebrity conductors working in the United States to campaign on his behalf. Leopold Stokowski (1882–1977), known for his dedication to Russian music, frequently included Scriabin's last three symphonies in his Philadelphia Orchestra programs from 1915 to 1932, and the *Poem of Ecstasy* became his specialty.[24] This revered conductor's vehement defense of Scriabin and commanding performances of his orchestral works bolstered the composer's reputation as worthy of the highest respect.

Charismatic conductors of Scriabin's music played a crucial role in impressing critics and audiences in America, and chief among them was Serge Koussevitzky (1874–1951). Koussevitzky entered Scriabin's life in 1908, at a time when the composer was wallowing in financial ruin. Koussevitzky had married into fabulous wealth and offered to publish the composer's works for life, including his unfinished *Mysterium*, and furnish him with an annual stipend. The would-be conductor and impresario saw Scriabin as a potential boon to his career. In turn, Scriabin regarded

Koussevitzky as his financial savior who supported him unconditionally, much like his benefactress Margarita Morozova had done for years. Koussevitzky conducted Scriabin's works across the United States for several decades, and featured the *Poem of Ecstasy* in his debut as the music director of the Boston Symphony Orchestra on 10 October 1924.[25] Olin Downes, new to the *New York Times* in 1924, fell under Koussevitzky's spell and considered him a powerful interpreter of the Russian composer's works. Downes raved how the *Poem of Ecstasy* was "gorgeously effective" in Koussevitzky's hands and had "swept his audience from its feet."[26] In addition to Koussevitzky and Stokowski, Scriabin's orchestral works benefited from the support of Albert Coates (1882–1953) in Los Angeles and London and Frederick Stock (1872–1942) in Chicago. These venerable conductors cemented the Russian composer's reputation in the United States as a legitimate heir to the venerable symphonic traditions of the nineteenth century.

EVANGELISTS OF THE SCRIABIN FAITH

While conductors performed orchestral works that promoted Scriabin's philosophical interests, pianists living in Chicago and New York championed his solo piano music and proselytized on his Theosophical beliefs. Chicago proved to be a hotbed of Theosophy in the early twentieth century. Following the death of Helena Blavatsky (1831–1891), who founded the Theosophical Society in America, Annie Besant (1847–1933) became the Society's figurehead, and in 1907 and 1909 she delivered a lecture series in Chicago and "won complete ascendancy" over a legion of neophytes.[27] Membership in the Theosophical Society around Chicago rose steadily in the 1910s, and the city hosted the Fortieth Annual International Convention in 1926 and the Third World Congress in 1929.[28] At this latter convention, Irish suffragist Margaret Cousins (1878–1954) performed a batch of Scriabin's preludes for four thousand attendees as a demonstration of how contemporary music could reinforce Theosophical principles.[29] Such explicit linkages between Scriabin's music and spiritual enlightenment would form the basis of his reputation in the United States during the 1920s.

Theosophical parlance became the lingua franca of Scriabin's early admirers in the United States. Devotees congregated in the piano studio of Djane Lavoie-Herz (1888–1982), who moved to Chicago in 1918 after studying for two years with Scriabin in Brussels at the height of his involvement with Theosophy.[30] In the 1920s, Lavoie-Herz formed a Chicago salon on Grand Boulevard (now Bellevue Place) that hosted such attendees as Henry Cowell, Dane Rudhyar, and Carl Ruggles. Scriabin's music often provided the group's daily bread.[31] In Lavoie-Herz's studio, students learned not only the technical secrets of interpreting Scriabin's music at the piano, but also how to harness the spiritual energy of the Russian composer's music. The American composer Ruth Crawford Seeger (1901–1953) was a protégé of Lavoie-Herz, and her early works bear Scriabin's imprint in their chords spaced in fourths and poetic expression marks (e.g., "mistico" in her Violin Sonata and Prelude No. 6).[32] Musicologist Carol Oja has described how patrons of Lavoie-Herz's studio formulated a concept of dissonance as a representation of spirituality, and within this ideological framework Scriabin's music set the standard.[33]

A firm advocate of Scriabin's music and Lavoie-Herz's theory of spirituality through dissonance was Gitta Gradova (neé Gertrude Weinstock [1904–1985]), who took top honors in the 1920s among some American critics as the "greatest interpreter" of Scriabin's music.[34] She readily assimilated the lingo bandied about by Theosophists, and spoke of Scriabin's works in a 1924 interview as "music of the astral body" that imparted "soul experiences."[35] Gradova's polished technique lent credence to this inflated rhetoric, prompting Henrietta Straus to rave in the journal *The Nation* that "she pierces those outer wrappings that make their appeal solely to the nerves and reveals the flame that was Scriabin himself."[36] Impressive performances from artists like Lavoie-Herz and Gradova raised awareness of Scriabin's music as surpassing mere entertainment, and offering a transcendental experience.[37]

Upstaging Gradova in her dedication to the music and its aesthetic ideals was Katherine Ruth Heyman (1877–1944), who delivered all-Scriabin recitals in New York in 1924 and 1927, and in Europe in 1927, 1934, and 1935.[38] Although she is not well known today, "Kitty" Heyman was one of the premiere female piano virtuosos of the early twentieth century. She received extensive training throughout Europe and the United States, and was well connected in the classical music scene in the early twentieth century. Heyman was also Scriabin's greatest advocate in America from the 1910s to the 1940s. Arthur Eaglefield Hull considered her to be the interpreter who expressed Scriabin's "spiritual message . . . more clearly than any other living pianist."[39] Her fanatical devotion to the composer knew no ends, and she earned distinction as the "high priestess of the Scriabin cult." Heyman claimed she had "met Scriabin on the moon and had an affair with him," "saw visions to his music," and translated the composer's coded messages from beyond the grave.[40] At "Conferences" held in her Upper East Side loft, she performed Scriabin's piano works and preached his gospel to such attendees as Charles Ives, Charles Griffes, and Elliot Carter.[41] As one of the most public proponents of the composer's music in America (she founded the Scriabin Circle in 1934 to raise awareness of his music and message), Heyman drew as much attention to the music's spiritual dimension as its musical beauty.

With Scriabin's piano music and aesthetic interests being promoted throughout Chicago and New York City by dedicated and capable pianists, his reputation as an innovative composer and spiritual guru became solidified in the decade after his death. Some American critics like Lawrence Gilman hailed him in 1921 as "one of the most fashionable of modern composers," even though they found his commitment to Theosophy "spurious."[42] Old Guard critics like Richard Aldrich and William J. Henderson still remained unconvinced of Scriabin's merits, but younger writers like Paul Rosenfeld were excited by what they had heard, and touted Scriabin as a progressive force in modern music.[43] By the late 1920s, however, Scriabin's halcyon days were numbered, and these enthusiastic supporters would soon be drowned out by the noisy protests of unsympathetic critics.

INEVITABLE DECLINE

As modernism crystallized as an ideological doctrine after the 1920s, musical tastes shifted, and various forms of spiritualism became discredited. Although Scriabin's reputation as a Theosophist had drawn attention to his music in the early 1920s, this association now hastened his decline. Blavatsky was discredited as a charlatan, and Eastern religions had become passé.[44] When the Great Depression struck in 1929, fulfilling basic needs further sidelined spiritual pursuits. As part of the New Deal, President Roosevelt instituted the Federal Music Project to support classical music in America. Roosevelt appointed the Russian-born violinist Nikolai Sokolov to be its director in 1935, and he held the post until 1938.[45] Sokolov had preferred late romantic French and Russian repertoire during his fifteen years as music director of the Cleveland Orchestra, but Scriabin's aging works did not satisfy the federal program's initiative to nurture gumptious and indigenous talent.[46]

By the 1930s, Scriabin's eclipse was complete. Writing from Paris in 1931, Leonid Sabaneev captured the consensus of opinion that would prevail over the next thirty-five years: "This belated romantic—a romantic to the marrow of his bones—made his appearance just when romanticism had come to be regarded as obsolete."[47] Once the tide of public opinion had turned against Scriabin, critics of all stripes jumped on the bandwagon of dissent, and had a field day pointing out the litany of faults that led to his downfall. Their outspoken views must have left a strong impression on readers. Yale professor David Smith sounded the alarm as early as 1922 by remarking that, "Scriabin's harmonic mannerisms, beautiful as they may be, mark a discouraging retrogression."[48] Paul Rosenfeld appreciated the Russian composer's music and dishearteningly wrote in 1936 that, "Scriabin's glory remains fairly complete in its eclipse. From time to time a zealous conductor repeats the unfortunate *Poème de l'Extase.* . . . Scriabin is 'romantic,' 'inflated,' 'mere color,' 'international in the invidious sense.' In fine, he is tabu."[49] Writing from Columbia University in 1941, musicologist Paul Henry Lang saw fit to declare that Scriabin's "whole art, nay, whole life, was a mere experiment, a supernatural dream, and whose mind, possessed by demonic forces, penetrated deeper and deeper into the mire of mystical speculations, hallucinations, and dementia."[50] Such disparaging remarks resonated deeply in the public consciousness and signaled how widespread the rejection of Scriabin's music had become.

Mounting resistance to Scriabin's music and aesthetics is well adduced by British critics, whose conservative sensibilities were rankled by the metaphysical overlay. Emblematic of Scriabin's precipitous decline after the mid-1920s is a jeremiad in the *Musical Times* by critic Alexander Brent-Smith, who bluntly stated, "it is because [Scriabin] offered muddle-headed reasoning seriously that the value of his later work is being suspected."⁵¹ Brent-Smith believed that the composer's philosophical pursuits derailed his artistic development: "Has, then, Scriabin's work any permanent value? Until he fettered himself with theories to prove his independence of theories—Yes. Afterwards his work was . . . sterile and futureless." Ernest Fennel and Robert Hull countered Brent-Smith's points in later issues of that journal, but despite their protests, Scriabin's stock was plummeting.⁵² Gerald Abraham mercilessly mocked "the whole of the later development of Skryabinesque harmony" as "a mere side-track in the history of music as a whole."⁵³ With smug satisfaction, he reported in 1933 that, "Scriabin is now thought very little of," a fitting end for a composer who was a "sad pathological case, erotic and egotistic to the point of mania."⁵⁴ Also writing from London was Franco-Greco musicologist Michel Calvocoressi, who in 1934 expressed his distaste for Scriabin's "music of colossal self-aggrandizement."⁵⁵

While some writers ridiculed Scriabin's aesthetics, others like Cecil Gray took umbrage with the composer's "monotonous and extraordinarily restricted" harmonic language. Siding with Abraham, Gray surmised that his "artistic achievement, apart from a few little piano pieces, is virtually nil." These writers complained that Scriabin's music lacked the organic, universal quality that distinguishes true art.⁵⁶ Such grievances betray a bias for Austro-German compositional techniques like developing variation and long-range harmonic motion, and compared to these standards of compositional technique, Scriabin becomes a veritable straw man.⁵⁷ Scriabin's flaccid rhythms especially came under fire (Soviet pragmatists voiced similar concerns over his music's lack of a consistent beat), as they often blur the barline and resist a consistent, measurable pulse. This atmosphere of murky stasis inspired many writers to reach for their most colorful analogies when disparaging the composer's late style. Cecil Gray jeered that Scriabin's music "merely heaves and undulates like an octopus in the flowing tide," while Paul Hume of the *Washington Post* wrote in a 1971 concert review that, "Listening to an entire program of [Scriabin's] piano music is terribly likely to leave you with the feeling that you have been sitting for an hour and a half in a tub of mucilage. Beautiful, multi-colored, rich, gooey glue from which you may never emerge."⁵⁸ These historians' widely read criticisms on modern music significantly marginalized the composer's position in music history.⁵⁹

Not everyone heaped scorn upon Scriabin after his heyday in the 1910s and early 1920s. For British critic Compton Pakenham, Stokowski's 1932 recordings of *Prometheus* and the *Poem of Ecstasy* triggered feelings of bittersweet nostalgia for "a day when [Scriabin] was very much in demand, when none of the regular lists of unsolicited suggestions reaching us was without its Scriabine [*sic*] item. But apparently those who wanted him have abandoned hope or found consolation in other fields."⁶⁰ "Those who wanted him" meant the performers whose conviction had made their interpretations so compelling. Scriabin's death knell sounded when their feverish passion for the music faded, a situation keenly recognized by Olin Downes. Downes acknowledged that Scriabin's "boudoir passion and parlor transcendentalism" had commanded attention, but by 1925 he admitted, "We are not dazzled or confused by Scriabin's style, which has become an old story."⁶¹ Downes still lauded the *Poem of Ecstasy* as a masterful balance of form and content. Yet only four years later under the same conductor, Downes gasped at how rapidly the work was "aging" and feared that Koussevitzky's interpretive secrets would soon be lost, because "no musician will take the '*Poeme l'extase*' very seriously when fifty more years have passed."[62]

That day arrived sooner than Downes had anticipated, not because Koussevitzky died, but because he grew disenchanted with Scriabin's music. In 1939, the conductor confessed to a journalist that, "Scriabin? I tell you frankly, it is now hard for me to play him at all." Five years later, his distaste grew even stronger: "I don't know exactly why, but I can't stand more of Scriabin. I will try him again next season. If he tires me then I will no more play him."[63] Koussevitzky kept his word and almost never played Scriabin's music again, even though he had built his reputation as a distinguished interpreter of this music. Koussevitzky knew that his popularity rested on his choice of repertoire, and his rejection of Scriabin was significant considering that the *Poem of Ecstasy* had made such an overwhelming impression at his Boston Symphony Orchestra debut in 1924. His 1949 silver anniversary program repeated his debut, but conspicuously omitted the piece with which his conducting career in America had been so effectively launched. When pressed about the omission, Koussevitzky admitted, "The public does not like him, and leading an orchestra is a matter of pleasing the public."[64] This public rejection of Scriabin's music by one of his formers supporters highlighted the composer's lowly status at mid-century.

The detached objectivism of postwar tastes nourished the anti-Scriabin sentiment through the 1950s. In 1961 the pianist Arthur Rubinstein lamented, "The public wants coldness, not warmth. Look at this vogue for pre-Bach . . .Where's the lyric sweep? The heart? Today *rejects* Scriabin and his romanticism."[65] But the long prohibition against the Russian composer's music had nearly run its course. By the late 1960s, the pendulum started to swing back in the composer's favor. Scriabin's early biographer, Leonid Sabaneev, had predicted as early as 1940 that if Scriabin's music were to ever reclaim its former glory, "the businesslike, prosaic, realistic atmosphere of our days must some day be illuminated by the fires of a reviving romanticism."[66] He was convinced it would happen, and it was a prophecy fulfilled. Just as aestheticism regained currency in the United States during the 1960s, Scriabin's music resurfaced under the guise of a romantic revival after languishing in obscurity for over four decades.

NEO-ROMANTICISM IN AMERICA

Post–World War II, Scriabin's works had long faded from memory, and Austro-German masterworks and new American scores dominated concert programs among U.S. orchestras.[67] Canonized masterworks were entrenched in the repertory, leading to a stagnant recycling of well-trodden pieces. The American critic Paul Hume bemoaned the atrophied state of concert programming in several reviews published in the late 1940s and early 1950s, and he woefully estimated in a 1951 article that non-canonized works constituted only 8 percent of the Philadelphia Orchestra's programs.[68] The situation barely improved by the mid-1960s, prompting the *New York Times'* chief music critic, Harold Schonberg, to grumble in late April 1966 that, "the repertory seems to be closing in rather than opening up. Year after year we hear the same things, and the overwhelming majority of what we hear stems from the Austro-German school . . . great and important areas of music are being neglected."[69] Hume and Schonberg both craved relief from this steady rotation of classics, as well as performers who took risks and could play off the cuff. Schonberg admonished a year later that, "the active repertoire is in a process of stagnation, much more than it ever has been in the history of music. It almost has boiled down to 50 or so popular classics plus a large amount of contemporary ephemera that emerges, flops around for awhile, and dies."[70] The desire for new music eventually allowed the more accessible works of Bernstein, Copland, and Ives to gain admission into the repertory, but these composers accounted for only a fraction of the names regularly featured on concert programs in the United States before the mid-1960s.

The value distinction between the core and peripheral repertory is well delineated in a famous *Sunday Times* article from 1925 written by the critic Ernest Newman, titled "The Virtuous and the Virtuoso."[71] The virtuous adopted Clara Schumann as their patron saint and represented the disciplined, cerebral approach to music; the virtuosi claimed Liszt as their patriarch and signified music's unchained, visceral side. While the virtuous allow the composer's voice to reign supreme, never flaunt their technique, and observe textual fidelity, virtuosi put personal stamps on every performance, revel in technical showmanship, and take liberties with the written score. The former camp had positioned itself as a bulwark against the demoralizing trends of the virtuosi, and since the 1940s, their ideology had prevailed, but by the 1960s a shift in cultural values was under way.

Peripheral repertory gained popularity in the mid-1960s through a revival of romantic music, which paved the way for Scriabin's eventual return to the repertory. In referring to the music reclaimed during this era as "romantic," I invoke a term used by contemporary critics and performers, yet some defining elements characterized this revived repertoire. All were considered a neglected work and/or composer, made considerable technical demands on the performer, and put a premium on harmonic chromaticism. The romantic revival launched in May 1968 when Butler University piano professor Frank Cooper staged a Festival of Romantic Music in Indianapolis.[72] Works virtually forgotten since the 1800s were dusted off and given inspired performances, and the festival's success sustained it annually until 1989.[73] A revival of romantic music may seem oxymoronic considering the enduring popularity of nineteenth-century works, but Cooper and other revivalists dug deep to unearth forgotten figures and historical rarities under the premise that these treasures were as valuable and virtuous as any canonized pieces.[74] Composers of yesteryear were examined with renewed vigor, and Scriabin was one of several figures whose legacies were revaluated, including Mahler, Berlioz, and Charles-Valentin Alkan. Although the romantic revival would inspire a reappraisal of Scriabin's historical value, not every participant had a canonic axe to grind. Many people enjoyed these rarities simply as guilty pleasures.

Texan pianist Raymond Lewenthal (1923–1988) emerged as a leader of the movement and he even coined the term "romantic revival." Fashioning himself as a modern-day Liszt, Lewenthal would sashay onto stages bedecked in a top hat, red-lined cape and cane, and his recitals were held in near total darkness.[75] Figure 8.1 shows Lewenthal in his typical concert attire. Lewenthal was among the first pianists to revive the Russian composer's music in the 1960s. His all-Scriabin recital on 17 May 1968 as part of the Festival of Romantic Music's inaugural proceedings earned glowing reviews from critics and rekindled interest in the composer.[76] His thunderous encore of *Hexameron*, a theme and variations for solo piano composed by Liszt, Chopin, Thalberg, and other romantic virtuosi, left an overwhelming impression of

Figure 8.1. Pianist Raymond Lewenthal, 1960s revivalist of Scriabin's music. *Courtesy of International Piano Archives, University of Maryland.*

the evening.⁷⁷ What was refreshing about the romantic revival was that it added a theatrical element that had been sorely lacking in concert music, and Lewenthal was an ideal spokesman. Not only did he bring a touch of flair to the concert experience; he also performed obscure and unforgiving works convincingly, and without insisting upon any composers' canonic promotion.

Performers like Lewenthal were important for rehabilitating Scriabin's public image, but equally influential were such critics as Harold Schonberg of the *New York Times*. Schonberg peered through the haze of skepticism and derision that had enveloped Scriabin, and he urged readers to keep an open mind about the composer's music, which he considered to be far ahead of its time in its use of modern harmony and instrumental color. In holding this opinion, Schonberg stood in defiance of the prevailing orthodoxy, which cast Scriabin as a washed-up romantic. Schonberg assiduously monitored Scriabin's return to the active repertory, and believed that this highly emotional and colorful music could invigorate the stagnant concert repertoire. Still, it took several years for the musical community to see his point of view.

The romantic revival was in full swing by 1968, but Scriabin's music first received renewed attention as early as 1965. Schonberg's review of Lorin Maazel's performance of the *Poem of Ecstasy* with the New York Philharmonic in March 1965 was the first article to suggest that a reappraisal of the Russian composer's music was overdue:

> The music is lush and as sexy as music can get. But it is not post-Wagnerian. Scriabin's harmonic ideas were too advanced for that, and his language is very original. Perhaps a re-examination of his work is in order.⁷⁸

The fact that Schonberg considered Scriabin a progressive when most critics and historians dismissed him as a bygone romantic spoke to the willingness of concertgoers to set aside preconceived notions about music of the past, and rediscover its unique charms and virtues. The Early Music revival was one of the first intimations of a revised attitude toward older repertoire, and the romantic revival emerged from this mind-set.⁷⁹

Maazel conducted the *Poem of Ecstasy* again in April 1965, prompting Schonberg to ruminate further on Scriabin's undeserved neglect. He lamented the dearth of performances of Scriabin's music in recent memory and proclaimed, "I happen to adore his music, all of it."⁸⁰ Yet he remained in the minority in his excitement over the return of this music. That year, he painted a stark portrait of the predominant critical attitudes toward Scriabin:

> Let a pianist present a group of early Scriabin preludes and etudes, and critics will go out of their way to condemn the music as nothing but diluted Chopin. Let one of the late piano pieces be programmed, and the musical intelligentsia are up in arms, inveighing against Scriabin's diffuseness, vagueness and fake philosophy. . . . This grieves those of us who consider Scriabin one of the most original, fascinating, enigmatic, revolutionary—and, yes, rewarding composers of the century.⁸¹

Clearly the *Neue Sachlichkeit* that had dominated postwar tastes had not fully dissipated, and five more years elapsed before Americans would share Schonberg's enthusiasm. But the situation was quickly improving. In 1966, Faubion Bowers announced that Scriabin had emerged from a "haze of public amnesia," and by 1969, he published his two-volume biography of the composer. Schonberg optimistically observed that, "There has been a major Scriabin renaissance in the last few years, but most attention has been focused on the problematic, mystical late works."[82] He had in mind the "Black Mass" Sonata (No. 9, Op. 68), *Vers la flamme* Op. 72, and the Five Preludes Op. 74. It is noteworthy that these ultra-chromatic pieces (1912–1915) were favored by performers considering that most of the music celebrated at Cooper's festivals was composed before 1880. But their harmonic spice and emotional verve appealed to broad musical tastes, if well executed, and their peculiar quality of otherworldliness resonated with an incipient awareness of elevated consciousness that would accord with the machinations of pop culture.

By 1969, critics across the nation took notice of Scriabin's budding popularity, and raised awareness of his growing stature. In a timely article titled "Why Alexander Scriabin?" various critics debated the significance and reasons for Scriabin's meteoric rise in popularity. *Chicago Tribune* critic Peter Gorner attributed the renewed attention directly to the romantic revival, observing that, "as the musical public continues to dislike what it hears coming from contemporary minds, and keeps seeking treasures in attics, Scriabin has been making the news."[83] Lester Trimble believed that Scriabin's music transcended the ephemeral trends of the romantic revival, and he considered Scriabin "the only *real* refreshment" of that movement.[84] Feeding the public frenzy was Bowers' biography, as well as his articles and record reviews in entertainment magazines. Four years later, he published a follow-up study, *The New Scriabin: Enigma and Answers* (1973), which capitalized on the composer's return to fame.[85] The highlight of 1969, however, was a performance of *Prometheus: Poem of Fire* at Yale University, replete with colored lights and incense pumped in from the air ducts (John Mauceri conducted the Yale Russian Chorus with lighting designed by Richard Gould).[86] Journalist Adrian Hope reported on this event in the October 1970 issue of *Life* magazine and gleefully noted how it spurred similar experiments in concert halls across the United States. Others would soon echo Hope's sentiments in characterizing Scriabin more as a prescient visionary than as an undervalued relic.

The romantic revival counteracted the preservationist mentality that had dominated the standard repertory, but good old-fashioned capitalism ensured its success. The keyboardist Igor Kipnis and archivist David Hall both agreed that a ripe market was the key catalyst for Scriabin's renewed success.[87] Statistics support this claim. In 1965, the *Schwann* record catalogue had only a few entries for Scriabin's music, but by 1970 it featured over thirty recordings, and over the next year, that figure doubled. Record executives were also keen to boost classical music sales, which had paled in comparison to those of popular music. Record companies explored increasingly abstract imagery for their classical music sets by using imaginative, colorful, and even sexually provocative jacket designs that made the record's packaging as attractive as the music on the disc. With his erotically charged scores like the *Divine Poem* and *Poem of Ecstasy*, Scriabin proved to be a marketing gold mine for performers seeking to carve out a niche for themselves, and for record companies looking to cash in on the next fashionable trend.

CENTENNIAL CELEBRATIONS AND REVIVALIST PERFORMERS

The romantic revival brought Scriabin's works back into concert halls and recording studios, but the centenary of his birth in January 1972 propelled his popularity to stratospheric heights. Critics across America remarked on the seemingly sudden hype over his music.[88] Critic Allen Hughes recognized that Scriabin's music appealed to the "senses rather than the intellect," acknowledging the importance of the virtuoso ideals of visceral stimulation and emotional hedonism that had gained currency through the romantic revival.[89] The public appetite for artworks that pushed music's expressive potential to its breaking point made objects of fascination out of Scriabin's recondite projects, such as his unfinished Prefatory Act, an eschatological work that the Russian composer Alexander Nemtin (1936–1999) reconstructed over twenty-eight years using sketch pages archived in the Scriabin Museum in Moscow.[90] Nemtin completed part one of the trilogy (*Universe*) in time for the 1972 centenary and recorded it for the Soviet label Melodiya the following year.[91] Another work of cosmic aspirations, *Prometheus: Poem of Fire*, had been completely absent from the *Schwann* record catalogue before the 1970s. As late as 1966, the British critic Alan Blythe had sneered:

> The structure seems non-existent, the philosophy behind it suspect if not lunatic, and the atmosphere it creates as steamy as the air in the Albert Hall that night. . . . Let us hear less in future of how Scriabin has been unjustly neglected by posterity: his semi-oblivion seems well justified if we are to judge by this empty score.[92]

However, the next five years saw three new recordings of *Prometheus* appear in U.S. record catalogues.[93] Taking stock of these new releases, critic Heuwell Tircuit remarked, "After years of neglect, one of the greatest nuts in the history of music has suddenly zoomed into near-star status."[94] Tircuit's cheeky description of Scriabin as "one of the greatest nuts" suggests that the composer's metaphysical preoccupations, a source of embarrassment only a few years ago, had now become a selling point. Such an interpretation was encouraged by commentators such as Robert Craft, who observed in the *New York Times* in 1970 that, "Judging from programs of younger pianists and conductors, a Scriabin revival—or resurrection, in the case of this messianist—is underway."[95] Comments such as these fueled curiosity about the composer's eccentric interests in the popular press, which tantalizingly blurred the line between madness and genius.

Several Scriabin-playing pianists joined Lewenthal in ushering his music back into circulation, and two distinct breeds emerged: those who paid deference to the composer by observing fidelity to the scores, and those who exploited the mystical, theatrical aspects of his music and occult lore. Among the leading exponents of the former approach was the Russian virtuoso Vladimir Horowitz, who released an all-Scriabin disc a full decade before the romantic revival. Scriabin's works formed a cornerstone of Horowitz's repertory throughout his career, and his interpretations never failed to transfix audiences. "Nobody plays Scriabin better than Mr. Horowitz," Schonberg gushed in a review of his 1965 "Historic Return" to Carnegie Hall after a twelve-year hiatus from concertizing. "Not only does he have complete affinity with the strange, mysterious world of Scriabin, but he also has the technique to make the complicated writing sound as clear as the strands of a Bach invention."[96] So spellbinding were Horowitz's renditions that he even made Scriabin's music seem fresh and arresting at the nadir of his reception. Reviewing a 1948 recital, Olin Downes reported:

> Scriabin has rather faded from the repertory in recent years, despite his once sensational reputation. But as Mr. Horowitz played . . . we were plunged back into the fevers of the period when Scriabin was considered the be-all and end-all of Russian piano music, and nobody who was anybody in the musical world could afford to laugh at him.[97]

A younger coalition emulated Horowitz in the self-effacing approach to Scriabin's piano music, including Vladimir Ashkenazy, who delivered all-Scriabin recitals in New York and London in 1972–1973. Another notable exponent was Austrian pianist Anton Kuerti, whom Bowers recognized in 1972 as "the foremost young Scriabin interpreter in America." Bowers also bestowed honorable mentions to Garrick Ohlsson, Alan Marks, Thomas Schumacher, and Justin Blasdale.[98] No fewer than five pianists recorded Scriabin's complete sonatas around the centenary, and the support and expertise of these pianists harnessed the full expressive power of Scriabin's solo piano works, and allowed audiences to hear this music as it should be played.[99]

Although this contingent of Scriabin-playing pianists was male-dominated, Hilde Somer and Ruth Laredo assumed prominent roles in the Scriabin revival, which paralleled Djane Lavoie-Herz's and Katherine Heyman's promotion of his music and mythos in the 1920s. Viennese-born Hilde Somer (1922–1979) toured America from 1969 to 1972, delivering all-Scriabin programs with lighting effects by Pablo Lights and Thomas Shoesmith of the Fillmore East's Joshua Light Show.[100] *Cosmopolitan* critic Nat Hentoff declared her first all-Scriabin album as thought provoking and trailblazing a record as The Beatles' *White Album*, high praise indeed for a classical album.[101] On 6 January 1972, Somer observed the anniversary of Scriabin's birth by packing Carnegie Hall with a capacity crowd of listeners both young and old who were eager to experience her multimedia production. Her visual and aural feasts enthralled the public (light shows had become ubiquitous at rock shows by the early 1970s), but most critics dismissed the colored lights as unsuited for Scriabin's music.[102] Representatives of the popular press like Stefan Kanfer of *Life* magazine, however, praised her light shows as the salvation for classical music. Somer's light shows prompted Kanfer to exclaim, "I have seen the recital's future, and it grooves . . . eighty-eight triggers and the screen becomes the roadmap to a psychedelic trip."[103] Such claims countered the opinions of influential voices like that of the Canadian pianist and recording advocate Glenn Gould, who prognosticated that music's future lay in recording studios, and the end user's ability to adjust the sound qualities to suit their own listening preferences. Gould also denigrated live concerts as antiquated rituals that promoted showmanship and pageantry over actual artistry.[104]

Somer was not alone in her campaign to bring a touch of theatricality to Scriabin's music in the Age of Aquarius. The American pianist Van Zandt Ellis (1944–1988) also performed Scriabin's music with lighting effects in the 1970s, and even had dancers accompany his performances.[105] Boston-based pianist Martha Anne Verbit, known for her penchant for unusual repertoire and eccentricity, adopted a similar approach to playing Scriabin's music during the revival years, when she regaled audiences with stories about the composer while playing his solo piano works, an event that she called "piano theater."[106] Many critics scoffed at such productions as gaudy and kitschy, but these performers' well-intentioned efforts aligned Scriabin's music with forward-thinking innovations in classical music, however ephemeral they may have been. These recitals livened up the moribund concert hall and enticed younger audiences.

Ruth Laredo (neé Meckler, 1937–2005) discovered Scriabin's music through Horowitz's recordings, and she debuted with a critically acclaimed album of the Russian composer's works for the Connoisseur label. Her first all-Scriabin record included the "White Mass" and "Black Mass" sonatas among other late works, and it was an instant sensation. Its commercial success emboldened Connoisseur to allow Laredo to record the composer's complete sonatas.[107] Even today, nearly fifty years after its initial release, many audiophiles consider Laredo's recordings of Scriabin's sonatas to be among the finest on record. Her command of Scriabin's technical and interpretive hurdles obviated the need for any gimmicks. Critic Bernard Holland commended Laredo's ability to conjure up the "mad and slightly evil quality" of Scriabin's works, but Laredo rejected the notion that his music conveyed any specific meanings: "I don't know what words like 'good' or 'ennobling' mean in terms of music," Laredo insisted, "but I know what beautiful means and Scriabin is beautiful."[108] As opposed to the more kitschy, sideshow productions that were popularized in the Age of Aquarius, Laredo approached the music in all seriousness and conviction. Allen Hughes remarked in a 1970 review of her first Scriabin album that, "She seems not to approach Scriabin as though he were a rare exotic, but as a vital and impulsive creator whose rapidly shifting ideas and moods are understandable, and in their own way, quite logical. Given this outlook, there is no need to be precious or mysterious and no necessity for exaggerating any of its elements. The result is mainstream, high-level music-making that makes the past half-century's neglect of Scriabin seem more inexplicable than ever."[109]

Perhaps the most salient indicator that Scriabin's music had achieved renewed respect in the 1970s was the attention that major conductors paid to his orchestral works. Eugene Ormandy, Seiji Ozawa, and Claudio Abbado all brought the *Poem of*

Ecstasy back into U.S. concert halls in honor of the centenary. When Abbado performed the tone poem at Philharmonic Hall in February 1971 with the Philadelphia Orchestra, Schonberg realized that Scriabin was undergoing a complete revaluation of his canonic standing:

> For a long time [Scriabin] was dismissed as a sentimental, mystic, a purveyor of neo-Chopin melodies (which he was in his early piano music), a self-indulgent colorist. Self-indulgence he did have, but also genius. His music is unique and it is good to see it beginning to take its proper place in history.[110]

In 1972, even hard-nosed modernists such as Pierre Boulez conducted the *Poem of Ecstasy*, evincing the hard-fought respect that Scriabin's music had earned from music professionals of all stripes. Schonberg remarked in astonishment that:

> The last piece in the world that one would ever expect to hear under [Boulez's] baton would be the decadent, juicy, over-rich, sensuous *Poem of Ecstasy*. [But] even avant-gardists find his music interesting, and that is only just. For Scriabin was one of the great avant-gardists before his death in 1915 and remained so until his abrupt plunge from favor in the 1930s.[111]

The qualities that Schonberg found so innovative in Scriabin's music were the same ideals celebrated in the music unearthed during the romantic revival: imagination and fantasy, harmonic innovation, and above all, technical virtuosity that pushed the limits of human ability. Yet Schonberg considered Scriabin far ahead of the pack of most turn-of-the-century composers, hence his vision of Scriabin as a forgotten pioneer of avant-gardism. One of the most remarkable aspects of Scriabin's revival is the diverse agendas that his music satisfied, from those who looked to the past to rediscover lost treasures, to those whose gaze was fixed firmly on music's future. The romantic revival and the Scriabin revival fulfilled both needs.

SCRIABIN MEETS AMERICAN PSYCHEDELICA

Just as the general curiosity about spiritualism and the occult benefited Scriabin's reception in the 1920s, a receptivity in the 1960s and 1970s toward spiritual enlightenment and alternative lifestyles and modes of thought provided an amenable atmosphere for the acceptance of Scriabin's music and aesthetics. Music served as an important vehicle for channeling the counterculture ethos, and the Monterey Pop (1967) and Woodstock Arts and Music festivals (1969)—both immortalized in documentary films that allowed millions of viewers unable to attend these events to witness their potent fusion of art and community—showcased music's pluralistic roles in culture and society: as a medium for political protest, as a focal point around which people with common ideals congregated, and as a vehicle for spiritual exploration.[112] The transition from the conservative values of American life in the 1950s to the political activism and artistic experimentation of the late 1960s parallels the overthrow of Victorian ideals by modernist impulses in the early twentieth century. Historian Daniel Singal framed the 1960s counterculture movement as modernism's "culminating moment."[113] Such a comparison between the values of these two eras seems logical considering the mutual celebrations of animal instinct, desire to eradicate dualisms, razing of social and cultural barriers, and quest for heightened consciousness. Singal argued that the 1960s counterculture "carried the Modernist embrace of natural instinct and primitivism to its seemingly inevitable conclusion."[114]

What could the youth generation of the 1960s have in common with the dandyish Russian composer? Scriabin's associations with mysticism and Theosophy, dutifully noted by critics like Schonberg and biographers such as Bowers, satisfied the counterculture members' curiosity about alternative spiritual practices. Drawing even closer to the counterculture lifestyle, his hazy and dizzying colorful late works bear qualities that resemble the altered states of perception that hippies sought to attain through meditation and hallucinogens. Another point of interest routinely mentioned in record liner notes and biographical sketches was the *Mysterium*, an apocalyptic rite intended to allow participants to transcend consciousness and reach utopia. Scriabin's idea for the piece was widely publicized from the 1910s through the modern day, and its folkloric fame allowed it to achieve an independent existence. Musicologist Simon Morrison sorted out the various strands of religious and philosophical thought that Scriabin funneled into his *Mysterium*, including:

> the Scriptures, the philosophies of Nietzsche and Schopenhauer, the ecumenical religious thought of Vladimir Solovyov, and the Theosophical doctrine of Helene Blavatsky. The performance was to be held for seven days and nights in India, during which time Scriabin planned to remove the barriers separating audience and performers and to create conditions favorable for spiritual communion (*sobornost*) and all-unity (*vseyedinstvo*).[115]

The *Mysterium*'s artistic syncretism and multimedia design had its 1960s analogue in "happenings," a term coined by the American painter Allan Kaprow (1927–2006).[116] This style of performance art bore less apocalyptic overtones than the Symbolist mystery plays Scriabin sought to enact, but happenings similarly aimed to dissolve the boundaries between performers and spectators, incorporate the natural environment into art (*Mysterium* was to be staged in the foothills of the Himalayas), and heighten the sensory awareness of its participants. Saxophonist Alexei Kozlov (b. 1935) recalled that in the 1970s, the basement of the Scriabin Museum in Moscow served as a popular site for happenings, where performers of all types would participate in a collective creative act.[117] Considering the spiritual uplift that counterculture advocates in America sought to achieve through meditation or hallucinogenic drugs, Scriabin's obsession with music's transformative properties must have seemed strikingly prescient for his era.

Exactly how popular Scriabin's music was among the 1960s youth counterculture is difficult to ascertain given the lack of any direct endorsements or documented statements from its members, but contemporary accounts of concerts at which his music was performed indicate that attendees who bore the outward markers of counterculture membership—in terms of fashion, demographics, and hygiene—patronized these events. Hilde Somer delighted at the throngs of hippies who attended her Scriabin light shows. A reviewer who attended one of her light shows in Chicago remarked that when the pianist was given congratulatory flowers at the end of her recital, they were handed to her by a young man who "had his hair bound in a ponytail at the neck. His ruffled shirt tucked into patched bells. And his bouquet was popping multicolored lights." "Scriabin would have liked that, you know," Somer commented to the reviewer. "He was, after all, the first mixed-media man."[118] At Martha Anne Verbit's 1971 all-Scriabin recital at the Phillips Collection in Washington D.C., the critic Robert Evett described how "The capacity crowd was young, the hair was long, the bell-bottomed trousers were the badge of uni-sex."[119] While these reviews represent the attendance at only a few events, similar observations by other reviewers suggest that counterculture members actively supported the Scriabin revival by attending concerts, and presumably comprising a fair portion of record-buying consumers.

Further evidence of how much the composer's music and aesthetic ideals resonated with counterculture values is provided by contemporary critics, who dipped into the counterculture lexicon to describe Scriabin's modern niche. Their writings reinforced the public image of Scriabin as a proto–Flower Child. In a review of Bowers' 1969 biography, Peter Gorner of the *Chicago Tribune* characterized Scriabin as "the first composer who may be rightly called a hippie, and this makes him especially meaningful today."[120] While this description is hardly applicable in every aspect of the hippie lifestyle, Scriabin's metaphysics overlapped enough with the mass media image of counterculture values that other critics made similar observations. Writing in a 1971 issue of *Atlantic Monthly*, Robert Evett dubbed Scriabin the "composer-in-residence to the Age of Aquarius," and astutely recognized that his centenary "would surely have passed unnoticed had it fallen a decade earlier."[121] Others drew explicit connections between Scriabin's music and psychedelic experiences: a *Harper's Magazine* reviewer insisted that the composer "thought of music in terms that can only be described as psychedelic," and in *Stereo Review*, record producer Paul Kresh considered his music "a kind of sonic methadone for a generation already partially wrecked on drugs."[122] Such comparisons were not confined to current affairs magazines. Don Heckman professed in the *New York Times* that Scriabin's music "throbs with an intensity reminiscent of the sensations aroused by hallucinogens."[123] These colorful pronouncements must have piqued the curiosity of consumers and concert-goers alike, regardless of their attitude toward the counterculture generation.

Record executives fully capitalized on the composer's budding reputation as a Flower Child. To rejuvenate lagging classical sales, Mercury A&R executive Joseph Bott and classical division director M. Scott Mampe launched an initiative to fortify new classical releases with a "strong modern-American look," in the words of Mercury publicist Margaret Turner.[124] Mercury's first effort in that vein was Hilde Somer's first all-Scriabin album (1968), which became a best seller largely due to the marketing of the composer; the album included a collectible daisy-shaped decal depicting Scriabin as the "First Flower Child," as seen in figure 8.2. "Perfectly legitimate," Somer told *Esquire* reviewer Martin Mayer, "because Scriabin *was* a kind of flower child—but clean, of course."[125] Record shops across America prominently displayed the decal as an eye-catching advertisement, the record was advertised in *High Fidelity* and *American Record Guide,* and college radio stations kept Somer's album on steady rotation.[126] The runaway success of her album prompted Mercury to release a second all-Scriabin album with Somer called *AΩ* (Alpha Omega, 1970), and in a 1973 *Piano Quarterly* article she endorsed Scriabin as "prophet of peace, love, and mysticism."[127] Channeling the charged rhetoric of Scriabin's 1920s supporters who ascribed to Theosophical ideals, Somer drew explicit parallels between psychedelic

Figure 8.2. The "First Flower Child" decal issued with Hilde Somer Plays Scriabin (Mercury SR 90500, 1968). *Courtesy of Universal Music Enterprises, a division of UMG Recordings, Inc.*

rock and Scriabin's music: "Long before the word 'psychedelic' was invented," she wrote, "long before Fillmore West (rock temple in San Francisco) and Fillmore East (in New York) were born, flourished and died, Scriabin was writing far out music to be played to the accompaniment of colored lights."[128] Somer's effusions were hardly subtle or shrewd, but they effectively reached the American public.

Not every commentator viewed Scriabin's newfound fame through rose-tinted glasses. His status as a proto–Flower Child stood at odds with the sentiment of British musicologist Hugh Macdonald, whose centennial tribute opened with the following salvo:

> Nothing is easier than to pour ridicule upon Skryabin's [sic] gradual and finally total self-delusion. Ever since the bubble of his persona was so rudely pricked in the 1920s . . . his quasi-religious convictions have been under relentless fire from the few critics who have paid him any attention at all, and must be eliminated from any possibility of serious consideration, now or even in the future.[129]

Many other critics shared Macdonald's rational, sober outlook. They believed that Scriabin's music retained its value as long as one ignored the metaphysical overlay. Other critics such as Paul Hume, however, argued that filtering out Scriabin's "distracting [and] useless" aesthetics only unmasked his paucity of musical invention. Hume shifted uncomfortably in his seat as he anticipated the spate of all-Scriabin recitals sure to flood concert programs in the coming year, grumbling that, "It will take strength of will and character to survive it."[130] Despite their vexation, these writers remained in the minority in their negative opinions of Scriabin. Their grievances did little to quell the fervor for Scriabin's works in the late 1960s and early 1970s.

THE CENTENARY DUST SETTLES

Scriabin's revivalists concerned themselves less with re-creating the values and conditions that shaped the composer's art during his lifetime than with recognizing affinities between his aesthetics and counterculture values. By putting Scriabin's significance in contemporary terms, they assimilated the composer's music and aesthetics into their own ideology. The uncanny convergence between the counterculture's sociological urges and the ideals that contemporary listeners apprehended in his music produced what philosophers have referred to as a *kairos*. For Plato and Aristotle, the term meant an opportune moment for persuasive rhetoric, but in terms of reception, it refers to a high water mark in an artwork's popularity.[131] Musicologist Carl Dahlhaus has suggested that a piece of music is most vital and meaningful during such apexes in public approval, which overturn the conventional wisdom that artworks are best understood by reconstructing the cultural codes and values active during the time they were written.

Compositions and their creators accumulate hermeneutic layers throughout their receptions by being adapted to the values and needs of different generations.

Dahlhaus argued that scrutinizing these highlights in an artwork's reception provides "a useful vantage point for surveying this historical process in its entirety and rendering it intelligible."[132] The remarkable compatibility that Scriabin's music and aesthetics had with the ideals of the 1960s counterculture illustrates just such a kairos, and demonstrated how deeply those values had permeated American culture and society. The resonance and significance of the event also confirmed that such qualities were not isolated to the ephemeral fads of popular culture or the hippie movement. They directly impacted the realm of high culture.

Although interpretive approaches to an artwork are evolutionary, conditions characteristic of a work's earlier reception can resurface at a later date and serve different sociological agendas. Thus, the popularity that Scriabin's music gained in the 1920s for its potential to provide spiritual enlightenment found renewed vigor during his revival years, when issues of canonic revaluation and the commodification of the counterculture zeitgeist remained important topics to critics, historians, and record companies. Although the mass market may have cast Scriabin as a proto–Flower Child, his music and legacy held other meanings for revivalists. Scriabin's multifaceted legacy allowed it to become topical in the late 1960s by dint of its adaptability to the competing agendas of a variety of figures who were immersed in the American music scene. To influential critics like Harold Schonberg, Scriabin was an undervalued harmonic innovator; to revivalist performers like Lewenthal, Horowitz, and Laredo, Scriabin was a neglected romantic; to fanatical virtuosi like Somer, he was a spiritual guru who heralded the psychedelic age. Scriabin's music not only fulfilled a void in the concert repertory; it also reflected the diversity of modern American life.

Every music revival offers an alternative to mainstream culture by reclaiming an idealized past, but Scriabin's resurrection after such a lengthy period of disfavor and neglect speaks to the public's avidity for his unique brand of art as well as the abundance of talented performers who championed his works in that era.[133] Their efforts are well documented in recordings and offer an enviable model for modern-day performers. Contemporary pianists, however, must ultimately make Scriabin's music applicable to the values of our current age. Like revivalist performers, their chief task should be to entice newer audiences to come to the concert hall. Only then can Scriabin's music thrive once more as it did during the 1920s and the 1960s in American history.

Part III

IN PERFORMANCE

Matthew Bengtson

9

From Musical Text to the Imagination

I can never forget my excitement upon purchasing the scores of Scriabin's piano music, and seeing it for the first time on the printed page. Having known some of these pieces only from recorded performances, I was full of anticipation to see how they looked in notation. I leafed slowly through these pages, and found myself mesmerized by their rhythmic and textural inventiveness, and fascinated by their unusual character indications. It seemed as if I had been initiated into a private world of secrets, potions, and spells: a kind of occult netherworld. Nowadays, we have long taken the availability of sheet music for granted. Even in the 1980s, when I was discovering Scriabin, scores and recordings of his music were already not difficult to find. It is easy to forget that this was not always the case. What a thrill of discovery must have awaited earlier generations of Scriabin enthusiasts in the West when scores of his music had finally become available for study and performance.

These scores represent the starting point for an extraordinary journey for a pianist, a process of interpretation that begins with getting notes into one's fingers and ends with performing acts of magic before an audience. This magic should ostensibly have the power to transport listeners to a higher spiritual plane. As John Bell Young described it, "the great Scriabin interpreter is a kind of translator capable of transforming himself from performer into conjurer."[1] Scriabin's ambition was to use music not merely to entertain his audience but to transform it, truly, to elevate its consciousness. To communicate Scriabin's art to an audience, one must attempt to conjure up or even cohabit this imaginative world.

The pianist bears an extra responsibility in Scriabin's music. The opportunity to play the role of conjurer is a thrill, but the mission can be daunting. A Scriabin performance, however attractive, well studied, and executed, will fail in its mission without the inspirational flight of fancy this music demands. For an audience unfamiliar with the music, an inferior performance would likely reflect badly on Scriabin himself rather than on the pianist. The great Scriabin interpreter Sviatoslav Richter remarked: "When I play well, Scriabin is liked. When I play badly, he is not. It's as simple as that."[2] More than proper execution, an intense temperament is crucial, one that matches the character of the music. As the Russian composer and critic Yuli Engel relates: "A clear, well-balanced talent alone could not convey the essential spirit of Scriabin's music in all its sharpness and power. Rather, a successful performance of Scriabin's works . . . ought to combine impulsiveness, whimsy, impetuosity, and an extreme, almost morbid, concentration of nervous intensity."[3]

How is it that a piano—a machine of hammers and strings—can be made to overtake one's emotions, and even spirituality, at the level to which this music aspires? In these pages, we will probe the answers to this question, considering the stylistic elements of Scriabin's piano *oeuvre*. In the coming chapters, we will investigate his wealth of melodic inspiration, trace the development of his famous mystical harmonies, and explore the myriad facets of sound and rhythm that form the signature elements of his distinctive compositional and performing style. We will also explore those aspects of playing technique that most characterize his approach to the keyboard, isolating the most important physical skill sets that a pianist needs to develop. Let us begin our overview with the musical scores, and progress from the objective details they contain to the imaginative world of Scriabin's fantasy.

SCRIABIN'S MUSICAL SCORES IN THEIR HISTORICAL CONTEXT

In the early years of the twentieth century, an array of exceptionally talented composers presented a wide variety of bold visions to the musical world. This era must rank among the most fertile periods in the history of musical creativity. Among these dynamic musical minds were some radical composers who pushed the limits of notation in an effort to convey their ideals. To them, ordinary musical notation seemed limited in its ability to convey a wide range of gestures and shapes. These composers began to expand their use of notation, asking more of both the performer and the instrument. Debussy, for example, expanded the notation of articulation to broaden a pianist's touch palette, thus refining the texture of the sound. Berg and Albéniz extended their use of dynamics, employing the extreme markings *pppp* and *ffff* in an attempt to squeeze the greatest range of resonances and timbres from the instrument. Schoenberg, while expanding the sense of consonance and dissonance, introduced new notations to clarify both the hierarchy of line and its metrical emphasis. Ives invented new fanciful markings to describe distant sound timbres, and explored an entirely new style of temporal organization, sometimes eliminating barlines altogether.

Scriabin was hardly any less ambitious in his aims than these contemporaries. However, compared to them, his notational practices were generally rather conservative. His publisher Mitrofan Beliaev, in receipt of the Second Sonata manuscript, complained, "There are, as usual, far too few markings."[4] Consider dynamics, for example. In performance, his music certainly requires an extremely wide range, but he saves extreme markings such as *ff* (and, very occasionally, *fff*) only for the biggest of climaxes. Even the grotesque death march of the Ninth Sonata is only marked with a single *forte*. As in Baroque and Classical styles, the performer's insight and understanding of the idiom is required to fill these imaginative gaps. Consider also the challenges of rhythm. Although Scriabin's rhythm as a performer was extraordinarily flexible, the notation of his music generally conforms to traditional norms.

In his brief performing career, Scriabin himself completed the process from the conception of ideas to the inspiration of live solo performance. A gold medal winner in piano performance from the Moscow Conservatory, and a pianist who focused exclusively on his own music, he was certainly the logical person to convey his musical message to the public. However, he was far from the only one who did so successfully. Not known for his praise of other musicians, he did respond with sincere appreciation to the performances of a small number of pianists who showed an affinity for his musical world, and who responded to his scores with imaginative fantasy. These pianists include Samuil Feinberg and Vsevolod Buyukly. As Scriabin pianists today, we must seek the kind of spark that lifts his inspiration from the printed page into a spiritual message. The colorful performance directives in the scores are the first place to look.

CHARACTER INDICATIONS

Colorful character indications in Italian and French form an important link in Scriabin's musical scores between pure notational facts and his imaginative inner world. We do not refer to ordinary performance directives (slow down, get louder, bring out the middle voice, etc.), but rather to programmatic suggestions that stimulate the poetic imagination. Jonathan Powell in *Grove Online* calls them "signposts for the psyche in its journey to lands previously unchartered and forbidden to musicians."[5] The pianist is called upon to respond with appropriate choices of sound, rhythm and texture. Scriabin's markings are among the most imaginative and evocative of any composer, and mark the endpoint of a Romantic tradition.

Scriabin began marking his scores in Italian, the traditional language of music, but even in his very early years had a penchant for unusual and evocative choices. For instance, the Prelude Op. 11 No. 1 in C (1893) was originally marked *Ondeggiante, carezzando* (undulating, caressing), a beautifully poetic description. However, seeing that Scriabin was a relatively unestablished composer, restraint and sober thinking prevailed prior to publication, most likely in the Beliaev firm, and this marking was ultimately downgraded to the neutral *Vivace*.[6] In his middle period, however, the lid came off and the genie was out of the bottle; colorful descriptions proliferated everywhere, including this same *Carezzando*. Some of his favorite indications during this period were *Festivamente* (festively), *Con fiducia* (with confidence), *Irato* (angry), *Fiero* (proud), *Affanato* (breathlessly), *Elevato* (lofty), and *Languido* (languid). For special moments, his vocabulary expanded to *Focosamente, giubiloso* (focused, jubilant) at the end of the Fourth Sonata, and *Con stravaganza* (extravagantly) in the Fifth. Scriabin's personal, ecstatic, and overtly erotic musical style had arrived. Not all musicians were convinced by this over-the-top language, however. It was just the kind of excess that would soon bear the brunt of Erik Satie's sharp satires, often in the form of deliberately absurd performance indications in his own music.

Scriabin's inventiveness with his markings could lead him down obscure linguistic byways in his attempts, as it were, to "eff the ineffable." In the *Poème* Op. 32 No. 1 he coins the poetic word *inaferando*. The Italian *afferrare*, according to Cassell's English-Italian dictionary, means to "grasp, seize or get hold of." The same dictionary also offers *inafferrabile* as "impossible to grasp or seize; out of reach" (and thus, elusive or ineffable). Scriabin's coinage is a concocted form, intended to imply a manner of playing: "play in an ineffable way." At the very least, the twists and turns of this linguistic labyrinth aptly illustrate a moving target that is "difficult to grasp."

Even one small designation in the score might help a pianist connect the musical dots into a coherent narrative vision. The passage of the Fifth Sonata beginning at m. 253 marked *con delizio* (with delight) is among the most overtly erotic in Scriabin's music. Every chord can be caressed and massaged with greater and greater innuendo until at the *molto rit.* in m. 270 the music turns a final suggestive corner. As the dynamics begin to fade out and the depths of the bass register are plumbed, we can imagine the lights being dimmed and sense that the real lovemaking is about to begin. After this section one finds another characteristic Scriabin marking: *con una ebbrezza fantastica* (with a fantastic drunkenness). This state of intoxication is clearly a reference to the cult of Dionysus. Like Nietzsche before him, and Nietzsche's followers, the Mystical Anarchists, Scriabin believed that dance and intoxication were a means to lift the human spirit, and could lead to a blinding moment of ecstasy (see chapter 7 for more information on these subjects). In this sonata, this consummation takes place at m. 401*ff*, and is one of the most overwhelming climaxes in all of Scriabin's music. In the Tenth Sonata, we find a similar pattern, beginning at m. 192 with the evocative French indication *avec une douce ivresse* (with gentle intoxication).[7] The sense of dizziness is depicted by a wobbling instability of tempo. It presages an awe-inspiring buildup to a terrific climax (*Puissant, radieux*) that lasts for several pages; it is as dazzling an evocation of light as one can find anywhere in the piano repertoire.

When Scriabin is generous with these evocative character indications, a pianist can readily envision a program for the work at hand. The Ninth Sonata, for example, is so densely littered with markings as to suggest the entire plot of a horror movie. Other works, however, offer fewer clues. For example, what is one to do in the Eighth Sonata, where there are scarcely any directions in sight in over thirty pages of music? A thorough knowledge of Scriabin's vocabulary of typical gestures will always help an interpreter to move from abstract notes on the page to the kinds of concrete images that demand a visceral response.

SCRIABIN'S VOCABULARY OF GESTURES

Among studies of instrumental music of the Baroque and Classical Eras, some of the most useful for performers are the ones that relate gestures of what was once considered pure absolute music to its contemporary culture.[8] Through such references, we can bridge the gap between ourselves and the audience of the composer's times. Many rhythmic and even melodic figures can link that music to *topoi* (topics, or literally, "places") with implied affective contexts. Especially significant *topoi* are contemporary dances (Minuets, Gavottes, etc.), which carry a whole vocabulary of related social connotations. Mozart, composing for an audience "in the know," used these kinds of references to great effect both in his instrumental music and in his operas.[9] Later, in the programmatic music of the nineteenth century, music took on a more explicitly descriptive character, as in the operas of Wagner, where connections between music and the characters and events of the opera are linked by the widespread use of *leitmotif*.

In Scriabin, where music is closely intertwined with philosophy, the impulse to connect musical material with extra-musical inspiration is especially strong. This impulse gains urgency in his late style, in which music is most explicitly linked to specific philosophical ideas. A sample *topos* from his early period is the song of the nightingale, a representative of erotic longing found in numerous Romantic composers, perhaps most famously in Schumann and Granados. Scriabin's trills and light filigree in the opening of the Fourth Sonata refer clearly to this tradition (see figure 9.1). This is a simple and conservative example by Scriabin's standards, but even Scriabin's fecund imagination settled on a fairly small collection of musical gestures throughout the development of his style. A proposal for a concrete programmatic understanding of Scriabin's late work has been put forward by musicologist Susanna

Figure 9.1. Nightingale sounds in Sonata No. 4 in F♯ major Op. 30, mm. 18–27. *Leipzig: Beliaev, 1904.*

Garcia.[10] Her *topoi* for Scriabin include the summons, the Eternal Feminine, the light motive, the flight motive, and the vertiginous dance.

Among Scriabin's most widespread and striking musical gestures are those that characterize the masculine and feminine poles of his gendered mystical universe.[11] Masculine assertiveness is represented by the *zov* (Russian for call, or summons), a rhythmic gesture in which a note, or group of short notes, leads to an accented long tone.[12] The trumpet summons in the *Poem of Ecstasy* (for example, at the final *Maestoso*) and *Prometheus* (for example, mm. 191–92) stand out as clear hallmarks of this style; they are some of the most memorable and readily identifiable moments of those works. The programmatic significance of the trumpet fanfare is analogous to the herald of the apocalypse. Fanfares in Scriabin's solo music should naturally be played with special emphasis in both rhythm and timing. Standing in stark contrast to the assertiveness of the *zov* is the seductive side of Scriabin's imagination. Garcia refers to this quality as "the Eternal Feminine," a cultural reference to Goethe's *Faust* that was further developed by Nietzsche, and which weighed heavily on Scriabin's cultural time and place. Music of the "Eternal Feminine" is marked by its rhythmic vagueness and sense of languor, and should naturally be played with great rhythmic freedom, undulating dynamics, and tenderness of sonority. The compelling juxtaposition of these opposing poles of attraction will help to emphasize and offset one another, and reveal a dynamic style in which sexual activity serves as a metaphor for creativity.

Two of Scriabin's preoccupations in his quest for spiritual ecstasy are the notions of light and flight. Satan, Lucifer, and Prometheus converge in ancient myth as bringers of light,[13] which represents a spiritual awakening. Fire, in particular, is a symbol of both defiance and a stage of enlightenment. Luminosity is typically represented in Scriabin's piano music by trills, tremolos, and bursts of explosive energy in the upper register. Flight is a metaphor for transcendence to a new plane of spiritual existence without gravity. Musical representations of the idea of flight permeate his musical idiom as irregular, fast, and spasmodic gestures, usually with an ascending contour.[14] The indication *ailé* (winged) is a widespread character indication in his late music. An explicitly labeled example is the short *Poème ailé* Op. 51 No. 3, which is chock-full of spasmodic 32nd note gestures that represent the sudden fluttering of wings.

Garcia's final *topos* is the "vertiginous dance." Scriabin labels it *danse délirante* (see the Sixth Sonata, m. 298). Scriabin and the Mystical Anarchists believed that spiritual ecstasy could be achieved through intoxicating spinning dances, part of the Dionysian cult ritual. The product of this ritual was "the dancer's collapse in exhaustion and an enhanced susceptibility to divine influence."[15] Although the delirious dance manifests itself as a specific formal and programmatic device in the sonatas and in *Prometheus*, the sense of vigorous acceleration and rhythmic drive had long been a significant part of Scriabin's style, both as a composer and as a pianist. One can hear it in his performance of the apparently innocent Mazurka Op. 40 No. 2, a work intended to charm and cajole rather than to shake the heavens. No elevated spirituality is in play here, but the Dionysian, ecstatic nature of his driving tempo reveals the high-strung, excitable nature of his musical personality through his career.[16]

This web of subjective associations between musical notes and philosophical ideas was enthusiastically received by Scriabin's close associates, inheritors of the Romantic tradition, in his later years.[17] They were accepted so enthusiastically, in fact, that the Symbolist movement expanded the list of correspondences to include colors, harmonies, touches, scent, movement, and language. Scriabin's art, powerful though it can be, is also exceedingly delicate, as it hinges on this tenuous vocabulary of relationships. In our own times, these kinds of connections have been deconstructed scientifically, and are generally viewed with a good deal of suspicion, or even cynicism. If this music is played by one who is contemptuous of such belief systems, its communicative power would surely be compromised. Although Scriabin's mystical ideas had their share of detractors even in his lifetime,[18] he did attract an enthusiastic following through his exceptional talent. Let us consider the advent of modern styles in composition and performance, and see how they have colored the lens through which we view Scriabin's art.

AFTER SCRIABIN'S DEATH: THE RISE OF MODERN PLAYING STYLES

World War I represented a decisive break in world history in many respects, and art music was no exception. In the devastation of this struggle, many of the ideals of Romanticism were destroyed and entirely new aesthetic trends would take over, led by Igor Stravinsky and his followers, by Erik Satie and *Les Six* in France, and by Sergei Prokofiev in Russia. These composers were all eager to shed the baggage of complex philosophies, many of which originated from the hated Germans.[19] They made polemics against the very idea of music's connection to a higher meaning. Clear attacks, lean textures, and motoric rhythms became the order of the day, not only in their piano music. The esoteric beliefs of Scriabin resembled too closely, in hindsight, just the sort of quixotic madness that had led to this brutal conflict.

Prokofiev, whose energetic rhythms and readily accessible style captured the spirit of the age, provided the remedy in Russia to Scriabin's subjective eroticism. Musicologist Nikolai Zhiliaev (1881–1938) offered the following comparison: "Prokofiev is a real barbarian compared to the fragile and sophisticated Scriabin." If Prokofiev was a "Scythian who captures wild animals with simple weapons," Scriabin was an "elf shooting at butterflies with moonbeams."[20] Some composers attempted to run against the powerful currents of change, but they were decidedly countercultural for their times. Among Russians, these composers include Rachmaninov, whose Romanticism exudes a nostalgia for a lost era, and Medtner, whose artistic goals were lofty but whose tastes for traditional craft seemed decidedly conservative, even old-fashioned.[21] On the other hand, there remained a number of idealistic followers of Scriabin, such as Stanchinsky, Obukhov, Roslavets, Lourié, Myaskovsky, Sabaneev, and Vyshnegradsky, but their music linked to Scriabin's world was considered too inimical to socialist purposes and was generally swept under the rug by the new regime.[22]

Virtuosity, however, was very much alive and well in the modernist musical aesthetic; indeed, it was an integral part of it. Masterworks in that style could demand every bit as much technical proficiency as anything the Romantics ever created. Witness, for example, Prokofiev's *Toccata* Op. 11, and Stravinsky's *Three Movements from Petrushka*. Beyond the realm of physical technique, however, interpretive demands on the performer were simplified, as rhythms had become stricter and the quality of sound more direct and immediate. A capable and well-prepared player in the modernist style will always tend to give a successful performance. On the other hand, in Scriabin's music (or in the music of Liszt or Schumann before him), technical proficiency is only the beginning of a long search for the music's deeper meaning. The interpretive simplicity of the modernist style may be a significant factor in its public success. In this process, however, the role of a performer is devalued from the status of coconspirator in the creative act to that of an executant.

Stravinsky reacted vigorously against the excesses of Romantic license at the expense of structural discipline. In doing so, he made a strong and highly influential distinction between execution and interpretation in the act of performance.[23] Ravel, in a conflict with the well-known left-handed virtuoso Paul Wittgenstein, famously confronted the pianist, denying him the liberties to which he had been accustomed. Wittgenstein protested, "Interpreters must not be slaves!" but Ravel retorted, "Performers are slaves!"[24] It is around this time that the tradition of the pianist-composer begins its sharp decline. Music conservatories have since tended to train performers more specifically for competitions, and less in the broader spectrum of skills, such as ear training and music theory, which would prepare a student to compose or improvise music. This trend has produced more accurate executants in a more limited repertoire, with less involvement in the creative process and the meaning behind the notes, whether the historical, biographical, or theoretical circumstances of composition, that is, precisely the factors that make music and musical performance an imaginative culture.

Performers, influenced by philosophical ideas such as *Neue Sachlichkeit* (New Objectivity), also began to apply them to other repertoires. Scriabin scholar Anatole Leikin refers to this modernist phenomenon as "the Great Freeze."[25] This apparently objective approach, where emotion and indulgence are mistrusted, has found mixed results. One could debate to what extent the music of Bach, Mozart, and Beethoven have been well served by this process, but their reputations as composers have suffered no damage. However, after the late-Romantic tradition had sharply diminished in performance style, Scriabin's music fell out of favor, and his reputation has suffered from performance styles that are not congruent with his aesthetic values. Boris Schloezer, the composer's brother-in-law and admirer, remarked that "[Scriabin's music] found no alliance with the spirit of post-war Europe where one perceives the need of calm, stability, the desire for order, a fear of experiments in every field, in politics, literature, poetry, and music."[26]

It would take until the latter half of the century until the historic performance practice movement would begin to reconsider approaches to Bach, Mozart, and

Beethoven with their cultural contexts, whether the characteristic inequalities of dance steps, their foundations in *stylus phantasticus* or *Affektenlehre*, and their relationship to the rhetorical declamation of the spoken word. These contexts can all help liberate musical expression from the click of the metronome. Not until the 1970s did the pendulum of aesthetic trends in composition begin to swing back toward Romantic warmth. Numerous recent studies have revisited and reevaluated early recordings and performance styles. This climate should foster a reappraisal of Scriabin's music, and allow for an understanding of a performance style to emerge that is congruent with his musical values.

SOME THOUGHTS FOR INTERMEDIATE PIANISTS AND TEACHERS

The most famous giants of music, the likes of Bach and Beethoven, will likely always dominate the life of the piano studio as well as the landscape of professional musical activity. However, certain composers, such as Kuhlau, Burgmuller, and Kabalevsky, have acquired widespread familiarity among piano teachers. With a deft combination of craft and charm, they serve important pedagogical needs of early intermediate students, and thus have found a niche in the repertoire. As students make the transition to the advanced level, however, assigning appropriate repertoire becomes a challenging dilemma. Scriabin's music, unfortunately, is seldom considered as suitable repertoire for students, and it is rarely attempted by amateurs. He taught piano students only for a short time, and surely did not compose with pedagogical thoughts in mind. According to conventional wisdom, Scriabin's music isn't appropriate for students because it is too complicated and difficult to play or understand. Further, Scriabin does not fit neatly into the traditional style periods.[27] As a Romantic, he is often passed over in favor of a long list of popular piano composers. As a representative of modernism, he is also bypassed, either as too close to the Romantic tradition, or else as being too quirky or individualistic to be a useful springboard for learning other musical styles. Assigning twentieth-century music is always a delicate proposition for a teacher, since there is always a fear that choosing the wrong piece might alienate younger musicians from exploring new musical terrains.

All this is a pity, because Scriabin's music could be a pedagogical treasure trove.[28] With a bit of exploring, we soon discover that many of his compositions are charming, attractive to a wide audience, and readily playable. They also offer an all-important pedagogical virtue: brevity. Scriabin may have written as many exquisite miniature piano pieces as any composer of Western music. Music teachers view excessively difficult pieces, quite properly, with suspicion and mistrust (and therefore many of Scriabin's etudes, and certainly the sonatas, should be assigned with great caution). However, overly long pieces constitute, in their own way, an equal menace to a student's long-term progress. Once a student has devoted enough preparation time to a particular work, it becomes psychologically too difficult to let it go, even when the final double bar is nowhere in sight. Odds are the final result will not be satisfying musically or a healthy learning experience. Short character pieces offer the opportunity to delve properly into all the artistic issues related to phrasing, declamation, touch, timing, and color, and also to the study of a work's form and harmony. Regrettably, in today's competitive climate, miniatures are passed over far too often in favor of more and more ambitious, larger, and more impressive pieces, obsessively prepared for live performances and competitions. All too often, these works fall beyond a student's experience, maturity, and comfort level.

Scriabin's miniatures offer numerous pedagogical benefits in the areas of technique, emotional expression, and harmonic understanding. The most challenging Preludes and Etudes give a tough technical workout, but one that is packaged compactly. An ambitious pianist will find these hurdles satisfying to overcome; once solved, the skills obtained will be applicable to a wide range of other music.[29] Scriabin's early works are often in remote key signatures. Gaining facility in these tonalities is an area where most students long remain uncomfortable and simply need more experience. Scriabin's music also offers an outlet to wear one's emotions on one's sleeve, projecting moods with generous Romantic expression. This is critical, since the ability to express typically lags behind the development of technique. Budding pianists in their adolescent years may especially relish this opportunity. Scriabin's later works may be a tougher sell for many, but they can be a great match for the right student. They challenge and expand the ear. With their roots in a Romantic idiom, they can help bridge the gap into the more dissonant musical styles of the twentieth century.

There are too many outstanding short pieces to introduce in this small space, but a few highlights can serve as a point of reference. The Etude Op. 2 No. 1 in C# minor makes an effective exercise in voicing and in casting a heavy, dark mood. Among those pieces with the most immediate appeal, we suggest the Mazurka Op. 3 No. 1, the Etudes Op. 8 Nos. 8 and 11, the Prelude Op. 22 No. 1, the Preludes Op. 37 Nos. 1 and 3, the Etude Op. 42 No. 4, the *Feuillet d'album* Op. 45 No. 1, and the *Danse Languide* Op. 51 No. 4. Full of charm and technically manageable, these pieces offer a friendly introduction to Scriabin's world. The Mazurkas Op. 3 are successful recital pieces, not overly demanding, and good tests for the flexible rhythmic declamation of stylized dance.

Scriabin's music can be effectively used for the development of technique. Especially for the development of the left hand, there is no more useful repertoire. In addition to the two pieces from Op. 9, many Preludes from Op. 11 and Op. 13, Op. 16 No. 1, and Op. 22 No. 1 are all helpful study material. Another important skill for developing pianists is right hand passagework, in which one must coordinate finger action with smooth movements of the wrist and arm to bring the fingers into proper striking position. Excellent test pieces are the Preludes Op. 11 No. 3, Op. 11 No. 23, Op. 13 No. 2, and Op. 15 No. 2. Polyrhythm is often a stumbling block for intermediate pianists, requiring focused attention; in the Etude Op. 8 No. 4 and Preludes Op. 11 No. 3, Op. 13 No. 4, and Op. 39 No. 3, this issue forms one of the biggest challenges. There are also many pieces for octaves and double notes. The

Preludes Op. 11 can make an attractive studio project, whereby students of diverse levels can be assigned pieces appropriate to their experience, and perform the entire cycle as a group. This cycle serves the same function as Chopin's Preludes Op. 28, at the same level of difficulty, but not so often played.

Among the later works, the collections Op. 57–59, Op. 63, Opp. 67, 69, 71, 73, and 74 are a rich repository of material. As introductions to twentieth-century style, they are generally briefer and no more demanding than Debussy's Preludes. Among them, only the Preludes Op. 67 No. 2, Op. 73 No. 2, and Op. 74 No. 5 pose burdensome technical difficulties. The Op. 57 pieces and the *Poème* Op. 69 No. 1 are among the most straightforward. The challenges of these late works include sound and texture, polyrhythms, harmonic understanding, accurate counting of rhythm, and imaginative characterization.

It is my hope that more pianists might explore Scriabin's miniature works at a formative developmental stage, and experience through performance the charms and beauties of his creative world that may have seemed inaccessible.

10

Technique

Before tackling issues of style and interpretation in Scriabin's music, a pianist has to confront its technical hurdles, which, in the most demanding pieces, can be formidable indeed. Scriabin's pianistic vocabulary was derived from the Romantic tradition, especially from Chopin and Liszt, and likely also influenced by the pianistic knuckle-busters he played as a student: Balakirev's *Islamey* and Liszt's *Reminiscences of Don Juan*. A large body of technical study material is designed to prepare a pianist's technical apparatus for the virtuosic demands of this repertoire: pieces by Hanon, Czerny, Clementi, Cramer, Duvernoy, Pischna, Moszkowski, Brahms, as well as Chopin and Liszt. These include Etudes for thirds, sixths, and octaves, for passage-work, velocity, and leaps, and for various other issues such as sonority, equality, and independence of fingers, and the execution of polyrhythms.

All of these skills are put to the test in Scriabin's piano music, but they are not the point of the music. Many of his miniatures belong to the compositional tradition that transforms technical hurdles into musical poetry. The classic sets of Etudes by Chopin and Liszt have set the standard for the genre of musically important technical studies. Liszt's choice of title, *Études d'exécution transcendante* (Studies of Transcendental Execution), is an appropriate testament to his purpose of creating technical studies with a nobility of poetic vision that transcends mere mechanical thinking. Scriabin's Etudes belong to this same category, and so do the most challenging of his Preludes, which can act as technical workouts as well as effective concert pieces. Special characteristics of Scriabinian technique include the expanded role of the left hand, widely spaced chords, flexible wrist technique, freedom of movement in spanning the keyboard, and an idiosyncratic style of trills. Also, since the two hands often cross one another or share registers, the pianist must often confront a dilemma about the appropriate division of labor between them. All these issues are confronted in this chapter.

EMANCIPATION OF THE LEFT HAND

Scriabin's 1891 right hand injury was a decisive event in his life in many ways (see chapter 3 for more details). It led him to focus more on composition than on performance, and prompted his first musings on spiritual matters. It also fundamentally shaped the nature of his approach to the instrument, first as a pianist and then as a composer. While recovering from his injury, he developed remarkable dexterity in his left hand from extensive practice. Soon he began composing music for the left hand alone: the Prelude and Nocturne, which were an immediate and impressive public success. These two pieces remain, to this day, clear standouts in the repertoire of music for the left hand alone. Scriabin's early reputation as a touring pianist-composer largely hinged on them. Especially on his American tour, he was known *primarily* as the composer of pieces for the left hand. Critics observed that—most unusually for a pianist—the extraordinary skill of his left hand had outstripped that of his right. César Cui wrote of a St. Petersburg concert, "His left hand is stronger than his right and sometimes smothers it. He played better with one hand in the Nocturne than he did with two hands in the other pieces."[1]

His instant success in this rare idiom surely tempted Scriabin to cash in on his reputation as a left-handed pianist to advance his career. He composed during this time a left-hand alone waltz that was said to use every virtuosic trick in the book. Riding high on his publicity, he would trot out this piece from time to time as an encore and dazzle his audiences. It is a great pity that this piece has been lost, but it may have been more a bag of parlor tricks than a serious musical composition.[2] Scriabin ultimately had second thoughts and discarded the piece. Although he was never one to shy away from writing difficult music, he considered technical wizardry and showmanship not as ends in themselves but rather as means toward the end of intense musical communication.

His attitude can be traced in these Op. 9 pieces and their relationship to the virtuoso tradition of left hand writing. Chopin's "Revolutionary Etude" Op. 10 No. 12, a bedrock of the tradition, seeks to improve the left hand in precisely those skills where it is traditionally weaker: strength and agility in rapid passagework. This Etude marks a key turning point in the piano repertoire at a time when rapid figurations were almost exclusively assigned to the right hand. Leopold Godowsky, the great Polish pianist, composer, arranger, and pedagogue, showed a special interest in the left hand's technical development.[3] In his arrangements of Chopin Etudes, for example, he reworked the already difficult "Thirds" Etude Op. 25 No. 6 in G♯ minor by giving the challenging part in thirds to the left hand. His rationale was that a pianist's left hand is not intrinsically weaker, but rather untrained. This Godowsky Etude makes a fascinating technical exercise for the rare pianist who can truly handle it, but it runs decidedly against the grain of traditional pianism.

Scriabin's left hand writing makes the most of what pianists naturally tend to do best. His style follows the laws of acoustics and the idiosyncrasies of piano sound. Everything begins with the overtone series, with its wide intervals in the bass register and narrower ones as it ascends to the soprano. The damper pedal can be used to sustain bass notes. When a composer follows the spacing of the overtone series, the left hand must cover a wider range of the keyboard than the right.[4] It must play bass notes and octaves, and provide harmonic support to fill the middle registers in the form of chords, arpeggios, and countermelodies. It may also occasionally cross over the right hand. The right hand typically plays more linear material: melodies or passagework. Scriabin's writing also exploits the shape of the left hand, taking advantage of the fact that the melody can be played by the thumb, the thickest and strongest finger. This style of composing is derived from the Chopin tradition, but in Scriabin, the richness of sonority, technical demands, and musical complexity of the left hand's role are all elevated to a new level.

As a concertizing pianist, my two hands are each trained to manage a wide range of technical problems, but there is no doubt where their natural predilections lie. My left hand stretches itself into a wide position more readily than my right.[5] It also has a better kinesthetic sense of distance, so it finds its targets more easily while leaping across registers. My right hand has more ready-made power and control in rapid passagework. Scriabin's pianism absolutely fits these typical characteristics.[6] In popular idioms too, the stride style—the foundation for much ragtime, blues, and jazz—uses the hands in just this way, with leaps in the left hand and more detail in a narrower range in the right hand. There is very little piano music written for the right hand alone, because it does not cover the range of the keyboard as naturally, and the thumb is in a disadvantageous position, on the bottom. Scriabin's success with and natural kinship for the left-hand alone idiom has inspired American composer Jay Reise (b. 1950) to arrange several of the most popular Scriabin Etudes as left-hand alone pieces: Op. 2 No. 1 in C♯ minor, Op. 8 No. 11 in B♭ minor, and also—quite improbably—Op. 8 No. 12 in D♯ minor. The last of these is an exceptionally demanding transcription, only performed to date by its dedicatee, the present author.[7]

After his successes in the left-hand alone idiom, Scriabin retained this playing style as a signature component of his two-handed music, giving the left-hand part both textural richness and polyphonic interest. The Preludes Op. 11 No. 1 in C major and No. 8 in F♯ minor are two early examples of the kinds of wide left-hand spans that would become the norm in Scriabin's writing. These parts need to be practiced well on their own, hands separately, to succeed when the hands are together. Even then, there are so many demands on one's tactile "radar" that memorization is a nearly indispensable step to assure the performer's comfort.

It is more common in Scriabin than any other composer that the left-hand part crosses above middle C. Indeed, from practicing his music, one quickly gains fluency in reading the ledger lines above the bass clef.[8] He liked to use the left hand's thumb as a strong tenor voice, like the cello's A string, which is especially expressive in the high register. There are many beautiful examples of this practice; I would mention especially *Fragilité* Op. 51 No. 1, the *Poème* Op. 59 No. 1, and the Etude Op. 65 No. 1.

The Etude Op. 8 No. 12 in D♯ minor is a well-known example of the kinds of left-hand technical obstacles a pianist will encounter. While the difficulties of the right hand's rapid-fire octaves capture our immediate attention, the left hand's part is equally demanding in its own way. Full of constant wide leaps, it can feel quite disorienting to play, and a significant amount of practice is necessary to navigate its numerous hazards. Other typically athletic left-hand parts from this period include the leaps of the Etudes Op. 8 No. 7 in C♯ minor and No. 9 in B♭ minor, the third movement of the First Sonata, a number of the Preludes Op. 11 (Nos. 1, 7, 19, 20, and 24), and the Prelude Op. 13 No. 6 in B minor, a brilliant left-hand study, in which both endurance and precision are required to manage the daunting leaps and vigorous rhythms.

Although most of Scriabin's left-hand parts aren't quite as fatiguing to execute as Op. 13 No. 6, they can often require uncommon skill and finesse. A beautiful example is the Prelude Op. 11 No. 11 in B major, a wonderful left-hand study I often recommend to students. It is very characteristic of Scriabin's approach to the piano, where the left hand clearly does the heavy lifting. It needs to dance gracefully over a range of three octaves, playing the bass, harmonic support and a gentle countermelody, all with impeccable textural refinement and layered dynamic control. Physical prerequisites for successful performance of this piece are a quiet, supple arm, an expert feel of keyboard geography (always anticipating the next arrival point before it comes), and quiet, efficient, and relaxed pivoting motions in the wrist. The hand will pivot both side to side and in and out, but always needs to stay very close to the keyboard. Not long after this Prelude, Scriabin would produce a companion gem in B major with another beautiful left-hand part (every bit as alluring but less technically demanding) in the Prelude Op. 16 No. 1. It is tempting to ask if the similarity of these two B major pieces might represent a synaesthetic's key-color association (as described in chapter 6 on color-hearing) or if they are simply a product of Scriabin's tactile memory at the keyboard.

CHORDS: ROLLED, BROKEN, STACKED, AND REPEATED

Scriabin's love of rich harmony and his predilection for widely spaced resonances produced many chords that can't be played at once by a single pair of hands. A performer is then confronted with a fascinating array of choices: textural choices (whether to roll or play as a series of blocks), distribution choices (how to assign notes to each hand), voicing choices (which parts to bring out), and timing choices (whether to roll the chord on, before, or around the beat). Given Scriabin's penchant for large chords, one might speculate that he had large hands like César Franck. However, he was in fact "a frail, diminutive man, standing just one inch over five feet, with small hands that could hardly play intervals wider than an octave."[9] Thus, Scriabin's own performing style was—like that of many of his contemporaries— rather liberal by modern standards in rolling chords, whether explicitly indicated by the score or not. He often rolled smaller chords for expressive effect when their size was not an issue.[10] Samuel Randlett, one of the earlier commentators, describes it as follows: "The romantic harp-like ripple of rolled chords fits into Scriabin's musical style quite beautifully and naturally.... The ripple is a part of the music, and for this reason it is often a mistake to play the notes of the chords simultaneously (even in the absence of an arpeggiation sign) by rearranging the distribution of the notes between the hands."[11] The issue of rearrangement in Scriabin's music, a large topic filled with nuanced considerations, is taken up below.

The art of performing widely spread chords is so critically important to successful interpretation of Scriabin's music that we must cover the issue in some detail. A pianist should strive to feel the luxury of the full resonance, to coordinate the action of fingers and pedal, and to conceal any physical challenges.[12] Artistic questions include the distribution of notes among the hands, and the decision to roll them or to organize them into a stack of blocked positions. If the chord must be rolled, how fast should the roll be, and in what order should those notes be played? Rhythmic placement is another important consideration, since a rolled chord, although defined to take place on a particular beat of the music, must unfold over nonmetric time. In Romantic style, the melody note will define the beat for the listener's ear. This note may not actually conclude the rolled chord, but may at times be found in the middle of it.

Let us consider the ends of three short Preludes as examples. The gigantic stacked chord at the conclusion of the Prelude Op. 37 No. 2 (figure 10.1a) puts an exclamation point on this lively work. Because of this character, a simple bottom-to-top roll is the most effective. In theory, this chord might be redistributed among the hands in a number of ways, but stacking the notes up to clang forth in solid blocks seems blunt and crude. As Randlett observed, the luxurious richness of the rolled chord (its ripple) is part of the music. In the tradition of Scriabin's own pianism, I prefer to allow the left hand to do most of the active work, rolling the four notes of the bass and then playing the soprano A♯, while the right hand remains statically in place playing only two notes (compare Op. 17 No. 5 below). One could certainly also spread the notes four in the left and three in the right (as printed), provided there is enough power in the right hand in this weak position with the fifth finger stretched on top. This straightforward method produces a warm and even sound, and tends slightly to emphasize the middle register where the two thumbs are located. It would not be a good idea to redistribute the bass part among two hands and then the treble three notes again among the two hands. All these changes of position would solidify and overly brighten the sound.

The other two Preludes, Op. 51 No. 2 (figure 10.1b) and Op. 67 No. 1 (figure 10.1c), are similar in character, each concluding softly and mysteriously with a large, resonant chord. The primary technical objective should be to avoid any unwanted accents. Thus, the two hands should retain the printed distributions to soften the overall sound. The artistic dilemma is the speed and coordination of the rolls of each hand. In this mysterious atmosphere, it is better for each hand to spread the chord more or less simultaneously, rather than from bottom to top. Typically, the left hand leads and the right hand follows.[13] Another possibility is to roll the right hand faster

Figure 10.1. Spacious final chords. The endings of: (a) Prelude Op. 37 No. 2 in F♯ major (Leipzig: Beliaev, 1904). (b) Prelude Op. 51 No. 2 in A minor (Leipzig: Beliaev, 1907). (c) Prelude Op. 67 No. 1 (Moscow: Jurgenson, 1913).

than the left; the advantages are that the melodic line can carry over more directly to the final destination in the soprano, and that the wider spacing of the left-hand part can be felt in its slower motion. Since the right hand arrives first, and the left hand finishes the roll after the beat (as in Baroque style), the last note of the left hand must be consciously de-emphasized.

In his earlier years, Scriabin would often write not just an oversized chord at the end of a piece, but whole chains of them, one for each melody note. He typically retains a broad spacing on each chord to maximize resonance, even at a high tempo, showing little concern for the practicalities of performance. It seems as if more hands are required. The formidable passage in the First Sonata shown in figure 10.2 provides a striking example. Not only are the chords stacked up beyond the size of anyone's hands, but polyrhythmic counterpoint is tossed in for good measure, all in full chords! Even a pianist who manages to survive this heroic battle is likely to emerge fatigued from the strain. Unfortunately, several more pages remain to conclude

Figure 10.2. Heavy and virtuosic chordal writing in Sonata No. 1 in F minor Op. 6, Mvt. I, mm. 128–38. *Leipzig: Beliaev, 1895.*

this demanding movement. Christoph Flamm comments on this problem in his informative introduction to the Bärenreiter edition:

> [Scriabin] writes increasingly wide-spaced and ultimately unplayable chords . . . to generate the expression of utmost tension while attempting to transcend the limits of the physically possible. This is precisely what he emphasized in a letter to his publisher at the same time that he was intent on proofreading analogous passages in the Op. 10 Impromptus: "As to the wide-spaced chords in the left hand, I've added the mark (*m.d.*) in only a few cases, whereas those that lack this mark are to be played with the left hand alone, for *the character of the sound depends on the manner in which they are executed* [emphasis mine]."[14]

Since this sonata was written at the time of a spiritual crisis, Scriabin put all his cards on the table, insisting that all the notes be retained, so as to express to the ultimate degree this triumphant moment in an otherwise anguished sonata.[15] This youthful enthusiasm, or excess, reaches an extreme point in the *Allegro de Concert* Op. 18, when the volume of notes seems to be well out of proportion with their inspiration. This chordal style is later taken up more successfully in the *Poème* Op. 32 No. 2, the *Poème tragique* Op. 34, and the Prelude Op. 37 No. 2 in F#, all brilliant works with a rich chromatic vocabulary. In them, we can detect an increase in compositional maturity, since an equally grandiose effect is achieved without an overreach in technical demands.

WRIST TECHNIQUE

Scriabin was always a nervous performer.[16] His skittish, impulsive energy may have detracted from his control on some occasions, but it gave an extra jolt of excitement; certainly, it was an essential part of his musical personality. From a technical point of view, a shot of adrenaline, well managed, can be a great advantage in playing his music, particularly for the shake of the arm and wrist that can be widely applied in his music for rapid-fire repetitions. Witness, for example, these quintuplets from the "delirious dance" of the Tenth Sonata (figure 10.3), a kind of nervous spasm that is perhaps an evocation of insects sparkling in the sunlight.[17] The complicated changes of time signature create a dizzying rhythmic pattern—very difficult to count accurately—that attempts to capture its quirky impulsiveness. To scintillate effectively, these must be played very rapidly and with small, percussive, birdlike attacks. The physical technique requires a flexible coordination of the arm and wrist to make a ricochet: a natural series of bounces off the keys that feeds off of its own momentum.

How is such a skill to be acquired? The literature on piano technique is extensive, and this section doesn't pretend to be a viable substitute for it, or for one-on-one interaction with an experienced teacher. However, it is fair to say that a strong wrist technique is indispensable for playing Scriabin's music at a high level. The wrist has to be both relaxed and expertly coordinated with the arm. One helpful description of this physical sensation is the staccato technique described in Gyorgy Sandor's *On Piano Playing: Motion, Sound and Expression*, summarized thus: "Essentially staccato motion is a throwing motion. The throw has to involve the entire arm, the hand, and the fingers."[18] The motion is initiated from a somewhat lower wrist position, where the flexed muscle stores energy like a coiled spring. A push of energy from the arm gives enough momentum to carry all the way through, as part of a coordinated larger motion. Some adrenaline or nerves (and maybe even a little extra caffeine) can help. A well-regulated, responsive piano action will give much-needed assistance. Some firmness is needed in the fingers to transfer the energy into the keys, but the wrist should be as loose and flexible as is practical.

Figure 10.3. Repeated chords in the "delirious dance" of Sonata No. 10 Op. 70, mm. 306–28. *Moscow: Jurgenson, 1913.*

Figure 10.4. Rapid octave runs in the Etude Op. 8 No. 12 in D♯ minor, mm. 1–5. *Frankfurt: Beliaev, 1895.*

For both expressive and technical reasons, it is usually preferable to cover as much musical territory as possible in a single thrust. For instance, in this well-known 16th-note run from the D♯ minor Etude, Op. 8 No. 12 (figure 10.4), the ricochet motion from the lower wrist position should start on the C×, and carry through in a single motion all the way to the A♯. Restarting with a new thrust on the E♯ might cause a false accent, since that "retake" slows down the arm. It would break the musical gesture into two small pieces. Patient practice is necessary to learn this technique and to acquire the endurance to sustain it. Pianists should beware of the instinct to force matters by tightening muscles, which can lead to an unpleasant sound at best, and injury at worst. If the wrist is consistently flexible in practice, speed and power can be gained over the long run. Practicing under tempo, taking breaks, varying activities, and regulating the length of practice sessions are all recommended practices to avoid risking muscular strain.

MOBILITY AND LEAPING TECHNIQUES

Critics of Scriabin's pianism may have found fault with the thinness of his tone, or his sometimes wayward rhythmic sensibility, but they did take note of his unusual agility in covering the keyboard. In the delightful Etude in Thirds Op. 8 No. 10, for example, the percussive leaping techniques in both hands make a boisterous and charming effect. The Waltz Op. 38 radiates fantastic energy by flying all over the keyboard, capturing through this virtuosity a dancer's sense of dizzying, vertiginous ecstasy. Scriabin's left hand parts usually cover a lot of ground, but when the right hand is moving about too, matters come to a head.[19] It seems to an audience that many hands are at work at once; only the most accomplished players can manage all this bustling activity. In the Op. 17 Preludes, for instance, contrast the challenge of No. 2 in E♭ (essentially an Etude for left hand octaves and leaps) with that of No. 5 in F minor (all of the above, plus a stern technical study in arpeggiated configurations in the right hand), all at a punishing *Prestissimo* tempo. Methodical practice is required to master this, but a pianist will gain thereby much knowledge of the keyboard's spatial relationships.

One of the most notorious cases of Scriabin's demanding writing can be found in figure 10.5, an intimidating passage from the Fifth Sonata. Although in some parts of the piece, these fanfarelike chords in the treble can be divided among the two hands, here they can be played only by the right hand, because the left hand has some tricky target practice of its own to negotiate. All of this, of course, takes place at a breakneck *Presto* tempo. No pianist who has tackled this piece will forget struggling over this passage, or ever perform a concert without imploring the gods for some good fortune to navigate it safely.[20] The passage, and others like it, should be practiced carefully, hands separately and together, with extremely firm fingers, each angled for geometric advantage to maximize the surface area of a successful strike. Some fingers (typically on white keys) may be very curved, while others (typically

Figure 10.5. Treacherous chordal leaps in Sonata No. 5 Op. 53, mm. 77–91. *Berlin: Éditions Russe de Musique, 1910.*

on black ones) may be quite flat. Finally, a panicky attitude, while understandable, is doomed to failure. The passage must be attacked with a cheeky confidence and aplomb that call to mind Scriabin's summons quoted at the opening of the piece: "to you I bring audacity!"

INTERPLAY BETWEEN HANDS AND THE DILEMMA OF DISTRIBUTION

Since Scriabin's piano writing often brings the hands into close contact with one another, there are many choices to be made about how to arrange notes among the hands. This issue can be a contentious one among performers and teachers, and many pianists struggle with making such decisions. On the one hand, a fine pianist friend once remarked to me, "His music is so unpianistic; before you can even start to play it you first have to rearrange everything!" On the opposite end of the spectrum, I observed the distinguished pianist Claude Helffer in masterclass telling a student, "Scriabin was a great pianist! You must play as it is written!" He would insist on putting the hands exactly as printed in the score, retaining some awkward-looking hand distributions. What are we to make of this age-old question in piano playing:

Observe the printed distribution or rearrange for convenience? Should our attitude be different in any way for Scriabin's music?

This debate is one instance of the fundamental philosophical question: What does a musical score mean? Particularly, what does a score of piano music mean? Is it proscriptive or descriptive? Is it a set of instructions for the player or rather a description of the layout of musical content? If the score is a set of instructions, then the bottom staff is generally intended for the left hand's music and the top one for the right, except for certain convergences, such as notes connected via beams, or stems-up and stems-down within one staff. If, instead, the score is a depiction of musical organization, the top staff might represent one musical strand while the bottom one represents another, as in a melody and accompaniment texture. This latter interpretation is a more flexible one, and there is a good deal of evidence (especially experiential evidence) that the great majority of common-practice period music fits it. Since notation has advanced from tablatures showing fingerings to staves and note-heads, musical content has become easier to visualize, and more removed from the mechanics of performance. Except for certain rare indications by composers, pianists have the freedom to select their own fingerings: a freedom that Debussy, for one, insisted on, in the preface to his Etudes. Hand distributions surely belong to the same category. Especially for performers with different hand shapes and sizes and varying sets of technical skills, this flexibility is most welcome in coping with music as demanding as Scriabin's.

There are, however, many sound reasons for attempting to retain the existing distributions as indicated in the score, even if they are at first more difficult to execute. Scriabin himself weighs in on the issue, saying to Sabaneev, "Do not laugh! I have often spent long hours considering whether the note stems ought to point up or down. . . . The emotional expression is entirely different, when the corresponding notes are played with the one hand or the other. . . . Take the opening of my Third Sonata. Could one really want to play [the C♯-F♯ octaves] with both hands? This is atrocious, a scandal! That sounds so serene and comfortable, but it has to be struck like lightning."[21]

The most natural way to preserve the character of each strand of music, and to delineate the relationship between these strands, is to assign each line of music consistently to its own hand. That applies both to independent polyphonic lines of music and to textural layers. Thus, in the B major Prelude, Op. 11 No. 11 (figure 10.6), even though some of the tenor notes fall into the right hand's range, it is more attractive for the pianist to feel the dynamic hairpin gesture (< >) in measure 2 by keeping it consistently in the left hand, maintaining a continuous melodic line. Each part stands to benefit from this arrangement. The left hand can more readily communicate the sense of wavy motion by experiencing it in its physique; meanwhile, the right hand can project a sense of breadth and calm. Particularly in m. 7, the moment of dissonance is all the more poignant when the thumbs play crossed, as written.[22] Many instances of this phenomenon can be found in Scriabin's writing.[23]

Figure 10.6. Keyboard arrangement in the Prelude Op. 11 No. 11 in B major, mm. 1–26. *Leipzig: Beliaev, ca. 1897.*

The style of interlocking thumbs is explored fully in the Prelude Op. 13 No. 5 in D major, a splendid study of legato double-notes and left-hand mobility and suppleness (see figure 10.7). The high tenor notes in the left hand must absolutely be retained as written. Both hands benefit: the right hand's legato sixths swell in a natural melodic shape, undisturbed, with *cantabile* projection, while the left hand is played a little lighter, and its expressive wide intervals help voice-lead the tenor A to G♯ in m. 2. Playing it as written may feel physically awkward at first, with all the rapid changes of position. The passage must be practiced until the left hand and arm can cover this territory as smoothly as possible. Opting to play the tenor E's with the right hand instead would spoil the natural division of labor and delineation of the parts.

Figure 10.7. Thumb crossings in the Prelude Op. 13 No. 5 in D major, mm. 1–11. Leipzig: Beliaev, 1897.

The *Drammatico* opening movement of the Third Sonata is full of interesting cases of chord execution where redistribution is a constant temptation. Let us focus here on the small transitional section in mm. 22–24, shown in figure 10.8, which features numerous interlocking chords. First of all, the crossed thumbs in m. 22 must be maintained because of the melodic integrity of the two parts. The tenor B on the third beat of m. 23 is less clear-cut. I prefer to distribute this as printed, to preserve the melodic shape of the tenor, especially since counterpoint is an especially strong

Figure 10.8. Chordal distribution in Sonata No. 3 in F♯ minor Op. 23, Mvt. I, mm. 22–26. *Leipzig: Beliaev, 1898.*

preoccupation for Scriabin at this moment of his career (see chapter 11 for details). However, the tenor B in m. 24 is another question. Since this B is motivically much less important than the tenor B on the previous beat, and is far more awkward to play as written, it can simply be played by the right hand. Similar lines of reasoning can apply to many other works, such as the Prelude in G minor Op. 27 No. 1, the Prelude in G♯ minor Op. 22 No. 1, and the *Feuillet d'album* Op. 45 No. 1.

Even when both hands are asked to share a certain piano key, it is often important to play it with the two hands, as printed. For example, the eloquent melody of the tumultuous Etude Op. 42 No. 5 (figure 10.9) shows Scriabin's sensitivity to tonal balance. In m. 21, the right hand has declaimed the melodic descending fifth, D♯ to G♯. The tenuto markings call for arm weight for sustaining power, without any hardness of attack. The left hand comes surging up to repeat this same G♯ twice during the period of melodic respite. The audience should perceive a conversational interplay of all three G♯ strikes, each with a different meaning; they certainly should not all sound as though they are part of the melody. This savvy keyboard writing

Figure 10.9. Note repetitions in the Etude Op. 42 No. 5 in C♯ minor, mm. 20–23. *Moscow: Muzgiz, 1924.*

style, which clearly separates the roles of the two hands, makes this easy to accomplish and a pleasure to play.

The clear and natural division of labor and ability to delineate layers of sound all explain the motto: "Play as it is written, unless there is an emergency!" Unfortunately, life is not so simple in Scriabin's virtuosic piano music, where there are many such "emergencies." An explicitly marked case can be found at the end of the stormy Prelude in F minor Op. 17 No. 5. Scriabin is eager to get both hands involved to generate the greatest amount of turbulence, more than a single hand could produce on its own. In the last two lines of this Prelude, the left hand is called in to help on numerous occasions, with the distribution indicated by *m.s.* The left hand is called on once again to play the soprano note of the final rolled chord, both for security and for tonal strength. The notation of these passages is a clear window into this pianist-composer's tactile sensibility at the keyboard.

If the style of such a passage can be taken as evidence of a pianistic orientation, there is a wide range of application in Scriabin's music. For example, in the Finale to the Second Sonata, the difficult perpetual motion figures in wide interval leaps would at times need to be divided between the hands, in order to play with the appropriate amount of rhythmic drive and derring-do. This division of labor is marked explicitly in m. 64 and m. 71, and could certainly be used at the ends of the arpeggios in m. 52 and in mm. 98*ff.* Even when not indicated in the score, redistribution is a good solution for the most ungainly technical challenges of widely spaced passagework, such as m. 5 or even mm. 29–30, which are difficult to play with the right hand alone at a *Prestissimo* tempo.[24]

Unfortunately, if redistribution solves one set of physical problems, it often creates a new set of challenges of balance and delineation. A thorough practice method in such cases is to work not only with separate hands, but in separate layers. For a relatively simple example, from the Second Sonata finale (figure 10.10), one can use the left hand to cover the tenor register E in the third quarter-note pulse. Then, practice in separate hands and separate layers, as follows: (1) right hand alone, feeling

Figure 10.10. Suggested fingering and distribution for Sonata No. 2 Op. 19 in G♯ minor, Mvt. II, m. 5.

the rhythmic gap that would be filled by the left, (2) left hand alone, not allowing the "foreign" note to interfere with the flow of octaves, either rhythmically or dynamically, (3) left hand octave layer alone, and finally (4) right hand eighths layer alone, with the left hand adding just the E and being sure it matches its right-hand neighbors in rhythm, dynamics, and length. Considering the trouble that is required to balance things properly after rearranging them, it is clear that this redistribution technique is best reserved "only for emergencies."

Franz Liszt, that restless innovator, was the most significant pioneer in finding novel ways to utilize the hands together at the keyboard. Bringing the two hands into the same register was just one of many kinds of creative new pianistic textures he explored.[25] This baton was passed on to the next generation of great pianist-composers: Busoni, Rachmaninov, Debussy, and Ravel, all of whom found their own Liszt-inspired new textures. Scriabin certainly belongs to this category and was as creative as any of them. The Seventh and Eighth Sonatas, for example, are veritable encyclopedias of multi-handed techniques, such as overlapping, crossing, and sharing registers. The melodic alternation of hands made famous by Liszt's concert Etude *Un sospiro* is employed in the Seventh Sonata's melody *vol joyeux* (m. 145), and still more elaborately, at m. 207 (*ondoyant*) (see figure 13.3a). The melody is thus permitted to soar, as if enveloped by the cascades of these winged gestures. The crossing of hands physically mimics the sensation of flight. In the Eighth Sonata, Scriabin's sheer textural inventiveness carries a great deal of musical interest (see for example the *Allegro* at mm. 356–70). The pianist must capitalize on this textural variety to carry the momentum of the piece forward in ecstatic heaving gestures. Performing this Sonata also requires a good deal of expertise in fingering and rearranging in the numerous cascades of fourths; each different harmony presents a different keyboard topography and thus demands a different fingering solution. Only at the *Allegro* in m. 226 is one hand required to play all these double-notes, but in a favorable tonality for facile execution.

Three passages from the Ninth Sonata will serve as interesting test cases for hand distribution. Each is notated on three staves, and the piano writing is ingeniously inventive and contrapuntal. In mm. 5–7 (figure 10.11a), the left hand should perform the lower two staves, and the right hand, the top staff only. This arrangement secures the integrity of voice-leading and is consistent with many examples we have already encountered of Scriabin's keyboard style. In mm. 105–09 (figure 10.11b), although the material is similar, the context gives the passage a very different meaning. In contrast to the inchoate, mysterious feeling at the opening of the piece, there is now a much more overt evil in the air. This passage occurs directly after the famous "poisonous" section (mm. 97*ff*; see chapter 3 for more detail). The addition of agitated syncopations in the treble also provokes a higher state of anxiety. It is an open question of interpretation whether a performer should communicate this tension by driving the tempo forward, or rather, try to express more tension by resisting that urge. That decision will have deep ramifications on the hand distribution one selects to perform this passage. When I learned this sonata first as a teenager, without a great

Figure 10.11. Considerations of hand distribution in Sonata No. 9 Op. 68, "Black Mass": (a) mm. 1–8, original material. (b) mm. 105–10, with easier hand distribution. (c) A difficult passage, and a proposed hand distribution solution, mm. 183–85. *Moscow: Jurgenson, 1913.*

deal of thought, I broke the middle staff into two hands, as marked. This is, indeed, the easiest arrangement to play, and a valid solution. It eliminates anxieties about the descending arpeggios, or of getting lost in the harmony changes while changing so many physical positions. However, more recently, in returning to this piece, I wondered if it wouldn't be more logical to play the lower two staves consistently with the left hand alone, so the independent parts could retain their proper shape. I spent some time working on this, but ultimately in the moment of performance, I would either revert to the fingering I knew, or else, unfortunately, get mixed up between the two versions. Pianists performing this piece should invest time from the start in learning each arrangement of hands, decide on a rhythmic pacing for the section, and then decide once and for all which one to employ.

The other passage to consider is the *Più vivo* at mm. 183–86 (mm. 183–85 are shown in figure 10.11c). Some rhythmic drive is essential in this section to relate the sordid tale of the *Black Mass*: an element that in my opinion is missing here, or at least inadequate, in many performances. The choice of fingering may be the root of the problem. Once again, Liszt's *Un sospiro* can inspire a solution. The right hand is better suited to performing the middle staff, with its anxious trills. The left hand can be used when needed to perform the melody in the top staff; ultimately the two hands will share that duty. The reader can observe my personal solution in the figure. Note that the tricky rhythms still have to be learned carefully, and this distribution doesn't make that any easier. However, the physical convenience of this solution makes it possible for the performer to manage a tempo that suits the mood of the moment.

In sum, Scriabin's music is by no means unpianistic, but is rather expert piano writing at the highest level. At any time, each hand might be called upon to share responsibilities with the other hand for particular voice parts or textural layers. It is ideal to keep textural layers consistently in the same hand, but when that is impractical, one should be willing to redistribute, and then practice to distinguish the layers clearly. These choices are ultimately personal decisions and will depend on one's physique, technical skill, and experience.

TRILLS

One signature ingredient of Scriabin's pianistic style is the trill, a device Scriabin used to help the piano achieve coloristic range and dynamic control that could transcend its usual limitations as an instrument. Although the coloristic use of the trill flourished first in Beethoven and continued in the nineteenth century, Scriabin took the device much further, especially in his later works. The many different kinds and qualities of trill in Scriabin's music require a variety of physical playing techniques. Trilling is one of the most individualistic of technical skills; many pianists find their own solutions to this challenge, and experimentation is required in order to discover new possibilities for oneself. This section is designed to stimulate that imaginative process." The most basic trill, executed by two alternating fingers in evenly subdivided rhythm, is rarely effective or appropriate in Scriabin. However, the delightful "Mosquito" Etude Op. 42 No. 3 in F# happens to be one of the very best technical studies in the repertoire for exactly that purpose. To perform it well, the pianist must change fingers in the midst of the trills while maintaining evenness of execution.

Our survey of advanced trill techniques begins with the most forceful category, the explosive trill. This trill would be appropriate at the demonic climaxes of the Sixth Sonata (m. 102, m. 106). A lot of firepower is needed to create the necessary combustion, and every single note should sear the keyboard with maximum power and clarity. Thus, I prefer to execute these not as trills at all, but rather as tremolos with two fists, each supporting multiple fingers. The right hand will attack the main note of the trill, pick up, shift to the higher note, and be joined by the left hand. The ordinary trilling method with two alternating fingers would never do; mere fingerwork cannot hold its own dynamically amid this ferocious music. Other explosive trills in Scriabin tend to appear in the high register, as in *Prometheus* and the Eighth Sonata, where the percussion of the initial attack helps excite the soundboard. When two hands are not available, at least the initial blow should be struck with the support of the arm, ideally onto a large surface (such as two fingers, or the side of the thumb).

Another useful nonstandard trilling technique is the three-fingered trill: thumb, third, and index fingers in a repeating 1323–1323 pattern. This method reduces the burden on each individual finger to restrike, and invokes the rotary power source of the wrist and arm. Once mastered, this fingering provides effortless sustained finger motion over long spans, and is applicable to music from any era. It is especially helpful for long trills that require some sustained moderate level of power, such as those in the early part of the Ninth Sonata (mm. 25*ff*). The principle of alternating fingers can also be applied to the cluster trills of the Sixth and Tenth Sonatas; these bursts of color should be sustained at a fairly even dynamic. I prefer an alternating fingering solution of 1–43–2–43–1–43–2–43, etc.

The majority of Scriabin trills, especially in his later music, are not sustained and even, but start with a burst of energy from a strong weighted attack, and gradually dissolve into indistinct murmuring vibrations and palpitations. Sustained, clear attacks throughout the duration of the trill are not expected or even desirable. Dynamics can be graduated both by arm weight and by flutter-pedal (see chapter 13 for more details). These kinds of trills, representing spasmodic flashes of light, are everywhere to be found in the Tenth Sonata, which has been nicknamed a "Trill Sonata." A full explication of the variety of tone colors in the trills of this sonata is an interesting project beyond our scope, but a technical means to approach them has been well described by pianist Scott Holden:

> As the trill accelerates, the fingers stay so close to the keys that they gradually extinguish themselves by no longer lifting enough to make the hammers reactivate. . . . Most trills in this sonata will start with a bit of an accent bathed in a deep pedal and then quickly fade away. On a good piano, the trill will sound as if it is still distantly palpitating, even

though the fingers have stopped moving. . . . The performer should never overpower or overarticulate the rhythmic precision of the trill.[26]

The wonderful variety of tonal color in these trills can be experienced in Vladimir Horowitz's spellbinding rendition of this sonata, a unique performance that, despite its occasional rhythmic eccentricities, is haunting for its uncanny sense of quivering ecstasy and otherworldly mystery.

11

Line and Melody

One of Scriabin's greatest strengths as a composer is the force of his convictions. No matter how complex or ambitious his style may be, the compositional affect he strives for is clear and compelling. Although numerous other composers attempted to probe the possibilities of his harmonic and rhythmic vocabulary, they were unable to achieve similar impact, primarily due to the lack of such a clear thread for the listener to follow.

One aspect of Scriabin's appealing directness is the wealth of his melodic invention. His melodic gifts are inherited from the tradition of Chopin, Schumann, and Tchaikovsky, and shared with his compatriot, Rachmaninov. Examples of Scriabin's melodic gifts are everywhere to be found in his music, evident already from his earliest miniature works. One immediately thinks of the wistful pathos of the famous Etude Op. 2 No. 1 in C♯ minor, and many of the early Preludes, such as Op. 16 No. 1 in B major and Op. 22 No. 1 in G♯ minor. Even some of the most thickly scored virtuosic Etudes, such as Op. 8 No. 12 in D♯ minor and Op. 42 No. 5 in C♯ minor, are—for all their pianistic extravagance and the sophistication of their voice-leading—still in essence models of melody and accompaniment. Even as his style changed, he never abandoned this melodic sensibility. A case in point is the Prelude Op. 74 No. 4. This Prelude in Scriabin's final opus is typically cited as a radical work approaching atonality, approximating the style of Alban Berg. However, it might equally be considered a throwback to traditional style: a four-part chorale texture with a melodic top voice. The English composer David Matthews had the eminently logical idea to arrange this piece for string quartet.[1] Despite the unstable, dissonant harmonic language, the melody is memorable and suits the human voice. These roots in traditional technique do not offend the senses as a stylistic anachronism; rather, they help to make an otherwise avant-garde piece comprehensible at first listening.

Attractive melodies are by no means exclusive to the miniature pieces; some of his most beautiful melodies can be found in the larger works, the symphonies and sonatas. The *Andante* of the Third Sonata features one of the most memorable: a broadly paced, eloquent theme given a special programmatic significance as "a sea of gentle feelings and melancholy. Love, sadness, vague desires, indefinite thoughts of fragile, shadowy delights."[2] The second theme of the First Sonata's opening movement, a splendid outpouring, is even more heart-rending when recalled in the stormy third movement, as shown in figure 11.1. This aural reminiscence makes a clear connection among the movements and lends thematic unity to the entire sonata.

Figure 11.1. Related melodies in the Sonata No. 1 Op. 6 in F minor (a) mvt. I, mm. 20–28 (b) mvt. III, mm. 34–39. *Leipzig: Beliaev, 1895.*

EXPRESSIVE PERFORMANCE OF EARLY PERIOD MELODIES

Scriabin's early period melodies are a splendid vehicle for Romantic expressivity. A pianist must dig deep to make a personal response, finding extremes of dynamic and rhythmic inflections that convey the intensity of these emotions. Performers thoroughly steeped in the Romantic style, with a knowledge of *cantabile* weighted tone production and an instinctive impulse for lyrical shaping, will make the best Scriabin players. The intuition for melodic declamation should come from an awareness of phrase dimensions, implied intervallic tensions in the melody itself,[3] and the underlying harmonic support. Expressive performance of this melodic material also requires freedom of rhythmic declamation, or *rubato*, a flexible rhythmic style from an Italian word meaning "stolen time." The characteristic rubato of the First Sonata's melodies, for instance, holds back the melodic eighths to give them extra time. In compensation, time is taken away from the longer held notes. The give and take between added time and stolen time should maintain a sense of overall balance. The effective pacing of accompaniment parts requires a pulse that flows rather steadily but not with the metronome; this pulse should be allied with, if not exactly synchronized with, the melodic shaping. As a consequence, the hands may often not strike together. Scriabin's recorded piano rolls show that the composer himself played in this manner.[4]

Some of Scriabin's melodies are flowery, fragrant, almost Puccini-like in their direct emotional appeal. This quality is essential to Scriabin's style and a far cry indeed from his reputation as a thorny, difficult composer. There are love songs to be found in his music, such as the Etude Op. 8 No. 8 in A♭, the second theme of the *Fantasie in B minor* Op. 28, and the rich themes from the third and fourth movements of the Third Sonata. While the emotional content of these themes is easy enough to understand, their performance can nevertheless present a difficult challenge. One wants to radiate the most expressive warmth while maintaining the dignity of the musical discourse, avoiding lapses into excessive sentimentality and poor taste. Vladimir Sofronitsky, Samuil Feinberg, and Sviatoslav Richter all excelled at treading this fine line in their Scriabin performances. Their renditions of the Fantasy's second theme can serve as models of great expressivity within a clear rhythmic pacing. They realize that the more bombastic sections of this work will give ample opportunity for dramatic excitement.

Surely one of the great masters of melodic shading was Vladimir Horowitz, who could bring a range of intensity and pathos to the simple melody of the Etude Op. 2 No. 1 that the best of opera singers could only envy. Horowitz performed this work countless times in his career, and gave it a variety of different readings, all full of freshness and spontaneity. This freedom is an important aspect of his style that exudes an air of authenticity in his Scriabin performances. I will use the CBS Masterworks recording as a primary reference.[5] Horowitz treats the opening hairpin (a < > marking) not with dynamics but rather with agogic inflections, i.e., variations from strict time that emphasize or de-emphasize certain notes by rhythmic placement. He marks the apex (high point) of the phrase—the downbeat of the second measure—by lingering on it, rather than arriving at a dynamic peak. Throughout his many performances of this work, he tends to prefer a dynamically strong opening and a broadly shaped diminuendo, with measure 2 being a rather soft chord.[6]

This diminishing dynamic curve is a highly effective way to sustain a melodic line, and seems especially suited to Russian melodies. At the outset of a new phrase, the pianist can begin stronger, with renewed energy, emulating the physicality of the breath in singing. Horowitz offers a wide variety of musical inflections in his performance that keep our rapt attention; in particular, his rhythm is highly plastic and flexible without compromising the continuity of the musical line. At m. 5, for instance, he pushes the tempo slightly to begin a four-bar phrase rather than another group of two. When the corresponding place arrives in m. 13, however, the dynamic indication calls for more intensity; he delivers this by taking a good deal of time into the downbeats of m. 14 and m. 15, with a significant dynamic drop to match it. All these devices prepare for the new tonality.

One can sense from this brief investigation the extent to which the musical text can be interpreted to bring the emotions of Scriabin's melodies to light. This liberty to express is surely one of the greatest pleasures in playing this music. Horowitz's rhetorical freedoms in this piece are effective because they correspond to the lengths of the phrases and the varying intensities of the harmonies. At times in his Scriabin performances, he does take some unusual liberties with rhythm, and occasionally also with the musical text, typically in the midst of some passages where Scriabin's pianism grows awkward. Horowitz generally prefers to focus on his unique strengths of pianistic color and melodic shaping. Such extraordinary strengths more than justified the means and bequeathed to us many powerful, viscerally communicative performances.

CHARACTERISTICS OF MELODY IN THE LATE STYLE

Although Scriabin would in his later works abandon sorrowful melodic outpourings in the conventional sense, his lyrical gifts remained an important stylistic attribute. His melodic writing had become more rarified. In his *Grove Music Online* article on Scriabin, Jonathan Powell describes this distinctive new melodic style as "full of suaveness and subtlety,"[7] citing the *Poème* Op. 69 No. 1. Another *Poème* Op. 71 No. 1, might serve equally as a case in point, offering fantastical menace as a counterpart to this lithe suaveness. Some late Scriabin melodies are so airy and supple that they rely a great deal on the interaction with the rest of the musical materials to achieve their desired character. For example, in the middle section of the Etude Op. 65 No. 1 in Ninths, shown in figure 11.2, the silky and serpentine right-hand line is, in its own way, an extraordinary melodic conception. However, it relies a great deal on its gossamer textural support, novel harmonic sensations, strange intervals of a ninth, and polyrhythmic interaction between the inner parts, to create its surreal mood.

Figure 11.2. Serpentine melody from the Etude Op. 65 No. 1 in Ninths, mm. 22–34. *Moscow: Jurgenson, 1912.*

Without these features, the melodic line itself, with its flaccid rhythmic profile, would communicate but little.

The secondary theme area in the late sonatas is a good place to search for Scriabin's rarified melodic style. In the tradition of Romantic sonata design, as laid out most notably by Adolph Bernhard Marx,[8] the second theme offers a lyrical or melodic contrast to the more assertive principal theme. In Scriabin's late sonatas, these secondary themes tend to share a complex, even vague, rhythmic profile, where duple and triple rhythms interact and beat accents are avoided. A good example is the second theme of the Ninth Sonata, shown in figure 13.10, to be played "with a nascent languor." Most notes of the melody are placed off the beat, and the alternation of duple and triple rhythms creates a vague impression. Even if a performer were to play this theme in strict rhythm (which would be none too stylish), taking dictation of this melody would be a tough task. Scriabin devotes as much time and space in this melody to seductive harmonic and rhythmic probing (between B♭ and C♭, mm.

35–38) as to the compelling arch of the melody itself (mm. 39–42). The smooth, stealthy way it emerges imperceptibly from the morass is Scriabin's evocative suggestion of an idea "being born" (*naissante*). It is tempting, and perhaps appropriate, to attribute to this an erectile quality. This extraordinary episode—undoubtedly one of a kind in the entire literature of music—bears the thumbprint of Scriabin's genius at its most radical and disturbing. A pianist needs to give plenty of time for the listener to experience all these sensations and to feel the ever-changing harmonic innuendo through varied balances and minute inflections of timing. The intricate rhythms should be well defined, but executed with suppleness and flexibility.

In the late sonatas, the characteristically hazy, floating texture of his second themes depicts what Susanna Garcia aptly calls the "Eternal Feminine."[9] Garcia's gendered reading of the sonatas is rooted in Scriabin's own writings, as well as the nineteenth-century German academic tradition of A. B. Marx. She observes that one of the driving forces in the development of these works is the way that confident "masculine" forces assert themselves and transform the apparently more pliable "feminine" materials in the course of the piece's argument. This process is facilitated by Scriabin's new melodic style. At this time, he tends to couch themes in smaller segments that are more flexible and subject to development through rhythmic distortion, sequence, and varied texture. It is revealing to compare the fragmentary melody marked *Avec une celeste volupté* in the Seventh Sonata (figure 12.16c), typical of Scriabin's late style, with its counterpart, the eloquent and more traditionally arch-shaped *Tragique* melody of the Eighth Sonata (figure 12.16b, m. 3). The difference in shape between these two melodic lines has important compositional ramifications as these works unfold. The Seventh Sonata's melody appears as a second theme, but in the Eighth Sonata, the melody is revealed in the work's introduction. Because of its length and clear profile, the grand melody of the Eighth Sonata is not as readily susceptible to rhythmic distortions and cumulative intensifications. Perhaps that is one reason why there are more languid, dreamy episodes in the Eighth than in the other late sonatas, giving this work a rather different character.

An important influence on the shape of Scriabin's late-style melodies was his obsession with the notion of unity (*edinstvo*) of artistic expression and mystical experience.[10] For example, he sought to unify visual, tactile, and olfactory sensations with musical ones. The attempt to unify the harmonic and melodic components of his music was thus a logical next step for him.[11] Clearly it had a great influence on his linear materials. A melody such as the one marked *le rêve prend forme* (the vision takes shape) of the Sixth Sonata (figure 11.3a), while always readily discernible as a melodic referent, would not be the kind of tune that one finds stuck in one's head after a concert. However, this idea serves a germinal function for almost all the materials of the piece, and appears in many different tempos, gestures, and moods, as can be seen readily by tracing the melodic contours in the figure.[12] This procedure is an apt application of "thematic transformation," a technique employed extensively by Liszt, in which musical materials retain their basic melodic shape but are altered in their rhythm and thus in their psychological profile. Certainly, thematic transforma-

Figure 11.3. Thematic transformations of melodic material in Sonata No. 6 Op. 62 (a) mm. 36–45 (b) mm. 69–87. *Berlin: Russischer Musikverlag, 1912.*

tion lends organic unity to a composition; however, the claim that such a germinating motive acts as a series for the work (in the Schoenbergian sense) is a doubtful one. Scriabin only transposes the pitch collection and distorts its rhythm; he employs none of the typical serial techniques, such as intervallic inversions and retrogrades.

VOICE-LEADING AND COUNTERPOINT

Scriabin's music is widely recognized for the imaginative force of his personality, but the meticulous quality of its construction is typically underestimated. This refined, almost dandyish character of his personality is amply evidenced by the elegant calligraphy of his musical manuscript,[13] his constant fear of infection, his taste in fine clothes, the careful grooming of his hair, and his signature moustache. Scriabin manages to make his fantastical ideas come to life in full force without concessions in the solidity of his compositional technique. The logic, or "principle," of his compositions was always important to him. Firm control of voice-leading and counterpoint is one important aspect of this craft. Anatoly Liadov, another composer sponsored by the timber merchant Mitrofan Beliaev, had a Classical, almost pedantic streak, but he praised Scriabin's voice-leading in his early works as the purest of all contemporary composers.[14] Scriabin's skill was refined at the Conservatory through his study with the composer and master pedagogue Sergei Taneyev, author of a substantial tome on counterpoint, and teacher of Rachmaninov and Medtner.[15] This powerful triumvirate of composers—Scriabin, Rachmaninov, and Medtner—all possessed in their own unique ways the rare knack for translating contrapuntal technique into highly idiomatic keyboard writing.

A serious interpreter of Scriabin's music cannot focus exclusively on its emotional and extramusical content without coming to terms with its structural features. He or she must be keenly aware of contrapuntal context, as in Bach or in Chopin, and follow the various interlacing linear threads, not merely as sequences of notes but as connected lines with their own inner tensions and dynamic impulses. For example, in the introduction to the Fourth Sonata (see figure 6.3), the primary melodic material is in the middle of the texture, but the high register forms a consistent linear thread of its own that should be clearly heard. The dynamic balance between the two parts should ebb and flow as the two individual parts have their own way. It is typical of Scriabin, like all natural contrapuntists, that the two important parts are distinct enough to be heard because of the contrast in their register and rhythmic values.[16] In the opening of the same Fourth Sonata's *Prestissimo volando*, we again observe Scriabin's careful attention to linear detail; the middle voices are full of small changes that are extremely difficult to play at this breakneck tempo. The best solution for a pianist, as often, is to practice the details methodically, internalizing the musical relationships in one's physical mechanism, and then focus on the larger lines and gestures in performance, hoping to glean as many of these smaller details as possible along the way.

Toward the end of his early period, in the late 1890s (roughly Opp. 20–27), Scriabin's music took on a highly technical, almost academic aspect in which contrapuntal craft is very impressive and easily audible at the surface. These years were his first intensive period of orchestral writing, and the time of his Conservatory professorship. All these experiences may have led to a time of obsession over polyphony and linear connections that influenced his piano writing. A pianist cannot help but feel this density of material, because the relative lack of filler material makes the music unusually difficult to play, even awkward at times. The powerful Prelude in G minor Op. 27 No. 1 provides a clear example. Although scored thickly in many octaves, it is full of tightly interlaced quasi-fugal entrances, in the manner of Schumann's Baroque-influenced Romantic writing. The top voice is the center of attention, but the answering details in the middle voice should not be lost in the process. Imitations in the deep bass should be clearly heard as closely related melodic shapes. Even the Mazurkas Op. 25, apparently slight salon pieces, show a great advance in linear sophistication compared to the Op. 3 set. In some cases, the cross voicings are quite challenging to play.[17]

The large-scale works of this period are also elaborately contrapuntal in character. Witness the imitative Scherzo movement and the fugal section in the Finale of the First Symphony. The *Fantasie* Op. 28—usually regarded as a late Romantic warhorse with grand gestures—offers many points of imitation and a high level of part writing, such as a wonderful canon in the *Più vivo* section (mm. 35*ff*) and an elaborate contrapuntal working out in the following section. The Third Sonata provides one of the clearest and most successful examples from this period. Its first movement feels to the pianist very much like a Bach fugue, both in its extraordinary density and in the felicitous way the various parts are distributed between the two hands. While Scriabin has written many handfuls of notes in this thickly scored movement, hardly any could be omitted, as material is recycled in various contrapuntal combinations in a tight web of motivic relationships. The final movement of this sonata, although not written in as straightforward part texture as the first, still reveals Scriabin's linear thinking in all registers through the progression of the chromatic inner lines within its turbulent harmonies.

Another prime example from this period is the Piano Concerto Op. 20. Scriabin was proud of the thematic unity he achieved when the materials of the piece are derived from the small cell of the opening. His demand for linear unity makes the solo part feel at times like a sort of Passacaglia, fitting into the orchestra, rather than presiding over it—a feature most often cited in the Brahms piano concertos (see figure 11.4a). At times, Scriabin's insistence on consistently crossing contrapuntal lines and rhythms leads the soloist into moments of great awkwardness, as shown in figure 11.4b. Faubion Bowers remarks, quite plausibly, that these prickly difficulties in the solo part have likely diminished the popularity of this otherwise attractive concerto.[18] The pianist cannot afford to ignore or overlook these details, but receives no plaudits for this activity that takes place largely under the audience's radar.

Figure 11.4. Piano soloist as melodic contrapuntist in the Piano Concerto in F♯ minor Op. 20, Mvt. I, (a) mm. 17–26 (b) mm. 94–101. *Leipzig: Beliaev, 1898. Reprinted by Broude Bros., New York City.*

As Scriabin's musical idiom advanced, Taneyev and Liadov—conservative personalities that they were—did not appreciate the more radical aspects of his late style. Scriabin did move away from some of the more turgid aspects of his music he wrote in the late 1890s, but he did not relinquish the linear craft that they admired. This can be observed even in the most pianistic textures such as the swirling passages of the Op. 42 Etudes. In the Sixth Sonata, in the extraordinary section marked *tout devient charme et douceur* ("everything becomes magic and sweetness"), fragments of melodic ideas swim about in every voice part as in a great aquarium (see figure 13.3b).[19] One of the most impressive examples of Scriabin's naturally flowing counterpoint is the grand *Lento* introduction to the massive Eighth Sonata (figure 11.5). Scriabin opens up from three to four staves in the interest of clarifying the web of five simultaneous melodic layers.

Even in his late style, Scriabin's insistence on linear rigor can create pianistic difficulties. In the Tenth Sonata, for example, the main motivic building blocks of the piece are stated in the introduction, figure 11.6a, a series of descending thirds. In

Figure 11.5. Layers of counterpoints across many staves in Sonata No. 8 Op. 66. Moscow: Jurgenson, 1913.

Figure 11.6. Falling thirds and thematic transformation in Sonata No. 10 Op. 70 (a) mm. 1–6 (b) mm. 39–42. *Moscow: Jurgenson, 1913.*

the symphonic main theme of the work, the chromatic soprano descent traces precisely these same intervals in a Lisztian thematic transformation, illustrated by the circled pitches in figure 11.6b. Scriabin intensifies the motivic focus on descending thirds with the alto voice's insistent A-F repetitions. This tight echo of important motivic material is a powerful exemplar of compositional design, and it is readily playable, even at a fast speed, by a pianist with well-trained, independent fourth and fifth fingers.[20] However, in the development section, where this material sequences through more remote tonalities, the pianism becomes downright awkward (as in m. 162). At such moments, a performer under pressure may well choose to focus on the excitement of the rhythmic drive and the overall dynamic shape of this section at the expense of a few details of part-writing clarity.

12

Harmony

Anyone who appreciates the imaginative use of harmony will find endless fascination in the music of Scriabin. His music has long been of special interest to music theorists, who have explored his harmonic language in countless books, articles, and dissertations. A working knowledge of his harmonic world is an emblem of a high-class Scriabin performer, since sensitivity to harmony is the essential underlying ingredient that informs all interpretive choices of sound, texture, and pacing. The tensions contained in these tonal relationships are mediators of the very substance of Scriabin's extra-musical aspirations, whether sadness, ecstasy, uncertainty, longing, or mystical transcendence.

Scriabin has long been heralded as among the bravest adventurers into unknown harmonic worlds. The stylistic environment of the Etude Op. 2 No. 1 in C♯ minor (1887) and the Five Preludes Op. 74 (1914) suggests almost two completely different composers in a span of less than thirty years. What is remarkable is not only the extent of the journey, but also its organic nature. Each opus leads naturally into the next, and the impression is a gradual evolution from one style into another.

Blessed with an exceptionally keen ear, Scriabin probed the world of harmony with the invested energy of an artist and the inquisitive mind of a scientist. He prided himself on creating novel sonorities that even the keen ears of his friend and amanuensis Leonid Sabaneev—himself a composer of significant talent—was unable to reproduce.[1] Many of these harmonies suggest a fascinating multiplicity of tonal implications, a web of innuendo suggested by Scriabin's remark, "You have to be able to walk around a chord."[2]

Although his mature harmonic language has achieved greater notoriety, the significance of harmony to musical expression is as germane to the earlier works as to the later ones. Some early salonlike pieces, such as the Mazurkas Op. 3, can easily sound thin and trivial if played without a keen sensitivity to harmony. These pieces can be brought to life by a performer who understands the harmonies and feels the emotions they represent, and gauges timings and balances accordingly. This sensibility above all distinguishes Samuil Feinberg's astonishingly vivid readings of the Mazurkas.

Scriabin's late music, on the other hand, often asks for a contemplation of sonority and resonance, and requires a keen sense of the amount of space they require to hover and comingle. Such qualities can be challenging to find in a piece such as the Sixth Sonata, which relies heavily on the dynamic tension of unstable lingering resonances. This intensity can be found with exceptional power in Sviatoslav Richter's outstanding live 1955 performance of the piece,[3] and is one of the main reasons his interpretation is so effective.

On a practical level, the savvy musician who studies Scriabin's harmonies will learn these demanding scores much more quickly, and avoid misreadings of accidentals in the text that are, unfortunately, far too widespread in commercial recordings. From this study, an intuition should develop that shapes an interpretation and provides an essential anchor in performance should one become lost at sea. Without it, public performance by memory is quite risky. An ambitious Scriabin pianist should be able to reproduce typical chords in all twelve key centers.

The literature of Scriabin analysis is rich and at times difficult. A thorough analysis of his harmony in all its facets is certainly beyond the scope of a single chapter. However, this subject is so critical to understanding Scriabin's achievement as a composer that we will take some time to "walk around" his chords, and especially to consider the cultural and philosophical significance of the harmonies he preferred. This chapter is, of necessity, the most detailed and technical in this book, but the equivalent of a full-year undergraduate course in tonal harmony should suffice to follow it.

THE ROOTS AND CHARACTERISTICS OF SCRIABIN'S EARLY HARMONIC LANGUAGE

Scriabin's early style is rooted in the harmonic practices of Tchaikovsky, Schumann, Chopin, and Liszt. His fascination with harmony was surely developed by an immersion in the music of these composers, all of whom had exceptionally sensitive ears for harmonic color. However, Scriabin's early works are not merely derivative; they have many distinctive characteristics of their own. A knowledgeable listener should be easily able to pinpoint his stylistic thumbprint. Let us trace a few of these characteristics in this section.

One earmark of his early style is a descending, chromatically inflected line, often representing a drooping sadness emblematic of his Russian heritage. This compositional technique can be found in the plaintive openings of several early pieces in E minor, such as the Mazurkas Op. 3 No. 7 and Op. 25 No. 3, and the Prelude Op. 11 No. 4. The last of these also highlights an augmented chord, which is one of his favorite sonorities (see figure 12.1a). The three descending tenuto notes that open the Piano Concerto Op. 20 exemplify this same tendency: a descending line arriving on a similarly dissonant, augmented-quality chord (see figure 12.1b). This searching chromaticism would continue to be an emblem of Scriabin's style during this time, in works such as the Prelude in B♭ Op. 17 No. 6, marked *Andante doloroso*.

a

b

Figure 12.1. Descending lines and augmented-quality chords in: (a) Prelude Op. 11 No. 4 in E minor, mm. 1–3 (Leipzig: Beliaev, ca. 1897). (b) Piano Concerto in F♯ minor Op. 20, mm. 1–9. *Leipzig: Beliaev, 1898. Reprinted by Broude Bros., New York City.*

As Scriabin's style matured, he treated descending lines more as a linear structural feature, and less as an explicit depiction of sorrow. He had begun to disapprove of music with depressive tendencies. Melodic shapes would begin to stretch upward, in a tense rivalry with the descending semitones. In the Mazurka in F-sharp minor Op. 25 No. 7, for example, we feel a strong tension between the chromatic descending lines and the yearning, ascending sevenths. In the Etude in C-sharp minor Op. 42 No. 5, chromatic descent of the soprano is once again offset by a corresponding ascent in the tenor, and by aspirational ascending arpeggios in m. 4—heaving gestures that suggest breathing (*Affanato*). An especially revealing case is the opening of the Fourth Sonata, where amid the chromatic descent of the tenor, the ear is primarily struck by the upward trajectory of the soprano's soaring line.

Chorale textures are another hallmark of early Scriabin. These also appear in both the middle period (e.g., the Preludes in B♭ Op. 35 No. 2 and Op. 39 No. 2 in D, each marked *Elevato*) and in the late works (such as the Prelude Op. 74 No. 4). His use of this traditional style suggests both the cultural inheritance of the Russian church and the pianistic heritage of Chopin.[4] One striking feature of this mode of expression is his use of open perfect fifths at cadences that give a haunting, archaic quality. These can be found for instance in the Op. 11 Preludes Nos. 12 and 16, at the ghostly conclusion to the whirlwind of the Prelude in A minor Op. 13 No. 2, and in the D-sharp minor variation of the second movement of the Concerto.

In contrast to the textbook chorale style, and especially the bleak open fifths, much of Scriabin's early language is notable for its lushness. He is especially fond of mixed and blended harmonies with added notes, as in the opening of the Prelude Op. 11 No. 1 (see figure 14.8a). This sonority could be analyzed as a kind of subdominant function over a tonic pedal, but the ear is mostly captivated by its luxurious quality: a mixture of six different diatonic pitches all lushly sustained in the pedal.[5] This attractive blended resonance—a hallmark of Scriabin's harmonic imagination—is especially common when sustained over sonorous pedal points.[6] The Prelude in B major Op. 16 No. 1 (figure 12.2) opens with another prime example of this suspended subdominant-quality harmony.[7]

Figure 12.2. Luxurious harmony that opens the Prelude Op. 16 No. 1 in B major. Leipzig: Beliaev, 1897.

AUGMENTED SIXTH CHORDS

Scriabin's harmonic language descended from the "Music of the Future" movement, represented by Liszt and Wagner. Along with certain specific chords, he inherited a tightly connected organic language in which pitch collections carry their own implications of voice-leading, and of tension and release. Late-Romantic composers who employed this rich vocabulary could manipulate the emotions of the audience in powerful ways by delaying or denying the resolutions that their chordal vocabulary demanded. Wagner is most often cited for this tendency, particularly in his opera *Tristan und Isolde*, which prolongs chromatic tensions over five hours of intense drama until its cathartic resolution in *Liebestod* (Death of love). Harmonic elements such as Neapolitan chords, half and fully diminished seventh chords, and augmented chords are widely exploited in this style, of which one could count César Franck, Hugo Wolf, Max Reger, and Richard Strauss among the foremost practitioners.

An essential element of Scriabin's chromatic harmony is the augmented sixth chord. The family of predominant chords with their resolutions is shown in figure 12.3, including the three traditional augmented sixths. An augmented sixth is a prime example of how intervallic tension is intensified in late-Romantic style. Modern theory textbooks typically describe an augmented sixth as a predominant function: a chord that progresses to the dominant in half steps. Augmented sixth chords act with greater urgency than other predominant chords, because they bring more chromatic pitches into play.

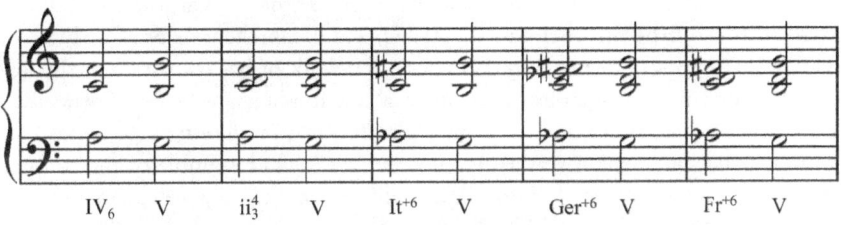

Figure 12.3. The family of predominant and augmented sixth chords.

Scriabin shows an unusually strong predilection for augmented sixths throughout his career, possibly more than any other composer. In a typical scenario, such as the end of the Prelude in A major Op. 15 No. 1, Scriabin will ratchet up harmonic tensions until arriving at an augmented sixth as the pinnacle, and gently release that stored-up energy in a concluding cadence. In the short Prelude in A minor Op. 11 No. 2, the main theme relies on this augmented sixth more than ten times for its color and its affect. The inverted version used in the penultimate measure is especially noteworthy for its poignant effect. Augmented sixths are used extensively in sequence in the theme from the First Sonata quoted in figure 11.1a. It is the harmonic language, and the augmented sixth especially, that lends this theme its yearning quality. The augmented sixth is a key player throughout the fascinating Mazurka in E♭ minor Op. 3 No. 10, a rarely played but powerful work in which the old-world elegance of the mazurka genre confronts a moody undercurrent of disturbing and unstable harmonies. The final C♭ major harmony, underlined by an ominous tolling of bells, makes for a poetically ambiguous ending that declines to answer the harmonic question posed by the German sixth chord in m. 209.

Scriabin's augmented sixths frequently are not used in the way they are typically described in modern theory texts, i.e., built on ♭vi and moving to V. Tchaikovsky's *Guide to the Practical Study of Harmony* (1871), a prominent source of the time, claims that an augmented sixth chord resolves not to the dominant, but directly to the tonic (i.e., ♭ii → I).[8] In this usage, the augmented sixth is treated as a version of a dominant but with the second scale degree (the bass note of a dominant four-three chord) lowered by a half step. Scriabin did not by any means invent this procedure, but he made it a personal hallmark. In light of Tchaikovsky's writing, we can see that this progression has deep roots in Russian traditions.[9]

Crucial to the flavor of an augmented sixth, and telling in terms of Scriabin's future development, is the role played by the interval of a tritone. This is especially true of the French sixth, which contains two tritones. A tritone, which spans six half steps, splits the octave's twelve into two equal parts, and is thus an intervallic inversion of itself. This mathematical property leads to an ambiguity in its use, or at least to a highly flexible arrangement, since this symmetry makes the tritone reversible. Since either pole can be considered as a root, resolutions in two different keys (also tritone-related) are possible. This feature, known as a "tritone link," is the crux of an elaborate analytical system for Scriabin's music by the Russian theorist, Varvara Dernova, one of the most serious, systematic, and comprehensive of all analyses of Scriabin.[10] Dernova's theory rests in turn on the work of her own teacher, the important Russian theorist Boleslav Yavorsky, a contemporary of Scriabin, who took the interval of the tritone and the principle of half-step resolution as the bedrock of a unique and comprehensive theoretical system.[11] A good example of the tritone's ambiguity is a French sixth built on ♭ii: it could be heard equally well as an inversion of a French sixth built on V. This V_7^{-5} chord is so widespread in Scriabin—even idiosyncratic—that we will give it a convenient label: the "French sixth dominant." The conclusion of the second movement of the First Sonata provides a clear enough example. A source, or at least relative, of the "tritone substitution" well known to jazz pianists, the tritone link relationship in this French sixth would become a bedrock of his later harmonic explorations, important for both its color and its extraordinary flexibility,[12] as detailed below.

VERTICAL THINKING AND NICKNAMED CHORDS

Largely due to the profound influence of the great French composer and theorist Jean-Philippe Rameau, the discipline of music theory has codified simultaneous sounding notes as chords, moments worthy to be heard frozen in time, with fixed roots and inverted positions. Rameau endured a great deal of criticism for distinguishing certain bass notations not simply as voice-leading phenomena "in the wild" but as different inversions of the same vertical entity consistently stacked in thirds. In the nineteenth century, that era of great advances in empirical science, there was a sort of arms race, in the wake of Rameau, to discover and classify new harmonic entities. Especially the composers of the "Music of the Future" movement invested themselves in inventing such novel combinations, in their Romantic quest to paint emotions, philosophy, and literature in bold new musical terms. In this environment, augmented sixth chords flourished, under the nicknames of Italian, French, and German. These monikers date from the early nineteenth century and are not based in any specific historical traditions, but are rather meant as colorful nicknames intended to describe the qualities of the great national schools of music.[13] Augmented sixths are thus an emblem of Scriabin's language, not only in their specific sounds and formal properties, but also in their relationship to musical culture and philosophy. They exemplify a broader trend in which sonorities that began life as the passing, ephemeral phenomena of voice-leading (such as a ♭6 in the figured bass of a Phrygian cadence) would become increasingly identified as autonomous vertical entities, proud chords with distinctive psychological significance of their own, objectified to the point of having colorful nicknames.

This Romantic trend only accelerated throughout the nineteenth century, and reached its climax in the music of Scriabin, where to listen vertically by isolating specific harmonic sounds—and indeed, to "walk around" those chords—can be a pleasurable exercise on its own. It is somewhat akin to viewing an oil painting and fixating on small areas of paint just to admire the unique colors. If these colors are distinctive enough to captivate one's imagination, it is a valid way to experience a work of art. The viewer (or listener) only needs to remember that these colors are parts of the picture, and not the picture itself. In fact, because Scriabin's harmonic ear was so keen and original, the misconception has arisen that he conceived of music *only* in terms of chords.[14] Chapter 11 should therefore be read as a necessary balance against the material of this chapter. Scriabin's unique vision, in his enduring battle cry for *edinstvo* (unity), was to combine the apparently distinct fields of harmony and melody into one greater whole.[15]

This delicate tension between horizontal and vertical ways of understanding music has extended to the present day in music theory. Horizontal thinking is most widely represented via the influential theories of Heinrich Schenker, and vertical ones perhaps most imaginatively by the pedagogical methods of Olivier Messiaen. Messiaen was wont to pick out specific chords on the piano, relish them for their coloristic properties, and train the ear to hear and recognize them out of context. It is no accident that Messiaen shares many characteristics with Scriabin, including a desire for mystical transcendence, an interest in color/harmony correspondences, a sense of timelessness in his music, and also certain technical features such as the octatonic scale (as detailed below). In popular music style, a lead sheet articulates harmonic rhythm, and a number of chords such as "sus4" have been codified as legitimate vertical sounds in a way that diverges from traditional analytical practices. Pitch-class (pc-set) set analysis, an analytical tool devised by Allen Forte and employed on Scriabin's music most notably by theorist James Baker,[16] investigates intervallic relationships systematically without reference to tonal structure. One of the controversial foundations of pc-set analysis is the implicit equivalence of pitch collections to their intervallic inversions.[17] Pc-set analysis does offer the distinct advantage in Scriabin's music of giving equal status to the horizontal and vertical dimensions, entirely in the spirit of the utopian interconnection that Scriabin had envisioned.

THE TRISTAN CHORD AND THE SCRIABIN SIXTH

Wagner held a central position in the race to discover and claim new harmonic territories. The most famous and influential of all these nicknamed chords is surely the Tristan chord, from his opera *Tristan und Isolde* (see figure 12.4a). Wagner's emphatic placement of this signature harmony from the opening of the Prelude, and his consistent and repeated articulation of it with powerful expressive force, elevates its significance from a single voice-leading accident to an autonomous harmonic event worthy of a special name. It has proven to be a key referential sound not just for this one opera but for the entire history of music. Numerous interpretations of the meaning of these musical lines have been advanced—including desire, love, suffering, and magical powers—but this harmony, the Tristan chord, is the meeting place where all these potent ideas meet and interact.

Scriabin's music, especially in his middle period, derives strongly from Wagner, building on both its harmonic language and its concomitant underpinnings of German philosophy. Unlike many of his musical contemporaries who sought to flee from this influence, Scriabin adored Wagner and even sought to outdo him; thus, Scriabin stands at the apogee of the Romantic movement. It stands to reason, then, that there are more nicknamed chords in Scriabin's music than in that of any other composer, so preoccupied he was with novel harmonic combinations. Among his signature harmonies, we can count the Tristan chord, the Scriabin Sixth, the *Extase* chord, the Mystic chord, and the "death harmonies" of the *Mysterium*.

As the representative of sexual longing, the Tristan chord is near and dear to Scriabin's expressive desires. This chord admits of many applications of harmony and voice-leading, and boasts a broad analytical literature. In simplest terms, the Tristan chord is a variant of a French sixth chord in A minor where the soprano's G♯ voice-leads to A.[18] This chord reveals itself most tellingly in Scriabin's music in the introduction to the Fourth Sonata (figure 12.4b). This passage can be interpreted poetically by way of Scriabin's own literary plan for the sonata:

> Oh, to be near to you, distant star!
> To drown in your trembling rays, you magnificent star!
> O deep, mad yearning! O sweet delight of desire!
> I wish only to desire eternally, yearning itself is my only wish.[19]

Even without the explicit interpretation by the poem, the Italian word *voglia* points to qualities of longing and desire. Scriabin's music mirrors his poem's wish "only to desire eternally" in the way it leaves the Tristan chord dangling and unresolved. Wagner did at least make a semi-resolution via a half-cadence to the dominant. In

Figure 12.4. Instances of the Tristan chord: (a) Wagner, opening of the Prelude to *Tristan und Isolde*. (b) Scriabin, Sonata No. 4 Op. 30, mm. 7–12 (Leipzig: Beliaev, 1904). (c) Prelude Op. 13 No. 1 in C major, mm. 38–43 (Leipzig: Beliaev, 1897). (d) Prelude Op. 27 No. 1 in G minor, ending, mm. 31–34 (Leipzig: Beliaev, 1904). (e) Prelude Op. 37 No. 4 in G minor, mm. 17–20 (Leipzig: Beliaev, 1904).

the Fourth Sonata, Scriabin either leaves the chord unresolved (m. 8, 27, and 31) or else resolves it indirectly, with the bass voice-leading upward instead (mm. 20–21 and 24–25).

The Tristan chord admits of many other resolutions and enharmonic reinterpretations, including the most obvious, a half-diminished chord. We will offer a few examples from Scriabin's most Wagnerian period. In figure 12.4c, the chord in the penultimate measure of the Prelude in C major Op. 13 No. 1 adds a bit of longing dissonance at the culmination of this otherwise optimistic Prelude. Both the middle register of the piano and the exact pitches (F-A♭-B—D♯) recall Wagner's own.[20] The powerful Prelude in G minor Op. 27 No. 1 (*Patetico*) opens discordantly with an enharmonic Tristan chord; in this work it usually leads to an unstable augmented chord. In the Coda, however (figure 12.4d), at the moment of truth, this tension exhausts itself, after a decidedly Tristanesque chromatic extension in the alto, to a G major conclusion. The Prelude in G minor Op. 37 No. 4 (*Irato impetuoso*, figure 12.4e) is a kind of companion harmonic laboratory to Op. 27 No. 1, offering a wide variety of harmonic interpretations in its resolutions of the Tristan chord.[21]

Considering Scriabin's innovative zeal, and his links to the "Music of the Future," it is no surprise that he would unveil a new augmented sixth with his own personal stamp. The chord identified in figure 12.5, the signature chord of the *Divine Poem*, has been dubbed by Scriabin scholar Hugh Macdonald the "Scriabin sixth,"[22] which we will abbreviate as Sc^{+6}. Beginning with the basic three tones (A♭, C, F♯) of the Italian sixth, where the French sixth adds a D, the German sixth a D♯/E♭, the Scriabin sixth adds instead an E-natural. In Scriabin's expressive world, this upward progression of added tones (D—D♯-E) would represent an increase in luminosity from the subdued French D to the brighter German E♭ to the grandiose Scriabin Sixth E. The Sc^{+6} can resolve only to a major tonic triad. The F♯/A♭ converge on G (a very strong attraction of semitones in contrary motion known as "concentric voice leading") while the other two tones are simply retained.[23] This rather inflated Sc^{+6} chord, extensively employed in the middle period, plays an important role in projecting the egoistic assertiveness of this music.

Figure 12.5. The "Scriabin sixth" as heard in m. 2 of the opening of the *Divine Poem* Op. 43.

The first entrance of the Sc^{+6} is presented with great fanfare, and—as Macdonald observes—with solemnity. The "resolution," however, is a surprise: a retrogression, so to speak, away from the expected motion toward the tonic ($Sc^{+6} \rightarrow IV_6$). Metaphorically, this represents a step away from clarity, back into uncertainty and the unknown. This powerful salvo opens up a wide tonal space and prepares a very large canvas for the symphony. Although Scriabin's chord is much less susceptible to enharmonic resolution possibilities than the Tristan chord, he makes use of many of these possibilities in his symphony,[24] whereas Wagner nearly always resolves his signature chord to the dominant.

The Sc^{+6} is often approached via a swelling gesture, from a major chord where scale degree 5 separates into $\sharp 4$ and $\flat 6$. In Scriabin's erotically tinged middle period language, this swelling is surely a metaphor for sexual attraction and the arousal of desire. There is an important influence from the music of Liszt, especially the *espressivo amoroso* (m. 339) from his *Mephisto Waltz No. 1*. For instance, in Scriabin's *Poème satanique* Op. 36, the fifth of the chord expands in mm. 54*ff* from B to the A♯/C and back, in an alluring, flirtatious manner. This typical motion is used in many contexts: for delicate expansions like these, for bold assertions of the ego (the *Poème* in D Op. 32 No. 2), and for mocking and subversiveness, as in the *Poème fantasque* Op. 45 No. 2, which relies almost exclusively on this device. The Sc^{+6} is also used to set up the end of a piece, with the effect of a kind of plagal cadence (IV $\rightarrow$ I) in which, ironically, the subdominant pitch itself has been completely eclipsed. The Fourth Sonata Op. 30 and the *Poème satanique* Op. 36 are just two examples of major works of this period that conclude with virtuosic resolutions of the Scriabin Sixth into a powerful, resonating, and triumphant tonic.

ALTERED AND MIXED-MODE DOMINANTS: THE LANGUAGE OF DESIRE

One of the most salient features of Scriabin's mature harmonic practice is a wide palette of dominant seventh (hereafter abbreviated V_7) chords that are altered,[25] suspended over tonic pedal-points, built on whole-tone foundations, used with ambiguous functionality, or simply unresolved. In Scriabin's music, there is almost every conceivable variety of $V_7^{\flat 5}$, $V_7^{9(\sharp 11)}$, $V_{13}^{\flat 9}$, $V_9^{\sharp 5}$, $V_7^{13(\sharp 11)}$ (etc.) an inquisitive harmonist could ever hope to find. The harmony of swing-era jazz has much in common with this vocabulary and may have been influenced by Scriabin's innovative style, whether directly or through its cross-fertilization with the music of contemporary composers, especially in France.[26]

The dominant seventh chord is the *locus classicus* for harmonic tension in tonal music. This tension is defined by its dissonant intervals (tritone, minor seventh) and tendency tones (the fourth and seventh scale degrees) that demand resolution to their resting points (the third and octave). The power of these tendencies to convey intense emotion, desire, and even sexual passion is a consistent leitmotif in commentaries on Scriabin's music. Musicologist Roy Guenther describes it as follows: "That all Skryabin's late-style should be thought of as 'dominant' in origin is logical and consistent, not only with the transitional style trait of prolonging the resolution tendency, but also with Skryabin's philosophy that creativity was for him an unceasing striving for an elusive goal."[27] The relationship between the yearning character of Scriabin's harmonies and his enormous creative ambitions is a central theme, most notably, of Richard Taruskin's classic essay "Scriabin and the Superhuman,"[28] of Kenneth M. Smith's monograph *Skryabin, Philosophy and the Music of Desire*,[29] and of Mitchell Morris's dissertation "Musical Eroticism and the Transcendent Strain: The Works of Alexander Skryabin, 1898–1908."[30] The reader is referred to these sources for a thorough exegesis on the relationship of harmonic tension to the philosophical immanent content of this music.

One of the most widely used altered dominants in Scriabin is the $V_{13}^{\flat 9}$, a potent harmonic cocktail that mixes the major mode of its 13th (the mediant of the key) with the minor quality of its ♭9 (the lowered submediant). The key of E♭ major may have been closely connected in Scriabin's imagination with this particular sonority. It lends much of the bittersweet quality to the poignant *Feuillet d'album* Op. 45 No. 1 (figure 12.6a),[31] and also to *Fragilité* Op. 51 No. 1 (figure 12.6b).[32] The liberal and inclusive nature of the jazz-style label $V_{13}^{\flat 9}$ is quite helpful here; in the context of such an intensely chromatic language, traditional musical notation is unable to describe every possible linear and vertical musical relationship at once. A composer is obligated to make a decision about the orthography (i.e., the choice among accidentals in spelling the chord). Here, Scriabin opts for B-natural, describing the linear motion of B to C, and pointing the pianist's eye to a G major harmony in the right hand. The listener hears vertically as well, interpreting the clash of B♭/B as a minor ninth, i.e., as the C♭ of a $V_{7}^{\flat 9}$ chord.[33] The $V_{13}^{\flat 9}$ is not only effective for such delicate effects, but gives an extra sense of intensity and heroic struggle in assertive, bombastic contexts such as the chordal flurries of the *Poème* in D Op. 32 No. 2 and the Prelude in F♯ Op. 37 No. 2.

The chord $V_{13}^{\flat 9}$ can be found frequently in the context of one of Scriabin's favorite voice-leading patterns where the ninth of the chord descends by a half step to ♭9, and sometimes on to the octave. This pattern is a style characteristic that runs consistently from his early period to his late, but its meaning changes considerably. The Poème Op. 32 No. 1 is a classic example: a $C\sharp_{13}$ chord where D♯ descends to D and finally to C♯, setting up the crooning main theme in the key of F♯. In the *Valse* Op. 38, this same descending chromatic line is the focus of the main theme. The expressive alto notes swell on the waltz's rhythmically emphasized second beats, and relax at the ends of measures. In the late style, the half-step descent from 9 → ♭9 will take on a new significance as a shift from one modal foundation to another, as detailed below.

Figure 12.6. Mixed-mode dominant harmonies: (a) *Feuillet d'album* Op. 45 No. 1 in E♭, mm. 15–19 (Leipzig: Beliaev, 1905). (b) *Fragilité* Op. 51 No. 1, mm. 1–9 (Leipzig: Beliaev, 1907).

WHOLE-TONE DOMINANTS AND THE *EXTASE* CHORD

An important feature of many of Scriabin's preferred dominant sonorities (e.g., $V_9^{\#5}$, $V_9^{\#11}$, the incomplete V_9, and $V_7^{\flat5}$) is their containment within a whole-tone scale formed on V. This family of chords is known as "whole-tone dominants."[34] Whole-tone fragments functioning as a dominant appear quite early in Scriabin's output, as an exotic or experimental element *à la* Mussorgsky, before being systematically explored in his later works. In figure 12.7a, a disorienting passage from the Prelude Op. 11 No. 16 in B♭ minor, conventional tonal implications are suspended until the powerful tonic arrival. This Prelude, something of an echo of the Finale of Chopin's "Funeral March" Sonata in the same key, is full of unsettling features. These include the ghostly parallel octaves, the changing time signature of 5/8–4/8, and numerous augmented chords. Even in such an environment, this whole-tone passage is particularly disturbing. It contributes a great deal to the work's exoticism and sense of the macabre. A similar strange and exotic effect can be found in the Piano Concerto's opening movement, where the already colorful altered secondary dominant ($V_7^{\flat 9(\flat 5)}$ / V) resolves to V by way of an entirely whole-tone sound built on a French sixth. In figure 12.7b, m. 126 of the solo part shows a rare instance in Scriabin's music (or anyone else's) of a textbook, fully written-out descending whole-tone scale.

A more mature example of Scriabin's whole-tone dominant practice can be found in the *Poème* Op. 52 No. 1, mm. 2–3 (figure 12.8). Floating in close proximity, many of Scriabin's favorite sonorities can be found here, all of them whole-tone based: an incomplete V_9 in the left hand in m. 2, an augmented chord in the right, and two French sixths in measure 3. This style—in which the entire whole-tone complex serves as a cache for dominant-quality chords—provides a broad and flexible vocabulary, since any member of the whole-tone scale can act as a new leading tone. Many unorthodox resolutions are possible. For instance, in the *Poem of Ecstasy*, the opening sonority, E♭-G-B-D♭-F (an incomplete V_9^{+5} on E♭), resolves in m. 5 directly to C major. In that work, the pressure of hovering dominant sonorities to arrive at a satisfactory resolution is very powerful. Boleslav Yavorsky remarks how "dominant (V) chords . . . produce 'a tension without relief' through which the listener 'thirsts for activity,' but 'the parch cannot be slaked'; there is 'no active resolution, no release into stability.'"[35] Considering the intensity of the pressure to resolve, the final conclusion on C major will be all the more satisfying, as Taruskin observes: "Scriabin's symphony consists in most general terms of a single fundamental gesture, an agonizingly prolonged structural anacrusis that at the very last moment achieves cataclysmic resolution/consummation. That consummatory gesture is the ultimate reality, the noumenon, for which sexual union, the creative act, the birth of the world . . . had been the conceptual or phenomenal metaphors."[36]

One of many unique sonorities Scriabin uses to prolong tension in the *Poem of Ecstasy* is a whole-tone dominant suspended over a tonic pedal, a heady concoction that occupies precisely that hazy middle ground between a dissonance and its resolution. It serves as a makeshift point of repose in a work that carefully avoids tension-destroying full cadences. In m. 19, we are prepared already for resolution to C major, but Scriabin resolves only the bass, leaving the rest suspended in air; he settles in m. 22 on a $V_9^{+5}/(I)$ chord. Richard Taruskin has dubbed this ensuing sound, one of the work's most characteristic sonorities, as the "*Extase* chord."[37] Figure 12.9a represents the sounding pitches at the conclusion of the clarinet melody in m. 25. This harmony reappears variously in the works of the Op. 50s in which tonality is weakened but still present, most notably as the final chord of *Désir* Op. 57 No. 1 (figure 12.9b), a work whose title makes explicit the chord's metaphorical meaning.

Figure 12.7. Whole-tone sounds: (a) Prelude Op. 11 No. 16 in B♭ minor, mm. 25–34 (Leipzig: Beliaev, ca. 1897). (b) Piano Concerto Op. 20, mm. 121–27. *Leipzig: Beliaev, 1898. Reprinted by Broude Bros., New York City.*

Figure 12.8. Whole-tone sonorities and floating rhythms: Prelude Op. 52 No. 1, mm. 1–21. *Berlin: Russischer Musikverlag, 1909.*

Harmony 267

Figure 12.9. *Extase* chords: (a) Pitches held in the *Poem of Ecstasy*, m. 22. (b) Conclusion of *Désir* Op. 57 No. 1. *Leipzig: Beliaev, 1908.*

ROOT MOVEMENT AND TONAL PLANNING IN THE MIDDLE PERIOD

A key to understanding this musical language, with its sometimes disorienting treatment of dominant functions, is the structural tonal planning of its bass progressions. Bass movement now typically occurs via tritones (i.e., the tritone link), sometimes by thirds, and sometimes by perfect fifths. This behavior can be most easily traced in the many miniatures of this period, for example, the *Danse languide* in G major Op. 51 No. 4 (figure 12.10), in which whole-tone dominants are housed within an entirely traditional formal framework. We arrive first at the key center of G in m. 4—perhaps a bit by surprise—via the tritone link A♭-D. The Neapolitan (♭II) function A♭ is very much the director of harmonic traffic in this piece, as it often is in middle-period Scriabin. This A♭ mediates between the tritone link to the dominant D (which finally connects to a safe harbor of G major) and various "points west" arrived at via other root movements by fifth, such as its own dominant, E♭, which begins the piece. In bars 5–8, aiming for D major, Scriabin sets up its Neapolitan (E♭), simply cycling the bass in fifths. Using fifth motions to the remote Neapolitan rather than to the tonic itself, Scriabin creates an internally consistent harmonic environment, in which the tonic is weakened by the absence of the traditional circle-of-fifth motions (ii-V-I) that would have firmly established it.

Although his focus on the Neapolitan is idiosyncratic, Scriabin retains many traditional features of tonal music. These include 4-bar phrase groups, parallel constructions, and the choice of the dominant (D major) as the first point of modulation. Even the remote key of the opening—a kind of secondary dominant—could be related to Schumann's harmonic practices. The short B section (mm. 8–12) emphasizes tritone relationships in sequence, but emerges—once again in traditional form—onto the dominant of D. In the Coda, Scriabin makes a coy move: a feint to continue the motion of circle of fifths still farther away from the tonic, in fact, to its opposite pole on the circle of fifths (E♭-A♭-D♭). This surprising move makes a flirtatious suggestion, which is marked by a new harmony, a major seventh chord, and

Figure 12.10. *Danse languide* Op. 51 No. 4. *Leipzig: Beliaev, 1907.*

a prolonged rest that appears to comment on the surprise. The laconic conclusion rejects this suggestion, returning to the dominant via the original tritone-link A♭–D, so that propriety can be restored via a clear G major cadence.

WEAKENING OF THE DOMINANT FUNCTION

The Fifth Sonata is a critical work in Scriabin's stylistic development in many respects, not least in its harmonic language. In it one can trace an application of dominant-family chords that grows increasingly radical and—as the introductory text suggests—audacious. Throughout the piece, Scriabin relishes the sonorous qualities of these harmonies, but systematically weakens their resolving tendencies. At *Languido* (figure 12.11), the initial sonority is entirely whole-tone except for the D♯. The musical tension that exists on this page is not geared so much toward the resolution of the dominant toward a tonic, but rather to the oscillation between the more alert D♯ and the inert, purely whole-tone D-natural—an ineffably fine but significant change of harmonic landscape. Richard Taruskin has described this style as "an almost infinitely extended, graded, and variegated dominant that in its ceaseless flux and nuance is almost palpably sensuous."[38] When Scriabin breaks away briefly from this suspended dominant, the harmony is still ambiguous, but clearly more stable and thus more directional, or, in his own language, willful (*con voglia*, mm. 17–18). The dynamic potential contained within that apparently innocent ascending gesture is unleashed in the ecstatic climax of mm. 433–40.

The second passage to consider is the *Meno vivo* second theme (figure 12.12), a small A-B-A design. Here too, the prevailing dominant harmony does not resolve directly to the tonic, but alternates with its corresponding French sixth dominant on F♭ in m. 123, in conjunction with another oscillation of semitones, D♭-D. The resolving tendencies in the French sixth dominant, very strong in traditional tonal music, are undermined by both the D♭-D motion and by its weak metrical positioning, for example, after the downbeat rest in m. 124. In m. 126, the soprano moves from F to G, making the environment more fully whole-tone and vague. The "b section" of this episode (mm. 128–33) offers real tonal activity in the form of bass movement by perfect fifth. The strongest point of arrival in m. 130, however, is no consonance, but rather a semi-resolution, an *Extase* chord. In the return of "a" (m. 134), the tonality is even more hazy, as the dominant sonority is now floating over a tonic pedal.

When this entire section returns in the development (mm. 271*ff*), the relaxing of harmonic gravity continues (figure 12.13). A resonant tonic pedal point is now present from the beginning and throughout. The ego—represented by the will to resolve—is being extinguished. With the addition of a new foreign pitch B♯, and then a shift in the soprano to G♯ (m. 277), we find a harmony akin to the famous "mystic chord," with its characteristic spacing in fourths: a chord to which we will return shortly below. This sonority's need to resolve—indeed, its very identity as a dominant—has been undermined, to the extent that the dominant pitch (F♯) itself isn't included among the five notes of the downbeat chord.

OCTATONICISM

The octatonic scale—the eight-tone scale formed by alternating whole and half steps—is without question one the most significant features of Scriabin's late style. Having been abroad for some time, in his return to Russia in 1909 he must have become acquainted with what was known as the "scale of Rimsky-Korsakov," as it

Figure 12.11. Sonata No. 5 Op. 53, mm. 13–46. *Berlin: Éditions Russe de Musique, 1910.*

Figure 12.12. Sonata No. 5 Op. 53, mm. 120–39. *Berlin: Éditions Russe de Musique, 1910.*

Figure 12.13. Sonata No. 5 Op. 53, mm. 271–83. Berlin: *Éditions Russe de Musique,* 1910.

was popularized in St. Petersburg at the time.[39] In the post-Promethean piano works of 1911–1915, it is fair to say that the octatonic scale reigns supreme, most notably in the Sixth, Seventh, and Ninth Sonatas.

The octatonic scale is a relative of the whole-tone scale in its properties of invariance, or periodicity. The whole-tone scale is called "symmetric" because—all its intervals being identical—a transposition of the scale by any number of its scale degrees yields an identical copy. The octatonic scale is periodic because it reproduces itself (is invariant) under transposition to every other scale degree. That is, a transposition by any number of minor thirds yields an identical copy. Both scales harbor a large number of tritones, and thus a big cache of ambiguous, self-reversible tritone links.

These invariant (self-reproducing) properties were later plumbed famously by Olivier Messiaen in his "modes of limited transposition."[40] His extra-musical aims of stasis, color/harmony correspondences, and mystical transcendence share so many points in common with those of Scriabin that it would be hard to deny a direct influence.

With so many tritones and diminished-seventh chords at hand, the octatonic scale excels at describing diabolical, nefarious materials. It also effectively depicts dynamic energies, such as fire, that are of special import to Scriabin's imaginative world. As Richard Taruskin has traced, octatonicism is an inheritance of the Russian tradition of fantastical harmony.[41] In the passage *avec une chaleur contenue* (with restrained warmth, see figure 13.8) from the Sixth Sonata, we can hear the scale unfurling, as if in a textbook, as a lyrical melody with an ardent but mysterious cast. The arrival chord here is extremely common and of special significance; it might be called the octatonic version of the mystic chord (i.e., with an m9, or E♭♭, above the D♭ bass, where a mystic chord—described in the next section—would have a M9, or E♭).[42] Tritones are exposed here in the left hand for the maximum bell-like sonorous effect. The octatonic scale also harbors that severest of dissonances, a set of two clashing tritones a half step apart in the bass. These grinding dissonances are laid bare most notably in the Codas of the Sixth and Seventh Sonatas. The lower three notes of this collection conveniently fit the left hand, and are virtually omnipresent in depicting the horrors of the Ninth Sonata, as well as in the unsavory arpeggiated interjections of the Poème Op. 71 No. 1.

The octatonic scale is quite versatile in its expressive capabilities; it is not merely a scale for depicting nightmares. Messiaen, for example, calls upon it in a major key in his *Vingt Regards sur l'Enfant Jesus* to represent the holiness of God the Father (*Le Theme du Père*). In Scriabin's music also, the moods called forth by this scale are diverse. In *Étrangeté* Op. 63 No. 2, for example, the pitch material is almost exclusively octatonic, but the character is marked as *gracieux, delicat* (graceful, delicate), and is thus not about shudders of fright. The *Poème* Op. 69 No. 2 is almost exclusively octatonic but is playful rather than menacing in character. Octatonicism is also an important element of the fantastical colorations of the *Poème* Op. 71 No. 2; it lends an aura of mystery to its sensuous landscape.[43]

THE MYSTIC CHORD: HISTORY AND SIGNIFICANCE

The most famous Scriabin sonority is well known in English-speaking countries as the "mystic chord" (See figure 12.14a). Especially in a book that deals with long-standing mythologies, this one requires special attention. The chord was first given special notice in print by Leonid Sabaneev, in a short and prominent 1912 article for *Der Blaue Reiter*.[44] Sabaneev did not explicitly nickname it "The Chord of *Prometheus*" in this article, as is often claimed. However, he certainly did lavish special attention on it, thus laying the grounds for its lasting recognition. He claimed this sonority as the basic principle of the composition, its higher unity. The mystic chord

Figure 12.14. The mystic chord (a) as described by Sabaneev in *Der Blaue Reiter* (b) as related to the overtone partials 8–9–10–11–13–14.

appeared most prominently in English under the pen of Arthur Eaglefield Hull in his book *Alexander Scriabin: The Great Russian Tone Poet*. Hull was certainly one of Scriabin's most important early apologists, whose writing likely did much to earn the composer (and the mystic chord) long-lasting recognition in the West. Both Sabaneev and Hull describe the chord as having been derived from the overtone series as a stack of fourths. Hull also claimed that Scriabin thereby invented a new style of composition, simply based on transpositions and rearrangements of this single device.

The moniker of "mystic chord" has stuck like glue; both the name and these early claims about his late style have been so oft-repeated as to have attained a kind of folk status in Scriabin lore. The mystic chord is likely to be the first fact a student learns about Scriabin's style in a music history class, without the benefit of much context, its purported ubiquity elevated almost to the point of caricature. Its colorful nickname sticks in the consciousness, quite like the whole-tone scales in the music of Debussy, which are significant, but hardly omnipresent, in the Frenchman's music. Hull and Sabaneev offer practically no analysis and little other supporting evidence to substantiate their ideas about this chord. Let us therefore delve into both the accuracy and relevance of their claims.

Title, "The mystic chord"

Hull wrote three rather similar commentaries on the chord in several prominent sources.[45] Although he is often credited with having invented this nickname in English, that is clearly not the case. Hull wrote, "He founded a new *chord* which his disciples have stupidly christened a 'mystery-chord.' There is no mystery about it. He simply selects the sounds he prefers from Nature's harmonic chord and—builds them up by fourths!"[46] While Hull does not mention these disciples by name, the honor appears to belong to Rosa Newmarch, one of the most energetic English propagandists for Russian music.[47] Newmarch was already in 1913 referring to the sonority as the "mystical chord."[48] Newmarch and then Hull may have been following the lead of Sabaneev, reiterating his claims, but their nickname is by no means an unreasonable one, given the extraordinary psychic powers the chord was meant to represent, which we discuss at the end of this chapter. The moniker credited to Sabaneev, "The Chord of *Prometheus*," may in fact be somewhat more appropriate, since this precise distribution of tones is encountered most often, and most consistently, in that work. The most authentic name of all for the chord, however, is none of these, but rather the one given by the composer himself, one discussed at the conclusion of this chapter: "the chord of the pleroma."

Derivation from the Overtone Series

Sabaneev and Hull both claim that Scriabin had derived the chord—whether directly or intuitively—from the partials of the harmonic series, and that therefore this chord had arisen from nature itself (see figure 12.14b). Apparently infatuated with this idea, Hull goes on to rhapsodize about Bach's *Well-Tempered Clavier* and the inadequacy of keyboard temperaments.[49] The overtone story is recounted by other contemporaries, including an article "In Memory of Scriabin" by the composer and critic Vyacheslav Karatigin (1875–1925). While the relationship to the series of overtone partials undeniably exists, the verdict of musicology has been decidedly hostile to its role in Scriabin's derivation of this sonority. An early critic of this finding was Igor Stravinsky, who was fascinated by Scriabin's music at the time of his death, but who disapproved of this analysis of his methods: "I swear," Stravinsky fulminated, "that with all my severest criticism of Scriabin, I showed him more respect than Karatigin with his overtones."[50] Richard Taruskin has led the modern-day charge against this theory, "[The mystic chord] has been described . . . by Sabaneyeff in the Blaue Reiter article . . . as originating in the higher partials of the harmonic series; but that curiously persistent notion merely begs the question, as any complex or dissonant harmony could be so described."[51] Simon Morrison, another leading musicologist of Russian music, also refers to the "long discredited notion that Skryabin derived his sonorities from the harmonic series."[52] Even Sabaneev himself remarked that, until he pointed it out to Scriabin, the composer himself was unaware of the connection.[53]

We do not know how exactly Scriabin came to this specific combination of pitches, but many have speculated. Taruskin, for example, presents a possible derivation of the mystic chord as a transposed inversion of the *Extase* chord, a kind of "walk around" of that harmony.[54] Personally, I imagine that this arrangement may have crystallized during the dominant-weakening procedures in the Fifth Sonata, as outlined in the previous section. It seems dubious to claim that "any complex or dissonant harmony" would so neatly contain exactly these lowest overtone partials. The overtone theory might, however, lead us in a helpful direction by recalling a mode sometimes called the "acoustic scale" (see figure 12.15b below), more conventionally known as the Lydian-Dominant or Lydian-Mixolydian. This mode is widespread especially at this time among many composers and in some folk traditions, though for reasons not related to overtone structures.[55] The extended dominant sonority $V_9^{13(\sharp 11)}$, a closer relative of Scriabin's past techniques, is constructed from these same pitches (see the opening of the Eighth Sonata, figure 12.16b). Since this mode of figure 12.15b has already so many nicknames, one more will perhaps not hurt, since it serves as a generator of much of Scriabin's pitch content. Let us call it for our purposes the "mystic mode."[56] We can then refer to a harmony derived from the pitches of the mystic mode as a "mystic-family chord." This methodology is appropriate since these kinds of harmonies are very common in Scriabin's piano music, while the traditional stack-of-fourths chord one encounters in *Prometheus* is rather rare.

Further Claims by Sabaneev

Sabaneev persisted in arguing the importance of the overtone series to the *Prometheus* chord, even though Scriabin himself was apparently unaware of the connection. He went on to make many other observations about it: "It incorporated all four 'consonant' triads of classical music: major, minor, diminished and augmented, combining them into a single unity.[57] This inclusion of all four conventional consonant harmonies in a single chord demonstrated the transcendence of traditional functional harmony (the motion from dissonance to consonance rather than their co-existence)."[58] Sabaneev jumps quickly from apparently scientific observations to extravagant claims that don't pass muster in our own sober times, but they are revealing about the kinds of belief systems that were common to Scriabin's time and place. Rebecca Mitchell argues that "in [Sabaneev's] analysis, the echo of a well-known Romantic trope can be heard: the microcosmic world of the individual and the macrocosmic external universe correspond, uncovered through the intuitive creativity of genius."[59]

Arrangement in Fourths

A consensus has arisen among theorists and historians alike that the tidy arrangement on the staff of the mystic chord in intervals of a fourth—undeniably true—is misleading, or at least of questionable significance. Among many uses of mystic-family chords, this exact arrangement of pitches is rather rare in Scriabin's music outside of *Prometheus* itself, where the interval of a fourth has real motivic significance in passages such as the muted trumpet calls in m. 21. The aural image of quartal harmony suggests a comparison, for instance, to the harmonic style of Hindemith, with which Scriabin's style could hardly be more radically contrasting. This contrast is in part due to the various qualities of fourths in the textbook mystic chord—including the two augmented fourths and one diminished one—and partly due to Scriabin's generally slower harmonic rhythm, an aspect of his style emphasized by Jim Samson.[60]

If quartal harmony were a foundational *raison d'être* of the mystic chord, a perfect or augmented fourth should nearly always be present in the bass register. However, when a tritone is used as the bass register in his piano music, he most frequently employs an octatonic harmony rather than a mystic chord. Perfect fourths in the bass are only found with any regularity in the Tenth Sonata. Mystic-family chords typically are spaced with the seventh over the bass. The augmented fourth (or lowered fifth, or ♯11) is more typically given to an upper register; indeed, the acoustic distribution of overtones—to which all good pianist-composers are sensitive—makes for a plausible explanation.

Scriabin does, however, employ small stacks of fourths rather frequently. This usually takes place in a middle or higher register, in a manner similar to some jazz voicings, for instance the opening of *Étrangeté* Op. 63 No. 2, and the tenor register voicings in the Etude Op. 65 No. 1. This spacing enables the music to float, in contrast to the solid impression given by blocks of thirds. It is fair, after all, that Scriabin should have received a bit of recognition as a proto-quartal composer. The Etudes Op. 65 reveal his interest in different chord spacings, and likely his awareness of Debussy's use of unusual intervals in works such as the Etude in Fourths, or the Prelude *Ondine*. A cursory glance at the "death harmonies" of the *Mysterium* proves that Scriabin was working in a typically systematic way, deliberately organizing harmonic structures in various different interval distributions.[61] These gigantic twelve-tone harmonies are arranged, with varied spacings, into the intervals of thirds, fourths, and fifths.

Evolving an Entire Composition from One Harmony

Hull writes, "[Scriabin] discovered many new chords or combinations; but, what is more remarkable, he invented practically a new style of composition. He takes a certain new chord which suits the particular feelings he wants to express, and evolves the whole composition out of this one extended harmony, using it on only a very few roots."[62] The notion may have derived from Sabaneev's claim about *Prometheus* that once this chord is heard as a consonance, "not a single dissonance is to be found in it."[63] This is an early example of the notion that Scriabin's late music—to say the same thing much less kindly—consists of a kind of improvisatory vamp on his favorite chord. The American analyst and composer George Perle states a similar idea much more formally, indeed grandly, claiming that Scriabin used a single set in a kind of pre-serial manner, as the common source of chords, melodies and harmonies.[64] This claim does at least have a basis in verifiable fact, since we know that Scriabin yearned for the unification of harmony and melody. Schoenberg's atonal music made similar claims to organic unity. Along these lines, Faubion Bowers has gone so far as to claim (offering no evidence, but likely responding to Perle) that the Seventh Sonata is "the first serial composition." But this is all too grand and too formal; in his article "Late Skriabin: Some Principles Behind the Style," Jay Reise writes off such speculations to "the influence of the post-Schoenbergian tendency towards over-systematization."[65] Serial composition implies a melodic ordering of tones and a degree of compositional control well in excess of what Scriabin had in mind.

Hull gives interesting examples of "foundation chords" in other works, but his procedure is speculative and lacks details about the process of composition he is claiming. As Reise observes, "There seems today to be a general consensus that the mystic chord is neither the key nor the generating element in Skriabin's method."[66] Reise proposes an alternative explanation of this style: not a simple, rigid system but rather a set of principles—a modal language of whole-tone and octatonic scales, careful attention to voice-leading in and out of these modes, and a system of tonal root movements that derive from the traditions of nineteenth-century chromatic tonal harmony.

A CONTEMPORARY VIEW OF MYSTIC HARMONY

Although the origins of mystic harmony can be traced in Scriabin's altered dominant language, in the late piano works, mystic-family chords no longer function as a dominant. They have become tonally inert, with no need for resolution. Modal thinking is quite helpful to explore the unique features of this style. Three modes or scales dominate the landscape: the whole tone, mystic, and octatonic (figure 12.15a-c), all of which harbor a great variety of altered dominant chords. These modes serve as the generators of harmonic and melodic material. As Reise observes, Scriabin does not stick rigidly to any of these modes in the course of most compositions but uses them flexibly, including foreign tones and moving smoothly from one to another with compact voice-leading. This process of voice-leading is facilitated by the many common tones among these modes. The substance that unites them all is the one harmony Scriabin had used extensively all his life: the French sixth chord. If there were any one Rosetta stone with the information to explain Scriabin's harmony for his whole life, it is surely this chord. In the textbook mystic chord, the lower four and most foundational notes form this French sixth. If the ninth above the bass is lowered, it becomes octatonic. If instead the thirteenth is lowered, it is whole-tone (figure 12.15d-f). Thus, the mystic chord acts as a kind of mediator, a convenient means of transit, hovering, as in midair, between the whole-tone and octatonic harmonic worlds.[67]

We have observed Scriabin's tendency to voice-lead 9 → ♭9 in his middle period, and he retains this trait in his late harmony. As in the subtle oscillations of the Fifth Sonata (which mediate between the mystic and whole-tone collections) this apparently small inflection represents a shift from the mystic to the octatonic scale. The 9 → ♭9 descent forms the subject of a number of Scriabin's melodic ideas, for exam-

Figure 12.15. Three modes: (a) Whole tone (b) Acoustic, or "Mystic" (c) Octatonic. The related versions of the mystic chord: (d) Whole tone (e) Standard (f) Octatonic.

ple, in *Prometheus* and the Eighth Sonata (see figures 12.16a and 12.16b). Scriabin spoke in radical terms about this detail: "Listen to the tragedy born out of such a dissolution . . . in two notes I alter hope into despair." In *Prometheus* he hailed this single descent as "the most tragic episode of my creative work."[68] These apparently overblown comments about a simple half-step descent suggest that he was well aware of this relationship of mystic harmony to octatonicism, and felt it in an unusually powerful way. In the Seventh Sonata, the process is reversed to ♭9 → 9 (figure 12.16c), so Scriabin considers this a moment of purity and celestial pleasure, a return out of the darkness of octatonicism to the light of the mystic mode. We can observe the struggle between A-natural and A♯ continuing for several measures.

This theory of modal transfer does a great deal to elucidate the celestial stillness of the Tenth Sonata's opening measures. An augmented chord, representing the whole-tone world, is set against a diminished triad, which represents the octatonic. The two descending thirds are offset by a leap up by third to B♭, followed by a winding search for the balance point: an A♭, harmonized by a French sixth. Scriabin was justifiably proud of the chromaticism of this breathtaking opening, for both its compositional logic and its uncanny expressive power. Playing this example, he liked to boast, "See how my music lies between the tones."[69]

The mystic chord's properties in tonal geometry were intended to represent the same thing in spiritual terms: a conduit, a nexus, a go-between, a mediator; these harmonies act as a link between the human and the divine. To borrow the language of Rebecca Mitchell, these are the "musical metaphysics" of mystic harmony. This harmony sought to achieve unity (*edinstvo*) and spiritual transcendence by eliminating the dualities of harmony and melody, consonance and dissonance, sound and color.[70] When Rachmaninov was amazed at the sound of the chord in *Prometheus*, he asked, "What are you using here?" Scriabin replied, "the chord of the pleroma." The pleroma is a Christian Gnostic term derived from the Greek for "plenitude," as Taruskin describes it: "the all-encompassing hierarchy of the divine realm, located entirely outside the physical universe."[71] Simon Morrison, in his article "Skryabin and the Impossible," traces the meanings of this harmony through its Symbolist roots through to his attempts to expand the principle further to achieve spiritual enlightenment in the *Mysterium*. "Skryabin conceived the 'chord of the pleroma' or 'mystic' chord as a musical symbol. It was to create a parallel, harmonic correspondence between external reality—what Ivanov called *realia*—and an internal, higher reality—*realiora*. It was to establish a relationship between the mobile, temporal world of perceptible phenomena and the immobile, nontemporal world of essences."[72]

This idea of the pleroma would be taken to its logical conclusion in the twelve-tone "death harmonies" in the sketches for the *Mysterium*. Many of these are constructed as extensions or combinations of the very sonorities described here: the French sixth, the Mystic chord, and the octatonic scale. These have been reproduced in Manfred Kelkel's massive tome on Scriabin.[73] In analyzing these structures, Morrison describes them as "inert acoustic structures modeled on traditional harmonies, but devoid of functionality."[74] The inclusion of all twelve pitches represents the ulti-

Figure 12.16. Inflections of the ninth of the chord: (a) *Prometheus* Op. 60, mm. 9–13 (Berlin: Russischer Musikverlag, 1913). (b) Sonata No. 8 Op. 66, mm. 1–4 (Moscow: Jurgenson, 1913). (c) Sonata No. 7 Op. 64, "White Mass," mm. 29–34 (Berlin: Russischer Musikverlag, 1913).

mate in stasis, universality, and timelessness. There can be no thought of resolution when there are no other pitches left to resolve to. It is here that Scriabin's spiritual vision shares much in common with (and indeed, may well have inspired) that of Schoenberg in *Jakobsleiter* and Ives in the *Universe Symphony*. All three composers sought to represent transcendental experience by means of the simultaneous use of all twelve chromatic pitches.[75]

Beyond these twelve-note maximal "pleroma" harmonies, there is indeed nothing further the twelve-note tonal system or its language of associated meanings would have to offer, besides the use of microtones, which were indeed explored by his follower Ivan Vyshnegradsky,[76] among others.

13

The Scriabin Sound

It is hardly too much to say that the whole of Scriabin's music springs from a love of piano sonority. The sonority comes first and, in a way, all else derives from it and is subservient to it.

—Samuel Randlett[1]

To play like Skryabin was absolutely impossible. His playing was unique: it could not be imitated by producing similar tone, or power or softness, and so on. For he had a special and entirely different relationship with the instrument, which was his own unrepeatable secret.

—Alexander Pasternak[2]

The mythology of the "Scriabin sound" has been fixed indelibly in my memory since a conversation I had with a Russian music student, who was ruminating on performances of Scriabin's music he had just heard by some aspiring young pianists. His broad hand gestures dragged trails of smoke from his cigarette through the air, as he granted some grudging approval of their technical skills. "But," he looked to me abruptly and removed his cigarette, gesturing rhythmically with his hand to make his point all the more emphatically, "they do not have the SOUND of Scriabin!"

What is this mythical, elusive "sound of Scriabin"? Surely, the expression is an oversimplification. It refers to more than just the timbre of the physical sound, but rather to the character of the whole. Music, after all, is always communicated through the coordinated interaction of sound in time, and it isn't possible to separate the two dimensions of the listening experience. Nevertheless, in Scriabin's music the timbre of the piano's sound does take on a special significance. In brief, some of the most salient characteristics of Scriabin's pianistic sound-world include:

Fast and decisive strikes of the key
Bright, scintillating sound bursts, often in the upper register
Ecstatic swirls of sound that avoid separation into definite metrical blocks
Cantabile tone projection in melodic playing
A muffled, indistinct sonority used for accompanying materials
Clear delineation of layers between important strands and supporting fabric
A limpid, floating, weightless sound to create languid moods
Attentive listening to pedaled resonances, and thus, especially:
Creative and varied use of pedal shadings to regulate balances and dynamics

Broadly speaking, Scriabin's sound in his early period belongs to the landscape of traditional Romantic pianism, with projected melodic *cantabile*, but less thick or heavy forte playing than in much of the Russian Romantic tradition. Some of his later works have much in common with the pianism of Debussy and Ravel, in whose music many of the points above also apply. Late Scriabin differs stylistically from these French counterparts more in rhythmic character and formal design than in the approach to the instrument. Scriabin, who found French impressionistic music too "passive,"[3] tends to require more vigorous contrasts, a wider dynamic range, and more assertive attacks. However, a rugged and overpowering style would be still less appropriate; reviews and reminiscences of Scriabin frequently comment on the elegance of his presentation and on a dearth of powerful dynamics.[4]

IN SEARCH OF A HISTORICALLY AUTHENTIC SCRIABIN SOUND

An authentic experience of Scriabin's piano sound is unfortunately inaccessible to today's musician. Recording technology that could have given an adequate sense of the tonal spectrum of his piano playing was not available until a number of years after his death. Whatever the merits of the piano roll recordings, their sound quality is certainly flat and unflattering. An image of Scriabin's own sound is thus a puzzle to be put together from several sources: these piano rolls, the musical scores, the playing of his most reputable followers and contemporaries who had heard him, and the firsthand reports of musicians and critics who heard his playing. These are nearly unanimous in observing a personal and distinctive quality of his playing, a quality that transcended almost magically the physical reality of a piano's means of sound production, or at least the type of piano sound one might have heard from his contemporaries. His professor Vasily Safonov recalled the playing of his favorite student: "Scriabin possessed in the highest degree what I always impressed on my students: the less like itself a piano is under the fingers of the player, the better it is."[5]

Reviewers of Scriabin's playing at times criticized his lack of powerful dynamics,[6] but one can ask whether this was truly a deficiency in his performance, or if such forceful touch was alien to his personality. One should also remember that Scriabin was a man of small stature, and perhaps not built naturally to produce a thunderous fortissimo. What many observed was his exquisite touch in soft playing and his ability to produce extraordinary effects: "Scriabin had an almost magical touch, especially bewitching when he played softly, superbly using his pedal for an ephemeral effect. He hated pianists who . . . played his compositions with the same approach and touch as if his piano pieces were Rachmaninov's or Tchaikovsky's."[7] Alexander Pasternak (1893–1982) commented on the effect of this weightless sonority on some listeners: "His enemies used to say that it was not real piano playing, but a twittering of birds or a mewing of kittens, meaning both his interpretation and the actual sound of the instrument."[8]

The recorded sources with the highest claims to authenticity are those of his immediate associates, and of those followers who had heard his playing. In this regard, two compact disc recordings of Scriabin's music are extremely valuable as a starting point. The first, "The Caswell Collection, Vol. 5 (1906–1926),[9] is a collection of performances by Scriabin himself, by Josef Lhevinne, Konstantin Igumnov, Alexander Goldenweiser, Austin Conradi, Lev Pouishnov, and Magdeleine Brard, all using the Welte-Mignon piano roll technology. The second, "Scriabine and the Scriabinians,"[10] includes recordings by Heinrich Neuhaus, Alexander Goldenweiser, Samuil Feinberg, Vladimir Sofronitsky, and Scriabin himself. The second of these recordings boasts Scriabin interpreters of higher stature, and performances of a uniformly high standard. However, on the Caswell disc, the sound quality of Scriabin's own rolls is superior. Among the pianists referenced here, Feinberg's recordings are of special interest from the standpoint of authenticity, since Scriabin had unusually high praise for his playing.[11] Sofronitsky is also of special interest; he married Scriabin's daughter Elena and cited Scriabin as his favorite composer. Although he never played for or heard Scriabin, his lifetime investment in and dedication to his music was enormous. Goldenweiser and Neuhaus arguably may have made a greater contribution to Scriabin's legacy as pedagogues than as performers: Neuhaus as the teacher of Sviatoslav Richter, one of the most important Scriabin pianists.

It is a great pity that we lack an authentic representation of the inimitable Scriabin sound, but the playing of these associates and followers was perhaps not inferior to the source. It is quite possible that Scriabin the pianist was a less than perfect conduit for the musical inspiration of Scriabin the composer. Critical responses to Scriabin's own playing run the gamut from wholesale approval to blanket condemnation. Composer and critic Yuli Engel found Scriabin's playing too dainty when a more powerful sound was called for: "Scriabin's tender and finely soft piano gifts were barely audible. You never felt there was any gunpowder, only smoke from a powder flash . . . But the powder charge *is* in Scriabin's music . . . only when we hear it played by other hands. . . . Others play his compositions more *powerfully*, and not just in the sense of force."[12] Perhaps the most forceful spokesperson for this contrarian viewpoint would be N. N. Cherkass, a leading piano teacher of his time, who penned a monograph, *Scriabin as Pianist and Piano Composer*.[13] Cherkass's overriding thesis is baldly stated: "Scriabin was a bad pianist."[14] One of Cherkass's primary objections was Scriabin's lack of a proper *legato*, a fact borne out by the surprisingly short articulations in the piano rolls that disregard the printed slurs. If Scriabin's best qualities were his touch sensitivity, or as Cherkass scientifically put it, "the dynamic relative shading [balance of tones] within a simultaneous concord of voices,"[15] we must lament after all that this evocative, evanescent sound is precisely what has been lost to posterity in his piano roll recordings.

QUALITIES OF TOUCH: LIMPID CARESSES

Virtuoso pianists are appreciative of Scriabin's highly idiomatic writing for the instrument, and luxuriate in his wash of sound that combines registers together so effectively. These characteristics may lead to the temptation to play in what we might pejoratively call an "impressionistic" manner,[16] that is, with light and shallow fingerwork, unsupported by the weight of the arm, relying on the pedal to combine sounds together. This style of playing, indiscriminately applied, is a common trait of inexperienced players, but it shouldn't be rejected *a priori* as a fault in every case. If used with good judgment in the right places, this technique can produce a hazy sonority ideal for some of Scriabin's languid moods, or an atmospheric background that supports a more prominent melodic strand.

An excellent example of this kind of delicate sonority can be found in *Caresse dansée* Op. 57 No. 2. Physical caresses are surely one of the most extravagant new experiences Scriabin sought to convey in his music. In this delightful *Poème*, the suggestive beckoning in the middle voice, moving by lurid half steps, depicts these intimate sensations, together with the rising and falling contour of the soprano. Only the top voice requires a bit of strength in the fingers. All the other parts should be stroked with the utmost tenderness in supporting it. In this rarefied air, pedal is needed only for occasional shadings. The *Poème* Op. 32 No. 1 is a prime example of Scriabin's languid, feminine mood that luxuriates in sonority, with unmistakably erotic overtones.[17] The pianistic style is similar to that of *Caresse dansée*, but with a duet of two prominent melodic lines.

QUALITIES OF TOUCH: INCISIVE STRIKES AND BELL-LIKE SOUNDS

When the sound environment is hazy, a flabby-fingered style can be effective, but in the majority of cases in Scriabin's music, that touch is not viscerally communicative enough to convey the clarity of his compositional design, the nervous intensity of his character, or the ambition of his ideas. It is especially important to understand that the dynamic indication of *pp*, widespread in Scriabin's music, does not imply a sluggish finger stroke, but rather a special overall mood, in which many qualities of touch should coexist. A small and decisive motion with firmer fingers is often appropriate, since it gives more rhythmic definition and excites a wider range of overtones.[18] This more active, chiseled style of playing seems to have involved also a quicker release of the fingers than was marked in the score. Anatole Leikin observes of the piano rolls: "Most of the time, Scriabin did not push down the key; instead, he struck it with a light, precise, quick finger strike.[19] [. . .] Scriabin habitually replaced longer notes with shorter time values, followed by rests. He disliked lingering on the keys; he preferred to continue the sound on the pedal while his hands hovered above the keyboard."[20]

The potency of Scriabin's magically weightless sonority can be measured by its bewitching effects on the talented Pasternak family, especially the Nobel Prize–winning novelist Boris Pasternak (1890–1960). Before developing his literary skills, Boris was affected by Scriabin's persona to the point that he enrolled in music school for a time, studying to be a composer himself.[21] Boris's mother, Roza, was herself a pianist of renown, a student of Rubinstein and Leschetitsky. Boris's father Leonid (1862–1945), a prominent Russian painter, knew Scriabin well and created some of the most recognizable and beloved images of Scriabin. He recalled that Scriabin's fingers seemed to extract sounds "not by falling on the keys, not by hitting them (which in fact they did) but in the opposite way, by pulling away from the keys and lightly soaring above them."[22] Boris's brother, Alexander (1893–1982), also commented, "As soon as I heard the first sounds on the piano, even if I was sitting with my eyes shut not looking at Scriabin's hands and fingers, I immediately had the impression that his fingers were producing the sound without touching the keys, that he was (as it were) snatching them away from the keyboard and letting them flutter lightly over it. This created an extraordinary illusion that his fingers in some strange way were drawing the sound *out* of the instrument."[23] Enchanting though this soaring touch could be, a number of critics and observers complained that it was insufficient to fill a large concert hall, and was more suitable for smaller venues.[24]

The effect of the early release of the key is perhaps greater on the performer's psychology than on the sound itself; the pianist feels where the control of the resonance is transferred from the finger to the pedal, in order to sense and convey the imagination of flight. A related and significant aspect of Scriabin's pianistic arsenal is what we might call the swirl of sound. It is made by a dense flurry of notes in a short time and space, as if from the energy of many tiny atoms colliding to create a solar wind.[25] This element of Scriabin's unique style is not captured by many pianists, and has proven elusive for some of the all-time greats. Sergei Prokofiev famously described Rachmaninov's performance of Scriabin's Fifth: "When Scriabin had played this sonata everything seemed to be flying upward; with Rachmaninov all the notes stood firmly planted on earth."[26]

The *Languido* section in the Fifth Sonata (m. 13, figure 12.11) is a prime laboratory for techniques of sound production. Although marked *pianissimo* and in a slow tempo, these keystrokes should be not hazy and delicate but rather fine, distinct touches, placed with rhythmic authority and then released, letting the piano resonate on its own like a vibraphone. Only the passage *molto languido* in mm. 29*ff* gives the opportunity to relax the fingers and to play more vaguely, like the caressing style; the indication *Accarezzevole* in m. 34 signifies this intent. Another case of dynamically soft but sharp attacks is in the Poème *Étrangeté* Op. 63 No. 2 (see figure 13.1). The poetic impression is highly refined and perhaps even miniaturized (*gracieux, delicat*), but the quality of fingerwork is the furthest thing from gentle. Every note in each hand should be articulated by talonlike fingertips, but with the smallest and most efficient of motions. The indication *aigu* (pointed) is highly significant, requiring a sudden, sharp attack, such as one finds also in the Poème Op. 69 No. 2 and in numerous passages of the Seventh Sonata. The spasmodic gestures in these several measures clearly relate to Scriabin's fascination with light and flight; if played with the requisite hardness of touch, these strange, surprising waves can reveal, as if through a prism, a whole kaleidoscope of tonal colors.

Clear and fast attacks can produce the kind of strikes commonly referred to by pianists as a "bell-like sound." The metaphor of a bell is widely used in pedagogy for apprehending keyboard touch and resonance; a similar striking motion is necessary to trigger its own percussive mechanism.[27] The American composer Dane Rudhyar, who was greatly influenced by Scriabin's musical language, traces the sound of bells to the world of mysticism. In his words, mystical music "is that music in which the element of tone predominates . . . each tone of a gong or bell is really a complex

Figure 13.1. Opening of *Etrangeté* Op. 63 No. 2, mm. 1–5. Berlin: Rossīĭskoe muzykal'noe izd-vo, 1912.

chord . . . Scriabin's works, after he . . . first was haunted by the great gong-tone . . . have been nothing but vast gong-combinations, modulations of some one throbbing, living Tone which is the soul and source of energy of the composition."[28] In pianistic terms, the technique for imitating a small bell is a fast, decisive attack commencing from very close to the target (the key), carried out with a firm, curved finger. Naturally, these small bell strokes are most effective in the higher registers where the hammers are lighter and the strings shorter and more tightly strung. The stroke of a larger bell, on the other hand, is slow, heavy, and broadly placed, most advantageous in the bass, usually with flatter fingers and with the support of the arm's weight.

Suddenness of attack can also be a significant aspect of sound production, irrespective of the dynamic range. A sudden attack emphasizes the mechanical noise of the hammer hitting the string. Many soft and slowly paced sections of Scriabin's music can benefit from a quick and dramatic strike, or from a sudden release. The Sixth Sonata, with its menacing summons, is full of such moments, such as the sudden *pp* dynamic in m. 6. A break in sustained sound here would disturb the musical tension, but a significant color change is required for the drama. The only effective solution seems to be an abrupt pedal release and a very swift, quiet, and precise re-attack.

Lively strikes are especially critical in realizing the "delirious dance" codas of the late sonatas that break the thematic material into tiny fragments. The frenzied, Dionysian rhythmic character of these passages requires vast reserves of physical energy to achieve the rhythmic clarity and vigor they require at such a breakneck speed, even at a quiet dynamic. The key strikes should be sharp and precise, but never heavy or deep. These passages must be rehearsed with the maximum strength of articulation in the fingers to prepare for the utmost in visceral energy that will be needed in performance.

PULSATING REPEATED CHORDS

Scriabin sought numerous means to transform and elevate the instrument's possibilities beyond a commonplace world of hammers and strings, with the inevitable decay of tone. Trills, discussed in chapter 10, are a good example. Another favored device is the use of repeated chords in both hands. Like trills, these pulsating chords are an inventive use of a piano's mechanism. This constant resupply of energy overcomes the instrument's natural tendency to decay, and thus gives the performer full rein on dynamics and color. Pianist Samuel Randlett writes, "The reason for Scriabin's lifelong fondness for repeated chord[s] is not far to seek: they produce a rhythmic vibration within a fundamentally static sonority."[29] The sense of visceral excitement in this texture can be found in Schubert's Lieder (such as "Ungeduld" from *Die schöne Müllerin*), in the climaxes of many of Chopin's works, and in many other pianist-composers such as Liszt, Fauré, and Rachmaninov. Traditionally, this texture might be used at the climax of a work, such as in Chopin's Barcarolle Op. 60 or Ballade in A♭ Op. 47. Scriabin employed it at the climactic endings of the D♯ minor Etude Op.

8 No. 12, the *Poème satanique* Op. 36, and the Fourth Sonata. But in his middle period, with his consistent emphasis on elevated, ecstatic expression, Scriabin sometimes used this texture as the foundation for entire pieces, as in the dynamic Poème Op. 32 No. 2 and the grandiose Poème *tragique* Op. 34. These quasi-orchestral passages of the middle period, inspired by Wagner, may rank among the greatest challenges of interpretation in Scriabin. It takes a certain amount of courage to write in this manner (and also to perform this kind of music in today's more cynical age) without appearing overly pretentious. An audience is not always willing or prepared to be receptive to such emotions.

At those precious moments when the performer feels the passion and has a vision for the piece, however, the impact can be electrifying. Here the element of taste is paramount, and we must remember that Scriabin, for all his assertiveness, was a very refined personality with a meticulous deportment, and was never known as a powerful player. Sound and rhythm must be effectively combined; rhythmic drive is preferable to excessive accumulated volume in such cases as a source of excitement, and a selective voicing is crucial to highlight important notes and to downplay others. All the great Scriabin pianists of the tradition do this effectively. It is a terrible mistake to play in a boorish way by banging out these chords too heavily, with too much pedal, or especially, too slowly.[30] The ending of the B minor *Fantasie* Op. 28, for instance, should be a thrilling, suffocatingly ecstatic passage for the audience, with its triumph in huge chords like César Franck. Unfortunately, it is also a glaring opportunity for the performer to misjudge the moment and overshoot the intended target.[31]

Scriabin relied less on repeated chords in his later years, but never abandoned them entirely, as we find in works such as the Etude Op. 65 No. 3 and the apocalyptic fanfares of the Seventh Sonata. However, when he did employ them, he often added the element of polyrhythm, increasing the intensity of the effect, for instance, in the final climax of the Fifth Sonata, and in the ghastly passage marked *joyeux, triomphant* in the Sixth Sonata (mm. 180–85). The spiritual feeling thus gains in intensity; it is no longer a single human's beating heart, but a vision of transformative ecstasy and brilliant light. The final and most brilliant step on the road is the chord tremolo employed in *Vers la flamme* Op. 72 and the climax of the Tenth Sonata Op. 70. How far we have come from the beating heart of Schubert's Lieder! A deeply held personal emotion has now become a cosmic and universal one.

TONAL LAYERING IN THE RUSSIAN HERITAGE

The origin of Chopin's beloved Nocturne genre in the style of pianist and composer John Field (1782–1837) is a well-known tale in the lore of the piano. The young Field was employed in the piano store of Muzio Clementi for his special expertise in demonstrating through his skilled improvisations the tonal capabilities of his instruments. In Field's style, assured melodic projection, especially in the soprano, is wrapped in a cloth of harmonic and textural support requiring an entirely different quality of touch. The Irishman's crucial role as the father of a great lineage of Russian pianists has been less widely acknowledged. Field traveled to St. Petersburg with Clementi, remaining there for most of his last three decades to concertize extensively and to train a line of outstanding Russian musicians beginning with Glinka. Field's most successful and devoted pupil was Alexander Dubuc (1812–1897, also spelled Dubuk, or Alexandre Dubuque), who wrote a memoir about Field.[32] Dubuc taught the leading Moscow teacher Alexander Villoing (1804–1878) as well as Nikolai Zverev (1832–1893) who in turn taught Scriabin, as well as Siloti, Rachmaninov, Goldenweiser, and many other important musicians.

The most significant of the nineteenth-century Russian virtuosi was Anton Rubinstein, who together with his brother, Nikolai, were students of Villoing. Anton Rubinstein's international career and influence was enormous, comparable to that of Liszt. Known as the "Russian Bear," he was widely known for his heart and for the exceptional beauty of his tonal production. His use of arm weight in tonal projection was likely a key to his success.[33] Scriabin's mother, Lyubov Petrovna Shchetinina (1850–1873), was a promising concert pianist whose life was cut short soon after her son's birth. She studied with Anton Rubinstein and the renowned pedagogue Theodor Leschetitsky (1830–1915).

Russian Romantic pianists, in the tradition of Field and Anton Rubinstein, have long excelled in isolating certain parts of the texture in preference to others, thus allowing melodies to float on an attractive cushion of sound. One can clearly hear this feature in the playing of all the great Scriabin interpreters. A fundamental example, and an ideal exercise in voicing for the intermediate-level pianist, is the popular Etude Op. 2 No. 1 in C♯ minor, where single notes in the melody are highlighted in *cantabile* style. Whole handfuls of accompanying chords sound muffled as harmonic support. In this style of playing, the shape of the hand and angle of attack are both significant factors that enable the melodic fingers to strike firmly, often from a high position, while the others only brush the keys, close to their targets. The need for such melodic projection can take extreme form, such as this momentous melodic declaration in the Eighth Sonata (see figure 13.2). With the support of the pedal, a full arm stroke on each note onto a wide finger surface (such as a sideways thumb) enables the middle register to intone deeply without any harshness.

In Scriabin's music, the delineation of textural strands is more than a matter of melody and accompaniment. His contrapuntal thinking affords the secondary parts varying degrees of melodic, motivic, and rhythmic (often polyrhythmic) interest. All of these require contrasting and internally consistent levels of the touches described above. The Prelude Op. 11 No. 11 in B major (shown in figure 10.6) is a wonderful exercise to develop this touch. The melody sings out in the right hand as one element, joined by a left-hand part that combines three more elements: a bass line, a tenor counterpoint (marked with staccato dots), and running 16ths. If played well, the listener should be able to distinguish clearly these four independent layers. The Seventh Sonata is full of these layering challenges, most especially the passage shown in figure 13.3a, where the main melody is set off clearly (*bien marquée*) within an el-

Figure 13.2. A momentous declaration in Sonata No. 8 Op. 66, mm. 158–64. *Moscow: Jurgenson, 1913.*

egant cloth of winged descents (marked *ailé,* "winged," and *ondoyant,* "undulating"), all of which retain their contrapuntal melodic identity in a complex polyrhythmic framework. The toughest pianistic demand is that the many notes in the "foreign" parts are clothed in an ethereal well-regulated pianissimo that allows the totality to be heard, without excessive congestion caused by the accumulation of sound. In addition to well-modulated qualities of touch, careful balances and attentive pedaling are required to pull this off successfully.[34]

Among the most demanding moments for tonal layering is the extraordinary passage *tout devient charme et douceur* from the Sixth Sonata (see figure 13.3b). Here the music is spread out onto three staves for better visualization, as it often is in Debussy. Each instrument of this metaphorical orchestra can be profitably practiced on its own with a keen focus on sound quality, or practiced together in smaller groups before being put back together. The slow melody in the soprano must be played with expressive tension and shape, with a very firm finger and a deliberate, deep stroke. The tenor and alto should be heard distinctly, but in a more fluid, less penetrating style than the soprano. The alto should be lightly marked in a melodic legato style, and the tenor with a thin but fast staccato attack that penetrates into the pedaled sonority. Finally, the higher alto and running left hand parts are not of melodic significance, but their watery contours should nevertheless be felt, since they give the passage its magical character. They are worthy to be practiced on their own to find the ultimate degree of evenness and remoteness. The pianist who can find the qualities of touch to delineate all these parts effectively inside the pedaled sound surely possesses the finesse to handle any page of music by Scriabin, or any other composer.

Figure 13.3. Textural layering in: (a) Sonata No. 7 Op. 64, mm. 207–11 (Berlin: Russischer Musikverlag, 1913). (b) Sonata No. 6 Op. 62, mm. 244–49 (Berlin: Russischer Musikverlag, 1912).

REGISTRAL CHARACTERS

Scriabin is exceptionally sensitive to the special timbral characteristics of different registers. His creativity in using these sonorities is unsurpassed. His fascination with such timbres is best exemplified in the Seventh Sonata, a *tour de force* in the colorful use of registers. In the coda, with its famous *en delire* (delirious) passage, we find sustained in the pedal the piano's lowest A, its highest C, and fistfuls of notes in between (see figure 13.4). These chords trigger an aural recollection of a stormy passage in the development (mm. 161 and 165), where strikes of lightning first lit up the treble. Standing in stark contrast are some ghoulish, indolent passages in the bass register (*subito più lento*, mm. 318–24). These recall a menacing summons in the bass (m. 25, and others) and an extended episode from the development (*poco meno vivo*, mm. 215–25) of great somnolence and morbidity. Scriabin's penchant for minor ninths in the bass—which also appear in many other works—highlights the mystery of that register. When the music is spread out widely across the keyboard, it is important for the pianist to highlight those extremes that give the music its special color and character.

Figure 13.4. Use of registers and "skyscraper chord" in the Coda of Sonata No. 7 Op. 64, "White Mass," mm. 320–33. Berlin: Russischer Musikverlag, 1913.

Bursts of brilliant light are a consistent feature of his late style. These flashes can usually be struck with alacrity, as in the brilliant flashes of the Tenth Sonata and *Vers la flamme*, the fiery sparkles of *Prometheus* (*flot lumineux*, mm. 414–48), the spasmodic gyrations of *Etrangeté* Op. 63 No. 2, and the Poème Op. 69 No. 2. This focus on high treble resonance can be found equally in earlier works, such as the melodic lines in the Coda to the Andante of the Sonata-Fantasie, which is discussed in chapter 3. The Piano Concerto Op. 20 is also full of many examples, such as the delicate arabesques at the end of the second movement, the ascending rockets that characterize the main theme of the third movement, and the stirring preparation for the chordal climax of the Finale (see figure 13.5). In any solo concerto, the high register is helpful for the soloist to be heard over the orchestra.

The depth and mysterious quality of the bass is equally dear to Scriabin, and is evocative of the traditions of his native Russia, where choirs are celebrated for the depth of their *basso profundo*. In Scriabin's writing, chorale textures and low registers frequently go hand in hand. A rich and resonant bass sound colors the Sonata No. 1 Op. 6 throughout, most tellingly in the Funeral March finale and in the second movement, with its religious sentiments. In a work as late as the Prelude Op. 51 No. 2, the depth, darkness, and chorale background suggest that Scriabin remained close to his Russian traditions in his later years. The entrance of the low A pedal point at the conclusion intensifies the gloom. This Russian flavor is apparent in the emotional depths of the climax of the C♯ minor Etude Op. 42 No. 5, where the very lowest A is hammered in a throbbing way. This low A is employed relatively often by Scriabin, perhaps most effectively at the conclusion of the whirling Coda of the Eighth Sonata, where the work's turbulent emotional arc is resolved most satisfyingly, to a point of utter exhaustion.

This audacious exploration of the piano's registers caused Scriabin at times to push for notes beyond its existing range. For example, in the very short Prelude Op. 39 No. 4, he writes a low G♯. Bösendorfer pianos of the time did offer tones below A, and some contemporaries such as Ravel, Bartók, and Busoni wrote music with the assumption that an expanded piano would someday become the standard. Hardly any piano ever built offers a note beyond a high C,[35] yet Scriabin asks for a D in the dizzying Coda of the Sixth Sonata (m. 365). Fortunately, there is enough activity at this point of the piece that omitting this D or just playing C in its place is a reasonable substitute in practice. Unlike the well-known case of Beethoven, the modern piano would never expand in its range to accommodate such visionary dreams as these.

Scriabin often intensifies the contrast between extreme registers by juxtaposing them closely. The effect is like a master painter who contrasts regions of light and shade on the canvas. For instance, in the Piano Concerto's third movement climax, the high register's brilliance is set off against the resonant depth of the low octaves. Here the instrument truly reaches the full glory of Tchaikovskian heroism. In the Tenth Sonata, the power and brilliance of the high tremolos is intensified when placed after a lugubrious probing of the murky low registers (*en s'eteignant peu a peu*,

Figure 13.5. Use of extreme registers in the Piano Concerto in F♯ minor Op. 20, mm. 140–41 up to rehearsal 9. *Leipzig: Beliaev, 1898; reprinted by Broude Bros., New York City.*

mm. 184–91). This style of buildup, a crescendo trajectory from low and foreboding to high and dazzling, is extended into an entire composition in *Vers la flamme* Op. 72. The sets of two pieces of Op. 59 and Op. 73 both make effective pairs when played as sets, in part because of their contrast of high vs. low registers.

COLOR

Scriabin's pianistic fame was based on his inimitable spectrum of tone colors. Fragile, mysterious, yet electrifyingly intense, they often did not even resemble a piano sound.

—Anatole Leikin[36]

One of the great pleasures of Scriabin's piano music is the multitude of opportunities it provides for creativity with pianistic tone color. Sensitivity to harmonic and textural colors—and the skill and daring to highlight them—is a key ingredient to successful performance of his music. As observed in the *New Harvard Dictionary of Music*, "[The color of a musical tone] is largely, though not exclusively, a function of the relative strengths of the harmonics (and sometimes non-harmonic frequencies) present in the sound."[37] A spectrograph can show, for instance, how those patterns vary from one woodwind instrument to another. Color can be modulated on a stringed instrument by such factors as bow speed, angle, and pressure, vibrato, and the choice of string. On the piano, the possibilities for coloristic change on a single note are limited, based primarily on the speed of the hammer at the point of attack. The physical noise of the hammer hitting the string is an important ingredient that should not be overlooked. Hard strikes of the hammer will enhance this noise element (articulation) and can be effective, in conjunction with the pedal, to excite the resonance of a particular part of the soundboard.

Pianos manufactured by different companies and in different eras all offer unique sets of case constructions, scale designs, stringing and hammers all tailored to suit the musical visions of their builders.[38] The firmness of the piano's hammers, especially, will have a crucial impact on a player's response and on the possibilities of the sound. Harder hammers will exaggerate the noise elements, excite the resonance of the soundboard, and create a stronger spectrum of high overtones. Softer hammers will help to camouflage these strikes and support limpid sounds.[39] In performance, tone color is less about the qualities of individual tones, and more about the myriad relationships they form in layers and combinations. These include the dynamic balances between registers, dynamic relationships from note to note (voicing), varieties of pedaled resonances (as described in the following section), and the gradations of texture in the hammer felt made possible by adjustments of the *una corda* pedal. A pianist who is adept as a colorist will have at his or her disposal a wide palette of these combinations as well as the judgment to apply them effectively.

One typical opportunity is a shift of registers. An imaginative pianist can make a great deal out of even a small change in the middle of the instrument. The descending sequence at the beginning of the Third Sonata is a case in point. If all the iterations of the theme are played in the same way, these repetitious statements would make for a monotonous effect on the listener. But each descent to the lower register brings with it a new tonality, growing ever darker and more mysterious, in keeping with the character of the movement (*Drammatico*). With each statement, the pianist can lower the dynamics, shift the voicing from the treble to the bass, decrease the intensity of attacks by relaxing the fingers, and gradually engage the *una corda* pedal. Finally, the pedaling of the left-hand motive can also be varied. At the very opening, the pedal might hold only the long note, and next time include a bit of the pickup octave (G♯ pickup to m. 9), and finally emphasize the bass note instead, with the higher note acting only as a harmonic resonance (B minor statement at m. 13).

Scriabin often highlights tonal color by abruptly juxtaposing assertive and languid moods. The angst-ridden Ninth Sonata is full of these exciting opportunities, especially the shifts in the opening section from shrieking *sforzando* to ghoulish *pianissimo* (mm. 19*ff*). A splendid moment from the earlier period occurs in the fiery *Prestissimo* of the Second Sonata (figure 13.6). The power of the bass is emphasized in the hammered triplet in m. 51; in this *fortissimo*, the arpeggio can be played with strong finger articulation throughout. At the double bar, the proverbial rug has been pulled out from under the listener; the bass is stroked as gently as possible and the arpeggio ripples with feathery lightness, emerging somewhat as it reaches the higher register. Only the top voice of the melody should sing out. The great majority of

Figure 13.6. Opportunity for color change in Sonata No. 2 Op. 19 in G♯ minor, Mvt. II, mm. 49–54. *Leipzig: Beliaev, 1898.*

298   Chapter 13

the contrast takes place in the bass and middle register. It is almost as if, in the bat of an eyelash, a Russian pianist performing a Tchaikovsky concerto has suddenly transformed into a French pianist playing a Fauré Barcarolle. In Scriabin's volatile style, such extremes of contrast should be sought out and exploited.

The *una corda* pedal should not be overlooked as a source of finely nuanced timbral contrasts; it can be used not only in blocks, but in minute adjustments to intensify the color. In figure 13.6, it can be applied after the double bar (where Scriabin in his own performance inserts a fermata) and removed just for the high D♯, and the top of the rising arpeggio. In the Seventh Sonata Coda (figure 13.7), the overall character (*avec une volupté radieuse, extatique*) might suggest some *una corda* pedal, but that can be taken off—partially or completely—at the height of the phrase in m. 254, and certainly at the onset of the trill in m. 255.

Scriabin's poetic character indications can also offer clues to pianistic tonal colors. In the first page of the Sixth Sonata, bars 11–15 (see figure 13.8) offer no less than four idiosyncratic character indications. All of them can be most readily interpreted as pianistic timbres in which the power of the key articulations is mollified. *Avec une chaleur contenue* calls for "restrained warmth." This indication may be interpreted as a cautionary signal to the pianist not to focus the sound too much on the upper voice. "Warmth" calls for keystrokes with enough weight to sustain the tone but with

Figure 13.7. Subtle changes of pedal in Sonata No. 7 Op. 64, "White Mass," mm. 252–60. *Berlin: Russischer Musikverlag, 1913.*

Figure 13.8. Expressive markings in Sonata No. 6 Op. 62, mm. 10–16. Berlin: Russischer Musikverlag, 1912.

not too much force, so as to conceal the attack of the hammer. The balance should favor the middle register more than usual. *Souffle mysterieux* is a most evocative marking, a "mysterious breath," an invitation to let go of clarity for a moment and to allow the "sinister" elements to blend together, for example, the half steps in the bass grace note and in the soprano's melodic line. *Onde caressante* (caressing wave) is a typical Scriabinesque indication, often used in the Seventh Sonata as well. It is perhaps an invitation to combine the arpeggiated harmony into the pedaled resonance, letting the trill float lightly and lazily on top of it. It may also influence the rhythm, as an invitation to linger a bit before the return of the opening bells (*concentré*), which should be played with a return to firm and sudden strikes.

PEDALED RESONANCES

Anton Rubinstein famously remarked that "the pedal is the soul of the piano," and this is never truer than in the music of Scriabin. Restlessly creative and imaginative since early childhood,[40] Scriabin must have discovered many creative pedaling techniques at an early age through his own process of experimentation. His teacher, Vasily Safonov, widely known as a demanding professor and a harsh taskmaster, admired his pedaling greatly. He recommended "Sasha-like pedaling" to his other students and often admonished them, "What are you looking at his hands for? Look at his feet!"[41]

The exceptionally refined quality of Scriabin's pedaling, and its special importance to the unique "Scriabin sound" as a whole, was noted by numerous contemporary listeners and critics. In Scriabin's final live performance, the critic Grigory Prokofiev wrote, "The tone is marvelous. . . . He achieves extraordinary effects. Don't forget he is a wizard with the pedal."[42] As Sabaneev describes it: "His virtuoso pedaling wrapped the tones with layers of resonances full of mystery. No pianists since him have been able to achieve this."[43] Samuil Feinberg, heavily influenced by Scriabin as a composer as well as a pianist, dealt with Scriabin's pedaling in some detail in his book, *Pianism as Art*:

> His creative work touches extreme boundaries, beyond which there is a mystery of sound that has not yet been discovered. . . . Scriabin approached this border by . . . an exquisite use of the pedal—so delicate and subtle that a simple pedal change may appear primitive or even rough. Accuracy in notating pedal marks—already difficult with Chopin's style—is thus almost inconceivable to achieve Scriabin's sound properly. As a result, he largely refused to enter pedal markings in his manuscripts.[44]

What were these unique pedal techniques? Did Scriabin invent them himself or simply have a sovereign command over all the standard methods? Maria Nemenova-Lunz, one of Scriabin's most dedicated and successful students, recalled: "Scriabin was a renowned wizard of the pedal, who used not just half and quarter pedals, but also what he called a 'pinpoint' pedal, a 'vibrating' pedal, and 'pedal mist.'"[45] Certainly, the limitations of piano roll technology leave us with less than even a crude approximation of what his wizardry might have produced.[46] Let us delve into some nuanced pedaling techniques that are crucial to effective Scriabin performance. Most of these methods involve sustaining a web of sound in which different elements of the texture are manipulated dynamically in unequal measure; they are thus congruent with the descriptions of Scriabin's own pedaling cited above.

The sophistication of elements involved in even a basic pedal change can be illustrated as a fundamental example in the Etude Op. 2 No. 1 in C♯ minor. Some overedited publications of this work unfortunately give a clear example how not to play it, by providing a bland pedaling recommendation with too many changes, such as figure 13.9a. Konstantin Igumnov, well-known Muscovite piano teacher, referred to this style of playing as the "sanitary pedal."[47] Scriabin did far better than this by omitting pedal markings altogether. The author's recommendation can be found in figure 13.9b, where one can find many features typical of Scriabin's refined hearing of pedaled sonority. The held quarter note in the alto of measure 3 provides a continuity of rich sound, deftly camouflaging what Feinberg considered the "roughness" of a simple pedal change. At the barline, the right hand holds all three notes of the previous bar all the way through as the left rolls its harmonic support. At the moment the pedal is depressed, all five notes should be sustained in the hand, as indicated in figure 13.9b; this core sonority is thus held in the pedaled sound all the way until the change at the third beat. Some blurring will certainly take place in the right hand, for instance the F♯-E-D♯ octaves of the melody; this bit of fog contributes to the overall mood and is no sign of carelessness. Overtones will clash less severely in the treble than they would in the bass. As the pedal is then finally changed, the

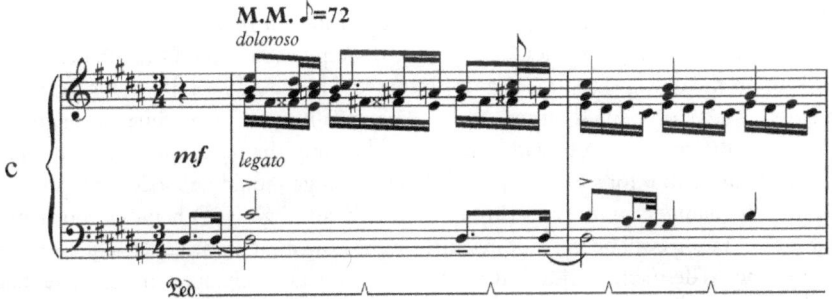

Figure 13.9. (a) Etude Op. 2 No. 1 in C♯ minor, mm. 3–4, "editor's pedaling." (b) Author's suggested execution of this passage. (c) Sonata No. 3 Op. 23 in F♯ minor, third movement, mm. 18–19, with author's suggested pedaling.

soprano is still held by the fingers, providing once again a continuity of sustained voices through the clearing of harmony. These fundamental techniques should be clearly understood and fully mastered by an intermediate student; it is a process that can require a good deal of time, care, and persistence.

A more advanced example of the pedal/finger coordination and right hand blending can be found in the *doloroso* episode from the Andante of the Third Sonata (see figure 13.9c, mm 18–19). In theory, this passage could be heard as a single chord with foreign tones blended in, but pedaling through an entire measure would permit too much accumulation of dissonance. The most basic editor's pedaling would be to change once every beat, as we saw in the previous example. While this pedaling allows for some degree of harmonic blending, it suffers from squareness, and tends to give an unwanted small emphasis on each beat. In Feinberg's formulation, it is "primitive." My suggested pedaling is given in the example. This flexible solution offers the maximum of mixed sonority to color each melody note and avoids metric regularity. Allowing some blurring of harmony—only to clear it after the new harmony is already established—is an important technique in Scriabin. Changing the pedal at musically "unimportant" moments such as these represents a kind of pianistic "breathing": a widespread metaphor in the literature.[48] It camouflages the changes and offers subtle color modulations under the surface. Measures 25–26 of this movement offer another attractive opportunity for blending where imagination trumps adherence to elementary rules. In the mid-register, the left hand's E certainly requires a pedal change for clarity, but in the low register, in measure 27, the change can be effectively omitted, creating a beautiful echo effect.

A passage from the Fifth Sonata (see figure 12.12) offers an interesting window into Scriabin's "pedal mist." In this sensuous atmosphere (*Accarezzevole*), the pedal will be used quite richly, but depending on the piano and the acoustical environment, some "breathing" of the kind described in the Third Sonata will likely be desirable. The crux of the matter is the oscillation of semitones G-F♯ (in mm. 120–21) and D♭-D (mm. 123–24), whose importance to Scriabin's harmony is discussed in chapter 12. One could simply keep the pedal down through this, but there are many other possibilities; a change might be desirable to provide respiration at the D-natural (end m. 123) or on the downbeat of m. 124, for instance. This could be a full change, half or quarter change, or a quick flutter. As this passage is iterated many times throughout the piece, the pianist can provide variety by changing the technique.[49] Two points, however, are critical for success. First of all, any change should be made very quickly, so that the dampers graze the strings only briefly and lightly. Otherwise, too many "ghost" vibrations will be lost. For instance, at the downbeat of m. 121, if a quarter- or half-change is desirable to clear out the alto F♯, a very rapid change can eliminate that and simultaneously retain the bass F (no longer held by the fingers), and give it an attractive slight diminuendo as the upper voices take control. The thicker bass strings are less likely to vanish as they are damped. Secondly, notes in the sustained harmony should be held in the fingers as much as possible to give flexibility in varying the sustained sound. That style (reminiscent of French harpsichord style) applies crucially to m. 123, where the slurred arpeggio marked in the bass clef should be played by both hands and all notes held by them, freeing the pedal to make whatever harmonic shadings it wishes. Unfortunately, in this case, a pedal change might sacrifice the sustained sound of the melody, but if that happens, if the pianist has voiced and shaped that melody well, it will exist nevertheless in the imagination.

Perhaps the most characteristic Scriabinian pedaling technique with the widest application is pedal fluttering. Dampers are brought as lightly as possible in contact with the vibrating strings; the idea is not to stop their vibrations but to slow them a bit with each successive contact, thus softening the tone. The foot can move quickly in a kind of vibrato (Nemenova-Lunz's "vibrating pedal"), lightly on top of the pedal's range of motion. The more rapidly and lightly it moves, the less perceptible these subtle dynamic changes will be. At first blush, this may seem a great deal of physical activity for a subtle change of sound, but only in this way can a pianist manipulate the fadeout of sustained harmony, gaining a dynamic control that is rare for a percussion instrument. Louder or thicker strings will continue to sustain, while softer or thinner ones will vanish more quickly.

The Poème Op. 32 No. 1 offers a characteristic opportunity for the fluttering technique. The *pianissimo* at m. 15 is a striking contrast of mood and sonority from the bass resonances of mm. 13–14. Surely at this *diminuendo*, Scriabin would have fluttered the pedal until much of the bass resonance had gone. The diminuendo fork likely carries an agogic significance as well—suggesting a lingering on this measure—in lieu of an actual fermata.[50] *Étrangeté* Op. 63 No. 2 highlights another typical and related technique (see figure 13.1). In m. 4, the second beat A can sound on its own, but the pedal change need not clear out the sharp vibrations of the upper register too directly. A very slow change or flutter, causing the sound to fade out gradually, would be an impressive effect. After some diminuendo, the pedal might at last change directly to clear the air, but this clarity is perhaps best withheld until a later moment. Pedal fluttering can often be effectively used in Scriabin's late music in conjunction with trills. There is probably no other pianistic texture in which a player can hope to enjoy fuller control over the instrument's developing dynamics.[51]

A passage from the Ninth Sonata Op. 68 (figure 13.10) illustrates a wide range of creative possibilities, and will conclude our pedaling workshop. The dramatic *subito piano* in m. 30 requires a very rapid and very full, clear change: not a smooth breathing pedal, but rather a sudden, drastic gulp of air that may represent Nemenova-Lunz's "pinpoint pedal." The next *subito piano* in m. 32 and 33 also needs to be controlled by the foot. Both chords are attacked in the left hand full force, but must be made to decay. I prefer to play the B♭-C♭ melody with two hands, to emphasize it, and to relegate the middle-register trichord to control by the foot. Flutter pedaling can now be employed quite aggressively (i.e., with deeper changes than are customary) because now the bass fades away rather than the upper register. The left hand must catch the trichord once again, without restriking the strings.[52] With this technique, the middle register seems to defy the laws of nature by outlasting the bass. After the bass register has vanished, the left hand can release the trichord again. The continuing flutter pedal will clear the air of all dust and debris, leaving only the soprano C♭ singing grotesquely onward.

The signal significance of Scriabin's interest in pedaled sonority continues to resonate in modern scholarship and composition. In her recent book, *The Spectral Piano: From Liszt, Scriabin, and Debussy to the Digital Age* (2014), pianist Marilyn Nonken profiles an influential contemporary artistic movement of composers—Murail, Grisey, Fineberg, Dufourt, and numerous others—who have taken the resonating properties of musical instruments as a fundamental basis for artistic exploration.

Figure 13.10. The sinuous second theme, following a passage that requires creative pedaling, in Sonata No. 9 Op. 68, "Black Mass," mm. 29–47. *Moscow: Jurgenson, 1913.*

Nonken writes of the idiosyncrasies of the piano's construction, and describes how she was "heartened to find a group of composers who considered these aspects of instrumental reality . . . as defining aesthetic concerns. . . . Their works were transcendent in performance because of, and not in spite of, the eccentricities of the instrument."[53] She describes lessons with her teacher Armand Basile on Scriabin's Tenth Sonata, in which she was taught to listen to the piano's resonance, or what she calls its "resonant stratigraphy," and "to hear the distinctive sound of each phrase and grasp specific acoustic phenomena relating to tone color observable only in real time."[54] Nonken profiles Scriabin as one of the spiritual forefathers of this movement, a "proto-spectral" composer who demands this kind of attentive listening:

> More so than Liszt, Scriabin explored the use of the pedals to create layered sonorities comprising individual tones resonating at different intensities. He used full, half, and quarter-pedalings to create a resonant stratigraphy: a multidimensional layering of sound, rich with harmonics bell-like in their variation, dissonance and decay. In the resonance, an acoustic shadow or after-image is perceived, a continuation of the sound that is at least as important as, if not more important than, its initial attacks.[55]

This "acoustic shadow" is indeed a telling feature of Scriabin's piano sound, and one that is still fresh to some of today's leading composers. In no small part, it highlights the characteristics that place him among the most imaginative exponents of the piano.

14

Rhythm

The impression that lingers is one of ravishment. He breaks the rhythmic flow and something new comes out each time. This suffuses the performance with freshness. . . . The secret is in the energetic rhythm.

—Grigory Prokofiev[1]

Scriabin's performances of his own music were unique not only for their sound, but also for their highly individualistic sense of rhythm. For today's Scriabin interpreter, these two issues of sound and rhythm are the most idiosyncratic to his style, and the most critical to successful interpretation. The mainstream performance style in Scriabin's time was a good deal more flexible than today's. Contemporary reports consistently suggest that Scriabin's style was unusually free, even by that standard. In reviews of his playing, the most frequently occurring word is "arrhythmical."[2] What are we to make of such a characterization? Could a pianist of international reputation truly have suffered from a defective sense of rhythm? If Scriabin's own rhythm was so erratic and unpredictable, how do we reconcile that against his criticism of other pianists' senses of rhythm?

This conundrum in Scriabin's music likely finds its roots in Chopin, in whose works the question of rhythmic flexibility is one of the most challenging and contentious issues of performance practice. Chopin's contemporaries already disagreed on the matter. On the one hand, Berlioz remarked, "Chopin was impatient with the constraints of meter; in my opinion he pushed rhythmic independence much too far. . . . Chopin *could* not play in time."[3] On the other hand, Chopin's student Friederike Müller-Streicher recalled, "Chopin required adherence to the strictest rhythm, hated all lingering and dragging, misplaced rubatos, as well as exaggerated *ritardandos*."[4] We must conclude that Chopin's playing struck a fine balance between Romantic freedom and Classical proportion, an ideal suggested by this reminiscence by the Anglo-German pianist-conductor Sir Charles Hallé: "A remarkable feature of his playing was the entire freedom with which he treated the rhythm, but which appeared so natural that for years it never struck me."[5] For Scriabin's playing to be so often characterized as "arrhythmical," it must have been a good bit freer than Chopin's. It's hard to imagine that, had Hallé been able to hear Scriabin, he could have failed to observe this freedom.

The crux of the Scriabin rhythmic dilemma was explained by the composer himself: "One can distort rhythm as much as one wants, but one should be able to convey how it is derived from the original rhythm."[6] In all probability, students and contemporaries who had heard Scriabin's quasi-improvised playing tried to imitate it, but the notated relationships had become unrecognizable in the process. Playing in the even tempo of the metronome, however, is entirely inimical to the spirit of Scriabin's music; that deserves to be censured as "arrhythmic," every bit as much as an exaggerated and disproportionate rubato. Scriabin delighted in the variability of rhythm, which he likened to phenomena of the natural world: "One can't notate rhythm precisely, because a piece of music . . . lives and breathes; it seems different today than tomorrow, just like the sea. How dull it would be if the sea looked exactly the same each day, for all time!"[7]

SCRIABIN'S PIANO ROLLS AND THEIR TRANSCRIPTIONS

Today's musicologist or performer has an abundance of resources for apprehending the rhythmic aspects of Scriabin's performance style. Piano rolls for Hupfeld and Welte-Mignon, readily available today, accurately preserve the rhythmic features of Scriabin's playing.[8] These piano rolls are an invaluable resource, opening a clear window into the composer-pianist's world. They offer the kind of information that a music lover covets in great composers from the distant past.

Scriabin's piano roll performances are available now not only in sound but also in musical notation. A transcription into modern notation by Pavel Lobanov (1923–2016) presents in parallel staves the original musical text (as published by Beliaev), the text of Scriabin's performance, and a graph that shows his tempo from beat to beat in metronome marks. This graph gives us a vivid visual representation of Scriabin's rubato. By following the curves of these tempo graphs, a listener can readily sense the ebb and flow of his performance. Lobanov's transcriptions represent a unique contribution to the field of historical performance style, not only for the music of Scriabin.[9] Until recently available only in Russian limited editions from the Scriabin Museum in Moscow, these transcriptions are now reproduced in *The Performing Style of Alexander Scriabin* (2011), a study by pianist and musicologist Anatole Leikin, which is important reading for a Scriabin scholar or aspiring pianist. Since Leikin's study is closely tied to the details of the Lobanov transcriptions, it is most valuable for its insights on rhythmic issues.

To our modern ears, Scriabin's style in these recordings may sound old-fashioned, even distorted. Faubion Bowers described them in 1969 as "a shock to today's listener."[10] For example, almost no modern pianists would feel at liberty to decorate the musical text, to play with the hands not together, to roll chords that are not indicated in the score, and to extravagantly accelerate or slow the tempo.[11] However, these are precisely the features of performance style that are notable and widespread in many early recordings of Romantic repertoire.[12] Scriabin allows himself all these freedoms and more, so his style must be approached with this set of norms in mind. This is by no means easy to do more than a hundred years after the fact, when our performance customs are so different.

It is also important to consider the circumstances under which the recordings were made, and the manner in which these rolls are translated into sound. Along the way, the engineers at Hupfeld and Phonola also had the ability to add or subtract tones from the performance, and even to correct mistakes.[13] Further, the process of generating actual sound from Scriabin's roll involves an additional performer or "playerist," who executes the composer's dynamic nuances and pedaling in real time. This playerist has interpretive and creative input. He or she requires training and skill, as well as taste and stylistic understanding, to perform this act. Engineers for the company are more motivated to create a polished product than to create an accurate historical record. Thus, two recordings of Scriabin's same piano roll can sound rather different from one another (as discussed in chapter 13). All these factors need to be weighed in judging the authenticity and value of Scriabin's recordings.

The dry sound quality of these recordings unfortunately does not give a fair opportunity to convince us of the musical merits of Scriabin's playing. It is difficult to listen selectively to certain aspects of a performance and ignore other, less desirable ones. Bowers describes it as "like analyzing a writer's personality from his typescript."[14] For these reasons, is all too tempting to write off these performances as weak or irrelevant. Leikin helps to bridge the imaginative gap in contextualizing these recordings. He provides a much-needed justification of the musical logic of those aspects of Scriabin's rhythm and phrasing that most differ from current practice. He is especially persuasive in pointing out that Scriabin's departures from the printed text were a consistent part of his conception of the piece. When he recorded the same work on multiple occasions, many of these same divergences are retained.

Understanding and appreciating Scriabin's piano rolls is only a first step toward finding a personal performance style. One must ask whether Scriabin the pianist was a more effective interpreter of his own music than some of the legendary pianists who followed him. After all, in evaluating a talented composer/performer of today, we would certainly compare (and at times prefer) performances by another musician. It is legitimate to prefer aspects of Scriabin performances from the recorded tradition by different artists. We must also ask how closely it makes sense today to emulate Scriabin's own style. A contemporary performer can only speak with authenticity to a contemporary audience through his or her own artistic temperament. *En route* to finding one's own style, however, imitating Scriabin's piano rolls may be, at some stage, a valuable step in the process.

A CASE STUDY OF RUBATO THROUGH PHRASING AND ANALYSIS

Scriabin's rubato may have had a magical effect on his audience, but it was rooted in musical logic, not in voodoo. The myriad forms and varieties of his rhythmic flexibility in performance are covered comprehensively in Leikin's detailed readings of the piano roll recordings.[15] To find such freedom, the modern pianist benefits from a composerly understanding of the work's character, harmonic content, and phrase structure. Armed with these fundamentals, a performance can assume interpretive risks. Because of the destabilizing element of risk, it is not easy to strike an ideal balance every time in live performance. This demand is one of the overriding challenges in performing Scriabin.

The ebb and flow of a piece of music can be found first and foremost through its phrase structure. Musical phrases are marked by cadences; this Latin-derived word literally means "falling," thus, a slackening of musical tension. Ends of phrases can be marked in performance by *diminuendo*, by relaxation of tempo, or both. In early twentieth-century Romantic performance style, the tendency to mark phrase endings by timing was quite pronounced. Samuil Feinberg's recordings make for a particularly interesting case study in rhythmic freedom. Among the early Scriabinists, his style of phrasing is the most freewheeling. A pianist of exceptionally wide accomplishment, Feinberg possessed a vast repertoire, and is well known as the first pianist to record the entire *Well-Tempered Clavier*. It is a supremely intelligent recording full of strong character that is deservedly ranked among the classics. His Romantic style of cadential phrasing, in the context of Bach's music, may sound to modern ears a little old-fashioned.[16] In his playing of Scriabin, however, that same phrasing strikes us as an exquisite lost art, urgently needing to be recaptured.

The Prelude in C♯ minor Op. 11 No. 10 (see figure 14.1) can serve as an example of how a simple compositional framework can be enlivened by flexible rhythm. Technically, this piece is suitable for an amateur. However, for pianists accustomed to playing strict time, capturing the push and pull that is endemic to this style is an exercise that may be viewed at first with some trepidation. The success or failure of a performance of this work will hinge significantly on this factor. The Prelude falls into a straightforward three-part form. Measures 1–8 consist of two four-bar units ending with a *rit.* and a fermata. Measures 9–12 are the contrasting four measure "B" section, ending with a big crescendo to an *fff* return of the opening "A" material. This return of A is also eight bars in length, like the opening, but now heavily notated with expressive indications.

Figure 14.1. Prelude Op. 11 No. 10 in C♯ minor. *Leipzig: Beliaev, ca. 1897.*

Decisions about the flow of tempo should be determined first and foremost by these landmarks. First, how should the opening section relate to the closing eight bars? Clearly the conclusion, with all its accent marks (>), is meant to be played in a declamatory fashion, much more heavily than the opening. This apotheosis of previously heard material is an abiding characteristic of Scriabin's style. How does the opening relate to the pacing of the climax? That is a prerogative of the performer; in the early Scriabin-playing tradition, there was already a significant difference of styles. The only choice that seems out of character is to play them at the same speed.

The first instinct from our experience with other composers might be to play the climax slowly and grandly, making the opening more fluid by comparison. But in Scriabin's music, it is stylish to accompany moments of impassioned ferocity like this with an energetic rhythmic push. The accent marks (>) in this case more probably refer to heaviness of attack rather than to emphatic rhythmic placement. Thus, the opening might be a little on the slower side, even hesitant, to contrast with the climax, and to highlight the eerie quality of its unresolved harmonies and widely spaced texture. The repeated *sf* and *sff* markings can be realized with rhetorical flourish, well out of strict time. This section of violent hammerblows will come off more effectively when the initial *fff* arrival is driven in tempo rather than held back; otherwise, the whole section becomes brutal and heavy-handed. The two fermatas and early *rit.* marking in m. 17 (compare the *rit.* in bar 8) all form an invitation to a Coda that is unusually broad and spacious for a Prelude of such modest dimensions.

The middle section should be timed in proportion to these landmarks and according to Scriabin's expressive indications. In bar 9, *con anima* (with spirit) seems to be an invitation to move the tempo forward, with the *portato* articulation suggesting lightness of texture in contrast with the slurs of the opening. The dynamic hairpins and *poco rit.* in bar 10 suggest small phrase segments, splitting up these four bars into two subgroups of two measures each. Again, these mini-phrasings will work more naturally when measure 9 is a little quicker than the opening. The listener should hear this quicker tempo as a structural marker for the B section.

With the Prelude's overarching structure in place, let us consider the internal relationships of the opening A section. The distinguishing features are the small phrased groups under the slurs and the extra *mf*, accented (>) middle voice. The slurs can be read as isolated units, motivically unified by their initial descent by thirds, but contrasting in their lengths. The effect is like a spoken dialogue. Extra time should be taken before and after each group, compensated by some acceleration within the slurred groups. The middle voice (*mf*, >), an entirely new personality in this dialogue, lends to the four bars an asymmetric 1+3 relationship. It requires some extra space of its own, like an interruption, and perhaps it needs to speak a little more slowly, allowing some time to react to the sudden intrusion. The rhythmic pull at the end of measure 1 can be offset by a slight push in measures 2–3. This sustains the phrase length of four measures and prepares a slight lingering in bar 4 to mark the first cadence. Gauging the extent of this cadential timing is a delicate point, because a further distinction must be made between this small relaxation and the more important demarcation in measure 8: a marked *ritard.* that forms the larger structural unit of the 8–bar A section (an antecedent-consequent relationship). A beautiful feature of the piano writing is the stretch to the left hand's tenth in measure 5. This interval requires just enough physical preparation time to make a natural phrasing. Pianists who cannot reach this tenth may require a little more time. This wide interval lends both color and harmonic support to the higher register, giving this second phrase even greater expressivity (and therefore also a different timing) than the first four bars. Melodic tension in the wide soprano intervals is a clue to this expressive timing; the soprano has climbed a full two octaves in the space of just a few notes.

THE *ZOV*, DOTTED RHYTHMS, AND THE *PORIV*

Although Scriabin's musical style developed a great deal over his career, many elements of his idiosyncratic vocabulary remained consistent. In chapter 9, idiomatic gestures that bear his unique stamp are outlined and related to his philosophical ideas. Most of these ideas are immediately distinguishable by their rhythmic profiles. The identification and effective projection of these motives is essential to idiomatic Scriabin performance.

One of Scriabin's favorite rhythmic motives throughout his life is the *zov* (a call, or summons), a powerful gesture of a short note leading to an accented long one. The openings of the Second and Third Sonatas (see figure 14.2) clearly relate to one another through this gestural language. This motivic link is an important clue how to execute the tricky rhythm of the Second Sonata's opening, a passage that can easily sound awkward or stilted. The questioning character of its harmony, the depth of its register, and the breadth of its tempo distinguish it from the fiery confidence of the Third Sonata. However, the assertive forward motion of the *zov* rhythm is a key ingredient. The pianist should differentiate it clearly from the watery triplet; the former should push forward, while the latter ought to fade away. The union of these two elements forms a single, coherent rhythmic shape.

Appearances of the *zov* should usually be quite strongly delineated. They are rarely effective in strict rhythm. If the pickup is a short note (as in the fanfares at the outset of the Seventh Sonata), the rhythm should feel sharp and angular. If the pickup is a long note (as in the two-note descending figure of *Vers la flamme* Op. 72), the pianist might regard it either energetically (and play it faster than marked) or else ominously (and play it slower). All notes in a *zov* gesture require emphasis, with the upbeat accented at least as strongly as the main note. Scriabin is fond of kingly, assertive gestures, marked *imperioso* or *impérieux*. These brands of royalty are self-important to the extent that they can disrupt metric flow. The music around them simply has to wait and accommodate their rhythmic space. A powerful example is *avec éclat* in m. 266 of the Seventh Sonata, where it is stylish to discard a literal rhythmic interpretation in order to play the fanfare with each hand fully supported by the arm, turning the mid-range of the piano into a blaring brass instrument.

Energetic dotted figures permeate Scriabin's rhythmic vocabulary, in the spirit of the *zov*. Scriabin gives renewed energy to simple triplet and quintuplet figures by writing dotted rhythms, as illustrated by figure 14.3. Although he was hardly the only composer to employ such figures, he used them so frequently that they became part of his distinctive rhythmic signature. For a stylistic performance, it is often effective to accelerate slightly the first group of notes, so that the expanded part of the dotted figure can occupy plenty of rhythmic space. The short note then can be played faster than notated.

The vitality of dotted rhythms was so critical to his style that Scriabin often chose to dot rhythms in performance that are not notated in the score. An informed modern pianist might consider this possibility, albeit with some discretion. For instance, the figure in the Prelude Op. 59 No. 2, m. 41, marked *avec défi* (with defiance), is

Figure 14.2. The *zov* rhythm in the openings of: (a) Sonata No. 2 Op. 19 in G♯ minor (Leipzig: Beliaev, 1898). (b) Sonata No. 3 Op. 23 in F♯ minor (Leipzig, Beliaev, 1898).

written as a rather bland triplet (see figure 14.4), but it seems to demand a dotted rhythm to project its character; one is even tempted to read this as an error in the manuscript.[17] Triplet figures in the Third Sonata opening movement are greatly varied in Scriabin's piano roll recording. Between the extremes of a smooth even triplet and a sharply dotted one, there are many rhythmic shades of gray that can be used to match the character of a particular passage. Leikin cites Scriabin's performance of the first movement of the Third Sonata as "a textbook demonstration as to how flexible the dotted rhythms can be, and indeed have to be. Depending on the expressive disposition of the moment, the dotted rhythms in his performance range widely, from incisively overdotted to normatively shaped."[18]

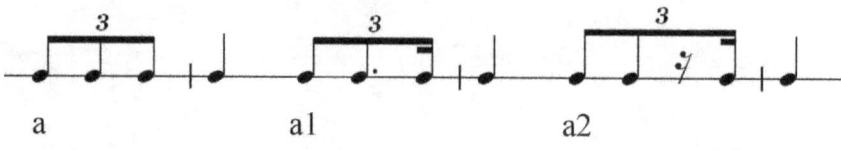

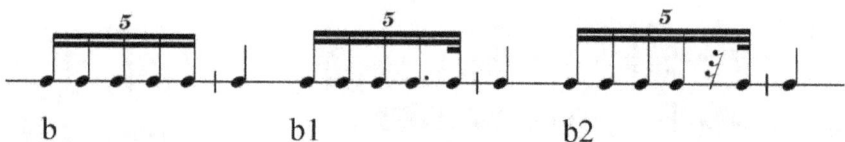

Figure 14.3. Scriabin's characteristic rhythmic dotting.

The "flight" gesture, or *poriv* (transporting burst) in Russian, represented the desire to achieve ecstasy through spiritual ascent, transcending what many artists felt to be a drab everyday reality.[19] In many cases, these figures come as abrupt, even spasmodic gestures. One form of the *poriv* is a rapid arpeggio figure that ascends and then returns down.[20] As with the performance of melodic lines, some acceleration and *crescendo* on the way up is an effective way of capturing its natural energy. More often a *poriv* is formed by a small group of rapid notes, such as the beginning of the dance in the Sixth Sonata, at m. 82, marked *avec entraînement* (sweeping), as shown in figure 11.3b. The Poème Op. 51 No. 3, appropriately entitled *Poème ailé* (Winged Poem), displays the *poriv* as a natural, unpredictable force with capricious changes of tempo. The charming Poème *Enigme* Op. 52 No. 2, though lighter in spirit, is another character piece cut from the same cloth. Initially marked *capricieusement*, it is also chock-full of tempo indications, time signature changes, dotted rhythms, arpeggios, and ascending gestures. The Sixth and Seventh Sonatas are full of these winged patterns that can be performed with a similar sense of caprice.

Figure 14.4. Autograph manuscript of Prelude Op. 59 No. 2, mm. 41–45. Holograph. *Reprinted from the Juilliard Manuscript Collection, Lila Acheson Wallace Library, The Juilliard School, with kind permission.*

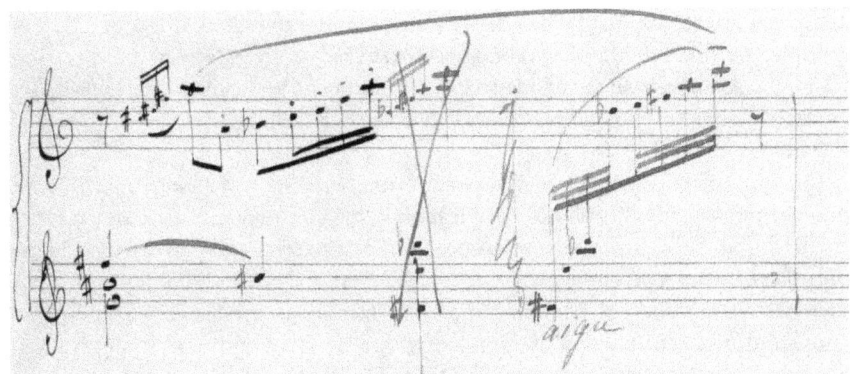

Figure 14.5. Autograph manuscript of *Etrangeté* Op. 63 No. 2, m. 25. Holograph. Reprinted from the Juilliard Manuscript Collection, Lila Acheson Wallace Library, The Juilliard School, with kind permission.

Scriabin's flight patterns pose interpretive questions in texture as well as in rhythm. The individual attacks of each note have gotten so close together that it can be difficult to distinguish between a rolled chord (with pitches held through), a series of grace notes, and a specifically notated fast rhythm with distinct notes. As usual with Scriabin, effective execution of these winged gestures should be discernible but not mathematically precise. Sometimes they can be clumped or chunked together: a kind of energetic rolled chord with pitches held through. The manuscript facsimile of the Poème *Étrangeté* Op. 63 No. 2, as shown in figure 14.5, reveals evidence (m. 25) of how the different possible notations of a *poriv* were competing in Scriabin's mind. One can observe his change in marking from a rolled chord to a rhythmically measured arpeggio, marked *aigu*. The new version seems to demand slower and clearer articulation than his original notation, and possibly more emphasis on the bass note.

COMPOSING OUTSIDE OF THE RHYTHMIC BOX

Flexibility in Scriabin's rhythm derives not only from performance style, but also from features of the compositions themselves. This assertion may be surprisingly contentious. Leikin quotes several prominent commentators who describe Scriabin's music as "dry and uninspired," citing its frequent use of sequence and habitual rooting in two- and four-bar phrase units.[21] He makes an astute comparison to Schumann's music—which has encountered similar criticism—and suggests that in both composers, it is entirely the performer's task to take a solid, even somewhat predictable and boxlike structure, and imbue it with an ebb and flow.[22] The above reading of the Prelude Op. 11 No. 10 would be an example of that process. However, these commentators—with whatever motivation—have cast Scriabin's rhythmic language in an unduly pessimistic light. Scriabin's style is a combination of traditional and progressive elements. Which of these one chooses to highlight is a question of attitude. Scriabin's rhythmic vocabulary is, of course, an essential aspect of his compositional style, but it receives relatively little comment in the literature, because his harmonic language, unique personality, and mystical beliefs have garnered most of the attention.[23]

One important source of rhythmic interest in Scriabin's style are groups of notes beamed across barlines, and those that lead into downbeat rests. These characteristics can be found, in conjunction with off-beat *sforzando* accents and polyrhythms, in the breathless *agitato* style of the early *Allegro appassionato* Op. 4 in E♭ minor, and in the Preludes Op. 11 No. 14 (E♭ minor) and 18 (F minor). In the Finales of the Second and Third Sonatas, this style is executed with greater strength and sophistication. Scriabin has a consistent preference for figures, especially triplets, that open with a two-note pickup. These can be found both in leaping figurations (Etude in B♭ minor Op. 8 No. 9, Impromptu in F♯ Op. 12 No. 1, and Prelude in E♭ Op. 17 No. 2), and in more lyrical contexts (Impromptu in F♯ minor Op. 14 No. 2 and the Etude in F♯ minor Op. 42 No. 2).

Although Scriabin rarely explores metric ambiguity as one finds in Schumann and Brahms, the Prelude Op. 11 No. 1 in C (see figure 14.8 below) is a shining exception—a work of singular rhythmic interest and novelty. Based in consistent 2+3 quintuplets with the characteristic two-note pickup, this Prelude undermines rhythmic solidity from the outset. The disoriented listener may well guess that the opening note is a downbeat. In the penultimate measure, the rhythmic dislocation is at last filled with the extra missing quarter note, restoring the downbeat to its rightful place. Even there, the indicated *accelerando* clouds our perceptions to the point that we may never notice the discrepancy. The piece ends so abruptly—especially in Scriabin's own lightning performance—that we are overwhelmed by its wave of sheer energy, unable to settle the metrical score in a fully rational way. Is this a case of the notorious "arrhythmia"?[24]

The opening movement of the First Sonata Op. 6 provides a powerful example of Scriabin's skill with rhythm. In this movement, it is the rhythm—even more than its chromatic harmony and pianistic virtuosity—that communicates his despair over his hand injury, in a musical drama of searing intensity. The meter of 9/8 is unusually common in his music since, like Chopin, he often prefers units of threes, both in the number of beats per measure and in the subdivisions of the beat.[25] His favored two-note pickup begins the work, but then immediately the hands seems to stumble over each other, as if vying to get ahead. The two hands only align on dissonances; at times one hand holds a tie while the other moves ahead. The *crescendo* pattern in m. 1 leads to a dramatic rest in the right hand of m. 2: a desperate gasp for air.

Rhythm is also an important element in the delivery of motivic pitch content. The main motive of the sonata, the three-note figure F-G-A♭, is reused with morbid obsessiveness in each movement. This motive bombards the listener from the very opening, striking at irregular time intervals. In the left hand, F-G come as the two pickups, and A♭ arrives again off-beat, only on the third eighth of the new measure. The right hand operates on a broader time scale: F in bar 1 downbeat, G in the second eighth of bar 2, and A♭ in the third beat of bar 2. The urgency of the two-note pickup is then felt through its immediate reentry in the left hand in a new register. It is crucial that the pianist press on, with no settling breath. After the first mark of punctuation in m. 8, the main motive is developed further in the right hand in mm. 9–10 with still more breathless, offbeat chords. This movement's second theme (m. 23*ff*), strongly contrasting in character, relates to the first theme in the syncopated placements of the left hand's chords.

The interaction of these F-G-A♭ motives at such different, irregular speeds reveals a powerful compositional technique. These tightly interlocked dislocations lend rhythmic drive and excitement to the unfolding of events through the movement. The marriage of thematic unity with rhythmic variety—the antiquated chant sound of the second movement, the galloping tarantella-like pulse of the third, and the throbbing, plodding dirge of the finale—is an admirable feature of this entire sonata.

Although rhythmic dislocation is central to the style of Scriabin's more turbulent pieces, rhythmic disturbances can also play a significant role in some of his lyrical works, even those deeply rooted in 4-bar phrase groups. The Mazurka Op. 25 No. 4 in E major illustrates this point. At face value, this piece may seem rather conservative in both harmony and form, but Scriabin must have held it in some regard in his later years, since he programmed it on his last Moscow recital in 1915 (see figure 14.6). The first bar of the theme is marked already with a *ritard* and *rubato* indication, with *a tempo* as soon as the second measure. This indication seems to encourage a little push in the running eighths of mm. 2–3, balanced by some relaxation in m. 4, where the sighing soprano may linger as it fades out. All these features lend a distinctive rhythmic shape to the theme as well as a prevailing mood of improvisatory freedom. A "dry and uninspired" four-bar unit it is not!

Since this mazurka follows a rondo design, it is fascinating to observe how these unusual features affect all aspects of the form, in particular the passages that transition back to the theme. In most rondos, *ritardando* is a traditional performance practice to prepare for the return of well-known melodic material. In Mozart's rondos, for example, a *ritard.* is often accompanied by a fermata and even an additional embellishment (*Eingang*). In this mazurka, however, Scriabin does not announce each return, but rather elides it. This dovetailing method changes our structural perceptions, bringing freshness to a simple rondo design that would seem otherwise quite outmoded at the turn of the twentieth century. An especially striking moment in the piece is the return of the theme after the climax in measure 137 (see figure 14.6b). The proportionally long middle section of the piece builds terrific momentum all the way to *presto* in a kind of written-out cadenza. After such an event, most composers would methodically prepare the return of the theme, until we are fully expecting it. Here, however, the main theme returns not after a *ritard.*, but rather right in the middle of one. Such striking features reveal Scriabin's individuality in one of the genres where he is closest to Chopin's tradition.

Figure 14.6. Unusual rhythmic pacing in the Mazurka Op. 25 No. 4 in E major (a) mm. 1–9 (b) mm. 129–44. *Leipzig: Beliaev, 1899.*

Scriabin's style embraced forward-looking characteristics such as changing meters and quintuple meters. These two features are often employed in conjunction with one another, forming a link to the sources of Russian folk music and chant. Quintuple meter is just common enough to be an element of the style, but rare enough to seem exotic and call attention to itself. In the Op. 11 Preludes, for example, he explored quintuple divisions in his time signatures: 15/8 in No. 14, 5/8 alternating with 4/8 in No. 16, and 5/8 alternating with 6/8 in No. 24. Two Preludes, Op. 33 No. 4 (5/4 meter) and Op. 67 No. 1 (5/8 meter), use groups of five to evoke Russian chant. Stravinsky picked up this thread, making the pointed use of rhythmic irregularity a defining characteristic of his style. When Scriabin changes meters—which he does more frequently in his later music—he is usually not after an angular effect, with downbeat accents, but rather a free and flexible prosody. Perhaps the most extraordinary example is the Poème Op. 52 No. 1 (see figure 12.8), in which (whether by accident or by design) the meter changes every bar until m. 21, where it settles on 15/16. The diverse assortment of 2/16, 5/16, 2/8, 3/8, 2/4, and 3/4 meters might look like a collection from Stravinsky's *Rite of Spring*. However, Scriabin's music sounds not jagged, folklike, and irregular, but fluid and free-formed.

Shifts of meter are important structural characteristics of the large-scale late works. The majority of them (*Prometheus* and the Sixth, Eighth, and Tenth Sonatas) are based in triple meters (3/4, 9/8, 6/8, 9/16), and achieve striking effects by switching to duple meter toward the end. Especially noteworthy are the simultaneous 2/8 and 3/8 meters at the end of the Sixth Sonata (where the two hands interact in an 8:3 polyrhythm) and the dance section (mm. 306–25) of the Tenth Sonata, where the changing meters alternate between 6- and 7-beat groups of sixteenth notes. The listener does not hear any specific numeric relationship but rather a breathless rhythmic game, portraying a state of intoxication. The Seventh and Ninth Sonatas share a basic 4/8 meter. The Seventh Sonata's frequent changes evoke not dance, but rather chant. The Ninth Sonata is more consistent in its use of 4/8 meter, giving the piece an oddly square character. Only the second theme breaks the pattern; it shifts flexibly between 6/8, 3/8, 4/8, and 5/8.

SUBDIVISIONS OF THE BEAT AND POLYRHYTHMS

Perhaps the most telling aspect of Scriabin's rhythmic language is the liquid effect he achieves by dividing the beat into various smaller units. He switches rapidly among duple, triple, quadruple, and quintuple subdivisions and often uses them simultaneously in polyrhythms. More than timbre, it is this treatment of rhythm that creates the impression of a floating sonority. Returning to the *Poème* Op. 52 No. 1, we can find in the first two lines duple and triple subdivisions at the eighth and sixteenth-note levels, a 2:3 polyrhythm in eighths and, in the first measure, a dotted triplet. Shortly thereafter, under the quintuplet pulses of 5/16 and 15/16, we find triplet eighths, forming a 3:5 polyrhythm. When each hand subdivides the basic beat into different units, the increased density of attacks fills the musical air with flotsam and jetsam—a confetti of sound that makes us forget the percussive nature of the piano.[26] Along with trills and repeated chords, polyrhythm belongs to the class of devices by which Scriabin attempts to transcend the piano's limitations. Polyrhythm also naturally suits a performance style with desynchronized hands and free rhythmic inflections.

Polyrhythms are present from Scriabin's earliest compositions, as a Chopinesque characteristic. For example, the *Impromptu à la Mazur* in F♯ Op. 7 No. 2 is very clearly in the Chopin tradition in form, genre, and style. However, as with so many other inherited stylistic features, Scriabin took polyrhythm much further. Amid the background of a folk dance in 3/4, he interjects in m. 33*ff* (see figure 14.7) some boldly destabilizing rhythmic elements: an asymmetrically grouped quadruplet in the left hand, and alternating right hand divisions of 6, 7, and 8.

Just as Scriabin reveled in the richness of his harmonies, he was also an innovator in polyrhythm. He especially relished polyrhythmic patterns against 5, of which 3:5 is perhaps most characteristic. These appear already in his early works (Op. 8 Nos. 2 and 4, Op. 11 Nos. 1 and 19, Op. 13 No. 4, Op. 15 No. 1, among others). Polyrhythms are perhaps the most important stylistic characteristic of the Op. 42 Etudes, especially the 3:5 relationship in Nos. 2, 6, and 8. In Nos. 2 and 6 especially, the busy accompaniments form a kind of pianistic wind on top of which the melody can soar. Ironically, it is only in Op. 42 No. 7 where we fully realize how far Scriabin has come. The 3:4 polyrhythm in that piece—an advanced pattern in Chopin's music—seems plain and almost old-fashioned in the context of the opus. The 3:5 relationship reappears in the late style as a key element in the transcendental sonority of *Guirlandes* Op. 73 No. 2.

Scriabin successfully explored most polyrhythmic combinations available up to the number 9, except for units of 7, which he generally avoided. Since he was after musical expression, not mathematical puzzles, he was selective in choosing the most natural among them to play. For example, he made a particular specialty of the exotic relationship 5:9—a logical outcome of his preference for 3 and 5 units. It is surprising that this complicated polyrhythm flows as smoothly as it does. He employed it first in the Etude Op. 42 No. 1, and subsequently—to greater musical effect—in the Tenth Sonata and in an extended passage of *Vers la flamme* Op. 72. Although he sometimes attempted more awkward relationships, for instance 5:8 (Sixth Sonata m. 247), 4:9 (Tenth Sonata m. 183), and 3:8 (Sixth Sonata mm. 330*ff*), he rarely repeated those experiments. Scriabin's polymetric language was the most advanced in its time, and made a strong impression on future generations of composers. It foretells the developments in the musical language of Boulez and Stockhausen, and later Xenakis, Feldman, and the "New Complexity" movement led by Ferneyhough and Finnissy. Elliott Carter, who is known for his innovative rhythmic language, has cited Scriabin as a significant early influence.[27]

Polyrhythms are one of the main stumbling blocks in Scriabin's music for pianists who encounter such difficult relationships there for the first time. These rhythms

Figure 14.7. An early example of complex polyrhythms: the Impromptu Op. 7 No. 2 in F♯ major, mm. 31–52. *Moscow: Jurgenson, 1894.*

should be first properly understood and accurately practiced. In the case of the most basic instances, 2:3, 3:4, and 3:5, these can be worked out by arranging into units of their least common multiple—beat subdivisions of 6, 12, and 15, respectively—to feel accurately the timing in the sequence of attacks. In case of the more difficult polyrhythms against 9, however, this method will be too burdensome. Choosing one unit (9) as fundamental and the other (5) as "irregular" will make the rhythm easier to conceptualize.[28]

Once these relationships are understood and internalized, the imagination can be given free rein in performance. Unlike composers such as Nancarrow and Ligeti, who are interested in hearing these rhythms as mathematical conflicts, Scriabin's rhythm ought to sound supple, airy, and flexible. There is a fine line between clarity of rhythm and pedantry. The freedom with which Scriabin surely imagined his polyrhythms can be seen in the Prelude Op. 11 No. 1 in C (figure 14.8). In mm. 19*ff*, figure 14.8b, the left hand is marked as a triplet quarter group equaling the five quintuplet eighths of the right (all of which equal two quarter-note beats). However, the notation is mathematically informal. A 3:5 polyrhythm is implied by the beaming, but the printed alignment suggests that the left-hand rhythm of m. 19 (and all the others) is meant to be executed according to the rather inelegant notation of figure 14.8c. Possibly, as this whirlwind accelerates (mm. 23*ff*), it may equalize into an even 3:5 relationship, but at such a tempo it is virtually impossible to hear such detail. In Scriabin's own performance style, where hands are often not together, the left hand often comes before the right in any case. This example could suggest how flexibly his notation might be interpreted elsewhere, and gives a clue to the appropriate balance between rhythmic discipline and freedom.

TEMPO

Throughout the nineteenth century, composers' reactions to the metronome ran the full gamut. Beethoven's initial enthusiasm to the invention famously turned to disgust. While some composers tried to offer markings, others treated the metronome with consternation or outright contempt. Brahms, for example, refused to supply markings, arguing that if the performer didn't have a sense of the music, the machine wasn't likely to do any good. Scriabin put metronome markings on his scores only under considerable pressure from his publisher Beliaev, who, not coincidentally, was responsible for his financial support during a critical period of his career. Beliaev, who clearly sensed the talent of his protégé, grew impatient with his poor proofreading (whether out of a genuine difficulty with secretarial work, or simple laziness), so his letters often took on a scolding tone. Beliaev was extremely strong-willed on the point of metronome indications, and insisted on them repeatedly in preparing manuscripts for publication.

Thanks to Beliaev's prodding, the majority of Scriabin's pieces do come with metronome markings. The conflict of their points of view, however, led to some contentious exchanges in their letters. Scriabin wrote, "Will send the Impromptus today. I put metronome marks as you suggest, although it is virtually useless to do so. In the second one, the tempo constantly changes."[29] Subsequently they get involved in another quibbling exchange. Beliaev asks, "When do the tempi change in the Concert Allegro?" "There isn't a metronome here, so I can't say." "If you make the slightest effort you can find a metronome. . . . I don't want to publish your works in a mess. . . . Rimsky's lesson to you has sailed right over your head!"[30] Following the early passing of Beliaev, Scriabin would no longer supply metronome marks in his freer-form later works.

Figure 14.8. Advanced rhythmic language in the Prelude Op. 11 No. 1 in C major (a) mm. 1–2 (b) mm. 17–25 (c) A more literal notation of the rhythm suggested in mm. 18–20. *Leipzig: Beliaev, ca. 1897.*

Scriabin's reluctance to write metronome markings might lead us not to take these indications seriously at all. However, they may be better guidelines to his performance than we might expect, provided we remember to turn off the metronome before beginning to play. The markings should be regarded as a floating, fluctuating tempo average. Some remarkable coincidences can be found in the apparently dry statistics. In the Prelude in A minor Op. 11 No. 2, marked at ♩=138, Scriabin's piano roll performing tempo of this piece ranges from ♩=36 to ♩=257, but the average tempo clocks in at precisely ♩=138![31] Similarly, in the Poème in F♯ Op. 32 No. 1, the printed marking is ♩=50. In the 1910 performance, the tempo (which varied from ♩=19 to ♩=110) averaged almost the same: ♩=51.[32]

Considering these factors, performers should not pass over these metronome markings too lightly, but they should not feel bound by them either. The performer's freedom to express and to make the music personal is after all a significant part of Scriabin's Romantic language. A wide variety of tempi can often be chosen for successful, and entirely different, performances of the same work.[33] An extreme case would be Vladimir Horowitz's reconsideration of the Ninth Sonata. In his 1953 recording, Horowitz rifles through the work in a mere 6½ minutes. In his more well-known 1965 version, rereleased on CBS Masterworks, he takes over 9 minutes.[34] Performances of the Seventh and Tenth Sonata on record range from 10 minutes to over 14. The faster performances seek to overwhelm us with the manic intensity of their rhythmic drive and sudden contrasts, while slower performances put their trust more in the communicative power of harmonic color to impact the listener.

A final word on tempo relates to the markings on the very fast end of the spectrum. These should be taken seriously and not regarded as quixotic. These tempi are corroborated by verbal accounts of the athleticism of his playing, and by his performances of the Etude Op. 8 No. 12 and the Prelude Op. 11 No. 14. Manic excitement is a key ingredient of the Scriabin personality; extremes must be embraced, and many pieces need to be fast and furious in order to make their proper effect. The Finales of the Second, Third, and Fourth Sonatas all demand this. Scriabin wrote to Beliaev about the tempo of the Second Sonata finale: "The second movement depends on the performer's technique . . . its speed breaks the limits of the metronome."[35] Scriabin regarded the *Presto* character of the Third Sonata finale as so important that he simplified the difficult left-hand part in his own performance in order to achieve the desired speed.[36] The most volatile of the early Preludes and Etudes demand the same lightning approach.[37]

In conjunction with radically fast tempi, the subject of accelerando deserves special attention. In much modern piano playing, there is a willingness to take extra time to be expressive, but a reluctance to push back elsewhere in return. Rhythmic acceleration is typically frowned upon as an error, a loss of control, and is discouraged in students. One striking feature of Scriabin's pianism is precisely this widespread tendency to accelerate. This trend did not die with Scriabin, but was carried on by some of his most successful interpreters. We hear it in Feinberg's recordings of the Mazurkas, with their whimsical excitement, and also in his ecstatic rendition of the Fourth Sonata. His headlong acceleration in the bridge passage to the second movement is a completely convincing solution to this interpretive puzzle. Rhythmic drive is overwhelming in Walter Gieseking's orgiastic 1947 live performance of the Fifth Sonata.[38] A good dose of this push at strategic moments was one of Sofronitsky's powerful qualities, especially in combination with his layered control of sound and range of expression. His astonishing interpretation of the Etude in G♯ minor Op. 8 No. 9 is impressive for its searing emotion.[39] It ranks among his numerous compelling Scriabin performances that strike one as definitive. In Scriabin's piano rolls, we also find many examples of acceleration. Some of the most striking can be found in the Poème Op. 32 No. 1, the Prelude Op. 22 No. 1, and the Mazurka Op. 40 No. 2. Musical clues where acceleration may be indicated include simplification of harmony, sequence, or repetitious quality, and a simplification of piano technique that encourages the music to move forward easily.

As a final thought: the ends of Scriabin's piano works are often not given to grand and satisfying conclusions, like that of the *Poem of Ecstasy*, that resolve tension and triumph over the odds. Rather, like the man himself, they tend to vanish suddenly. The Fifth Sonata is a notorious example, but the tendency is already evident in the early Preludes (Op. 11 No. 1, Op. 13 No. 2), and especially in Scriabin's own performances of the music. Particularly noteworthy are the Prelude in E♭ minor Op. 11 No. 14, with his addition of one extra chord, and the Etude in D♯ minor Op. 8 No. 12. In Scriabin's own performance of this Etude (originally marked with a *ppp* ending) he does not send us down heroically in flames, holding our ears from the horrible din of a sustained chord. Rather, with two *secco* chords, he races to the finish and abruptly blows out the candle!

EPILOGUE

Scriabin has long retained the image of an irrational mystic, ungrounded in the realities of the world or even in common sense. However, the visionary side of his personality is balanced by a meticulous, obsessive formal perfectionism. Although Scriabin's music has the imaginative power to transport us, it is completely lucid writing. The performer's fundamental challenge is to capture the excitement of Scriabin's imaginative magic while remaining faithful to this craftsmanship. To attain this ideal, one must find a rhythmic vocabulary full of plasticity but also inherent musical logic, and a sound quality that is at times ethereal, enthralling, or ecstatic. The understanding of Scriabin's harmony and its relationship to its philosophical underpinnings is the surest guide.

In performing Scriabin, there is no substitute for an immersion in his style through practice, experimentation, self-education, and listening to the greatest masters. An impressive list of pianistic giants—both Russian and otherwise—have tackled this music and produced a rich recorded legacy. In these recordings, we can find outstanding qualities to admire and emulate, such as Scriabin's rhythmic drive, Sofronitsky's extraordinary weightless sonorities, Feinberg's exquisite phrasing, Richter's intensity, and Horowitz's imagination with pianistic color.

Scriabin's music presents all kinds of challenges in every interpretive dimension. The intellect and imagination are fully engaged, no two performances are alike, and very different approaches to the music are entirely possible. Whether in rhythm, sound, pedaling, or the response to his subjective expressive markings, a daring imagination is the key to success, but one that resonates in sympathy with Scriabin's world. Small wonder that, in live concerts as well as in recordings, it's easy to find many interpretations of his music that seem to miss the mark, alongside some extraordinarily good ones.

How exciting that, in an era where much standard piano repertoire has been performed and recorded practically to exhaustion, in Scriabin's music, there is a great deal that remains to be said.

Notes

PREFACE

1. Among the items I have collected over the years are historical postcards of Scriabin, one of which features a famous portrait by German artist Robert Sterl (1867–1932). This portrait adorns the cover of this book. In a letter of 19 February 1911, Scriabin wrote to his mistress Tatyana and exclaimed, "What a portrait Sterl did of me! I know that you'll be endlessly pleased. He put so much into it! He made some kind of ideal being with a soft oval face and an extremely complicated expression in the eyes; I would very much like to be that way!" Scriabin, *Pisma* [Letters], ed. Kashperov (Moscow: State Publishers, 1965), 561. Also see my article, "Postcards from the Edge: Scriabin in Popular Trade," *Journal of the Scriabin Society of America* (Winter 2009–2010): 7–19.
2. Powell, "Skryabin, Aleksandr Nikolayevich," in *Grove Music Online* (accessed 14 September 2009).
3. Online at http://juilliardmanuscriptcollection.org/composers/scriabin-aleksandr/.
4. Simon Morrison, "The Spirit Ascends," *Times Literary Supplement* (18 November 2015); online at http://www.the-tls.co.uk/tls/public/article1634388.ece_.
5. The film trailer is currently available online. For more information on the event and its participants, see www.scriabininthehimalayas.com.
6. The only background knowledge one needs to follow the musical discussions in this book is a basic understanding of sonata-allegro form, which is pervasive in Scriabin's music and can be gleaned from any number of textbooks or Internet websites. As a starting point, readers can consult a succinct explanation of sonata form written by William Wieland, professor of music at Northern State University in South Dakota, online at https://www3.northern.edu/wieland/theory/form/sonata.htm For a more in-depth discussion of the form, readers should consult Charles Rosen's *Sonata Forms*, revised edition (New York: W.W. Norton, 1988).

7. For other recording recommendations, see John Bell Young, "Scriabin On Disc" (27 December 2001), *Music & Vision* online at http://www.mvdaily.com/articles/2001/12/scriabn1.htm.

8. The chapter on Scriabin's 1960s revival in America is a revised version of an article that was originally published as "A Russian Mystic in the Age of Aquarius: The U.S. Revival of Alexander Scriabin in the 1960s," *American Music* 30/2 (Summer 2012): 194–227.

9. Abraham, Review of *Scriabin: A Biography*, by Faubion Bowers, *Music & Letters* 52/3 (July 1971): 311–14.

10. Bowers, *Scriabin: A Biography*, second ed. (Mineola, NY: Dover, 1996), 2:138.

CHAPTER 1: EN GARDE OR AVANT-GARDE? EXPLODING THE SCRIABIN MYTH

1. Dernova, *Garmoniia Skriabina* (Leningrad: Muzyka, 1968); Baker, *The Music of Alexander Scriabin* (New Haven: Yale University Press, 1986); Eberle, *Zwischen Tonlitat und Atonalitat: Studien zur Harmonik Alexander Skrjabins* (Munich: Katzbichler, 1978); Steger, *Der Weg der Klaviersonate bei Alexander Skrjabin* (Munich: Wollenweber, 1979); and Perle, "Scriabin's Self-Analyses," *Music Analysis* 3 (1984).

2. Kelkel, "Les esquisses musicales de l'Acte Préalable de Scriabine," *Revue de Musicologie* 17 (1971): 40–48.

3. Bowers, *Scriabin: A Biography of the Russian Composer*, 2 vols. (Palo Alto: Kondransha, 1969); second revised ed. (Mineola, NY: Dover, 1996); Belza, *Aleksandr Nikolaevich Skryabin* (Moscow: Muzyka, 1982); Rubtsova, *Aleksandr Nikolaevich Skryabin* (Moscow: Muzyka, 1989).

4. Cooper, "Aleksandr Skryabin and the Russian Renaissance," *Studi musicali* 1 (1972): 327–56; Taruskin, "Putting Scriabin (and Schoenberg) Together: Un Acte Prealable," unpublished MS, 1993); Matlaw, "Scriabin and Russian Symbolism," *Comparative Literature* 31 (1979): 1–23; Brown, "Skriabin and Russian 'Mystic' Symbolism," *19th-Century Music* 3 (1979): 42–51; Schloezer, *Scriabin: Artist and Mystic*, trans. Nicolas Slonimsky (Berkeley and Los Angeles: University of California Press, 1987).

5. Bowers, *Scriabin: A Biography*, 1:92, citing Lapshin, *Artistic Creation* (Petrograd, 1923).

6. Bakst, *A History of Russian-Soviet Music* (New York: Dodd & Mead, 1966), 264, 271.

7. Varvara Dernova (1906–??). Soviet musicologist and protégé of Boleslav Yavorsky, she became the leading Scriabin theorist of the twentieth century. She developed Yavorsky's theory of tritone links, duplex modes, and enharmonic sequences and applied it to the late works of Scriabin. See her *Garmoniia Skriabina* [Scriabin's Harmony] (Leningrad: Muzyka, 1968). Translated by Roy J. Guenther in "Varvara's Dernova's *Garmoniia Skriabina*: A Translation and Critical Commentary" (Ph.D. diss., Catholic University of America, 1979). Also see Roy J. Guenther, "Varvara Dernova's System of Analysis of the Music of Skryabin," in Gordon D. McQuere, ed., *Russian Theoretical Thought in Music* (Ann Arbor: UMI Research Press, 1983).

8. Baker, *The Music of Alexander Scriabin* (New Haven: Yale University Press, 1986), 270.

9. Adorno, *Introduction to the Sociology of Music*, trans. E. B. Ashton (New York: Seabury Press, 1976), 5.

10. Lang, *Music in Western Civilization* (New York: Norton, 1941), 1025.

11. Lang, ibid.

12. Nietzsche, ibid., 23–25.

13. See discussion of Mussorgsky, 33–34.
14. Lang, *Music in Western Civilization*, 994.
15. Bowers, *Scriabin: A Biography*, 2:227.
16. For a description of authorial intent, see Mikhail Bakhtin, *Speech Genres and Other Late Essays*, ed. Caryl Emerson and Michael Holquist, trans. Vern W. McGee (Austin: University of Texas Press, 1986).
17. Bakhtin, ibid. Cited from "Response to a Question from Noviy Mir," 4.
18. Harnoncourt, *Baroque Music Today: Music as Speech. Ways to a New Understanding of Music*, trans. Mary O'Neill (Portland: Amadeus Press, 1988).
19. Bernice Glatzer Rosenthal, "The Transmutation of the Symbolist Ethos: Mystical Anarchism and the Revolution of 1905," *Slavic Review* 26 (1977): 626.
20. The Russian word *dyeistviye* is often translated as "act." Action is the intended meaning here because it suggests an ongoing experience in favor of a single, momentary coup.
21. Nietzsche, "Greek Music Drama." Lecture delivered in Basel, 18 January 1870. Text from *Erste Jaresgabe der Gesellshaft der Freunde des Nietzsche-Archivs* (Leipzig: Hadl Verlag, 1926), trans. James L. Fessenden, unpublished MS, p. 9.
22. Barthes, *Image/Music/Text*, trans. Steven Heath (New York: Hill & Wang, 1978), the "Grain of the Voice." By this, Barthes refers not only the particular timbre, quality, or distinctive use of the human voice, but its inscription in the body of the Other, that is, to its reincarnation as substance in the listener/receiver.
23. Caryl Emerson and Robert William Oldani, *Modest Mussorgsky and Boris Godunov* (Cambridge, UK: Cambridge University Press, 1994). Citing a letter from Mussorgsky to Vladimir Nikolsky, 28 June 1870, in *Modest Petrovich Musorgsky, Literaturnoe nasledie*, ed. Aleksandra Anatolevna Orlova and Mikhail Sammoylovich Pekelis, 2 vols. (Moscow: Muzyka, 1971–1972): 1:103; and *The Mussorgsky Reader: A Life of Modest Petrovich Mussorgsky in Letters and Documents*, ed. and trans. Jay Leyda and Sergei Bertensson, reprint (New York: Da Capo Press, 1970), 122.
24. Boleslav Yavorsky, *Stroenie muzykal'noi rechi: Materialy i zemetki* (Moscow, 1908), Sec. 2, p. 4. Cited in "The Theories of Boleslav Yavorski," by Gordon D. McQuere, in *Russian Theoretical Thought in Music* (Ann Arbor, MI: UMI Research Press, 1983), 129.
25. Boleslav Yavorsky, "Konstruktsiia melodicheskovo protessa," in *Struktura melodii* (Moscow: State Academy of Artistic Sciences, 1939), 35. Cited in "The Theories of Boleslav Yavosky," in McQuere, et al.
26. Boleslav Yavorsky, *Stroenie*, Sec. 2, p. 4. Ibid.
27. Asafiev, *Intonatsiia* I, p. 163. Cited in "Boris Asafiev and Musical Form as Process," in McQuere, op cit.
28. The idea of "great time" was introduced by Bakhtin in his final essay, "Toward a Methodology for the Human Sciences (1974). "The mutual understanding of centuries and millennia, of peoples, nations, and cultures, provides a complex unity of all humanity, all human cultures . . . and a complex unity of human literature. . . . All of this is revealed only on the level of great time. . . . Contexts of understanding. The problem of *remote contexts*. The external renewal of meetings in all new contexts. *Small time* (the present day, the recent past, and the foreseeable—desired—future) and great time: infinite and unfinalized dialogue in which no meaning dies." *Speech Genres and Other Late Essays*, 169, 10.
29. Marc Silverman, "Scriabin's Black Mass Sonata: Structure and Language" (D.M.A. diss., Manhattan School of Music, 1983), 62, 65. Cited in Dmitri Rachmanov, "Alexander Scriabin's 'White Mass' Sonata: Style and Structure" (D.M.A. diss., Manhattan School of

Music, 1989), np. Silverman refers to this characteristic of Scriabin's musical aesthetic as "crescendo form" (Silverman op. cit., pp. 62, 65, ibid.).

30. Bowers, *Scriabin: A Biography*, 2:70. Letter to Leonid Sabaneev.

31. R. C. Zaehner, *Mysticism: Sacred and Profane* (Oxford University Press, 1957). By panenhenic, Zahner refers to the mystic's sense of being at one with the world while continuing to recognize its phenomenal existence. Pan-en-hen-ism is, strictly speaking, "all-in-one-ism."

32. Quoted in Schloezer, *Scriabin: Artist and Mystic*.

33. Andrei Bely, *St. Petersburg*, trans. John Cournos (New York: Grove Press, 1989).

CHAPTER 2: LIFE, LEGACY, AND MUSIC

1. Schloezer, "Two More Russian Critiques: Sergei Prokofiev," *Music & Letters* 8/4 (October 1927): 427.

2. Gervais, "Skriabin, Alexander Nikolayevitch," in *Grove's Dictionary of Music and Musicians*, Vol. 7, ed. Eric Blom (London: Macmillan, 1954), 831.

3. "The Most Recent Trends in Russian Music," in Stuart Campbell, *Russians on Russian Music, 1880–1917* (Cambridge: Cambridge University Press, 2007), 225–28.

4. Sabaneev, "Liszt and Scriabin," originally published in *Muzyka* 45 (8 October 1911), reprinted in the *Journal of the Scriabin Society of America* 6/1 (2001–2002), trans. Don Louis Wetzel. Quote on p. 91. Cf. Zsolt Gárdonyi, "Paralipomena zum Thema 'Liszt und Skrjabin,'" in Gárdonyi, Zsolt, and Siegfried Mauser, eds., *Virtuosität und Avantgarde: Untersuchungen Zum Klavierwerk Franz Liszts* (Mainz: Schott, 1988), 9–31.

5. For whatever reason, Scriabin left Opp. 50 and 55 unfilled in his catalogue.

6. A 1917 article proclaimed that, "there are already the Moscow Scriabin Society, the Petrograd Scriabin Society, and it is hard to tell how many others. The avowed purpose of these societies is to enlighten the musical public as to the true nature of Scriabin's works and as to his particular place in the history of modern Russian music . . . no Russian piano-recital is considered complete nowadays without the name of Scriabin somewhere on the program." See "Men and Matters of Moment," *Russian Review* 3–4 (1917): 115.

7. Brent-Smith, "Some Reflections on the Work of Scriabin" [Part I]," *Musical Times* 67/1001 (1 July 1926): 694, 593.

8. Myers, "Scriabin: A Reassessment," *Musical Times* 98/1367 (January 1957): 35.

9. Mann, "The Divine Poem," *London Times* (25 February 1972), 11F.

10. Rebecca Mitchell provides a concise summary of Scriabin's philosophical development in *Nietzsche's Orphans: Music, Metaphysics, and the Twilight of the Russian Empire* (New Haven: Yale University Press, 2016), 67–85. Also see Cyril Scott, *Music: Its Secret Influence Throughout the Ages* (New York: Samuel Weiser Inc., 1958).

11. Reviewer David Murray howled, "the publication of [Schloezer's] book . . . is as silly as the book itself, and no more comprehensible. What can have possessed the Oxford University Press?" *Musical Times* 129/1743 (May 1988): 248. For other reviews of Schloezer's *Artist and Mystic* book, see Gerald Seaman, *Slavonic and East European Review* 67/1 (January 1989): 153–54; Christopher J. Barnes, *Modern Language Review* 85/3 (July 1990): 815–16; Roy Guenther, *Notes* 47/3 (March 1991): 758–59.

12. Schloezer, *Scriabin: Artist and Mystic* (Berkeley: University of California Press, 1987), 118.

13. Scriabin published the poem at his own expense. In a 1907 letter, he stated that, "I do not wish the text [of the poem] to be printed in the score. Conductors who propose to perform the work may always be told that explanatory comment is to be found there; but in general they should start by approaching it as pure music." Quoted in C. C. J. von Gleich, *Die Sinfonischen Werke von Alexander Skrjabin* (Bilthoven: A. B. Creyghton, 1963), 19.

14. Bowers, *The New Scriabin: Enigma and Answers* (New York: St. Martin's Press, 1973), 108.

15. Bowers, ibid., 118.

16. Cooper, *Ideas and Music* (London: Barrie and Rockliff, 1965), 127. Also see his "Scriabin's Mystical Beliefs," *Music & Letters* 16/2 (April 1935): 110–15.

17. A case in point is the British filmmaker Ken Russell's radio play *The Death of Alexander Scriabin* (first aired in 1995), which depicts a fictitious meeting between Scriabin and the famous occultist Aleister Crowley (played by Oliver Reed, one of Russell's favorite actors) in St. Basil's Cathedral in Moscow, Russia. Both men were indeed in Russia during that time, and in the radio play, Crowley encounters Scriabin playing his "Black Mass" Sonata while sacrificing a goat in St. Basil's Cathedral at midnight on Walpurgis Night. Scriabin and his wife, Vera, also appear in a recent book of fictional fantasy by Sean Michael Welch titled *1897: Aliens! Vampires! Zombies!* (Permuted Press, 2015). Other recent works of popular fiction that feature Scriabin include *The Last Encore* by Julia Butler (Creative Vision Incorporated, 2014) and *Silhouettes of Time*, a collection of short stories by Maya Mitra Das (Azalea Art Press, 2016).

18. Ferguson, *An Illustrated Encyclopedia of Mysticism and the Mystery Religions* (New York: Seabury Press, 1977), 126–27.

19. Several history books offer overviews of the major events that shaped the first decades of the twentieth century, when Old World values were vanquished by technological advancements and scientific discovery. For a summary of significant world events that shaped early twentieth-century culture, see Peter Conrad, *Modern Times, Modern Places: Life and Art in the Twentieth Century* (New York: Alfred A. Knopf, 1999).

20. *Oxford American Dictionary and Language Guide* (New York: Oxford University Press, 1999), 1046. Blavatsky also wrote under the pseudonym of Radha Roy.

21. Several Theosophical publications offer testimony to Scriabin's semblance of thought with Theosophy. See Sybil Marguerite Warner, "Scriabin: Musician and Theosophist," http://www.theosophyforward.com/theosophy-and-the-society-in-the-public-eye/503-scriabin-musician-and-theosophist. The Irish Indian suffragist Margaret Cousins (née Gillespie) and her husband, the literary critic James Cousins, wrote several publications and promoted Scriabin's connection with Theosophy in the 1920s and 1930s. See Margaret E. Cousins, "Scriabine: A Theosophist Master Musician," *The Theosophist* 46/2 (November 1924): 238, 246. Reprinted as *Scriabine: A Theosophist Master Musician* (Theosophical Publications/Kessinger Publishing, LLC, 2005).

22. See Bowers, *The New Scriabin*, 192.

23. Gawboy, in an unpublished paper titled "What Can Theosophy Tell Us About Skryabin's *Prometheus, Poem of Fire?*" read at the Annual Meeting of the American Musicological Society, San Francisco, CA, 9 November 2011; and Baker, "Scriabin's Music: Structure as Prism for Mystical Philosophy," in *Music Theory in Concept and Practice*, eds. Baker, Jonathan Bernard, and David W. Beach (University of Rochester Press, 1997).

24. See Edmund B. Lingan, "Katherine Tingley's Theosophical Theatre: Greek Revivalism and New Religion in Lomaland, USA," *Journal of Dramatic Theory and Criticism* 26/1 (Fall

2011): 5–25. Remnants of Lomaland are located on the campus of Point Loma Nazarene University.

25. Schloezer, *Scriabin: Artist and Mystic*, 69.
26. Carlson, "Fashionable Occultism," 3.
27. Russiapedia, http://russiapedia.rt.com/prominent-russians/music/aleksandr-scriabin.
28. Hull, *Scriabin: A Great Tone Poet* (London: Kegan Paul, 1921), 254.
29. The *Mysterium* has inspired a book of fiction by Georgiana Peacher, titled *Skryabin Mysterium: Dream Mind of Alexander Scriabin* (Xlibris, 2004). The *Mysterium* is also depicted in Issue 3 of the graphic novel trilogy *Suffrajitsu: Mrs. Pankhurst's Amazons* (2015). The *Mysterium* also plays a central role in the supernatural serial podcast, *The Black Tapes*.
30. A comprehensive account of the *Mysterium*'s gestation, first as an unfinished opera, and later as the unfinished Prefatory Act, is found in the second half of Schloezer's *Artist and Mystic* book.
31. Morrison, *Russian Opera and the Symbolist Movement* (Berkeley and Los Angeles: University of California Press, 2002), 203.
32. Schloezer, *Scriabin: Artist and Mystic*, 180.
33. Ibid., 292.
34. See Anton Rovner, "Alexander Nemtin: The Fulfiller of Scriabin's Musical and Philosophical Legacy," *21st-Century Music* (October 2000): 8–16.
35. Daniel Bosshard, *Thematisch-chronologisches Verzeichnis der musickalischen Werke von Alexander Skrjabin* (Mainz: Ediziun Trais Giats Ardez, 2003). This thematic catalogue offers a spoil of resources that are not cited on any Internet databases.
36. Gunst, *A. N. Scriabin i ego tvorchestvo* (Moscow: Sklad izdaniia v Rossiyskom muzykal'nom izd-vie, 1915), 5–8.
37. Quoted in Taruskin, *Stravinsky and the Russian Traditions: A Biography of the Works through Mavra* (Berkeley: University of California Press, 1996): 1:793.
38. Ivanov-Boretski, "Puti muzyki i revoliutsii," *Muzykal'naia nov'* 1 (1923): 17, 18.
39. The *London Times* observed, "There is already a fairly vigorous reaction from Scriabin, led not by such old-fashioned folks as ourselves . . . but by leaders of a new movement. For them Stravinsky is the man." "Scriabin and Stravinsky: Permanence in Music," *The Times* (11 June 1921), 8.
40. Asafiev, *A Book About Stravinsky*, trans. Richard French (Ann Arbor: UMI Research Press, 1982), 22.
41. Quoted in Harlow Robinson, *Sergei Prokofiev: A Biography* (New York: Viking Press, 1987), 57–58.
42. Werth, *Musical Uproar in Moscow* (London: Turnstile Press, 1949), 32.
43. Stanislav Markus ed., *Aleksandr Nikolaevich Skriabin, 1915–1940: sbornik k 25-letiiu so dnia smerti* (Moscow: Gosudarstvennoe muzykal'noe izdatel'stvo, 1940).
44. "A Scriabin Cycle," *Soviet Literature* 12 (December 1946): 70.
45. Arthur Eaglefield Hull put into perspective the jarring manner in which Scriabin's late music was introduced to the British public: "What would have been the fate of Beethoven's works in England had we been introduced to the Ninth Symphony and the later quartets, with no other preparation than perhaps the knowledge of a few of the undistinctive works of a precocious childhood. . . . Yet this is exactly the way Scriabin has been forced on us."
46. Kalisch, "London Concerts," *Musical Times* (1 December 1919): 694.
47. Rosenfeld, "Scriabine," *Seven Arts* 2 (August 1917): 638–45; also see *Musical Portraits* (New York: Harcourt, Brace & Co., 1920; second ed., 1968), 177–89; "Scriabin and Mrs.

Grundy," *New Republic* 79/1018 (6 June 1934): 104; and "Scriabin Again," in *Discoveries of a Music Critic* (New York: Harcourt, Brace & Co., 1936), 158.

48. Gilman, "Mr. Scriabin's 'Divine Poem,'" *Harper's Weekly* 51/2623 (30 March 1907): 474.

49. Schloezer, "Scriabine," *Modern Music: League of Composers' Review* 1/3 (Nov. 1924): 15.

50. H. C. Colles, "London Critic Finds Scriabin 'Cloying,'" *New York Times* (30 September 1923), R3.

51. Review of Alfred Swan's *Scriabin*, *Musical Times* 64/964 (1 June 1923): 405.

52. Fennell, "A Word for Scriabin," *Musical Times* 67/1003 (1 September 1926): 833; and White, "Alexander Scriabin," *Chesterian* 13/104 (July 1932): 213.

53. Abraham, *A Hundred Years of Music*, fourth ed. (London: Duckworth, 1974), 225, 255; and *This Modern Stuff: A Fairly "Plaine and Easie" Introduction to Contemporary Music* (London: D. Archer, 1933), 42.

54. Michael Kennedy, *Adrian Boult* (London: Hamish Hamilton, 1987), 157.

55. See Robert A. Stradling and Meirion Hughes, *The English Musical Renaissance, 1840–1940: Constructing a National Music* (Manchester, NY: Manchester University Press, 2001), 104, 190.

56. Cooper, "Music—Scriabin," *London Mercury* 31/182 (December 1934): 209; and Hull, "The Orchestral Method of Scriabin," *Chesterian* 16/11 (November–December 1934): 34.

CHAPTER 3: THE SOLO PIANO MUSIC

1. Cui's remark originally appeared in Paul Rosenfeld's 1917 article on Scriabin in *Seven Arts*, Vol. 2, 639.

2. Harold Schonberg, "'Amoral Little Mystic,'" *New York Times* (11 April 1965), X11.

3. Some important sources for Scriabin's early piano music include Donald Garvelmann, *Youthful and Early Works of Alexander and Julian Scriabin*; and Daniel Bosshard, *Alexander Skrjabin: Jugendwerke für Klavier* (Ediziun Trais Giats Ardez, 1997).

4. For more on left hand alone piano music, see Theodore Edel, *Piano Music for One Hand* (Bloomington: University of Indiana Press, 1994). Hans Brofeldt also designed a website that offers a comprehensive resource on the subject: http://www.left hand-brofeldt.dk/.

5. See Eckart Altenmüller, "Alexander Scriabin: His Chronic Right-Hand Pain and Its Impact on His Piano Compositions," *Progress in Brain Research* (February 2015), online http://publicationslist.org/data/eckart.altenmueller/ref214/Altenm%C3%BCller_Scriabin2015.pdf.

6. The labels of "repeated-note arpeggios" and "repeated chords" were proposed by Samuel Randlett, who catalogued an assortment of Scriabin's signature pianistic figurations in his 1966 dissertation, "The Nature and Development of Scriabin's Pianistic Vocabulary." He condensed his findings and published them in a series of articles, which appeared as "Elements of Scriabin's Keyboard Style," *Piano Quarterly* 1970–1971, issues 74 (Introduction, pp. 20–25); 75 (Part 1 cont., pp. 18–23); 76 (Part 1, pp. 22–25); 77 (Part 1 cont., pp. 24–27), and 78 (Part 1 cont., pp. 26–30).

7. Hull, *A Great Russian Tone-Poet: Scriabin* (London: Kegan Paul, 1921), 116.

8. William Newman, *The Sonata Since Beethoven* (Chapel Hill: University of North Carolina Press, 1969), 746–47. Critic Alfred Swan observed, "On the music that now comes from the Russian centres [*sic*], traces of the later Scriabin are scattered with a free hand, but it

cannot be said that the seed has fallen on fertile soil." "The Present State of Russian Music," *Musical Quarterly* 13/1 (January 1927): 36–37.

9. Copland, *What to Listen for in Music* (New York: McGraw-Hill, 1967), 118.

10. Kenneth Hamilton, *Liszt: Sonata in B Minor* (Cambridge: Cambridge University Press, 1996), 66. Liszt dedicated the work to fellow composer Robert Schumann, who had fallen ill and was sent to an insane asylum. Liszt had a copy of the score delivered to Schumann's wife Clara Wieck, who was herself a renowned pianist. But Wieck's tastes diverged diametrically from Liszt's, and in private she deemed the sonata to be "frightful" and "appalling."

11. On the stylistic affinities between Prokofiev's and Scriabin's first sonatas, both in F minor, see Ellon Carpenter, "Scriabin and Prokofiev: Their First Published Piano Sonatas," *Journal of the Scriabin Society of America* 31/1 (Winter 2008–2009): 42–65.

12. Bowers, "Centennial Reflections," *Clavier* 11/1 (January 1972): 19.

13. See Garvelmann, *Youthful and Early Works of Alexander Scriabin*, 11–19. Although it was not published until after his death, this early *Sonata-fantasie* was his first completed sonata. Scriabin wrote the piece when he was fourteen and dedicated it to Natalya Sekerina.

14. Ye. Rudakova and A. I. Kandinsky, *Scriabin: His Life and Times*, trans. Tatyana Chistyakova (Neptune City, NJ: Paganiniana Publications, Inc., 1984), 69. Original source: Yuli Engel, "Scriabin: A Biographical Essay," [in Russian] *Muzykal'niy sovremennik*, op. cit., p. 21.

15. Faubion Bowers stated that the program of the Third Sonata included the commentary "written not by Vera, ironically, to whom the sonata rightfully belongs as common property of their first year of marriage, but by Tatyana, his second wife." *Scriabin: A Biography*, 1:254.

16. Liner notes by Simon Nicholls, from *Scriabin: The Complete Piano Sonatas*, Marc-André Hamelin, piano (Hyperion, 1995).

17. The link with César Franck is not far-fetched when we consider that upon his arrival in the United States for a concert tour in late December 1906, Scriabin was interviewed by several reporters and asked his opinions on modern music. He replied that Debussy was a "fine, subtle delicate talent," but his music had "no unity, no architecture." The one composer Scriabin did admire was César Franck. See "'The Russian Chopin'—Alexander Scriabine, Composer, Pianist and Dreamer," *Boston Evening Transcript* (22 December 1906), 22. Hugh Macdonald also pointed out some compositional similarities between Scriabin's middle-period works and the music of Franck in his 1978 book, *Skryabin*.

18. The Henle editions of the sonatas offer more information about the early versions of this sonata.

19. Hull, *A Great Russian Tone Poet: Scriabin*, 134.

20. Kenneth Smith, "Erotic Discourse in Scriabin's Fourth Sonata," *British Postgraduate Musicology* 7; http://britishpostgraduatemusicology.org/bpm7/smith.html.

21. Valentina Rubtsova, preface to the Henle edition of the Fifth Sonata. This preface also discusses the lengthier genesis of the Fifth Sonata, which contradicts the received wisdom asserted by Bowers that the piece was written in six days.

22. Kashperov, ed. *Pisma: Aleksandr Nikolaevich Skriabin* (Moscow: Muzyka, 1965), letter of December 1907.

23. Bruno Monsaingeon, trans. Stewart Spencer, *Sviatoslav Richter: Notebooks and Conversations* (Princeton: Princeton University Press, 2001), 139.

24. Richard D. Sylvester, *Rachmaninoff's Complete Songs: A Companion with Texts and Translations* (Bloomington: Indiana University Press, 2014), 236.

25. Jim Tushinski, *Van Allen's Ecstasy* (Lethe: Southern Tier Editions, 2004).

26. Bowers, *Scriabin: A Biography*, 2:229.

27. Sabaneev, *Reminiscences* (Moscow: Muzgiz, 1925), 109.

28. Claude Herndon, "Skryabin's New Harmonic Vocabulary in His Sixth Sonata," *Journal of Musicological Research* 4 (1983): 353–68; and Cheong Wai-Ling, "Scriabin's Octatonic Sonata," *Journal of the Royal Musical Association* 121/2 (1996): 206–28.

29. Susanna Garcia pointed out that the dramatic forces in Scriabin's sonatas preserve the nineteenth-century model of dramaturgy as outlined by A. B. Marx, which lends the late sonatas a musical road map that makes them intelligible through their dense harmonic veil. For more on Marx's views on sonata form, see Scott Burnham, "The Role of Sonata Form in A. B. Marx's Theory of Form," *Journal of Music Theory* 33/2 (Autumn 1989): 247–71.

30. Sabaneev, "A. N. Skriabin: ego tvorcheskii put' i principy chudozhestvennogo voploscheniya" (Scriabin: His Creative Path and Principles in his Artistic Expression), in *Muzykal'niy sovremennik* Nos. 4–5 (1916): 128. Quoted in the preface to the Seventh Sonata by Valentina Rubtsova (the Henle edition).

31. Quoted in Bowers, *Scriabin: A Biography*, 2:231.

32. Bowers, *The New Scriabin: Enigma and Answers* (New York: St. Martin's Press, 1973), 180.

33. See Young, "Celebrating the Scriabin Centennial with Pianist Matthew Bengtson," http://www.mattbengtson.com/news-fanfareinterviewjuly2015.html.

34. Sabaneev, *Reminiscences*, quoted in Peter Sabbagh, *The Development of Harmony in Scriabin's Works* (Universal Publishers, 2001), 7.

35. Garvelmann, in the liner notes to Michael Ponti, *Scriabin: 12 Piano Sonatas* (Vox SVBX 5461, 1974).

36. Heyman, *The Relation of Ultramodern to Archaic Music* (Boston: Small, Maynard and Sons, 1921), 120.

37. Bowers, *Scriabin: A Biography*, 2:244.

38. Hull, *A Great Russian Tone Poet*, 157.

39. Quoted in the Henle edition of the Ninth Sonata—preface by Valentina Rubtsova.

40. Leiber, "Conjure Wife," *Unknown Worlds* 7 (April 1943): 46.

41. Dubal, *Evenings With Horowitz: A Personal Portrait* (Pompton Plains and Compton: Amadeus Press, 1991), 280.

42. Bowers, *The New Scriabin*, 180.

43. On interpretation in this sonata, see Scott Holden, "Finding the Essence of Late Scriabin in His Tenth Sonata," in *The Pianist's Craft: Mastering the Works of Great Composers*, ed. Richard P. Anderson (Lanham, MD: Rowman & Littlefield, 2011), 169–88.

44. See Barbara Milewski, "The Mazurka and National Imaginings: Poland, Frederic Chopin, Karol Szymanowski" (Ph.D. diss., Princeton University, 2002); and idem, "Chopin and the Myth of Folk," *19th-Century Music* 23/2 (Autumn 1999): 113–35.

45. Young, review of Eric Le Van, http://www.mvdaily.com/articles/2005/01/levan1.htm.

46. Duncan took a special interest in Scriabin's music in 1921, during her first winter in the Soviet Union. She actually met the composer in person on an earlier visit. "Revolutionary" was written in 1923 when Duncan was living in Russia; it represents a fight for freedom against oppression. "The Crossing at St. Petersburg" was an ode to the famine that was taking place in Russia in the early 1920s. "Mother" (1921) was a tribute to all mothers who had suffered any loss. Duncan's two children, Patrick (aged 6) and Beatrice (aged 4), were killed in 1913 when the chauffeured car in which they were riding plunged off the bridge into the Seine River in Levallois-Perret outside Paris, France. Their governess, Annie Sim, also died in the accident. See Andrea Mantell Siedel, *Isadora Duncan in the 21st Century: Capturing the Art and Spirit of the Dancer's Legacy* (Jefferson, NC: McFarland & Co., 2016), 196–201.

47. Quoted in Mikhail Yanovitsky, "Scriabin Etudes, Op. 8 as a Set," *Journal of the Scriabin Society of America* 7/1 (Winter 2002–2003): 20. Originally in *Pisma*, ed. Alexei Kashperov (Moscow: Muzgiz, 1965), 91–92.

48. Scriabin wrote to Beliaev about this alternate version, "You have probably already received the etudes. You will find among them a second version of the D♯ minor which I don't want published just yet. Let it remain with you for a while because there's something about it that doesn't satisfy me. Yes, truth to tell, this has all happened because of my fiddling with it." Garvelmann, *Youthful and Early Works of Alexander and Julian Scriabin*, 130–36. This quote appears on p. 130.

49. Garvelmann, ibid., 130.

50. For more information on the key relationships as an ordered set, and how they relate to the etudes of Chopin and Liszt, as well as works by Mussorgsky and Tchaikovsky, see Mikhail Yanovitsky, "Scriabin Etudes, Op. 8 as a Set," op. cit.

51. Writing in reference to the famous D♯ minor Etude Op. 8 No. 12, W. J. Henderson of the *New York Sun* mused on the composer's tendency for using remote keys, noting that, "Let us be original in keys at any cost. D sharp minor is something to hold close to one's heart." See "The Russian Symphonists," *New York Sun* (21 December 1906), 6.

52. On Scriabin and Natalya's relationship, see http://www.interlude.hk/front/universe-delightalexander-scriabin-natalya-sekerina/. Accessed 3 August 2016.

53. Donald Garvelmann pointed out that this piece inspired Polish composer Karol Szymanowski to write his Etude Op. 4 No. 3 in the same key. See his liner notes to Scriabin's complete piano music, Michael Ponti, piano. Also see Stephen Downes and Paul Cadrin, eds. *The Szymanowski Companion* (Ashgate, 2015); and Agnieszka Chwilek, "The Scriabin Theme in the First Phase of Karol Szymanowski's Creative Development," *Musicology Today* (2008): 26–38.

54. See Ju-Hee Kim, "A Performer's Guide to the Piano Etudes Op. 42 of Alexander Scriabin" (DMA diss., University of Nebraska, 2005).

55. Quoted in Rudakova and Kandinsky, *Scriabin: His Life and Times*, 84.

56. Somer, "Scriabin's Preludes and Etudes," *Piano Quarterly* 24/94 (Summer 1976): 47.

57. *Pisma*, ed. Kashperov, 594.

58. Edwin Evans, "Scriabin," *Fortnightly Review* 103 (1915): 1077.

59. Heyman, *The Relation of Ultramodern Music to Archaic*, 123–24. Likely for this reason the American pianist Allen Tanner referred to No. 3 of the set as "Broken Glass."

60. See Willi Apel, *The History of Keyboard Music to 1700*, trans. Hans Tischler (Bloomington and Indianapolis: Indiana University Press, 1972), 44–46, 213–20.

61. See Sun H. Kang, "An Analytical Study of Scriabin's Preludes, Op. 11" (DMA diss., Dongduk Women's University, 2002); Seong-Ae Lim, "The Influence of Chopin in Piano Music on the Twenty-Four Preludes for Piano, Op. 11 of Alexander Scriabin" (DMA diss., Ohio State University, 2002); Hwa-Young Lee, "Tradition and Innovation in the Twenty-Four Preludes, Opus 11 of Alexander Scriabin" (MM, University of Texas at Austin, 2006); Cully Bell, "Scriabin's Preludes Opus 11: A Pedagogical Guide" (DMA, University of Cincinnati, 2012); and Daniel P. González, "The Complete Piano Preludes of Alexander Scriabin: The Evolution of His Revolutionary Compositional Style" (DMA, University of Maryland, 2013). My comments on the Preludes Op. 11 are partially indebted to the observations found in dissertations by Kang and Lee.

62. In a letter of 23 March 1896, Scriabin responded to Beliaev's assertion that the preludes he had delivered failed to meet the terms of their agreement. To this, Scriabin replied, "With

regard to the missing preludes, I don't quite understand you, dear Mitrofan Petrovich. You say that one should not force one's creativity, and I would have had to practically wring it out of myself, because they're not here." *Pisma*, p. 132.

63. Two recent studies focus on Scriabin's middle-period preludes: Soonbok Kee, "Elements of Continuity in Alexander Scriabin's Musical Language: An Analysis of Selected Piano Preludes" (DMA, University of Cincinnati, College-Conservatory of Music, 2008); and Jeremy Nowak, "Development of Middle-Period Style in the Preludes of Alexander Scriabin" (MM, Texas Tech University, 2014).

64. Sabaneev, *Reminiscences of Scriabin* (Moscow: Klassika XXI, 2000), 326.

65. Bowers, *Scriabin: A Biography*, 2:265.

66. See Polina Dimova, "The Frozen Desert and The Crystal City: Figurations of Alexander Scriabin's Music in Evgenii Zamiatin's 'The Cave' and *We*," *Ulbandus Review* 16 (2014): 48–70; and Eugene Zamyatin and D. S. Mirsky, "The Cave," *The Slavonic Review* 24 (June 1923): 145–53.

67. Quoted in Bowers, *Scriabin: A Biography*, 2:264.

68. Taruskin, *Music in the Early Twentieth Century: The Oxford History of Western Music* (Oxford: Oxford University Press, 2005), 200–205. George Perle was the first theorist to propose interval cycles as an organizational method in Scriabin's late works in his article "Scriabin's Self-Analyses," *Music Analysis* 3/2 (July 1984): 101–22. Perle remarked that Scriabin's harmonic experiments "leads him not into 'atonality,' but rather a new kind of 'tonality' in which symmetrical partitionings of the semitonal scale (by means of interval cycles) generate new, totally consistent, referential harmonic structures."

69. See Keith T. Johns with Michael Saffle, eds., *The Symphonic Poems of Franz Liszt* (Stuyvesant, NY: Pendragon Press, 1996). For more on Scriabin's late *poèmes* for piano, see Elise Hae-Ryung Yun, "Alexander Scriabin's Late Piano Poems: Language, Thought and Performance" (Ph.D. dissertation, New York University, 1998).

70. Macdonald, *Skryabin*, 40.

71. Bowers, "Richter on Scriabin," *Saturday Review* 48 (12 June 1965), 59.

72. In a letter of 16 November 1903 to Vera, Scriabin remarked, "Imagine! Belyasha [Beliaev] was beside himself over Satan!! I had to repeat the last part three times for him." Kashperov, ed., *Pisma*, 292.

73. See Cheong Wai-Ling, "Scriabin's Octatonic Sonata," *Journal of the Royal Musical Association* 121/2 (1996): 206.

74. Macdonald, *Skryabin*, 39. In his article on the Tenth Sonata, Scott Holden suggests that to achieve Scriabin's *crystalline* tone, the pianist must use a "high and fast attack with a shallow depth [which] will produce a ringing tone without core. When played in rapid succession, this makes a leggiero sound, especially if tiny amounts of space are placed between each note." "Finding the Essence of Late Scriabin in His Tenth Sonata," 182.

75. Quoted in the Henle edition of *Vers la flamme*, with a preface by Valentina Rubtsova.

76. Rowen, "Transcending Imagination; Or, An Approach to Music and Symbolism during the Russian Silver Age" (Ph.D., dissertation, UCLA, 2015), esp. 124–45. Rowen discusses the performative aspects of *Vers la flamme* in terms of Horowitz's famous recording, as well as the Apollonian and Dionysian dialectic as derived from Nietzsche.

77. In March 2015, a Chinese pianist named Henry Chau was sentenced to life in prison after killing his parents and consuming their remains in a cannibalistic ritual. At his trial, Chau confessed that he had repeatedly listened to *Vers la flamme* every night for a month before the killings. Chau had become obsessed with the idea that the world would be con-

sumed in a ball of flame; listening to *Vers la flamme* "enhanced the images of flames in his mind that he believed would signal the impending end of the world." Julie Chu, "Son Who Chopped up Parents and Kept Heads in the Fridge Jailed for Life in Hong Kong," *South China Morning Post* (24 March 2015), online at www.scmp.com/news/hong-kong/article/1745300/son-who-killed-and-dismembered-parents-gruesome-hong-kong-murders. Retrieved on 16 September 2015.

78. Leikin, "Controlled Pyrotechnics," *San Francisco Classical Voice* (12 February 2008), http://www.sfcv.org/reviews/controlled-pyrotechnics.

79. Quoted in Sergei Bertensson and Jay Leyda, *Rachmaninoff: A Lifetime in Music* (Bloomington: University of Indiana Press, 2001), 196.

80. Darren Leaper with William Jones, "Alexander Borovsky—The Forgotten Scriabinist and His Own Reminiscences of Scriabin," article published online by the Scriabin Association, http://www.scriabin-association.com/alexander-borovsky/. Borovsky's unpublished memoirs contain observations about Scriabin's playing style, which are currently being published by Jones. See http://alexanderkborovsky.blogspot.com/.

81. Borovsky's unpublished memoirs, courtesy of William Jones. Cited in Leaper, op. cit.

82. Among the other casualties was a pianist named Romanovsky, who was similarly scolded in the press for his performances of Scriabin's works. Prokofiev confessed in a diary entry of 1916 that, "I am very glad I had hissed Romanovsky when he played [Scriabin's Sonata No. 4 Op. 30] in September, he had bashed his way through it then without the slightest understanding." Prokofiev, *Diaries 1915–1921 Behind the Mask*, trans. Anthony Phillips (New York: Faber & Faber, 2006), 85.

83. Edward Stanley Mitchell trained at Trinity College under Frederick John Easthope Martin. According to his obituary, he had keen interests in bridge, railways, and tennis. *Royal College of Music Magazine* 46/3 (1950): 111. He died on September 29, 1950.

84. R. C. Longworth, "When Titans Crumble," *Chicago Tribune* (30 April 1989), 364.

85. John Allison, "John Ogdon: A Pianist Possessed," *The Telegraph* (26 April 2014), online at http://www.telegraph.co.uk/culture/music/classicalmusic/10782874/John-Ogdon-a-pianist-possessed.html.

86. Joseph Horowitz, "Disks: 26 Scriabin Pieces," *New York Times* (15 March 1979), C11. Most accounts report that Sofronitsky's handkerchiefs were snow-white, which would make sense considering the pianist's drug of choice. Solomon Volkol wrote that, "People held their breath when Sofronitsky brought his famous white handkerchief to his nose, right on stage. This meant that the pianist felt the need for an additional snort of cocaine. This behavior was a challenge to the strict norms of Soviet life. For the pianist and his admirers, it was a desperate declaration of the right to spontaneity and rebellion." *St. Petersburg: A Cultural History* (New York: Free Press, 1995), 365.

87. Paperno, *Notes of a Moscow Pianist* (Amadeus Press, 2003), 49.

88. A film clip exists from the Moscow Conservatory in 1945, showing Fyodorova taking a lesson from Neuhaus on Scriabin's Prelude Op. 13 No. 2 in A minor online at https://www.youtube.com/watch?v=tSYZ_UWu78Y.

89. Robert Rimm, *The Composer-Pianists: Hamelin and the Eight*, 89–98.

90. Several of Feinberg's recordings are commercially available and demonstrate that his interpretations still set the standard for today. A good starting point is the website: http://www.forte-piano-pianissimo.com/samuilfeinberg.html.

91. David Dubal, *Evenings with Horowitz: A Personal Portrait*, 5–6.

92. See John W. Clark, "Divine Mysteries: On Some Skriabin Recordings," *19th-Century Music* 6/3 (Spring 1983): 264–68.
93. Henahan, "Who Will Replace the Old Guard of Soviet Music?" *New York Times* (27 October 1985), 19.
94. See Schonberg "Battle of the Blands—Pianists Today Can't Get Handle on Romantic Music," *Houston Chronicle* (3 August 1986), 24; and idem, "Do Today's Pianists Have the Romantic Touch?" *New York Times* (6 July 1986), H1.
95. Feinberg, *Pianizm kak iskusstvo* (Pianism as Art), 111.

CHAPTER 4: SYMPHONIES AND ORCHESTRAL WORKS

1. Holloway, *On Music: Essays and Diversions, 1963–2003* (Brinkworth, UK: Claridge Press, 2003), 292.
2. Volkov, ed., *Testimony: The Memoirs of Dmitri Shostakovich*, trans. Antonina Bouis (New York: Limelight Editions, 2004), 62.
3. Gerald Abraham wrote in a 1931 article that Scriabin "employed the orchestra only when his ideas took shapes that transcended the limits of a keyboard and a pair of hands. The additional resources offered by the orchestral palette were merely an incidental advantage. Consequently his scoring is essentially old-fashioned and has no particular attractions for ears accustomed to brilliant scoring even in works of minor importance." Abraham, "Scriabin Reconsidered," *Musical Standard* (September 1931): 216.
4. The remark about Brahms' First Symphony being "Beethoven's Tenth" originated with Hans von Bülow (1830–1894). He was a pupil of Liszt and from 1857–1863 was married to Liszt's daughter, Cosima. See Alan Walker, *Hans von Bülow: A Life and Times* (Oxford: Oxford University Press, 2010), 289.
5. Rimsky-Korsakov's *Principles of Orchestration* (1891), ed. Maximilian Steinberg (reprint, New York: Dover, 2013), remains a touchstone in the literature.
6. Rimsky-Korsakov, *Chronicle of My Musical Life*, trans. Judah Joffe (London: Eulenberg Books, 1974), 319. Stravinsky recalled that Rimsky-Korsakov called Scriabin "the narcissus" behind his back and said of his music, "*mais, c'est du Rubinstein*" [but, it's just Rubinstein], meaning hackneyed and unoriginal.
7. "What Is Orchestration" (March 8, 1958), in Jack Gottlieb, ed., *Leonard Bernstein: Young People's Concerts* (reprint, Pompton Plains, NJ: Amadeus Press, 2005), 61. "The Young People's Concerts" aired on CBS from 1958–1972.
8. Gottlieb, ed., *Young People's Concerts*, 75.
9. Alexei Kashperov, ed., *Skriabin: Pisma* [Letters] (Moscow: Muzyka, 1965), 155. For more on Beliaev, see Michel Montagu-Nathan, "Beliaev—Maecenas of Russian Music," *Musical Quarterly* 4/3 (July 1918): 450–65.
10. *Scriabin, Piano Concerto in F♯ minor Op. 20 and Anton Rubinstein, Piano Concerto No. 4 in D Minor Op. 70, in Full Score*, ed. Joseph Banowetz (Mineola, NY: Dover, 2002), vi.
11. Norris, "The Development of the Russian Piano Concerto in the Nineteenth Century" (Ph.D. diss., University of Sheffield, 1988), 140.
12. Sabaneev, *Vospominaniia o Skriabine* [Reminiscences of Scriabin] (Moscow: Klassika XXI, 2000), 254–55.
13. Israel Nestyev, *Prokofiev*, trans. by Florence Jonas (Stanford, CA: Stanford University Press, 1960), 80.

14. W. J. Henderson deemed the first two movements of the Piano Concerto "very pretty and fragile piece[s] of salon music." But the finale he found borderline offensive: "not either pretty or polite, and it compels the pianist to smite the keyboard very rudely indeed . . . such a roaring affrightened the ladies, especially those who sat in the front seats." "The Russian Symphonists," *New York Sun* (21 December 1906), 6. Bowers quotes reviews from every major critic in attendance that night at Carnegie Hall in *Scriabin: A Biography*, 2:145–46.
   15. On Scriabin's Volga tour, see Ellen von Tiderböhl, "Memories of Scriabin's Volga Tour (1910) [Pts. I and II]," *Monthly Musical Record* (1 May and 1 June 1926): 137–38; 168–69; and "A Musical Journey Down the Volga," *Etude* 44 (December 1926): 905–6.
   16. "London Concerts," *Musical Times* 55 (1914): 257.
   17. "Moscow Pays Fitting Tribute to Memory of Alexander Scriabin," *Musical Courier* 72 (13 January 1916), 36.
   18. Bowers, *Scriabin: A Biography*, 1:261.
   19. Henry C. Lahee, *Annals of Music in America* (Boston: Marshal Jones Co., 1922), 264.
   20. Vasily Yastrebtsev, *Reminiscences of Rimsky-Korsakov*, ed. and trans. by Florence Jonas (New York: Columbia University Press, 1985), 327. Pushkin's verse comes from chapter six of *Eugene Onegin*.
   21. Bowers, *Scriabin: A Biography*, 1:270.
   22. Karatigin, "The Most Recent Trends in Russian Music," in *Russians on Russian Music, 1880–1917*, ed. Stuart Campbell (Cambridge: Cambridge University Press, 2007), 226.
   23. Text from the score of the Symphony No. 1 (Melville, NY: Belwin Mills, Kalmus Miniature Scores No. 1481, n.d.), trans. Xenia Tashlitsky.
   24. Kashperov, ed., *Pisma*, 231–32.
   25. Hull, *A Great Russian Tone-Poet: Scriabin*, 41.
   26. John L. Holmes, *Composers on Composers* (Westport, CT: Greenwood Press, 1990), 133.
   27. The definitive text on the subject of musical topics is Leonard Ratner, *Classic Music: Expression, Form, and Style* (New York: Schirmer, 1980).
   28. Elaine Sisman, *Mozart: The "Jupiter" Symphony* (Cambridge: Cambridge University Press, 1993), 71.
   29. Bowers, *Scriabin: A Biography*, 1:282.
   30. Ibid.
   31. Rudakova and Kandinsky, *Scriabin: His Life and Times* (Neptune City, NJ: Paganiniana Publications, 1984), 76. Original text in "Reminiscences," Stanislav Markus, ed., in *Alexander Nikolaevich Skriabin, 1915–1940: Sbornik k 25–letiiu so dnia smerti* (Moscow, Leningrad: Gosudarstvennoe muzykal'noe izdatel'stvo, 1940), 23.
   32. Bowers, *Scriabin: A Biography*, 1:283.
   33. Scriabin's Second Symphony became a specialty of Semkow's, and his expertise in the piece led to his first recording contract with Columbia Records in 1969 (Columbia MS 7285).
   34. Vivien Schweitzer, "A Swirling Symphony from the Vault," *New York Times* (31 January 2009), C9. Information was also taken from the New York Philharmonic performance history's online archives. Available at http://www.archives.nyphil.org. Accessed on 18 November 2015.
   35. A particularly illuminating discussion of Tatyana's life and relationship with Scriabin was written by Marina Lobanova and can be found online at: http://mugi.hfmthamburg.de/en/Artikel/Tatiana_Schloezer-Skrjabina.
   36. Christopher Barnes, *Boris Pasternak: A Literary Biography, Volume I (1890–1928)*, second ed. (Cambridge: Cambridge University Press, 2004), 45. Pasternak documented his

reminiscences of Scriabin in three autobiographies, *Safe Conduct* (1931); *Childhood: 1905* (1941); and *I Remember: Sketch for an Autobiography* (1959).

37. Hugh Macdonald, *Skryabin* (Oxford: Oxford University Press, 1978), 33.

38. Taruskin's *Music in the Early Twentieth Century*, vol. 4 of his Oxford History of Western Music series, outlines similarities between Scriabin's *Divine Poem* opening and Wagner's *Tristan* prelude (pp. 208–12).

39. Macdonald, *Skryabin*, 41.

40. "The Russian Symphony," *New York Times* (15 March 1907), 9.

41. Gilman, "Mr. Scriabine's '*Divine Poem*,'" *Harper's Weekly* (30 March 1907): 474.

42. On Stock's performances of Scriabin, see Edward Moore, "Stock Plays Symphony by Scriabin," *Chicago Tribune* (20 January 1923), 15; and Ruth Miller, "Two Novelties Mark Program of the Orchestra," *Chicago Tribune* (2 April 1921), 15. The 1926, 1929, and 1932 seasons were the only years that the *Divine Poem* went unperformed.

43. De Vries, *Comfort Me With Apples: A Novel* (Boston; Toronto: Little, Brown and Co., 1956), 61.

44. Sabaneev, *Vospominaniia o Skriabine* (Moscow: Klassika, 2000), 265. Cf. Rebecca Mitchell, *Nietzsche's Orphans: Music, Metaphysics, and the Twilight of the Russian Empire*.

45. *Nexus: Book Three of the Rosary Crucifixion* (Paris: Obelisk Press, 1961), 368. Faubion Bowers used Miller's description as the title of a series on Scriabin, on which he commentated for the Canadian Broadcasting Company in 1972. Featuring the top interpreters of the day (Laredo, Ogdon, Abbado, et al.), the series covered every Scriabin opus over the course of fourteen installments recorded from 28 June to 27 September 1972. Filed in the Rogers and Hammerstein Archives of Recorded Sound, New York Public Library. The fourteen reel-to-reel tapes run from *LT-10–2460 through *LT-10–2473.

46. Krehbiel, "Elman and Russian Orchestra," *New York Tribune* (11 December 1908), 7.

47. Henderson quoted in Slonimsky, *Lexicon of Musical Invective*, 172–73.

48. Anatole Leikin, *The Performing Style of Alexander Scriabin* (Farnham and Burlington, VT: Ashgate, 2013), 3.

49. Lourié, *Serge Koussevitzky and His Epoch* (New York: Alfred A. Knopf, 1931), 161.

50. Other dance and ballet scores created from the *Poem of Ecstasy* include adaptations by Sokolow (New York, 1956), Petit (Milan, 1968), Beatty (Stockholm, 1972), and others. Ballets created to Scriabin's music include John Neumeier's *Dämmern* (Twilight, Frankfurt, 1972) and R. North's *Scriabin Preludes and Studies* (London Contemporary Dance Theatre, 1978).

51. Newmarch, "'Prometheus': The Poem of Fire," *Musical Times* 55 (1 April 1914): 229.

52. Herbert Antcliffe, "Prometheus in Music," *Musical Quarterly* 12/1 (1926): 110–20; and Paul Bergatnolli, *Prometheus in Music: Representations of the Myth in the Romantic Era* (Farnham and Burlington, VT: Ashgate, 2007).

53. "Scriabine and Delville," *Theosophist* 57/4 (January 1936): 358.

54. Blavatsky, *The Secret Doctrine: The Synthesis of Science, Religion, and Philosophy*, Vol. 2 (1888), "Stanzas of Dzyan," Stanza III, verse 5.

55. Not everyone agreed on the effectiveness of this strategy. Hull grumbled, "surely some less brutal policy than the plan of playing the work twice over at one concert could have been found. Who would want to hear, say, the Ninth Symphony of Beethoven through *twice running*?" "The Five Symphonies of Scriabin," *Monthly Musical Record* (1 February 1916): 36.

56. Corder, "On the Cult of Wrong Notes," *Musical Quarterly* 1/3 (July 1915): 383; and "'Prometheus' for First Time Given Setting of Colors," *Musical America* 21/21 (27 March 1915), 2.

57. Rudakova and Kandinsky, *Scriabin: His Life and Times*, 73.

58. Howard Pollack, *Skyscraper Lullaby: The Life and Music of John Alden Carpenter* (Washington, D.C.: Smithsonian Institution Press, 1995), 105–10.

59. Maurice Rosenfeld, "Give 'Prometheus' American Premiere," *Musical America* (13 March 1915), 16. *Prometheus* drew hisses from the audience and Stock only repeated this piece in 1930 and 1937.

60. Judith Tick, *Ruth Crawford Seeger: A Composer's Search for American Music* (New York: Oxford University Press, 1997), 45, 379n. The 1926, 1929, and 1932 seasons were the only years Stock did not conduct a performance of the *Divine Poem*.

61. Smith, "Stock Master of Rich Toned Orchestration," *Chicago Tribune* (15 Nov. 1942), H9.

62. Works and performance dates for Stokowski are: *Divine Poem*—19–20 November 1915; 5–6 January 1917; 11 January 1917; *Poem of Ecstasy*—26–27 October 1917; 15–16 March 1918; January 1919; 11 February 1919; and *Prometheus*—7–8 April 1922; 18 April 1922; 3–4 October 1930 (all with Harold Bauer, piano); and 11–12 March 1932 (Sylvan Levin, piano).

63. "Play 'Poem of Ecstasy,'" *New York Times* (12 February 1919), 11.

64. "Stokowski Rebukes Audience," *Musical America* (22 February 1919). The "useless" quote originally appeared in *Arts and Decoration* (November 1922) and was cited in Oliver Daniel, *Stokowski: A Counterpoint of View* (New York: Dodd & Mead, 1982), 225.

65. Bowers, *Scriabin: A Biography*, 2:243.

66. Baughan, "On the Modern Language of Music," *Musical Times* 55/854 (1 April 1914): 227.

67. Newman, "Scriabine's *Prometheus*," *The Nation* (18 February 1913): 781–82.

68. Krehbiel, "Coates Makes Farewell Bow as a Conductor," *New York Tribune* (3 January 1921), 8. Also see "Scriabin Stirs Interest," *Los Angeles Times* (23 November 1930), B17.

69. Gerald Cumberland, "The Welsh Music Festival," *Musical Times* (1 July 1920): 478.

70. Bowers, *The New Scriabin*, 7.

71. Irene Downes, ed., *Olin Downes on Music: A Selection of His Writings During the Half-Century 1906 to 1955* (New York: Simon and Schuster, 1957), 217. Rumors of Koussevitzky's sloppy baton technique, inability to recognize wrong notes or errors in transposition, and difficulty in score-reading have circulated since the 1920s and were encouraged by Nicolas Slonimsky, whose book *Perfect Pitch* [New York: Oxford University Press, 1988] contemptuously described how Koussevitzky relied on rehearsal pianists to prepare for performances, and how he could not decipher Stravinsky's *Rite of Spring* score until Slonimsky re-barred the work in colored pencil. Downes defended Koussevitzky against accusations of dilettantism in a Sunday *New York Times* article, which as biographer Moses Smith observed, did Koussevitzky more harm than good. See Downes, "A Conductor's Musicianship," *New York Times* (25 November 1928), X8; and Smith, *Koussevitzky* (New York: Allen, Towne & Heath, 1947), 170. Leon Botstein argued that opprobrium toward Koussevitzky stemmed from jealousy over his wealth and fame. "On Conductors, Composers, and Music Directors: Serge Koussevitzky in Retrospect," *Musical Quarterly* 86/4 (2002): 583–90.

72. Koussevitzky conducted the *Poem of Ecstasy* with the BSO eleven times (premiering it on 21 October 1910), the *Divine Poem* four times, and *Prometheus* three times. For full dates, see H. Earle Johnson, *Symphony Hall: Boston* (Boston: Little, Brown & Co., 1950), 383.

73. Downes, "Koussevitzky Gets Ovation in Boston," *New York Times* (11 Oct. 1924), 18.

74. Pianist Mark Weinbaum recalled a colorful exchange from the 1940s that illustrates Koussevitzky's hostility toward Scriabin. After an exceptional performance, a young admirer congratulated him and remarked, "'What a pity, Dr. Koussevitzky, that you never play Scriabin.' Instantly the conductor's face turned red. His eyes flashed as he shouted, 'Who are you to tell me what and whom to play!' There was a hush in the room. Taken aback, the young man tried to apologize. But that was of no use. Finally he fled under a torrent of unintelligible shouts." See Weinbaum, "S. A. Koussevitzky," *Russian Review* 16/4 (Oct. 1957): 64–65. For both sides of the Scriabin/Koussevitzky debate, see Faubion Bowers and Diana Cavallo, "A 60-Year-Old Controversy Flares up Again," *High Fidelity Magazine* (June 1969): 54–61.

75. "Inspired Prophet," *New York Times* (19 February 1950), X7.

76. "Changes in Taste," *New York Times* (4 June 1939), X5.

77. Robert Evett, "The Man with the Astral Body," *Atlantic Monthly* (October 1971): 128.

78. Jean Vermeil, *Conversations with Boulez: Thoughts on Conducting* (Portland: Amadeus Press, 1996), 48.

79. Stravinsky, *Poetics of Music: In the Form of Six Lessons*, trans. Arthur Knodel and Ingolf Dahl (Cambridge: Harvard University Press, 1998), 122. "The idea of *interpretation* implies the limitations imposed upon the performer or those which the performer imposes upon himself . . . which is to transmit the music to the listener. The idea of *execution* implies the strict putting into effect of an explicit will that contains nothing beyond what it specifically commands." Emphasis added.

80. Holland, "Translating a Language of Ecstasy," *New York Times* (8 August 1999), AR29.

81. Young, "An All-Consuming Philosophical and Spiritual Agenda," published by *Music & Vision*, available at http://www.mvdaily.com/articles/2000/01/scriabin.htm.

82. Lenaghan, "Scriabin and Boulez: A Place for Emotion," *New York Times* (29 August 1999), AR2.

CHAPTER 5: MADNESS AND OTHER MYTHS

1. *Horowitz: A Reminiscence*, directed by Patt Jaffe; produced by Peter Gelb; performed by Vladimir Horowitz, piano (C Major Entertainment, 1993).

2. Quoted in Nicolas Slonimsky, *Lexicon of Musical Invective: Critical Assaults on Composers Since Beethoven's Time* (New York: W. W. Norton, 2000), 174.

3. "Color Music: Scriabin's Attempt to Compose a Rainbow Symphony," *Current Opinion* 58 (May 1915): 332.

4. Abraham, *A Hundred Years of Music*, fourth ed. (London: Duckworth, 1974), 224–25.

5. Calvocoressi, *Music and Ballet: Recollections of M. D. Calvocoressi* (London: Faber and Faber, 1934), 246, 248; and Lambert, *Music Ho! A Study of Music in Decline* (New York: Charles Scribner's Sons, 1934), 309.

6. Lang, *Music in Western Civilization* (New York: W. W. Norton, 1941), 1025.

7. Garvelmann, *Scriabin: Complete Piano Music*, Michael Ponti, piano (Vox: SVBX 5462).

8. Deutsch, *Zweck: A Novel and Mostly Reliable Musical History* (London: Troubadour, 2016). To his credit, Deutsch acknowledges that the myth of Scriabin being related to Molotov was untrue.

9. Deutsch, ibid., 148.

10. Sabaneev's two other books on Scriabin include *Skriabin i iavlenie tsvetnogo slukha v sviazi so svetovoi simfoniei "Prometei"* [Scriabin and the Occurrence of Synaesthesia in Con-

nection with the Light Symphony, "Prometheus"] (St. Petersburg: Muzyka, 1916), and *A. N. Skriabin* (Moscow: Rabotnik Prosveshcheniia, 1922). See also S. W. Pring, "L. Sabaneev," *Musical Times* 68/1018 (1 December 1927): 1090.

11. Sabaneev actually clarified one of the long-standing myths in the literature concerning the relationship of the *luce* part in *Prometheus*. In her 2012 article "Scriabin and the Possible," cowritten with lighting designer Justin Townsend, Anna Gawboy observed that, "While the majority of the concert-going public now assume Scriabin's synesthesia was neurological in origin, Sabaneev indicated that Scriabin deliberately constructed his system of tone-color correspondence for its artistic and spiritual effects." She noted that in performance, this myth has fostered the idea of the *luce* part as a tonal palate of shifting colors, but her reading of the piece incorporates more subtle shifts of light and color.

12. Ivanova-Scriabina, "Critique of Subjectivity: An Examination of *Vospominaniya o Skriabine* [Reminiscences of Scriabin] by Leonid Sabaneyev," Scriabin Association, online at http://www.scriabin-association.com/critique-of-subjectivity-an-examination-of-vospominaniya-o-scriabine-reminiscences-of-scriabin-by-leonid-sabaneyev-by-alina-ivanova-scriabina-moscow/. Accessed 28 May 2016. The negative connotation of the phrase "Sabaneevschina" evokes clear parallels with Zhdanovschina, one of the darkest periods in Russian music history.

13. A. Scriabin, I. Nikonovich, *Vospominaiia Sofronitskogo* [Remembering Sofronitsky], (Moscow, 2008), 89.

14. Margarita Morozova gave some understanding of Scriabin's powers of persuasion when she wrote that, "when he spoke, his eyes were so dreamlike, they sparkled with joy ... what he said, those various thoughts and fantasies that were in him, and that belief in the victory of the creative strength of humanity opened some sort of unending horizon to me, and I felt that the limits of my spiritual life expanded. This called forth such elation, such a desire to live and act. It was unlike anything I have ever experienced before." Morozova, *Vospominaniia o Skriabine*, 1:49. Quoted and translated in Rebecca Mitchell, *Nietzsche's Orphans: Music, Metaphysics, and the Twilight of the Russian Empire* (New Haven: Yale University Press, 2016), 97.

15. Sabaneev, "Sergei Prokofiev," *Music & Letters* 8/4 (Oct. 1927): 425. The "appendicitis" quote is from the same article.

16. Larry Sitsky, *Music of the Repressed Russian Avant-Garde, 1900–1929* (Westport, CT: Greenwood Press, 1994), 292, 299.

17. Quoted and translated in Mitchell, *Nietzsche's Orphans*, 219.

18. Sabaneev, "Scriabin: On the Twenty-Fifth Anniversary of His Death," *Musical Times* 81/1168 (June 1940): 256.

19. Sabaneev, *Modern Russian Composers*, trans. Judah Joffe (New York: International, 1927), 48, 50. The "paranoiac" quote and following material also come from this book.

20. Sabaneev, "Scriabin and the Idea of a Religious Art," *Musical Times* 72 (1 September 1931): 790. The following "Scriabinist" quote is from the same article.

21. Sabaneev, *Vospominaniia o Skriabine*, reprint (Moscow: Klassika 21, 2000), 368.

22. Quoted in Mitchell, *Nietzsche's Orphans*, 186.

23. Sabaneev, "Scriabin: On the Twenty-Fifth Anniversary of His Death," 257.

24. Sabaneev, "A. N. Scriabin—A Memoir," *Russian Review* 25/3 (July 1966): 260, 263.

25. Ivanova-Scriabina, "Critique of Subjectivity: An Examination of *Vospominaniya o Skriabine*," op. cit.

26. Don Louis Wetzel's Ph.D. dissertation includes an informative discussion of the enmity between Schloezer and Sabaneev. See "Alexander Scriabin in Russian Musicology and its Background in Russian Intellectual History" (University of Southern California, 2009), 134ff.

27. Aside from his polymathic abilities, Slonimsky was better positioned than anyone to translate Schloezer's book. He roomed with Boris and Tatyana Schloezer and her surviving children when civil war broke out in Russia in 1919. Slonimsky recounted the tale of their encounter in the Translator's Foreword to *Scriabin: Artist and Mystic* (see n28).

28. Schloezer, *Scriabin: Artist and Mystic*, translated by Slonimsky (Berkeley: University of California Press, 1987), 62.

29. Emerson, Review of *Scriabin: Artist and Mystic*, by Boris de Schloezer, *The Slavic and East European Journal* 33/2 (Summer 1989): 316.

30. Schloezer, "Scriabine," *Modern Music: League of Composers Review* 1/3 (Nov. 1924): 14.

31. Another example of scholarship that identifies Theosophy as a dominant influence is Maria Carlson's article, "Fashionable Occultism: The World of Russian Composer Aleksandr Scriabin," *Journal of the International Institute* 7/3 (Summer 2000): online at http://quod.lib.umich.edu/j/jii/4750978.0007.301/--fashionable-occultism-the-world-of-russian-composer?rgn=main;view=fulltext.

32. Schloezer, *Scriabin: Artist and Mystic*, 69. Blavatsky's key texts were *Isis Unveiled* and the *Secret Doctrine*.

33. Schloezer, ibid., 67

34. Schloezer, ibid., 69

35. To take but one example, in 1929, the Theosophical Society's third World Congress took place in Chicago, and Irish suffragist Margaret Cousins (1878–1954) performed a batch of Scriabin's preludes for four thousand attendees as a practical demonstration of how modern music could reinforce Theosophical principles. James and Margaret Cousins, *We Two Together* (Madras, India: Ganesh, 1950), 499; and W. L. Hubbard, "Besant Pleads for Art to Save Nation from Decay," *Chicago Tribune* (22 September 1907), B1.

36. Quoted in Maria Lobanova, *Mystiker, Magier, Theosoph, Theurg: Alexander Skryabin und seine Zeit* [Mystic, Mage, Theosophist, Theurgist: Alexander Scriabin and His Time] (Hamburg: Bockel Verlang, 2004), 15.

37. One can immediately grasp this aspect of Bowers' personality by listening to a series of interviews of Bowers by Donald Garvelmann in 1969, and an interview of Bowers and Vladimir Ashkenazy by Robert Sherman on "The Listening Room" for station WQXR in 1973. These broadcasts have been uploaded to YouTube by pianist and historian David Dubal.

38. Bowers, *Scriabin: A Biography*, second ed. (New York: Dover, 1996), 1:69.

39. Bowers, *Scriabin: A Biography*, first ed. (Tokyo and Palo Alto: Kodansha International, 1969), 2:192. All subsequent citations from Bowers' biography are from the second revised edition unless otherwise noted.

40. Reviews of Bowers' books offer a detailed list of errata. See Gerald Abraham, review of *Scriabin: A Biography of the Russian Composer 1871–1915*, by Faubion Bowers, *Music & Letters* 52/3 (July 1971): 311–14; and Irwin Freundlich, review in *Piano Quarterly* (Winter 1970–1971): 26–28.

41. See Marco Mula and Michael R. Trimble, "Music and Madness: Neuropsychiatric Aspects of Music," *Medicine, Music, and the Mind* 9 (2009): 83–86; Vladan Starcevic, "The Life and Music of Alexander Scriabin: Megalomania Revisited," *Australasian Psychiatry* 20/1 (2010): 57–60; and Emanuel Garcia, "Rachmaninov and Scriabin: Creativity and Suffering in Talent and Genius," *Psychoanalytic Review* 91/3 (June 2004): 433–42.

42. Michael Steen, *The Lives and Times of the Great Composers* (New York: Oxford University Press, 2005), 798.

43. Bowers: *Scriabin: A Biography*, 1:68–69.

44. See Antoinette Burton, *The Postcolonial Careers of Santha Rama Rau* (Durham: Duke University Press, 2007), 104. Later in life, Bowers openly admitted his homosexuality, and it was also discussed in Shirō Okamoto's book, *The Man Who Saved Kabuki: Faubion Bowers and Theatre Censorship in Occupied Japan* (Honolulu: University of Hawaii Press, 2001). Ms. Burton interviewed Ms. Rau in August 2003 and asked her about the passages in Okamoto's book related to Bowers' homosexuality. The quote included in the text is from that interview.

45. Bowers, "Homosex: Living the Life," *Saturday Review* (12 February 1972), 23–28. Also see Bowers, "The Importance of Being Homosexual," *Village Voice* (27 May 1971), 17–21, 24, 76.

46. See Asafiev, *Skriabin: 1871–1914—Opit Kharacteristiki* (St. Petersburg: Svetozvar, 1921); Mikhailov, *A. N. Skriabin* (Moscow: Muzyka, 1983); Viktor Delson, *Skriabin* (Moscow: Muzyka, 1971); and Valentina Rubtsova, *Alexander Nikolaevich Skriabin* (Moscow: Muzyka, 1989).

47. Stuart, "Fifty Years of Music Criticism," *Tempo* 19 (Spring 1951): 14; and Schwarz, *Music and Musical Life in Soviet Russia, 1917–1970* (New York: W. W. Norton, 1972), 62.

48. Bowers, *Scriabin: A Biography*, 1:86.

49. Schwarz, *Music and Musical Life in Soviet Russia*, 62.

50. Lunacharsky, *Revolutionary Silhouettes*, trans. Michael Glenny (New York: Hill & Wang, 1967), 18.

51. Lourié, *Sergei Koussevitzky and His Epoch*, 120.

52. Hull's Scriabin articles include "A Survey of the Pianoforte Works of Scriabin," *Musical Quarterly* 2/4 (October 1916): 601, 614; "The Five Symphonies of Scriabin," *Monthly Musical Record* (1 February 1916): 36; "The Pianoforte Sonatas of Scriabin [Pt. I]," *Musical Times* 57/885 (1 November 1916): 492–95; [Pt. II] *Musical Times* 57/886 (1 December 1916): 539–42.

53. Swan, *Scriabin* (London: William Clowes & Sons, 1923), 111. Swan, *Russian Music and its Sources in Chant and Folk-Song* (New York: Norton, 1973), 171.

54. Newmarch, "Scryabin and Contemporary Russian Music," *Russian Review* 2/1 (1913): 158; idem, "'Prometheus': Poem of Fire," *Musical Times* 55/854 (1 April 1914): 227–31; "Alexander Scriabin," *Musical Times* (1 June 1915): 329–30; and "Scriabin, Alexander Nicholaevich," in *Grove's Dictionary of Music and Musicians*, Vol. 4, ed. H. C. Colles (New York: Macmillan, 1937), 702–03.

55. "The Revival of the Leeds Festival," *Musical Courier* (2 November 1922): 5.

56. Hull, "Scriabin: A Comment," *Musical Times* 67/1005 (1 November 1926): 994.

57. American composer George Antheil related a story from 1922 when Stravinsky's mother visited her son in Berlin. She nearly reduced Stravinsky to tears in her chastising over him not following in Scriabin's footsteps. When Stravinsky finally broke down and admitted his hatred for Scriabin's music and desire to be nothing like Scriabin, Anna shook her head and said to him, "Now, now Igor! You have not changed one bit all these years. You were always like that—always contemptuous of your *betters*!" Quoted in Antheil, *Bad Boy of Music* (London: Hutchinson, 1949), 36–37.

58. The British pianist John Ogdon wrote an unpublished work entitled "Death of Scriabin: Kaleidoscope Part 4," a solo piano piece with stage directions. The manuscript score is archived at the Royal Northern College of Music and includes the following sections (1) The Pimple; (2) The Carbuncle; (3) The Furuncle; (4) His Help from Rosa Newmarch; (5) His Cry: "I will be Brave Like an Englishman"; (6) The Burial—and Wait of his First Wife; (7) The Memorial Concert. To my knowledge, the work was never performed in public.

59. "One of the Last Bolsheviks, 'Iron Pants' Molotov Dies," *Wilmington Morning Star News* (11 November 1986), 4A.

60. See online blog, The Sunday Papers, "Tolstoy-Scriabin-Molotov Mystery Edition," http://www.indymedia.ie/article/80990.

61. Add to the rumor mill the idea that the firstborn of Scriabin and Tatyana was a deformed animal. In his *Reminiscences*, Sabaneev reported that the scandal that ensued when Scriabin and Tatyana had their first child prompted whisperings that they had conceived not "a little mouse or frog, but some sort of unknown creature," the body of which had been preserved and donated to a local museum. Cf. Mitchell, *Nietzsche's Orphans*, 64. This quote comes from the classic poem "The Tale of Tsar Saltan" (1831) by Alexander Sergeevich Pushkin, which was originally published in a children's book of fairy tales. In the poem, two women are so jealous of the tsarina that they trick the tsar into thinking their son is a freak of nature. Thanks to Xenia Tashlitsky for this reference.

CHAPTER 6: ON SYNAESTHESIA OR "COLOR-HEARING"

1. "'Prometheus' For First Time Given Setting of Colors," *Musical America* (27 March 1915): 1.

2. Ortmann, "Theories of Synaesthesia in the Light of a Case of Color-Hearing," *Human Biology* (1933): 205.

3. Rita Steblin, *A History of Key Characteristics in the 18th and Early 19th Centuries* (Rochester, NY: University of Rochester Press, 2002).

4. Rachmaninov, ed. Oskar von Riesemann, *Rachmaninoff's Recollections* (New York: Routledge Revivals, 2015), 157.

5. Schloezer, *Scriabin: Artist and Mystic* (Berkeley and Los Angeles: University of California Press, 1987), 96.

6. Sabaneev, "Scriabin and the Phenomenon of Colored Hearing in Connection with the Light Symphony *Prometheus*," *Muzykal'niy sovremennik* 4–5 (Petrograd, 1916): 169–75. In Russian.

7. Several different variants of Scriabin's color wheel were devised by Scriabin, Myers, Sabaneev, Vanechkina, Galeyev, and random Internet authors in various grades of accuracy. The fact that we can trace subtle differences of hue among primary and close secondary sources is further evidence that Scriabin's color-hearing was not synesthetic according to our current definitions. The color wheel included in this chapter is based on Galeyev's formulation, as found in the Dover score of *Prometheus*, with notes by Bowers. My thanks to Anna Gawboy for making this observation.

8. Sabaneev, *Vospominaniia o Skriabine* (Moscow: Muzsector Gosizdata, 1925), 48.

9. Annie Besant and C. W. Leadbetter, *Thought-Forms* (London: Theosophical Publishing Society, 1905), 75.

10. Dann, *Bright Colors Falsely Seen: Synaesthesia and the Search for Transcendental Knowledge* (New Haven: Yale University Press, 1998), 71.

11. Gawboy and Townsend, "Scriabin and the Possible," *Music Theory Online* 18/2 (June 2012): http://www.mtosmt.org/issues/mto.12.18.2/mto.12.18.2.gawboy_townsend.html. Retrieved on 25 August 2015.

12. Cytowic eventually revised his opinion in *Wednesday Is Indigo Blue*.

13. Levitin, interviewed by Elliott Forrest, on "The Arts File: Synesthesia, Scriabin and Seeing Music" (22 October 2010); www.wqxr.org/#!/story/99054–synesthesia-scriabin-and-seeing-music/. Retrieved on 4 July 2015.

14. Myers, "Two Cases of Synaesthesia," *British Journal of Psychology* 7/1 (May 1914): 112–17. It was not Myers' first report on the subject; see his "A Case of Synaesthesia," *British Journal of Psychology* 4/2 (September 1911): 228–38. The meeting between Myers and Scriabin took place on 24 March 1914. In his letter to his mistress Tatyana the day before the visit, Scriabin mentions that he was invited to Cambridge by two professors. The other person was likely C. W. Valentine, who collaborated with Myers on several synaesthesia studies. In his two-volume biography of Scriabin (in the original and the revised second edition), Bowers misidentifies him as "Professor Charles Mayer."

15. The key of F♯ major presents an interesting link in terms of Liszt's influence on Scriabin. The musicologist Alan Walker wrote in his three-volume biography of Liszt that, "It cannot be an accident that so much of [Liszt's] 'divine' or 'beatific' music unfolds in the key of F♯ major," and he lists the *Bénédiction de Dieu dans la solitude*, *St. Francis of Assisi Preaching to the Birds*, the "Paradiso" section of the *Dante* Sonata, and *Les Jeux d'eaux à la Villa d'Este*, the last two pieces from Books 2 and 3 (respectively) of the *Années de pèlerinage*. Walker, *Franz Liszt: Volume Two—The Weimar Years, 1848–1861* (New York: Alfred Knopf, 1989), 154n. Scriabin also chose the key of F♯ major for his most transcendent works, including the Fourth and Fifth Piano Sonatas (Sonata No. 3 is in F♯ minor), the *Poème* Op. 32 No. 1, *Feuillet d'album* Op. 58, and at least one piece from the sets of Opp. 33, 37, 39, 40, and 42. It is no coincidence that his most famous work, the Etude Op. 8 No. 12, is in the key of D♯ minor, which is the relative minor of F♯ major. The exalted feeling of these pieces is literally heightened by playing mainly on the piano's black keys (an F♯ major chord consists of notes played only on the black keys).

16. Samuel, *Olivier Messiaen—Music and Colour—Conversations with Claude Samuel*, trans. E. Thomas Glasow (Portland: Amadeus Press, 1994), 40–41.

17. Bowers, *Scriabin: A Biography*, second ed. (Mineola, NY: Dover, 1996), 1:149.

18. Peacock, "Synesthetic Perception: Alexander Scriabin's Color Hearing," *Music Perception* 2/4 (Summer 1985): 483–505. Idem, "Instruments to Perform Color-Music: Two Centuries of Technological Experimentation," *Leonardo* 21/4 (1988): 397–406.

19. Hoffmann was likely referring to color metaphorically and not reporting on his actual perception, but the ubiquity of this quote in the literature has led to its widespread use as early evidence of the condition. My thanks to Anna Gawboy for this observation.

20. Gawboy, "Alexander Scriabin's Theurgy in Blue: Esotericism and the Analysis of 'Prometheus: Poem of Fire' Op. 60" (Ph.D. dissertation, Yale University, 2010).

21. Gawboy and Townsend, "Scriabin and the Possible," *Music Theory Online* 18/2 (June 2012). A documentary about Gawboy's and Townsend's collaboration at Yale can be found at www.youtube.com/watch?v=V3B7uQ5K0IU. Also see Danuta Mirka, "Colors of a Mystic Fire: Light and Sound in Scriabin's *Prometheus*," *American Journal of Semiotics* 13/1–4 (Fall 1996): 227–48.

22. Hugh Macdonald, "Lighting the Fire: Skryabin and Colour," *Musical Times* 124/1688 (October 1983): 600–602. The term "color organ" was first used by British painter Alexander Rimington (1854–1918), who constructed one in his home around 1885 and attracted much attention with it, piquing the curiosity of Richard Wagner and Sir George Grove.

23. Vanechkina and Galeyev, "Was Scriabin a Synaesthete?" *Leonardo* 34/4 (2001): 357–61. Available online at http://prometheus.kai.ru/skriab_e.htm. Retrieved on 17 July 2015.

The article misidentifies Myers as "Mayers," but it also contains a valuable bibliography of sources not often cited in the English-language literature.

24. Baker, "*Prometheus* and the Quest for Color-Music: The World Première of Scriabin's *Poem of Fire* with Lights, New York, March 20, 1915," in *Music and Modern Art*, ed. James Leggio (New York: Routledge, Taylor Francis Books, 2002), 61–96.

25. Infamous in this regard is Baker's application of Schenkerian analysis and pitch-class set theory in *The Music of Alexander Scriabin* (New Haven: Yale University Press, 1986). For a critique of Baker's approach, see Richard Taruskin, review of *Scriabin: Artist and Mystic*, by Boris de Schloezer and *The Music of Alexander Scriabin*, by James Baker in *Music Theory Spectrum* 10 (Spring 1988): 143–69. To his credit, Baker also drew upon theoretical analysis to explore more interpretive aspects of the music in his article, "Scriabin's Music: Structure as Prism for Mystical Philosophy," in *Music Theory in Concept and Practice* (Rochester: University of Rochester Press, 1997), 53–96.

26. Highlights of this literature include John Runciman, "Noises, Smells and Colours," *Musical Quarterly* 1/2 (April 1915): 149–61; "Scriabin and 'Color Music,'" *American Monthly Review of Reviews* 51/6 (June 1915): 747–49; "Color Music: Scriabin's Attempt to Compose a Rainbow Symphony," *Current Opinion* 58 (May 1915): 332–33; Sabaneev, "The Relation Between Sound and Colour," *Music & Letters* 10/3 (July 1929): 266–77; Wilson Lyle, "Alexander Scriabin—Innovator of Sound and Colour," *Musical Opinion* (April 1965): 401–03; Hugh Macdonald, "Lighting the Fire: Skryabin and Colour," *Musical Times* 124/1688 (October 1983): 600–602; and John Gage, *Color and Culture: Practice and Meaning from Antiquity to Abstraction* (Berkeley and Los Angeles: University of California Press, 1999).

27. Gawboy and Townsend, "Scriabin and the Possible," *Music Theory Online* 18/2 (June 2012), op. cit. The title of their article plays off of the title of Simon Morrison's seminal article, "Skryabin and the Impossible," *Journal of the American Musicological Society* 51/2 (Summer 1998): 283–330.

28. Gawboy, "Symphony of Light and Sound," *Live it Up!* (2012–2013), 31.

29. Rothstein, "Music: Scriabin's 'Fire,'" *New York Times* (14 March 1983), C13.

30. "'Prometheus' For First Time Given Setting of Colors," 1.

31. British critic E. A. Baughan reported that over half of the audience left after Wood's first performance because "their musical morals had been outrageously assaulted," and the second hearing barely eased the burden put upon the remaining listeners. Wood's supporters hailed the concert as a triumph, but other witnesses were skeptical. Baughan, "On the Modern Language of Music," *Musical Times* 55/854 (1 April 1914): 231–34.

32. Henderson, "Scriabin's 'Prometheus' in New York," *Chicago Tribune* (28 March 1915), VIII4.

33. Edward Rice Doyle, "Will Colour Music Become an Art?" *The Bookman* 41 (1915): 399–400; and G. W. Harris, "Color Music," *The Independent* 82 (17 May 1915): 292–93.

34. "'Color Music' Tried Here for the First Time," *New York Times* (28 March 1915), SM15.

35. Henderson, quoted in "'Prometheus' For First Time Given Setting of Colors," 1.

36. Bowers, "Listen with Your Eyes," *Village Voice* (11 December 1969), 43.

37. Alexander Scriabin, "*Poem of Ecstasy*' and '*Prometheus: Poem of Fire*' in Full Score (New York: Dover, 1995), 115.

38. A comprehensive list of all documented performances of *Prometheus* with lights can be found in I. Vanechkina, "On the Performances of A. Scriabin's 'Lighting Symphony': Myths and Reality," *Leonardo*, at http://prometheus.kai.ru/perform_e.htm. Retrieved on 6

September 2015. Among other notable performances in the West were those by the Milwaukee Symphony Orchestra under Paul Chihara in 2000, and the London Philharmonic with Vladimir Jurowski in 2014.

39. Macdonald, "Lighting the Fire," 601. Yale University also performed *Prometheus: Poem of Fire* in Woolsey Hall on 22 November 1969, but it is the 1971 performance that lives in infamy. The original program from the 1969 concert, along with photos and press clippings about the event, can be found online at http://yso.yalecollege.yale.edu/gallery/november-22–1969–woolsey-hall-scriabin-prometheus-poem-fire-debussy-khamma-premiere. The lighting display was overseen by a graduate student in architecture named Richard Gould. Woolsey Hall reached absolute capacity during the 1969 performance, which was free and open to the public. The Yale University Orchestra intended to take their show on the road to the Soviet Union, but "diplomatic difficulties" shelved the plans. "Symphony to Add Color," *Yale Daily News* 90 (19 Feb. 1971), 1. An even greater opportunity was lost when the famous February 1971 performance was slated to be filmed by CBS for an educational TV show called "Camera Three." Two days before the performance, however, producer Merrill Brockway pulled the plug on the project, citing insufficient lighting for a proper filming. Walter Frisch, "'Prometheus' Transcends," *Yale Daily News* 91 (22 Feb. 1971), 3.

40. Rothstein, "Music: Scriabin's 'Fire,'" C13.

41. Bowers, "Review of The University of Iowa's Performance of Scriabin's *Prometheus*, September 24, 1975, Hancher Auditorium," *High Fidelity/Musical America* (January 1976), MA20–MA21.

42. Macdonald, "Lighting the Fire," 602.

43. "Recordings," *High Fidelity/Musical America* 21/1 (January 1971): 64. Somer's annotated scores of Scriabin's music, along with her personal correspondence and other music-related items, are currently unsorted and archived in the archives at Yale University.

44. Linda Winer, "Multimedia Recitalist," *Chicago Tribune* (30 Jan. 1970), Sect. 2, p. 13.

45. Lincoln Ballard, "A Russian Mystic in the Age of Aquarius: The U.S. Revival of Alexander Scriabin in the 1960s," *American Music* 30/2 (Summer 2012): 194–227.

46. Anthony Tommasini, "The Colors and Sounds of Scriabin," *New York Times* (4 November 2011), online at http://www.nytimes.com/2011/11/05/arts/music/spectral-scriabin-at-baryshnikov-arts-center-review.html. Corinna Da Fonseca-Wollheim, "Electric Lights Orchestrate an Extrasensory Sound," *Wall Street Journal* (23 October 2010), online at http://www.wsj.com/articles/SB10001424052702304741404575564081843945998. Retrieved on 2 September 2015.

47. Swed, "Music Review: Spectral Scriabin," *Los Angeles Times* (18 March 2012), online at http://latimesblogs.latimes.com/culturemonster/2012/03/music-review-spectral-scriabin-.html. Retrieved on 3 September 2015. An interview with Tipton and Andjaparidze can be found online at http://www.pri.org/stories/2010–10–25/alexander-scriabin.

48. Bell, "Music Review: Eteri Andjaparidze and Jennifer Tipton with 'Spectral Scriabin' at the Broad Stage," *Culture Spot LA* (25 March 2012). Retrieved on 4 September 2015. Online at http://culturespotla.com/2012/03/music-review-eteri-andjaparidze-and-jennifer-tipton-with-spectral-scriabin-at-the-broad-stage/.

49. Nonken, *The Spectral Piano: From Liszt, Scriabin, and Debussy to the Digital Age* (Cambridge: Cambridge University Press, 2014); and idem, "Messiaen to Murail, or, What Sounds Become," in *Perspectives on the Performance of French Piano Music*, ed. Scott McCarrey and Lesley A. Wright (Farnham: Ashgate Publishing, 2014), 192.

50. "Hilde Somer Tries Out Scriabin's Multimedia Concept," 63.

51. Friedrich Kerst and Henry Krehbiel, eds. *Beethoven: The Man and the Artist, as Revealed in His Own Words* (Boston: Indy Publishing, 2008), 15.
52. Bowers, *Scriabin: A Biography*, 1:226.
53. Bowers, *Scriabin: A Biography*, 1:341.
54. Translated in Alexander Skrjabin, Piano Sonata No. 4 in F♯ major, Opus 30, G. Henle Verlag 1110, ed. Valentina Rubtsova (Munich, 2014), 17.
55. Lawrence Gilman, "Music of the Month: A Mystical Tone Poet," *The North American Review* 225/799 (June 1922): 842–43.
56. Bowers, *Scriabin: A Biography*, 2:135.
57. Frances Maes, *A History of Russian Music: From Kamarinskaya to Babi Yar* (Berkeley and Los Angeles: University of California Press, 2002), 215.
58. Susanna Garcia, "Scriabin's Symbolist Plot Archetype in the Late Piano Sonatas," *19th-Century Music* 23/3 (Spring 2000): 273–300.
59. Bowers, *The New Scriabin: Enigma and Answers* (New York: St. Martin's Press, 1973), 180.
60. Bowers, *The New Scriabin*, 179.
61. Sabaneev, *Modern Russian Composers*, trans. Judah Joffe (Freeport, NY: Books for Libraries Press, 1971), 167.
62. Gawboy, "Alexander Scriabin's Theurgy in Blue: Esotericism and the Analysis of 'Prometheus: Poem of Fire' Op. 60," [Op. cit]; and Christopher Dillon, "Scriabin's Synaesthesia and its Significance in *Prometheus: Poem of Fire*, Op. 60, and in Other Selected Late Works," (DMA treatise, Peabody Conservatory of Music, 2002).
63. Lazaros C. Triarhou, *Scriabin for Neuroscientists: A Study in Syn-Aesthetics* (CreateSpace Independent Publishing Platform, 2015). In summary, Triarhou asserted that, "In Scriabin's case, the term 'synaesthesia'—often associated with the composer—may more accurately pertain to philosophical aesthetics (*aisthetike*) than psycho-physiological sensation (*aisthesis*). Scriabin's amalgam of music, spectacle and intuition at the dawn of the previous century antedates the multimedia actuality of our era." At the time of this writing, I have not had the opportunity to review Triarhou's work.

CHAPTER 7: SCRIABIN'S RUSSIAN ROOTS AND THE SYMBOLIST AESTHETIC

1. Orga, liner notes to *Symphony No. 3/Poem of Ecstasy*, Moscow Symphony Orchestra, Igor Golovschin, conductor (Naxos 8.553582, 1997).
2. "What Germany Thinks of the Late Scriabine," *Musical Courier* (9 June 1915): 32.
3. Schonberg, "Scriabin: His Message Is Just Beginning to Be Clear," *New York Times* (16 January 1972), D13.
4. Stravinsky, *Poetics of Music: In the Form of Six Lessons*, trans. Arthur Knodel and Ingolf Dahl (Cambridge: Harvard University Press, 1998), 98.
5. Plekhanov, *Literatura i estetika* (Moscow, 1958), 2:95; quoted in Ralph Matlaw, "Scriabin and Russian Symbolism," *Comparative Literature* 31 (1979): 1.
6. Lunacharsky, trans. Wetzel, "On Scriabin," *Journal of the Scriabin Society of America* 8/1 (Winter 2003–2004): 43.
7. Grout, *A History of Western Music*, third ed. (New York: W. W. Norton, 1981), 410.

8. See Richard Taruskin, "Some Thoughts on the History and Historiography of Russian Music," *Journal of Musicology* 3/4 (Autumn 1984): 321–39; Marina Frolova-Walker, "On *Ruslan* and Russianness," *Cambridge Opera Journal* 9/1 (1997): 21–45; and Rutger Helmers, *Not Russian Enough? Nationalism and Cosmopolitanism in Nineteenth-Century Russian Opera* (Rochester, NY: University of Rochester Press, 2014).

9. In 1926, the Soviet ideologist Yuri Keldysh lashed out against composer Boris Shekhter's "Skriabinesque excesses," and grumbled that, "he almost completely adopts Skriabin's musical language in his compositions." Davidenko, quoted in Neil Edmunds, *The Soviet Proletarian Music Movement* (Oxford: Peter Lang, 2000), 246, 250. Other composers influenced by Scriabin include Anatoly Alexandrov, Nikolai Roslavetz, Leonid Sabaneev (especially his Piano Sonata Op. 15 [1915] and Sonata for Violin, Cello and Piano Op. 20 [1923/24]), and Samuil Feinberg, especially in his Sixth Piano Sonata (1923). See Larry Sitsky, *Music of the Repressed Russian Avant-Garde, 1900–1929* (Westport, CT: Greenwood Press, 1994); and Sanda Hîrlav Maistorovici, "Alexander Scriabin, Founder of a School of Composition?" *Musicology Today* 1/25 (Jan.–March 2016): 75–78.

10. Engel, "Views and Reviews," *Musical Quarterly* 10/4 (October 1924): 629–30.

11. Slonimsky, *Russian and Soviet Music and Composers*, Vol. 2, ed. Electra Yourke (New York: Routledge, 2004), 39.

12. Taruskin proposed an alternative to the idea that Scriabin lacked a school of composers by arguing for Scriabin's inclusion in the Beliaev circle, or *Beliayevski kruzhok*. This guild of pre-Revolutionary Russian composers included Glazunov, Liadov, and Scriabin. It gained attention in the 1880s when Mitrofan Beliaev channeled his timber fortune into recruiting and promoting the leading composers from the St. Petersburg and Moscow Conservatories (Glazunov was his first investment). In its exclusive roster of native talent, the Beliaev circle was the natural successor to the Mighty Handful. See Taruskin, *Stravinsky and the Russian Traditions*, 47–71; and *Defining Russia Musically: Historical and Hermeneutical Essays* (Princeton: Princeton University Press, 1997), 82–90.

13. Taruskin, *Defining Russia Musically*, 47.

14. Stravinsky, *Poetics of Music*, 93. On Stravinsky's connection with Russian music, see Taruskin, "Just How Russian was Stravinsky?" *New York Times* (16 April 2010), online at http://www.nytimes.com/2010/04/18/arts/music/18stravinsky.html?_r=0.

15. Taruskin has demonstrated that as Stravinsky matured, he went to great lengths to conceal his former admiration of Scriabin. Stravinsky's earlier praise of the elder composer's works was not reciprocated. Taruskin asserted that, "Every word Stravinsky ever published on the subject [of Scriabin] is false and biased and must be dismissed from consideration (p. 791). See "Stravinsky and Scriabin" in *Stravinsky and the Russian Traditions: A Biography of the Works through Marva* (Berkeley and Los Angeles: University of California Press, 1996).

16. Frolova-Walker, "On *Ruslan* and Russianness," 21.

17. Young, "Scriabin Defended Against His Devotees: A Critical Examination of the Russian Composer in the Context of Russian Religion, History, and Culture," online at http://www.criticalmass.johnbellyoung.com/scriabin-defended-against-his-devotees-a-critical-evaluation-of-the-composer-in-the-context-of-russian-history-religion-and-culture/.

18. Engel, "The Music of Skryabin," in Stuart Campbell, ed., *Russians on Russian Music, 1880–1917* (Cambridge: Cambridge University Press, 2003), 200. Engel added that, "this is in no wise a reproach to Skryabin; it is not a failing and not a virtue but simply an organic property of his gift."

19. Anonymous, "Scriabine—The Man and Musician," *American Review of Reviews* 64/6 (December 1921): 657.

20. Bowers, quoted in the foreword to Donald Garvelmann, *Youthful and Early Works of Alexander and Julian Scriabin* (New York: Music Treasure Publications, 1970).

21. Bowers, *Scriabin: A Biography*, second ed. (Mineola, NY: Dover, 1996), 2:227.

22. "A. Scriabin i I. Gofman o Shopene" [Scriabin and Josef Hofmann on Chopin], *Russkaia muzykalnaia gazeta* 13 (28 March 1910): 353–54. Cited in Rebecca Mitchell, *Nietzsche's Orphans*, 255.

23. Rachmaninov, "National and Radical Impressions in the Music of To-day and Yesterday," *The Etude* 37/10 (October 1919): 615.

24. Boris Schloezer, "An Abridged Analysis" (1928), trans. Ezra Pound in Edwin Corle, ed., *Igor Stravinsky; A Merle Armitage Book* (New York: Duell, Sloan & Pearce, 1949), 33.

25. Sabaneev, "Scriabin and the Idea of a Religious Art," *Musical Times* 72/1063 (Sept. 1931): 790.

26. Leonard, *A History of Russian Music* (New York: Macmillan, 1957), 225, 219.

27. Swan, *Russian Music and its Sources in Chant and Folk-Song* (New York: Norton, 1973), 152, 170; and Abraham, *Studies in Russian Music* (London: W. Reeves, 1936), 2.

28. Morgan, *Twentieth-Century Music: A History of Musical Style in Modern Europe and America* (New York: Norton, 1991), 55.

29. Bowers, "Richter on Scriabin," *Saturday Review* 48/24 (12 June 1965): 58.

30. Sitsky, *Music of the Repressed Russian Avant-Garde, 1900–1929*, x.

31. Abraham, "Elements of Russian Music," *Music & Letters* 9/1 (January 1928): 53.

32. Engel, "The Music of Skryabin," in *Russians on Russian Music, 1880–1917*, ed. Campbell, 199.

33. Leikin, "From Paganism to Orthodoxy to Theosophy: Reflections of Other Worlds in the Piano Music of Rachmaninov and Scriabin," in *Voicing the Ineffable: Musical Representations of Religious Experience*, ed. Siglund Bruhn (Hillsdale, NY: Pendragon Press, 2002), 38.

34. Clifton Callender, "Voice-Leading Parsimony in the Music of Alexander Scriabin *Journal of Music Theory* 42/2 (Autumn 1998): 219–33; and Jay Reise, "Late Skriabin: Some Principles Behind the Style," *19th-Century Music* 6/3 (1983): 220–31.

35. See Taruskin, Review of *Scriabin: Artist and Mystic*, by Boris de Schloezer and *The Music of Alexander Scriabin*, by James Baker, *Music Theory Spectrum* 10 (Spring 1988): 166.

36. For instance, in *Music of the 20th Century*, William Austin excoriated Scriabin's method of composing through "sheer repetition and sequence," which "in the course of five minutes or more . . . has appalling results" (pp. 71–72).

37. Abraham, "Elements of Russian Music," 56. In a letter from 1868 to Rimsky-Korsakov, Mussorgsky commented that, "When a German thinks, he reasons his way to a conclusion. Our Russian brother, on the other hand, starts with the conclusion and then might amuse himself with reasoning. That's all I have to say to you about symphonic development." Quoted in Taruskin's review of Baker and Schloezer, *Music Theory Spectrum* (1988), 166.

38. Macdonald, *Skryabin* (Oxford: Oxford University Press, 1978), 10, 12.

39. Abraham, *On Russian Music: Critical and Historical Studies of Glinka's Operas, Balakirev's Works, etc., with Chapters Dealing with Compositions by Borodin, Rimsky-Korsakov, Tchaikovsky, Mussorgsky, Glazunov, and Various Other Aspects of Russian Music* (London: W. Reeves, 1939).

40. Cheong Wai-Ling, "Scriabin's Octatonic Sonata," *Journal of the Royal Musical Association* 121/2 (1996): 206–28.

41. See Taruskin, *Defining Russia Musically*, 342–45.

42. See Gerald Abraham, "The Whole-Tone Scale in Russian Music," *Musical Times* 74/1085 (July 1933): 602–4; and Mary Woodside, "Leitmotiv in Russia: Glinka's Use of the Whole-Tone Scale," *19th-Century Music* 14/1 (Summer 1990): 67–74.

43. Jay Leyda and Sergei Bertensson, *Sergei Rachmaninoff: A Lifetime in Music* (Bloomington: Indiana University Press, 2001), 369.

44. Taruskin, Review of Schloezer and Baker, *Music Theory Spectrum*, 164.

45. Schwarz, *Music and Musical Life in Soviet Russia, 1917–1970* (New York: Norton, 1972), 323.

46. *Rachmaninoff's Recollections*, as told to Oskar Von Reismann; and Leyda and Bertensson, *Sergei Rachmaninoff: A Lifetime in Music*, 184.

47. For more on the bell references in this piece, see Timothy Shafer, "Color and Gesture in the Piano Music of Franz Liszt," in Richard P. Anderson, ed., *The Pianist's Craft: Mastering the Works of Great Composers* (Lanham; Toronto: Scarecrow Press, 2012), 106–12.

48. Other notable examples in piano music in which bell sounds are prominent include Grieg's *Klokkenklang* Op. 54 No. 6 (Bell Ringing), which features open fourths and fifths and pedal points that allow the sonorities to intermingle in an Impressionist manner. Debussy's *Cloches à travers les feuilles* (Bells Through the Leaves, 1907) and Ravel's *La Vallee des cloches*, the sixth movement from his piano suite *Miroirs* (1904–1905) similarly imitate bells. In these works, bell-like effects are achieved by repeated notes, à la Liszt.

49. Bowers, *Scriabin: A Biography*, 1:255.

50. Quoted in Morrison, *Russian Opera and the Symbolist Movement*, 221.

51. Igor Nikonovich, "Vospominaniia Sofronizkogo" [Remembering Vladimir Sofronisky], *Klassika* XXI, 88.

52. Randlett, "Gongs and Moires," *Clavier* 11/1 (January 1972): 10.

53. This literature includes Martin Cooper, "Aleksandr Skryabin and the Russian Renaissance," *Studi musicali* 1 (1972): 327–56; Brown, "Skriabin and Russian 'Mystic' Symbolism," *19th-Century Music* 3 (1979): 42–51; Matlaw, "Scriabin and Russian Symbolism," *Comparative Literature* 31 (1979): 1–23; Vladimir Padwa, "Symbolism in Alexander Scriabin's Music," in *The Symbolist Movement in the Literature of European Languages*, ed. Anna Balakian (John Benjamin's Publishing, 1984), 493–98; Ye. L. Krzhimovskaia, "Skriabin i Russkii Simvolizm," *Sovetskaia Muzyka* 2 (1985): 82–86; and Maria Carlson, "Fashionable Occultism: The World of Russian Composer Aleksandr Scriabin," *Journal of the International Institute* 7/3 (Summer 2000): online.

54. Taruskin, *Defining Russia Musically*, 107.

55. In his *Reminiscences*, Sabaneev stated that the composer "was none other than a symbolist in music, and all those premises which are now considered as traditional regarding Symbolists in poetry and literature are completely and even more categorically applicable to him." Marina Kostalevsky, "Ivanov on Skrjabin," *Russian Literature* 44 (1998): 318. In less flattering terms, Stravinsky characteristically described Scriabin as a "pseudo-esoteric symbolist." Vera Stravinsky and Robert Craft, *Stravinsky in Pictures and Documents* (London: Hutchinson, 1979), 605.

56. Malcolm Brown, "Skriabin and Russian 'Mystic' Symbolism," *19th-Century Music* 3 (1979): 46. Cf. Maria Carlson, "Fashionable Occultism: The World of Russian Composer Aleksandr Scriabin," *Journal of the International Institute* 7/3 (Summer 2000): online.

57. For specific examples of this technique, see Susanna Garcia, "Scriabin's Symbolist Plot Archetype in the Late Piano Sonatas," *19th-Century Music* 23/3 (Spring 2000): 273–300.

58. Maria Carlson, "Fashionable Occultism," op cit.

59. Marvick, "Two Versions of the Symbolist Apocalypse," 294 (see n60).

60. Marvick, "Two Versions of the Symbolist Apocalypse: Mallarmé's *Livre* and Scriabin's *Mysterium*," *Criticism* 28/3 (Summer 1986): 302. Powell's 2001 *New Grove* entry also assigned Scriabin a place in the Symbolist pantheon alongside Mallarmé in their celebration of the creative act as self-identification with the divine.

61. The writings of the Russian Symbolists, however, were never used as sung lyrics in Scriabin's music. For an example of the Symbolist influence on French music, consider the connection between Baudelaire's poetry and Debussy's piano prelude "Les sons et les parfums tournent dans l'air du soir," as explained by Paul Roberts in his book, *Images: The Piano Music of Claude Debussy* (Portland: Amadeus Press, 1996), 71–80.

62. Brown, "Skriabin and Russian 'Mystic' Symbolism," 44.

63. For more on the concept of ecstasy and spiritual transcendence in Scriabin's music, see Mitchell Morris, "Musical Eroticism and the Transcendent Strain: The Works of Alexander Skryabin, 1898–1908" (Ph.D. dissertation, University of California, Berkeley, 1998).

64. See James West, *Russian Symbolism: A Study of Vyacheslav Ivanov and the Russian Symbolist Aesthetic* (London: Methuen & Co., 1970), 170.

65. See Michael Wachtel, *Russian Symbolism and Literary Tradition Goethe, Novalis, and the Poetics of Vyacheslav Ivanov* (Madison, WI: University of Wisconsin Press, 1994), 67. The phrases "only a parable" and "nur Gleichnis" come from Goethe's *Faust II*.

66. Morrison, *Russian Opera and the Symbolist Movement*, 185.

67. Ibid., 189.

68. Matlaw, "Scriabin and Russian Symbolism," 5.

69. Sabaneev, *Vospominaniia o Skriabine* (Moscow: Muzyka, 1925), 162.

70. Matlaw, "Scriabin and Russian Symbolism," 5. Also see Ivanov, *Svet vechernii* (London: Clarendon Press, 1962), 193.

71. Translated and quoted in Rebecca Mitchell, *Nietzsche's Orphans*, 99.

72. Victoria Adamenko, *Neo-Mythologism in Music* (Hillsdale, NY: Pendragon Press, 2007), 154.

73. Marina Kostalevsky, "The Birth of Poetry from the Spirit of Criticism: Ivanov on Skrjabin," *Russian Literature* 44/3 (1 October 1998): 323.

74. Grout, *A History of Western Music*, third ed. (New York: W. W. Norton, 1981), 410.

75. For more on the Orpheus myth in pre- and post-Revolutionary Russian culture, see Rebecca Mitchell, *Nietzsche's Orphans*, 61–67, 211–13.

76. Robert Bird and Michael Wachtel, eds. *Selected Essays* (Evanston: Northwestern University Press, 2001), 213.

77. Karatygin, "Lektsiia-konsert pamiati A. N. Skriabina," *Rech* (1915): 4.

78. See Bernice Glatzer Rosenthal, ed., *The Occult in Russian and Soviet Culture* (Cornell: Cornell University Press, 1997), 128.

79. Delson, *Skriabin: Ocherki zhizni i tvorchestva* [Essays on His Life and Creative Works] (Moscow: Muzyka, 1971), 379.

80. Russian scholars Irina Vanechkina and Bulat Galeyev were the first to publish on the affinities between Ciurlionis and Scriabin. See "Scriabin and Chiurlionis: On the Way to the Light-Music Synthesis," http://prometheus.kai.ru/scr-chiur_e.htm. Cf. Nathalie Lorand, "Symbolist Visions: the Role of Music in the paintings of M. K. Ciurlionis," *Lithuanian Quarterly Journal of Arts and Sciences* 49/2 (Summer 2003): online at http://www.lituanus.org/2003/03_2_04.htm.

81. Bely met Scriabin at the home of Margarita Morozova, the composer's patron. Amused at the composer's fastidious appearance and effete mannerisms, Bely had little desire to cultivate his company. On Scriabin's capricious attitude toward philosophy, Bely remarked "All the while the little white fingers of his pale little hand kept jabbing out chords of some kind in the air: his pinkies took the 'Kant' note, his middle finger would trace the 'Culture' theme, and all at once—whoops!—a leap of the index finger over a whole row of keys to the one marked 'Blavatsky.'" *Mezhdu dvukh revolutsii* (Leningrad: State Publishers, 1934), 348–49. Quoted in Taruskin, *Defining Russia Musically*, 317.

CHAPTER 8: THE REVIVAL IN 1960s AMERICA

1. Quoted in Leonid Sabaneev, "Scriabin and the Idea of a Religious Art," *Musical Times* 72 (1 September 1931): 790.

2. Macdonald, *Skryabin* (London: Oxford University Press, 1978), 10. Australian pianist Ernest Hutcheson similarly advised that, "If we ignore Scriabin's philosophy completely, we can enjoy his music better." *The Literature of the Piano: A Guide for Amateur and Student* (New York: Knopf, 1964), 333.

3. Tompakova, *Zovushchii k svyetu: Aleksandr Skriabin v Anglii* [Calling to Light: Alexander Scriabin in England] (Moscow: Muzyka, 1999); and Thomas, "The Impact of Russian Music in England (1893–1929)," (Ph.D. diss., University of Birmingham, 2005). Other sources that discuss Scriabin's reception include Richard Taruskin, *Defining Russia Musically* (Princeton: Princeton University Press, 1996), esp. pp. 311–16; Margarita Pryashnikova and Olga Tompakova, eds., *Letopis' zhizni i tvorchestva A. N. Skriabina* [Chronicle of the Life and Creative Work of A. N. Scriabin] (Moscow: Muzyka, 1985); Don Louis Wetzel, "Alexander Scriabin in Russian Musicology and its Background in Russian Intellectual History" (Ph.D. diss., University of Southern California, 2009); and Lincoln M. Ballard, "Defining Moments: Vicissitudes in Alexander Scriabin's Twentieth-Century Reception" (Ph.D. diss., University of Washington, 2010).

4. Gray, *A Survey of Contemporary Music*, second ed. (London: Humphrey Milford, 1927), 158, 159.

5. Cooper, "Ecstasy for Ecstasy's Sake," *The Listener* (10 October 1957): 563.

6. "Wagner: Thoughts in Season," *Hudson Review* 13/3 (Autumn 1960): 338.

7. Machlis, *Introduction to Contemporary Music* (New York: Norton, 1961), 132.

8. "Josef Hofmann's Recitals," *New York Times* (25 March 1898), 6.

9. Henry C. Lahee, *Annals of Music in America* (Boston: Marshal Jones, 1922), 264.

10. "The Latest Russian Pianist," *New York Times* (28 January 1906), 7.

11. "'The Russian Chopin'—Alexander Scriabine, Composer, Pianist and Dreamer," *Boston Evening Transcript* (22 December 1906), 22.

12. Pryashnikova and Tompakova, *Letopis' zhizni i tvorchestva A. N. Skriabina*, 150.

13. "M. Scriabine's Recital," *New York Times* (4 January 1907), 7.

14. Letter of 9 January 1907 from Scriabin to Tatyana Schloezer, in Kashperov, ed., *Pisma: Aleksandr Nikolaevich Skriabin* (Moscow: Muzyka, 1965), 458; "M. Scriabine's Recital," *New York Times* (4 January 1907), 7; "Mr. Scriabine's Recital," *New York Tribune* (31 January 1907), 7.

15. "A Russian Concert," *New York Times* (1 March 1907), 9; and Hansell Baugh, "Scriabin in America," *The New Freeman* 3/4 (8 April 1931): 86–88.

16. Henderson, "More Scriabine Music," *The Sun* (15 March 1907), 9.

17. Henderson, "In the World of Music," *The Sun* (10 March 1907), 10. All Henderson quotes in that paragraph are from the same review. In another article, Henderson stereotypically wrote that Russian music predictably featured "tunes characteristic of their race and national disposition, and one is never at a loss to fancy that he hears the sobbing of the melancholy winds across the steppes echoed in the sorrowful hearts of people of minor moods." "Some Russian Novelties," *The Sun* (1 March 1907), 9.

18. Informing these critics' opinions were the moral bonds and sacrosanct truths of the Victorian Age. Daniel Singal has cogently described how modernism loosened those standards in favor of new modes of perception that embraced individual desires and contradictory impulses. "Towards a Definition of American Modernism," in *Modernist Culture in America*, ed. Singal (Belmont, CA: Wadsworth, 1991); and Singal, *The War Within: Victorian to Modernist Thought in the South, 1919–1945* (Chapel Hill: University of North Carolina Press, 1982).

19. Mark Grant, *Maestros of the Pen: A History of Classical Music Criticism in America* (Boston: Northeastern University Press, 1998), 58–62.

20. "The Russian Symphony," *New York Times* (15 March 1907), 9.

21. Gilman, "Mr. Scriabine's 'Divine Poem,'" *Harper's Weekly* 51/2623 (30 March 1907): 474.

22. Quoted in Faubion Bowers, *Scriabin: A Biography*, 2:161.

23. Shortly after these reviews appeared, Scriabin abruptly left the U.S. after his mistress Tatyana arrived to accompany him. The financial burden of her presence loomed less than the fear of exposure; only a year earlier, Russian writer Maxim Gorky (1868–1936) was discovered cohabitating in a New York hotel with a woman who was not his wife, and both parties were unceremoniously evicted. ("Gorky and Actress Asked to Quit Hotels," *New York Times* [15 April 1906], 1; and "Out of Third Hotel, Gorky is Now Hiding," *New York Times* [16 April 1906], 1.) Scriabin well knew of this scandal and warned Tatyana about the dangers if she traveled to the U.S., but she took matters into her own hands. Soon after her arrival in New York in April 1907, Scriabin in a panic cabled Alexander Glazunov to borrow six hundred rubles and fled with Tatyana to Paris. See Scriabin's letter of 21 March 1907 to Glazunov in Kashperov, *Pisma*, 464.

24. Stokowski, "Play 'Poem of Ecstasy,'" *New York Times* (12 February 1919), 11.

25. With the Boston Symphony Orchestra, Koussevitzky conducted *Poem of Ecstasy* eleven times, the *Divine Poem* four times, and *Prometheus* three times. H. Earle Johnson, *Symphony Hall, Boston* (Boston: Little, Brown & Co., 1950), 383.

26. Downes, "Koussevitzky Gets Ovation in Boston," *New York Times* (11 October 1924), 18.

27. "Annie Besant Here to Win Converts," *New York Times* (1 August 1909), 4. Besant's lectures were published as *Theosophical Lectures: Chicago 1907* (Theosophical Society, 1907).

28. Judith Tick, *A Composer's Search for American Music* (New York: Oxford University Press, 1997), 44–45.

29. James and Margaret Cousins, *We Two Together* (Madras, India: Ganesh, 1950), 499; and W. L. Hubbard, "Besant Pleads for Art to Save Nation from Decay," *Chicago Tribune* (22 September 1907), B1.

30. Djane and her husband, Siegfried, each published articles on Theosophical ideals in Scriabin's music. See Siegfried Herz, "The Art of Alexander Nikolaevitch Skriabin," *The Etude* 44 (May 1926): 345–46, 399; and Djane Lavoie-Herz, "Scriabine's Prometheus," *Musical Canada* 10 (May 1915): 3.

31. Judith Tick, "Ruth Crawford's 'Spiritual Concept': The Sound-Ideals of an Early American Modernist," *Journal of the American Musicological Society* 44/2 (1991): 232–33.

32. In an interview of 29 November 1984, Vivian Fine confided that "Ruth's music before Charlie [Seeger] was influenced by Scriabin, mainly in the chords, the fourths, the augmented fourth plus perfect forth." Tick, "Ruth Crawford's 'Spiritual Concept,'" 232–33.

33. Oja, *Making Music Modern: New York in the 1920s* (New York: Oxford University Press, 2000), 144–52.

34. "Contemporary American Musicians," *Musical America* (10 January 1925): 23; and Thomas Cottle, *When the Music Stopped: Discovering My Mother* (Albany: State University of New York Press, 2004), 25.

35. "Contemporary American Musicians," 23; and Tick, "Ruth Crawford's 'Spiritual Concept,'" 233.

36. Quoted in Cottle, *When the Music Stopped*, 38.

37. Photographer Ansel Adams also studied Theosophy and found a psychic connection with Scriabin's music, which to him "speaks spiritual messages." Anne Hammond, *Ansel Adams: Divine Performance* (New Haven: Yale University Press, 2002), 12.

38. Heyman founded the Scriabin Circle in New York in 1934. For reviews of her all-Scriabin recitals see "Scriabin Memorial," *New York Times* (14 April 1924), 14; "Miss Heyman Plays All-Scriabin Recital," *New York Times* (7 April 1935), N4; "Katherine Heyman Heard in Recital," *New York Times* (6 March 1937), 9; "Miss Heyman in Recital," *New York Herald-Tribune* (6 March 1937).

39. Quoted in New York Public Library Clippings file, "Some Press Comments of her Former Tour in the West" (1917).

40. See Bowers, "Memoir with Memoirs," *Paideuma* 2/1 (Spring 1973): 61; and Hillary Poriss, "Women, Musical Canons and Culture: Katherine Ruth Heyman," *Journal of the Scriabin Society of America* 2 (Winter 1997–1998): 14–31.

41. Carter acknowledged that Heyman's *The Relation of the Ultramodern to Archaic Music* (which contained a chapter on Scriabin) "was almost required reading for this somewhat Blavatskian circle." "Documents of a Friendship with Ives," in *The Writings of Eliot Carter*, eds. Else and Kurt Stone (Bloomington: Indiana University Press, 1977), 333. For more on the Scriabin-Ives connection, see Lincoln Ballard, "Scriabin and Ives: An Unanswered Question?" *Journal of the Scriabin Society of America* (2004): 37–61.

42. Gilman, "Scriabin—The Man and Musician," *American Review of Reviews* 64/6 (December 1921): 657.

43. See Aldrich's reviews of the *Divine Poem* in the *New York Times* on 7 January 1922 (p. 19) and of the *Poem of Ecstasy* on 17 February 1922 (p. 16).

44. In 1931, C. E. Bechhover Roberts published an exposé biography of Blavatsky, *The Mysterious Madame* (New York: Brewer, Warren & Putnam) that depicted her as "one of the most accomplished, ingenious and interesting charlatans of history." See P. W. Wilson's review, "Founder of Modern Theosophy," *New York Times* (17 May 1931), 67.

45. William Young and Nancy Young, *Music of the Great Depression* (Westport, CT: Greenwood Press, 2005), 193–200.

46. William Osborne, *Music in Ohio* (Kent, OH: Kent State University Press, 2004), 237; and Kenneth J. Bindas, *All of This Music Belongs to the Nation: The WPA's Federal Music Project and American Society, 1935–1939* (Knoxville: University of Tennessee Press, 1995), 16–17.

47. Sabaneev, "Scriabin and the Idea of a Religious Art," *Musical Times* 72/1063 (1 September 1931): 789.

48. Smith, "The 'Reds' of Music," *New York Times* (26 November 1922), 102.

49. Rosenfeld, *Discoveries of a Music Critic* (New York: Harcourt, Brace, and Co., 1936), 158.

50. Myers, "Scriabin: A Reassessment," *Musical Times* 98/1367 (January 1957): 35. A critic and historian of twentieth-century music, Myers (1892–1985) worked for the *Times* and *Daily Telegraph* from 1920–1934. Lang, *Music in Western Civilization* (New York: Norton, 1941), 1025.

51. Brent-Smith, "Some Reflections on the Work of Scriabin [Pt. I]," *Musical Times* 67/1001 (1 July 1926): 593.

52. Fennel, "A Word for Scriabin," *Musical Times* 67/1003 (1 September 1926): 833; and Hull, "Scriabin: A Comment," *Musical Times* 67/1005 (1 November 1926): 993–94.

53. Smith, "The 'Reds' of Music," *New York Times* (26 November 1922), 102. Abraham, *A Hundred Years of Music*, fourth ed. (London: Duckworth, 1974), 225, 255.

54. Abraham, *This Modern Stuff: A Fairly "Plaine and Easie" Introduction to Contemporary Music* (London: D. Archer, 1933), 42. Also see his chapter on Scriabin in *Masters of Russian Music* (London: Duckworth, 1936). Program notes quoted in Martin Cooper, "Music—Scriabin," *London Mercury* 31/182 (December 1934): 201.

55. Calvocoressi, *Music and Ballet: Recollections of M. D. Calvocoressi* (London: Faber and Faber, 1934), 246, 248.

56. Gray, *A Survey of Contemporary Music*, second ed. (London: Humphrey Milford, 1927), 158, 159.

57. For more on how Scriabin's distinctively Russian compositional practices deviate from those of the Austro-German tradition, see Richard Taruskin, "Review of James Baker, *The Music of Alexander Scriabin* and Boris de Schloezer, *Scriabin: Artist and Mystic*," *Music Theory Spectrum* 10 (Spring 1988): 164–66.

58. Gray, *A Survey of Contemporary Music*, 155; and Hume, "A Tub of Glue," *Washington Post* (25 January 1971), D8.

59. Abraham offered similar assessments of Scriabin in "Scriabin Reconsidered," *Musical Standard* (September 1931): 214–16; *Studies in Russian Music* (London: Scholarly Press, 1936), and *This Modern Stuff: An Introduction to Contemporary Music* (London: Citadel Press, 1946).

60. Pakenham, "Recorded Music," *New York Times* (19 June 1932), X5.

61. Downes, "Critical Scales Show Changing Valuations," *New York Times* (3 May 1925), X6.

62. Downes, "Boston Symphony Orchestra," *New York Times* (23 November 1928), 30.

63. "Inspired Prophet," *New York Times* (19 February 1950), X7.

64. Bowers, "Keynote Address at The Scriabin Museum, Moscow (January 7, 1992)," *Journal of the Scriabin Society of America* 1/1 (Winter 1996–1997): 8.

65. Quoted in Bowers, *Scriabin: A Biography*, 1:84.

66. "Scriabin: On the Twenty-Fifth Anniversary of His Death," *Musical Times* 81/1168 (June 1940): 257.

67. Joseph Horowitz, *Classical Music in America: A History of its Rise and Fall* (New York: Norton, 2005), 277, 488.

68. "Repertoires Need Freshening," *Washington Post* (12 October 1947), L3; "What Your Orchestra 'Owes' You," *Washington Post* (20 February 1949), L1; "Critic Raps Ormandy Program," *Washington Post* (12 April 1951), B2; and "Music in a Rut," *Washington Post* (25 November 1951), B4.

69. Schonberg, "Unobserved Anniversary," *New York Times* (24 April 1966), X13.

70. Schonberg, "Twilight of Romanticism?" *New York Times* (2 April 1967), 111.

71. Originally published on 21 June 1925, reprinted in *More Essays from the World of Music: Essays from the Sunday Times* (New York: Da Capo Press, 1958), 160–63. Schonberg and his successor at the *Times*, Donal Henahan, recycled its themes in later articles. See Schonberg, "About Virtuosity," *New York Times* (28 April 1963), 135; and Henahan, "Does Virtuoso Mean Virtuous?" *New York Times* (30 November 1969), D35.

72. Schonberg, "Music: Festival at Butler," *New York Times* (21 May 1968), 43; and anon., "Festivals: Romantic Revival," *Time Magazine* 93/22 (30 May 1969): 105.

73. Schonberg, "The Romantics—Are They for Now?" *New York Times* (19 May 1968), D21.

74. Howard Klein, "Should We Dig Up the Rare Romantics? Yes," *New York Times* (23 November 1969), M1. Klein noted, "One argument runs that we have eroded away with too much exposure [to] the great peaks of the Romantic period, now we must be content with the foothills of inspiration . . . The only true argument, therefore, should be that we overlooked noble summits and now should give equal time to the rivals of Beethoven, Berlioz, Wagner, Schumann, Chopin, and Liszt." For a counterview, see Glenn Gould, "Should We Dig Up the Rare Romantics? . . . No, They're Only a Fad," *New York Times* (23 November 1969), 57.

75. Alan Rich observed, "The romantic revival is better off with a prophet of Lewenthal's ability to drive his points home with wit and insight than the baroque revival was a decade ago with the blabbermouths and pedants who falsified the music with their barococo pronouncements and devitalized it with their bloodless performances." "Schubert Would Have Approved," *New York Magazine* (8 December 1969): 66.

76. Robert Finn, "A Festival of Romantic Music Revives Forgotten Composers," *Cleveland Plain-Dealer* (26 May 1968), E26. Lewenthal's program was ordered: Left Hand Prelude Op. 9 No. 1, Five Preludes Op. 74, Twenty-Four Preludes Op. 11 [Intermission] *Vers la flamme* Op. 72, B minor *Fantasie* Op. 28. Encore: *Hexameron*.

77. Charles Staff, "Tonal Splendor, Brilliance Produced by Lewenthal," *Indianapolis News* (18 May 1968), 8.

78. Schonberg, "Music: Maazel Returns," *New York Times* (26 March 1965), 28.

79. Harry Haskell, *The Early Music Revival: A History* (London: Thames and Hudson, 1988), 131–50.

80. Schonberg, "'Amoral Little Mystic,'" *New York Times* (11 April 1965), X11.

81. Ibid.

82. "Visions to Put the Acid Set to Shame," *New York Times* (13 April 1969), D17.

83. Gorner, "Scriabin's Case has Another Day in Court before New Values," *Chicago Tribune* (14 September 1969), G4.

84. James Goodfriend, ed., "Why Alexander Scriabin? Seven Critics Zero in on a Current Target," *Stereo Review* 30 (January 1973): 69.

85. Both Bowers books received mixed reviews. Considering the dearth of English-language sources, they were landmark achievements, but Gerald Abraham and Miloš Velimirović frowned upon their lack of citations, incomplete index, and factual errata. Abraham, review of *Scriabin: A Biography of the Russian Composer*, by Bowers, *Music & Letters* 52/3 (July 1971): 311–14; and Velimirović, review of *Scriabin: Enigma and Answers*, by Bowers, *Slavic Review* 34/2 (June 1975): 443–44.

86. Edward Rothstein, "Music: Scriabin's 'Fire,'" *New York Times* (14 March 1983), C13; and Bowers, "Listen with Your Eyes," *The Village Voice* (11 December 1969), 36.

87. Kipnis added, "If enough people express enthusiasm over a particular composer, others jump on the bandwagon: performers, listeners, and not least, record companies." Goodfriend, "Why Alexander Scriabin," 69.

88. Notable Western publications not previously cited include: Edmund Rubbra, "The Resurgence of Scriabin," *The Listener* (26 February 1970): 289; Don Heckman, "Scriabin: 'Ice, Cocaine, Rainbow,'" *New York Times* (10 October 1971), D28; Robert Evett, "The Man with the Astral Body," *Atlantic Monthly* (October 1971): 128–31; Henry-Louis de la Grange, "Prometheus Unbound," *Music and Musicians* 233 (January 1972): 34–41; Schonberg, "Scriabin: His Message Is Just Beginning to Be Clear," *New York Times* (16 January 1972), D13; and Schonberg, "Music of Scriabin Never Entirely Out of Repertory," *Nashua Telegraph* (23 February 1972), 22. The winter 1970–1971 issue of *Piano Quarterly* and the January 1972 issue of *Clavier* magazine were also dedicated to the Scriabin centenary.

89. Hughes, "Scriabin Thought Young," *New York Times* (15 March 1970), 129.

90. Liner notes for *Scriabin/Nemtin Universe*, Kiril Kondrashin, cond. and Aleksei Lyubimov, piano (Rus Disc 11004, 1973); reprinted in the *Journal of the Scriabin Society of America* 3/1 (Winter 1998–1999): 30–32.

91. Anton Rovner, "Alexander Nemtin, The Fulfiller of Scriabin's Musical and Philosophical Legacy," *21st-Century Music* 7/10 (October 2000): 8–16. The second part, *Mankind*, was composed from 1976 to 1980, and the third part, *Transfiguration*, was completed in 1996.

92. Blythe, "Hot Air," *Music and Musicians* 15/2 (1966): 42.

93. In order of release, they were Eugene Ormandy (cond.) and Vladimir Sokoloff (piano) with the Philadelphia Orchestra (RCA Red Seal SB 6854/RCA Victor LSC-3214, 1971); Lorin Maazel (cond.) and Vladimir Ashkenazy (piano) with the London Philharmonic (Decca SXL 6527, 1972); and Donald Johanes (cond.) and Alfred Mouledous (piano) with the Dallas Symphony Orchestra (Candide 31039, 1972).

94. "A Scriabin Collection—Among the New Albums," *San Francisco Examiner*, Sunday insert, *This World* (20 February 1972), 32.

95. Craft, "Time for a Revival—or Resurrection," *New York Times* (5 April 1970), 280. This article was revised as "Toward the Flame" in *Prejudices in Disguise* (New York: Knopf, 1974), 181–84. Cf. "Scriabin Centenary" in the same collection (pp. 185–90).

96. Schonberg, "Still Horowitz, Still the Master," *New York Times* (10 May 1965), 38.

97. Downes, "Horowitz Draws Throng to Recital," *New York Times* (3 February 1948), 30.

98. "Anton Kuerti—'A Pianistic Supernova,'" *New York Times* (27 February 1972), D26. Other internationally renowned Scriabin pianists active in the U.S. and England during the 1960s and 1970s included John Ogdon, Roger Woodward, Michael Ponti, Lazare Berman, and Roberto Szidon.

99. These included Ruth Laredo (Nonesuch, 1970); John Ogdon (EMI, 1971); Roberto Szidon (Deutsche Grammophon, 1971); Robert Cornman (Charlin, 1972); and Michael Ponti (Vox, 1974). Glenn Gould also planned to record Scriabin's complete sonatas for Columbia, but abandoned the project after recording the Third and Fifth Sonatas.

100. "Recordings," *High Fidelity/Musical America* 21/1 (January 1971): 64. Also see Donal Henahan, "Piano Debut Here for Miss Verbit," *New York Times* (20 March 1971), 16; and Channing Gray, "Verbit: 'I Just Hate Dull,'" *Providence Journal* (5 May 1989), D7.

101. Hentoff, "Cosmo Listens to Records," *Cosmopolitan* (March 1969): 18.

102. "Hilde Somer Tries Out Scriabin's Multimedia Concept," *New York Times* (18 Dec. 1969), 63.

103. Kanfer, "Mixed Media to the Rescue," *Life* (20 February 1971): 15.

104. Kanfer, "Mixed Media to the Rescue," 15. Gould's most persuasive defense of this view is "The Prospects of Recording," *High Fidelity* 16/4 (April 1966): 46–63.

105. *New York Magazine* concert listings (8 April 1974), 28.

106. Donal Henahan, "Piano Debut Here for Miss Verbit," *New York Times* (20 March 1971), 16; and Channing Gray, "Verbit: 'I Just Hate Dull,'" *Providence Journal* (5 May 1989), D7.

107. Liner notes to *Scriabin*, Ruth Laredo, piano (CS 2034 and 2035); and Holland, "Ruth Laredo's Difficult Cup of Tea," *New York Times* (20 September 1987), H31.

108. Holland, "Ruth Laredo's Difficult Cup of Tea," H31.

109. Hughes, "Three Pianists Who Avoid Ruts," *New York Times* (9 August 1970), 90.

110. Schonberg, "Abbado: Big Sonorities, With Control," *New York Times* (4 February 1971), 29.

111. Schonberg, "Scriabin Handsomely Led by Boulez," *New York Times* (14 October 1972), 39.

112. *Monterey Pop* (1968), directed by D. A. Pennebaker and produced by John Phillips and Lou Adler; and *Woodstock: The Director's Cut* (1970), directed by Michael Wadleigh and edited by Martin Scorsese and Thelma Schoonmaker. *Woodstock* won an Academy Award for Best Documentary Feature in 1970.

113. Singal, *Modernist Culture in America* (Belmont, CA: Wadsworth Press, 1991), 20–21.

114. Singal, "Towards a Definition of American Modernism," *American Quarterly* 39/1 (Spring 1987): 21.

115. Morrison, *Russian Opera and the Symbolist Movement*, 185.

116. Noah Wardrip-Fruin and Nick Montfort, *The New Media Reader* (MIT Press, 2003), 83.

117. See Robert Adlington, *Sound Commitments: Avant-Garde Music and the Sixties* (Oxford: Oxford University Press, 2009), 266.

118. Linda Winer, "Multimedia Recitalist," *Chicago Tribune* (30 Jan. 1970), Sect. 2, p. 13.

119. Somer, "To Alexander Scriabin, the Prophet of Peace, Love and Mysticism," *Piano Quarterly* 21/81 (Spring 1973): 32; and Evett, "The Man with the Astral Body," *Atlantic Monthly* (October 1971): 131.

120. Gorner, "Scriabin's Case has Another Day in Court before New Values."

121. Evett, "The Man with the Astral Body," 128, 131.

122. Discus, "Wild Romantics," *Harper's Magazine* 238/1429 (June 1969): 102; and Kresh in Goodfriend, "Why Alexander Scriabin," 71.

123. Kresh, "Scriabin: 'Ice, Cocaine, Rainbow,'" D28. Robert Craft similarly commented that the final pages of *Poem of Ecstasy* imparted for younger listeners "a psychedelic exaltation of the kind imputed to the fungus of immortality, *ling chih*." "Towards the Flame," in *Prejudices in Disguise* (New York: Knopf, 1974), 185.

124. Jack Hiemenz, "Scriabin and His Demons," *High Fidelity* 20 (September 1970): 19–20.

125. Mayer, *Esquire* 72/2 (August 1969): 52.

126. In an analogous act of modernization, two years later Mercury released *The Naked Carmen*, which featured highlights from Bizet's opera performed by popular singers of the era in contemporary vocal styles. The free-loving Carmen was portrayed as a model for women's liberation, and the album even included instructions on how to stretch rubber bands across the folded cover and insert a colored light bulb to create an "Electric Spanish Cigar-Box

Guitar, Light Show, and Sound Sculpture." The history of *The Naked Carmen*, complete with interviews from the original creative team and performers, can be found online at http://www.echonyc.com/~jhhl/nakedc.html (accessed 2 December 2010).

127. *Piano Music of Alexander Scriabin: AΩ*, Hilde Somer, piano (Mercury SR 90525, 1970); and "To Alexander Scriabin, the Prophet of Peace, Love and Mysticism," 32. Mercury exploited the composer's occult mythos in *AΩ*. The "White Mass" and "Black Mass" Sonatas appeared on opposite sides of the LP, the album art contrasted angelic faces with gargoyles, and the cover featured an illustration of warring mythical beasts and a quote by Henry Miller: "Scriabin is cosmic fire—pure hallucinogenics promising rainbow nirvana." Liner notes by composer Arthur Cohn described the "occult music" on the album as laden with "esoteric mysticism" and "sexual connotation."

128. Somer, "To Alexander Scriabin, the Prophet of Peace, Love and Mysticism," 32.

129. Macdonald, "'Words and Music by A. Skryabin,'" *Musical Times* 113/1547 (January 1972): 22.

130. Hume, "Like a Banana Split, Scriabin is a Matter of Taste," *Washington Post* (25 July 1971), K8; and "An Unusual Program," *Washington Post* (13 October 1971), B10.

131. *Kairos* referred to the ways that a given time, place, audience, or context can enhance or constrain rhetorical persuasion. Plato employed this term in *Phaedrus* and Aristotle wrote about it in *Rhetoric*. See James L. Kinneavy and Catherine R. Eskin, "Kairos in Aristotle's *Rhetoric*," *Written Communication* 17 (2000): 432–44; and Phillip Sipiora and James S. Baumlin, *Rhetoric and Kairos: Essays in History, Theory, and Praxis* (Albany: State University of New York Press, 2002), 2–12.

132. Dalhaus, "Problems in Reception History," in *Foundations of Music History* (New York: Cambridge University Press, 1983), 158.

133. Schonberg, "Cycles and Revivals in Music," *New York Times* (8 April 1978), D12; and Bernard Jacobson, "The 'In' Composers: Mahler, Ives, Nielsen, Sibelius, Vivaldi, Berlioz—Are They Permanent Classics or Just Temporary Fads?" *High Fidelity/Musical America* 19/7 (July 1969): 54–57.

CHAPTER 9: FROM MUSICAL TEXT TO THE IMAGINATION

1. John Bell Young, "Scriabin Defended Against his Devotees: A Critical Evaluation of the Composer in the Context of Russian History, Religion, and Culture," http://www.criticalmass.johnbellyoung.com/scriabin-defended-against-his-devotees-a-critical-evaluation-of-the-composer-in-the-context-of-russian-history-religion-and-culture/.

2. "Richter on Scriabin," an interview with Faubion Bowers in the *Journal of the Scriabin Society of America* 2/1 (Winter 1997–1998): 8.

3. Yuli Engel, "Teatr i muzyka" [Theater and Music], *Russkie vedomosti* 62 (5 March 1906): 3, quoted in Anatole Leikin, *The Performing Style of Alexander Scriabin* (Burlington, VT: Ashgate, 2011), 279–80.

4. Faubion Bowers, *Scriabin: A Biography*, second ed. (New York: Dover, 1996), 1:246.

5. Jonathan Powell, "Skryabin, Aleksandr Nikolayevich," in *Grove Music Online* (accessed September 10, 2016).

6. See, for example, Alexander Skrjabin, *24 Préludes Opus 11* (Munich: G. Henle Verlag, 1996), 40.

7. Scriabin's shift from Italian to French markings may have been a product of his own travels, his own readings of theosophical literature in French, or perhaps a cultural reference to French influence on the Russian Silver Age. See Richard E. Overill, "Alexander Scriabin's Use of French Directions to the Pianist," http://www.scriabin-association.com/articles/alexander-scriabins-use-of-french-directions-to-the-pianist/.

8. The classic text on this subject is Leonard Ratner's *Classic Music: Expression, Form, and Style* (New York: Schirmer Books, 1980).

9. See Wye Jamison Allanbrook, *Rhythmic Gesture in Mozart: Le Nozze di Figaro & Don Giovanni* (Chicago: University of Chicago Press, 1983).

10. Susanna Garcia, "Scriabin's Symbolist Plot Archetype in the Late Piano Sonatas," *19th-Century Music* 23/3 (Spring 2000): 273–300.

11. Garcia describes the significance of this polarity in Scriabin's mystical universe in ibid., 281.

12. Garcia, who calls it the "Divine Summons," observes, "fanfares share an annunciatory and gestural shape rather than intervallic content." Ibid., 278.

13. Thus began the first program booklet for *Prometheus*. See Bowers, *Scriabin: A Biography*, 2:206–07.

14. Garcia, "Scriabin's Symbolist Plot," 284.

15. Ibid., 285. There is an unmistakable echo of Stravinsky's *Rite of Spring*, premiered in 1913. It is enlightening to perceive the clear parallels at this time between these two musicians, typically regarded as polar opposites.

16. I omit here Garcia's first rubric, the "notion of mystic unity," which is less convincing, particularly since most of these sonatas do not begin with mystic family chords (see chapter 12 for more details). The sonata whose opening harmonies most closely resemble the mystic chord is the Eighth, which she does not consider in her article, and which does not follow as clearly her proposed plot archetype.

17. These associates included most notably Tatyana and Boris de Schloezer, Sabaneev, the Morozovas, and the poet Vyacheslav Ivanov. For more on Scriabin's close circle of friends, confidantes, and admirers, see Rebecca Mitchell, *Nietzsche's Orphans: Music, Metaphysics, and the Twilight of the Russian Empire* (New Haven: Yale University Press, 2016), 85–103.

18. See, for example, the comments of Symbolist poet Andrei Bely, as in chapter 7, "Scriabin's Russian Roots and the Symbolist Aesthetic." The attitude of a successful Scriabinist is expressed beautifully by Leonid Sabaneev: "He infected all of us around him with an enthusiasm for his beliefs and the beauty of his dreams. Even if you did not believe him, you at least wanted to." Quoted in Bowers, *Scriabin: A Biography*, 2:8.

19. The most influential of these philosophers are Goethe, Kant, Schopenhauer, and Nietzsche. See Mitchell, *Nietzsche's Orphans*, 257, for an explanation of the powerful influence of German philosophy on the Russian intelligentsia in this period.

20. Zhiliaev, "Sergei Prokofiev," *K novym beregam* 1 (April 1923): 19. Soviet critic Nikolai Briusov argued that, "For the revolution in music to occur, this new style should eradicate all characteristics of the former style and construct a completely new order. We must build order out of chaos. We will be participants in the fight for a new and even bigger change ahead" (Zhiliaev, 14). See "Po tu storonu Skriabina," *K novym beregam* 2 (May 1923): 13–15. Cf. Viktor Beliaev, "Skriabin i budushchee muzyki," *K novym beregam* 2 (May 1923): 9–13.

21. See Mitchell, *Nietzsche's Orphans*, 104–36, regarding the conflict between Medtner's ideals and aspirations and the *Zeitgeist*.

22. See Larry Sitsky, *Music of the Repressed Russian Avant-Garde, 1900–1929* (Westport, CT: Greenwood Press, 1994) for more information on these composers.

23. Igor Stravinsky, *Poetics of Music in the Form of Six Lessons* (Cambridge: Harvard University Press, 1942), 122*ff.*

24. See, for example, Benjamin Ivry, *Maurice Ravel: A Life* (New York: Welcome Rain Publishers, 2000), 166–67.

25. Leikin, 283–84.

26. Boris de Schloezer, "Scriabine," in *Modern Music*, published by the *League of Composers' Review* 1:3 (Nov. 1924): 15.

27. This is also a problem at a higher level for many auditions and competitions, where repertoire choices are shaped by the desire to adhere to these traditional categories.

28. An entirely similar point of view was espoused by Edward Mitchell, one of the most significant early Scriabin pianists in England. His article "Scriabin and the Pianoforte Teacher" contains a commentary and many specific recommendations. See Edward Mitchell, *Scriabin: The Great Russian Tone Poet: A Complete Catalogue of His Piano Compositions with Thematic Illustrations* (London: Hawkes & Son, 1929).

29. These pieces certainly had this effect for the present author. When I began tackling these etudes they were much more difficult than any repertoire I had ever attempted before. The extra push needed to overcome these hurdles greatly accelerated my technical development.

CHAPTER 10: TECHNIQUE

1. César Cui, quoted in Faubion Bowers, *Scriabin: A Biography* (New York: Dover, 1996), 1:197. In this highly laudatory review, Cui noted another unusual phenomenon for a composer-pianist: "in contrast with what usually happens, the composer carried the performer."

2. Scriabin recalled, "[In America] my Nocturne for the Left Hand was so successful that I always had to play it as an encore. So I remembered that long ago, I had written another piece for the left hand alone. It was a complicated waltz in the manner of Johann Strauss, full of virtuoso passages and octaves, and it was a dreadful piece!" Leonid Sabaneev, *Erinnerungen an Alexander Skrjabin* [Reminiscences of Scriabin] (Berlin: Ernst Kuhn, 2005), 158. All translations from the German of Sabaneev's *Erinnerungen* are mine.

3. For more on Godowsky, see the profile in Robert Rimm, *The Composer-Pianists: Hamelin and the Eight* (Portland, OR: Amadeus Press, 2002), 47–84.

4. See Samuel Randlett, "Elements of Scriabin's Keyboard Style," *Piano Quarterly* (Spring 1971): 19–20, for some well-chosen examples.

5. It is unclear whether this happens because practicing widely spaced parts improves this hand's flexibility, or perhaps because muscular strength and flexibility typically run in inverse proportions.

6. The Prelude Op. 67 No. 2, a very tricky left hand study, is the exception that proves the rule. In the extraordinary cadenza to the Nocturne Op. 9 No. 2, where the rapid passagework is obviously difficult, Scriabin takes care to separate the thumb from the other fingers, which can more comfortably cover smaller spaces.

7. Reise's three transcriptions are published in the *Journal of the Scriabin Society of America* 8/1 (Winter 2003–04): 105–08, Vol. 11/1 (Winter 2006–07): 89–92, and Vol. 13/1 (Winter 2008–09): 92–5. A live performance of the Op. 8 No. 12 transcription can be found at the author's website and YouTube channel.

8. Scriabin avoided switching to the treble clef in the left hand where possible. In works such as the Poème Op. 59 No. 1 and Etude Op. 65 No. 1, he ventures with ledger lines above the bass clef all the way to the E a tenth above middle C.

9. Anatole Leikin, *The Performing Style of Alexander Scriabin* (Burlington, VT: Ashgate, 2011), 14.

10. A good example can be found in his performance of the Prelude in A minor Op. 11 No. 2, transcribed by Pavel Lobanov, reproduced in Leikin, 96–103. Although Leikin correctly observes that many of Scriabin's rhythmic displacements are designed to highlight voice-leading (e.g., the left hand in mm. 14–15), the rolled chords in mm. 64 and 67 are not so much to clarify line as to highlight a new harmony, to create a new texture, and to make an attractively transparent sound.

11. Samuel Randlett, "Elements of Scriabin's Keyboard Style," *Piano Quarterly* (Spring 1971): 20. This article contains a detailed discussion of chord spacing (pp. 18–21). Randlett's series of *Piano Quarterly* articles from 1970–71, "Elements of Scriabin's Keyboard Style," form one of the earliest and most systematic investigations into the components of Scriabin's pianism.

12. Chopin's Etude Op. 10 No. 11 in E♭ is one of the best technical studies to rehearse this skill. There is no doubt that Chopin's preference for widely spread hand positions played a critical role in Scriabin's sensibility.

13. Data from Scriabin's piano rolls strongly confirms this traditional order; for instance, in the Prelude Op. 10 No. 2, "in the overwhelming majority of cases, the LH runs ahead of the RH (40 out of 45 displacements)" (Leikin, 57).

14. Scriabin's letter of late Dec. 1894 or early Jan. 1895, quoted in Alexander Skrjabin, *Sämtliche Klaviersonaten I* BA9616, ed. Christoph Flamm (Kassel: Bärenreiter, 2011), xlii.

15. The concluding bars of the Fourth Sonata use a similar physical impossibility to express a radiant sense of triumph. It is certainly better for a performer here to focus on rhythmic drive and accumulated sound in the pedal rather than trying to play every one of the printed notes. It is possible to leave out different pitches in successive attacks of the left-hand chords, so that in the end, all pitches have been captured evenly in the accumulated pedal resonance.

16. The ordeal of Scriabin's concertizing is described in Leikin, 40–41, and in the colorful reminiscences of Matthew Pressman, director of the Rostov music school, as related in Bowers, *Scriabin: A Biography*, 2:217–18.

17. "My Tenth Sonata is a sonata of insects. Insects are born from the sun . . . they are the sun's kisses." Sabaneev, *Erinnerungen an Alexander Skrjabin*, 301.

18. Gyorgy Sandor, *On Piano Playing: Motion, Sound and Expression* (New York: Schirmer Books, 1995), 94. The staccato motion is covered in 93–107.

19. The high degree of mobility and athleticism in Scriabin's early period works may have been a strong influence on Prokofiev, who took this element even further in his most virtuosic works, especially the concerti.

20. One is reminded of Walter Gieseking's description of Ravel's virtuosic pieces, which are "so tricky, so risky, and demanding such an extreme virtuosity that there will always be an element of good luck in succeeding to play them correctly, not only technically, but with the right expression, in spite of all difficulties." Walter Gieseking, "On Playing Ravel," booklet to *The Solo Piano Works of Maurice Ravel* (Angel Records 5S-3541, 1955).

21. Sabaneev, *Erinnerungen an Alexander Skrjabin*, 185–86. Examples of changed hand distributions can be found, for example, in the autograph manuscript to Étrangeté Op. 63 No. 2; see http://juilliardmanuscriptcollection.org/composers/scriabin-aleksandr/.

22. Randlett writes about thumb crossing, "The pianist who plays the notes exactly as they are written, with thumbs interlocked, will find it relatively easy to keep the parts separated into their proper tonal levels . . . the voicing of the chords is subject to an extremely subtle control." Randlett, "Elements of Scriabin's Keyboard Style," *Piano Quarterly* (Winter 1971–1972): 26. Interlocking thumbs are also commonly found in the music of Schumann, Ravel, Albéniz, and many other great pianist-composers.

23. In this Prelude, I personally would not redistribute anything until m. 24, when the left-hand waves are more disjointed, and quite difficult to hear as belonging organically together in any case. The tenor A-naturals, taken by the right hand, voice-lead naturally to the alto G♯ in mm. 25*ff*.

24. Among countless other examples, we might mention the Fifth Sonata, m. 115. Without redistributing, rhythmic drive will be lost and the musical focus on the important overriding rhythmic gesture—the right hand's trumpet fanfare—will be compromised. The Seventh Sonata, also full of imperious fanfares, requires the same pianistic approach, for instance in passages such as mm. 12*ff*.

25. An explication of Liszt's pianistic innovations can be found in the chapter "Liszt and the Keyboard" in Alan Walker, *Franz Liszt, Volume One: The Virtuoso Years, 1811–1847*, revised edition (Ithaca: Cornell University Press, 1987), 285–318.

26. Scott Holden, "Finding the Essence of Late Scriabin in His Tenth Sonata," in Richard Paul Anderson, ed., *The Pianist's Craft: Mastering the Works of Great Composers* (Lanham, MD: Scarecrow Press, 2012), 178–79.

CHAPTER 11: LINE AND MELODY

1. See "David Matthews: Complete String Quartets, Volume Three" (Toccata Classics OTCC 0060, 2014).

2. Sigfried Schibli, *Alexander Scriabin und seine Musik: Grenzüberschreitungen eines prometheischen Geistes* (Munich and Zurich, 1983), 174, as quoted in Alexander Skrjabin, *Sämtliche Klaviersonaten I* BA9616, ed. Christoph Flamm (Kassel: Bärenreiter, 2011), lii.

3. The affective quality of intervallic tensions refers to a concept known in Russian as *intonatsiia*; see John Bell Young's description in chapter 1.

4. For a detailed look at the desynchronization of hands in Scriabin's performance, see Anatole Leikin, *The Performing Style of Alexander Scriabin* (Burlington, VT: Ashgate, 2011), esp. pp. 26 and 52–53.

5. *Alexander Scriabin*, Vladimir Horowitz, piano (CBS Masterworks MK 42411, 1987).

6. There is considerable research to advocate for the agogic interpretation of hairpins in Romantic music, especially involving a lingering tempo, even though the practice has not gained traction in much modern playing and pedagogy. See for instance David Hyun-su Kim, "The Brahmsian Hairpin," *19th-Century Music* 36/1 (Summer 2012): 46–56, and Roberto Poli, *The Inner Life of Musical Notation: Defying Interpretive Traditions* (Milwaukee: Amadeus Press, 2010) for two recent discussions.

7. Jonathan Powell, Skryabin [Scriabin], Aleksandr Nikolayevich, *Grove Music Online*, accessed August 20, 2015, http://www.oxfordmusiconline.com/.

8. Adolph Bernhard Marx, *Die Lehre von der Musikalicher Komposition*, in four volumes (Leipzig: Breitkopf und Härtel, 1837, 1838, 1845, and 1847). See Birgitte Plesner Vinding

Moyer, "Concepts of Musical Form in the Nineteenth Century: With Special Reference to A. B. Marx and Sonata Form" (Ph.D. diss., Stanford University, 1986).

9. Garcia describes this as "a fluid, improvisatory rhythmic style, exhibiting such devices as arpeggiated chords, ties that regularly obscure downbeats, and a rhythmic preference for triplets, [which] encourages a mood of passivity and languor by negating a strong metrical and harmonic sense." Susanna Garcia, "Scriabin's Symbolist Plot Archetype in the Late Piano Sonatas," *19th-Century Music* 23/3 (Spring 2000): 281.

10. See Rebecca Mitchell, *Nietzsche's Orphans: Music, Metaphysics, and the Twilight of the Russian Empire* (New Haven: Yale University Press, 2015), 67–89, for a detailed exegesis on Scriabin's philosophical activities and his obsession with the trope of unity.

11. See, for example, ibid., 81.

12. Susanna Garcia traces this procedure as a typical appearance of a flight motive, "usually a rhythmically compressed fragment of the erotic theme . . . (imparting) a sense of activity and motion on material that earlier appeared in a static and languorous form" (Garcia, 284).

13. The neatness of Scriabin's calligraphy, and its implications on Scriabin's clarity of intent and lucidity of procedure is the spin-off for an excellent article by Simon Nicholls at http://www.scriabin-association.com/the-texts-of-scriabins-works-some-observations-of-a-performer-researcher-teacher/.

14. Liadov went on to grumble, "in some of his most recent works he has penetrated into such thickets that I simply refuse to analyze those works." See Sergei Prokofiev, *Prokofiev by Prokofiev: A Composer's Memoir* (New York: Doubleday, 1979): 238. Also of interest is critic Grigorii Prokofiev's review in the *Russian Musical Gazette*: "Even in his most off moments we still know that we are in the presence of a great talent and an artist. . . . Try correcting his musical grammar or logic, and you will find the mistakes in *you*, not him." Quoted in Faubion Bowers, *Scriabin: A Biography* (Mineola, NY: Dover, 1996), 2:196.

15. Sergei Ivanovitch Taneyev, *Convertible Counterpoint in the Strict Style*, trans. G. Ackley Brower (Boston: Bruce Humphries, 1962).

16. See Leikin, 32–33, for more on Scriabin's linear thinking. Leikin considers that this way of thinking enters Scriabin's performance style also in the way he spreads chords.

17. See, for example, Op. 25 No. 2, mm. 5–8, Op. 25 No. 5 mm. 89–96, and Op. 25 No. 7 mm. 65–72.

18. See Bowers, *Scriabin: A Biography*, 1:239.

19. Descending chromatic lines in mm. 33–39 of this sonata recall similar descending lines in the Finale of the Third. See also mm. 167*ff*, where the suavely written left hand part, while being natural to play, offers both melody and accompaniment all on its own.

20. From a pianistic standpoint, this writing resembles the idea from Chopin's Etude Op. 10 No. 2 in A minor, but in a more convenient descending shape.

CHAPTER 12: HARMONY

1. See Larry Sitsky, *Music of the Repressed Russian Avant-Garde, 1900–1929* (Westport, CT: Greenwood Press, 1994), 291–300, for details on Sabaneev the composer.

2. Varvara Dernova, "Garmoniya Skryabina," translated in Taruskin, "Scriabin and the Superhuman," in *Defining Russia Musically*, 330. An example of a walk-around is proposed in Taruskin, 338–40. Presumably, Scriabin means a chord that can be "walked around" is highly flexible in function when inverted, transposed, or reinterpreted enharmonically.

3. See "Richter—Volume Ten" (Melodiya BMG Richter Edition 74321 29470-2, 2005).

4. Notable examples of chorale style can be found in the second and fourth movements of the Sonata in F minor Op. 6, the Prelude in C Op. 13 No. 1, the Preludes Op. 16 No. 3, No. 4, and Op. 22 No. 2, and notably the second movement theme of the Piano Concerto Op. 20.

5. Numerous instances of commingling many pitches in one pedal are explored in Anatole Leikin, *The Performing Style of Alexander Scriabin* (Burlington, VT: Ashgate, 2011), 35.

6. A few more of many such examples can be found in the Prelude for the Left Hand in C♯ minor Op. 9 No. 1 and in the Prelude in E♭ major Op. 11 No. 19.

7. See also the coda of the Sonata-fantasy in G♯ minor Op. 19 (m. 46*ff* and m. 122*ff*), the opening of the Fourth Sonata's *Prestissimo*, and the *Presto con allegrezza* m. 47 of the Fifth Sonata, among others.

8. Tchaikovsky writes simply, "The augmented chord of the sixth resolves into the tonic triad," in Chapter XXVII, paragraph 99a, in *Guide to the Practical Study of Harmony*, trans. Krall and Liebling (Canoga Park, CA: Summit Publishing, 1970), 106. How ironic, then, that the most widely quoted example of an augmented sixth resolving directly to the tonic in the standard repertoire would be by Tchaikovsky's nemesis Brahms, in the Chaconne theme of the Finale to his Fourth Symphony.

9. Prokofiev's First Sonata—in dark and stormy F minor like Scriabin's First—ends with this same progression, and thus reveals further its stylistic debt to Scriabin and his Russian progenitors.

10. See Roy J. Guenther, "Varvara Dernova's Garmoniia Skriabina: A Translation and Critical Commentary" (Ph.D. dissertation, Catholic University of America, 1979), and Guenther, "Varvara Dernova's System of Analysis of the Music of Skryabin," in *Russian Theoretical Thought in Music*, ed. Gordon D. McQuere (Ann Arbor: UMI Research Press, 1983), 165–216. See also Jay Reise, "Late Skriabin: Some Principles Behind the Style," *19th-Century Music* 6/3 (Spring 1983): 220–31, for another evaluation of Dernova's work.

11. See Gordon D. McQuere, "The Theories of Boleslav Yavorsky," 109–64, in McQuere, *Russian Theoretical Thought in Music*.

12. The symmetrical relationships observed via this tritone relationship foretell the envisioning of tonal harmony in terms of geometrical space. See Dmitri Tymoczko, *A Geometry of Music: Harmony and Counterpoint in the Extended Common Practice* (New York: Oxford University Press, 2011). The tritone substitution in particular is discussed in 360–65.

13. In his historical survey of augmented sixths, Mark Ellis writes, "These geographical names appear to have originated in the early nineteenth century and reflect only the vaguest of actual national usage. John Calcott's *Grammar of Music* . . . identifies by name these national variants . . . in London in 1806." Mark Ellis, *A Chord in Time: The Evolution of the Augmented Sixth from Monteverdi to Mahler* (Burlington, VT: Ashgate, 2010), 1.

14. Carl Dahlhaus, *Nineteenth-Century Music* (Berkeley: University of California Press, 1989), 382. In his critique of Scriabin's style, 382–84, Dahlhaus cites a number of ideas traced to Scriabin's thought that have since been called into question; see the section on the Mystic Chord for details.

15. "For me there is no more difference between melody and harmony. Both are one and the same." Leonid Sabaneev, *Erinnerungen an Alexander Skrjabin* [Reminiscences of Scriabin] (Berlin: Ernst Kuhn, 2005), 55.

16. See James Baker, *The Music of Alexander Scriabin* (New Haven: Yale University Press, 1986).

17. After accepting inversional equivalence, one can quickly spot surprising relationships such as the intervallic identity of the mystic and *Extase* chords. This fact must have inspired a fascinating thought experiment, whereby Scriabin scholar Luigi Verdi published an intervallically inverted version of *Désir* Op. 57 No. 2. See *Journal of the Scriabin Society of America* 9/1 (Winter 2004–05): 100.

18. One discourse from the vast cultural and analytical literature on the Tristan chord that relates closely to Scriabin is Richard Taruskin's article "Scriabin and the Superhuman: A Millennial Essay," 324–28, in Taruskin, *Defining Russia Musically* (Princeton: Princeton University Press, 1997).

19. Translated in Alexander Skrjabin, *Piano Sonata No. 4 in F♯ major, Opus 30*, G. Henle Verlag 1110, ed. Valentina Rubtsova (Munich, 2014), 17.

20. This enharmonic chord acts very differently from the Tristan chord, being not an augmented sixth but rather a relative of the viio7 of the previous measure.

21. For example, in mm. 1–2, the resolution of the chord is at best indirect. In m. 9 and m. 11, partial resolution is offered through an augmented chord (as in Op. 27 No. 1), but in mm. 4, 6, and 20, the resolution is quite blunt (as in Op. 13 No. 1).

22. See Hugh Macdonald, *Skryabin* (Oxford: Oxford University Press, 1978), 37.

23. The concentric semitone voice-leading makes this a perfect fit for the theories of Boleslav Yavorsky. See Gordon D. McQuere, "The Theories of Boleslav Yavorsky," in McQuere, *Russian Theoretical Thought in Music*, 109–64.

24. For example, at the end of the development section, he uses the chord as retrogression ($Sc^{+6} \rightarrow IV_6$), passing chord ($IV_6 \rightarrow Sc^{+6} \rightarrow I6/4$), and final cadence ($Sc^{+6} \rightarrow I$).

25. That is, the 5ths, 9ths, or 13ths are chromatically adjusted, borrowed from mixed modes.

26. See Stuart Isacoff, "Scriabin's Mystic Chord," originally in "Jazz and Keyboard Workshop" as reprinted in *Journal of the Scriabin Society of America* 1/1 (Autumn 1996): 25–28.

27. Roy J. Guenther, "Varvara Dernova's System of Analysis of the Music of Skryabin," in *Russian Theoretical Thought in Music*, ed. Gordon D. McQuere (Ann Arbor: UMI Research Press, 1983), 180.

28. Richard Taruskin, "Scriabin and the Superhuman: A Millennial Essay," in *Defining Russia Musically*, 324–28.

29. Kenneth Smith, *Skryabin, Philosophy and the Music of Desire*, Royal Musical Association Monographs (Surrey, England: Ashgate 2013), where especially pp. 108*ff* chart philosophical ramifications in detail.

30. Mitchell B. Morris, "Musical Eroticism and the Transcendent Strain: The Works of Alexander Skryabin, 1898–1908" (Ph.D. diss., University of California, Berkeley, 1998).

31. It is employed in sequence in measures 13, 15, and 17, and then prominently in the Coda in m. 23.

32. The tendency for this harmony and tonality to coincide may be an argument in favor of Scriabin's key-color imagination, or perhaps—more cynically—for the tendency of his fingers to feel certain configurations on the keyboard. We have already observed the wailing chromatic descent pattern recurring in the key of E minor and the angry, turbulent nature of the G minor pieces with their Tristanesque harmonies. There are similar correspondences in his music to be traced also in C major, F♯ major, and B major.

33. For more on Scriabin's orthography, see Cheong Wai-Ling, "Orthography in Scriabin's Late Works," *Music Analysis* 12/1 (March 1993): 47–69; and David Tomasacci, "A Theory of

Orthography and the Fundamental Bass for the Late Oeuvre of Scriabin" (Ph.D. diss., Ohio State University, 2013).

34. The Scriabin Sixth is also a whole-tone sonority, though not a dominant: an early piece of evidence of Scriabin's tendency toward modal thinking. The V7♯5 chord was singled out for a statistical study by the Soviets for its extraordinary frequency of use in middle-period Scriabin; see Bowers, *Scriabin: A Biography,* 1:89. The methodology strikes one as a precursor of our data age.

35. Boleslav Yavorsky, as cited in Bowers, *The New Scriabin: Enigma and Answers* (New York: St. Martin's Press, 1973), 141–42.

36. Taruskin, "Scriabin and the Superhuman: A Millennial Essay," 336.

37. Ibid., 338.

38. Ibid., 336.

39. See Taruskin's article "Chernomor to Kashchei: Marmonic Sorcery, or, Stravinsky's 'Angle,'" *Journal of the American Musicological Society* 38 (1985): 72–142, for the historical sources of this scale in Russian music of this time—particularly in Rimsky-Korsakov—and for its impact especially on Stravinsky. The scale is widespread at this time also in Debussy, Ravel, Bartók, and many others.

40. Olivier Messiaen, *The Technique of My Musical Language,* trans. John Satterfield (Paris: A. Leduc, 2001).

41. See Taruskin, "Chernomor to Kashchei: Marmonic Sorcery, or, Stravinsky's 'Angle,'" for details.

42. This octatonic version of the mystic chord is far more widespread in the piano music than the standard version with a major ninth. For example, it concludes the Sixth Sonata, opens the Seventh Sonata, and forms the evocative fiery ending of *Flammes sombres* Op. 73 No. 2.

43. For more on Scriabin's octatonicism, see, for example, Ellon D. Carpenter, "Scriabin's Octatonic Motives," *Journal of the Scriabin Society of America* 8/1 (Winter 2003–2004): 45–58.

44. Sabaneev, "Prometheus von Skrjabin," in *Der Blaue Reiter,* ed. Wassily Kandinsky and Franz Marc, new documentary edition by Klaus Lankheit (Munich: R. Piper and Co., 1965), 107–24. In English, "Scriabin's 'Prometheus'" in *The Blaue Reiter Almanac,* ed. Wassily Kandinsky and Franz Marc, new documentary edition by Klaus Lankheit (New York: Viking Press), 127–40. Also of interest is Sabaneev's article "Prometheus—A Preview," from *Muzyka* 1 (27 November 1910), translated with commentary by Don Louis Wetzel in *Journal of the Scriabin Society of America* 5/1 (Winter 2000–01): 97–105.

45. These are *Musical Quarterly* 2/4 (Oct. 1916), "The Pianoforte Sonatas of Scriabin," in *Musical Times* (1 December 1916): 539–42, and "The Mystic Chord," in *A Great Russian Tone-Poet: Scriabin* (London: Kegan Paul, 1921), Chapter IX.

46. Hull, *Musical Quarterly* 2/4 (Oct. 1916): 609.

47. For more on Newmarch, see P. Ross Bullock, *Rosa Newmarch and Russian Music in Late Nineteenth and Early Twentieth-Century England* (Farnham, England, 2009).

48. Newmarch wrote, "It is considered that these chords composed entirely of harmonies have a certain 'mystical' quality akin to the tone of a big bell in its lower registers, and that they excite a kind of radio-tension, stringing up the nerves, when they ascend to the higher registers." *Russian Review* 2/1, 160. She cites the "mystical chord" again on p. 166 and once more in the *Musical Times* of 1914, repeating similar phrases. This proselytizing by Newmarch

and Hull to raise awareness of Scriabin's works and revolutionary style gives a good sense of his impact in England in his last years.

49. See the colorful dialogue recounted in Olga Monighetti's memoirs, in Bowers, *Scriabin: A Biography*, 2:201–03, in which Scriabin laments the limitations on tuning imposed on a piano. See also Leonid Sabaneev, *Erinnerungen an Alexander Skrjabin* [Reminiscences of Scriabin] (Berlin: Ernst Kuhn, 2005), 185–88.

50. "Stravinsky . . . had an excellent grasp of Scriabin's methods, which had their basis not in 'odd-numbered overtones' (a widespread canard of the day) but in the same Russian common practices as Stravinsky's own." Taruskin, in *Stravinsky and the Russian Traditions: A Biography of the Works through Mavra* (University of California Press, 1996), 796. This chapter "Stravinsky and Scriabin" is an excellent source regarding Stravinsky's conflicted relationship with Scriabin's legacy.

51. Taruskin, "Scriabin and the Superhuman," 342.

52. Morrison, "Skryabin and the Impossible," *Journal of the American Musicological Society* 51/2 (July 1998): 314, fn61.

53. According to Rebecca Mitchell, "While Maria Lobanova argues that Scriabin's sketches for *Prometheus* demonstrate that this was Scriabin's approach, Sabaneev claimed that Scriabin was unaware of this connection until he drew the composer's attention to it." Mitchell, *Nietzsche's Orphans: Music, Metaphysics, and the Twilight of the Russian Empire* (New Haven, CT: Yale University Press, 2016), 257. See Marina Lobanova, "Zahlen, Mystik, Magie: Neueste Erkentnisse zu Skrjabins Promethee," *Das Orchester* 50/1 (January 2002): 8; Sabaneev, *Vospominaniia o Skriabine* [Reminiscences of Scriabin] (Moscow: Klassika-XXI, 2000), 114, as cited in Mitchell.

54. Taruskin, "Scriabin and the Superhuman," 339–40. The intervallic identity between the inverted "Extase chord" and the Mystic chord is made apparent by the methodology of pc-set analysis, where this almost whole-tone collection is known as 6–34. See Allen Forte, *The Structure of Atonal Music* (New Haven: Yale University Press, 1973).

55. Sabaneev, to his credit, also presents the harmony as deriving first from a mode, particularly in the *Muzyka* article. His version has only six pitches, omitting the fifth, as in figure 12.14a.

56. Thanks to Jay Reise for suggesting this coinage.

57. Sabaneev, "'Prometei' Skriabina," *Muzyka* 13 (26 February 1911): 286–94, here 289–90, as cited in Mitchell, *Nietzsche's Orphans*, 257, fn107.

58. Mitchell, *Nietzsche's Orphans*, 88–90.

59. Ibid., 88.

60. Jim Samson, *Music in Transition: A Study of Tonal Expansion and Atonality, 1900–1920* (New York: Norton, 1977).

61. The death harmonies of the *Mysterium* are quoted and discussed in Manfred Kelkel, *Alexandre Scriabine: Sa vie, l'ésotérisme et le langage musical dans son oeuvre*, 3:173–200, and Morrison, "Scriabin and the Impossible," 313ff.

62. Hull, *A Great Russian Tone-Poet: Scriabin*, 105.

63. Sabaneev, "Scriabin's 'Prometheus'" in *The Blaue Reiter Almanac*, 135. It is true that *Prometheus* itself is quite tightly connected to this specific harmony, to the point that the *luce* part makes a harmonic analysis of a piece in terms of mystic chord roots. See Gawboy and Townsend, "Scriabin and the Possible," *Music Theory Online* 18/2 (June 2012): para. 19. Online at http://mtosmt.org/issues/mto.12.18.2/mto.12.18.2.gawboy_townsend.html. Accessed 28 October 2016.

64. Likely Bowers was referring to Perle, *Serial Composition and Atonality: An Introduction to the Music of Schoenberg, Berg, and Webern*, 5th rev. ed. (Berkeley 1981), 41–43. But as Taruskin points out, most of Perle's observations about the "derived heptatonic" could be made of any cycle-of-thirds piece. See Taruskin, "Chernomor to Kashchei: Harmonic Sorcery, or Stravinsky's 'Angle,'" *Journal of the American Musicological Society* 38/1 (1985): 129. On Perle's article, see also Samson, *Music in Transition*, 209.

65. Reise, "Late Skriabin: Some Principles Behind the Style," *19th-Century Music* 6/3 (Spring 1983): 221.

66. Ibid.

67. For more detail on Scriabin's use of modes and passage among them, see Luigi Verdi, "Harmonic Spaces in Skrjabin's Late Music," *Journal of the Scriabin Society of America* 9/1 (Winter 2004–05): 101–06, and Cheong Wai-Ling, "Scriabin's 'White Mass': A Dialogue Between the 'Mystic' and the Octatonic," *Journal of the Scriabin Society of America* 5/1 (Winter 2000–2001): 69–93.

68. Bowers, *Scriabin: A Biography*, 2:244.

69. Ibid.

70. See Mitchell, *Nietzsche's Orphans*, 80–85.

71. The story is related in Taruskin, "Scriabin and the Superhuman," 341.

72. Morrison, "Skryabin and the Impossible," 314.

73. Kelkel, 3:173–200.

74. Morrison, "Skryabin and the Impossible," 315.

75. See Taruskin, "Eschatological Torsos," in "Scriabin and the Superhuman," 349–59, and Ballard, "Scriabin and Ives: An Unanswered Question?" *Journal of the Scriabin Society of America* 9/1 (Winter 2004–05): 37–62.

76. See Sitsky, 248–53, for information on Vyshnegradsky.

CHAPTER 13: THE SCRIABIN SOUND

1. Randlett, "Elements of Scriabin's Keyboard Style," *Piano Quarterly* (Winter 1970–1971): 21.

2. Alexander Pasternak, "Skryabin: Summer 1903 and After," *Musical Times* (December 1972): 1173.

3. Nataliya Sukhina, "Alexander Scriabin (1871–1915): Piano Miniature as Chronicle of his Creative Evolution. Complexity of Interpretive Approach and its Implications" (Ph.D. diss., University of North Texas, Denton, 2012), 31.

4. Scriabin's student Maria Nemenova-Lunz recalled, "One often hears from the school of 'shattering pianism' how Scriabin lacked strength. It is true that he did not have a 'frightening fortissimo.' He did not much like 'materialistic' sonority. He always said that the deepest *forte* must always *sound* soft." Quoted in Bowers, *Scriabin: A Biography*, 2:145–46. Nemenova-Lunz (1879–1954, also spelled as "Nemenova-Luntz") later served as professor at the Moscow Conservatory (1922–1954). She is the author of memoirs on Scriabin as teacher and pianist (*Muzykal'nyi sovremennik* 4, 1916). According to Heinrich Neuhaus, Scriabin asked her once to repeat a measure 50 times! See Christopher Barnes, trans. and ed., *The Russian Piano School* (London: Kahn and Averill, 2007), 115.

5. Alfred J. Swan, *Russian Music and its Sources in Chant and Folk-Song* (London: John Baker, 1973), 148. Liszt made similar remarks in his teachings.

6. See, for example, Grigory Prokofiev's review in the *Russian Musical Gazette* on Scriabin's last Moscow performance in 1915: "His ethereal sounds cannot quite fill the hall." Quoted in Bowers, *The New Scriabin: Enigma and Answers* (New York: St. Martin's Press, 1973), 197.

7. Victor I. Seroff, *Rachmaninoff* (New York: Simon and Schuster, 1950), 169.

8. Alexander Pasternak, "Skryabin," 1173.

9. Caswell Collection, Vol. 5 (1906–1926). Pierian Recording Society: PIR0018.

10. "Scriabine and the Scriabinians," Harmonia Mundi LDC 288032, 1992.

11. Vladimir Horowitz also played for Scriabin, at the age of 11, and although clearly he had not reached artistic maturity, Scriabin's observation of his talent can be interpreted as a sign of artistic approval or kinship. See David Dubal, *Evenings with Horowitz: A Personal Portrait* (Secaucus, NJ: Carol Publishing Group, 1991), 4–6. Among Scriabin's students, one of the finest performers and interpreters of his music was Yelena Bekmann-Shcherbina (1882–1951).

12. Quoted in Bowers, *Scriabin: A Biography*, 2:233.

13. N. Cherkass, *Skryabin kak pianist i fortepiannyi Kompozitor* (Petrograd, 1916), as described in Bowers, *The New Scriabin*, 199–202.

14. Quoted in Bowers, *The New Scriabin*, 200. This entire chapter "In Performance" (195–204) contains an interesting profile of Scriabin's pianism. In evaluating Cherkass's critique, we must consider he was a highly conservative pedagogue and likely reluctant to accept a new style of pianism that violated long-standing dogmas.

15. Bowers, *The New Scriabin*, 202.

16. The term is employed here not in the sense of a proper French performance style, but rather in the negative sense of what Debussy considered "a convenient term of abuse," which he himself disavowed. This flaccid style without clear and clean fingerwork is also rarely appropriate or effective in the interpretation of Debussy's music.

17. These gendered terms are explored elsewhere in Susanna Garcia, "Scriabin's Symbolist Plot Archetype in the Late Piano Sonatas," *19th-Century Music* 23/3 (Spring 2000): especially 287–89, and in Kenneth Smith, *Skryabin, Philosophy and the Music of Desire* (Surrey, England: Ashgate, 2013).

18. For a detailed description of these qualities of attack, varying depth and key speed, see Holden, "Finding the Essence of Late Scriabin in His Tenth Sonata," in Richard Paul Anderson, ed., *The Pianist's Craft: Mastering the Works of Great Composers* (Lanham, MD: Scarecrow Press, 2012), 182.

19. Leikin, *The Performing Style of Alexander Scriabin* (Burlington, VT: Ashgate, 2011), 42.

20. Ibid., 37.

21. See Christopher Barnes, and Boris Pasternak, "Pasternak as Composer and Scriabin-Disciple," *Tempo* 121 (1977): 13–25.

22. Leonid Pasternak, "Summer of 1903," *Novy Mir* 1 (1972): 209–10, trans. Leikin, 37.

23. Alexander Pasternak, "Skryabin: Summer 1903 and After," 1173. Also of interest is Pasternak's analysis of Scriabin's posture: "The character of his playing was inseparably connected with the way he sat at the instrument. He always sat somewhat farther from the keyboard than is usual, leaning back, his head up. That is why it seemed like his fingers were not actually touching the notes. All this ensured the lightness and resonance which were the essence and charm of his playing, and that twittering of little birds which was so necessary to him" (1174).

24. Sabaneev wrote, "His tone was so intimate that at the back of a large hall in *pianissimo* you could no longer hear it." Leonid Sabaneev, *Erinnerungen an Alexander Skrjabin* [Remi-

niscences of Scriabin] (Berlin: Ernst Kuhn, 2005), 52. A London critic wrote sardonically of his delicate performance of dainty miniatures, which "it would only be possible to enjoy in comfort if one could kidnap the composer and insist upon a recital all to oneself by firelight." Anon., "M. Scriabine's 'Wrong Notes': Studies for a Firelight Recital," *London Times* (27 March 1914), 13.

25. Playing these difficult notes is only the starting point to achieving this sense. These swirling textures can be found in the finale to the Second Sonata, the arpeggio figurations in the *Fantasie* Op. 28, and the Etudes Op. 42. The recording of these Etudes by Arthur Greene (Prague: Supraphon, 1996) exemplifies this ecstatic swirled sound and retains a clear control of polyphony.

26. Prokofiev, quoted in David Gutman, *Prokofiev* (London: Alderman Press, 1988), 52.

27. See Marilyn Nonken, *The Spectral Piano: From Liszt, Scriabin and Debussy to the Digital Age* (Cambridge: Cambridge University Press, 2014), 43–44, for a historical sketch that traces this way of listening to the days of acoustical research. See chapter 7 for more on bells.

28. Dane Rudhyar, "The Mystic's Living Tone," *Modern Music* 7/3 (April–May 1930): 33–35.

29. Samuel Randlett, "Elements of Scriabin's Keyboard Style" in *Piano Quarterly* (Winter 1970–1971): 22. He also offers a selection of examples of the phenomenon in *Piano Quarterly* (Summer 1971), 22–26. As with the trill, Beethoven may have been a spiritual father of this technique, although his specific pianistic means were different. See the discussion of his "pulsating vibration" in Konrad Wolff, *Masters of the Keyboard* (Bloomington: Indiana University Press, 1990), 128–39.

30. The volume aspect is the most difficult among these, and is the most open to interpretation in particular cases. If the chords are put too much in the background to the melody, some visceral excitement may be lost. For example, in the big *fff appassionato* climax in the *Fantasie* Op. 28, mm. 129–32, the chords need to be struck firmly to achieve the density of attacks needed for an effective climax.

31. As often also in Liszt's music, this kind of error has had the unfortunate tendency of injuring the composer's image while enhancing the performer's reputation with uneducated audiences. A model example for how to treat these passages can be found in Margarita Fyodorova's magisterial performance of the *Poème tragique* Op. 34, a work rarely performed and still more rarely done justice. Live recording in Florida, 1992: https://www.youtube.com/watch?v=Os_nVHqwE8I.

32. Alexander Dubuc, *Memories of John Field, with an Introduction by M. Balakirev*, Knizhka Nedeli ("Weekly Booklets"), Moscow, 1898, cited in Patrick Piggott, *The Life and Music of John Field 1782–1837* (London: Faber and Faber, 1973), 272.

33. An introduction to Anton's Rubinstein's career and pianism can be found in Reginald Gerig, *Famous Pianists and Their Technique* (Bloomington: Indiana University Press, 2007), 290–96.

34. John Bell Young's unique reading of the Seventh Sonata is notable for the clarity of its layered counterpoints, and this particular passage especially shines. John Bell Young, *Prisms: Scriabin, Tolstoy, Mahler, Downs, Block* (Americus Records, AMR 19991013, 1999).

35. One rare exception is the recent Australian-built Stuart and Sons piano.

36. Leikin, *The Performing Style of Alexander Scriabin*, 104.

37. "Tone color" in *The New Harvard Dictionary of Music*, ed. Don Randel (Cambridge: Harvard University Press, 1986), 863.

38. Scriabin owned a Bechstein piano, still at the Scriabin Museum in Moscow. He also played Bechsteins most frequently in his later years, most notably in his acclaimed London concerts.

39. A bright piano can make soft dynamics hard to control. However, an instrument with overly soft hammers can leave a pianist with limited resources, especially in Scriabin. I once felt very dissatisfied with my playing of the Sixth Sonata on a small and mellow piano, where it was difficult to find variety in the sound. Shortly thereafter, on a concert grand that was brighter than I would usually prefer, the opening bell strikes had the stern and ominous quality they needed because of the increased complexity of tone offered by this larger instrument.

40. "At seven Shurinka [the young Alexander] began to make toy pianos. . . . He always gave them away to the first visitor who admired them. And as soon as he completed a perfect one, his interest lapsed. . . . Shurinka also wrote playlets." Bowers, *Scriabin: A Biography*, 1:111–12.

41. Safonov is here quoted by Heinrich Neuhaus in *The Art of Piano Playing* (London: Barrie and Jenkins, 1973), 166.

42. Bowers, *The New Scriabin*, 197.

43. Sabaneev, *Erinnerungen an Alexander Skrjabin*, 52.

44. Samuel Feinberg, *Pianism as Art*, second ed. (Moscow: State Music Publishing House, 1969), 107–8, quoted in Rimm, 109–10.

45. Maria Nemenova-Lunz, "Iz vospominaniy uchenitsy" [From Reminiscences of a Student], typescript; State Scriabin Museum, no. 8, pp. 5, 8–9, as cited in Leikin, 15.

46. See Leikin, *The Performing Style of Alexander Scriabin* for many detailed insights on Scriabin's pedaling choices on these rolls, of which perhaps the most interesting are his decisions at times to use little or no pedal.

47. Konstantin Igumnov, quoted by Heinrich Neuhaus in Barnes, *The Russian Piano School*, 166. I recall feeling disappointment in one lesson for a student's unimaginative pedaling of this work. It turned out that he was literally following the editor's suggestions.

48. When Debussy heard the elderly Liszt play the piano, he "recalled that Liszt used the pedal sparingly, 'like a form of breathing.'" Alan Walker, *Franz Liszt: The Final Years, 1861–1886* (Ithaca: Cornell University Press, 1996), 476. See Nonken, *The Spectral Piano*, 44 in relation to pedal "breathing" in Scriabin's music.

49. Another case of the same phenomenon can be found in the Eighth Sonata, mm. 258–61.

50. See also the Prelude for the Left Hand Op. 9 No. 1, mm. 16–18, where every marked rest should probably entail a gradual fadeout by sensitive fluttering rather than an abrupt silence. In this way, the release to a single note A in m. 18 completes a convincingly tapered dynamic shape.

51. Prominent examples include the Seventh Sonata (*extatique* in mm. 252*ff*, and at the ending), the final measures of the Eighth Sonata (*doux, languissant*) and the numerous sustained cluster-trills in the Tenth Sonata, such as the passage *avec élan lumineux vibrant* from mm. 258*ff.*

52. This technique is also significant in the French tradition, in Debussy and subsequently in the detailed pedal indications of Boulez, Takemitsu, and many others.

53. Nonken, *The Spectral Piano*, 10.

54. Ibid., 2.

55. Ibid., 44.

CHAPTER 14: RHYTHM

1. Review in the *Russian Musical Gazette*, 1915, quoted in Bowers, *The New Scriabin: Enigma and Answers* (New York: St. Martin's Press, 1973), 197.
2. Intensive statistical studies of Scriabin's reviews were performed by Tatyana Shaborkina, longtime director of the Scriabin Museum in Moscow; see her 1940 article "Notes on Scriabin the Performer," as quoted in Bowers, *Scriabin: A Biography* (New York: Dover, 1996), 1:92. The list is quite revealing: "arhythmical," "nervous," "magical," "wizard-like colors," "pedalization," "tonal lights," "pauses," and "silences full of thought" (Bowers, *The New Scriabin*, 197). See *Birzhevye vedomosti* (14 February 1894), and César Cui, 'Nachinayushchy kompozitor,' *Nedelya* (12 March 1895), as cited in Anatole Leikin, *The Performing Style of Alexander Scriabin* (Burlington, VT: Ashgate, 2011), 28.
3. Jean-Jacques Eigeldinger, *Chopin: Pianist and Teacher* (Cambridge: Cambridge University Press, 1986), 50.
4. Ibid., 49. See also Eigeldinger, 181–83, for more information on her. Chopin's student Karol Mikuli had a similar experience, and remarked, "in keeping time Chopin was inexorable . . . the metronome never left his piano" (ibid., 49).
5. James Methuen-Campbell, *Chopin Playing, From the Composer to the Present Day* (New York: Taplinger, 1981), 30.
6. Comment to Sabaneev on the playing of Evgeny Gvozdkov in Sabaneev, *Erinnerungen an Alexander Skrjabin* [Reminiscences of Scriabin] (Berlin: Ernst Kuhn, 2005), 334. Weighing the evidence in Eigeldinger's book, it seems unlikely that Chopin would have sanctioned "distorting rhythm as much as one wants." Thus, Scriabin's views could be considered somewhat more liberal than those of Chopin. Chopin's students criticized the rhythmic practices of the pianists in this era. Eigeldinger goes so far as to label "generations of pianists subsequent to Chopin's" as "victims of a pseudo-tradition," who "submitted his music to agogic distortions in the name of the vague and convenient term 'rubato.' This practice was in vogue from before the second half of the nineteenth century up to the 1930s." Eigeldinger 118, fn92.
7. Scriabin, quoted in Sabaneev, *Erinnerungen an Alexander Skrjabin*, 187. The metaphor of breathing is a clear echo of comments about his pedaling; see chapter 13, "The Scriabin Sound."
8. "The Caswell Collection, Vol. 5 (1906–1926), Pierian Recording Society: PIR0018, and *Scriabine and the Scriabinians*, Harmonia Mundi LDC 288032, 1992.
9. In some music, the entire notion of an *Urtext* edition is a questionable construct, since no final and definitive version exists. In such cases, an edition such as this one, giving variants, represents the ideal scenario. This phenomenon tends to occur in works where ornamentation plays a prominent role, such as Bach's French Suites, or varied ornamentations in Mozart and Chopin.
10. Bowers, *The New Scriabin*, 198.
11. In Scriabin's recordings, "a four- or five-fold differential between the slowest and the fastest tempo within the same piece is common." Leikin, *The Performing Style of Alexander Scriabin*, 27.
12. See Neal Peres da Costa, *Off the Record: Performing Practices in Romantic Piano Playing* (Oxford: Oxford University Press, 2012).
13. See Leikin, 5–18, and also da Costa, *Off the Record*, 9–40.
14. Bowers, *Scriabin: A Biography*, 1:91.

15. See Leikin, 27–31. These include marking off formal sections with a different tempo (29), quickening the tempo for ascending melody, relaxing it for a descent (29), combining *cresc.* with *accel.* and *rit.* with *dimin* (52). I would add: holding the tempo to highlight an interesting harmony, or to announce an assertive fanfare (*zov*), pushing the tempo to depict a burst of energy (*poriv*), holding the tempo for a melody, and pushing it for a less interesting accompaniment, and finally, pushing the tempo to sustain the middle of the phrase, and holding it at the cadence.

16. Freedom of rhythmic declamation is among a handful of apparently old-fashioned liberties that have made something of a comeback in some Bach performances on both modern and early instruments.

17. The rhythm in the *Stichvorlage* is quite plainly a series of eighths, but the spacing of the pitches is unequal. A missing dot in the corresponding rhythm four bars later, the disagreement with the rhythm of the corresponding m. 12, and the blatant carelessness of the E♯/E♭ clash in the following measure are all factors that call this rhythm into question.

18. Leikin, *The Performing Style of Alexander Scriabin*, 38.

19. The airplane was the ultimate expression of the Italian Futurists' obsession with movement, speed, and power. These influences were keenly felt by the Russian avant-garde, both in the art of the Cubo-Futurists (Burliuk, Larionov, Goncharova, Malevich) and in literary works such as Merezhkovsky's *Icarus*. Tragically, the airplane would prove not to be a vehicle for spiritual ascent, but rather a lethal weapon of death in the Great War.

20. See for instance: Prelude in G minor Op. 37 No. 4, Etude in E♭ Op. 42 No. 8, Prelude in E♭ Op. 45 No. 3, Prelude in D♭ Op. 48 No. 3, and Prelude Op. 59 No. 2.

21. Leikin, 2. He quotes William W. Austin, *Music in the 20th Century* (New York: Norton, 1966), 68, 71–72; Richard Anthony Leonard, *A History of Russian Music* (New York: Macmillan, 1957), 220; and David Burge, *Twentieth-Century Piano Music* (New York: Schirmer Books, 1990), 56. Along these lines, one might quibble with Scriabin's "bookish" adherence to sonata forms (see Aaron Copland's critique in chapter 3). Leikin accepts the characterization of the compositions, remarking that "[examples of irregularity] constitute a relatively small portion of Scriabin's oeuvre. . . . Scriabin achieved phrase asymmetry and metric elasticity through performance rather than notation" (Leikin, 28).

22. See Leikin, 280–81, for some parallels and for Scriabin's personal interest in Schumann's music.

23. A noteworthy exception is the article "Numerical Symbolism in Some of Scriabin's Late Piano Works" by musicologist Luigi Verdi in *Journal of the Scriabin Society of America* 10/1 (Winter 2005–2006): 41–55, in which the author proposes an extremely detailed relationship between beat patterns and mathematical theories of Scriabin's early teacher Georgi Konyus. Intriguing though this hypothesis is, its wider applicability to Scriabin's earlier output is doubtful.

24. In this cycle of Op. 11 Preludes that clearly models Chopin's Op. 28, one can also hear an echo of the quintuplets and polyrhythms from the climax of Chopin's C major Prelude.

25. The Sixth Sonata, m. 168 is an extreme case: a 3/4 meter, whose quarters are split into triplet eighths, each of which is subsequently divided into still more sets of threes.

26. One of the most forbidding cases of rhythmic complexity is found in the Seventh Sonata, m. 29*ff.* The mixture of 6/8 and 3/4 meters already serves to undermine the idea of a regular accented pulse, but the syncopations in the left hand make it especially difficult to keep together. Thinking in 6/8 meter is a helpful strategy.

27. See David Schiff, *The Music of Elliott Carter* (Ithaca: Cornell University Press, 1998), 21.

28. To be as accurate as possible, one can give each note a percentage of the beat: 11 percent for 1/9 of a beat, 20 percent for 1/5 of a beat, etc., and then draw vertical lines to indicate alignments and the sequence of attacks.

29. Letter of Scriabin to Beliaev of 4 January 1895, quoted in Bowers, *Scriabin: A Biography*, 1:194.

30. Bowers, *Scriabin: A Biography*, 1:242–43. Belaiev is referring to Rimsky's harsh response to Scriabin's errors in the Piano Concerto manuscript. See chapter 4 for more details.

31. Leikin, *The Performing Style of Alexander Scriabin*, 56.

32. Ibid., 64.

33. Scriabin was enthusiastic about the multifarious expressive possibilities of his music. The short Prelude Op. 74 No. 2 was a special favorite piece at the end of his life, and he liked to vary the affect as he played it multiple times. See Sabaneev, *Erinnerungen an Alexander Skrjabin*, 351–53, and Bowers, *Scriabin: A Biography*, 2:265.

34. *Vladimir Horowitz Plays Scriabin* (1953–1956), IDIS 6602, and *Alexander Scriabin* (CBS Masterworks MK 42411, 1987), both with Vladimir Horowitz, piano.

35. Bowers, *Scriabin: A Biography*, 1:250.

36. Christoph Flamm wrote that "the published text sets down something akin to an abstract ideal that must, if necessary, be adapted to the technical skills of the performer in order to attain the desired expression." See Alexander Skrjabin: *Complete Piano Sonatas I*, ed. Christoph Flamm (New York: Bärenreiter, 2011), liv.

37. These include the Preludes Op. 11 Nos. 14, 18, 24; Op. 13 No. 2; and Op. 17 No. 5; and Etudes Op. 8 No. 12; Op. 42 No. 1; Op. 42 No. 8; Op. 49 No. 1; and Op. 56 No. 4. As always, it is sometimes possible to have too much of a good thing, and occasionally excessive speed can diminish from a work's excitement rather than add to it. Arguably, even the great Richter occasionally overshoots the mark, as in his Prelude Op. 13 No. 4, Etude Op. 42 No. 8, and Prelude Op. 59 No. 2.

38. Walter Gieseking, previously unissued public performances and broadcasts, from the collection of Deutsches Rundfunkarchiv (Music and Arts LC 1070).

39. Vladimir Sofronitsky, Melodiya LP D08779.

Glossary and Pronunciation Guide

Common usage has promoted Anglicized spellings of Russian names, which are used throughout this book for the sake of simplicity (e.g., Alexander vs. Aleksandr; Scriabin vs. Skryabin; Tchaikovsky vs. Chaikovski). This pronunciation guide is intended to be an intuitive and phonetic rendering of the original Cyrillic. Biographical sketches of the figures cited below focus on their relationship with Scriabin and their historical significance.

PRONUNCIATION KEY

ē	long "e," as in "*e*vil"
e	schwa, as in "op*e*n"
ô	as in "*o*ften"
o	as in "g*o*at"
g	hard "g," as in *g*ive

Altschuler [ALT-shoe-ler], *Modest* [mo-DEST] *Isakovich* [ee-SAH-kov-each] Модест Исакович Альтшулер (1873–1963)—Russian cellist and conductor who founded the Russian Symphony Society in New York City in 1903 and delivered the American premieres of Scriabin's symphonies. Most notable was Altschuler's world premiere of *Prometheus: Poem of Fire* with the color organ on 20 March 1915, at Carnegie Hall in New York City. Altschuler also advised Scriabin on orchestrating the *Poem of Ecstasy*.

Arensky [a-REN-skee], *Anton* [an-TÔN] *Stepanovich* [step-AHN-ov-each] Антон Степанович Аренский (1861–1906)—Russian composer, pianist, and conductor. Both of his parents were highly musical, and he graduated from the St. Petersburg Conservatory and composed many instrumental and vocal works. Arensky was Scriabin's teacher in harmony and counterpoint at the Moscow Conservatory, where he taught from 1882 until his early death in 1906. He famously refused to sign Scriabin's diploma in 1892 upon his graduation from the Moscow Conservatory.

Beethoven [BAY-toe-ven], *Ludwig van* [LUDE-vig fawn] (1770–1827)—German pianist and composer whose symphonies and piano sonatas imparted some influence on Scriabin in terms of their programmatic content and their development of germinal themes and motives. Scriabin claimed to dislike Beethoven's "muscular" works. Scriabin's solo piano sonatas are arguably the most consistent body in that genre since Beethoven's 32 solo piano sonatas.

Beliaev [be-lya-EYE-ev], *Mitrofan* [mee-trô-FAN] *Petrovich* [pet-ROVE-each] Митрофан Петрович Беляев (1836–1904)—Munificent patron of Russian music from 1894 until his death in 1904. His publishing firm was based in Leipzig and published the music of many Russian composers, including Scriabin. Beliaev made his fortune as a timber merchant and served as a surrogate father to Scriabin, providing counsel to help Scriabin with professional and personal difficulties. He established the Glinka Prize in 1892, which Scriabin won several times. His hulking frame made an almost comical contrast to Scriabin's dainty figure.

Blavatsky [blah-VAT-skee], *Helena* [yell-YEN-na] *Petrovna* [pet-ROVE-na] Елена Петровна Блаватская (1831-1891)—Russian-born occultist, spiritual medium, and cofounder of the Theosophical Society in 1875. She authored several books on Theosophy that directly influenced Scriabin's thinking and were noted influences on his *Poem of Ecstasy* and *Prometheus: Poem of Fire*, including *The Secret Doctrine* and *The Key to Theosophy*. Blavatsky's writings also provided inspiration for Scriabin's apocalyptic *Mysterium*.

Bowers, Faubion [FOE-bee-en] (1917–1999)—Oklahoma-born biographer who wrote two widely read books on the composer, *Scriabin: A Biography* (2 volumes, 1969) and *The New Scriabin: Enigma and Answers* (1973). Bowers served as aide-de-camp to General Douglas MacArthur in World War II, and was also a historian of Japanese kabuki theater. From 1951 to 1966, he was married to Santha Rama Rau, who wrote a screenplay for the novel, *A Passage to India*.

Chopin [SHOW-pan], *Frédéric* [FREH-drihk] (1810–1849)—Polish pianist-composer and a founding father of the Romantic style of pianism. Chopin cultivated a style that featured lush, chromatic chords supporting a lyrical, vocal-like melody. Aside from his two Piano Concertos and some scattered works, Chopin (like Scriabin) wrote almost exclusively for solo piano, and his published works favored the standard dance forms of the waltz, polonaise, and mazurka. Chopin was Scriabin's favorite composer as a child, and he emulated the Polish master in his attraction to salon-type forms and structures. Rather than showcasing virtuosity in their music, as Liszt did, Chopin and Scriabin focused on wistful charm and poetic expression.

Ciurlionis [Chur-lee-OWE-nees], *Mikalojus* [mik-a-LOW-is] (1875–1911)—Lithuanian painter of the Symbolist style who was also a musical prodigy (flute and piano) and composed nearly 400 pieces of music. Initially trained as a musician, Ciurlionis gained greater fame as a painter. Professing to be a synaesthete (a person with cross-modal sensory perception), Ciurlionis was as committed as Scriabin to dissolving the boundaries between the fine arts and achieving a synthetic art. Just as many of Scriabin's piano pieces utilize titles more suited to poetry, the canvases of Ciurlionis bear such titles as Nocturne, Fugue, Sonata, and Prelude.

Glazunov [gla-zu-NÔV], *Alexander Konstantinovich* [cons-tan-TEEN-ov-each] Александр Константинович Глазунов (1865–1936)—Russian conductor, pianist, professor of composition and orchestration at the St. Petersburg Conservatory, and its director from 1905 to 1930. Glazunov was also patronized by Beliaev early in his career, and he became one of the chief executors of Beliaev's publishing house following Beliaev's death in 1904. Among his notable pupils was Dmitri Shostakovich.

Haydn [HIGH-din], *Joseph* [YO-zef] (1732–1809)—Austrian composer nicknamed "Papa" who wrote 106 symphonies and compositions for nearly every major genre, both vocal and instrumental. He served as the Kapellmeister (Court Composer) for the Esterházy family from 1762 until his death in 1809. Haydn revolutionized chamber music and was known for interjecting humorous episodes and other surprises into his music, which introduced a new level of audience engagement in the Classic era. Haydn's oratorio *Die Schöpfung* (The Creation, 1797–1798) included one of the best-known representations of light in music.

Heyman [HAY-men], *Katherine Ruth Willoughby* (1877–1944)—American pianist, champion of Scriabin's music in the 1920s–1940s, founder of the Scriabin Circle and the Scriabin Society of America, and author of *The Relation of Ultramodern to Archaic Music* (1921), which includes important chapters on Debussy and Scriabin. Among her piano students was Faubion Bowers. An eccentric personality, Heyman was widely known as the "high priestess of the Scriabin cult," and her live performances of the composer's music were electrifying.

Horowitz [HÔ-roe-wits], *Vladimir* [vla-DEEM-ear] *Samoylovich* [sam-OYL-ov-each] Владимир Самойлович Горовиц (1903–1989)—Russian pianist who was among the greatest piano virtuosos of the twentieth century, and who tirelessly championed Scriabin's music, even in the decades when it was unfashionable to do so. Horowitz specialized in romantic repertory and recorded many of Scriabin's piano works, often playing them as encores. He performed for Scriabin as a young man in 1914 and was famously advised by the composer to become a "cultured" (i.e., well-rounded) artist.

Hull, Arthur Eaglefield (1876–1928)—British writer, critic, organist, and composer. Hull became the editor of the *Monthly Musical Record* and contributed widely to musical life in England in the early twentieth century. He wrote the first English-language biography of Scriabin, *A Great Russian Tone Poet* (1916), and famously coined the term "mystic chord" to describe the signature sonority so prominently featured in Scriabin's late compositions.

Ivanov [eve-AN-ôv], *Vyacheslav* [VYA-che-slav] *Vsevolodovich* [VSE-vo-lod-ov-each] Вячеслав Всеволодович Иванов (1866–1954)—Russian philosopher, Symbolist poet, and religious historian. In addition to sharing a view of art as revelatory and transcendent, Scriabin and Ivanov bonded over their admiration for ancient theater and art's important role in the coming revolution. One of the composer's closest late associates, Ivanov assisted Scriabin in the writing of his Prefatory Act, the precursor to the composer's *Mysterium*. After Scriabin's death, Ivanov was one of the staunchest defenders of his legacy.

Karatigin [car-a-TEE-gin], *Vyacheslav* [VYA-che-slav] *Gavrilovich* [gav-REEL-ov-each] Вячеслав Вячеслав Гаврилович Каратыгин (1875–1925)—St. Petersburg music critic and modern music advocate. He first learned music from his mother, who was a professional pianist. From 1907 to 1917, he was active as a music critic, and also taught aesthetics and music history at the Petrograd Conservatory from 1916. As a critic, he welcomed the music of Scriabin, Stravinsky, and Prokofiev at a time when many Russian critics saw them as negative influences. He advocated the idea of a "musical revolution." A prolific writer, he published monographs on Mussorgsky, Chaliapin, and Scriabin, and also wrote piano pieces and songs.

Koussevitzky [koo-se-VEET-skee], *Serge* [SURGE] *Alexandrovich* [all-ex-AN-drove-each] Сергей Александрович Кусевицкий (1874–1951)—Double bass player, conductor, and wealthy impresario who patronized Scriabin and published his compositions from 1910 to 1915. Koussevitzky married the heiress to a tea fortune, and continued to perform Scriabin's orchestral works long after the composer's death (and their personal falling out in 1911). Despite his lack of training in conducting, he earned distinction as one of the premier interpreters of Scriabin's symphonic works, especially the *Poem of Ecstasy*.

Lavoie-Herz [la-voy-HAIRTS], *Djane* [dee-ANN] (1889–1982)—Pianist and pedagogue who studied with Alfred La Liberté and Scriabin (both piano and Theosophy) in Brussels. Renowned for her interpretations of Scriabin, Liszt, and Brahms, Lavoie-Herz lived in Toronto and moved to Chicago in 1919, where she established a salon for modern music and taught composition. Among her pupils were Ruth Crawford Seeger and Vivian Fine.

Liadov [LYA-dôv], *Anatoly* [an-na-TOE-lee] *Konstantinovich* [cons-tan-TEEN-ov-each] Анатолий Константинович Лядов (1855–1914)—Russian composer, conductor, pianist, and professor at the St. Petersburg Conservatory. He was born into a family of Russian musicians and was two generations older than Scriabin. Despite his lukewarm reaction to Scriabin's symphonies, he led the Russian premieres of his first two symphonies. Liadov was a defender of Scriabin's early music, and his older compositions, such as the Four Pieces Op. 64, bear the influence of Scriabin's late style.

Liszt [LIST], *Franz* (1811–1886)—Hungarian virtuoso pianist, conductor, and arch-Romantic composer. Liszt was allied with Wagner and Berlioz in the "War of the Romantics" as an advocate of a progressive style of music known as "Music of the Future." Along with Chopin and Wagner, Liszt exerted a powerful influence on Scriabin, especially in terms of his virtuosic piano technique and visionary approach to piano writing. The diabolical and programmatic aspects of his music left a decisive influence on Scriabin, as did Liszt's advanced harmonic vocabulary. Liszt's single-movement symphonic poems for orchestra were direct models for the *Poem of Ecstasy* and *Prometheus: Poem of Fire*.

Lobanov [lo-BAHN-ôv], *Pavel* [PAH-val] *Vasilevich* [va-SEE-lye-veech] Павел Васи́льевич Лоба́нов (1923–2016). Pianist, scientist, sound engineer, teacher at Gnesin Institute from 1949–1983, and researcher at the Scriabin Museum in Moscow from 1992–2009. For several years, he was a recording engineer at the nationalized record label, Melodiya. Like Sabaneev, Lobanov admirably combined the traits of a scientist and a musician in his approach to Scriabin's music. He studied with Vladimir Sofronitsky, who was a family friend, and transcribed Scriabin's piano roll recordings into musical notation complete with tempo graphs.

Lunacharsky [lu-na-CHAR-skee], *Anatoly* [an-na-TOE-lee] *Vasilevich* [va-SEE-lye-veech] Анато́лий Васи́льевич Лунача́рский (1875–1933)—Soviet politician and the first Soviet People's Commissar of Education. A highly cultured man and prolific writer, Lunacharsky was a key facilitator in the Bolshevik takeover of Russian culture after the 1917 Revolution. He campaigned to preserve Russia's pre-Revolutionary cultural heritage, including its art, music, and architecture. He sought to narrow the gap between the bourgeoisie and the proletariat by exposing the lower classes to culture that had been exclusive to the privileged classes. Lunacharsky was a vigilant supporter of Scriabin, who he saw as a beacon of light and inspiration for the Russian people.

Morozova [mo-ROE-zo-va], *Margarita Kirillovna* [kear-EEL-ov-na] Маргари́та Кири́лловна Моро́зова (1873–1958)—Philanthropist, publisher, wife of art collector Mikhail Morozov, and patron of many Russian Symbolist artists, including Scriabin (1904–1908). She studied piano with Scriabin and Nikolai Medtner. Her relationship with Scriabin fizzled over her lack of enthusiasm for his newest works and his decision to accept Tatyana Schloezer as his mistress. After the composer's death, Morozova helped finance the Scriabin State Museum and financially supported his struggling family.

Pasternak [pas-ter-NAK], *Boris* [bah-REES] *Leonidovich* [lay-o-NEED-ov-each] Бори́с Леони́дович Пастерна́к (1890–1960)—Composer, poet, and author of the critically acclaimed novel, *Dr. Zhivago*, which won the Nobel Prize for Literature in 1958. Pasternak encountered Scriabin often as a young boy and left priceless accounts of the composer in his three autobiographies, *Safe Conduct* (1931), *Childhood* (1941), and *Essay in Autobiography* (1956).

Prokofiev [pro-COUGH-yev], *Sergei* [sayre-GAY] *Sergeyevich* [sayre-GAY-ôv-each] Серге́й Серге́евич Проко́фьев (1891–1953)—Russian pianist-composer who was a generation behind Scriabin and attended the St. Petersburg Conservatory. Prokofiev was influenced by Scriabin's music in his youth, but like Stravinsky, he downplayed this influence later in life. Prokofiev's symphonic poem, *Dreams*

Op. 6 (1910), is dedicated to Scriabin and is influenced by the elder composer's *Rêverie*.

Rachmaninov [rock-MON-ee-nôv], *Sergei* [sayre-GAY] *Vasilievich* [va-SEE-lye-veech] Сергей Васильевич Рахманинов (1873–1943)—Russian pianist and composer, and Scriabin's classmate at the Moscow Conservatory. Following his friend's sudden death, Rachmaninov undertook an extensive concert tour across Russia to honor Scriabin's legacy and raise funds for the late composer's struggling family. This concert tour jump-started Rachmaninov's international career as a concert pianist. His style never abandoned the lush romanticism of the late nineteenth century, and his solo piano works and Piano Concertos Nos. 2 and 3 remain staples of the modern repertory.

Richter [REEKH-ter], *Sviatoslav* [svyat-o-SLAV] *Teofilovich* [tay-o-FEEL-ov-each] Святослав Теофилович Рихтер (1915–1997)—Soviet pianist who was widely recognized as one of the greatest interpreters of Scriabin's music. Rarely did he perform outside of Russia, but he left a substantial recorded legacy and did much to keep Scriabin's music in circulation in the twentieth century. His live recordings exude an aura of electricity and mystery rarely captured on recorded media.

Rimsky-Korsakov [RIM-skee COARSE-a-kôv], *Nikolai* [nee-co-LIE] *Andreyevich* [an-DRAY-ôv-each] Николай Андреевич Римский-Корсаков (1844–1908)—Composer, conductor, and professor at the Moscow Conservatory, and Scriabin's teacher. A brilliant orchestrator known for his colorful and imaginative scores, he advised Scriabin on matters of orchestration in his early symphonic works and conducted many public performances of Scriabin's works. He recognized Scriabin's extraordinary talents from early on, but did not approve of the composer's egocentricity.

Sabaneev [sah-bôn-YEAH-yev], *Leonid* [lay-o-NEED] *Leonidovich* [lay-o-NEED-ov-each] Леонид Леонидович Сабанеев (1881–1968)—Russian scientist, composer, and music critic. He was Scriabin's friend and amanuensis during the last five years of his life. His *Vospominaniia o Skriabine* (Reminiscences of Scriabin) and other writings left behind valuable observations on the composer's thought process and artistic goals, especially those from 1910 to 1915. An important early witness to Scriabin's evolution of thought and musical culture, Sabaneev was a highly biased observer whose opinions and observations should be accepted conditionally.

Safonov [sah-PHONE-ôv], *Vasily* [va-SEE-lee] *Ilyich* [eel-YEECH] Василий Ильич Сафонов (1852–1918)—Russian conductor, pianist, and professor of piano at the Moscow Conservatory. He was Scriabin's mentor and piano teacher at the Conservatory, where he was its director from 1889 to 1918. He led the Russian premieres of Scriabin's early symphonies, and also conducted many other works with orchestras around Russia and Europe. Safonov often conducted with the New York Philharmonic, where his contacts expedited early performances of Scriabin's symphonies.

Schloezer [SHLET-zer], *Boris* [bah-REES] *Fyodorovich* [FYO-doe-rove-each] Борис Фёдорович Шлёцер (1881–1969)—Russian-born music and art critic who lived in Paris for many years and was music editor for *La Revue Musicale*. As Scriabin's brother-in-law, he spent much time around him and authored one book on the composer, *Scriabin: Artist and Mystic* (trans. Nicolas Slonimsky), which emphasizes the mystical, philosophical aspects of his personality and creativity, in strong contrast to Sabaneev's negatively tinged writings on the composer.

Schloezer [SHLET-zer], *Tatyana Fyodorovna* [FYO-doe-rove-na] Татьяна Фёдоровна Шлёцер (1883–1922)—Scriabin's mistress from 1904 until his death in 1915. They first met in November 1902 in Moscow. Her mother, Maria, was an accomplished pianist who studied with Theodor Leschetitzky, and taught Tatyana the rudiments of pianism. Tatyana endured many hardships both social and financial in her illegitimate union with Scriabin. She strongly encouraged his fondness for philosophy and the occult, and helped write some of the program notes to his sonatas and symphonies. Scriabin fathered three children with Tatyana: Ariadna (1905–1944), Julian (1908–1919), and Marina (1911–1998).

Skriabina, Vera Ivanovna [eve-AN-ov-na] *Isakovich* [ee-SAH-kov-each] Вера Ивановна Исакович (1875–1920)—Scriabin's first wife, whom he met at the Moscow Conservatory. They were married in 1897, but her practical, headstrong nature clashed with the composer's personality, and she refused to grant him a divorce. Scriabin fathered four children with Vera: Rimma (1898–1905), Elena (1900–1990), Maria (1901–1989), and Lev (1902–1910). A distinguished pianist in her own right, Vera performed her husband's works long after their marriage had ended.

Slonimsky [SLOW-neem-skee], *Nicolas Leonidovich* [lay-o-NEED-ov-each] Николай Леонидович Слонимский (1894–1995)—Russian-born polymath who cultivated careers as a conductor, author, pianist, composer, and lexicographer. He studied conducting with Albert Coates and Eugene Goosens, and built most of his career in America, where he taught at the Boston Conservatory and wrote articles for the *Boston Evening Transcript*. In spite of his talent as a pianist, Slonimsky is best known for his voluminous writings of music criticism, including the chronology *Music Since 1900* (1937) and the *Lexicon of Musical Invective* (1953). Slonimsky translated Schloezer's *Scriabin: Artist and Mystic* (1987) into English.

Sofronitsky [sof-roe-NEAT-skee], *Vladimir* [vla-DEEM-ear] *Vladimirovich* [vla-dee-MEAR-ov-each] Владимир Владимирович Софроницкий (1901–1961)—Russian pianist noted for his interpretations of Scriabin's piano music. In 1920, he married Scriabin's daughter, Elena, after meeting her at the Petrograd Conservatory. Sofronitsky was widely recognized as one of the most persuasive and powerful interpreters of Scriabin's piano works, despite never having met his idol. He taught at the Leningrad Conservatory from 1936 to 1942, and taught at the Moscow Conservatory from 1942 to 1961.

Solovyov [so-lo-VYOFF], *Vladimir* [vla-DEEM-ear] *Sergeyevich* [sayre-GAY-ôv-each] Владимир Сергеевич Соловьёв (1853–1900)—A founding father of Russian

Symbolist poetry and Ivanov's teacher. Solovyov's theory that art should serve a revelatory function particularly attracted Scriabin. Solovyov recognized art as having a transcendent, revelatory quality. His theories of theurgy and all-unity had a particularly profound impact on Ivanov and, in turn, on Scriabin in his preparations for the *Mysterium*.

Somer [ZUH-mer], *Hilde* [HILL-duh] (1922–1979)—Austrian pianist known for her performances of contemporary music, Brazilian music, and especially Scriabin's music with colored lights in the 1970s. She studied with Claudio Arrau, Rudolph Serkin, and Wanda Landowska. Somer was one of the primary champions of Scriabin's music during his revival in the early to mid-1970s, and her performances of his music are largely forgotten and underappreciated.

Stravinsky [stra-VIN-skee], *Igor* [EE-gore] *Feodorovich* [FYO-do-rove-each] Игорь Фёдорович Стравинский (1882–1971)—Russian orchestral composer whose lengthy career covered many different styles, from late Romanticism to Neo-Classicism and serialism. Stravinsky first achieved worldwide fame in 1913 with his ballet *Vesna svyashchennaia* (Rite of Spring) and other ballets produced by Diaghilev and the Ballet Russes. An early admirer of Scriabin, Stravinsky's appreciation for the composer was not reciprocated, and he later downplayed his youthful enthusiasm for Scriabin. His early ballets, such as *The Firebird* and *Petrushka*, contain strong stylistic affinities with Scriabin's *Divine Poem* and *Poem of Ecstasy*.

Taneyev [ta-NAY-yeff], *Sergei* [sayre-GAY] *Ivanovich* [eve-AN-ôv-each] Сергей Иванович Танéев (1856–1915)—Composer, conductor, pianist, and professor of counterpoint and harmony at the Moscow Conservatory, where he taught until 1905. He served as the director of the Moscow Conservatory from 1885 to 1889, and was a master of the art of writing counterpoint, a subject on which he authored thick textbooks.

Vrubel [VROO-bel], *Mikhail* [mi-KALE] *Alexandrovich* [all-ex-AN-drove-each] Михаил Александрович Врубель (1856–1910)—Russian painter of the Symbolist and Art Nouveau styles who achieved international fame with his *Demon* series of paintings, particularly his *Demon Seated* (1890). He initially studied law like his father, but found his calling in painting and illustration. He formally studied painting at the St. Petersburg Academy of Arts under Pavel Chistyakov. Vrubel developed a deep appreciation for older artistic traditions and sought to reconcile modern sensibilities with the styles of the past. His last decades were spent in Moscow, where he experienced a nervous breakdown from which he never recovered.

Wagner [VAH-gner], *Richard* [RICK-hard] (1813–1883)—German composer who sided with Liszt and Berlioz as advocates of "Music of the Future." Wagner almost exclusively focused on composing a new style of opera he termed "music drama," and was committed to the idea of a total artwork, or *Gesamtkunstwerk*, that sought to reunite the various branches of the fine arts (music, poetry, and drama) into a synthetic whole. Notable is Wagner's interest in ancient mythology, as exemplified in his four-opera cycle, *Der Ring des Nibelungen* (The Ring of the Nibelung), and his use of short melodic ideas, or leitmotifs, that symbolized characters, emotions, and objects. Wagner profoundly influenced Scriabin's incorporation of poetry and philosophy into his symphonies and sonatas. His works also imparted a strong stylistic influence on Scriabin, especially his Prelude to *Tristan und Isolde* (1865).

Zverev [ZVAI-rev], *Nikolai* [nee-co-LIE] *Sergeyevich* [sayre-GAY-ev-each] Николáй Сергéевич Звéрев (1832–1893)—Russian piano teacher who taught piano and musicianship at the Moscow Conservatory. He studied with Alexander Dubuque and was a strict disciplinarian whose pupils typically lived in his home with him, among them Rachmaninov and Scriabin. His home was a musical hub in Moscow and attracted the leading musicians of the age, including Anton Rubenstein, Taneyev, Arensky, Safonov, and Tchaikovsky.

Bibliography

BOOKS AND DISSERTATIONS

Baker, James. *The Music of Alexander Scriabin*. New Haven: Yale University Press, 1986.
Bosshard, Daniel. *Thematisch-chronologisches Verzeichnis der musickalischen Werke von Alexander Skrjabin*. Mainz: Ediziun Trais Giats Ardez, 2003.
Bowers, Faubion. *The New Scriabin: Enigma and Answers*. New York: St. Martin's Press, 1973.
Bowers, Faubion. *Scriabin: A Biography*. Second rev. ed. Mineola, NY: Dover, 1996.
Delson, Viktor. *Skriabin: Ocherki zhizni i tvorchestva* [Essays on His Life and Creative Works]. Moscow: Muzyka, 1971.
Feinberg, Samuil. *Pianizm kak iskusstvo* [Pianism as Art]. Second ed. Moscow: State Publishing House, 1969.
Garvelmann, Donald. *Youthful and Early Works of Alexander and Julian Scriabin*. New York: Music Treasure Publications, 1970.
Gershenzon, Mikhail, ed. *Russkie propilei: Materialy po istorii russkoe mysli i literatury*. Vol. 6. Moscow: Sabashnikovykh', 1919.
Guenther, Roy. "Varvara Dernova's *Garmoniia Skryabina*: A Translation and Critical Commentary." Ph.D. dissertation, Catholic University of America, 1979.
Heyman, Katherine Ruth. *The Relation of the Ultramodern to Archaic Music*. Boston: Small Maynard and Co., 1921.
Hull, Arthur Eaglefield. *A Great Russian Tone-Poet: Scriabin*. London: Kegan Paul, 1921.
Kashperov, Alexei, ed. *Pisma: Aleksandr Nikolaevich Skriabin*. Moscow: Muzyka, 1965.
Kelkel, Manfred. *Alexandre Scriabine: sa vie, l'esoterisme et le langage musical dans son oeuvre*. Paris: Champion, 1978.
Leikin, Anatole. *The Performing Style of Alexander Scriabin*. Farnham and Burlington, VT: Ashgate, 2011.
Macdonald, Hugh. *Skryabin*. London: Oxford University Press, 1978.
Markus, Stanislav, ed. *Aleksandr Nikolaevich Skriabin, 1915–1940: Sbornik k 25-letiiu so dnia smerti*. Moscow, Leningrad: Gosudarstvennoe Muzykal'noe izdatel'stvo, 1940.

Metzger, Heinz-Klaus and Rainer Riehn. *Aleksandr Skrjabin und die Skrjabinisten*. München: Edition Text + Kritik, 1983.
———. *Aleksandr Skrjabin und die Skrjabinisten II*. München: Edition Text + Kritik, 1983.
Mitchell, Rebecca. *Nietzsche's Orphans: Music, Metaphysics, and the Twilight of the Russian Empire*. New Haven, CT: Yale University Press, 2016.
Mitchell, Edward. *Scriabin: The Great Russian Tone Poet*. London: Hawkes & Sons, 1927.
Morrison, Simon. *Russian Opera and the Symbolist Movement*. Berkeley: University of California Press, 2002.
Pavchinsky, Sergei E. *A. N. Skriabin: sbornik statei: k stoletiiu so dnia rozhdeniia (1872–1972)*. Moscow: Sovetski kompozitor, 1973.
Powell, Jonathan. *After Scriabin: Six Composers and the Development of Russian Music*. Ph.D. dissertation, University of Cambridge, 1999.
Rimsky-Korsakov, Nikolai. *My Musical Life*. Translated by Judah Joffe. New York: A. A. Knopf, 1942.
Rudakova, Ye. and A. I. Kandinsky. *Scriabin: His Life and Times*. Neptune City, NJ: Paganiniana Publications, 1984.
Sabaneev, Leonid. *Modern Russian Composers*. New York: International Press, 1927.
———. *Alexander Skrjabin: Werk und Gedankenwelt*. Berlin: Kuhn, 2006.
———. *Vospominaniia o Skriabine*. Moskva: Klassika-XXI, 2000.
Schibli, Sigfried. *Alexander Skryabin und seine Music*. Munich: R. Piper, 1983.
Schloezer, Boris. *Scriabin: Artist and Mystic*. Translated by Nicolas Slonimsky. Berkeley: University of California Press, 1987.
Steger, Hanns. *Materialstrukturen in den fünf späten Klaviersonaten Alexander Skjabins*. Regensburg: Gustav Bosse Verlag, 1977.
Swan, Alfred. *Scriabin*. London: William Clowes & Sons, 1923.
Vanechkina, I. L. and B. M. Galeyev, eds. *Poèma ognya: Kontseptsia svetomuzykal'nogo sinteza A. N. Skriabina*. Kazan: Izdatel'stvo Kazanskogo Universiteta, 1981.
Widmaier, Sebastian. *Skrjabin und Prometheus*. Karlsruhe: Hanke-Verlag, 1986.
Williams, Edward. *The Bells of Russia: History and Technology*. Princeton: Princeton University Press, 1985.

ARTICLES IN NEWSPAPERS, BOOKS, AND JOURNALS

Abraham, Gerald. "Scriabin Reconsidered." *Musical Standard* (Sept. 1931): 214–16.
Antcliffe, Herbert. "The Significance of Scriabin." *Musical Quarterly* 10/3 (July 1924): 333–45.
Baker, James. "Scriabin's Music: Structure as Prism for Mystical Philosophy." In *Music Theory in Concept and Practice*, 53–96. Rochester: University of Rochester Press, 1997.
Belza, Igor. "Alexander Scriabin." *Soviet Literature* 2 (1947): 62–65.
Bowers, Faubion and Diana Cavallo. "A 60-Year-Old Controversy Flares Up Again." *High Fidelity Magazine* (June 1969): 54–61.
Brent-Smith, Alexander. "Some Reflections on the Work of Scriabin [Pts. I & II]." *Musical Times* 67/1001 and 1002 (1 July and 1 August 1926): 593–95; 692–95.
Brown, Malcolm. "Skriabin and Russian 'Mystic' Symbolism." *19th-Century Music* 3 (1979): 42–51.

Carlson, Maria. "Fashionable Occultism: The World of Russian Composer Aleksandr Scriabin." Reprinted in *Journal of the Scriabin Society of America* 12/1 (Winter 2007–2008): 54–63.
Cooper, Martin. "Scriabin's Mystical Beliefs." *Music & Letters* 16/2 (April 1935): 110–15.
———. "Aleksandr Skryabin and the Russian Renaissance." *Studi musicali* 1 (1972): 327–56.
Evans, Edwin. "Scriabin." *Fortnightly Review* 103/582 (June 1915): 1071–80.
Garcia, Emanuel. "Rachmaninoff and Scriabin: Creativity and Suffering in Talent and Genius." *Psychoanalytic Review* 91/3 (June 2004): 433–42.
Garcia, Susanna. "Scriabin's Symbolist Plot Archetype in the Late Piano Sonatas." *19th-Century Music* 23/3 (Spring 2000): 273–300.
Goodfriend, James, ed. "Why Alexander Scriabin?" *Stereo Review* 30 (Jan. 1973): 68–71.
Grange, Henry-Louis de la. "Prometheus Unbound." *Music and Musicians* (Jan. 1972): 34–43.
Heckman, Don. "Scriabin: 'Ice, Cocaine, Rainbow.'" *New York Times*, 10 October 1970, D28.
Herndon, Claude. "Skryabin's New Harmonic Vocabulary in His Sixth Sonata." *Journal of Musicological Research* 4 (1983): 353–68.
Hope, Adrian. "Fiery Music of a Mystic." *Life* 69/16 (16 October 1970): 72–76.
Hughes, Allen. "Hilde Somer, Pianist, Tries Out Scriabin's Multimedia Concept." *New York Times*, 18 December 1969, 63.
Hull, Arthur Eaglefield. "The Five Symphonies of Scriabin." *Monthly Musical Record* 46 (1 February 1916): 36.
———. "A Survey of the Pianoforte Works of Scriabin." *Musical Quarterly* 2/4 (October 1916): 601, 614.
———. "The Pianoforte Sonatas of Scriabin [Pts. I & II]." *Musical Times* 57, Nos. 885 and 886 (November 1 and December 1, 1916): 492–95; 539–42.
Lavoie-Herz, Siegfried. "The Art of Alexander Nikolaievitch Skriabin." *The Etude* 44 (May 1926): 345–46, 399.
Livingston, Tamara. "Music Revivals: Towards a General Theory." *Ethnomusicology* 43/1 (Winter 1999): 66–85.
Lunacharsky, Anatoly. "On Scriabin." Translated by Don Louis Wetzel. *Journal of the Scriabin Society of America* 8/1 (Winter 2003–2004): 37–44.
Lyle, Wilson G. "Alexander Scriabin—Innovator of Sound and Colour." *Musical Opinion* (April 1940): 401–03.
Macdonald, Hugh. "Words and Music by A. Skryabin." *Musical Times* 113/1547 (January 1972): 22–27.
Macdonald, Hugh. "Lighting the Fire: Skryabin and Colour." *Musical Times* 124/1688 (October 1983): 600–602.
Marvick, Louis. "Two Versions of the Symbolist Apocalypse: Mallarmè's *Livre* and Scriabin's *Mysterium*." *Criticism* 28/3 (Summer 1986): 287–306.
Matlaw, Ralph. "Scriabin and Russian Symbolism." *Comparative Literature* 31 (1979): 1–23.
Mirka, Danuta. "Colors of a Mystic Fire: Light and Sound in Scriabin's *Prometheus*." *American Journal of Semiotics* 13, nos. 1–4 (Fall 1996): 227–48.
Montague-Nathan, M. "Belaiev—Maecenas of Russian Music." *Musical Quarterly* 4/3 (July 1918): 450–65.
Newmarch, Rosa. "Scryabin and Contemporary Russian Music." *Russian Review* 2/1 (1913): 153–69.
Newmarch, Rosa. "Scriabin's *Prometheus*." *Music Student* (1915): 196.

———. "'Prometheus: Poem of Fire." *Musical Times* 55/854 (1 April 1914): 227–31.
———. "Alexander Scriabin." *Musical Times* 56/868 (1 June 1915): 329–30.
Peacock, Kenneth. "Synaesthetic Perception: Alexander Scriabin's Color Hearing." *Music Perception* 2/4 (Summer 1985): 483–506.
Perle, George. "Scriabin's Self-Analyses." *Music Analysis* 3/2 (1984): 101–23.
Poriss, Hilary. "Women, Musical Canons and Culture: Katherine Ruth Heyman." *Journal of the Scriabin Society of America* 2/1 (Winter 1997–1998): 14–31.
Reise, Jay. "Late Skriabin: Some Principles Behind the Style." *19th-Century Music* 6/3 (Spring 1973): 220–31.
Rodgers, John. "Four Preludes Ascribed to Yulian Skriabin." *19th-Century Music* 6/3 (Spring 1983): 213–19.
Rosenfeld, Paul. "Scriabine." *Seven Arts* 2 (August 1917): 638–45.
Rubbra, Edmund. "The Resurgence of Scriabin." *The Listener* (26 February 1970): 289.
Rudyar, Dane. "Djane Lavoie-Herz and Her Work." In *Rudhyar Archival Project* [database online]; originally published in the *Musical Observer* (March 1926). Available from http://www.khaldea.com/rudhyar/djanelavoieherz.html. Accessed 15 July 2007.
Runciman, John. "Noises, Smells, and Colours." *Musical Quarterly* 1/2 (April 1915): 149–61.
Sabaneev, Leonid. "Scriabin and the Idea of a Religious Art." *Musical Times* 72/1063 (1 September 1931): 789.
———. "A. N. Scriabin - A Memoir." *Russian Review* 25/3 (1966): 257–67.
Sabaneev, Leonid and S. W. Pring. "Scriabin: On the Twenty-Fifth Anniversary of His Death." *Musical Times* 81/1168 (June 1940): 256–57.
Sabaneev, Leonid. "Religious and Mystical Trends in Russia at the Turn of the Century." *Russian Review* 24/2 (October 1965): 354–68.
Schloezer, Boris. "Scriabine." *Modern Music: The League of Composers' Review* 1/3 (November 1924): 14–18.
Scriabine, Marina. "Alexandre Scriabine." *Le Cahiers Canadiens de la Musique* 3 (1971): 23–26.
Smith, Kenneth. "Erotic Discourse in Scriabin's Fourth Sonata." *British Postgraduate Musicology* 7 (2005). Available from http://www.bpmonline.org.uk/bpm7/smith.html. Accessed 2 March 2007.
Stanley, Louis. "Scriabin in America." *Musical America* 74 (15 February 1954): 33, 178, 218, 220.
Stell, Jason. "Music as Metaphysics: Structure and Meaning in Skryabin's Fifth Piano Sonata." *Journal of Musicological Research* 23 (2004): 1–37.
Tiderböhl, Ellen von. "A Further Note on Alexandre Nikolaewitsh Scriabin." *Monthly Musical Record* 45/534 (1 June 1915): 154.
———. "Memories of Scriabin's Volga Tour (1910) [Pts. I and II]." *Monthly Musical Record* (1 May and 1 June 1926): 137–38; 168–69.
———. "A Musical Journey Down the Volga." *Etude* 44 (December 1926): 905–6.
Vanechkina, Irina and Bulat M. Galeyev. "Was Scriabin a Synesthete?" *Leonardo* 34/4 (August 2001): 357–61.
Verdi, Luigi. "Numerical Symbology in Some of Skrjabin's Late Piano Works." *Journal of the Scriabin Society of America* 10/1 (2005–2006): 41–55.
Wai-Ling, Cheong. "Scriabin's Octatonic Sonata," *Journal of the Royal Music Association* 121/1 (1996): 206–28.

Wood, Ralph. "Skryabin and His Critics." *Monthly Musical Record* (November–December 1956): 222–25.
Yuenger, Blanche. "A Scriabin Jubilee." *Chicago Tribune*, 10 January 1972, B10.
Ziegler, Sister Mirelda. "Scriabin: The Mystical Centenarian." *Music Journal* 30/2 (February 1972): 28–29, 57.

Index

Abbado, Claudio, 98, 101, 110, 198–99
Abraham, Gerald, 30, 114, 164–66, 190, 339n3, 360n85
accents, 77–78, 212, 222, 227, 237, 243, 310–12
accident, 34
acoustic scale, 275, *278*
acoustic shadow, 305
Acte préalable (Prefatory Act), 2, 26, 59, 172, 196, 332n30
action (*dyeistviye*), 8, 11, 329n20
Adams, Ansel, 358n37
aesthetics, 2, 3, 203, 214; culture and, 8; emotions and, 4; light and, 142; mysticism and, 3, 22, 185; of Symbolism, 174–76, 179–80; synaesthesia and, 351n63
Affektenlehre. *See* Doctrine of Affections
airplane, 378n19
Aldrich, Richard, 185, 188
Alexander Scriabin's Ragtime Band, 53
Alexander Scriabin: The Great Russian Tone Poet (Hull, A.), 34, 274
Alexandrov, Anatoly, 37
Alexandrovich, Nikolai (father), 16, 130
Allegro appassionato Op. 4, 36, 316
Allegro de Concert Op. 18, 225

Altschuler, Modest, 66; as champion of Scriabin's music, 94, 97, 102; Russian Symphony Orchestra Society and, 85, 92, 97, 98, 102, 184; Symphony No. 3 in C minor Op. 43, *Le Divin Poème* (*Divine Poem*) and, 92–93; Symphony No. 4, *Poème de l'Extase* (*Poem of Ecstasy*) in C major Op. 54 and, 94, 97, 186; Symphony No. 5, *Prometheus: Poem of Fire in F♯ major* Op. 60 and, 142, 155
Andjaparidze, Eteri, 145–46, 155
Années de pèlerinage (*Years of Pilgrimage*) (Liszt), 170
A. N. Skriabin i ego tvorchestvo (Scriabin and His Creative Work) (Gunst), 27
Antheil, George, 346n57
Apollon, 176
Arensky, Anton, 75, 84, 88
Aristotle, 203, 363n131
arm weight, use of, 232, 288, 290
arpeggiated chords, 297, 314, 316, 367n9, 375n25
arrangement in fourths, 276–77
Asafiev, Boris, 10, 28, 48, 126, 161, 163
Ashkenazy, Vladimir, 26, 70, 72, 197
atonality, 6, 337n68

attack, 213, 225, 232, 237, 283, 288, 311, 315, 320
auditory gravitation, 10
augmented fourths, 358n32
augmented sixth chords, 91, 254–56, *255*, 257, 369n8, 369n13; French Sixth chord, 256, 258, 260, 264, 269, 278
Austro-German music, 166, 190, 191–92
avant-garde, 1, 199, 378n19
AΩ, 202, 363n127

Bach, Johann Sebastian, 36; French Suites, 377n9; as master of counterpoint, 84; preludes of, 59; solo concertos, 76; WTC, Books I and II, 59–60, 275, 309
Baker, James, 4–5, 140–41, 257
Bakhtin, Mikhail, 6–7, 10, 329n28
Balakirev, Mily, 20, 218
Ballade in A♭ Op. 47 (Chopin), 288
Ballade No. 10 in D♭ major (Chopin), 56
Balmont, Konstantin, 169–70, 174
Baltimore Symphony Orchestra, 142
Baltrušaitis, Jurgis, 174
Barcarolle Op. 60 (Chopin), 288
Barere, Simon, 31
Baroque era, 6
Barthes, Rolande, 9
Bartók, Béla, 50
Basile, Armand, 305
Bastei, 61
Battle of Borodino, 12
Baudelaire, Charles, 175, 355n61
the Beatles, 197
Bechstein piano, 375n38
Beethoven, Ludwig van: *Creatures of Prometheus*, 98; Fifth Symphony, 148; influence on piano sonata, 39; influence on Scriabin, 148; light and, 148; "Moonlight" Sonata Op. 27 No. 2, 39; Ninth Symphony, "Chorale," 37, 75, 82, 184–85, 332n45; "Ode to Joy," 82; Scriabin's criticism of, 138–39; Sixth Symphony, "Pastorale," 87, 148; Sonatas of, 36, 38, 39; symphonies of, 138–39; Third Symphony, "Eroica," 98; trills and, 152, 375n29

Beliaev, Mitrofan, 43, 324; death of, 17–18, 89; Glinka Prize and, 42; letters to, 54–55, 336n48, 337n62; Liadov and, 246, 368n14; as patron of Scriabin, 75, 81, 84, 99; publishing house of, 55; on Symphony No. 1 in E major Op. 26, 84
Beliaev circle, or *Beliayevski kruzhok*, 352n12
Bell, Theodore, 146
Bella, Rudolf, 68
bells: bell-like tone quality, 169, 285–88; in First Sonata, 38; influence on Russian composers, 168–69; intended for *Mysterium*, 46, 172; as musical influence on Scriabin, 169–70; Rachmaninov and, 168–69, *170*; in Russian music, 168–73, 354n48; in Seventh Sonata, 46, 48; in Sixth Sonata, 45; in Sonata No. 1 in F minor Op. 6, 38, 171, *172*; in Sonata No. 3 in F♯ minor Op. 23, 171–72; in Sonata No. 5 in F♯ major Op. 53, 172; in Sonata No. 6 Op. 62, 172, *173*; in Sonata No. 7 Op. 64 "White Mass," 173; symbolic qualities of, 168, 169; timbre of, 169; ubiquity of bells in Russian life, 46, 168–69; in *Vers la Flamme* Op. 72 (*Toward the Flame*), 173; *zvon*, 169
The Bells Op. 35 (Rachmaninov), 169
Bely, Andrei, 64, 180, 355n81, 364n18
Benois, Alexandre, 178
Berg, Alban, 161, 239
Berlioz, Hector, 49, 87, 89, 92
Bernstein, Leonard, 76, 192
Besant, Annie, 23, 187
biographers, 27–32
birthday, 15, 29
The Birth of Tragedy from the Spirit of Music (Nietzsche), 20, 83, 93
Bizet, Georges, 362n126
Blanc-Gatti, Charles, 138
Der Blaue Reiter, 117
Blavatsky, Helena Petrovna, 23–24, 98–99, 121–22, 142, 187, 189, 200, 358n44
Blumenfeld, Felix, 97
Blythe, Alan, 196
Bolshoi Theater, 143

Book About Stravinsky (Asafiev), 28
Boris Godunov (Mussorgsky), 46, 169
Borodin, Alexander, 169
Borovsky, Alexander, 69
Boston Evening Transcript, 184
Boston Symphony Orchestra, 88, 108, 187, 191
Botstein, Leon, 342n71
Bott, Joseph, 201
Boulez, Pierre, 108–10, 199, 322
Boult, Adrian, 30
bourgeois culture, 28
Bowers, Faubion, xii–xiii, 277, 341n45; Abraham criticism of, 360n85; biography of, 30, 195; career as writer, 123; criticism of, 82; education and background of, 122–23; heterosexual affairs, 123; homosexuality and, 125, 346n44; myths created by, 122–26; on Scriabin interpreters, 197; sensationalism of, 124; Theosophy and, 24; writing style of, 123–24
Brahms, Johannes, 36, 75, 77, 247, 316, 369n8
Brassin, Louis, 67
Brent-Smith, Alexander, 19, 189–90
Bright Colors Falsely Seen: Synaesthesia and the Search for Transcendental Knowledge (Dann), 136–37
Bülow, Hans von, 339n4
Buyukly, Vsevolod, 209
By the Stars. See Po zvezdam
bytovoi romans (urban romance style), 165
Byzantine chant, 7

cadential phrasing, 309
cadenzas, 77
calligraphy, 246, 368n13
Calvocoressi, Michel, 190
La Campanella (Liszt), 170
Canon in D minor, 34
cantabile, 241, 283, 290
Caresse dansée Op. 57 No. 2, 285
Carnegie Hall, 97, 102, 131, *132*, 133, 140–41, 155, 183
The Cave. See Peshchera
centennial celebrations, 29, 196–99

character indications (expression marks), 188; color and, 298–99, *299*; French, 364n7; Italian, 209, 364n7; of *Poème ailé* Op. 51 No. 3, 212; poetic, 188, 209–10, 298; in Sonata No. 5 in F♯ major Op. 53, 210; in Sonata No. 6 Op. 62, *299*; Sonata No. 7 Op. 64 "White Mass," 151; in Sonata No. 9 Op. 68 "Black Mass," 209; of Sonata No. 10 Op. 70, "Trill," 210; unusual, 90, 207
Chau, Henry, 337n77
Chekhov, Anton, 68
Cherkass, N. N., 284–85, 374n14
Chicago Symphony Orchestra, 85, 93, 101, 103, 109, 110
childhood, 27, 78, 299
children, 40, 121, 347n61
Chopin, Frédéric, 36, 377n9; Ballade in A♭ Op. 47, 288; Ballade No. 10 in D♭ major, 56; *Barcarolle* Op. 60, 288; Etude Op. 10, 56, 61, 219, 366n12, 368n20; Etude Op. 25, 55, 61, 219; "Funeral March" Sonata, 264; hand positions and, 366n12; imagination of, 52; mazurka and, 51–52; musical style of, 17, 35; nationalism and, 37, 160, 163; as pervasive influence on Scriabin, 16–17, 37, 38, 52, 55, 78–79, 180, 184, 194, 218, 254, 317, 320; Piano Concerto in F♯ minor Op. 20 and, 78; Prelude Op. 11 and, 378n24; Prelude Op. 28, 35, 59, 60, 61, 78–79, *79*; rhythms of, 306–7, 377n4, 377n6; Sonata No. 2 in B♭ minor, 20; tempo rubato and, 306–7
chorale textures, 253–54, 294, 368n4
chords, 221; arpeggiated, 297, 314, 317, 367n9, 375n25; foundation, 277; French sixth, 256, 258, 260, 264, 269, 278; nicknamed, 256–58; repeated, 288–89, 320, 336n6; resonance of, 223; rolled, 222; skyscraper, 293; of Sonata No. 1 in F minor Op. 6, 223, 224, 225; of Sonata No. 4 in F♯ major Op. 30, 366n15; spacing of, 223, 224; stacked, 222, 223; Tristan, 258–61, *259*,

370n18, 370n20; walk-arounds, 257, 368n2. *See also specific types*
Christianity, 11
Chuev, Felix, 130
Cincinnati Symphony Orchestra, 81, 183
circle of fifths, 136, 267
Ciurlionis, Mikalojus, 64, 179–80, 355n80
Clark, Edward, 30
Clarke, Martha, 68
Classical Era, 76
clavier à lumières, 98, 139
Clementi, Muzio, 289–90
Cleveland Orchestra, 189
Les cloches de Genève (Liszt), 170–71, *171*
C♯ *minor Prelude* (Rachmaninov), 34, *171*
Coates, Albert, 92–93, 105, 106, 128, 151, 187
Cold War, 130
color, 296–99; character indications and, 298–99, *299*; circle of fifths and, 136; colored light performances, 131–36, *132*, 140–47, 155, 195, 349n38, 350n39; color-tonal correspondences, *136*, 347n7; creativity and, 138; dynamics and, 297; harmony and, 257; key signatures and, 370n32; numbers and, 180; pianism and, 296; in Sonata-Fantasie (No. 2) in G♯ minor Op. 19, 297; in Sonata No. 6 Op. 62, *299*; in Sonata No. 7 Op. 64 "White Mass," 298, *298*; thinking, 138; trills and, 236, 237, 238. *See also* synaesthesia
color-hearing. *See* synaesthesia
color organ. *See tastiera per luce*
color-tonal correspondences, *136*, 347n7
Columbia Records, 340n33
Comfort Me With Apples (De Vries), 93
Comissiona, Sergei, 142
compositional language, 1, 7
compositional process, 58
compositional techniques, 41, 75, 84, 163, 190
compositional vocabulary, 2, 4
conductors, 86, 102–10
Conjure Wife (Leiber), 49
Cooper, Frank, 192

Cooper, Martin, 31
Copland, Aaron, 37, 192
Corder, Frederick, 101
cosmopolitanism, 28, 162
counterculture, American, 93, 144, 183, 199–203, 204
counterpoint, 8; Bach as master of, 84; in Etude Op. 42, 249; in Piano Concerto in F♯ minor Op. 20, 247, *248*; in Sonata No. 4 in F♯ major Op. 30, 246; in Sonata No. 6 Op. 62, 249, 368n19; in Sonata No. 8 Op. 66, 249, *249*; in Sonata No. 10 Op. 70, "Trill," 249–50, *250*
Couperin, Francois, 59
Cousin, Victor, 22
Cousins, Margaret, 187, 345n35
Craft, Robert, 196
Cranko, John, 97
The Creation (Haydn), 148
creative act, 20
creative personality, 1
creativity, 64, 74, 86, 123, 138, 212, 262, 299
Creatures of Prometheus (Beethoven), 98
criticism, 19, 29–30, 101, 189; of double performances, 105; of harmony, 190; of Piano Concerto in F♯ minor Op. 20, 340n14; Russian style and, 162–63; of Symphony No. 1 in E major Op. 26, 102, 185; of Symphony No. 3 in C minor Op. 43, *Le Divin Poème* (*Divine Poem*), 90, 92, 185–86; of Symphony No. 4, *Poème de l'Extase* (*Poem of Ecstasy*) in C major Op. 54, 97, 114, 151, 191; of Symphony No. 5, *Prometheus: Poem of Fire* in F♯ major Op. 60, 101, 114, 142, *143*. *See also specific critics*
Cross, Lowell, 144
Crowley, Aleister, 331n17
Cubo-Futurists, 378n19
Cui, Cesar, 33
culture, 5, 8, 28, 123, 162, 174, 177, 195, 365n7. *See also* counterculture, American
cycle-of-thirds, 372n64
Cytowik, Richard, 133, 137

Dahlhaus, Carl, 203–4
dance music, dance rhythms, 76, 78, 85, 162, 319–20
danger, 68
Dann, Kevin, 136–37
Danse languide Op. 51 No. 4, 18, 267, *268*
death, 178, 186; cause of, 128–29; Koussevitzky and, 126; Moscow Conservatory and, 126; myth about Easter, 27, 66, 68–69, 117, 124, 130; myths about, 128–29; popularity after, 126; Rachmaninov memorial tour after, 68–69, 126; Schloezer, B., and, 120; unpopularity after, 19, 27–32, 189–91
death harmonies, 258, 277, 279
The Death of Alexander Scriabin (Russell), 331n17
Debussy, Claude, 208, 217, 229, 334n17, 354n48, 355n61; Etude in Fourths, 277; impressionistic interpretation and, 374n16; intervals of, 277; light and, 150; *La Mer*, 150; *Nuages*, 82; *Prélude à l'après-midi d'un faune*, 82; Prelude Ondine, 277; whole-tone scale of, 274
Delville, Jean, 99, *100*
Demon (series of paintings, Vrubel), 179
"Demon," 179
Dernova, Varvara, 256, 328n7
Désir Op. 57 No. 1, 167, 264
desire, dominant seventh chords and, 261–63
Deutsche, Stephen, 115
Deutsche Grammophon, 109
Deutscher, Isaac, 127
development, 76, 86
Devil, as artistic symbol, 65–66, 178–79
De Vries, Peter, 93
diachronic point of view, 159
Dionysus, 20, 93, 176, 210, 212
Disney, Walt, 103
dissonance, 88, 98, 188, 239, 273, 302
distribution of notes among the hands, 221, 222, 228–36, *235*
Divine Poem. *See* Symphony No. 3 in C minor Op. 43, *Le Divin Poème*
Divine Will, 175
divisi strings, 89

Dixon, James, 105
Doctrine of Affections (*Affektenlehre*), 134, 148, 215
dominant function, 268–69, *270–72*
dominant seventh chords, 62, 261–67, *263*, *265–67*, 370n34
Don Giovanni (Mozart), 36
dotted rhythms, 79, 312–14, *314*, 316
double notes, 216
double performances, 105
Downes, Olin, 29, 108, 190–91, 197
dramaturgy, 335n29
"Dream of a Witches' Sabbath," 49, 92
Dr. Zhivago, 1, 89
Dubuc, Alexander, 290
Duncan, Isadora, 54, 335n46; "The Crossing at St. Petersburg," 54, 335n46; "Mother," 54, 335n46; "Revolutionary," 54, 335n46
duple meters, 243, 319
dyeistviye. *See* action
dynamics, 9, 208–9, 234, 283–85, 373n4, 374nn23–24; color and, 297; melody and, 241–42; pedal techniques and, 303; of piano, 296, 375n39; piano rolls and, 308; in Sonata No. 5 in F♯ major Op. 53, 286–87; of Sonata No. 6 Op. 62, 288; volume, 375n30

Early Music revival, 194
early period melody, 241–42
ecstasy, 4–5, 21, 93, 175–76
edinstvo. *See* unity
Édition Russe de Musique, 43, 83
education, 22, 27. *See also* Moscow Conservatory
Einstein, Albert, 135
Elbe Sandstone Mountains, 61
"Elements of Russian Music" (Abraham), 165
Ellington, Duke, 134
Ellis, Van Zandt, 198
Elman, Mischa, 97
Emerson, Caryl, 121
emotions, 4, 95, 165, 208, 216, 242
Engel, Carl, 161
Engel, Yuli, 27, 162, 208

England, 29, 126, 127, 332n45
Enigme Op. 52 No. 2, 314–15
Enlightenment, 9, 134
equal-tempered tuning, 116
eroticism, 42, 68, 165, 176, 195–96, 261, 368n12
Eternal Feminine, 212, 244
Étrangeté Op. 63 No. 2, 273, 277, 287, *287*, 294, 303, *315*
Etude in Fourths (Debussy), 277
Etude Op. 2 No. 1, 220, 239, 290, 335n46; harmony of, 251; Horowitz and, 113, 241–42; pedal techniques in, 300, *301*; recordings of, 54
Etudes Op. 8: key signatures of, 55, 348n15; No. 1-5, 55; No. 7, 55, 221; No. 8, 55, 241; No. 9, 55–56, 221, 316–17, 325; No. 10, 56, 227; No. 11, 55, 56, 220; No. 12, 35, 54, 55, 56, 73, 220–21, *226*, 227, 239, 289, 324, 335n46, 336n51, 379n37; recordings of, 56; Scriabin letter to Beliaev about, 54–55, 336n48
Etudes Op. 10 (Chopin), 56, 61, 219, 366n12, 368n20
Etudes Op. 25 (Chopin), 55, 61, 219
Etudes Op. 42, 375n25; counterpoint in, 249; No. 1, 56–57, 320–22, 379n37; No. 2, 57; No. 3, 57, 153, 237; No. 4, 57, 183; No. 5, 54, 57, 183, 232, *232*, 239, 253, 294, 335n46; No. 6, 57; No. 7, 57; No. 8, 57, 379n37; polyrhythms in, 320–22; recordings of, 57; rhythm in, 56–57, 320–21; Skriabina, V., and, 56–57
Etude Op. 49 No. 1, 58, 379n37
Etude Op. 56 No. 4, 58, 379n37
Etudes Op. 65: letter to Sabaneev about, 58; No. 1 in Ninths, 58–59, 220, 242, *243*, 277, 365n8; No. 2 in Sevenths, 58–59; No. 3 in Fifths, 58–59, 289; recordings of, 59
execution, interpretation and, 109, 214, 343n79
expression, 379n36
expression marks. *See* character indications
expressive performance, 241–42

Extase chord, 258, 263–67, *267*, 269, 275, 369n17, 372n54

falling sixth intervals, 86
falling thirds, *250*
family, 16, 40, 121, 130, 290, 347n61
fanfares (*zov*), 367n24; Garcia on, 364n12; in Sonata-Fantasie (No. 2) in G♯ minor Op. 19, 312, *313*; in Sonata No. 3 in F♯ minor Op. 23, 312, *313*; of Sonata No. 7 Op. 64 "White Mass," 289, 312; of Symphony No. 4, *Poème de l'Extase* (*Poem of Ecstasy*) in C major Op. 54, 212; of Symphony No. 5, *Prometheus: Poem of Fire in F♯ major* Op. 60, 212; of *Vers la Flamme* Op. 72 (*Toward the Flame*), 312
Fantasia, 103, 134
Fantasy in B minor Op. 28, 35–36, 53, 241, 247, 289, 375n25, 375n30
Faust (Goethe), 212
Federal Music Project, 189
Feinberg, Samuil, 53, 71–73, 209, 252, 284, 300, 309, 325–26
feminine, 66, 212, 244
Fennell, Ernest, 30, 190
Ferguson, John, 22
Festival of Romantic Music, 192, 193
Feuillet d'album Op. 45 No. 1, 232, 262
Feuillet d'album Op. 58, 18
fiction, appearances in, 331n17
Field, John, 289–90
Fifth Symphony (Beethoven), 148
filigree, 81
finales, 85
fin de siècle intelligentsia, 22
fingers, 218, 227–28, 236–38, 250, 365n6. *See also* hands
Firebird (Stravinsky), 109, 165
"First Flower Child," 145, 201, *202*
First Viennese School, 161
Flamm, Christoph, x, 224
Flammes sombres Op. 73 No. 2, 371n42
Fleming, Alexander, 129
flight, 234, 314, 315, 368n12
Flight of the Bumblebee (Rimsky-Korsakov), 152

floating rhythms, 266
fluttering pedal techniques, 302–3, 376n50
folk dances, 78, 85, 162, 320
folk music, 27, 128, 160, 163, 164, 166, 319
folk mythology, 51
Fonteyn, Margot, 97
Formalism, as a critical and theoretical approach to Scriabin's music, 7–8, 109
formal traditions, 41
Forte, Allen, 257
foundation chords, 277
fourths, arrangement in, 276–77
Fragilité Op. 51 No. 1, 18, 220, 262
Franck, César, 41, 221, 289, 334n17
Francke, J. E., 184
Der Freischütz (Weber), 92
French sixth chords, 256, 258, 260, 264, 269, 278
French Suites (Bach), 377n9
Freud, Sigmund, 125
Frolova-Walker, Marina, 162
fugue, 84, 85
full pedal technique, 305
"Funeral March" Sonata (Chopin), 264
Futurists, 378n19
Fyodorova, Margarita, 66, 71

Galeyev, Bulat, 140
Garcia, Susanna, 211–12, 244, 364n12, 364nn15–16, 367n9, 368n12
Garvelmann, Donald, 48
Gawboy, Anna, 99, 140, 141, 144, 344n11, 348n21
Gergiev, Valery, 85
German sixth chords, 255, 260
Gesamtkunstwerk, 25, 135, 177, 183
gestures, 38, 45, 211–13
Gielen, Michael, 145
Gieseking, Walter, 325, 366n20
Gilels, Emil, 63, 73
Gilman, Lawrence, 29–30, 92
Glazunov, Alexander, 74, 75, 166, 357n23
Glinka, Mikhail, 162, 166–67, 290
Glinka Prize, 42, 82, 90, 97, 100
Godowsky, Leopold, 34, 219
Goethe, Johann Wolfgang von, 98, 212

Goldenweiser, Alexander, 35, 71
Golovanov, Nikolai, 29
Gordon, David, 53
Gorky, Maxim, 357n23
Gould, Glenn, 41, 198, 361n99
Gould, Richard, 39, 350
Gradova, Gitta, 188
Granados, Enrique, 211
Grant, Mark, 185
Gray, Cecil, 183, 190
Great Depression, 189
Great Freeze, 214
Great Time, 10, 329n28
Greek Music Drama, 5, 7, 8
Grout, Donald, 160, 177
Grove, George, 348n22
Guide to the Practical Study of Harmony (Tchaikovsky, V.), 256, 369n8
Guirlandes Op. 73 No. 1, 320
Gunst, Evgen, 27, 34

hairpins, 241–42, 367n6
half pedal technique, 305
half-step resolution, 256
Hallé Orchestra, 93
hands: crossings, 67, 220, 234; desynchronization of, 241, 320, 367n4; distribution of notes among, 221, 222, 226–36, *235*; division of labor among, 218, 233; flexibility, 365n5; injury to right, 20, 38, 219; interlocking thumbs, 231, 367n22; interplay, 228–36; leaping technique, 218, 220, 221, 227–28, *228*; Liszt and, 234; muscular strength of, 227, 365n5; positions, Chopin and, 366n12; redistribution of parts between, 222, 233, 234, 367n23nn24; right hand passagework, 216; roles of, 233; score and, 228–29; in Sonata No. 3 in F♯ minor Op. 23, 229, 231; thumb crossings, *231*, 366n22; trills technique, 237; wrist technique, 216, 218, 225–27. *See also* left hand
happenings, 144, 200
harmonic blending, 302
harmonic experiments, 337n68
harmonic innuendo, 244

harmonic language, 2–3, 11, 56, 251, 252–54
harmonic mannerisms, 189
harmonic paradox, 9
harmonic style, 45, 46
harmony, 221; color and, 257; criticism of, 190; death, 258, 277, 279; dissonance and, 239; of Etude Op. 2 No. 1, 251; of Glinka, 166–67; jazz, 261; of Liszt, 252, 254; of Mazurka Op. 3, 251–52; melody and, 47, 279; mystic, 278–81; in Piano Concerto in F♯ minor Op. 20, 253, *253*; of Prelude Op. 74, 251; in Russian music, 166–67; of Schumann, R., 267; sensitivity to, 251; of Sonata No. 6 Op. 62, 252; of Symphony No. 3 in C minor Op. 43, *Le Divin Poème* (*Divine Poem*), 91; of Symphony No. 4, *Poème de l'Extase* (*Poem of Ecstasy*) in C major Op. 54, 94, 167; in Symphony No. 5, *Prometheus: Poem of Fire in F♯ major* Op. 60, 50, 100–101; tonality and, 370n32; of Wagner, 18
Harnoncourt, Nikolaus, 7
Haydn, Joseph, 36, 148
Hayers, Sidney, 49
Heckman, Don, 201
Helffer, Claude, 228
Henahan, Donal, 73
Henderson, William J., 97, 142–43, 188, 340n14, 357n17
Hentoff, Nat, 197
Hexameron, 193
Heyman, Katherine Ruth W., 48, 69–70, 123, 188, 197
high art (*stile antico*), 84
Hinduism, 22, 23, 180
History of Russian-Soviet Music (Bakst), 4
History of Western Music (Grout), 160
Hoffmann, E. T. A., 139, 348n19
Hofmann, Josef, 183
Holden, Scott, 237–38
homosexuality, 125, 346n44
horizontal thinking, 257
Horowitz, Vladimir, 73, 326; Etude Op. 2 No. 1 and, 113, 241–42; live recordings of, 41; melody and, 241; recordings of, 72, 197, 198, 241, 324; Sonata No. 9 Op. 68 "Black Mass" and, 50, 72, 324; Sonata No. 10 Op. 70, "Trill" and, 238; talent of, 374n11; tempo choices of, 50, 324; tempo rubato and, 242; *Vers la Flamme* Op. 72 and, 72, 155, 337n76
Horowitz: A Reminiscence, 113
Hrdliczka, Gertrud, 88
Hughes, Allen, 196
Hull, Arthur Eaglefield, 24, 34, 36, 84, 94–95, 127, 188, 332n45; mystic chord and, 274–75; on Sonata No. 9 Op. 68 "Black Mass," 49
Hull, Robert, 31, 190
Hume, Paul, 191, 203

Ideal Creative Power, 42
Igumnov, Konstantin, 300, 376n47
An Illustrated Encyclopedia of Mysticism and the Mystery Religions (Ferguson), 22
imagination, 114, 156, 211, 257
Imagists, 9
imitation, 84, 161
Imperial Mariinsky Theater, 101
impressionistic interpretation, 285, 374n16
Impressionists, 176
Impromptu a la Mazur Op. 7 No. 2, 320
Impromptu Op. 7 No. 2, *321*
Impromptu Op. 10, 224
Impromptu Op. 12, 172, 316
Impromptu Op. 14 No. 2, 316
improvisation, 16, 367n9
incisive strikes, 285–86
influences on musical style, 15–18, 79
injury to right hand, 20, 38, 219
insanity, 19, 31, 101, 113–15, 118, 121, 196
interlocking thumbs, 231, 367n22
International Symphony, 110
interpretation, 70, 109, 110, 214, 229, 285, 343n79, 374n16
interval cycles, 337n68
intervallic inversions, 246, 258
intervallic retrogrades, 246
intervallic space, 10
intervallic tension, 241, 255, 367n3
intervals: of Debussy, 277; falling sixth, 86; forbidden, 58; *intonatsiia* and, 9–10; of

mystic chord, 22; smallest possible, 155; tritones, 256, 267, 273, 369n12
intonatsiia (Russian intonation theory), 9–10, 367n3
Introduction to Contemporary Music (Machlis), 183
Islamey (Balakirev), 20, 218
Italian sixth, 260
Ivanov, Vyacheslav, 25, 174–78, 180
Ivanov-Boretski, Mikhail, 28
Ives, Charles, 26, 50, 188, 192, 281

Der Jacobsleiter (Schoenberg), 26
jazz, 53, 220, 256, 261, 277
Jenkins, Cyril, 106
Joshua Light Snow, 145
journals, 21
"Jupiter" Symphony (Mozart), 75
Jurgenson, Pyotr, 16

kairos, 203, 363n131
Kalafati, Vasily, 86
Kamarinskaya (Glinka), 162
Kanfer, Stefan, 197–98
Kant, Immanuel, 18
Kaprow, Allan, 200
Karatygin, Vyacheslav, 16, 28, 83, 178, 275
Kashir, 44
Kelkel, Manfred, 2
Kerman, Joseph, 183
key signatures: color and, 370n32; of Etudes Op. 8, 55, 348n15; of Liszt, 348n15; piano sonatas and, 48; synaesthesia and, *136*, 138, 221, 347n7, 348n15
Kissin, Evgeny, 80
Komen, Paul, 63
Konyus, Georgi, 378n23
Konyus, Lev, 90, 95
Korsakovskaya gamma (Rimsky-Korsakov), 167
Koussevitzky, Serge, 98, 101; background of, 106; baton technique of, 342n71; championing of Scriabin's music, 43, 107; death and, 126; disillusionment with Scriabin's music, 31, 108, 191; Downes enthusiasm for, 108, 187, 190–91; legacy as a conductor, *107*,

107–8, 342n71; *Mysterium* and, 186–87; performing Piano Concerto in F♯ minor Op. 20, *107*; reputation of, 107–8; Symphony No. 4, *Poème de l'Extase* (*Poem of Ecstasy*) in C major Op. 54 and, 97, 107–8, 187, 191; Volga tour of, 80, 107; wealth and patronage of, 186–87
Kozlov, Alexei, 200
Krehbiel, Henry, 97, 106, 185
Kreisler, Johannes, 139
Kreisleriana (Hoffmann), 139
Kresh, Paul, 201
kujawiak, 51

Lang, Paul Henry, 6, 189
language, 177
Lapshin, I. I., 3
Laredo, Ruth, ix, 72, 197, 198
large-scale forms, 86
laser light shows, 147
The Last Romantic, 113
Latin music, 53
Lavoie-Herz, Djane, 187–88, 197
László Somogyi, 144
leading tones, 95
leaping technique, 218, 220, 221, 227–28, *228*, 316
learned style, 84–85
LED lights, 156
left hand: development, 216, 220–21; emancipation of, 219–21; Left-hand alone waltz (lost), 219, 365n2; Nocturne for left hand alone Op. 9 No. 2, 34–35, 183, 219, 365n2, 365n6; piano music of, 220–21; Prelude for left hand alone Op. 9 No. 1, 219, 369n6, 376n50; role of, 218; technique of, 219; thumb of, 220, 365n6; treble clef in, 365n8. *See also* hands
left-hand alone waltz (lost), 219, 365n2
legacy, 15, 31, 69, 103, 158; fringe interests and, 182; Ivanov as proselyte of, 177; multi-faceted, 204; mysticism and, 22; mystique about, 115; Piano Concerto in F♯ minor Op. 20 and, 76; Piano Sonatas and, 33; Schloezer, B., and, 120; synaesthesia and, 131, 137

legato, 65–66, 231, 285, 291
The Legend of the Invisible City of Kitezh and the Maiden Fevroniya (Rimsky-Korsakov), 169
Leiber, Fritz, 49
Leikin, Anatole, 68, 165, 214, 296, 307
Leitmotif, 42, 175, 211, 261–62
Lentulov, Aristarkh, 143
Leonard, Richard, 164
Lermontov, Mikhail, 179
Lermontova, Varvara, 119
Leschetitsky, Theodor, 16, 290
Lewenthal, Raymond, as Romantic revivalist, 70, *193*, 193–94, 197, 360n45
Lhévinne, Josef, 20, 34–35, 183
Liadov, Anatoly, 77, 83–84, 87, 100, 102, 246, 249, 368n14
Das Lied von der Erde (Mahler), 6
Life magazine, 195
A Life for the Tsar (Glinka), 162, 166
lifestyle, 129
light, 5, 10, 287; aesthetics and, 142; Beethoven and, 148; colored light performances, 131–36, *132*, 140–47, 155, 195, 349n38, 350n39; construction of, 147–55; Debussy and, 150; fire, 212; laser light shows, 147; LED, 156; as musical metaphor in Scriabin's music, 42, 46, 50, 67–68; passages in his music that depict light, 47, 148, 294; in Piano Concerto in F♯ minor Op. 20, 294; in Sonata No. 4 in F♯ major Op. 30, 149, *150*; in Sonata No. 6 Op. 62, 152; in Sonata No. 7 Op. 64 "White Mass," *151*, 151–52; in Sonata No. 9 Op. 68 "Black Mass," 152, *153*; in Sonata No. 10 Op. 70, "Trill," 152–53, *153–54*, 294; symbolism of, 148–49; in Symphony No. 3 in C minor Op. 43, Le Divin Poème (Divine Poem), 149; in Symphony No. 4, Poème de l'Extase (Poem of Ecstasy) in C major Op. 54, 150–51; in Symphony No. 5, Prometheus: Poem of Fire in F♯ major Op. 60, 50, 294; techniques used by Scriabin to create the impression of, 45, 148, 155; technology and, 147; trills as

luminosity, 67, 152, *153–54*; as used in performances of Scriabin's piano music, 210; in Vers la Flamme Op. 72 (Toward the Flame), 154, 294
Lights, Pablo, 145
linguistic theory, 9
Liszt, Franz, 192; Années de pèlerinage (Years of Pilgrimage), 170; La Campanella, 170; daughter of, 339n4; hands and, 234; harmony of, 252, 254; influence on Scriabin, 16–17, 37, 38, 41, 42, 146, 218; as inventor of symphonic poem, 64; key signatures of, 348n15; Les cloches de Genève, 170–71, *171*; Mephisto Waltz No. 1, 65, 261; pedal techniques of, 305, 376n48; pianistic technique, 17; Piano Sonata in B minor, 37–38, 334n10; Les Préludes, 64; "Prometheus," 98; Réminiscences de Don Juan, 20, 218; as representative of "Music of the Future," 254; similarities to Scriabin, 16, 29, 33, 34; Un Sospiro Concert Etude, 234, 236; tone poems and, 64; Transcendental Études, 55, 218; use of thematic transformation, 244
liturgical chant, 11
Le Livre (The Book) (Mallarmé), 26, 180
Lobanov, Pavel, 307
Loewe, Carl, 64
Lomaland, 23–24
London Symphony Orchestra, 97, 105, 144
Los Angeles Philharmonic, 106, 110
Lourié, Arthur, 97, 120, 127
Lucifer, 98, 99, 179, 186, 212
Lunacharsky, Anatoly, 120, 127, 160
Lydian-Dominant, 275
Lydian-Mixolydian, 275
lyrical shaping, 241

Maazel, Lorin, 194
Macdonald, Hugh, 66, 144–45, 166, 182, 203, 260
Machlis, Joseph, 183
madness. See insanity
"Magic Fire Music," 67
The Magic Flute (Mozart), 23
Mahler, Gustav, 6, 82, 87, 161

Mallarmé, Stéphane, 26, 175, 180, 355n60
Mann, William, 19
"Mannheim Steamroller," 75
The Man Who Tasted Shapes (Cytowik), 133
Margulis, Vitaly, 41, 72
Marx, Adolph Bernhard, 243, 244
masculine, 66, 212, 244
Masonic symbolism, 23
Matthews, David, 239
Mazurkas Op. 3, 16, 52–54, 247, 251–52, 255
Mazurkas Op. 25, 35, 53–54, 172, 247, 252–53, 317, *318*
Mazurkas Op. 40, 54, 212, 325
mazurkas, 51–52, 252
McGill University, 137
Medtner, Nikolai, 37
Meichik, Mark, 44
melody: dynamics and, 241–42; early period, 241–42; emotions and, 242; harmony and, 47, 279; Horowitz and, 241; performance of, as hallmark of Scriabin's compositional style, 241–42; of Sonata No. 6 Op. 62, 244, *245*; of Sonata No. 7 Op. 64 "White Mass," 244; of Sonata No. 8 Op. 66, 244
Mephisto Waltz No. 1 (Liszt), 65, 261
La Mer (The Sea) (Debussy), 150
Messiaen, Olivier, 42, 131, 138, 257, 273
metric ambiguity, 316
metronome marks, 322, 324
middle-period preludes, 61–62
Mighty Five (*Moguchaya kuchka*), 33, 61, 64, 162, 167
Millar, Preston, 142
Miller, Henry, 94, 341n45, 363n127
Milton, John, 148
minor ninths, 293
minor seconds, 155
Mir Iskusstva (World of Art), 174
mist pedal technique, 300
Mitchell, Edward, 70
Mitchell, Rebecca, 118, 276, 279
mobility techniques, 227–28
modal thinking, 278
modernism, 189, 200, 357n18

modernity, 143
modern playing styles, 213–15, 364n20
Modern Russian Composers (Sabaneev), 118
Moguchaya kuchka. *See* Mighty Five
Molotov, Vyacheslav, 115, 130, 343n8
Molotov cocktail, 130
Molotov Remembers: Inside Kremlin Politics, 130
Monteaux, Pierre, 108
Monterey Pop Festival, 199
"Moonlight" Sonata Op. 27 No. 2 (Beethoven), 39
Morceaux Op. 2, 16
Morozova, Margarita, 43, 89, 187, 344n14, 355n81
Morris, Mitchell, 262
Morrison, Simon, x, 25, 176, 200, 275, 279
Moscow Conservatory: alumni of, 34, 71, 102, 134; death and, 126; Scriabin's tenure as professor of piano, 35, 52; Scriabin's training at, 16, 17, 20, 75, 164, 166; teaching staff, 17, 71, 74, 75, 81, 84, 89, 90, 166
Moscow Scriabin Society, 330n6
mothers, 335n46
motives, 9–10, 11, 175, 317
moustache, 129, 246
Mozart, Wolfgang Amadeus, 23, 36, 75, 78, 317, 377n9
Mozer, Alexander, 139
Mravinsky, Yevgeny, 110
Müller-Streicher, Friederike, 306
Musical America, 142
musical cognition, 8
Musical Contemporary. *See Muzykal'niy sovremennik*
musical criticism, 9
musical imagery, 4
musical imagination, 8
musical meaning, 5
Musical Uproar in Moscow (Werth), 28
The Music of Alexander Scriabin (Baker), 4–5
"Music of the Future" movement, 254, 257, 260
musicology, 3

Mussorgsky, Modest, 9, 46, 124, 166, 169, 170, 263–64
Muti, Riccardo, 88, 110
Muzyka, 116
Muzykal'niy sovremennik (*Musical Contemporary*), 27
Myaskovsky, Nikolai, 37, 97
Myers, Charles S., 137–38, 348n14
Myers, Rollo, 19
Mysterium, 24, 36; bells intended for, 46, 172; death harmonies in, 258, 277, 279; description of, 25–27; influences on (Theosophy, Symbolism), 25; Koussevitzky and, 186–87; philosophy and, 200; relation to *Acte préalable*, 26; religion and, 25; Sabaneev and, 118; Schloezer, B., and, 120; similarity to contemporary projects, 46, 48–49, 50, 63
mystical anarchy, 210, 212
mystic chord, 30, 258, 269; *Extase* chord and, 275, 372n54; history and significance, 273–78; Hull, A., and, 274–75; intervals of, 22; Newmarch on, 371n48; octatonicism, octatonic scale and, 273, 371n42; overtones, overtone series and, 274–76, 372n50; Sabaneev and, 116, 119, 273, *274*, 276, 372n53, 372n63; Seventh Sonata and, 46, 47; in Sonata No. 7 Op. 64 "White Mass," 46, 47, *280*; in Sonata No. 8 Op. 66, *280*; in Sonata No. 10 Op. 70, "Trill," 279; Symphony No. 5, *Prometheus: Poem of Fire in F♯ major* Op. 60 and, 100–101, *280*; tonal geometry of, 279
mystic harmony, *278*, 278–81
mysticism, 1–2, 11, 115, 183, 200; aesthetics and, 3, 22, 185; compositional language and, 7; definition of, 22; Lapshin on, 3; legacy and, 22; as pathological, 2, 7; Seventh Sonata and, 46
mystic mode, 275–76
mystic unity, 364n16
myths: afterlife of Scriabin's music, 126–28; about children, 347n61; created by Bowers, 122–26; created by Sabaneev, 116–19, 344n11; created by Schloezer, B., 119–22; about death, 128–29; of Easter death, 27, 67, 68–69, 117, 124, 130; Prometheus, 3, 12, 98–99

The Naked Carmen, 362n126
Nápravník, Eduard, 101
nationalism, 27, 37, 160–65, 173
Neapolitan Sixth chords, 255, 267
Nemenova-Lunz, Maria, 43
Nemtin, Alexander, 26, 59, 196
neo-romanticism, in U.S., 191–96
nervousness, 57, 63, 73, 114, 115, 124, 208, 225, 377n2
Nesterov, Mikhail, 178
Neue Sachlichkeit (New Objectivity), 214
Neuhaus, Heinrich, 71, 117, 122
"New Complexity" movement, 320
New Deal, 189
Newman, Ernest, 192
Newmarch, Rosa, 128, 274, 371n48
New Objectivity. See *Neue Sachlichkeit*
The New Scriabin: Enigma and Answers (Bowers), 195
New York Philharmonic, 85, 88, 102, 106, 143, 184
New York University, 139
Nexus: Book Three of the Rosary Crucifixion (Miller), 94, 341n45
nicknamed chords, 256–58
Nietzsche, Friedrich, 3, 8, 18, 115; Dionysian principle and, 20, 93; influence on Scriabin, 20, 200, 210; mystical anarchy, 210, 212; philosophical theories of, 20, 83, 93, 210, 212; Symphony No. 1 in E major Op. 26 and, 83; Symphony No. 4, *Poème de l'Extase* (*Poem of Ecstasy*) in C major Op. 54 and, 93; on synaesthesia, 5
Nietzsche's Orphans: Music, Metaphysics, and the Twilight of the Russian Empire (Mitchell, R.), 118
Night of the Eagle (Leiber), 49
Nikisch, Arthur, 88, 106–7
Ninth Symphony, "Chorale" (Beethoven), 37, 75, 82, 184–85, 332n45

"Nobody Knows the Trouble I've Seen," 86
Nocturne for left hand alone Op. 9 No. 2, 34–35, 183, 219, 365n2, 365n6
Nocturne Op. 5, 16
Nonken, Marilyn, 146, 303
Norton, Eliot, 162
notation, 208, 300, *301*, 307, 315, *323*
Le Nozze di Figaro (Mozart), 36
Nuages (Debussy), 82
numbers, 25, 180

oberek, 51
occult associations, 21–22, 49, 67–68, 165, 199, 331n17
occult lore, 22, 197
octatonicism, octatonic scale, 45, 46, 167, 257, 269–73, *278*; dissonance and, 273; in *Étrangeté* Op. 63 No. 2, 273; mystic chord and, 273, 371n42; in Poème Op. 69 No. 2, 273; in Poème Op. 71 No. 1, 273; in Poème Op. 71 No. 2, 273; Rimsky-Korsakov and, 270, 272, 371n39; in Sonata No. 6 Op. 62, 273, 371n42; in Sonata No. 7 Op. 64 "White Mass," 273, 371n42; in Sonata No. 9 Op. 68 "Black Mass," 273; whole-tone scale and, 272
octaves, 216
"Ode to Joy" (Beethoven), 82
"Oeaohoo," 99
Ogdon, John, 70, 346n58
Ohlssohn, Garrick, 80
Olcott, Henry Steel, 23
Old Guard of New York music critics, 142, 185, 188
On Piano Playing: Motion, Sound and Expression (Sandor), 225
open fifths, 254
"open" work, 180
orchestration, 75–76, 86, 339n3; of Symphony No. 4, *Poème de l'Extase (Poem of Ecstasy)* in C major Op. 54, 94; of Symphony No. 5, *Prometheus: Poem of Fire in F♯ major* Op. 60, 99–101
Orga, Ates, 158
ornamentation, 377n9

Ornstein, Leo, 50
Orthodox chant melodies, 27, 128, 166
Orthodox Church, 168
Ortmann, Otto, 133
Ossovsky, Alexander, 102
Other, 329n22
overtones, overtone series, 138, 219–20, 274–76, 372n50
Oxford University Orchestra, 145
Ozawa, Seiji, 143

Paganini, Niccolò, 170
Pakenham, Compton, 190
Paperno, Dmitri, 71
Paradise Lost, 148
Paris Academy of Music, 120
passion, 289
Pasternak, Alexander, 282, 284
Pasternak, Boris, 1, 71, 89, 286
Pasternak family, 286
patriotism, 160–61
Pavchinsky, Sergei, 90
Peacock, Kenneth, 139
pedaled resonances, 299–305
pedal techniques, 369n5; breathing metaphor for, 302, 376n48, 377n7; damper, 220; dissonance and, 302; dynamics and, 303; editor's notation of, *301*; in Etude Op. 2 No. 1, 300, *301*; fluttering, 302–3, 376n50; French, 376n52; of Liszt, 305, 376n48; mist, 300; notation of, 300; pinpoint, 300; in Poème *Étrangeté* Op. 63 No. 2, 303; in Poème Op. 32 No. 1, 303; in Prelude for left hand alone Op. 9 No. 1, 376n50; quarter, half, and full, 305; sanitary, 300; of Sonata No. 3 in F♯ minor Op. 23, 301–2; in Sonata No. 9 Op. 68 "Black Mass," 303, *304*; trills and, 303, 376n51; vibrating, 300; virtuosity of, 300
penmanship, 246, 368n13
Pentatone, 85
perfectionism, 325
performance, 214, 241–42, 307, 308, 309, 320
performance art, 180

The Performing Style of Alexander Scriabin (Leikin), 307
Perle, George, 277, 337n68
personality, 15, 113, 123, 246, 364n18
Peshchera (*The Cave*) (Zamyatin), 63
Petrograd Scriabin Society, 330n6
Petrushka (Stravinsky), 160, 165, 167, 214
Philadelphia Orchestra, 92–93, 110, 186, 192, 199
philosophy: beliefs, 31; criticism of Scriabin for his interest in, 3; German, 258; influences on Scriabin, 3–4, 6, 18–20, 25, 184, 356n81; music and, 6; *Mysterium* and, 200; poème form and, 18; Symphony No. 1 in E major Op. 26 and, 83, 85; Symphony No. 3 in C minor Op. 43, *Le Divin Poème* (*Divine Poem*) and, 19, 90, 185; Symphony No. 4, *Poème de l'Extase* (*Poem of Ecstasy*) in C major Op. 54 and, 19, 93; Symphony No. 5, *Prometheus: Poem of Fire in F♯ major* Op. 60 and, 19; synaesthesia and, 351n63. *See also* mysticism
phrase structures, phrasing, 309–11, 378n21
physical demands, 68
pianism, 73, 222, 286, 296, 373n4, 374n14
Pianism as Art (Feinberg), 73, 300
pianists, 68–73, 215–17
piano (instrument), 33; Bechstein, 375n38; construction of, 305; dynamics of, 296, 375n39; hammers of, 296, 375n39; manufacturing of, 296; resonance of, 305; timbre of, 282; tuning, 371n49
Piano Concerto in F♯ minor Op. 20, 39, 340n14, 368n4; Brahms and, 77; Chopin and, 78; compositional principle in, 77–78; counterpoint in, 247, *248*; criticism of, 340n14; dance music, dance rhythms in, 78; expression markings of, 78; harmony in, 253, *253*; Koussevitzky performing, *107*; legacy and, 76; light in, 294; opening movement of, 264; premieres of, 76, 80; Prokofiev, S., on, 80; recordings of, 80; Rimsky-Korsakov and, 77, 379n30; themes of, *78*; triple meters in, 78; use of registers in, *295*; variations of, 78, *79*; whole-tone sounds in, *265*
Piano Concerto No. 2 in B♭ major (Brahms), 77
Piano Concerto No. 2 in C minor Op. 18 (Rachmaninov), *170*
Piano Concerto No. 21 in C minor, K. 491 (final mvt.) (Mozart), 78
piano rolls, 366n13, 376n46; dynamics and, 308; imitation of, 309; performance style and, 308; recordings, 284, 286, 308, 309, 377n15; technology, 300; transcriptions of, 307–9; Welte-Mignon, 56, 60
piano sonatas. *See* sonatas
Picture of Dorian Gray (Wilde), 68
Pictures at an Exhibition (Mussorgsky), 166, 170
pinpoint pedal techniques, 300
Planck, Max, 135
Plato, 174–75, 203, 363n131
playing style, 220, 282, 374n23
pleasure, 92, 93–94
Plekhanov, Georgi, 160
pleroma. *See* mystic chord
Pletnev, Mikhail, 85
Podgaetsky, Alexei, 48
Poe, Edgar Allen, 169
poème, philosophy and form of, 18
Poème ailé Op. 51 No. 3, 212
Poème fantasque Op. 45 No. 2, 261
Poème-Nocturne Op. 61, 65–67
Poème Op. 32: No. 1, 53, 210, 262, 285, 303, 325; No. 2, 225, 262, 289; No. 5, 53
Poème Op. 52, No. 1, 264, 319
Poème Op. 59 No. 1, 220, 365n8
Poème Op. 69, 242, 273, 287, 294
Poème Op. 71, 242, 273
Poème satanique Op. 36 (*Satanic Poem*), 17, 49, 65–66, 69, 183, 261, 289
Poème symphonique in D minor, 70
Poème tragique Op. 34, 18, 225, 289, 375n31
Poem of Ecstasy (poem), 21, 94

Poem of Ecstasy (symphony). *See* Symphony No. 4, *Poème de l'Extase* in C major Op. 54
poetic expression marks in Scriabin's music. *See* character indications
Poetics of Music: In the Form of Six Lessons (Stravinsky), 109, 343n79
poetry, 18, 22, 64, 149, 166, 180
Poland, 51
polyphony, 84, 247, 375n25
polyrhythms, 56–57, 289, 316, 378n24; conceptualizing, 322, 378n28; development, 216–17; in Etude Op. 42, 320–21; execution of, 218; in *Impromptu à la Mazur* in F♯ Op. 7 No. 2, 320; in Impromptu Op. 7 No. 2, *321*; performance style and, 320; in Poème Op. 52 No. 1, 320; in Prelude Op. 11, 322; in Sonata No. 10 Op. 70, "Trill," 322; in *Vers la Flamme* Op. 72 (*Toward the Flame*), 322
Ponti, Michael, 66, 72–73
pop culture, 123, 195
popularity, 195, 196; after death, 126; in England, 126, 127; Stravinsky's jealousy of, 346n57; unpopularity after death, 19, 27–32, 189–91
poriv (transporting burst), 152, 314, 316
portato chords, 149, *150*, 154, *154*
Portsmouth Point, 30
posthumous reputation, 19, 27–32
posture, 374n23
Powell, Jonathan, ix, 51, 242
powers of persuasion, 344n14
Po zvezdam (*By the Stars*) (Ivanov), 176
Prefatory Act. *See Acte préalable*
Prélude à l'après-midi d'un faune (Debussy), 82
Prelude for left hand alone Op. 9 No. 1, 219, 369n6, 376n50
Prelude in C♯ minor Op. 3 No. 2 (Rachmaninov), *171*
Prelude *Ondine* (Debussy), 277
Prelude Op. 10 No. 2, 366n13
Preludes Op. 11, 81; Chopin and, 378n24; No. 1, 60, 172, 209, 220–21, 254, 316, *323*; No. 2, 60, 255, 324, 366n10; No. 3, 216; No. 4, 60–61, 252–53, *253*; No. 7, 61, 221; No. 8, 220; No. 10, 309, *310*, 311, 316; No. 11, 61, 221, 229, *230*, 290, 316; No. 12, 254; No. 14, 61, 316, 319, 325, 379n37; No. 16, 61, 254, 264, *265*, 319; No. 18, 61, 379n37; No. 19, 61, 221, 369n6; No. 20, 61, 221; No. 23, 61, 216; No. 24, 61, 221, 319, 379n37; polyrhythms in, 322; Rachmaninov and, 60; recordings of, 61; rhythms in, 319, *323*; writing of, 60
Preludes Op. 13, 60, 81; No. 1, 172, *259*, 260, 368n4; No. 2, 216, 254, 379n37; No. 4, 379n37; No. 5, *231*; No. 6, 221
Preludes Op. 15, 60, 81, 216, 255
Preludes Op. 16, 60, 81, 221, 239, 254, *254*, 368n4
Preludes Op. 17, 60, 81, 227, 233, 253, 316, 379n37
Preludes Op. 22, 232, 239, 325, 368n4
Prelude Op. 27 No. 1, 232, 247, *259*, 260
Preludes Op. 28 (Chopin), 35, 59, 60, 61, 78–79, *79*
Prelude Op. 33 No. 4, 319
Prelude Op. 35 No. 2, 253
Preludes Op. 37, 57, 172, 216, 222, *223*, 225, *259*, 260, 262
Preludes Op. 39, 216, 253, 294
Prelude Op. 45, No. 3, 378n20
Preludes Op. 48, 62
Prelude Op. 51 No. 2, 222, *223*, 294
Prelude Op. 52 No. 1, *266*
Prelude Op. 56, No. 4, 379n37
Prelude Op. 59, No. 2, 62, 313, *314*, 378n17, 379n37
Preludes Op. 67, 222, *223*, 319, 365n6
Preludes Op. 74, 18, 62–64, 165–66, 195, 239, 251, 379n33
preludes, definition of, 59
Les Préludes (Liszt), 64
Preparation for the Final Mystery, 26
primitivism, 200
Prince Igor (Borodin), 169
Le Printemps (The Spring), 64

Prokofiev, Grigorii, 69, 306, 368n14
Prokofiev, Sergei, 34, 37, 76, 80, 97, 213; as musical antithesis to Scriabin, 28; on Piano Concerto in F♯ minor Op. 20, 80; *Scythian Suite*, 117; sonatas of, 38, 369n9; *Toccata* Op. 11, 214
Promenade Concerts, 88
"Prometheus" (Liszt), 98
Prometheus-2, 143
Prometheus Institute in Kazan, 140, 143
Prometheus myth, 3, 12, 98–99
psychedelica, in U.S., 199–203
psychology, 23
public perception, 114, 115, 158, 194
public persecutions, 28
Puccini, Giacomo, 241
Pushkin, Alexander Sergeevich, 347n61

"Quartet Fridays," 75
quater pedal technique, 305
Queens Hall Orchestra, 93
quintuplets, 316, 378n24

Rachmaninov, Sergei, 44, 56, 66, 76; bells and, 168–69, *170; The Bells* Op. 35, 169; C♯ minor Prelude, 34; depression of, 124; memorial tour after Scriabin's death, 68–69, 126; nationalism and, 163; Piano Concerto No. 2 in C minor Op. 18, 124, 170; Prelude in C♯ minor Op. 3 No. 2, 171; Prelude Op. 11 and, 60; preludes of, 60; Romanticism of, 213; Sonata in D minor Op. 28, 37; Symphony No. 5, *Prometheus: Poem of Fire in F♯ major* Op. 60 and, 286; synaesthesia and, 134–35
ragtime, 53
Rameau, Jean Philippe, 59, 256–57
Randlett, Samuel, 173, 221–22, 282, 288
RAPM (Russian Association of Proletarian Musicians), 28
Rau, Santha Rama, 125
Ravel, Maurice, 214, 354n48, 366n20
realism, 28, 164
reception, 27–32, 29, 92–93, 199, 332n45
recital pieces, 216

record companies, 204
recordings. *See specific works*
redistribution of parts between the hands, 222, 233, 234, 367nn23–24
registers, use of, *293*, 293–96, *295*
Reise, Jay, 220, 277–78
The Relation of the Ultramodern to Archaic Music (Heyman), 48
religion, 11, 20–21, 23, 25, 177
Réminiscences de Don Juan (Liszt), 20, 218
Reminiscences of Scriabin. See Vospominaniia o Skriabine
remote contexts, 329n28
remote keys, 336n51
repeated chords, 288–89, 320, 333n6
repeated-note arpeggios, 333n6
repetition, 76, 166
The Republic (Plato), 174–75
reputation, 182–83, 189, 191, 214
resolutions, 264
resonance, 223
resonance, pedaled, 299–305
resonant stratigraphy, 305
Rêverie in E major Op. 24, 80–82
Rêverie at Music Hall, 183
reviews. *See* criticism
Rhein, John von, 110
rhetoric, music and, 84–85
rhythmic declamation, 378n16
rhythmic dislocation, 317, 318
rhythmic language, 11, 316
rhythms: breathing, 377n7; changing meters, 319; characteristic, 306, 317, 319; of Chopin, 306–7, 377n4, 377n6; composing outside the box, 316–20; dance music, dance rhythms, 76, 78, 85, 162, 320; distortion of, 377n6; dotted, 79, 312–14, *314*, 316; in Etudes Op. 42, 56–57, 320–21; flexibility of, 306, 309; floating, *266*; in mazurka, 51; in Mazurka Op. 25 No. 4, *318*, 318–19; metric ambiguity, 317; motives and, 317; notation of, 307, 316, *323*; ornamentation, 377n9; pacing, *318*; placement, 222; in Poème Op. 52 No. 1, 319; in Prelude Op. 11, 319, *323*; in Prelude Op. 33, 319; in Prelude Op.

67, 319; sense of, 306; in Sonata No.
1 in F minor Op. 6, 317–18, 378n25;
in Sonata No. 6 Op. 62, 319–20; in
Sonata No. 7 Op. 64 "White Mass,"
320, 378n26; in Sonata No. 8 Op. 66,
319; in Sonata No. 9 Op. 68 "Black
Mass," 243–44, 320; in Sonata No. 10
Op. 70, "Trill," 319–20; speech and,
52; of Stravinsky, 319; subdivisions
of beat, 320–22; in Symphony No. 5,
Prometheus: Poem of Fire in F♯ major Op.
60, 319; triplet, quintuplet, 62, 368n9.
See also fanfares; polyrhythm; tempo;
tempo rubato
Richter, Sviatoslav, 44, 65, 71, 73, 155,
164, 208, 252, 379n37
right hand passagework, 216
Rimsky-Korsakov, Nikolai, 55, 75, 81, 86,
339n6; *Flight of the Bumblebee*, 152;
Korsakovskaya gamma, 167; *The Legend
of the Invisible City of Kitezh and the
Maiden Fevroniya*, 169; octatonicism,
octatonic scale, 270, 272, 371n39; Piano
Concerto in F♯ minor Op. 20 and, 77,
379n30; *Sadko*, 159–60; synaesthesia
and, 134–35
Rite of Spring (Stravinsky), 50, 167, 319,
342n71, 364n15
Rochester Philharmonic, 105
Rodzinski, Artur, 110
rogue figure or outsider, status as, 158–60,
163, 168
rolled chords, 222
Romanov dynasty, 158
Romanovsky, 338n82
Romantic artist, 82, 86, 189, 191, 213
Romantic expression, 216, 241–42
Romanticism, 6, 213, 360n74
Romantic performance style, 309
Romantic revival, 191–93, 195, 204,
360nn74–75; centennial celebrations
and, 196–99
Romantic tradition, 215, 218, 283
rondo form, 79, 319
Roosevelt, Franklin Delano, 189
root movement, 267–68
Rosenfeld, Paul, 29, 188

Rosicrucianism, 180
Roslavetz, Nikolai, 352n9
Rothstein, Edward, 142
Royal College of Music, 70
Royal Philharmonic Society, 85
Rubinstein, Anton, 37, 76, 143, 179, 290,
299, 339
Rudhyar, Dane, 287
Russell, Ken, 331n17
Russian Association of Proletarian
Musicians. *See* RAPM
Russian chant, 7, 319
Russian church, 254
Russian heritage, 289–92
Russian intonation theory. *See intonatsiia*
Russian music, 158; bells in, 168–73,
354n48; characteristics of, 165; emblems
of, 165–68; emotion and, 165; folk
music traditions of, 11, 51, 160, 165,
275, 319; harmony in, 166–67; history,
330n6; musical traditions of, 72, 160,
256, 273, 294; nationalism in, 160–65;
quintessential traits of, 165, 167,
168, 170, 173; scales in, 167; stylistic
qualities of, 4
Russian musical traits, lack of, 37, 165
Russian Orthodox Church, 20, 180
Russian Piano School, 71
Russian Revolution, 27, 63, 102, 126, 128,
143, 169, 177
Russian style, 162–65
Russian Symphony Orchestra Society, 85,
92, 97, 98, 102, 184, 185
Russian tradition, 256
Ryndam, 184

Sabaneev, Leonid, 15, 45, 49, 121, 347n61,
354n55, 364n18; career as music critic,
117; disillusionment with Scriabinism,
118, 119; education of, 116; *Mysterium
and*, 118; mystic chord and, 116, 119,
273, 274, 276, 372n53, 372n63; myths
created by, 116–19, 344n11; Schloezer,
B., feud with, 120; Scriabin letter to,
58; Symphony No. 5, *Prometheus: Poem
of Fire in F♯ major* Op. 60 and, 344n11;
view of Scriabin as deranged, 118, 119

Sacks, Oliver, 134
Sadasky, Vassily, 110
Sadko (Rimsky-Korsakov), 159–60
Safonov, Maria, 31
Safonov, Vasily, 75, 80, 85, 88, 89, 102, 184, 283, 299
Samson, Jim, 276
Samuel, Claude, 138
Sandor, Gyorgy, 225
sanitary pedal techniques, 300
Satan, 98, 186, 212
Satanic Poem. *See Poème satanique* Op. 36
Satie, Erik, 210, 213
Sayn-Wittgenstein, Carolyne, 40
Scarlatti, Domenico, 36
Schenker, Heinrich, 257
Schiller, Friedrich, 82
Schloezer, Boris, 2, 19–20, 24, 30, 119–22, 330n11, 345n27
Schloezer, Pavel, 89
Schloezer, Tatyana (mistress and common law wife), 40, 69, 89, 327n1, 334n15, 345n27; children with, 121, 347n61; letter to Lunz, 43; living with, 17; in U.S., 357n23
Schoenberg, Arnold, 26, 73, 161, 208
Schonberg, Harold, 73, 159, 192, 194–95, 197, 199–200, 204
Schools of composers, or "Isms," 160–62, 180
Schopenhauer, Arthur, 18, 20, 200
Schumann, Clara, 192
Schumann, Robert, 247, 267, 316, 334n10
Schwab, Charles, 102
Schwann record catalogue, 196
science, 23, 331n19
scores, 77, 208–9, 228–29
Scriabin, Alexander Nikolaevich. *See specific entries*
Scriabin, Nikolai (brother), 130
Scriabin and His Creative Work. *See A. N. Skriabin i ego tvorchestvo*
Scriabin: Artist and Mystic. *See Skriabin: Lichnost, Misteriia*
Scriabin Association, 338n80
Scriabin Circle, 188

Scriabin for Neuroscientists: A Study in Syn-Aesthetics (Triarhou), 351n63
"Scriabin in the Himalayas," xi, xvii
Scriabin Museum, 2, 196, 200, 307
Scriabin sixth chord, 258–61, *260*, 370n34
Scriabin Society, 119, 178
Scriabin Society of America, 330n4, 334n11
Scriabin sound, 282, 283–85, 299–300
Scriabin: The Great Russian Tone Poet (Mitchell, E.), 70
Scythian Suite (Prokofiev, S.), 117
The Sea. *See La Mer*
Second Symphony, "Resurrection" (Mahler), 82
Second Viennese School, 161
The Secret Doctrine (Blavatsky), 99, 122
Seeger, Ruth Crawford, 187–88, 258n32
Sekerina, Natalya, 39, 334n13
self-aggrandizement, 114, 183, 190
semitonal scale, 337n68
Semkow, Georg, 88, 340n33
sensuality, 92
sentimentality, 241
serialism, 246, 277
Serpinskaia, Nina, 176–77
Seven Arts, 29
sexual freedom, 93–94
sexuality, 20, 92, 115, 123; creativity and, 212; eroticism, 42, 68, 165, 176, 195–96, 261, 368n12; spirituality and, 22
sexual orientation, 125
Shapira, Elyakum, 144

sharpened fifths, 167
Shchetinina-Scriabina, Lyubov Petrovna (mother), 16, 290
sheet music, 207
Shoesmith, Thomas, 145
Shostakovich, Dmitri, 76
silence, 45
Silver Age of Russian culture, 5, 174, 177, 365n7
Sim, Annie, 335n46
single-movement sonatas, 37–38
Sisman, Elaine, 85
Sitsky, Larry, 164

Les Six, 213
Sixth Symphony, "Pastorale" (Beethoven), 87, 148
Skriabin (Sabaneev), 116
Skriabina, Lyubov, 87
Skriabina, Vera Isakovich (wife), 17, 39, 40, 56, 65–66, 77, 86, 88–89, 331n17, 334n15
Skriabin: Lichnost, Misteriia (Schloezer), 19–20, 121, 330n11
Skryabin (Macdonald), 182
Skryabin, Philosophy and the Music of Desire (Smith, K.), 262
skyscraper chord, *293*
Slonimsky, Nicolas, 19–20, 342n71, 345m27
small time, 329n28
Smith, Kenneth M., 262
Smith, Moses, 342n
Socialist Realism, 162
Sofronitsky, Vladimir, 29, 70–71, 117, 173, 325–26, 338n86
Sokolov, Nikolai, 189
solo concertos, 76
Solovyov, Vladimir, 175
Somer, Hilde, 72, 145, 147, 197, 198, 201–2
Somov, Konstantin, 178
Sonata-Fantasie (No. 2) in G♯ minor Op. 19, 36, 39–40, 69, 208–9, *233*, 294, 334n13; color in, 297; fanfares in, 312, *313*; tempo in, 325
Sonata in D minor Op. 28 (Rachmaninov), 37
Sonata No. 1 in F minor Op. 6, 221, 223, *224*, 225, 368n4, 369n9; augmented sixths in, 255; bells in, 38, 171, *172*; chorale textures in, 294; chords of, 223, *224*, 225; opening movement of, 240, *240*; recordings of, 39; rhythms in, 317–18, 378n25
Sonata No. 2 in B♭ minor (Chopin), 20
Sonata No. 3 in F♯ minor Op. 23, 35, 53, 184, 240–41, 334n15; bells in, 171–72; chordal distribution in, *232*; fanfares in, 312, *313*; hands in, 229, 231; pedal techniques of, 301–2; recordings of, 40, 41; tempo in, 325; use of registers in, 296–97
Sonata No. 4 in F♯ major Op. 30, 21, 41–43, 45, 56, 89, 338n82; chords of, 366n15; climactic ending of, 289; counterpoint in, 246; light in, 149, *150*; poem as inspiration for, 149, 258; portato chords in, 149, *150*; tempo in, 325; trills in, 211, *211*; Tristan chord in, *259*, 260
Sonata No. 5 in F♯ major Op. 53, 41, 45, 56, 69, 73, 227, *228*, 334n21, 367n24; bells in, 172; character indications in, 210; climactic ending of, 289; dominant function in, 268–69, *270–72*; dynamics in, 286–87; recordings of, 44; Symphony No. 4, *Poème de l'Extase* (*Poem of Ecstasy*) in C major Op. 54 and, 43–44; tempo in, 325
Sonata No. 6 Op. 62, 22, 36, 44–45, 65, 66; bells in, 172, *173*; character indications in, *299*; Coda of, 294; color in, *299*; counterpoint in, 249, 368n19; dynamics of, 288; harmony of, 252; light in, 152; melody of, 244, *245*; octatonicism, octatonic scale in, 273, 371n42; rhythms in, 319–20; tonal layering in, 291, *292*; trills in, 152, 237
Sonata No. 7 Op. 64 "White Mass," 38, 62, 234, 367n24; bells in, 173; character indications in, 151, *151*; color in, 298, *298*; fanfares of, 289, 312; light in, *151*, 151–52; melody of, 244; mystic chord and, 46, 47, *280*; octatonicism, octatonic scale in, 273, 371n42; recordings of, 47; rhythms in, 320, 378n26; as serialism, 277; Sonata No. 9 Op. 68 "Black Mass" and, 46, 48; tonal layering in, 290, *292*, 375n34; use of registers in, *293*
Sonata No. 8 Op. 66, 47–48, 49, 234, 279; Coda of, 294; counterpoint in, 249, *249*; melody of, 244; mystic chord in,

280; recordings of, 48; rhythms in, 319; tonal layering in, 290, *291*; trills in, 237
Sonata No. 9 Op. 68 "Black Mass," 17, 41, 46–47, 65, 67, 73, 195; character indications in, 209; Crowley and, 331n17; distribution of hands in, 234, *235*, 236; Horowitz and, 50, 72, 324; Hull, A., on, 49; Leiber and, 49; light in, 152, *153*; nickname of, 48; occult associations and, 22, 49; octatonicism, octatonic scale in, 273; opening four-note motto of, 49; pedal techniques in, 303, *304*; premiere of, 48; recordings of, 50; rhythm in, 243–44, 320; Sonata No. 7 Op. 64, "White Mass" and, 46, 48; trills in, 152, *153*, 237
Sonata No. 10 Op. 70, "Trill," 36, 47, 48, 50–51, 337n74; character indications of, 210; climactic ending of, 289; counterpoint in, 249–50, *250*; Horowitz and, 238; light in, 152–53, *153–54*, 294; mystic chord in, 279; perfect fourths in, 276; polyrhythms in, 322; recordings of, 51; rhythms in, 319–20; tremolos in, 294; trills in, 237; wrist technique in, 225, *226*
sonatas, 20, 335n29; design, 243; form, 38, 45, 327n6, 378n21; history of, 36–38; key signatures and, 48; legacy and, 33; of Prokofiev, S., 38; rash of sonatas after 1903; in Russian music, 37; Scriabin's contribution to, 29, 33, 36; single-movement, 37–38; three-part, 37
"Sons of the Flames of Wisdom," 99
Un Sospiro Concert Etude (Liszt), 234, 236
sound quality, 291. *See also* touch
Sovremennye zapiski, 163
spatial relationships, 227
Spectralism, 146
The Spectral Piano: From Liszt, Scriabin, and Debussy to the Digital Age (Nonken), 146, 303
speech, 9, 52
spirituality, 7, 22, 188, 199, 281
The Spring. See Le Printemps
Sputnik, 140
stacked chords, 222

stagnancy in the standard repertory, 191, 194
Stalin, Josef, 1, 130
Stamitz, Johann, 74–75
Star of David, 99
St. Basil's Cathedral, 331n17
Steinhart, Alexander Lang, 101
stereo sound, 125
Sterl, Robert, *107*, 327n1
stile antico. See high art
Stock, Frederick, 30, 93, 101, 103, 106, 187
Stokowski, Leopold, 92–93; championing of Scriabin's music, 30, 186; defense of Scriabin's music, 103–5; recordings of, 190; reputation of, 103; Symphony No. 4, *Poème de l'Extase* (*Poem of Ecstasy*) in C major Op. 54 and, 103–5, *104*, 186–87
stolen time (rubato), 241
St. Petersburg Conservatory, 37, 71, 75, 86
Strauss, Richard, 87, 92, 352n15
Stravinsky, Igor, 28, 123, 213; *Firebird*, 109, 165; interest in Scriabin's music, 275, 372n50; jealousy of Scriabin's popularity, 346n57; mother of, 128–29, 346n57; nationalism and, 162, 163; *Petrushka*, 160, 165, 167, 214; *Poetics of Music: In the Form of Six Lessons*, 109, 343n79; rhythms of, 319; *Rite of Spring*, 50, 167, 319, 342n71, 364n15
The Structure of Musical Speech (Yavorsky), 10
Stuart, Charles, 126
stylistic influences. *See* influences on musical style
subdivisions of beat, 320–22
subjectivism, 28
Sudbin, Yevgeny, 80
Supreme Being, 11
Survey of Contemporary Music (Gray), 183
Swan, Alfred, 30, 128, 164, 333n8
Symbolism, 2, 6, 7; aesthetic tenets of, 174–76, 179–80; apocalyptic, 175, 177; history of, 174, 175, 180; influence of, 24, 121, 180; *intonatsiia* and, 10; Ivanov and, 174–78; Masonic, 23; Morozova

and, 89; music and, 20, 181; mystery plays of, 200; poetry of, 22, 64, 141, 152, 174, 175, 179, 180, 354n55; *poriv*, 152; synesthesia and, 5; tradition, 180, 181; in visual arts, 50, 175, 176, 178, 179–80. *See also specific artists*
symbols, 2, 3, 23; Devil, as artistic, 65–66, 178–79
Symphonic Allegro in D minor, 75, 90
Symphonie fantastique (Berlioz), 49, 87, 92
symphonies, 74–76
Symphonies (Bely), 64
Symphony No. 1 in C minor Op. 68 (Brahms), 75
Symphony No. 1 in E major Op. 26, 21, 82–85, 90, 102, 184–85, 247
Symphony No. 2 in C minor Op. 29, 56, 85–88, *87*, 102
Symphony No. 3 in C minor Op. 43, *Le Divin Poème* (*Divine Poem*), 42, 56, 57, 59, 110; Altschuler and, 92–93; criticism of, 90, 92, 185–86; expression marks of, 90; Glinka Prize for, 90; harmony of, 91; length of, 89; light in, 149; "Luttes," *91*, 92; opening motto, 90, *91*, 92; Pasternak, B., on, 89–90; philosophy and, 19, 90, 185; premieres of, 18, 29, 88, 92–93, 102; reception of, 92–93; recordings of, 93; Scriabin sixth in, 260, *260*; Stock annual performance of, 93, 103; title of, 18, 64; *Tristan und Isolde* and, 90; words and text of, 90
Symphony No. 4, *Poème de l'Extase* (*Poem of Ecstasy*) in C major Op. 54, 43–44, 59, 74, 87, 110, 198, 331n13; Altschuler and, 94, 97, 186; Boulez and, 199; Coates performances of, 106, 128, 151, 187; conclusion of, 325; criticism of, 97, 114, 151, 191; "Ego Theme gradually realizing itself," *95*; eroticism and, 176; exposition of, 62; expression markings of, 94; fanfare of, 212; Glinka Prize (2nd place) for, 97; harmony of, 94, 167; "Human love," *96*; "Human striving after the ideal," *95*; Koussevitzky and, 97, 107–8, 187, 191; light in, 150–51; Maazel's performance of, 194; Miller on, 94, 341n45; Nietzsche and, 93; orchestration of, 94; philosophy and, 19, 93; *Poem of Ecstasy* accompanying poem, 21, 94; premieres of, 18, 93, 97, 102, 186; recordings of, 98; sharpened fifths in, 167; "Soaring flight of the spirit," *96*; Sonata No. 5 and, 43–44; Stokowski and, 103–5, *104*, 186–87; Taneyev on, 97; tension in, 264, *267*; themes, 94, *95–96*; title of, 64, 94; "Will to rise up," *96*
Symphony No. 5, *Prometheus: Poem of Fire in F♯ major* Op. 60, 64, 66, 341n55; Altschuler and, 142, 155; with colored lights, 131–36, *132*, 140–47, 155, 195, 349n38, 350n39; cover illustration for score of, *100*; criticism of, 101, 114, 142, 143; Delville and, 99, *100*; double performances of, 105; Dover score of, 347n7; fanfare of, 212; forgotten score of, 140; harmony in, 50, 100–101; Ivanov and, 177; light in, 50, 294; mystic chord and, 100–101, *280*; Newmarch program notes for, 128; "oohs" and "aahs" as methaphors in, 12; orchestration of, 99–101; philosophy and, 19; premieres of, 29, 101, 102, 103, 131, *132*, 133, 140–41, 142; Rachmaninov and, 286; recordings of, 101, 196; rhythms in, 319; Sabaneev and, 344n11; story of, 98; synaesthesia and, 139–41; Theosophy and, 23, 25, 98–99, 105, 145, 186; tonal plan of, 139; trills in, 237; Wood and, 105; Yale University, performances with color lights, 140, 144, 195, 350n39
synaesthesia, 182; aesthetics and, 351n63; associative, 140; color thinking, 138; color-tonal correspondences, *136*, 347n7; criticism of Scriabin's claims, 133, 136, 140; definition of, 5, 140; discovery and debate about, 134–37; Doctrine of Affections and, 134; history of, 134–37, 141; key signatures and, *136*, 138, 221, 347n7, 348n15; laws of, 135; legacy and, 131, 137; literature on

Scriabin's, 137–41; manifestations of, 344n11; neurology and, 156, 351n63; Nietzsche on, 5; people endowed with, 134; philosophy and, 351n63; Rachmaninov and, 134–35; Rimsky-Korsakov and, 134–35; stimuli of, 133–34; Symbolism and, 5; Symphony No. 5, *Prometheus: Poem of Fire in F♯ major* Op. 60 and, 139–41; as universal and innate, 135

synchronic point of view, 159

Synesthesia: A Union of the Senses (Cytowik), 137

Szidon, Roberto, 38, 39, 44, 51, 361nn98–99

Szigeti, Joseph, 56

Szymanowski, Karol, 336n53

"The Tale of Tsar Saltan," 347n61

Taneyev, Sergei, 75, 97, 166, 246, 249

Taruskin, Richard, 64, 161–62, 166, 174, 262, 264, 352n12, 352n15

tastiera per luce (color organ), 99, 142–43, 149, 155–56, 157, 186, 348n22

Tchaikovsky, Piotr, 37, 76, 97, 127, 163

Tchaikovsky, V., 256, 369n8

Tchaikovsky Competition, 70

teachers, 215–17

technical challenges, 51, 54, 55, 57, 62, 156, 217, 222, 233, 236, 290–91, 309, 326

technique development, 216

technology, 143, 147, 156, 331n19

tempo: acceleration of, 308, 314, 317, 325, 377n15; choices of Horowitz, 50, 324; flexibility of, 242; flow of, 310; graphs, 307; lingering, 308, 367n6; metronome markings, 322, 324; speed, 379n37

tempo rubato, 86; arrhythmia, 306–7, 317, 378n24; compared to Chopin, 306–7; definition of, 241; Feinberg and, 309; Horowitz and, 242; phrasing and analysis, 309–11; in Scriabin's piano rolls, 241; tempo graphs, 307

tenutos, 77, 253

textural layering. *See* tonal layering

thematic transformation, 244, *245*, 246

Theory of Relativity, 135

Theosophical Society, 23, 187, 345n35

Theosophy, 182, 200; Adams and, 358n37; allure of, 23–24; Besant and, 23; Blavatsky as leader of, 98–99, 142; Bowers and, 24; definition of, 23; influence on Scriabin, 19, 23–25, 98–99, 121–22, 180, 187–88; music and, 24; numbers and, 25; principles of, 345n35; Schloezer, B., on, 121–22; Symphony No. 5, *Prometheus: Poem of Fire in F♯ major* Op. 60 and, 23, 25, 98–99, 105, 145, 186

Third Symphony (Mahler), 87

Third Symphony, "Eroica" (Beethoven), 98

This is Your Brain on Music: The Science of a Human Obsession (Levitin), 137

Thomas, Gareth, 182

three-movement design, 74

three-part sonatas, 37

thumb crossings, *231*, 366n22

Thus Spoke Zarathustra (Nietzsche), 20

timbre, 69, 169, 179, 282, 293, 329n22

timing, 221, 244

Tingley, Katherine, 23

Tipton, Jennifer, 145–46, 155

Tircuit, Heuwell, 196

Titan, 98, 99

Toccata Op. 11 (Prokofiev, S.), 214

Tommasini, Anthony, 146

Tompakova, Olga, 182

tonal attraction, 9–10

tonal balance, 232. *See also* voicing

tonality, harmony and, 370n32

tonal layering, 289–92, 375n34

tonal planning, 267–68

tonal structure, 257

tone: color, 50, 69, 344n11; crystalline, 66, 337n74; overtones, overtone series, 138, 219–20, 274–76, 372n50; poems, 64, 97; quality, 68

topics, or *topoi*, 84–85, 211

Toscanini, Arturo, 113

touch, qualities of, 285–88

"Toward a Methodology for the Human Sciences," 329n28

Toward the Flame. See *Vers la Flamme* Op. 72
Townsend, Justin, 140, 141, 144, 344n11, 348n21
transcendence, 2, 30, 93, 257, 273, 279; ecstasy and, 175–76; ego and, 95; music and, 20; Symphony No. 1 in E major Op. 26 and, 85
Transcendental Études (Liszt), 55, 218
transcriptions, of piano rolls, 307–9
transfiguration of man, 11
transporting burst. *See poriv*
treble clef, in left hand, 365n8
tremolos, 81, *154*, 237, 289, 294
Triarhou, Lazaros C., 156, 351
trills, 45, 81, 218, 288, 320; Beethoven and, 152, 375n29; coloristic use of, 236, 237, 238; fingering of, 236–38; hands technique for, 237; as luminosity, 45, 67, 152, *153–54*, 212; meaning of, 50, 152; non-standard techniques in, 237; pedal techniques and, 303, 376n51; in Seventh Sonata, 47; in Sonata No. 4 in F♯ major Op. 30, 211, *211*; in Sonata No. 6 Op. 62, 152, 237; in Sonata No. 8 Op. 66, 237; in Sonata No. 9 Op. 68 "Black Mass," 152, *153*, 237; in Sonata No. 10 Op. 70, "Trill," 237; in Symphony No. 5, *Prometheus: Poem of Fire in F♯ major* Op. 60, 237; technical skills required for, 236–37
triple meters, 76, 78, 243, 319
triplets, 313, 316
Tristan chord, 258–61, *259*, 370n18, 370n20
Tristan und Isolde (Wagner), 90, 255, 258, *259*, 341n38
tritone interval, 256, 267, 273, 369n12
Trubetskoi, Sergei, 21
Tsar Kolokol, 168
Tushinski, Jim, 44
"Two Cases of Synaesthesia," 137–38

una corda pedal, 296–97, 298
unification theory, 12
United States (U.S.), 31, 183–87, 191–96, 199–203, 357n23. *See also* counterculture, American

unity (*edinstvo*), 200, 244, 257, 279, 368n10
Universe Symphony (Ives), 26, 281
University of Brussels, 120
University of Iowa, 105, 144
unpopularity after death, 19, 27–32, 189–91
urban romance style. *See bytovoi romans*
use of fourths, 22, 42, 46, 48, 55, 65, 187–88, 234
Ushakoff, Alex, 144

Valse Op. 1, 16
Van Allen's Ecstasy (Tushinski), 44
Van der Stucken, Frank, 81, 183
Vanechkina, Irina, 140
Vedanta, 180
Venok Skriabina, 178
Verbit, Martha Anne, 48, 198
Verdi, Luigi, 369n17
Verlaine, Paul, 175
Vers la Flamme Op. 72 (*Toward the Flame*), 49, 65, 67, 195; bells in, 173; Chau and, 338n77; fanfares of, 312; Horowitz and, 72, 155, 337n76; light in, *154*, 294; polyrhythms in, 320; portato chords in, 154, *154*; recordings of, 68; tremolo chord in, 289; use of registers in, 296
vertical thinking, 256–58
vibrating pedal technique, 300
Victorian Age, 357n18
Villoing, Alexander, 290
virtuosity, 214, 227, 300, 366n20
vocalism, 165
voglia, 258
voice, 329n22
voice leading, 62, 166, 234, 246–50, 260, 278, 370n23
voicing, 221, 366n22. *See also* tonal balance
Volga tour, 80, 107
Vospominaniia o Skriabine (*Reminiscences of Scriabin*) (Sabaneev), 45, 49, 116–19, 120–21, 135, 347n61, 354n55
Vrubel, Mikhail, 178–79, 180
Vyshnegradsky, Ivan, 213, 281

Wagner, Richard, 92, 211, 348n22; Gesamtkunstwerk, 25, 177, 183; harmony of, 18; influence on Scriabin, 18, 62, 86, 89–91, 260, 289; nationalism and, 163; *Tristan und Isolde*, 90, 255, 258, 259, 341n38; *Die Walküre*, 67
walk-arounds, 257, 368n2
Walton, William, 30
Waltz Op. 38, 227
Wang, Yuja, 68
Warlich, Hugo, 97
Weber, Carl Maria von, 92
Webern, Anton, 161
Wednesday is Indigo Blue (Cytowik), 133
Weinbaum, Mark, 343n74
Well-Tempered Clavier, Books I and II (WTC) (Bach), 59–60, 275, 309
Welte-Mignon piano rolls, 56, 60
Werth, Alexander, 28
Westinghouse, George, 102
"What Makes Music Symphonic," 76
White, Terrence, 30
White Album (the Beatles), 197
White Light Festival, 145
whole-tone dominant, 263–67, *265–67*, 370n34
whole-tone scale, 167, 263, 272, 274, *278*
Wieck, Clara, 334n10
Wilde, Oscar, 68
Williams, Pharrell, 134
Winkler, Alexander, 81
witchcraft, 22
Wittgenstein, Paul, 34, 214
women's liberation, 362n126
Wonder, Stevie, 134
Wood, Sir Henry J., 29, 80, 88, 93, 101, 105, 142, 349n31
Woodstock Arts and Music Festival, 199
Woolsey Hall, 350n39
The World as Will and Representation (Schopenhauer), 20
World of Art. See *Mir Iskusstva*
World War I, 27, 29, 34, 63, 128, 174, 177, 213
World War II, 103
wrist technique, 216, 218, 225–27
writings, 21, 294
WTC. See *Well-Tempered Clavier*, Books I and II

Yale University, 140, 144, 195, 350n39
Yavorsky, Boris, 9, 10, 264
Years of Pilgrimage. See *Années de pèlerinage*
Young People's Concerts, 76

Zamyatin, Evgenvy, 63
Zeltzer, Mark, 71
Zhdanov, Andrei, 28
Zhdanov, Nikolai
Zhdanovschina trials, 28
Zhiliaev, Nikolai, 213
Zhukov, Igor, 72
zov. See fanfares
Zverev, Nikola, 290
zvon, 169
Zweck: A Novel and Mostly Reliable Musical History (Deutsch), 115

About the Authors

Lincoln Ballard received his Ph.D. in Music History from the University of Washington in 2010 under the guidance of Stephen Rumph, and his research has primarily focused on popular music and twentieth-century art music. Ballard specializes in the music of Alexander Scriabin, and his dissertation offered the first comprehensive study of Scriabin's posthumous reception history in Russia and in the West. His writings have been published in peer-reviewed journals such as *American Music*, the *Journal of the Scriabin Society of America*, *Performance Practice Review*, and *Popular Music*. Ballard has taught music history and appreciation at the University of Washington, University of Puget Sound, Southwestern College, and Cascadia Community College.

Critically acclaimed as a "musician's pianist," **Matthew Bengtson** has a unique combination of musical talents ranging from pianist, harpsichordist, and fortepianist to composer and analyst. An advocate of both contemporary and rarely heard music, he performs an unusually diverse repertoire, ranging from William Byrd to numerous contemporary composers. He has performed extensively in the United States, Mexico, and continental Europe, and can be heard on the Roméo, Arabesque, Griffin Renaissance, Albany, Musica Omnia, and Navona record labels. In 2015, the 100th anniversary of Scriabin's death, he toured with numerous all-Scriabin recitals, performing the complete sonatas in Philadelphia and Chicago. He was the featured soloist in the multisensory celebration "Scriabin in the Himalayas" in Ladakh, India. His recordings of the complete sonatas have garnered numerous rave reviews: "Only Horowitz and Richter can compare to what Bengtson achieves on this disc. Has Scriabin ever been played better?" (*American Record Guide*). In *Fanfare*, he has been called "a Scriabinist for the 21st century . . . upon whom future generations can rely for definitive interpretations." Mr. Bengtson is a graduate of Harvard University in computer science and of the Peabody Conservatory in piano performance. He is assistant professor of piano literature at the University of Michigan School of Music, Theatre and Dance. www.mattbengtson.com.

John Bell Young's recordings of the music of Scriabin, Friedrich Nietzsche, and others on the Newport Classics, Americus, and Sony Classical labels have earned international critical acclaim. He has performed throughout the United States, Europe, Asia, and South America. His principal teachers were Constance Keene, Margarita Fyodorova, Olga Barabini, and Bruce Hungerford. He has coached with Claudio Arrau, John Browning, Shura Cherkassky, Vladimir Feltsman, and Ernst Levy. Young is a prominent music critic whose columns have appeared in the *American Record Guide*, *Opera News*, *Clavier*, *Classical DisCDigest*, the St. Petersburg *Times*, have appeared in and the popular online publications, *Tower of Babel* and *Music & Vision*. Young is also a frequent adjudicator for international piano competitions. His 2002 CD, entitled *Prisms*, which features the music of Scriabin, Mahler, Michel Block, Leo Tolstoi, and Hugh Downs, was released by Americus Records in 2000. In October 2002, Americus Records released his recording of Richard Strauss' melodrama, *Enoch Arden*, for narrator and piano, where he is joined by the distinguished film and stage actor Michael York. Mr. Young is also the founder and CEO of Identity Marketing for Concert Artists, Inc, a consultant agency that produces recordings for numerous labels and concert artists.

www.ingramcontent.com/pod-product-compliance
Lightning Source LLC
Chambersburg PA
CBHW022056150426
43195CB00008B/155